Lecture Notes in Computer Science 747

Edited by G. Goos and J. Hartmanis

Advisory Board: W. Brauer D. Gries J. Stoer

Michael Clarke Rudolf Kruse
Serafín Moral (Eds.)

Symbolic and Quantitative Approaches to Reasoning and Uncertainty

European Conference ECSQARU '93
Granada, Spain, November 8-10, 1993
Proceedings

Springer-Verlag

Berlin Heidelberg New York
London Paris Tokyo
Hong Kong Barcelona
Budapest

Series Editors

Gerhard Goos
Universität Karlsruhe
Postfach 69 80
Vincenz-Priessnitz-Straße 1
D-76131 Karlsruhe, Germany

Juris Hartmanis
Cornell University
Department of Computer Science
4130 Upson Hall
Ithaca, NY 14853, USA

Volume Editors

Michael Clarke
Department of Computer Science, Queen Mary and Westfield College
Mile End Road, London E1 4NS, United Kingdom

Rudolf Kruse
Department of Computer Science, Technical University of Braunschweig
Bültenweg 74-75, D-38106 Braunschweig, Germany

Serafín Moral
Departamento de Ciencias de la Computación e I.A.
Facultad de Ciencias, Universidad de Granada
Campus de Fuente Nueva, 18071 Granada, Spain

CR Subject Classification (1991): I.2.3

ISBN 3-540-57395-X Springer-Verlag Berlin Heidelberg New York
ISBN 0-387-57395-X Springer-Verlag New York Berlin Heidelberg

© Springer-Verlag Berlin Heidelberg 1993
Printed in Germany

Typesetting: Camera-ready by author
Printing and binding: Druckhaus Beltz, Hemsbach/Bergstr.
45/3140-543210 - Printed on acid-free paper

Preface

This volume contains the papers accepted for presentation at ECSQARU-93, the European Conference on Symbolic and Quantitative Approaches to Reasoning and Uncertainty, held at the University of Granada, Spain, from November 8 to 10, 1993.

In recent years it has become apparent that an important part of the theory of Artificial Intelligence is concerned with reasoning on the basis of uncertain, incomplete, or inconsistent information. Classical logic and probability theory are only partially adequate for this and a variety of other formalisms both symbolic and numerical have been developed, some of the most familiar being non-monotonic logic, fuzzy sets, possibility theory, belief functions, and dynamic models of reasoning such as belief revision and Bayesian networks.

These are new and active areas of research with many practical applications and many interesting theoretical problems as yet unresolved. Several European research projects and working groups have been formed and it soon became apparent that there was a need for a regular European forum where work in this area could be presented and discussed by specialists. The first conference was held at Marseille in 1991 (LNCS 548). This, the second of a regular biennial series, has again been sponsored by the major European research project in this area, DRUMS (Defeasible Reasoning and Uncertainty Management Systems, ESPRIT BRA 6156), involving 21 European partners and by the newly-formed European Society for Automated Practical Reasoning and Argumentation (ESAPRA).

The executive Scientific Committee for the conference consisted of Philippe Besnard (IRISA, Rennes), Rudolf Kruse (University of Braunschweig), Henri Prade (IRIT, Toulouse) and Michael Clarke (QMW, University of London). We gratefully acknowledge the contribution of the many referees, too many to list individually, who were involved in the reviewing process. Finally we would like to thank the University of Granada for providing all the necessary facilities and Serafín Moral of the University of Granada who was responsible for the local organisation.

August 1993   Michael Clarke, Chairman

Table of Contents

$\mathcal{RES}$: A formalism for reasoning with relative-strength defaults

Z. An   M. McLeish
Department of Computing and Information Science
University of Guelph
Guelph, Ontario
N1G 2W1, Canada

Areas: Common Sense Reasoning, Knowledge Representation, Probabilistic Reasoning.

Abstract

$\mathcal{RES}$ is a system for reasoning about evidential support relationships between statements[1, 2]. In $\mathcal{RES}$, the preferences of these supports are represented symbolically, by directly comparing them, instead of by numerical degrees. Z^+ is a formalism for reasoning with variable-strength defaults[5] which provides a mechanism to compute a minimum admissible ranking for models (subject to the consistency condition) from the given integer strengths of defaults.

In this paper, we combine the two systems. We show that the same consistency condition of Z^+ can be applied to $\mathcal{RES}$ even though the preferences of rules are represented as a relation in $\mathcal{RES}$. A similar procedure is devised which can produce the admissible relative strengths (a relation) and can produce the relation on models with respect to the strengths of the rules they violate. A consequence relation is defined and a procedure to answer queries concerning it is devised. The resulting system, also called $\mathcal{RES}$, is then compared to Z^+. We show that, while $\mathcal{RES}$ is very similar to Z^+ and displays comparable reasoning processes most of the time, they are not the same and $\mathcal{RES}$ is more in agreement with common sense in some situations. Comparing $\mathcal{RES}$ to the stratified ranking system [6] shows that $\mathcal{RES}$, as presented, also shares some limitations with Z^+.

1 Introduction

It has been widely acknowledged that all defaults are not created equal [5, 11] and that defaults differ in many aspects such as in their importance and their firmness. It has been widely agreed also that a language or a mechanism must be devised for expressing this valuable knowledge. The only problem remaining is what aspects about this knowledge should be represented and how.

The general way of representing this knowledge is by the strengths of defaults. Thus it will be very desirable if we can have a standard measurement of such strengths. As a matter of fact, there are many cases where such a measurement is available. These situations have been studied extensively in the literature. Different measurements have been proposed and both quantitative and qualitative reasoning with those measurements have been investigated[3, 8, 12, 13]. There are cases, however, where a normal measurement is not available or is not suitable. At the same time, there are also cases where the desirable reasoning patterns are amenable to some other representations simpler and more primitive than such measurements.

$\mathcal{RES}$ is a system for reasoning about evidential support relationships between statements, where the preferences of these supports are represented symbolically, by directly comparing these supports, instead of by numerical degrees. That is, we begin with a set of arguments and a relation on this set which reflects the strengths of the arguments. Here, by an argument we mean the relationship between statements e and p, representing that when e is found to be true, there is a justification to conclude that p is true. It has been shown that $\mathcal{RES}$, in a defined sense, can represent all the information in a probability distribution, belief function, or possibility distribution and can reflect many reasoning patterns[1, 2].

The $\mathcal{RES}$ system as presented has a serious problem in that it doesn't have a built-in way to scale up. In $\mathcal{RES}$, the two statements in an argument $\langle e, p \rangle$, *i.e.* e and p, are required to belong to separated first order logics. Conclusions reached cannot be used as evidence to trigger further reasoning. In this paper, we try to remedy this fault of $\mathcal{RES}$ by applying the Z^+ mechanism [5]. The arguments will be treated as rules as in Z^+, but instead of associating integers with rules, preferences among rules will be represented as a relation, called the *base relation*. A procedure will be proposed which can form the relative strengths of the rules given the base relation and can produce a relation on the models of the language with respect to the relative strengths of the rules which are falsified in these models (subject to the same consistency condition). In this way, we extend the reasoning capability of $\mathcal{RES}$.

In the following section, the presentation of Z^+ formalism in [5] is parallelled but in relative terms. We define some important terms and present the two procedures mentioned above. The resulting system will also be denoted as $\mathcal{RES}$. Examples are presented showing that $\mathcal{RES}$ can display similar reasoning processes as Z^+ in many cases. In section 3, $\mathcal{RES}$ is compared to Z^+ showing that they are not completely the same and in some situations $\mathcal{RES}$ can display reasoning processes more defensible than these displayed by Z^+. $\mathcal{RES}$ is also compared to the stratified ranking system, showing that $\mathcal{RES}$ shares some limitations with Z^+. In the last section, the conclusions are summarized.

2 Relative Rule Strength and Plausible Conclusions

As with Z^+, we consider a set of rules $\Delta = \psi_i \rightarrow \phi_i$ where ψ_i and ϕ_i are propositional formulas over a finite alphabet of literals, "$\rightarrow$" denotes a new connective. But different from Z^+, the preferences of such rules are represented as a relation. That is, we have a relation S over Δ (denoted as "$\leq$"). These relations are required to be reflexive and transitive and are called *base relations*.

Following the terms with Z^+, we will call a truth valuation of the literals in the language *a model*. For a formula ψ of the language, M is said to be *a model for ψ*, denoted as $M \models \psi$, iff ψ is true in M. A model M is said to *verify* a rule $\psi \rightarrow \phi$ if $M \models \psi \wedge \phi$, to *falsify* $\psi \rightarrow \phi$ if $M \models \psi \wedge \neg\phi$, and to *satisfy* $\psi \rightarrow \phi$ if $M \models \psi \supset \phi$. A rule $\psi \rightarrow \phi$ is *tolerated* by Δ iff there exists a model M such that M verifies $\psi \rightarrow \phi$ and satisfies all the rules in Δ.

With these terms, the formalism Z^+ can be presented using relative terms. One should notice the parallel between the following presentation with that of Z^+ in [5].

Definition 1 A relation R on the models of the language is called a priority relation if it is reflexive and transitive.

Such a relation is supposed to have the same role as that of the ranking in Z^+. That is, $M_1 \preceq M_2$ is to be read as M_1 is no more abnormal than M_2[1].

---

[1]The reverse of the relation, representing normality, might be more intuitive and more consistent with the term priority relation[4]. We use this direction so the following presentation can be in parallel with that of Z^+.

In the following, we will also use $M_1 \prec M_2$ to denote $(M_1 \preceq M_2) \wedge (M_2 \not\preceq M_1)$ and other notations conventionally.

Definition 2 *A model M^+ for ψ is said to be* a minimal model for ψ *under priority relation R^+ iff there is no model M for ψ such that $M \prec M^+$.*

A priority relation R on models of the language is said to be admissible with regard to a default set Δ *iff for every rule $\psi_i \rightarrow \phi_i$, if M_+^+ is a minimal model for $\psi_i \wedge \phi_i$ and M_-^+ is a minimal model for $\psi_i \wedge \neg\phi_i$, then $M_+^+ \prec M_-^+$.*

The minimal priority relation admissible to Δ will be denoted as R_0^+.

Notice that the base relation, which carries the preference information among the rules, is not used in the definition above. In fact, the minimal priority relation defined above is composed of the preference relationships which are derivable from the specificity considerations on the rules[10].

From the definition, we can define a set of defaults to be *consistent* if it admits at least one priority relation. A theorem similar to **Theorem 1** in [5] can be reached. This is actually very easily seen, as **Theorem 1** in [5] has established that whether a set of default rules is consistent is completely independent of the strengths of the rules.

But we need to incorporate a base relation S into a priority relation when S is not empty. To do this, we need to define the relative strengths of rules first.

Definition 3 *Let R_0^+ be the minimal admissible priority relation of Δ and let S be a base relation on Δ. A relation S^+ on Δ is called* the relative strengths *derived from Δ and S provided that for any two rules r_i and r_j, $r_i \geq r_j \in S^+$ (meaning r_j is no stronger than r_i) iff*

1. *for every minimal model M_2 falsifying r_j, and every model M_1 falsifying r_i, $M_2 < M_1$; or*

2. *we can have neither $r_i \geq r_j \in S^+$ nor $r_j \geq r_i \in S^+$ from the step above and $r_i \geq r_j \in S$.*

The definition specifies that the relative strength is reached by first adding the relationships which are derivable from the specificity considerations. After that, relationships from the base relation are added if the two rules in those relationships are not comparable so far. If these two rules have become comparable already from specificity considerations, their relationships from S, if existing, will be blocked and not be reflected in S^+.

A priority relation on models reflecting both Δ and S can be defined as follows:

Definition 4 *The priority relation R^+ of Δ and S, denoted as "$\preceq$", is a relation on models in which $M_1 \preceq M_2$ iff*

- M_1 *doesn't falsify any rule; or*
- *for any rule r_i which is falsified by M_1, there exists a rule r_j which is falsified by M_2 such that $r_j \geq r_i \in S^+$. That is, for any rule falsified by M_1, there exists a stronger rule which is falsified by M_2.*

Obviously, $R^+ \supseteq R_0^+$. We can also define a consequence relation using R^+.

Definition 5 *A formula ϕ is called* a plausible conclusion *of ψ, denoted as $\psi \vdash \phi$, iff ϕ is true in all minimal models for ψ.*

The similarity between absolute strength and relative strength doesn't stop here. Similar procedures can be devised for constructing the priority relation and for testing whether a pair of formulae belongs to the consequence relation with regard to a set of default rules and a base relation. These procedures are presented below:

Procedure RS

Input: A consistent set Δ of default rules. A base relation S on Δ.

Output: The priority relation on models and the relative strength relation S^+ on Δ.

Part I

1. Let RZ^+ be an empty set, Δ_1 be Δ, and S_0^+ be an empty relation on Δ.

2. While $RZ^+ \neq \Delta$ do:
   (a) Let Δ_0 be the set of rules tolerated by Δ_1 and $RZ^+ = RZ^+ \cup \Delta_0$.
   (b) $S_0^+ := S_0^+ \cup \{r_i > r_j | r_i \in \Delta_0, r_j \in RZ^+$, there exists at least one model M which verifies r_i and falsifies r_j, and there doesn't exist any other model M' which verifies r_i and falsifies only part of those rules falsified by M.$\}$.
   (c) $\Delta_1 := \Delta_1 - \Delta_0$.

3. Let S_t^+ be the transitive closure of S_0^+.

Part II

1. S^+ is a relation on Δ such that for any rules $r_i, r_j \in \Delta$, $r_i \geq r_j \in S$ iff
   - $r_i \geq r_j \in S_t^+$; or
   - $r_i \geq r_j \notin S_t^+, r_j \geq r_i \notin S_t^+$, and $r_i \geq r_j \in S$.

2. R^+ can be calculated as shown in Definition 4.

Procedure PC

Input: A consistent set Δ, the relation R^+ from Δ, and a pair of consistent formulas ψ and ϕ.

Output: Answer YES/NO/AMBIGUOUS depending on whether $\psi \vdash \phi$, $\psi \vdash \neg\phi$, or neither.

1. If Δ is empty, then RETURN(AMBIGUOUS)[2].

2. TEST1 whether there is a model M such that $M \models \psi \wedge \phi$ and M satisfies Δ.

3. TEST2 whether there is a model M such that $M \models \psi \wedge \neg\phi$ and M satisfies Δ.

4. CASES on the results of TEST1 and TEST2:
   - IF TEST1=Yes and TEST2=No then RETURN($\psi \vdash \phi$).
   - IF TEST1=No and TEST2=Yes then RETURN($\psi \vdash \neg\phi$).
   - IF TEST1=Yes and TEST2=Yes then RETURN(AMBIGUOUS).
   - IF TEST1=No and TEST2=No then let MIN be the set of all minimal rules with respect to R^+. Set Δ to be $\Delta - MIN$ and go back to step 1.

Example 1 *Flying birds.*

Let $\Delta = \{b \rightarrow f, p \rightarrow \neg f, p \rightarrow b\}$ and S be an arbitrary relation on Δ. The rules in Δ stands for the "birds fly", "penguins don't", and "penguins are birds" respectively.

As $b \rightarrow f$ is tolerated by Δ but $p \rightarrow b$ and $p \rightarrow \neg f$ are tolerated only by $\Delta - (b \rightarrow f)$, from part I of the RS procedure we reach that $S_t^+ = \{p \rightarrow \neg f > b \rightarrow f, p \rightarrow b > b \rightarrow f\}$.

When we are asked whether $p \vdash f$ or $p \vdash \neg f$ is in the consequence relation, the first round of the PC procedure will produce "No" answers for both tests. This will lead to the removing of rule $b \rightarrow f$ as it is the weakest. The second round will then

---

[2] This test is actually necessary even for Z^+.

return with the answer $p \vdash \neg f$. It should be noticed that the answer $p \wedge b \vdash \neg f$ could be reached in the same manner.

It should be noticed also that it is the specificity considerations embodied in the RS procedure which renders minimal models falsifying the rule $b \rightarrow f$ to be preferred to minimal models falsifying rule $p \rightarrow b$ and/or $p \rightarrow \neg f$. In this example, the base relation S can be anything (including the empty relation) and the result would not change as the relationships in S will be blocked anyway.

In the following, an example is presented in which the base relation matters.

Example 2 *The Nixon diamond.*

Let $\Delta = \{q \rightarrow p, r \rightarrow \neg p\}$ where the rules are read as "Quakers are pacifists" and "Republicans are not pacifists". The part I of the procedure RS will find that both rules are tolerated by Δ and will produce an empty relation for S_t^+. Part II of the procedure will then make S^+ to be the same as S, the base relation which is the input.

If we know an individual to be either a Republican or a Quakers but not both, the result is obvious. In the case of the "Nixon-diamond" where Nixon is both a Republican and a Quakers, what conclusion should we make?

Now the base relation S can be one of the four cases depending on which rule is preferred.

1. $S = \phi$. That is, we have no knowledge as to which rule is stronger (which might be an honest representation of somebody's knowledge of this matter.) For the first round, the PC procedure will produce "No" answers for both tests and make Δ empty as both rules are minimal. After that, the answer "AMBIQUOUS" will be returned.

2. $S = \{r \rightarrow p \geq q \rightarrow \neg p\}$. This time, models violating $r \rightarrow p$ is preferred to those violating $q \rightarrow \neg p$ which makes $r \wedge q \vdash p$ the returned answer.

3. $S = \{q \rightarrow \neg p \geq r \rightarrow p\}$. The relationship is reversed from the above case, so is the answer.

4. $S = \{r \rightarrow p \geq q \rightarrow \neg p, q \rightarrow \neg p \geq r \rightarrow p\}$. The relationships in both directions are presented. This is a verbose way to say that the two rules are of the same strength. The process of the first case is then repeated which produces the answer "AMBIGUOUS".

4 Relative vs. Absolute

The difference between the relative method and the method using integers is that, for the relative method, the resulting relation on both rules and models can be partial. The integer method always displays a universal relation. That is, using integers will render every pair of rules or models comparable.

This might not always be an advantage. For a simple example, case 1 of example 2 cannot be represented honestly, even though the result and the reasoning process of case 1 is identical to those of case 4.

There are situations where adhering to numbers will cause some problems which are more serious. In Example 3, we show that the Z^+ ranking will change the relationship between rules in an undesirable way. In Example 4, we show that the fact that integers are comparable universally will block some intuitive reasoning.

Example 3 *English speaking.*

Let $\Delta = \{r_1 : c \rightarrow e, r_2 : q \rightarrow \neg e, r_3 : q \rightarrow c, r_4 : le \rightarrow e\}$ be the set of default rules and let the integer strengths of these rules be $\delta_1, \delta_2, \delta_3, \delta_4$ respectively, where δ_i are non negative integers. Rules in Δ stand for "Canadians speak English", "Quebecois don't speak English", "Quebecois are Canadians", and "People who learnt English speak English" respectively. It can be noticed that this default set is isomophic to the "Flying Birds" problem except for the last rule.

Figure 1: Relationships of relevant models

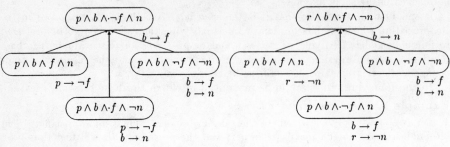

Suppose that we are querying a person who is a Quebacois and who learnt English. What should be our conclusion? The Z^+ ranking of the rules will be computed to be $\delta_1, \delta_1 + \delta_2 + 1, \delta_1 + \delta_3 + 1$ and δ_4 respectively. As $q \wedge le \wedge c \wedge e$ will violate r_2 and $q \wedge le \wedge c \wedge \neg e$ will violate r_4, the result will be dependent on whether $\delta_1 + \delta_2 + 1$ is larger than, smaller than, or equal to δ_4. For example, if we set $\delta_3 = \delta_4 = 2$ and $\delta_1 = \delta_2 = 1$ (for good reasons), the answer will be that this person does not speak English.

However, this conclusion can hardly be justified. Recall that it is the specificity considerations which have increased the ranks of r_2 and r_3 and this specificity should, obviously, have nothing to do with r_4. But now the conclusion is reached by overruling r_4 with those considerations, even though we are told that r_4 is firmer than r_2 at the outset. This is surprising as removing rule r_1 will reverse the answer!

It should be noticed that this kind of reasoning is not justifiable by referring back to probabilistic reasoning on which the Z^+ system is based. In fact, no matter what δ_i is, this set of rules embodies a conflict in probabilistic assertions. Asserting infinitesimal probabilities to all the rules will lead to the conclusion that $q \wedge le$ is impossible.

Using $\mathcal{RES}$, the procedure will not affect the relationship between r_2 and r_4 and thus the result will be decided depending on the input relationship between r_2 and r_4. We can justify conclusions like this very simply as follows: Because there are minimal models which violate only one of these rules, the conclusion should be made by considering which rule is preferred.

This line of reasoning is reflected faithfully in the RS procedure. Here, part I enforces the specificity by changing only the relationships between r_1 and r_2, r_3 and keeps the relationship between r_2 and r_4 untouched.

Example 4 *Flying birds and nesting ones.*

Let $\Delta = \{b \rightarrow f, p \rightarrow \neg f, p \rightarrow b, b \rightarrow n, r \rightarrow \neg n, r \rightarrow b\}$ and S be an empty relation.

In this example, another set of rules asserting a bird property and its exception is added to the rules of Example 1. The additional rules stand for "Birds nest", "Robins don't" and "Robins are birds".

This doubling of rules shows a good feature of the relative strength system. It will produce the relationships between models as shown in Figure 1. In those models, either $p \wedge b$ or $r \wedge b$ is true. In the figure, an arrow will lead from one model to another if the later model is more normal than the former and the rules below a model are those violated in the model.

These relationships are suitable for the relative strength system to display desirable reasoning processes. For example, we have $f \wedge n$ given b, $\neg f \wedge n$ given $p \wedge b$, $f \wedge \neg n$ given $r \wedge b$, and $\neg f \wedge \neg n$ given $p \wedge r \wedge b$.

This extended set of rules, as already noticed in [5], will cause problems for the Z^+ formalism of default strengths. By arranging the integers assigned to those rules carefully, we can have either "penguins nest" or "robins fly". But no matter what integers are assigned to those rules, we cannot have both at the same time.

To see how this happens, we need to consider the two dashed links in Figure 1. To have "penguins nest" we need the dashed link on the left part. The only way to do this with integer strengths is to make the integer assigned to $b \rightarrow n$ greater than that to $b \rightarrow f$.

Symmetrically, to have that "robins fly" will need to assign a bigger integer to $b \rightarrow n$ than to $b \rightarrow f$.

We can do neither (make them equal), either (one bigger than another), but not both.

The analysis has made it obvious that this problem is caused by the fact that all integers are comparable universally. This fact will make the model which violates both $b \rightarrow f$ and $b \rightarrow n$ to be equally minimal as it is one model which violates only one of these two rules. Using relative strengths of rules overcomes this problem. Models violating both rules are set to be more abnormal than models violating only one of these rules, no matter which rule it is. This is done by keeping the two rules *not* comparable.

In the following example, we show that $\mathcal{RES}$ also shares some limitations with Z^+.

Example 5 *(Dead battery) [6])*

The rule set is $\Delta = \{tk \rightarrow cs, tk \wedge bd \rightarrow \neg cs, lo \rightarrow bd\}$ encodes the information that "Typically if I turn the ignition key the car starts", "Typically if I turn the ignition key and the battery is dead the car will not start", and "Typically if I leave the head lights on all night the battery is dead". The relation on the defaults is empty. That is, there is no knowledge concerning the strength of the rules.

For this example, $\mathcal{RES}$ system falls short just as Z^+ does. The problem is that the desirable conclusion "$lo \wedge tk \vdash \neg cs$" cannot be reached. This is because both the Z^+ ranking procedure and the RS procedure embody only the specificity considerations, and there are no reasons from specificity considerations to prefer $lo \rightarrow bd$ to $tk \rightarrow cs$.

To reach the desired conclusion, other considerations are needed. In [6], another kind of ranking, called stratified ranking, is described. Stratified ranking, among other things, embodies the considerations of the direction of causal relationships. Using stratified ranking, the situation presented in this example can be elegantly handled.

Stratified ranking, on the other hand, has problems of its own. As it adheres to the probabilistic ϵ-semantics more closely than Z^+, it cannot incorporate some rule preferences.

5 Conclusions

In this paper, we have shown that the same consistency condition of defaults in Z^+ can be applied to the $\mathcal{RES}$ system where preferences among rules are represented as a relation among those rules. Similar procedures have been devised so that the relation representing the relative strengths of rules and the priority relation on models can be computed and queries concerning the consequence relation can be answered, as with system Z^+.

However, $\mathcal{RES}$ is not completely the same as Z^+ and can display some good features which are lacking in Z^+. We have shown that there are problems with Z^+: Ranks are calculated which might change relationships between rules in an undesirable way; The fact that integers are universally comparable might exclude some desirable reasoning processes. Both problems are solved very simply in $\mathcal{RES}$.

$\mathcal{RES}$ also shares some limitations with Z^+. It falls short in some common sense reasoning situations such as those where the direction of causal relationships is important.

It will be interesting to see how other common sense reasoning considerations can be incorporated with relative strengths. For example,

- Comparing $\mathcal{RES}$ to studies on preferential relations and reasoning based on them[7, 9];

- Extending the concept of argument in $\mathcal{RES}$ to be composed of a set of rules instead of only one. As an argument is directed by definition, this might provide a way to incorporate the causal relation considerations.

Acknowledgement
We would like to thank Professor Pearl at UCLA for his directions.

References

[1] Z. An, D. Bell, and J. Hughes. $\mathcal{RES}$—a relation based method for evidential reasoning. In *Proc. 8th Conf. on Uncertainty in AI*, pages 1–8, 1992.

[2] Z. An, D. Bell, and J. Hughes. Relation based evidential reasoning. *Int. J. on Approximate Reasoning*, accepted, in preparation.

[3] P. P. Bonissone et al. Uncertainty and incompleteness: Breaking the symmetry of defeasible reasoning. In M.Henrion, R.D.Shachter, L.N.Kanal, and J.F.Lemmer, editors, *Uncertainty in Artificial Intelligence*, volume 5, pages 67–85. 1990.

[4] C. Boutilier. What is a default priority? In *Proc. CCAI 1992*, pages 140–147, 1992.

[5] M. Goldszmidt and J. Pearl. System-Z^+: A formalism for reasoning with variable-strength defaults. In *Proc. AAAI-91*, 1991.

[6] M. Goldszmidt and J. Pearl. Rank-based systems: A simple approach to belief revision, belief update, and reasoning about evidence and actions. In *Proc. Conf. Knowledge Representation*, 1992.

[7] B. Grosof. Generalizing prioritization. In J. Allen, J. Fikes, and E. Sandewall, editors, *Principles of Knowledge Representation: Proc. of the 2nd. Int. Conf.* Morgan-Kauffmann, 1991.

[8] J. Y. Halpern and M. O. Rabin. A logic to reason about likelihood. *Artificial Intelligence*, 32:379–405, 1987.

[9] S. Kraus, D. Lehmann, and M. Magidor. Nonmonotonic reasoning, preferential models and cumulative logics. *Artificial Intelligence*, 44:167–207, 1990.

[10] H. Kyburg Jr. The reference class. *Philosophy of Science*, pages 374–97, 1983.

[11] V. Lifschitz. Circumscriptive theories: a logic-based framework for knowledge representation. *Journal of Philosophical Logic*, 17:391–441, 1988.

[12] J. Pearl. *Probabilistic Reasoning in Intelligent Systems: Networks for Plausible Inference*. Kaufman, 1988.

[13] G. Shafer. *A Mathematical Theory of Evidence*. Princeton University Press, 1976.

A Semantics for Open Normal Defaults via a Modified Preferential Approach[*]

Franz Baader[1] and Karl Schlechta[2]

[1] Lehr- und Forschungsgebiet Theoretische Informatik, RWTH Aachen,
Ahornstraße 55, D-52074 Aachen, baader@informatik.rwth-aachen.de
[2] Université de Provence, Case G, 3, Place Victor Hugo, F-13331 Marseille Cedex 3,
ks@gyptis.univ-mrs.fr

Abstract. We present a new approach for handling open normal defaults that makes it possible
1. to derive existentially quantified formulae from other existentially quantified formulae by default,
2. to derive universally quantified formulae by default, and
3. to treat cardinality formulae analogously to other formulae.
Differing from previous approaches that do not satisfy all these properties, we will not view open defaults as schemata for certain instantiated defaults. Instead they will be used to define a preference relation on models. In modification of the usual approaches to preferential semantics we shall consider limits instead of minimal models.

1 Introduction

In many cases, default information expresses properties of ("almost all") individuals of a given class. Thus "Birds normally can fly" speaks about a default property of the class of all birds, and not about the individual bird Tweety. On the technical level, in Reiter's Default Logic [11], this means that most of the "naturally" occurring defaults are so-called *open defaults*, i.e., default rules with free variables. On the other hand, Reiter's definition of an extension—which describes the semantics of a default theory—makes sense only if considered for closed defaults.

To bridge this gap, Reiter assumes that open defaults stand for all their ground instances. The aim is to apply defaults not only to individuals that are explicitly given by ground terms, but also to those implicitly present because of the theory. Therefore, Reiter proposes to Skolemize the world description (i.e., the facts one starts with) and the consequents of defaults before building ground instances. Unfortunately, it turns out that the Skolemization step has the very unpleasant effect that the consequences of a default theory may depend on the *syntactic* form of the world description one starts with (see [1] and the full paper [3] for examples).

[*] This work was done while both authors were at the German Research Center for AI (DFKI), Saarbrücken, and was supported by BMFT grant ITW-9201.

Another problem of Reiter's treatment of open defaults has been pointed out by Lifschitz [8]. If one does not assume that all individuals of the universe are named by ground terms, one cannot deduce universally quantified formulae by default. To overcome this problem, Lifschitz proposes a modification of default logic in which free variables are not treated as metavariables for ground terms. In principle, he considers models of different cardinality separately, and fixes the universe for a given cardinality. Then he introduces new object constants representing all elements of the universe, and instantiates the defaults with these new constants. Since the new constants are assumed to represent *all* elements of the universe, one can now deduce some universally quantified formulae by default. However, this way of proceeding also has some strange effects: since models of different cardinalities are considered separately, formulae concerning the cardinality of the universe are treated differently from other formulae. In addition, defaults with prerequisites are not handled in the same way as defaults without, and the problem of applying defaults to implicit individuals is not solved either. A detailed discussion of the problems of Reiter's and Lifschitz's approach can be found in the full paper [3].

In the following we propose a new treatment of open defaults that tries to avoid these problems. We restrict our attention to normal defaults, i.e., defaults where the justification and the consequent are identical. Open normal defaults will not be instantiated by ground terms or new object constants, but will be used to define a preference relation on the models of the world description. To move to a "better" (or preferred) model we sometimes have to change the cardinality of the universe of the model, which means that we do not consider models of different cardinality separately. Unlike the usual approaches to preferential semantics we cannot always take the *best* models to construct our semantics. The reason is that we may get infinite chains of models that become better and better. Instead of dismissing such a chain because it contains no optimal model we will consider something like the limit (i.e., end segments) of the chain.

The definition of this new approach is given in Section 2, and illustrated by examples in Section 3. In Section 4 we point out that the nonmonotonic consequence operator we get has "nice" proof-theoretic properties such as cumulativity.

2   A Semantics for Open Normal Defaults

We consider normal defaults in the sense of Reiter, i.e., default rules of the form $\alpha : \beta/\beta$, where α, β are first-order formulae. Such a rule is called "open" if α or β contain free variables.

The restriction to normal defaults is justified by the fact that these are the most natural types of default rules. The main reason for using non-normal defaults is that they can sometimes encode priorities between (otherwise normal) defaults [12]. As pointed out by Brewka [5], it is preferable to treat priorities directly (see, e.g., [4, 2]), and not by an ad hoc encoding. In the present paper we do not take priorities between open defaults into account. This will be a subject of further research.

The aim of the modified preferential semantics presented below is to overcome the problems of previous approaches pointed out above, i.e., it should be able to

1. derive existentially quantified formulae from other existentially quantified formulae by default,
2. derive universally quantified formulae by default, and
3. treat cardinality formulae analogously to other formulae.

Approaches that instantiate defaults by new object constants or ground terms, without Skolemizing existential quantifiers, are problematic with respect to the first requirement. For this reason we shall not consider defaults as schemata for certain instantiated defaults. Instead they will be used to define a preference relation on the models of the world description. Intuitively speaking, a model M_2 will be better than M_1 with respect to a given default d if M_2 contains "less counterexamples" to d than M_1. To satisfy the third requirement from above, we cannot assume that the models we compare have the same universe. Since we are not interested in set-theoretic niceties, we shall frequently talk about sets of models even though these will most probably only be classes.

Before we can give a formal definition of the preference relation, we have to introduce some notation. An open normal default $d = \alpha : \beta/\beta$ will be written as $\alpha(\underline{x}) : \beta(\underline{x})/\beta(\underline{x})$, where the tuple $\underline{x} = (x_1, \ldots, x_n)$ consists of the free variables occurring in α, β. Now let $\underline{x} = (x_1, \ldots, x_n)$ be a tuple of variables, and let ϕ be a formula having some of these variables as its free variables. Assume that M is a model with universe $\mathcal{U}_M$, and ν is a valuation that replaces the x_i by the elements u_i of $\mathcal{U}_M$. We say that $\phi(u_1, \ldots, u_n)$ holds in M iff $\nu(\phi)$ is true in M.

Definition 1 (positive and negative examples). Let $(\mathcal{W}, \mathcal{D})$ be a default theory, and let $d = \alpha(\underline{x}) : \beta(\underline{x})/\beta(\underline{x}) \in \mathcal{D}$ be an open default containing n free variables. For a model M of $\mathcal{W}$ with universe $\mathcal{U}_M$, a tuple $\underline{u} \in \mathcal{U}_M^n$ is a *positive example* for d in M iff $\alpha(\underline{u})$ and $\beta(\underline{u})$ both hold in M. It is a *negative example* for d in M iff $\alpha(\underline{u})$ holds in M, but $\beta(\underline{u})$ does not hold in M.

To move to a preferred model we require that we do not lose any positive example, and that at least one negative example is changed into a positive one. In addition, we disallow the introduction of new negative examples since changing one negative example into a positive one while introducing a lot of new negative examples would not capture the intuition behind the notion of a preferred model

Definition 2 (d-preferred models). Let $(\mathcal{W}, \mathcal{D})$ be a default theory, d be a default in $\mathcal{D}$, and M_1, M_2 be models of $\mathcal{W}$. We say that M_2 is *d-preferred* to M_1 $(M_1 \succ_d M_2)$ iff the following conditions hold:

1. The set of positive examples for d in M_1 is a subset of the set of positive examples for d in M_2.
2. At least one negative example for d in M_1 is positive for d in M_2.

3. M_2 does not contain new negative examples for d.

The fact that one may first apply a default d_1, then a default d_2, etc., is captured by going from a model M_1 of $\mathcal{W}$ to a d_1-preferred model M_2, from there to a d_2-preferred model M_3, etc.

Definition 3 (preferred models). For a default theory $(\mathcal{W}, \mathcal{D})$, the preference relation $\succ$ between models of $\mathcal{W}$ is defined to be the transitive closure of the union of all relations $\succ_d$ for $d \in \mathcal{D}$. As usual, the reflexive closure of $\succ$ is denoted by $\succeq$.

In general, this preference relation will not be antisymmetric, and even if it is antisymmetric there may be infinitely decreasing chains. Thus there may exist models of $\mathcal{W}$ that are not above a minimal model, and it may even be the case that there are no minimal models.

The usual treatment of preference relations (see, e.g., [14, 7]) is to consider just the minimal models. In Section 3 we shall give an example that demonstrates that this is not the adequate way to treat our preference relation. For this reason we shall now define a modified preferential semantics.

Definition 4 (dense sets). Let $>$ be a transitive relation on a set $\mathcal{S}$, and let $\geq$ denote its reflexive closure. Let $\mathcal{A}$ be a subset of $\mathcal{S}$.

1. $\mathcal{A}$ is $>$-*complete* in $\mathcal{S}$ iff for all $s \in \mathcal{S}$ there exists $a \in \mathcal{A}$ such that $s \geq a$.
2. $\mathcal{A}$ is $>$-*closed* in $\mathcal{S}$ iff for all $a \in \mathcal{A}$ and $s \in \mathcal{S}$, $a > s$ implies $s \in \mathcal{A}$.
3. $\mathcal{A}$ is $>$-*dense* in $\mathcal{S}$ iff it is both $>$-complete and $>$-closed in $\mathcal{S}$.

If it is clear from the context we will often omit the prefix $>$.

The rôle of minimal models in normal preferential semantics is now taken over by dense sets ("limits").

Definition 5 (modified preferential semantics). Let $(\mathcal{W}, \mathcal{D})$ be a normal default theory, and let $\succ$ be the preference relation on models of $\mathcal{W}$ defined by this theory. We say that a closed formula ϕ is a *default consequence* of $(\mathcal{W}, \mathcal{D})$ iff there is a $\succ$-dense set in the set of all models of $\mathcal{W}$ such that ϕ is true in all elements of this dense set.

If every model of $\mathcal{W}$ lies above some minimal model[2] then the set of minimal models is dense. Moreover, any dense set must contain all minimal models. This shows that in this case our modified preferential semantics coincides with the usual approach of taking minimal models.

The definition of a preferential semantics based on dense sets makes sure that the nonmonotonic consequence relation has nice proof-theoretic properties (see Section 4). But before considering these abstract properties we shall give concrete examples that motivate the way our preferential semantics was defined.

---

[2] This property is called smooth in [7] or stoppered in [10].

3 Examples

In the following, P, Q will always be unary predicate symbols, and x, y variable symbols. The first example demonstrates that, as in Lifschitz's approach, one can derive universally quantified formulae by default.

Example 1 (universally quantified formulae by default).

defaults: $d = \ : P(x)/P(x)$.
world description: empty.

A model where all elements of the universe are in P is minimal with respect to $\succ_d$ because it contains no negative examples. In addition, any model where $\neg P$ is not empty can be modified to a d-preferred model where all elements of the universe are in P. Thus the set of minimal models is dense, and any dense set must contain all minimal models. Obviously, the formula $\forall x.\ P(x)$ holds in all minimal models. □

If the world description implies that there is a counterexample for the default, one can no longer derive that all elements are in P. But as in Lifschitz's approach one can deduce that all elements different from the counterexample are in P.

Example 2 (at least one counterexample).

defaults: $d = \ : P(x)/P(x)$.
world description: $\exists x.\ \neg P(x)$.

First, one can show that models where all but one element of the universe are in P are $\succ_d$-minimal models (see [3] for details). Second, it is easy to see that any model where $\neg P$ has more than one element can be modified to a d-preferred model with exactly one element in $\neg P$. Finally, the formula $\exists x.\ (\neg P(x) \wedge \forall y.\ (x \neq y \to P(y)))$ holds in all minimal models. □

This example demonstrates why the third condition in the definition of d-preference is necessary. Assume that d-preference was defined just using the first and the second condition. Then one could move from a model having exactly one element in $\neg P$ to a better one by first putting this one element into P, and then augmenting the universe by a new element that is put into $\neg P$. It is easy to see that this way one would deduce by default all formulae saying that the universe contains at least n elements (for each cardinality n).

While these formulae are no desirable default consequences in the above example, one should like to deduce them (for finite cardinalities) in the next example: If the world description implies the existence of infinitely many elements of $\neg P$, a default that says that normally all elements are in P should allow one to derive that P is also infinite.

Example 3 (infinitely many counterexample).

defaults: $d = \ : P(x)/P(x)$.

world description: For each finite cardinality n a formula saying that $\neg P$ contains at least n elements.

For all finite cardinalities n, the formula saying that P has at least n elements is a default consequence of this theory. To prove this it suffices to show that the set of all models of the world description for which P is infinite is a dense set (see [3] for details). □

In the above example, no model can be minimal with respect to $\succ_d$. Since any model of the world description must contain infinitely many negative examples, one can always change one of these to a positive example, thus obtaining a d-preferred model. Thus a minimal-model approach would not be appropriate. The next example demonstrates that, unlike Lifschitz's approach, ours is able to deduce existentially quantified formulae by default.

Example 4 (existentially quantified formulae by default).

defaults: $d = P(x) : Q(x)/Q(x)$.
world description: $\exists x.\ P(x)$.

By an argument very similar to the one used in Example 1 one can show that $\forall x.\ (P(x) \to Q(x))$ is a consequence of this theory. Together with $\exists x.\ P(x)$ this yields $\exists x.\ Q(x)$ as a default consequence. □

In the presence of a counterexample, e.g., if the world description consists of the formula $\exists x.\ (P(x) \land \neg Q(x))$, one can still deduce an appropriate universally quantified formula, namely

$$\exists x.\ (P(x) \land \neg Q(x) \land \forall y.\ (x \neq y \to (P(y) \to Q(y)))).$$

But the existential formula $\exists x.\ Q(x)$ can no longer be obtained. This is reasonable since P could have just one element, which then must be in $\neg Q$. However, if the world description contains an additional formula saying that P has more than one element, we again get $\exists x.\ Q(x)$.

It should be noted that in Example 4 one would get the same result if the formula $\exists x.\ P(x)$ was replaced by $P(b)$ for a constant b. In particular, in the presence of a counterexample, one would not conclude $Q(b)$ because b could be this counterexample. This shows that our approach does not assume that named individuals (i.e., individuals described by ground terms) are more normal than other individuals. This assumption is, however, made by approaches that instantiate defaults with ground terms.

In [3] it is also demonstrated that our approach is sceptical (i.e, from contradictory defaults we do not draw default conclusions), and that—unlike Lifschitz's approach—ours does not treat cardinality formulae differently from other types of formulae.

4 Proof-Theoretic Properties

The modified preferential approach we have presented in Section 2 satisfies most of the proof-theoretic properties considered by Gabbay [6], Makinson [9], and Kraus, Lehmann and Magidor [7]. It should be noted that this does not really depend on the specific preference relation $\succ$ defined in Section 2, but on the way the relation is used to define the semantics. The properties are usually formulated as rules for a nonmonotonic consequence relation $\vdash\!\!\!\sim$.

Definition 6. Assume that we have a fixed set $\mathcal{D}$ of default rules. For closed formulae α, β, the expression $\alpha \vdash\!\!\!\sim \beta$ means that β is a consequence of the default theory $(\mathcal{D}, \{\alpha\})$.

Theorem 7. *The nonmonotonic consequence relation defined in Section 2 satisfies the properties "Right Weakening," "Reflexivity," "And," "Or," "Left Logical Equivalence," and "Cautious Monotony," and thus also "Cumulativity."*

See [7] for the definitions of these properties and [3] for the proof of the theorem.

The next example demonstrates that "Rational Monotony" is not always satisfied (as was to be expected).

Example 5. We consider the fixed set of defaults $\mathcal{D} = \{\ : P(x)/P(x)\}$. The closed formulae α, β, γ are defined as

$$\alpha \equiv \exists x.\ \neg P(x)$$
$$\beta \equiv \exists x.\ (\neg P(x) \wedge \forall y.\ (x \neq y \rightarrow P(y))),$$
$$\gamma \equiv \forall x.\ \neg P(x).$$

We have seen in Example 2 that β is a consequence of the default theory $(\mathcal{D}, \{\alpha\})$. Thus we know that $\alpha \vdash\!\!\!\sim \beta$. In addition, the argument in Example 2 shows that $\neg\gamma$ is not a default consequence of $(\mathcal{D}, \{\alpha\})$, i.e., $\alpha \not\vdash\!\!\!\sim \neg\gamma$.

However, β is not a consequence of the theory $(\mathcal{D}, \{\alpha \wedge \gamma\})$, i.e., $\alpha \wedge \gamma \vdash\!\!\!\sim \beta$ does not hold. Obviously, models of γ cannot contain positive examples for the default $d = \ : P(x)/P(x)$. For this reason we know that the preference relation $\succ_d$ is empty on the set of all models of $\alpha \wedge \gamma$. This implies that the set of all models of $\alpha \wedge \gamma$ is the only dense set. But β does not hold in all models of $\alpha \wedge \gamma$. $\qquad\qquad\square$

5 Conclusion

In the approach for handling open normal defaults presented in this paper the defaults of a given default theory induce a preference relation $\succ$ between models of its world description. We have shown by examples that this avoids some of the drawbacks of approaches that view open defaults as schemata for certain instantiations.

Differing from the usual preferential approaches, our nonmonotonic consequence relation is not defined with reference to $\succ$-minimal models. Instead we have introduced the notion of $\succ$-dense sets. In Section 4 it was shown that, because of this modified preferential approach, our nonmonotonic consequence relation has most of the "nice" proof-theoretic properties mentioned by Gabbay [6], Makinson [9], and Kraus, Lehmann and Magidor [7].

In the present paper, we did not take priorities among defaults into account. A possible solution to this problem could be to restrict the preference relation $\succ_d$ for a default d in the following way: If d' is of higher priority than d then going from a model M_1 to a d-preferred model M_2 must not delete positive examples or introduce new negative examples for d'.

References

1. F. Baader and B. Hollunder. Embedding defaults into terminological knowledge representation formalisms. In *Proceedings of the 3rd International Conference on Knowledge Representation and Reasoning*, Cambridge, Mass., 1992.

2. F. Baader and B. Hollunder. How to prefer more specific defaults in terminological default logic. To appear in *Proceedings of the IJCAI'93*, Chambery, France, 1993.

3. F. Baader and K. Schlechta. A semantics for open normal defaults via a modified preferential approach. Research Report RR-93-13, DFKI Saarbrücken, 1993.

4. G. Brewka. Preferred subtheories: An extended logical framework for default reasoning. In *Proceedings of the IJCAI'89*, pages 1043–1048, Detroit, Mich., 1989.

5. G. Brewka. *Nonmonotonic Reasoning: Logical Foundations of Commonsense*. Cambridge University Press, Cambridge, 1991.

6. D. Gabbay. Theoretical foundations for non-monotonic reasoning in expert systems. In K.R. Apt, editor, *Proceedings of the NATO Advanced Studies Institute on Logics and Models of Concurrent Systems*, pages 439–457, La Colle-sur-Loup, France, Springer Verlag, 1985.

7. S. Kraus, D. Lehmann, and M. Magidor. Nonmonotonic reasoning, preferential models and cumulative logics. *Artificial Intelligence*, 44(1-2):137–207, 1990.

8. V. Lifschitz. On open defaults. In *Proceedings of the Symposium on Computational Logics*, Brüssel, Belgium, 1990.

9. D. Makinson. General theory of cumulative inferences. In M. Reinfrank, J. de Kleer, M.L. Ginsberg, editors, *Proceedings of the Second International Workshop on Non-Monotonic Reasoning*, pages 1–18, Springer Verlag, Berlin, 1989.

10. D. Makinson. General patterns in nonmonotonic reasoning. To appear in D. Gabbay and C. Hogger, editors, *Handbook of Logic in Artificial Intelligence and Logic Programming*, vol. II: Nonmonotonic and Uncertain Reasoning, Oxford.

11. R. Reiter. A logic for default reasoning. *Artificial Intelligence*, 13(1-2):81–132, 1980.

12. R. Reiter and G. Criscuolo. On interacting defaults. In *Proceedings of the IJCAI'81*, 1981.

13. K. Schlechta. Some results on classical preferential models. To appear in *J. of Logic and Computation*, 2(6), 1992.

14. Y. Shoham. Nonmonotonic logics: Meaning and utility. In *Proceedings of the IJCAI'87*, pages 388–393, Milan, Italy, 1987.

Possibilistic Logic: From nonmonotonicity to Logic Programming

Salem Benferhat, Didier Dubois, Henri Prade

I.R.I.T. (Univ. P. Sabatier) 118, route de Narbonne
Toulouse 31062 Cédex France
email: {Benferha, Dubois, Prade}@irit.fr

Abstract: Links between preferential semantics of possibilistic logic, semantics of prioritized circumscription, and one of the semantics used in logic programming, namely the perfect model semantics of stratified logic programs, are presented.

1. Introduction

The relationship between logic programming and nonmonotonic reasoning has been discussed in several papers, e.g. Przymusinski [1988]. Besides, the connection between nonmonotonic logic and possibilistic logic [Dubois et al., 1993] has been laid bare, and more recently a natural way to represent default rules in the framework of possibilistic logic has been proposed in [Benferhat et al., 1992]. It has been shown that possibilistic logic can easily encode Pearl[1990]'s System Z. Besides, possibilistic logic programming has been outlined [Dubois et al., 1991].

In this paper, we give the connection between possibilistic logic and the perfect model semantics for stratified logic programs proposed by [Przymusinski, 1988]. In the same paper, it has been shown that this declarative semantics is equivalent to four of the most important approaches to nonmonotonic reasoning, namely: circumscription, default logic, autoepistemic logic and closed world assumption. Of course, since most of the developments of possibilistic logic have been done in the propositional case, we restrict ourselves to propositional logic programs. Let us point out that our approach to study the expressiveness of possibilistic logic in the context of logic programming is very similar to the one used in [Bidoit and Froidevaux, 1987] with default logic.

The paper is organized as follows. Section 2 recalls the main ideas underlying possibilistic logic. Section 3 restates how to represent default rules in the framework of possibilistic logic. Section 4 goes one step further on the connection between nonmonotonic reasoning and possibilistic logic by exploring the relationship between possibilistic logic and circumscription. Section 5 shows that perfect models can be encoded in the framework of possibilistic logic. Section 6 provides an illustrative and comparative example.

2. Possibilistic Logic

In this paper we only consider a fragment of possibilistic logic called Necessity-valued possibilistic logic, and we focus our interest on its semantics. See [Dubois et al., 1993] for a complete exposition of possibilistic logic. In possibilistic logic, a knowledge base Σ is organized in several layers $\Sigma = B_1 \cup \ldots \cup B_n$, such that all the formulas in B_i have the same level of priority or certainty and are more reliable than the ones in B_j where $j > i$. This ordering is modelled by attaching a weight $\alpha \in (0,1]$ to each formula with the convention that $(\phi\ \alpha_i) \in B_i$, $\forall i$ and $\alpha_1 = 1 > \alpha_2 > ... > \alpha_n > 0$. The α_i's are interpreted as lower bounds of necessity measures [Dubois et al., 1993]; this gives birth to the semantics recalled here.

The priorities used in a knowledge base induces a complete ordering on the set of classical interpretations Ω encoded by a so-called possibility distribution. Formally, a possibility distribution π is a function from Ω to the interval $[0,1]$. A possibility distribution π is said to be normalized if there exists an interpretation ω such that $\pi(\omega)=1$. This corresponds to the consistency of the prioritized knowledge base Σ. The possibility distribution π associated with Σ can be computed from the prioritized knowledge base, by associating with each interpretation ω, the value 1 minus the highest ranked formula of $\Sigma = B_1 \cup ... \cup B_n$ falsified by ω, namely:

$$\forall \omega \in \Omega, \quad \pi(\omega) = 1 - \max\{\alpha_i / \ (\phi\ \alpha_i) \in \Sigma \ \ \omega \models \neg\phi\}$$

Given a possibility distribution π, a ranking of the formulas can be defined in terms of a possibility measure Π, as follows:

$$\Pi(\phi) = \max\{\pi(\omega), \ \omega \models \phi\}$$

Now, let us introduce the notion of a consequence relation using the notion of a preferential entailment in the sense of Shoham [1988]. Let Σ be a prioritized knowledge base and let π be its associated possibility distribution.

Def. 1: An interpretation ω is *preferred* to interpretation ω' iff $\pi(\omega) > \pi(\omega')$.

Def. 2: An interpretation ω is a *possibilistic preferential model* of Σ if $\pi(\omega) > 0$ and there is no interpretation preferred to ω.

We denote the set of the preferential models of Σ by $\text{Pref}_\pi(\Sigma)$. A preferential model ω of Σ is not necessarily a classical model of Σ, indeed we may have Σ inconsistent and $\text{Pref}_\pi(\Sigma)$ not empty. Of course, each classical model of Σ is also a possibilistic preferential model of Σ, and in the case where Σ is consistent, $\text{Pref}_\pi(\Sigma)$ coincides with the set of classical models of Σ. In the consistency case, we have $\text{Pref}_\pi(\Sigma) = \{\omega \in \Omega, \pi(\omega) = 1\}$. It must be noticed that the set $\text{Pref}_\pi(\Sigma)$ can be empty, and we then say that the knowledge base $\Sigma = B_1 \cup ... \cup B_n$ is totally inconsistent, which means that B_1 is inconsistent.

Def. 3: A formula ϕ is a *possibilistic consequence* of Σ, denoted $\Sigma \models_\pi \phi$, iff $\text{Pref}_\pi(\Sigma)$ is not empty and each possibilistic preferential model of Σ entails ϕ.

Consequence relation between formulas can also be defined (e.g. [Dubois et al., 1993]). First, we give the notion of the preferred model of a formula:

Def.4: An interpretation ω is the *possibilistic preferential model* of a formula ϕ iff (i) $\omega \models \phi$, (ii) $\pi(\omega) > 0$, (iii) if $\omega' \models \phi$ then $\pi(\omega) \geq \pi(\omega')$.

Def. 5: A formula ψ is *π-entailed by a formula* ϕ wrt the knowledge base Σ, denoted by $\phi \models_\pi \psi$, iff $\Pi(\phi) > 0$ and each possibilistic preferential model of ϕ also satisfies ψ.

The next section summarizes the properties of $\models_\pi$ and recalls how to represent default rules in the framework of possibilistic logic (see [Benferhat et al., 1992] for details).

3. Representing default rules in possibilistic logic

Possibilistic entailment is a nonmonotonic inference relation (e.g. [Dubois et al., 1993]). It has also be shown in [Benferhat et al., 1992] that the $\models_\pi$ satisfies most of the properties proposed in [Kraus et al., 1990] and [Gärdenfors and Makinson, 1992] for nonmonotonic consequence relations. Namely, the following properties: Cut, (left) Or and Cautious Monotony, Left Logical Equivalence, Right Weakening, (right) And and Rational Monotony are satisfied by π-entailment. However, only a restricted form of Reflexivity is satisfied (if $p \neq \bot$, $p \models_\pi p$), and π-entailment only satisfies the restricted form of Supraclassicality (if $p \neq \bot$, then $p \models q$ implies $p \models_\pi q$). But, a Nihil ex Absurdo (NA) property defined as: $\neg(\bot \models_\pi p)$ is satisfied by $\models_\pi$, which means that rather to deduce everything from inconsistent premises we deduce nothing. It must be noticed that even without full Supraclassicality and Reflexivity, a representation theorem for nonmonotonic inference similar to the one presented in [Gärdenfors and Makinson, 1992] holds [Benferhat et al., 1992]. This is not surprising, indeed we have:

Prop. 1: Let Σ be a consistent prioritized knowledge base, and let $\vdash_C$ be a comparative expectation inference relation [Gärdenfors and Makinson, 1992] where the stratification represents an expectation ordering. Let ϕ be a given formula and Σ' a new knowledge base constructed by putting ϕ in a higher and new layer, namely $\Sigma' = \{\{\phi\}, \Sigma\}$. Then,

$$\text{If } \phi \neq \bot \text{ then } \phi \vdash_C \psi \text{ iff } \phi \models_\pi \psi$$

In this framework, a default rule "generally ϕ is ψ" is simply interpreted by "the best models satisfying ϕ must also satisfy ψ". Namely, if $R = \{\phi_i \rightarrow \psi_i\}$ is a set of default rules, then we construct a set of constraints:

$$C = \{\text{Max}\{\pi(\omega), \omega \models \phi_i \wedge \psi_i\} > \text{Max}\{\pi(\omega), \omega \models \phi_i \wedge \neg\psi_i\}\}$$

In general, C induces only a partial ordering on the set Ω of interpretations. In possibilistic logic, the minimum specificity principle (which is at the basis of the semantics) gives us a way to complete a partial ordering. The idea is to assign to each interpretation the highest possible possibility value with respect to constraints in C. We have [Benferhat et al., 1992]:

Prop. 2: Let π be the possibility distribution built from the partial ordering given by C and the minimum specificity principle. Then the π-entailment is equivalent to the 1-entailment described in System Z [Pearl, 1990].

4. Prioritized circumscription and possibilistic semantics

Circumscription [McCarthy, 1980,1986] has been one the first approaches proposed to formalize nonmonotonic reasoning. We only consider the propositional case here, and we focus on the semantical aspect of circumscription, but first we need some conventions and notations. Let S be the set of propositional symbols. If ω is an interpretation, then $E_p(\omega)$ denotes the "extension" of p in ω, and is equal to the empty set if ω falsifies p and equal to the set $\{t\}$ if ω satisfies p.

Def. 6: Let Σ be a knowledge base and Z and V two disjoint lists of propositional symbols. A model ω_1 is said to be less than ω_2 iff:
• all propositional symbols of S other than Z and V have the same extensions in ω_1 and ω_2
• The extension of each element of Z in ω_1 is contained in its extension in ω_2.

Then, a model ω is said to be a Circ-model of Σ if there is no model less than ω, and a consequence relation is defined: a formula ϕ is said to be a Circ-consequence of Σ, denoted by $\Sigma \models_{Circ} \phi$, iff each Circ-model of Σ satisfies ϕ. Prop. 3 is useful to establish the connection between prioritized circumscription and possibilistic logic:

Prop. 3: Let Σ be a consistent knowledge base, and let $Z=\{p\}$ the propositional symbol to be circumscribed, and let $V=S-Z$. Let Σ' be a prioritized knowledge base with two layers, the first contains Σ, and the second contains $\neg p$. Then a model ω is a Circ-model of Σ iff it is a possibilistic preferential model of Σ'.
Proof:
• If Σ entails p, each classical model ω of Σ, we have $E_p(\omega)=\{t\}$, and therefore ω is also a Circ-model. Since Σ is consistent and entails p, then Σ' is equivalent to Σ, which means that $\text{Pref}_\pi(\Sigma')$ is identical to the set of classical models of Σ, and thus to the set of Circ-models of Σ.
• If Σ entails $\neg p$, the set of Circ-models is still identical to the set of classical models, and for each ω, $E_p(\omega)$ is empty. Since p contradicts Σ, the knowledge base Σ' again is equivalent to Σ, and then $\text{Pref}_\pi(\Sigma')$ is identical to the set of Circ-models of Σ.
• If Σ neither entails p nor entails $\neg p$, the Circ-models ω of Σ are those for which $E_p(\omega)=\varnothing$. Adding $\neg p$ to Σ means restricting the models of Σ to those which falsifies p, and therefore $\text{Pref}_\pi(\Sigma')$ is identical to the set of Circ-models of Σ. $\square$

The idea in prioritized circumscription [Lifschitz, 1985] is to introduce an ordering among propositional symbols in Z which defines in what order the extensions are to be minimized. Here, we further assume that the ordering is complete and strict, and that $Z= S = \{p_1>...>p_n\}$.
We first select models of Σ which have the extension of p_1 minimized. Then we select the resulting models by choosing the ones minimizing the extensions of p_2, and so on until p_n. The remaining models are called $Circ_{p_1>...>pn}$-models of Σ. Then we have:

Prop. 4: Let $\Sigma_0=\Sigma$. Let $\Sigma_i = (\Sigma_{i-1}, \{\neg p_i\})$ a 2-layer knowledge base with Σ_{i-1} in the first stratum. Then $Circ_{p_1>...>pn}$-models of Σ and $\text{Pref}_\pi(\Sigma_n)$ are identical.

Proof of Prop. 4 is a direct consequence of Prop. 3. This result explains the connection between circumscription and possibilistic logic first suggested in [Dubois et al., 1989], where a possibilistic knowledge base $\{(\phi_i\ \alpha_i)\ i=1,n\}$ is shown to be semantically equivalent to $\{(\phi_i \vee ab_i\ 1)\} \cup \{(\neg ab_i\ \alpha_i)\}$ and where possibilistic entailment comes down to minimize abnormality.

Prop. 4 only gives a connection between possibilistic semantics and a particular case of circumscription where (i) the ordering between propositional symbols is strict and complete, and (ii) all propositional symbols are minimized. Let us first relax the second assumption, namely we do not circumscribe all the propositional symbols S but just a subset Z of it, but letting varying all the rest of propositional symbols (S-Z), then we can show that Prop. 4 is still valid. We can also relax the first assumption to a total pre-order, then Prop. 4 can be generalized by only claiming the existence of a possibilistic knowledge base having the same models as the prioritized circumscription. However its construction is less straightforward.

5. Possibilistic semantics and Perfect models

We only consider a finite propositional language for the sake of simplicity. The kind of logic programs P considered in this paper are of the form:

$$P= \{C \leftarrow A_1,...,A_n, \neg B_1,...,\neg B_m\}$$

where A_i, B_i, C are propositional symbols. A Herbrand model ω of P is represented by a set of propositional symbols, and is said to be minimal if there is no other model which is included in ω. If for each clause in P we have m=0, then P has exactly one minimal Herbrand model [Lloyd, 1987]. If m≠0, then P has several minimal models in general . The idea in [Przymusinski, 1988] is to select some minimal Herbrand models from a given ordering between propositional symbols. The selected models are called the perfect Herbrand models and are defined in the following way:

Def. 7 (Perfect models) : Let P be a propositional logic program, and let < be an ordering between propositional symbols. Let ω and ω' be two models of P. We say that a model ω' is preferred to the model ω, denoted by $\omega' <_p \omega$, if for each propositional symbol A for which $\omega' \models A$ and $\omega \models \neg A$ there is another propositional symbol B<A such that $\omega \models B$ and $\omega' \models \neg B$. A model ω is said to be the perfect model of Σ if there is no models preferable to ω.

The following proposition gives a relationship between the notion of a perfect model and a possibilistic preferential model:

Prop. 5: Let P be a propositional logic program, and let $\{A_1,...,A_n\}$ be an ordering on propositional symbols. Let $\Sigma = \{P, \neg A_1,...,\neg A_n\}$ be a prioritized knowledge base[1]. Then each perfect model of P is also a possibilistic preferential model of Σ. The converse is false.

Proof:
• Recall that the possibilistic preferential models are the classical models of the consistent sub-base $\{P, \neg A_1,...,\neg A_i\}$ where $\{P, \neg A_1,...,\neg A_{i+1}\}$ is inconsistent. Assume that ω is a perfect model of P but is not a possibilistic preferential model of Σ then there exists an element p_j of a stratum j≤i such that $\omega \models p_j$. Let ω' be a possibilistic preferential model of Σ, then we have $\omega' \models \neg p_j$ and $\forall k<j$ we have also $\omega' \models \neg p_k$ therefore $\omega' <_p \omega$ which contradicts the fact that ω is a perfect model of Σ.

---

[1] A_i is a set of propositional symbols with a priority equal to i, and $\neg A_i$ is the set of the negation of propositional symbols having the priority i.

• The converse is false. Indeed, assume that ω and ω' are possibilistic preferential models of Σ, then we have $\forall j \leq i$, $\forall p \in A_j$ $\omega \models \neg p$ and $\omega' \models \neg p$. Assume also that $\forall p \in A_{i+1}$ $\omega \models \neg p$ and $\omega' \models \neg p$. Now suppose that $\forall p \in A_{i+2}$ $\omega \models \neg p$ while there exists an element q of A_{i+2} such that $\omega' \models q$ therefore $\omega <_p \omega'$ and ω' is not a perfect model. $\square$

The previous proposition is not entirely satisfactory, since we want to construct from a propositional program logic P some possibilistic knowledge base Σ such that the perfect models are identical to the set of possibilistic models. For this aim we consider a particular case of ordering relation on propositional symbols.

Prop. 6: Let P a propositional logic program. We assume that the ordering on propositional symbols is complete and strict, namely we have $p_1 < ... < p_n$. Then there exists a prioritized knowledge Σ such that the perfect models of P are the possibilistic preferential models of Σ.

We now recall the definition of stratified logic programs. Let $P = \{C \leftarrow A_1, ..., A_n, \neg B_1, ..., \neg B_m\}$ be a propositional logic program. We define a dependency graph G for the program P [Przymusinski, 1988] as a directed graph whose vertices are the propositional symbols. An edge is drawn from A to B if and only if there exists a clause where B is its head and A is one of its premise, and if the premise is negative then the edge is said to be negative. Once the dependency graph of P is constructed, we define an ordering relation between propositional symbols. A propositional symbol A is said to be better than B, denoted by A<B, if and only if there exists at least one directed path leading from A to B and passing through at least one negative edge. Then a propositional program is said to be stratified if there is no cycle in the dependency graph of P passing through negative edges. There is another definition of a stratified logic program:

Def. 8 [Apt et al., 1988]: A logic program P is said to be stratified, if it is possible to decompose the set of propositional symbols S into k disjoint lists $S_1, ..., S_k$, called strata, such that for each clause of $C \leftarrow A_1, ..., A_n, \neg B_1, ..., \neg B_m$ we have:
- Stratum (Ai) $\leq$ Stratum (C)
- Stratum (Bi)< Stratum (C).

It is clear that there exists programs which are not stratified (and therefore they have no perfect models) (e.g., $P = \{q \leftarrow \neg p, p \leftarrow \neg q\}$).
Prop. 7 shows the equivalence between the perfect models and the possibilistic preferential models *in the case of stratified logic programs*.

Prop. 7: Let P a logic program. If P is stratified then there exists a prioritized knowledge base Σ such that each perfect Herbrand models of P is a possibilistic preferential model of Σ, and the converse is true.
Proof:
The proof is easy since it has been shown in [Bidoit & Froidevaux, 1987] that each stratified logic programs has a unique perfect model. The equivalence between perfect models and possibilistic models for a stratified logic program can be shown by the following algorithm which gives a stratification $S_0 ... S_k S_{k+1}$, such that for each $i \leq k$ the stratum S_i contains exactly one propositional symbol. Let $P = \{C \leftarrow A_1 ... A_n \neg B_1 ... \neg B_m\}$ be a logic program. Let $C = \{B_i < C, A_i \leq C\}$ the

corresponding set of constraints. The following algorithm looks for a strict and total ordering between propositional symbols and gives the stratification $S_0...S_kS_{k+1}$.

- Let i=0, Stop=false
- Repeat a-b until stop
    a• Let p a propositional symbol which does not appear in the right side of any constraint of $\mathcal{C}$,
    b• If p does not exist then stop=true
        else b1• Remove from $\mathcal{C}$ constraint containing p.
        b2• $S_i=\{p\}$, i=i+1;
- S_{k+1}=set of propositional symbols in $\mathcal{C}$ □

6. Illustrative Example:

Let us apply the three formalisms used in this paper to the penguin example. Thus, we consider $\Sigma=\{$"generally, birds fly", "generally, penguins are birds", "all penguins are birds"$\}$. We denote by $\Omega=\{\omega_0: \neg b \wedge \neg f \wedge \neg p, \omega_1: \neg b \wedge \neg f \wedge p, \omega_2: \neg b \wedge f \wedge \neg p, \omega_3: \neg b \wedge f \wedge p, \omega_4: b \wedge \neg f \wedge \neg p, \omega_5: b \wedge \neg f \wedge p, \omega_6: b \wedge f \wedge \neg p, \omega_7: b \wedge f \wedge p\}$ the set of classical interpretations, and p,b,f denote respectively penguins, birds and fly, and we are interested in knowing if penguins fly.

• Possibilistic approach: In the possibilistic logic, the previous knowledge base imposes three constraints to construct the possibility distribution π, namely we have: $\max(\pi(\omega_6),\pi(\omega_7)) > \max(\pi(\omega_4),\pi(\omega_5))$, $\max(\pi(\omega_5),\pi(\omega_1)) > \max(\pi(\omega_3),\pi(\omega_7))$, $\max(\pi(\omega_5),\pi(\omega_7)) > \max(\pi(\omega_1),\pi(\omega_3))$. Using the minimum specificity principle, these constraints induce a unique possibility distribution π, such that $\{\omega_0,\omega_2,\omega_6\}$ are the most possible, $\{\omega_4,\omega_5\}$ are less possible, and $\{\omega_1,\omega_3,\omega_7\}$ are the least possible ones. Using this possibility distribution it is easy to check that birds which are penguins do not fly ($\pi(\omega_5)>\pi(\omega_7)$).

• Perfect models: the knowledge base is encoded in the following logic program $P=\{f \leftarrow \neg ab_1\ b, b \leftarrow p, ab_1 \leftarrow \neg ab_2\ p, p \leftarrow \}$. The ordering < on propositional symbols must satisfy the following constraints: $\{b \leq f, ab_1 < f, p \leq b, p \leq ab_1, ab_2 < ab_1\}$. The logic program is stratified and for example accepts $\{p,ab_2,b\}<\{ab_1\}<\{f\}$ as a stratification. The program P has a unique perfect model $\{p,b,\neg ab_2,ab_1,\neg f\}$, and therefore we deduce that penguins do not fly.

• Prioritized circumscription: we have seen in the two previous formalisms, that the ordering (between interpretations or between propositional symbols) is extracted directly from the *syntax* of the knowledge base, while in the formalism of circumscription the priorities are given by the user. Therefore, in this example the result depends on the priorities introduced by the user, namely if ab_1 is more prioritary than ab_2 then we deduce that penguins fly, if ab_1 and ab_2 have the same priority we deduce nothing, and we deduce penguins do not fly in the last case. However, once the priorities are given, circumscription offers a very powerful framework.

7. Concluding remarks

We have pointed out how the possibilistic semantics can be used in order to rank defaults, according to their specificity, as system Z does, for plausible reasoning purposes. It would be then interesting to compare the ordering thus obtained with the one given by the logic programming stratification when we consider positively headed defaults. Moreover, the possibilistic, or equivalently Z, ordering may be refined either by taking advantage of an explicit ordering as in System Z^+ [Goldzmidt and Pearl, 1991], or by taking into account more constraints (e. g. "all p are not $\neg f$" will be encoded by $\prod(p \wedge f)=0 \Leftrightarrow \forall \omega \models p \wedge f, \pi(\omega)=0$).

Besides, some logic programs have no perfect models. To cope with this problem we may think of adding, to each clause, a number which gives the priority of the clause in the logic program. Different kinds of prioritized logic programs have been proposed; see, e.g., [Subrahmanian, 1989], [Dubois et al., 1991]. Combining the explicit ordering with the one given by the stratification may help us to give a solution to unstratified logic programs. Indeed, if we consider the previous example: $P=\{q \leftarrow \neg p, p \leftarrow \neg q\}$, we have p<q, q<p. Then if we have also the ordering p<q given by the user, then the constraint q<p would be rejected.

References

[Apt et al., 1988] K. Apt, H. Blair, A. Walker, Towards a Theory of Declarative knowledge, in: Foundation of Deductive Databases and Logic Programming, (ed. J. Minker) Morgan Kaufmann, 89-148.

[Benferhat et al, 1992] S. Benferhat , D. Dubois, H. Prade, Representing default rules in possibilistic logic. KR'92 , 673-684.

[Bidoit and Froidevaux, 1987] Minimal subsumes default logic and circumscription in stratified logic programming, In LICS, New-York, 89-97.

[Dubois et al.,1989]D.Dubois,J.Lang, H.Prade. Automated reasoning using possibilistic logic: semantics, belief revision, and variable certainty weights. UIA'89, 81-87.

[Dubois et al., 1991] D. Dubois, J. Lang, H. Prade. Towards possibilistic logic programming. ICLP'91, 581-595.

[Dubois et al., 1993] D. Dubois, J. Lang, H. Prade. "Possibilistic logic". To appear in Handbook of Logic for Artificial Intelligence (D.M. Gabbay, ed.), vol. 3, 439-513.

[Gärdenfors and Makinson, 1992]. Non-monotonic inference based on expectations. Artificial Intelligence, to appear.

[Goldszmidt and Pearl 1991]. System-Z^+: a formalism for reasoning with variable-strength defaults. AAAI-91, 399-404.

[Kraus et al., 1990]S. Kraus, D. Lehmann, M. Magidor. Non-monotonic reasoning, preferential models and cumulative logics. Artificial Intelligence, 44: 167-207.

[Lifischitz, 1985] Computing Circumscription, IJCAI'85, Los-Angeles.

[Lloyd, 1984]   Foundations of Logic Programming. Springer-Verlag 1984.

[McCarthy, 1980] Circumscription - A form of non-monotonic reasoning. Artificial Intelligence, 13:27-39.

[McCarthy, 1986] Application of circumscription to formalize commonsense reasoning. Artificial Intelligence, 28:89-116.

[Pearl, 1990] System Z: A natural ordering of defaults with tractable applications to default reasoning. TARK'90, 121-135.

[Przymusinski, 1988] On the relationship between Logic programming and Non-monotonic Reasoning. AAAI'88, 444-448.

[Shoham, 1988] Reasoning About Change – Time and Causation from the Standpoint of Artificial Intelligence. Cambridge, Mass.: The MIT Press.

[Subrahmanian, 1989] Mechanical proof procedures for many-valued lattice-based logic programming. Research report, Computer Science Dept., Syracuse Univ., N. Y., USA.

Learning Membership Functions

Francesco BERGADANO
Department of Mathematics
University of Catania
Catania, Italy

Vincenzo CUTELLO
Fuzzy Logic R & D Group
Co.Ri.M.Me.* Research Center
Catania, Italy

Abstract. An efficient method for learning membership functions for fuzzy predicates is presented. Positive and negative examples of one class are given together with a system of classification rules. The learned membership functions can be used for the fuzzy predicates occurring in the given rules to classify further examples. We show that the obtained classification is approximately correct with high probability. This justifies the obtained fuzzy sets within one particular classification problem, instead of relying on a subjective meaning of fuzzy predicates as normally done by a domain expert.

1 Introduction and preliminaries

In his seminal paper [12] L. Zadeh introduced fuzzy sets assuming well given membership functions, with the understanding that the degrees of membership define the meaning of linguistic terms. Subsequently, many researchers have worked on problems related to the measurement and acquisition of fuzzy membership functions (see [9] for an excellent survey on this research work).

The goal of our investigation is to introduce a theoretical framework for acquiring membership functions which are *probably, approximately correct* in the sense of Valiant [10] and targeted to some specific high level and non-fuzzy classification problem. As such, the present work also addresses the problem of learning classification rules from examples [6]. Valiant's framework makes this problem more precise by requiring (1) that the learned classification system is approximately correct with high probability and (2) that the induction procedure is polynomial. For performance-sensitive applications, such strong requirements are appropriate. However, only very simple classifiers are learnable in this sense [4, 7, 8]. Here, we take a less ambitious, but more practical view: we assume that a system of classification rules is given, but require the induction system to learn the membership functions of the fuzzy predicates occurring in that system. We will show that this can be done in polynomial time while making the classification system predictive; a more extensive description with all the

---

*Consorzio per la Ricerca sulla Microelettronica nel Mezzogiorno, Universitá di Catania and SGS-Thomson

needed details is found in [1].

To clarify the above consider the following examples.

Example 1.1 Suppose we are given a classification system for the concept of *well functioning car*.

Such a concept is intuitively fuzzy. However, for all practical purposes we want to have a criterion that can always be applied when we want to decide whether the car needs some repairing or not.

One possible and simple criterion can be the following

(c1) If the engine temperature is high and the car speed is medium-high then the car is NOT well functioning; or

(c2) if the oil level is low then the car is NOT well functioning.

The above criterion can be formalized as follows:

$$High(Eng\_temp(x)) \wedge Med\_High(Speed(x)) \rightarrow NWF(x)$$
$$Low(Oil\_lev(x)) \rightarrow NWF(x)$$

where, $High, Med\_High, Low$ are fuzzy predicates with some obvious intended meaning. □

Example 1.2 Suppose now we are concerned with the well-functioning of an air conditioning system. In this case we may have the following criterion:

(c1) If the temperature is high and the temperature decreasing is small then the system is NOT well functioning; or

(c2) if the temperature is low and the temperature increasing is small then the system is NOT well functioning; or

(c3) if the temperature is medium and the temperature decreasing is big then the system is NOT well functioning; or

(c3) if the temperature is medium and the temperature increasing is big then the system is NOT well functioning:

$$High(t(x)) \wedge small - (\Delta t(x)) \rightarrow NWF(x)$$
$$Low(t(x)) \wedge small + (\Delta t(x)) \rightarrow NWF(x)$$
$$Medium(t(x)) \wedge big - (\Delta t(x)) \rightarrow NWF(x)$$
$$Medium(t(x)) \wedge big + (\Delta t(x)) \rightarrow NWF(x)$$

where, $t(x)$ is the temperature, $High, Low, Medium, small+, small-, big+$ and $big-$ are fuzzy predicates and $\Delta t(x)$ represent the temperature variation. □

Clearly, the truth values for such fuzzy predicates depend heavily upon the semantic of the system. For instance, for a temperature of 40 degree centigrades, $High(40)$ has a very low value in example 1.1, whereas it has a big value in example 1.2.

In both examples, we have a non-fuzzy classification predicate NWF and fuzzy classification rules. The values of the antecedents of the rules are computed using the min-max semantics. For each disjunct the minimum truth value is computed and then the maximum of all these values, α, is taken. Depending on such a value α we have a $(0-1)$-value for NWF.

We introduce a threshold value θ, which will be called *security parameter*, so that

- if $\alpha \geq \theta$ then $NWF(x) = 1$;

- if $\alpha < \theta$ then $NWF(x) = 0$.

As we mentioned above, we want to learn membership functions for the systems in the two examples according to the Valiant approach (Probably Approximate Correct learning or PAC-learning). Therefore, we suppose that we are given a set of positive and negative examples for NWF and we want to be able to say that with high probability we will produce membership functions so that the classification systems obtained will make mistakes with very low probability.

2   Problem Setting

Let $\mathcal{C}$ be a given concept class over a universe $\mathcal{U}$. Therefore, $\mathcal{C}$ is a collection of $(0-1)$-valued unary predicates. Each element of $\mathcal{U}$ is a k-uple of real numbers whose intented meaning is to characterize specific subparts of the system under study. Let $C \in \mathcal{C}$ and suppose a system S_m of classification rules for C is given in the following form:

$$
\begin{aligned}
Q_1^1(p_{Q_1^1}(x)) \quad &\wedge \cdots \wedge Q_{n_1}^1(p_{Q_{n_1}^1}(x)) \to C(x) \\
\cdots \qquad &\cdots \qquad\qquad \cdots \\
Q_1^m(p_{Q_1^m}(x)) \quad &\wedge \cdots \wedge Q_{n_m}^m(p_{Q_{n_m}^m}(x)) \to C(x)
\end{aligned}
\tag{2.1}
$$

where

- the predicates Q_i^j are taken from a set $\mathcal{P}=\{Q_1, ..., Q_n\}$ of given unary predicates;

- for all Q_j, p_{Q_j} is a projection function that returns the parameter which is of significance for Q_j.

- for every component k, the predicates $Q_1, ..., Q_{m_k}$ corresponding to k (i.e. such that p_{Q_i} returns the value of the k-th component) define a linguistic hierarchy [13].

Notice that

- it is possible that the same predicate occurs in different rules.

- Concerning linguistic hierarchies we have that the membership functions must be ordered in the following sense: if $j > i$ then for every $0 \leq \alpha \leq 1$ we have $\{x|Q_i(x) > \alpha\} \prec \{x|Q_j(x) > \alpha\}$, where $\prec$ is a suitably defined order relation.

Therefore we can say that $x \in \mathcal{U}$ is a member of the concept C if and only if the disjunction

$$\bigvee_{j=1}^{m} \bigwedge_{i=1}^{n_j} Q_i^j(p_{Q_i^j}(x))$$

is true. Since we are allowing some predicates in $\mathcal{P}$ to be fuzzy whereas C is not we make the following assumptions:

- A security parameter $0 < \theta < 1$ is given;

- $C(x)$ is true if and only if

$$\bigvee_{j=1}^{m} \bigwedge_{i=1}^{n_j} Q_i^j(p_{Q_i^j}(x)) > \theta$$

and where the truth value above is computed according to the min-max semantic, i.e.

$$\bigvee_{j=1}^{m} \bigwedge_{i=1}^{n_j} Q_i^j(p_{Q_i^j}(x)) = \max_{j=1,\ldots,m} \left(\min_{i=1,\ldots,n_j} (Q_i^j(p_{Q_i^j}(x))) \right).$$

Given a set F=$\{\mu_1, \ldots, \mu_n\}$ of membership functions associated to the predicates in $\mathcal{P}$, the fuzzy classification system (FCS for short) (2.1) will be denoted by S_m^F. The notation S_m will then denote the collection of all possible FCS's S_m^F, which in turn can be characterized as the collection of all sets F of membership functions.

For the time being, we will suppose that the unknown membership functions we are trying to learn are *convex* (see [5], pp. 17). In particular, the above implies that membership functions do not have local maxima. Moreover, concerning the linguistic hierarchies the convexity hypothesis implies that for every predicate Q the set $\{x|Q(x) > \alpha\}$ is an interval of the real line for every α. So, we can suppose that the order relation $\prec$ is the standard order relation on real intervals:

$$[a, b] \prec [c, d] \text{ iff } a \leq b \text{ and } c \leq d.$$

Such FCS's will be called *convex* fuzzy classification systems.

By definition, S_m is connected to a non fuzzy predicate, i.e. non fuzzy concept C. Our goal is to learn the membership functions from positive and negative examples of the concept C.

Again, we stressed the hypothesis that a classification system S_m^F will be used with respect to the fixed threshold value θ. The obtained truth value will be denoted by $S_m^F(x)$. In the end, x is classified as a positive example of C if $S_m^F(x) > \theta$.

For an element x we define $error(S_m^F, x)$ to be true if the obtained classification is wrong, i.e. if $C(x)$ is true and $S_m^F(x) \le \theta$ or $C(x)$ is false and $S_m^F(x) > \theta$.

Given a set E of positive and negative examples of C, drawn from an unknown, but fixed distribution D over the universe $\mathcal{U}$, we define

$$\underline{\text{global errors}} \quad Errors \;=\; \{x \in X \,|\, error(S_m^F, x)\}$$

$$\underline{\text{observed error}} \;\; Err_o \;=\; \frac{|Errors \cap E|}{|E|}$$

$$\underline{\text{expected error}} \;\; Err \;=\; \sum_{x \in Errors} D(x)$$

When learning the unknown membership functions we have two goals:

(1) keeping Err_o low, because we want the rule system to perform well on the given examples. Otherwise we could not expect future classifications to be correct.

(2) guaranteeing that Err is sufficiently close to Err_o, so that observed correct behavior of the system does not turn out to be completely meaningless with respect to future performance.

The next section addresses goal (2) and section 4 describes an algorithm designed to achieve goal (1).

3 PAC-learnability and number of examples

We now give a formal definition of PAC-learnability of a concept class (see, e.g., [2, 3, 8, 11] for more details).

Let $\mathcal{C}$ be a class of concepts over a universe $\mathcal{U}$. Every element $C \in \mathcal{C}$ is therefore a subset of $\mathcal{U}$. Let D be a probability distribution on $\mathcal{U}$.

Given a concept $C \in \mathcal{C}$, for every $\epsilon > 0$ a concept C_1 is an ϵ-approximation of C if

$$\sum_{C(x) \neq C_1(x)} D(x) < \epsilon.$$

DEFINITION 3.1 *Given a concept class $\mathcal{C}$ over a universe $\mathcal{U}$ we say that the class $\mathcal{C}$ is PAC-learnable if and only if there exists an algorithm $\mathcal{A}$ such that for every probability distribution D on $\mathcal{U}$, every $C \in \mathcal{C}$, every $\epsilon, \delta > 0$, with probability at least $1 - \delta$, algorithm $\mathcal{A}$ produces an ϵ-approximation of C in time polynomial on $1/\epsilon, 1/\delta$ and the size of C.* □

Let us now introduce a combinatorial parameter which will provide us with a necessary and sufficient condition for PAC-learnability.

Let $\mathcal{U}$ be a nonempty set and $\mathcal{C}$ be a collection of subsets of $\mathcal{U}$.

DEFINITION 3.2 *Let $U \subseteq S \subseteq \mathcal{U}$. We say that U is selected by C in S if and only if there exists $C \in \mathcal{C}$ such that*

$$U = C \cap S.$$

DEFINITION 3.3 *Let $S \subseteq \mathcal{U}$. We say that S is shattered by $\mathcal{C}$ if and only if for all $U \subseteq S$, U is selected by $\mathcal{C}$ in S.*

We then define the VC dimension of $\mathcal{C}$ as

$$vc(\mathcal{C}) = \max\{|S| : S \text{ is shattered by } \mathcal{C}\}.$$

The above combinatorial notion was introduced in [11].

As proven in [2], the number of examples needed by a consistent PAC-learning algorithm for the concept class $\mathcal{C}$ is bounded by

$$\max(\frac{4}{\epsilon} \ln \frac{2}{\delta}, \frac{8d}{\epsilon} \ln \frac{13}{\epsilon}),$$

where $d = vc(\mathcal{C})$.

Theorem 1 *[1] Let S_m be a class of convex FCS's of type (2.1). Let $C \subseteq \Re^k$. We then have*

$$vc(S_m) < 2m + 1.$$

The following corollary immediately follows from the above theorem and the result in [2].

COROLLARY 3.1 *S_m is PAC-learnable.* ∎

4 A Simple Learning Procedure

The general idea is as follows:

- given ϵ and δ draw at least

$$\max(\frac{4}{\epsilon} \ln \frac{2}{\delta}, \frac{16m}{\epsilon} \ln \frac{13}{\epsilon}),$$

  examples from the distribution D;

- determine the hypercubes of $\Re^k$ where there are positive examples only (the *positive hypercubes*);

- use one rule of S_m to cover each positive hypercube.

We assume that the correct fuzzy classification system S_m^F lies within the hypothesis space S_m, i.e. we want to learn a class of concepts *by* the same class [4, 7]. Moreover, we need to make another, less usual assumption. Every rule of the correct system S_m^F must be represented by some positive example, and separated from the other rules by some negative example. An equivalent way of saying this is that there are exactly m positive hypercubes, if we draw the above given number of examples. This is reasonable, as we may suppose that the classification rule is given by an expert who will not include a rule in S_m if it is totally useless relatively the *world* (i.e. the probability distribution of events) he/she lives in. However, the assumption makes the learning algorithm depend on the example distribution, while our previous bound on the VC-dimension is distribution-free. Designing an algorithm to work efficiently in the general case is a main issue for our future work. We will now give a learning algorithm for convex FCS, that will work if the above assumptions are satisfied.

Learning algorithm
Input: θ, ϵ, δ and $N = \max(\frac{4}{\epsilon} \ln \frac{2}{\delta}, \frac{16m}{\epsilon} \ln \frac{13}{\epsilon})$ examples in $\mathbb{R}^k$;
Output: with probability at least $(1 - \delta)$, membership functions for predicates in S_m which are ϵ-approximations of the unknown ones.

for every component k do

    project the m positive hypercubes on the k-th component,
        obtaining m_k positive intervals $\{[a_1, b_1], ..., [a_{m_k}, b_{m_k}]\}$

    define P_j^k as the trapezoidal fuzzy set $(a_{j-1}, a_j, b_j, b_{j+1})$,
        where $a_0 = a_1$ and $b_{m_k+1} = b_{m_k}$.

define θ so that no negative examples are covered.
end Algorithm.

When projecting the m positive hypercubes on the k-th component, we obtain m_k positive intervals, where the number of predicates in the linguistic hierarchy for the k-th component that occur in S_m is also m_k. This follows from the fact that every rule is represented by some positive example (there are m hypercubes) and the correct classification system belongs to the hypothesis space S_m.

By construction $\theta = 1$ guarantees that no negative examples are covered. Therefore it is possible to lower θ until the above continues to be true.

The algorithm is clearly polynomial, as the number of needed examples is polynomial. The main loop in the algorithm is for every component k and there are at most m hypercubes and therefore at most m positive intervals for every component.

Acknowledgements: This work is supported in part by the EC Esprit BRA Project DRUMS-2.

References

[1] F. Bergadano and V. Cutello. Pac learning of fuzzy systems. *Tech Report, University of Catania*, 1993.

[2] A. Blumer, A. Ehrenfeucht, D. Haussler, and M.K. Warmuth. Learnability and the Vapnik-Chervonenkis dimension. *Journal of ACM*, 36(4):929–965, 1989.

[3] L. Devroye. Automatic pattern recognition: a study of the probability of error. *IEEE Trans. on P.A.M.I.*, 10(4):530–543, 1988.

[4] M.J. Kearns. *The Computational complexity of Machine Learning*. MIT press, 1990.

[5] G.J. Klir and T.A. Folger. *Fuzzy sets, uncertainty and information*. Prentice Hall, Englewood Cliffs, NJ, 1988.

[6] R.S. Michalski. A theory and methodology of Inductive Learning. *Artificial Iintelligence*, 20(3), 1983.

[7] B.K. Natarajan, editor. *Machine Learning. A theoretical approach*. Morgan Kaufmann, 1991.

[8] L. Saitta and F. Bergadano. Error probability and valiant's learning framework. *IEEE Trans. on P.A.M.I.*, 15(1):145–155, 1993.

[9] I.B. Turksen. Measurement of membership functions and their acquisition. *Fuzzy sets and systems*, 40:5–38, 1991.

[10] L. Valiant. A theory of the learnable. *Commmunications of the ACM*, 27(11):1134–1142, 1984.

[11] V. Vapnik and A.Y. Chervonenkis. On the uniform convergence of relative frequencies of events to their probabilities. *Theory of probability and its applications*, 16(2):264–280, 1971.

[12] L.A. Zadeh. Fuzzy sets. *Information and Control*, 8:338–353, 1965.

[13] L.A. Zadeh. The concept of a linguistic variable and its application to approximate reasoning: Part i. *Information Sci.*, 8:199–249, 1975.

The Use of Possibilistic Logic PL1 in a Customizable Tool for the Generation of Production-Rule Based Systems

Guilherme Bittencourt   Maurício Marengoni   Sandra Sandri

Instituto Nacional de Pesquisas Espaciais - INPE
C.P. 515 - São José dos Campos - 12200 - SP - Brazil
Tel.: 55 (123) 41 8977 r. 650 Fax: 55 (123) 21 8743
E-mail: sandri@lac.inpe.br

Abstract. A theoretical framework is proposed, in which possibilistic logic can be uniformly used to treat uncertainty associated with production rules, when knowledge is represented in either logic or frames. This model is being implemented in the uncertainty module of a tool designed to allow the construction of expert system shells.

1 Introduction

The analysis and interpretation of images from different sources - remote sensing satellites, synthetic aperture radars, aerial photos, etc - involve several specialized activities, ranging from almost automatic tasks to highly complex manipulations, usually performed manually or with the help of a variety of computing systems. Some of these tasks can be efficiently performed by rule-based expert systems [1]. The separation of control and knowledge usually present in such systems led naturally to the development of building tools: knowledge representation languages [2, 3], including hybrid representation languages [4, 5] ; and expert system shells [6, 7, 8].

The coding of the domain knowledge into a shell's knowledge representation language is the most important bottleneck in the use of such a technology. Besides the inherent difficulties of extracting the expertise hidden inside expert brains and representing it in an artificial formalism, this expertise, in many cases, is not a sound, complete and coherent body of knowledge, but usually pervaded with noise, uncertainty and inconsistency. To represent this "less than certain" knowledge, it is necessary that, embedded into the knowledge representation language, some uncertainty formalism is available.

From the expert system development point of view, it is important that the adopted uncertainty model be easy to understand by domain experts, in such a way that the informations provided by them correspond as closely as possible to their intuitions. One of such models is the possibilistic framework, in which numerical quantification is used as a way of ordering competing hypothesis. Its main operations are fairly easy to be dealt with from the developer point of view, and its comprehension do not require any special mathematical skills from the average user.

In this paper, we present the initial configuration of the uncertainty management module of a tool designed to allow the construction of customized expert system shells [9]. The tool is capable of handling three knowledge representation formalisms

— logic, frames and semantic nets, and integrates a modular graphical interface with a shell building tool. In this paper we propose an environment where possibilistic logic PL1 can be uniformly used to treat uncertainty associated with production rules and knowledge represented in logic or frames.

2 Tool Architecture

The tool architecture includes two management modules - the tool interface and the shell generator - and three Lisp function package libraries - the kernel, the knowledge acquisition interface, and the expert system interface (see Fig. 1).

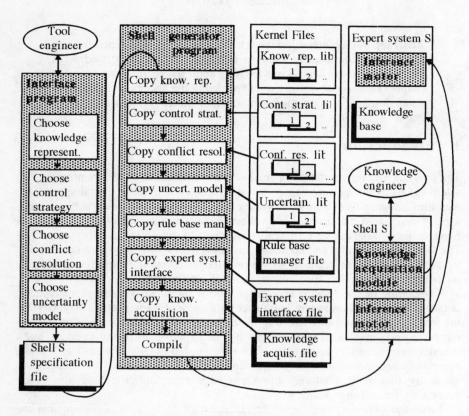

Fig. 1. Tool Architecture

The tool is used as follows. First of all, the tool engineer interacts with the *tool interface*, choosing his shell specifications from menus. He may choose as many knowledge representation models as he wishes, an uncertainty model, a control strategy, and a conflict resolution mechanism. Based on these choices the tool itself specifies the remaining items. These specifications are used by the *shell generator* to select, from the package libraries, the packages containing the functions needed to build an expert system shell satisfying the specifications. These packages are integrated in a stand alone system, which is then optimized in order to eliminate unnecessary tests, and then compiled. Finally, the compiled version of the specified shell and the knowledge acquisition package are used to develop an expert system to solve the intended problem. An expert system created by this shell consists of the inference motor and a knowledge base generated by the interaction between a knowledge engineer and the knowledge acquisition interface shell (see Fig. 1).

3 Knowledge Representation

All the knowledge contained in the knowledge base of an expert system generated by the tool is encoded in rules of the type *if* <expression> *then* <expression>. Each expression is a conjuction of items, each of which may be either a graphical comand or a term representing a piece of knowledge, encoded in a knowledge representation model (logic, frames, etc...). How the terms are classified and interpreted depends on the knowledge representation formalism used and on the control strategy adopted. A typical rule of an image classification expert system can be informally stated as:

If the texture of region x is of type t1 then x is a bear soil region.

In a cycle, if forward-chaining is used, the left hand side of the rule is matched against the facts known to the system and a list of valid substitutions is returned. Each substitution is applied to the right-hand side of the rule, generating a new fact.

Each of the knowledge representation formalisms dealt with in the tool is defined by a formal language, a reasoning mechanism, and an interface between the formalism and the rule bases. In its present version the tool deals with 3 paradigms : logic, frames [11] and semantic nets [12]. In this work we concentrate on the first two paradigms.

The *logical formalism* consists of a collection of independent facts and is thus adequate to domains where the knowledge is largely unstructured. The main drawback of the formalism is the inefficiency of the inference method: automatic deduction. The tool manipulates rules written in both propositional and first-order logic. The facts however can only be propositional or grounded formulae. In this formalism the rule above is represented by :

If (Texture(x, t1)) then (Bear-soil(x)),

where *x* is a variable, *t1* is a constant and *Texture* and *Bear-soil* are predicates.

The *frame formalism* [11] consists of a hierarchy of data structures called frames, composed of a set of slots to which values can be associated. These values can be either any relevant information about the concept represented by the frame, or another frame. Efficient inference mechanisms are integrated into the formalism: inheritance through the frame hierarchy, facets that control the type of value adequate for each slot, default values that can be used when no information is available, procedural attachment to allow the execution of external functions. The formalism is adequate to taxonomically structured domains where the inheritance mechanism can be efficiently explored. Here our rule is represented by :

If (x (texture t1)) then (x (class bear-soil)),

where *x* is a variable to be matched with a frame, *texture* and *class* are slots of *x*, with values *t1* and *bear-soil* respectively.

4 Uncertainty Management

All the pieces of knowledge given to the system, - the rules extracted from experts and the facts forwarded by the user -, may be inherently pervaded with uncertainty. On the other hand, several knowledge representation models may coexist in a single application. The uncertainty models furnished by the tool should then be such as to deal with different knowledge representation models in a uniform manner. Moreover, these models should be of fairly easy comprehension by the average experts, knowledge engineers and expert system users. Possibililistic logic is one of such models.

The only uncertainty model available so far in the tool is based on a special kind of possibilistic logic, called necessity-valued logic [10], or PL1. In this logic, to each first-order formula φ, representing a statement in a knowledge base, we associate a constraint $N(\varphi) \geq \alpha$, where N is a necessity measure (see [13] for a detailed study in possibility theory, and [10] for a survey in possibilistic logic). The constraint $N(\varphi) \geq \alpha$ in PL1 is represented by the pair $(\varphi\ \alpha)$, called a *necessity-valued formula* (nvf). The quantity α is called the *valuation* of formula φ. In necessity-valued logic we make extensive use of the following properties :

$$N(\varphi \vee \neg\varphi) = 1 \qquad ; \text{ if } \varphi \models \psi \text{ then } N(\psi) \geq N(\varphi)$$
$$N(\varphi \wedge \psi) = \min(N(\varphi), N(\psi)) \qquad ; \quad N(\varphi \vee \psi) \geq \max(N(\varphi), N(\psi))$$

In PL1, the *graded modus ponens* [10], introduced in [13], replaces the classical modus ponens rule:

$$(\varphi\ \alpha), (\varphi \rightarrow \psi\ \beta) \vdash (\psi\ \min(\alpha, \beta))$$

where $\rightarrow$ denotes the classical logical implication.

The use of logic PL1 in the rules formalism of the tool is quite straighforward, independently of the knowledge representation model. Let us suppose that we have a set of n facts φ_i, and a rule R = *If φ_1 and φ_2 and ... and φ_n then ψ_1 and ... and ψ_k*, where both the facts and the rule are pervaded with uncertainty, and the φ_i's and the ψ_i's are represented in a given uncertainty model. Let us suppose that for each fact φ_i we have $N(\varphi_i) \geq \alpha_i$. The facts can then represented by n nvf's $(\varphi_i\ \alpha_i)$. Let us suppose that for rule R we have $N(R) \geq \beta$. Rule R stands in fact for k formulae $(\varphi_1 \wedge ... \wedge \varphi_n \rightarrow \psi_i\ \beta)$, $1 \leq i \leq k$, one for each conclusion ψ_i.

Using the n facts referenced in the premise, we obtain a global nvf $(\varphi_1 \wedge ... \wedge \varphi_n\ \alpha)$, where $\alpha = \inf_{1 \leq j \leq n} \alpha_j$. Since these facts match the left hand side of the rules generated from R we obtain as result k nvf's $(\psi_i\ \min(\alpha, \beta))$, $1 \leq i \leq k$. If the use of several rules yields m nvf's $(\psi\ \delta_l)$, $1 \leq l \leq m$, for a given conclusion ψ, the final global nvf relative to ψ will be $(\psi\ \delta)$, where $\delta = \sup_{1 \leq l \leq m} \delta_l$.

In what it refers to facts, the treatment of uncertainty using PL1 yields no problem when the facts are represented in logic. Indeed, we only have to represent each fact by a nvf $(\varphi\ \alpha)$, and build the knowledge base with only the meaningful ones, i.e. those where $\alpha > 0$. In knowledge representation models in which the concept of inheritance is present, such as frames and semantic nets, the treatment of facts is not so simple.

5 Logic PL1 and Frames

We show below how the logic PL1 was used in the frame formalism, in our system. We consider that uncertainty in this formalism has three ways of manifestation.

The first manisfestation of uncertainty to be dealt with is how much we believe in the value attached to a given slot in a given frame. In other words, it concerns how much we believe that an objet has a certain property. For instance, we have to find a way of stating that although all birds are oviparous, not all of them are capable of flying.

Here, we propose to simply attach a pair $(c\ \alpha)$ to a slot s in a frame f, where c is the value of c in f, and α is a valuation in logic PL1. This is represented by the nvf $(\varphi(f,s,c)\ \alpha)$, meaning that there is a necessity of at least α that $\varphi(f,s,c)$ = "the value of slot s of frame f is c" is true. For instance, for the bird problem presented above, we could attach the nvf (oviparous 1) to the slot "reproduction" in frame "bird", and a nvf (True .9) for the slot "flies".

The second manifestation of uncertainty refers to how much we believe that a frame g inherits all the properties of its father frame f, which are not explicitly specified in g itself. In other words, it refers to how much a class is a true sub-class of another one. For instance, when constructing a frame structure concerning elephants, we may not be completely sure that Clyde is really a gray elephant, although it is our best guess. On the other hand, we cannot state that all circus elephants are royal elephants, although most of them are so. Note that these two cases characterize distinct kinds of uncertainty (the first one is more a matter of personal belief, the second one is derived from statistics). Here, however, we give them an uniform treatment.

We deal with the second manifestation of uncertainty by attaching a valuation to each link between two frames. This is done in the following manner. In each frame g with father f, we create a slot s_0 = "father" which represents in fact the link between frames f and g. To slot s_0 in g we then attach the pair $(f\ \alpha)$, where α is the valuation on the link between f and g. Formally, this is represented by the nvf $(\varphi(g,s_0,f)\ \alpha_0)$, meaning that there is a necessity of at least α_0 that $\varphi(g,s_0,f)$ = "frame g inherits the attributs of frame f" is true.

Finally, the third manifestation of uncertainty refers to the rules in the knowledge base. We will see further on that the valuation attached to a rule will influence the valuations in the slots referenced in the conclusion of the rule.

5.1 Search of the Value of a Slot

We now discuss how we obtain the value and valuation concerning a given slot and frame. For that, we need some more notation. Let U be the set of all the frames that exist in a given moment of the processing of an application. Let g be a frame in U. Then

. S(g) is the set of slots in g.
. F(g) is the family of g defined by :
  i) $g \in F(g)$,
  ii) if $h \in F(g)$, and $k \in U$ is the father of h, then $k \in F(g)$.

First of all, let us recall the basic mechanism of inheritance in the frame paradigm, when no uncertainty is involved. A slot s concerning a particular frame f will not be created on a frame g descending from f, unless the user so specifies explicitly. If g does not have slot s, the value for s in g is the same as the value for s in f, i.e. the value in g is "inherited" from f.

When logic PL1 is used in the frame paradigm, three situations are possible, when we search the pair (value valuation) of a slot s on a frame g :

i) s is a slot of g, i.e. $s \in S(g)$.

In this case the system simply yields the pair $(c \; \alpha)$ attached to s in g. For instance, in Figure 2, the system yields the value "forest" and valuation .9 as the answer to the question "what is the type of area-1 ?" .

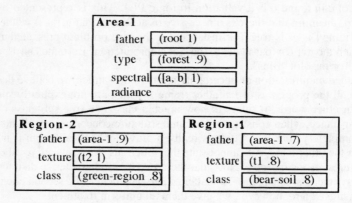

Fig.2. Frames in an image classification application

ii) s is not a slot of g, but s belongs to a frame h in the family of g, i.e. $s \in S(h)$, $h \in F(g)$, $h \neq g$.

Let $(c \; \alpha)$ be the pair attached to s in h. In this case the system yields c as the value, but the valuation will take into account not only α but also all the valuations on the links between g and h, represented by the slot s_0 = "father". Let $(k_{0i} \; \gamma_{0i})$ be the pair attached to slot s_0 in frame i. Formally, the system yields the pair $(c \; min(\alpha, \; \gamma))$, where $\gamma = min_{\; i \in F(g) - F(h)} \; \gamma_{0i}$. For instance, in Figure 2 the system yields the value "forest" and valuation .7 as the answer to the question "what is the type of region-1 ?" .

iii) s is not present in any frame in the family of f. In this case the system disregards the query.

5.2 Creation and Modification of Frames

A frame f can be created before a session of the expert system. In this case, the user determines the nvf's $(c_i \; \alpha_i)$ to be attached to each slot s_i in S(f). The system makes sure that slot s_0, corresponding to the link, is created. It also verifies that all valuations α_i take their values in [0, 1].

Frame f can also be created or modified during run time, by performing the actions contained in the right-hand side of a rule R under execution (here we only consider the case in which inference is done using the forward-chaining mechanism [14]).

The creation of frame f occurs if the right-hand side of rule R contains a clause referencing the (yet inexistant) frame f and slot s_0. Otherwise the system considers the action as a modification of frame : if the slot already exists the new value completely overrides the older one ; otherwise the new slot is simply created with the new value. In either case (creation or modification), the valuation to be attached to a slot is calculated using the valuation from the rule, the specific valuation for the slot (given in the conclusion of the rule) and the valuation calculated for the premise of the rule.

The treatment given to the creation and the modification of a frame f by a rule is uniform. Let R be a rule $R = If\ \varphi_1\ and\ \varphi_2\ and\ ...\ and\ \varphi_n\ then\ \psi_1\ and\ ...\ and\ \psi_k$, where both the φ_i's and the ψ_i's reference slots in frames. Rule R stands in fact for k formulae $(\varphi_1 \wedge ... \wedge\ \varphi_n \rightarrow \psi_i\ \beta)$, $1 \leq i \leq k$, where β is the valuation of rule R (see Section 4). The φ_i's and the ψ_i's are given by clauses of the type (f (s (c α))), where f is a frame, s is a slot, and (c α) the nvf attached to s in f.

Let (c α_i) be the pair (value valuation) given to slot s_i by the right-hand side of R, and δ be the valuation obtained by the system for the left-hand side of R. Then the pair (c min(δ, β, α_i)) will be attached to slot s_i in f.

Note that valuations α_i and β are known to the system before the execution process starts. Therefore, it seems unnecessary to have the rule valuation β, since it could be incorporated directly in the slots valuations. In other words, instead of (c$_i$ δ_i) we could attach (c$_i$ min(δ_i, β)) to slot s in f. We have chosen to keep the rule valuation β in our framework because it can help the conflict resolution module to order the rules. For instance, if in an application we want that a single rule be fired per cycle, we can choose the rule R_k which has the highest valuation min(δ_k, β_k), where δ_k stands for the valuation calculated for the left-hand side of R_k, and β_k stands for the rule valuation of R_k.

As an example of the use of rules, let us suppose that in our base we have a frame "region-1" having the slot "father" with nvf (area-1 .7) and the slot "texture" with nvf (t1 .8). Let $R = If\ (x\ (texture\ t1))\ then\ (x\ (class\ (bear-soil\ .9))$, be a rule in the system with rule valuation $\beta = 1$. Substituting x as "region-1" in rule R yields the nvf (t1 .8) in the left-hand side of the rule. Following the notation given above we have $\beta = 1$, $\delta = .8$, and $\alpha = .9$. The application of the rule will then produce nvf (bear-soil min(.8, 1, .9)), which thus gives nvf (bear-soil .8) as the final result (see Fig. 2).

6 Conclusion

We have presented the first developments of the uncertainty management module of a tool for the generation of expert system shells that is capable of handling different knowledge representation paradigms.

We presented here the way our tool uses logic PL1 to deal with uncertainty in the logical and the frame knowledge representation models. For the future, we also intend to extend the treatment of uncertainty with PL1 to semantic nets. Differently from frame inheritance, semantic nets allows for explicit exception links resulting in much more complex inheritance algorithms.

Logic PL1 is the single uncertainty model provided by the tool so far ; in the future, we intend to enrich the tool with other uncertainty models.

A meteorological radar image interpretation system [15] has been developed using a frame-based expert system shell generated by the tool. Although part of the knowledge base in this application is uncertain in nature, no uncertainty is yet treated. A study on the use of possibilistic logic in this system is underway, and the outlooks are quite promising.

Acknowledgements
This work was partially supported by FAPESP, contract No. 91/3532-2

References

1. Buchanan B.G., Shortliffe E.H., *Rule-Based Expert Systems, the MYCIN Experiments of the Stanford Heuristics Programming Project*. Addison Wesley, 1984.
2. Bobrow D.G., Winograd T., "An Overview of KRL, A Knowledge Representation Language". Cognitive Science, Vol. 1, No. 1, pp. 3-46, 1977.
3. Laurent J.-P., Thome F., Ayel J., Ziebelin D., "KEE, Knowledge Craft et Art: Evaluation comparative de trois outils de développement de systèmes experts". Revue d'Intelligence Artificielle, Vol. 1, No. 2, pp. 25-53, 1987.
4. Bittencourt G. "A Hybrid System Architecture and its Unified Semantics". In Proc. 4th Int. Symp. on Methodologies for Intelligent Systems (Z.W. Ras, ed); North-Holland, pp. 150-157, Charlotte, NC, 1989.
5. Calmet J.; Tjandra O.; Bittencourt G. "MANTRA: A Shell for Hybrid Knowledge Representation". *Proc. 3rd Int. Conf. on Tools for Artif. Intel.*, San José, Ca, 1991.
6. Brownston L., Farrel R., Kanr E., Martin N., *Programming Expert Systems in OPS-5, An Introduction to Rule-Based Programming*. Addison Wesley, Reading, Ma, 1985.
7. Buchanan B.G., Feigenbaum E.A., "DENDRAL and Meta-DENDRAL: Their Applications Dimension". *Artificial Intelligence*, Vol. 11, No. 1-2, pp. 5-24, 1978.
8. Van Melle W., Shortliffe E.H., Buchanan B.G., "EMYCIN A Domain Independent System that Aids in Constructing Knowledge-Based Consultation Programs". In *State of the Art Report on Machine Intelligence*, New York, Pergamon, Infotech, 1981.
9. Bittencourt G., Marengoni M., "A Customizable Tool for the Generation of Production-Based Systems". *Proc. 8th Int. Conf. on Artificial Intelligence in Engineering*, pp. 337-352, Toulouse, France, 1993.
10. Dubois D., Lang J., Prade H., *Possibilistic Logic*. Report IRIT/91-98/R, IRIT, Toulouse, France, 1991.
11. Minsky M., "A Framework to Represent Knowledge". In *The Psychology of Computer Vision*, (P. Winston, ed), McGraw-Hill, pp. 211-277, 1975.
12. Quillian, M.R., "Semantic Memory". In *Semantic Information Processing*, (M.L. Minsky, ed), pp. 216-270, M.I.T. Press, Cambridge, Ma, 1968.
13. Dubois D., Prade H. (with the collaboration of H. Farreny, R. Martin-Clouaire, C. Testemale), *Possibility Theory - An Approach to the Computerized Processing of Uncertainty*. Plenum Press, 1988.
14. Davis R., King J., "An Overview of Production Systems". *Machine Intelligence*, vol 8, pp. 300-332, 1977.
15. Silva, F. de A.T.F. da, "A Hybrid Formalism for Representation and Interpretation of Image Knowledge". *Proc. Int. Soc. for Photogrammetry and Remote Sensing Congress*, Washington, DC, 1992.

Probabilistic Network Construction Using the Minimum Description Length Principle

Remco R. Bouckaert

Department of Computer Science, Utrecht University,
P.O. Box 80.089, 3508 TB Utrecht, The Netherlands,
E-Mail: remco@cs.ruu.nl

Abstract

This paper presents a procedure for the construction of probabilistic networks from a database of observations based on the minimum description length principle. On top of the advantages of the Bayesian approach the minimum description length principle offers the advantage that every probabilistic network structure that represents the same set of independencies gets assigned the same quality. This makes it is very suitable for the order optimization procedure as described in [4]. Preliminary test results show that the algorithm performs comparable to the algorithm based on the Bayesian approach [6].

1 Introduction

Probabilistic networks offer a sound and efficient formalism for representing uncertainty. Efficient algorithms are known for making inferences with knowledge in probabilistic networks [13, 11, 8]. In several domains it have been demonstrated that probabilistic networks are feasible for diagnostic systems [2, 7, 18, 1]. So, probabilistic networks also offer a practical formalism for representing uncertainty.

Constructing probabilistic networks from experts is a time consuming task. Since more and more large databases become available, the automated construction of probabilistic networks from databases is an important issue. Automatic constructed networks may be used to decrease time needed for knowledge elicitation from an expert.

Theory developed so far can be divided into non Bayesian approaches and Bayesian approaches. Non Bayesian approaches [5, 20, 14, 19, 21] rely on treshold values (e.g., p-values). Furthermore, the algorithms that use conditional independence information need a lot of observations to make statistical tests for identifying this kind of independence reliable. No prior probabilities can be assigned to arcs or sets of arcs in these algorithms and they output only one model without quantifying its likelihood with respect to other structures.

Contrary to this, the Bayesian approach [6, 9] flaws these drawbacks. It does not rely on treshold values and returns the probability of a network structure given the database. It is possible to output more than one structure and performs well with few observations. Furthermore, prior probabilities may be assigned to network structures in order to express preference of some network structures above other. In [6] an algorithm based on the Bayesian approach is presented. Later in this paper we will see what the disadvantages of this algorithm are.

In Section 2, we recall some definitions concerning probabilistic networks. In Section 3, the Bayesian approach is presented. In Section 4, we present the minimum description length principle and some of its properties, a recovery algorithm and some preliminary results. We end with conclusions in Section 5.

2 Probabilistic Networks

A *probabilistic network* B is a pair (B_S, B_P) where the *network structure* B_S is a directed acyclic graph (DAG) and B_P is a set of conditional probability tables. Let U be the set of variables considered. For every variable $x \in U$, B_P contains a conditional probability table $P(x|\pi_x)$ that enumerates the probabilities of all values of u given the values of variables in its *parent set* π_u in the DAG. The distribution represented by this network is $\prod_{x \in U} P(x|\pi_x)$ [13].

For a joint probability distribution P over a set of variables U, we call X and Y *conditionally independent* given Z, written $I(X, Z, Y)$, if $P(XY|Z) = P(X|Z)P(Y|Z)$ for all values of the variables in XYZ. $I(X, Z, Y)$ is called an *independency statement*.

In a DAG, a trail is a path that does not considers the direction of the arcs. We can read some independency statements from a DAG using blocked trails and d-separation: A trail in B_S between two nodes x and y is *blocked* by a set of nodes Z if at least one of the following two conditions hold:
• the trail contains a head-to-head node e and $e \notin Z$ and every descendant of e is not in Z.
• there is a node e in the trail with $e \in Z$ and e is not a head-to-head node in the trail.
In a DAG B_S, let X, Y and Z be sets of nodes. We say that X is *d-separated* from Y given Z if every trail between any node $x \in X$ and any node $y \in Y$ is blocked by Z.

If X and Y are d-separated by Z in B_S, then the independency statements $I(X, Z, Y)$ holds in the distribution represented by B_P. A DAG B_S is an *I-map* of the set of independency statements that hold in a distribution P if $<X, Z, Y>$ in B_S implies $I(X, Z, Y)$ holds in P; B_S is a *minimal I-map* if no arc can be removed from B_S without destroying its I-mappedness.

3 Network Construction: The Bayesian Approach

In this paper, we are interested in retrieving a network structure given a database of observations of the variables in U. In the remainder of this paper we assume that the database variables are discrete, cases in the database occur independently given the probabilistic network model, and there are no cases that have variables with missing values. Furthermore, we assume the density function $f(B_P|B_S)$ is uniform, i.e., no probability table is preferred for a given structure before the database has been seen.

The Bayesian approach is based on maximizing the probability of the network structure given that data D, i.e., calculate $\max_{B_S} P(B_S|D)$. In order to compare the quality of two network structures B_{S_1} and B_{S_2} we have to calculate

$$\frac{P(B_{S_1}|D)}{P(B_{S_2}|D)} = \frac{\frac{P(B_{S_1}, D)}{P(D)}}{\frac{P(B_{S_2}|D)}{P(D)}} = \frac{P(B_{S_1}, D)}{P(B_{S_2}, D)}.$$

So, it is sufficient to calculate $P(B_S, D)$, for which Cooper and Herskovits give the following formula.

Theorem 3.1 *(Cooper & Herskovits[6]) Let U be a set of n discrete variables, where a variable x_i in U has r_i value assignments $(v_{i1}, ..., v_{ir_i})$. Let D be a database of N cases, where each case contains a value assignment for each variable in U. Let B_S denote a network structure containing just the variables in U. Each variable x_i in B_S has a set of parents, which we represent by the list π_i. Let w_{ij} denote the jth unique instantiation of π_i relative to D. Suppose there are q_i such unique instantiations of π_i. Define N_{ijk} to be the number of cases in D in which variable x_i has the value v_{ik} and π_i is instantiated as w_{ij}. Let $N_{ij} = \sum_{k=i}^{r_i} N_{ijk}$. It follows that:*

$$P(B_S, D) = P(B_S) \prod_{i=1}^{n} \prod_{j=1}^{q_i} \frac{(r_i - 1)!}{(N_{ij} + r_i - 1)!} \prod_{k=1}^{r_i} N_{ijk}!. \tag{1}$$

With this formula a greedy algorithm K2 (see below) has been formulated that for a given ordering of the nodes calculates the parent set for every node independently. This is done by adding the node to the parent set that maximally improves $P(B_S, D)$ until no node can be added such that $P(B_S, D)$ increases.

Algorithm K2

Let the variables be ordered $x_1 \ldots x_n$, $\forall_{i \in [1..n]} \ \pi_i := \emptyset$
for i:=1 **to** n **do**
    repeat
        $y := \max_y \{P(B_{S_y}, D)/P(B_S, D) \mid y \in \{x_1 \ldots x_{i-1}\} \backslash \pi_i,$
                                    B_S is the structure defined by π_i,
                                    $B_{S_y} = B_S$ where $\pi_i = \pi_i \cup \{y\}\}$
        if $P(B_{S_y}, D)/P(B_S, D) > 1$ **then** $\pi_i := \pi_i \cup \{y\}$
      until $P(B_{S_y}, D)/P(B_S, D) \leq 1$ **or** $\pi_i = U_i$

A drawback of this algorithm is that an ordering on the nodes is required. In [4] an algorithm has been presented for optimizing a node ordering in order to remove arcs. It is based on the independencies represented by the network structure. However, the algorithm in [4] relies on manipulating the ordering and transform networks into other networks that represents the same set of independencies. In order to use this algorithm, it would be nice to have a measure of the quality of a structure that is the same for all network structures that represent the same set of independencies. Unfortunately, this is not the case for the measure of Theorem 3.1.

Consider the database D over the binary variables $U = \{a, b\}$ in Table 1. Let S_1 be the structure $a \to b$ and S_2 be the structure $b \to a$. Both structures represent the same set of independencies (namely none) but $P(P_{S_1}, D) = 6.4 P(P_{S_2}, D)$ if we assume $P(S_1) = P(S_2)$.

4   A Minimum Description Length Approach

Another way to judge the quality of a network structure is by the minimum description length principle [15, 16] which minimizes the complexity of the model and maximizes the fitness. This principle results in the following measure.

a	b
0	0
0	0
0	0
0	1
1	0
1	0
1	1
1	1

$S_1 : a \rightarrow b \quad P(P_{S_1}, D) = P(S_1)\frac{(2-1)!}{(8+2-1)!}4!4!\frac{(2-1)!}{(4+2-1)!}\frac{(2-1)!}{(4+2-1)!}3!1!2!2!$

$S_2 : b \rightarrow a \quad P(P_{S_2}, D) = P(S_2)\frac{(2-1)!}{(8+2-1)!}5!3!\frac{(2-1)!}{(5+2-1)!}\frac{(2-1)!}{(3+2-1)!}3!1!2!2!$

Table 1: A database of observations over two binary variables and two network structures.

Theorem 4.1 *Let U, B_S, D, N, n, r_i, q_i, N_{ijk}, and N_{ij} be as defined in Theorem 3.1. Let $Q(B_S, D)$ be the quality of a network structure for database D defined by*

$$Q(B_S, D) = \log P(B_S) - NH(B_S, D) - \frac{1}{2}k \log N \qquad (2)$$

where $k = \sum_{i=1}^{n} q_i(r_i - 1)$ and $H(B_S, D) = \sum_{i=1}^{n}\sum_{j=1}^{q_i}\sum_{k=1}^{r_i} -\frac{N_{ijk}}{N}\log\frac{N_{ijk}}{N_{ij}}$. Then,

$$\log P(B_S, D) = Q(B_S, D) + O(1)$$

with respect to N.

Detailed proofs of this and the other theorems can be found in [3]. Approaches, like [12, 10], based on information criterea apply the same quality measure as $Q(B_S, D)$ where the $\log N$ term is replaced by another function and the prior on belief network structures is assumed uniform. Formula 2 is interesting because it tells something about the behavior of $P(B_S, D)$. Let's have a closer look at this formula. It consist of three parts.

The first part $\log P(B_S)$ is a term in which prior probabilities on network structures are represented. For example, suggestions by experts about the presence of arcs in a network may be modeled by this term. Also, restrictions on directions of arcs can be represented by $\log P(B_S)$. The latter may be important when an optimal ordering of the nodes is searched for. The term is not part of the original MDL-principle so in a sense $Q(B_S, D)$ is not pure MDL.

The second term $H(B_S, D)$ represents the conditional entropy of a structure. Entropy is a non negative measure of uncertainty which is maximal when uncertainty is maximal (uniform distribution) and zero when there is complete knowledge (no uncertainty). The more information is given the lower the entropy. Therefore, it is clear that adding nodes to a parent set will decrease the entropy term in the formula.

In the third term $\frac{1}{2}k \log N$, k is the number of independent probabilities that have to be estimated for obtaining the probability tables B_P for a given structure B_S. The term represents the error introduced by estimating all these probabilities

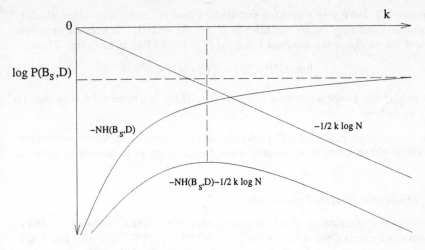

Figure 1: Relation between $\log P(B_S, D)$ and the number of independent probabilities in a probabilistic network

from the database D. This term induces automaticly the principle of Occams razor: network structures with fewer arcs are preferred above probabilistic networks with more arcs that are of equal quality. So, simpler models are preferred above complex ones unless the entropy of the more complex model is much lower than the simpler one. Figure 1 gives an impression of the interaction between the entropy term and the third term when $P(B_S)$ is assumed uniform for all networks structures. This principle gives a natural stopping criterion for heuristics that search for network structures.

Theorem 4.2 *Let D be a database over a set of variables U and B_S be a network structure. Assume $P(B_S)$ is uniform. For every network structure $B_{S'}$ that represent the same set of independencies we have*

$$Q(B_S, D) = Q(B_{S'}, D).$$

This theorem says that every network that represents the same set of independencies has the same quality according to the Formula 2. We saw in Section 3 that this is not true in general for Formula 1. Therefore, this formula has an advantage for applying transformations on the node ordering for network structure construction above the formula of Cooper and Herskovits. Furthermore, it heirs all advantages of the Bayesian approach: it does not depend on treshold values, extra information can be incorporated and likelihood of one model compared to another model is given.

4.1 Asymptotic Properties

Let θ be a total ordering on the variables in U. We say that a network structure B_S obeys the ordering if for every arc $a \to b$ in B_S $\theta(a) < \theta(b)$. For large number of observations we have the following property.

Theorem 4.3 *Let P_D be a positive distribution that generates a database D. Let θ be a complete ordering on the variables in U Let B_S and $B_{S'}$ be network structures obeying θ where B_S is the minimal I-map of P_D. Let $P(B_S)$ be uniform. Then,*

$$\lim_{N \to \infty} Q(B_{S'}, D) - Q(B_S, D) < 0$$

if and only if $B_{S'}$ is not a minimal I-map of P_D. If B'_S is a minimal I-map then the limit goes to zero.

So, the measure proposed will prefer the original network structure overwhelmingly above other network structures when the number of observations grows to infinity.

4.2 Heuristic Search Procedure

As shown in [17] the number of network structures over n nodes can be calculated by the recursive formula $G(0) = 1$, $G(n) = \sum_{i=1}^{n}(-1)^{i+1}\binom{n}{i}2^{i(n-1)}G(n-i)$. For $n = 10$ there are approximately 4.2×10^{18} network structures. So, it is computational not feasible to regard all network structures. Therefore, we assume an ordering on the nodes is given. This leaves only $\sum_{i=2}^{n} 2^{i-1} = 2^n - 2$ structures to be considered. Since, this is still not polynomial we apply the following greedy algorithm that considers only at most $O(n^3)$ different structures. It is a transformation of K2 where the probability of a network structure and a database is replaced by the quality measure of Theorem 4.1 under the assumption that every network structure is equiprobable.

Algorithm K3

Let the variables be ordered $x_1 \ldots x_n$, $\forall_{i \in [1..n]}\ \pi_i := \emptyset$
for i:=1 **to** n **do**
    repeat
        $y := \max_y\{Q(B_{S_y}, D) - Q(B_S, D) \mid y \in \{x_1 \ldots x_{i-1}\}y \backslash \pi_i,$
                           B_S is the structure defined by π_i,
                           $B_{S_y} = B_S$ where $\pi_i = \pi_i \cup \{y\}\}$
        if $Q(B_{S_y}, D) - Q(B_S, D) > 0$ **then** $\pi_i := \pi_i \cup \{y\}$
    until $Q(B_{S_y}, D) - Q(B_S, D) \leq 0$ **or** $\pi_i = U_i$

Since, the terms $Q(B_{S_y}, D)$ and $Q(B_S, D)$, have a lot of terms in common that cancel out in $Q(B_{S_y}, D) - Q(B_S, D)$ the quality of a network compared to one with one arc more can be efficiently calculated.

4.3 Preliminary Results

The algorithm was tested on random generated probabilistic network with binary variables. First, a random network structure without cycles B_S with ten nodes was generated. Then, a set of conditional probability tables consistent with B_S were generated. With this probabilistic network a set of observations was generated and both K2 and K3 were applied to these observations with the same (original) node ordering.

obs.	K2 vs. Original			K3 vs. Original			K3 vs. K2		
	extra	missing	sum	extra	missing	sum	extra	missing	sum
100	2.2	3.3	5.5	0.8	4.7	5.5	0.0	2.8	2.8
200	1.6	2.3	4.9	0.1	2.6	2.7	0.0	1.8	1.8
300	1.4	1.8	3.2	0.3	3.5	3.8	0.0	2.8	2.8
400	1.4	1.9	3.3	0.2	2.7	2.9	0.0	2.0	2.0
500	1.8	1.5	3.3	0.1	2.1	2.3	0.0	2.3	2.3

Table 2: Test results.

In Table 2 the average results over ten trials are presented. The first column represents the number of observations generated. Two network structures are compared by showing the number of arcs that can be found in the first network but not in the other (columns labeled 'extra') and the number of arcs found in the second network but not in the first (columns with 'missing'). The columns 'sum' contain the total of wrong placed arcs (mismatch = extra arcs + missing arcs).

The first three columns show the comparison of the generated network structures and the structures found by K2. The next three show the comparison of generated structures and K3 and the last three columns the comparison of K2 and K3. As could be expected, the number of mismatched arcs decrease when the number of observations increase.

K3 shows a tendency to stop adding arcs earlier than K2 does. This is expressed by the zeros in the two but last column. This could be expected by a close observation in the derivation of the approximation in Theorem 4.1 [3]. The table suggests that K3 performs comparable to K2, so it may be a useful algorithms for network structure recovery. It is not quite clear why the sum of mismatched arcs is less on average for K3 compared with K2.

5 Conclusions

A formula for the quality a network structure given a database based on the minimum description length approach is presented. An algorithm for the recovery of network structures based on this measure is compared with the K2 algorithm that is based on the Bayesian approach. Preliminary test results suggest that these algorithms performs comparable.

The presented formula based on the minimum description length principle heirs all positive properties of the formula presented by Cooper and Herskovits [6] that is based on the Bayesian approach. Furthermore, it assigns the same quality to every network structure that represents the same set of independencies. This makes the approximation very suitable for the node order optimization procedure described in [4].

Acknowledgements

I want to thank the referees for their work and comments.

References

[1] S. Andreassen, M. Wolbye, B. Falck, and S.K. Andersen. Munim - a causal probabilistic network for interpretation of electromyographic findings. In *Proceedings of the IJCAI*, pages 366–372, Milan, Italy, 1987.

[2] I. Beinlich, H. Seurmondt, R. Chavez, and G. Cooper. The alarm monitoring system: a case study with two probabilistic inference techniques for belief networks. In *Proceedings Artificial Intelligence in Medical Care*, pages 247–256, London, 1989.

[3] R.R. Bouckaert. Belief network construction using the minimum description length principle. Technical Report RUU-CS-93-??, To appear, Utrecht University, The Netherlands, 1992.

[4] R.R. Bouckaert. Optimizing causal orderings for generating dags from data. In *Proceedings Uncertainty in Artificial Intelligence*, pages 9–16, 1992.

[5] C.K. Chow and C.N. Liu. Approximating discrete probability distributions with dependency trees. *IEEE Trans. on Information Theory*, IT-14, pages 462–467, 1986.

[6] G.F. Cooper and E. Herskovits. A bayesian method for the induction of probabilistic networks from data. *Machine Learning*, pages 309–347, 1992.

[7] D. Heckerman, E. Horvitz, and B. Nathwani. Towards normative expert systems: Part I, the pathfinder project. *Methods of Information in Medicine*, 31:90–105, 1992.

[8] M. Henrion. An introduction to algorithms for inference in belief nets. In *Proceedings Uncertainty in Artificial Intelligence 5*, pages 129–138, 1990.

[9] E. Herskovits. *Computer-based probabilistic-network construction*. PhD thesis, Section of Medical Informatics, University of Pittsburgh, 1991.

[10] S. Højsgaard and B. Thiesson. Bifrost- block recursive models induced from relevant knowledge, observationsm and statistical techniques. Technical Report R 92-2010, Institute for Electronic Systems, University of Aalborg, Denmark, June 1992.

[11] S.L. Lauritzen and D.J. Spiegelhalter. Local computations with probabilities on graphical structures and their applications to expert systems (with discussion). *J.R. Stat. Soc. (Series B)*,Vol. 50, pages 157–224, 1988.

[12] S.L. Lauritzen, B. Thiesson, and D.J. Spiegelhalter. Diagnostic systems created by model selection methods – a case study. In *Proceedings 4th International Workshop on AI and Statistics*, 1993.

[13] J. Pearl. *Probabilistic Reasoning in Intelligent Systems: Networks of Plausible Inference*. Morgan Kaufman, inc., San Mateo, CA, 1988.

[14] G. Rebane and J. Pearl. The recovery of causal polytrees from statistical data. In *Proceedings Uncertainty in Artificial Intelligence*, pages 222–228, 1987.

[15] J. Rissanen. Stochastic complexity and modeling. *Annals of Statistics*, 14(3):1080–1100, 1986.

[16] J. Rissanen. Stochastic complexity. *Journal of the Royal Statistical Society B*, 49(3):223–239, 1987.

[17] R.D. Robinson. Counting unlabeled acyclic digraphs. In *Proceedings of the fifth Australian Conference on Combinatorial Mathematics*, pages 28–43, Melbourn, Australia, 1976.

[18] M.A. Shwe, B. Middleton, D.E. Heckerman, M. Henrion, E. Horvitz, H. Lehmann, and G. Cooper. Probabilistic diagnosis using a reformulation of the internist-1/qmr knowledge base: I the probabilistic modal and inference algorithms. *Methods of Information in Medicine*, 30:241–255, 1991.

[19] P. Spirtes, C. Glymour, and R. Scheines. *Causation, Prediction, and Search*. To appear, 1993.

[20] T. Verma and J. Pearl. Causal networks: Semantics and expressiveness. In *Proceedings Uncertainty in Artificial Intelligence*, pages 352–359, 1988.

[21] N. Wermuth and S.L. Lauritzen. Graphical and recursive models for contingency tables. *Biometrika*, 72:537–552, 1983.

IDAGs: a Perfect Map for Any Distribution

Remco R. Bouckaert
Department of Computer Science, Utrecht University,
P.O. Box 80.089, 3508 TB Utrecht, The Netherlands,
E-Mail: remco@cs.ruu.nl

Abstract

The notion of relevance that is very important in knowledge based systems can be efficiently encoded by conditional independence. Although directed acyclic graphs (DAG) are powerful means for representing conditional independencies in probability distributions it is not always possible to find a DAG that represents all conditional independencies and dependencies of a distribution. We present a new formalism that is able to do this for positive probability distributions. The main issue is to augment a DAG with a special kind of arcs that induce independencies. Furthermore, an efficient algorithm is presented for building these extended DAGs.

1 Introduction

In typical inference tasks the necessary volume of information would become unmanageable if no assumptions about relevance and irrelevance were made. Relevance shows a monotonic and nonmonotonic behaviour: It is relevant to know if someone has drunk a lot of beer the other day for deciding he has a head-ache. However, if you know he has a hang up, it becomes irrelevant to know whether the person has drunk too much. Also, it is not relevant to know if someone is allergic for deciding he has a cold. However, if the person is sneezing, it does become relevant to know if this person is allergic because it may explain the sneezing.

Conditional independence in probability distributions reflects this monotonic and nonmonotonic behaviour and it has a firmly established theoretical base in probability theory [3]. These properties make conditional independence a natural way to encode irrelevancies in knowledge based systems. Directed acyclic graphs (DAG) are powerful means for representing conditional independencies in probability distributions [5, 7, 9, 10]. Furthermore, efficient algorithms are known for making inferences with DAGs [6, 8, 9]. However, DAGs are not expressive enough to represents all independencies of any distribution and meanwhile represents all dependencies of the distribution.

In this paper, a new formalism is presented that can represent all independencies and dependencies of positive distributions. The main idea is to augment DAGs with arcs that induce independencies between nodes. They act in a fashion that very much resembles the way justifications in truth maintenance systems [4] encode relevancies. These arcs contain a monotonic part as well as a nonmonotonic part. In Section 2, we describe terms and definitions concerning conditional independence and DAGs. In Section 3, we introduce the new formalism, an extension of the DAG-formalism. We conclude with some suggestions for further research.

2   Conditional independence

For a joint probability distribution P over a set of variables U, we call X and Y *conditionally independent* given Z, written $I(X, Z, Y)$, if $P(XY|Z) = P(X|Z)P(Y|Z)$ for all values of the variables in XYZ (In this paper we write capital letters to denote sets of variables or nodes and lower case letters to denote single variables or nodes. All variables or sets of variables mentioned are elements or subsets of U unless stated otherwise); $I(X, Z, Y)$ is called an *independency statement*. The *independency model M* of a distribution P over U is the set of all valid independency statements in P. In this paper we assume the distribution is positive $(P > 0)$. Therefore, the following rules called *independency axioms* apply [3, 9]:

symmetry	$I(X, Z, Y)$	$\Leftrightarrow I(Y, Z, X)$
decomposition	$I(X, Z, WY)$	$\Rightarrow I(X, Z, W)$
weak union	$I(X, Z, WY)$	$\Rightarrow I(X, ZW, Y)$
contraction	$I(X, ZW, Y) \wedge I(X, Z, W)$	$\Rightarrow I(X, Z, WY)$
intersection	$I(X, ZW, Y) \wedge I(X, ZY, W)$	$\Rightarrow I(X, Z, WY)$

These independency axioms can be considered rules of inference. For example, if $I(X, Z, Y)$ holds in a distribution then by the symmetry axiom, $I(Y, Z, X)$ holds in the distribution also.

A DAG is a directed graph that does not contain paths starting and ending at the same node. A *trail* in a DAG is a path that does not consider the direction of the arcs. A *head-to-head node* in a trail is a triple of consecutive nodes x, y, z such that $x \to y \leftarrow z$ in the DAG. A *probabilistic network* is a pair (G, Γ) where G is a DAG and Γ is a set of conditional probability tables. For every variable $u \in U$, Γ contains a conditional probability table $P(u|\pi_u)$ that enumerates the probabilities of all values of u given the values of its parents π_u in the DAG. The distribution represented by this network is $\prod_{u \in U} P(u|\pi_u)$ [9]. Independency statements that hold in the distribution represented by a probabilistic network can be read from the structure of the DAG using the notions of blocked trail and d-separation [5, 9].

Definition 2.1 *Let G be a DAG. A trail in G between two nodes x and y is **blocked** by a set of nodes Z if at least one of the following two conditions hold:*
• *the trail contains a head-to-head node e and $e \notin Z$ and every descendant of e is not in Z.*
• *there is a node e in the trail with $e \in Z$ and e is not a head-to-head node in the trail.*

Definition 2.2 *In a DAG G, let X, Y and Z be sets of nodes. We say that X is **d-separated** from Y given Z, written $<X, Z, Y>$, if every trail between any node $x \in X$ and any node $y \in Y$ is blocked by Z.*

A DAG G is an *I-map* of an independency model M if $<X, Z, Y>$ in G implies $I(X, Z, Y) \in M$; G is a *minimal I-map* of M if no arc can be removed from G without destroying its I-mappedness. G is a *D-map* of M if $I(X, Z, Y) \in M$ implies $<X, Z, Y>$ in G; G is a *perfect map* of M if it is both an I-map and a D-map of M.

It is not always possible to find a perfect map of a distribution. For example, if we have a bell that rings when the outcome of the flipping of two coins is the same

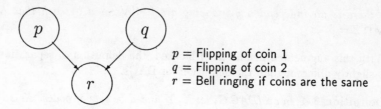

p = Flipping of coin 1
q = Flipping of coin 2
r = Bell ringing if coins are the same

Figure 1: A DAG representing the coins and bell example

[9]. Let p and q denote the variables that represent the outcome of the coins and r the ringing of the bell. Just to keep the distribution positive, put the bell in a noisy factory such that it is not always clear if it rings or not. The variables are pairwise independent so the independency model M is $\{I(p, \emptyset, q), I(p, \emptyset, r), I(q, \emptyset, r) + \text{sym.}\}$. But, given the third variable they are dependent. This nonmonotonic behaviour cannot perfectly be represented by a DAG. The best we can do is represent the model by a minimal I-map as in Figure 1.

3   IDAGs

In this section we present a new formalism for representing an independency model with a graph. In order to do so we need to introduce a new type of arc called independency inducing arc.

Definition 3.1 *An* **independency inducing arc** *(IIA) is an ordered triple* $\mathcal{P}$, $\mathcal{M}$, $\mathcal{N}$, *written* $(\mathcal{M}|\mathcal{N} \to \mathcal{P})$, *of which* $\mathcal{P} = (a, b)$ *is an unordered pair of nodes and* $\mathcal{M}, \mathcal{N} \subseteq U \backslash \{a, b\}$ *are two disjoint sets of nodes.*

Like for justifications in truth maintenance systems [4], the set $\mathcal{M}$ represents the monotonic part and the set $\mathcal{N}$ the nonmonotonic part of the arc, as will be shown. A DAG can be extended with these arcs, resulting in an IIA-directed acyclic graph (IDAG). In other words, you can regard an IDAG having embedded a DAG.

Definition 3.2 *An* **IIA directed acyclic graph** *(IDAG)* $G = (U, A, Q)$ *is an ordered tuple in which* U *is a set of nodes,* A *is a set of arcs such that* (U, A) *is a DAG and* Q *is a set of independency inducing arcs.*

A set of probability tables can be added to the IDAG in a similar way this is done with DAGs. We speak of trails in an IDAG to denote trails in the embedded DAG. Like for DAGs, a criterion can be formulated for reading independency statements from the IDAG.

Definition 3.3 *Let* G *be an IDAG. A trail* $t(a, b)$ *in* G *is* **I-blocked** *by a set of nodes* Z *if at least one of the following conditions hold:*
• *the trail contains a head-to-head node* e *and* $e \notin Z$ *and every descendant of* e *is not in* Z.
• *there is a node* e *in the trail with* $e \in Z$ *and* e *is not a head-to-head node in the trail.*

52

- *there is an independency inducing arc* $(\mathcal{M}|\mathcal{N} \to a,b)$ *such that* $\mathcal{M} \subseteq Z$ *and* $\mathcal{N} \cap Z = \emptyset$.

With this augmented definition of blocked, the definition of separation for IDAGs is slightly different than the definition for DAGs.

Definition 3.4 *In an IDAG G, let X, Y and Z be sets of nodes. X is **I-separated** from Y given Z, written $<X, Z, Y>$ if every trail between any node $x \in X$ and any node $y \in Y$ is I-blocked by $XYZ\backslash\{x,y\}$.*

With these definition the semantics of IIAs is fixed. The semantics of an IIA $(\mathcal{M}|\mathcal{N} \to a,b)$ is that it forces the nodes a, b independent given a set of nodes Z if all nodes in $\mathcal{M}$ are in Z, but only if no nodes in $\mathcal{N}$ are in Z. However, an IIA is ignored if at least one these conditions does not hold. So, IIAs never make nodes dependent, unless they are dependent in the embedded DAG. This nonmonotic behaviour causes the IDAGs to be a very powerful formalism for representing independency models.

Note that we use the same notation for I-separation as for d-separation. The context will make clear which kind of separation is meant. Using the notion of I-separation the definitions of I-mappedness, D-mappedness and perfect mappedness apply to IDAGs.

Since d-separation obeys intersection ($<X, ZW, Y>$ and $<X, ZY, W>$ imply $<X, Z, WY>$ [9]) we have that if for all $x \in X$ and $y \in Y$ $<x, XYZ\backslash\{x,y\}, y>$ in a DAG then $<X, Z, Y>$ follows from applying intersection several times. In IDAGs that do not contain IIAs, the set of I-separation statements is equal to the set of d-separation statements in the embedded DAG. So, I-separation can be regarded an extension of d-separation.

We give three examples of IDAGs. The model of the coins and bell example in Section 2 can be described by the IDAG as shown in Figure 2. This IDAG is the DAG of section 2 with two IIAs namely $(\emptyset|p \to q,r)$ and $(\emptyset|q \to p,r)$. In the figure these IIAs are depicted as rectangles with the two relevant sets divided by a '|'. We have a perfect map of the independency model since not only $I(p,\emptyset,q)$ but also $I(p,\emptyset,r)$ and $I(q,\emptyset,r)$ (and symmetric statements) are represented.

Consider the situation in which we have two males and two females who have mutual heterosexual contacts [9]. Let the variables m_1, m_2, f_1 and f_2 represent if respectively male 1, male 2, female 1 and female 2 have any venereal disease

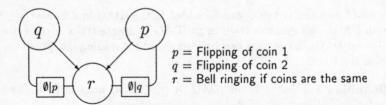

p = Flipping of coin 1
q = Flipping of coin 2
r = Bell ringing if coins are the same

Figure 2: An IDAG that is a perfect map of the coins and bell example.

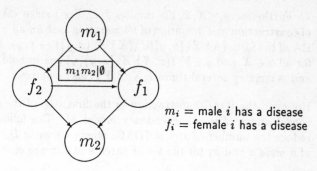

Figure 3: IDAG that is a perfect map of $M = \{I(f_1, m_1 m_2, f_2), I(m_1, f_1 f_2, m_2) +$ sym.$\}$.

or not. The independency model $M = \{I(f_1, m_1 m_2, f_2), I(m_1, f_1 f_2, m_2) +$ sym.$\}$, corresponding to this situation, cannot be perfectly represented by a DAG. However, as shown in Figure 3, this can be done with an IDAG by adding the IIA $(m_1 m_2 | \emptyset \to f_1, f_2)$ to the DAG.

Another case where no DAG that is a perfect map of the distribution may exist is when a distribution that has a perfect map is marginalized over some variables. Let the DAG in Figure 4 be a perfect map. Then, for the distribution marginalized over a no DAG exists that is a perfect map since it is not possible to represent both $I(a, \emptyset, d)$ and $I(b, \emptyset, e)$ and have a trail $cbde$ in a DAG. The IDAG also depicted in Figure 4 does represent the distribution perfectly.

Theorem 3.1 *Let M be an independency model of a positive probability distribution. Then an IDAG exists that is a perfect map of M.*

Proof: An IDAG can be generated from an independency model M by taking a fully connected DAG and add, for every independence statement $I(a, Z, b)$ in M, an IIA $(Z | U \backslash (Z \cup \{a, b\}) \to a, b)$. We have to show that for this IDAG $I(X, Z, Y) \Leftrightarrow <X, Z, Y>$.

$I(X, Z, Y)$ implies that for all $x \in X$ and $y \in Y$ $I(x, XYZ \backslash \{x, y\}, y)$ using weak union and symmetry. By method of construction for every statement $I(x, XYZ \backslash \{x, y\}, y)$ there is an IIA $(XYZ \backslash \{x, y\} | U \backslash (XYZ \backslash \{x, y\}) \to x, y)$. Therefore, by definition of I-separation we have $<X, Z, Y>$.

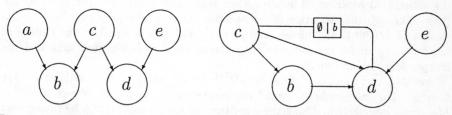

Figure 4: A DAG that is a perfect map and an IDAG that is a perfect map of its marginalisation.

Furthermore, $<X, Z, Y>$ implies $I(X, Z, Y)$ since $<X, Z, Y>$ means by method of construction and definition of I-separation that for all $x \in X$ and $y \in Y$ there is an IIA of the form $(XYZ \backslash \{x, y\} | U \backslash (XYZ \backslash \{x, y\}) \rightarrow x, y)$. By method of construction for all $x \in X$ and $y \in Y$ $I(x, XYZ \backslash \{x, y\}, y)$ has to hold. By applying intersection and symmetry several times $I(X, Z, Y)$ can be derived. □

However, the IDAG construction in the first step of the proof would take $\binom{n}{2} 2^{n-2}$ consultations of the independency model M. The following rules can be used to reduce the number of arcs in IDAGs where we write D_a for the set of descendants of a node a and π_a for the set of parents of a in the embedded DAG.

- Intersection
$(\mathcal{M} \cup \{d\} | \mathcal{N} \rightarrow a, b)$ and $(\mathcal{M} | \mathcal{N} \cup \{d\} \rightarrow a, b)$ can be replaced by $(\mathcal{M} | \mathcal{N} \rightarrow a, b)$.
- Arc removal
$b \rightarrow a$ can be removed if an IIA $(\mathcal{M} | \mathcal{N} \rightarrow a, b)$ exists with $\mathcal{M} \cap D_a = \emptyset$ and $\mathcal{N} \cap \pi_a = \emptyset$.
- IIA removal
$(\mathcal{M} | \mathcal{N} \rightarrow a, b)$ can be removed if $\pi_a \subseteq \mathcal{M}$ and $D_a \subseteq \mathcal{N}$.

Note that by definition of IIAs $\mathcal{M}$ and $\mathcal{N}$ are disjoint subsets of $U \backslash \{a, b\}$. Therefore, the conditions for IIA-removal imply that no arc $b \rightarrow a$ exists and that b is not a descendant of a. The transformation rules above do not influence the model represented by the IDAG if the IDAG is a perfect map of an independency model.

Theorem 3.2 *Let M be an independency model of a positive distribution and G be an IDAG that is a perfect map of M. Let G' be an IDAG that is equal to G after application of intersection, arc removal or IIA removal. Then, the independency model represented by G' is M.*

Sketch of a proof: The intersection rule follows from the definition of I-separation: $(\mathcal{M} \cup \{d\} | \mathcal{N} \rightarrow a, b)$ implies for all sets S such that $\mathcal{M} \cup \{d\} \subseteq S \subseteq U \backslash \mathcal{N}$ $I(a, S, b)$ is in M. $(\mathcal{M} | \mathcal{N} \cup \{d\} \rightarrow a, b)$ implies for all sets S such that $\mathcal{M} \subseteq S \subseteq U \backslash (\mathcal{N} \cup \{d\})$ $I(a, S, b)$ is in M. Therefore, for all sets S such that $\mathcal{M} \subseteq S \subseteq U \backslash \mathcal{N}$ we have $I(a, S, b)$ is in M. This can be described by the single IIA $(\mathcal{M} | \mathcal{N} \rightarrow a, b)$.

The arc-removal rule follows from the following. Let M_G^{DAG} be the independency model that is the closure of the set of statements $\{I(a, \pi_a, U \backslash D_a \pi_a) | a \in U\}$ under the independency axioms, then M_G^{DAG} is exactly the set of independency statements represented by the embedded DAG of the IDAG G (follows from [11]). Let M_Q be the model that contains all independency statements $I(a, C, b)$ represented by the IIAs. Through the definition of I-separation, the model represented by G is the closure of $M_G^{DAG} \cup M_Q$ under intersection. And this is equal to the closure of $M_G^{DAG} \cup M_Q$ under the independency axioms since G is a perfect map and the independency axioms apply.

Let $M_{G'}^{DAG}$ be similar defined as M_G^{DAG} for G' where G' is G without the arc $b \rightarrow a$. The independency model represented by G' is the closure of $M_{G'}^{DAG} \cup M_Q$ under intersection. Using the conditions of arc-removal, it can be shown that $I(a, \pi_a \backslash \{b\}, U \backslash (\pi_a D_a \backslash \{b\}))$ is in the model of G. Since this model is equal to M

and M is closed under the independency axioms, the model represented by G' is also equal to M.

The IIA-removal rule follows from the observation that any independency statement $I(a, S, b)$ represented by the IIA is also represented in the embedded DAG. □

As noted before, the method of construction described in the proof takes exponential consultations of the independency model. So, it is useful to search for a less complex method of construction. A minimal I-map can be constructed from an independency model M using the notion of causal input lists [10] in $O(|U|^2)$ consultations of M.

Definition 3.5 *Let M be the independency model of a distribution P over U. Let θ be a total ordering on U. A **causal input list** L_θ over M is a set of independency statements that for all $x \in U$ contains one statement $I(x, \pi_x, U_x \backslash \pi_x)$ where $U_x = \{y | \theta(y) \prec \theta(x)\}$ and π_x the smallest subset of U_x such that $I(x, \pi_x, U_x \backslash \pi_x) \in M$. π_x is called the **parent set** of x.*

The DAG G_θ associated with a causal input list L_θ has parent sets of the nodes corresponding to the parent sets in L_θ. This DAG is a minimal I-map of M [10]. The model M_θ represented by G_θ is equal to the closure of L_θ under the independency axioms (follows from [10]).

A less complex way to construct an IDAG which is a perfect map of an independency model M is to start with a DAG G_θ generated from a causal input list L_θ of M and add IIAs where necessary. Obviously, IIAs that will be absorbed using one of the reduction rules need not be considered. Furthermore, the information that the embedded DAG is a minimal I-map can be used to exclude more triples (namely the triples that are coupled [2]).

4 Further Research

In this paper we have presented a formalism for representing any positive distribution perfectly. The formalism uses a DAG augmented with independency inducing arcs and the d-separation criterion is augmented accordingly. Furthermore, an efficient algorithm for constructing IDAGs from DAGs that are minimal I-maps is presented.

Efficient algorithms for inference based on lazy evaluation of the network may be developed that use the independencies induced by IIAs. For inference the probabilities of every variable given a finding has to be calculated. It is clear that only the probabilities of the variables for which the finding is relevant will change. The more independencies there are, the fewer calculations have to be made. And IIAs are a method to add more independencies to a network. Especially in large IDAGs, these algorithms may yield a lower complexity than the algorithms currently known for inference in probabilistic networks. Relevance plays an important role in explanation of results inferred. Therefore, explanation algorithms based on independencies may be revisited accordingly.

Furthermore, in [1] an algorithm has been presented that optimizes the causal ordering θ by applying simple operations on θ with consequences for the DAG G_θ

and independency model M_θ. The strategy is to apply such an operation only if the represented independency model after the operation contains the one before the operation. This strategy has been shown to yield a local minimum. In order to find the global minimum, we believe the IDAG formalism can be of great help, since after an operation on an ordering θ, IIAs can be added in order to let the new independency model contain the old one.

Conditional independence reflects irrelevancy for all values of variables. However, variables may be dependent for certain values of variables. For example, the decision if someone is pregnant is not influenced by the result of a pregnancy test if the sex of the tested person is male, while it is influenced if the sex is female. So, the relevancy of the test result for being pregnant is dependent on the value of sex. It may be useful to look at formalisms and efficient inference and explanation algorithms that explore these independencies.

Acknowledgements

I want to thank the referees for their work and comments.

References

[1] R.R. Bouckaert. Optimizing causal orderings for generating dags from data. In *Proceedings Uncertainty in Artificial Intelligence*, pages 9–16, 1992.

[2] R.R. Bouckaert. Conditional dependencies in probabilistic networks. In *Proceedings 4th International Workshop on AI and Statistics*, 1993.

[3] A.P. Dawid. Conditional independence in statistical theory. *Journal of the Royal Statistical Society B*, 41(1):1–31, 1979.

[4] J. Doyle. A truth maintenance system. *Artificial Intelligence*, 12:231–272, 1979.

[5] D. Geiger. *Graphoids: a qualitative framework for probabilistic inference*. PhD thesis, UCLA, Cognitive Systems Laboratory, Computer Science Department, 1990.

[6] M. Henrion. An introduction to algorithms for inference in belief nets. In *Proceedings Uncertainty in Artificial Intelligence 5*, pages 129–138, 1990.

[7] S.L. Lauritzen, A.P. Dawid, A.P. Larsen, and H.G. Leimer. Independence properties of directed markov fields. *Networks*, Vol 20, pages 491–505, 1990.

[8] S.L. Lauritzen and D.J. Spiegelhalter. Local computations with probabilities on graphical structures and their applications to expert systems (with discussion). *J.R. Stat. Soc. (Series B)*,Vol. 50, pages 157–224, 1988.

[9] J. Pearl. *Probabilistic Reasoning in Intelligent Systems: Networks of Plausible Inference*. Morgan Kaufman, inc., San Mateo, CA, 1988.

[10] J. Pearl, D. Geiger, and T. Verma. The logic of influence diagrams. In R.M. Oliver and J.Q. Smith, editors, *Influence Diagrams, Belief Nets and Decision Analysis*, pages 67–87. John Wiley & Sons Ltd., 1990.

[11] T. Verma and J. Pearl. Causal networks: Semantics and expressiveness. In *Proceedings Uncertainty in Artificial Intelligence*, pages 352–359, 1988.

Learning Non Probabilistic Belief Networks*

Luis M. de Campos and Juan F. Huete

Departamento de Ciencias de la Computación e I.A., Universidad de Granada
18071-Granada, Spain

Abstract. Probability intervals constitute an interesting formalism for representing uncertainty. In order to use them together with belief networks, we study basic concepts as marginalization, conditioning and independence for probability intervals. Then we develop some algorithms for learning simple belief networks (trees and polytrees), based on this kind of non purely probabilistic information.

1 Introduction

Belief networks are useful and well founded knowledge representation tools for reasoning with uncertainty in Artificial Intelligence. Belief networks encode independence relationships among variables in a graph, and use them to perform inference by means of local methods. Belief networks have been mainly studied from a probabilistic point of view, in the sense that the underlying uncertainty formalism is probability theory. So, probabilistic propagation algorithms are very well developed ([8, 9]) although there is also a solid work in their non probabilistic counterparts ([4, 11, 13]). However, although there is a lot of works about the problem of learning probability-based belief networks ([1, 5, 6, 9, 10, 12],...), the situation is very different for the non probabilistic case. The objective of this paper is the learning of graphical structures from non purely probabilistic information, more concretely, from probability intervals.

Most of the probabilistic algorithms for learning belief networks ([9, 10, 12],...) suppose that implicitly we have a joint probability distribution (or an estimation of this distribution obtained from a set of data). Then we can formulate questions about independence relationships among variables, and use this distribution to get the answers. Although it is almost always possible to extract a probability distribution from a set of data, there are several reasons for using also non-probabilistic techniques: first, the number of data can be small, and therefore the probabilistic estimation may be not very reliable; second, data can be incomplete or partially unknown, and third, some data may have been obtained from subjective judgments (of experts) that may not be necessarily expressed in terms of probabilities.

We will suppose that we have information on a finite set of variables $X_1, X_2, \ldots, X_n$, in the form of probability intervals $[l(x_1, \ldots, x_n), u(x_1, \ldots, x_n)]$, and we

---
* This work has been supported by the European Economic Community under Project Esprit III b.r.a. 6156 (DRUMS II)

want to build a graph that represents (or estimates) the relationships among the variables, in the light of the available information. We will not study here the way in which we can get probability intervals. It suffices to say that they could be obtained directly from experts, or from empirical information (a set of examples) using statistical techniques as confidence intervals. Moreover we will restrict ourselves to study simple structures as trees or polytrees, although the methodology developed here could be extended to more complex structures. Propagation in these networks can be done by using techniques studied in [4, 13].

The paper is organized as follows: in Sect. 2 we study probability intervals. This is the uncertainty formalism that will be used later. Section 3 studies the concepts of independence and dependence between variables. Two algorithms for learning simple belief networks from a set of probability intervals are proposed in Sect. 4. Finally, several future lines of research are considered in Sect. 5.

2 Probability Intervals

Let us consider a variable X taking its values in a finite set $D_x = \{x_1, x_2, \ldots, x_n\}$ and a family of intervals $[l_i, u_i], 0 \leq l_i \leq u_i \leq 1, i = 1, \ldots, n$. We can interpret these intervals as a set of bounds of probability by defining the set $\mathcal{P}$ of probability distributions on D_x as $\mathcal{P} = \{P \in \mathcal{P}(D_x) \mid l_i \leq p(x_i) \leq u_i\}$, where $\mathcal{P}(D)$ denotes the set of probabilities defined on a domain D. As $\mathcal{P}$ is obviously a convex set, we can consider probability intervals as a particular case of convex sets of probabilities ([7]).

In order to avoid for the set $\mathcal{P}$ to be empty, it is necessary to impose one condition to the intervals $[l_i, u_i]$, which is:

$$\sum_i l_i \leq 1 \leq \sum_i u_i \ . \tag{1}$$

A set of probability intervals verifying (1) is called proper. We will always use proper probability intervals, because non proper intervals are useless.

In addition to a convex set $\mathcal{P}$, we can also associate with the proper intervals $[l_i, u_i]$ a pair (l, u) of lower and upper probabilities (also called a probability envelope or a pair of representable measures) through $\mathcal{P}$ by means of $l(A) = \inf_{P \in \mathcal{P}} P(A)$, $u(A) = \sup_{P \in \mathcal{P}} P(A)$, $\forall A \subseteq D_x$. So, probability intervals can be also considered as particular cases of lower and upper measures, where the set of associated probabilities is defined only by restrictions affecting the individual probabilities $p(x_i)$.

In order to maintain consistency between both views of probability intervals, it would be interesting that the restriction of $l(.)$ and $u(.)$ to the singletons (sets with only one element) be equal to the original bounds, that is to say, that $l(\{x_i\}) = l_i$, $u(\{x_i\}) = u_i$, $\forall i$. These equalities are not always true: in general, we have only the inequalities $l(\{x_i\}) \geq l_i, u(\{x_i\}) \leq u_i, \forall i$. The conditions that the intervals $[l_i, u_i]$ must verify in order to get the previous equalities are:

$$\sum_{j \neq i} l_j + u_i \leq 1 \text{ and } \sum_{j \neq i} u_j + l_i \geq 1, \forall i \ . \tag{2}$$

A set of probability intervals verifying condition (2) is called reachable. Given the proper probability intervals $[l_i, u_i], i = 1, \ldots, n$, and their associated convex set of probabilities $\mathcal{P}$, we define a new set of probability intervals $[l'_i, u'_i]$ by means of

$$l'_i = l_i \vee \left(1 - \sum_{j \neq i} u_j \right) , \quad u'_i = u_i \wedge \left(1 - \sum_{j \neq i} l_j \right) , \quad \forall i . \qquad (3)$$

It can be proved that the set of probabilities associated to $[l'_i, u'_i]$ is also $\mathcal{P}$. So, as the narrower intervals $[l'_i, u'_i]$ constitute a more accurate representation of the probabilities in $\mathcal{P}$ than $[l_i, u_i]$, and moreover they verify conditions (2), we will perform the substitution when it is necessary, thus always using reachable probability intervals.

Reachable sets of probability intervals guarantee that the values of the lower and upper associated measures (l, u), $l(x_i)$ and $u(x_i)$, coincide with the initial probability bounds l_i and u_i. The values of $l(.)$ and $u(.)$ for the other subsets of D_x which are not singletons can be calculated by means of the following expressions:

$$l(A) = \sum_{x_i \in A} l_i \vee \left(1 - \sum_{x_i \notin A} u_i \right) , \quad u(A) = \sum_{x_i \in A} u_i \wedge \left(1 - \sum_{x_i \notin A} l_i \right) \quad \forall A \subseteq D_x . \quad (4)$$

For general lower and upper probability measures we need to give all the values $l(A)$ or $u(A)$ in order to have a complete specification of these measures, that is, we need $2^{|D_x|}$ values. For several distinguished kinds of measures, as probabilities or possibilities, it suffices to have the $|D_x|$ values of these measures for singletons, and the rest of values may be calculated as $P(A) = \sum_{x_i \in A} p(x_i)$, $\Pi(A) = \bigvee_{x_i \in A} \pi(x_i)$ for probabilities P and possibilities Π, respectively. For probability intervals, we need to specify only $2|D_x|$ values (l_i and u_i) instead of $2^{|D_x|}$.

2.1 Marginals of Probability Intervals

Now let us consider two variables X and Y taking values in the sets $D_x = \{x_1, x_2, \ldots, x_n\}$ and $D_y = \{y_1, y_2, \ldots, y_m\}$ respectively, and a set of reachable bidimensional probability intervals $[l_{ij}, u_{ij}], i = 1, \ldots, n, j = 1, \ldots, m$, defined on the cartesian product $D_x \times D_y$, representing the joint available information on these two variables. We want to define the marginals of these probability intervals. To do that, we can use the interpretation of a set of probability intervals as a pair of lower and upper measures (l, u). Given (l, u), the marginal measures (l_x, u_x) on D_x (for the marginals on D_y is analogous) are defined as $l_x(A) = l(A \times D_y)$, $u_x(A) = u(A \times D_y)$, $\forall A \subseteq D_x$. Alternatively, we could use the interpretation of probability intervals as convex sets of probabilities, and define the marginal of $[l_{ij}, u_{ij}]$ on D_x as the set $\mathcal{P}_x$ of marginal probabilities of the probabilities in the convex set $\mathcal{P}$ associated to $[l_{ij}, u_{ij}]$, that is to say, $\mathcal{P}_x = \{P \in \mathcal{P}(D_x) \mid \exists Q \in \mathcal{P} \text{ such that } p(x_i) = \sum_j q(x_i, y_j), \forall i\}$. In our case both definitions are equivalent, in the sense that $\mathcal{P}_x$ is just the set of probabilities associated to (l_x, u_x), that is to say, $l_x(A) = \inf_{P \in \mathcal{P}_x} P(A)$, $u_x(A) = \sup_{P \in \mathcal{P}_x} P(A)$, $\forall A \subseteq D_x$. Moreover, it can be proved that these marginal lower and upper measures are in fact the probability intervals $[\sum_j l_{ij}, \sum_j u_{ij}]$ $\forall i$, and using (3) the equivalent reachable expression is $[l_i, u_i]$, where

$$l_i = \sum_j l_{ij} \vee \left(1 - \sum_j \sum_{k \neq i} u_{kj} \right), \ u_i = \sum_j u_{ij} \wedge \left(1 - \sum_j \sum_{k \neq i} l_{kj} \right), \ \forall i \ . \quad (5)$$

Observe that the calculus of the marginal on one variable is very easy: we only sum the values l_{ij} and u_{ij} on the other variable; next the equivalent but reachable intervals are obtained using the formulas (5).

2.2 Conditioning of Probability Intervals

To define the conditioning of probability intervals we will again use their interpretation as lower and upper measures, because there are several definitions of conditioning in this framework. We will use the definition of conditioning proposed in [3]: Given a pair of lower and upper measures (l, u) defined on a domain D, and a subset $B \subseteq D$, the conditional lower and upper measures given that we know B, $(l(.|B), u(.|B))$ are defined as

$$l(A|B) = \frac{l(A \cap B)}{l(A \cap B) + u(\overline{A} \cap B)}, \ u(A|B) = \frac{u(A \cap B)}{u(A \cap B) + l(\overline{A} \cap B)}, \ \forall A \subseteq D \ .$$

In our case, we have a set of bidimensional probability intervals $[l_{ij}, u_{ij}]$, and we want to calculate the conditional probability intervals given that we know the value of one variable, say $Y = y_j$. Then, taking into account the expressions for the lower and upper measures associated to probability intervals given in (4), the conditional probability intervals can be written as $[l_{i|j}, u_{i|j}]$, where

$$l_{i|j} = \frac{l_{ij}}{l_{ij} + \left(\sum_{k \neq i} u_{kj} \wedge \left(1 - \sum_k \sum_{h \neq j} l_{kh} - l_{ij} \right) \right)} \quad (6)$$

$$u_{i|j} = \frac{u_{ij}}{u_{ij} + \left(\sum_{k \neq i} l_{kj} \vee \left(1 - \sum_k \sum_{h \neq j} u_{kh} - u_{ij} \right) \right)} \quad (7)$$

So, the calculus of the conditional probability intervals is also very easy. Moreover, these intervals are always reachable, and therefore it is not necessary to transform them in reachable intervals by using (3).

3 Defining Independence and Measuring Dependence

In probability theory, independence between two variables holds when the bidimensional probability measure coincides with the product measure obtained by multiplication of the marginals. This condition is equivalent to the equality between the marginal and each conditional probability.

For probability intervals we will adopt the second perspective. Thus, our view of independence is related to the quantity of information that we have on a variable before and after conditioning to another variable: if we do not get additional information after conditioning then we assert the independence.

In order to precise the meaning of "not to get additional information", we will use again the lower and upper probabilities interpretation of probability intervals. Given two pairs of lower and upper measures (l_1, u_1) and (l_2, u_2), defined on the same domain D, we say that (l_2, u_2) is less informative than (l_1, u_1) if and only if (l_1, u_1) is included (see [2]) in (l_2, u_2), that is to say, if

$$l_2(A) \leq l_1(A), \ \forall A \subseteq D \text{ or equivalently } u_2(A) \geq u_1(A), \ \forall A \subseteq D . \qquad (8)$$

For probability intervals, the inclusion of $[l_i, u_i]$ in $[l_i', u_i']$ holds if and only if

$$l_i' \leq l_i \leq u_i \leq u_i', \ \forall i . \qquad (9)$$

Now we are ready to formalize the concept of independence for probability intervals. Let $[l_{ij}, u_{ij}]$, $i = 1, \ldots, n$, $j = 1, \ldots, m$, be a set of reachable bidimensional probability intervals defined on $D_x \mathrm{x} D_y$, which represents the available knowledge about two variables X and Y. Then we say that X and Y are independent (with respect to $[l_{ij}, u_{ij}]$) if and only if the marginal intervals defined in (5) are included in the conditional intervals defined in (6) and (7), that is to say:

$$l_{i|j} \leq l_i \leq u_i \leq u_{i|j} \text{ and } l_{j|i} \leq l_j \leq u_j \leq u_{j|i}, \ \forall i, j . \qquad (10)$$

This definition of independence between two variables can be easily generalized to deal with conditional independence of two variables given a third variable (or a set of variables). It is very easy to see that for probability measures (10) reproduces the usual concept of probabilistic independence.

In addition to define independence for probability intervals, we also want to study some method to measure the degree of dependence. The degree of dependence between two variables, $Dep(X, Y)$, should measure the gain of information on one variable obtained after conditioning to the other variable: the more dependent X and Y are then the greater $Dep(X, Y)$ should be. One of these $Dep(.,.)$ measures could be defined according to the following idea: if $l_{i|j}$ is lesser than l_i (or $u_{i|j}$ is greater than u_i) then there is no contradiction with the definition of independence. However, the greater than l_i is $l_{i|j}$ (or the lesser than u_i is $u_{i|j}$) then the more the deviation of the independence conditions is, and therefore the greater $Dep(X, Y)$ should be. Moreover, this deviation must be weighted by the plausibility of the corresponding result $Y = y_j$.

So, if we define $Dep(X|Y)$ as

$$Dep(X|Y) = \sum_j u_j \left[\sum_i [(u_i - u_{i|j}) \vee 0] + \sum_i [(l_{i|j} - l_i) \vee 0] \right]. \qquad (11)$$

then the degree of dependence between X and Y, $Dep(X, Y)$, is

$$Dep(X, Y) = Dep(X|Y) + Dep(Y|X) . \qquad (12)$$

It can be easily seen that X and Y are independent if and only if $Dep(X, Y) = 0$.

4 Learning Simple Networks

Once we have a concept of independence for probability intervals, and a way for measuring dependence, many of the probabilistic algorithms for learning belief networks can be easily generalized to deal with probability intervals. We will consider here only algorithms for learning simple networks like trees or polytrees. Let us suppose that we have n variables $X_1, X_2, \ldots, X_n$, and a set of n-dimensional probability intervals $[l(x_1, x_2, \ldots, x_n), u(x_1, x_2, \ldots, x_n)]$. We want to build a graph that represents (or estimates) the relationships among these variables, in the light of the available information. For example, a tree approximation can be obtained by using the following generalization of the Chow-Liu's algorithm ([5, 9]):

- *For $i = 1$ to $n - 1$ and For $j = i + 1$ to n do*
  - *Calculate the reachable marginal probability intervals $[l_i, u_i]$, $[l_j, u_j]$.*
  - *Calculate the conditional probability intervals $[l_{i|j}, u_{i|j}]$, $[l_{j|i}, u_{j|i}]$.*
  - *Calculate the degree of dependence $Dep(X_i, X_j)$.*
- *Rank the $n(n-1)/2$ values $Dep(X_i, X_j)$ in decreasing order.*
- *Repeat*
  - *Select the next value $Dep(X_i, X_j)$.*
  - *If the branch X_i—X_j, together with the previously introduced branches does not form a cycle, insert it in the tree.*
- *until $n - 1$ branches have been inserted.*

If we want to obtain a polytree approximation, we can use an extension of the Rebane and Pearl's algorithm ([9, 10]):

- *Use the previous algorithm to obtain a tree structure.*
- *For all the patterns X_i—X_k—X_j found in the tree, do*
  - *Test the condition $Dep(X_i, X_j) < \epsilon$. If it is true, give to the branches the direction $X_i \rightarrow X_k \leftarrow X_j$ (head-to-head pattern).*
- *Give direction to the remaining branches, but do not produce more head-to-head patterns.*

In this algorithm ϵ is a threshold used to detect independences. So, the inequality $Dep(X_i, X_j) < \epsilon$ means that X_i and X_j are considered as independent variables (see [1]).

Let us consider an example: We have four variables X, Y, Z and T, all of them can take two values, say 1 and 2. The available information about these variables is given by the set of probability intervals, $[l(x, y, z, t), u(x, y, z, t)]$ shown in table 1. We must obtain the reachable marginal and conditional probability intervals for all the pairs of variables, in order to calculate the degrees of dependence. For example, for the variables X and Y, the bidimensional, marginal and conditional intervals are given in tables 2, 3 and 4 respectively. To calculate the degree of dependence between X and Y, we use the formulas (11) and (12), obtaining $Dep(X, Y) = 0.1307$. By repeating this process for all the pairs of variables, we get

$Dep(X,Y) = 0.1307,\; Dep(X,Z) = 0.9232,\; \mathrm{Dep}(X,T) = 0.2084$
$Dep(Y,Z) = 0.4470,\; Dep(Y,T) = 0.1706,\; \mathrm{Dep}(Z,T) = 0.3093$

Therefore, the estimated tree structure is

$$X-Z-Y$$
$$\mid$$
$$T$$

If we want to estimate a polytree structure and, for example, fix the threshold ϵ to $\epsilon = 0.15$, we obtain the following polytree

$$X \to Z \leftarrow Y$$
$$\downarrow$$
$$T$$

Table 1. Probability intervals on X, Y, Z, T

x y z t	$l(x,y,z,t)$	$u(x,y,z,t)$	x y z t	$l(x,y,z,t)$	$u(x,y,z,t)$
1 1 1 1	0.0556	0.0956	2 1 1 1	0.0000	0.0380
1 1 1 2	0.1564	0.1964	2 1 1 2	0.0220	0.0620
1 1 2 1	0.0000	0.0228	2 1 2 1	0.0000	0.0260
1 1 2 2	0.0052	0.0452	2 1 2 2	0.0340	0.0740
1 2 1 1	0.0682	0.1082	2 2 1 1	0.0000	0.0308
1 2 1 2	0.1858	0.2258	2 2 1 2	0.0052	0.0452
1 2 2 1	0.0000	0.0326	2 2 2 1	0.0000	0.0344
1 2 2 2	0.0934	0.1334	2 2 2 2	0.1096	0.1496

Table 2. Bidimensional intervals

x y	$l(x,y)$	$u(x,y)$
1 1	0.2172	0.3600
1 2	0.3474	0.5000
2 1	0.0560	0.2000
2 2	0.1148	0.2600

Table 3. Marginal intervals

x	$l(x)$	$u(x)$	y	$l(y)$	$u(y)$
1	0.5646	0.8292	1	0.2732	0.5378
2	0.1708	0.4354	2	0.4622	0.7268

Table 4. Conditional intervals

y	$l(y\mid X=1)$	$u(y\mid X=1)$	y	$l(y\mid X=2)$	$u(y\mid X=2)$
1	0.3028	0.5089	1	0.1772	0.6353
2	0.4911	0.6972	2	0.3647	0.8228
x	$l(x\mid Y=1)$	$u(x\mid Y=1)$	x	$l(x\mid Y=2)$	$u(x\mid Y=2)$
1	0.5206	0.8654	1	0.5719	0.8133
2	0.1346	0.4794	2	0.1867	0.4281

Remark: The original probability intervals $[l(x,y,z,t), u(x,y,z,t)]$ were obtained from a probability distribution with a polytree structure identical to that obtained, but allowing a deviation of 0.02 for each probability value (that is, from each p_i we obtained $[p_i - 0.02, p_i + 0.02]$).

5   Concluding Remarks

We have studied probability intervals as a formalism for dealing with uncertainty in Artificial Intelligence, and we have generalized some algorithms for learning belief networks from this kind of non probabilistic pieces of information. However, a lot of work remain to be done. Future research should include: A deeper study of independence in non probabilistic formalisms, and methods to measure dependence degrees; Study of ways to extract probability intervals from raw data, and merge this empirical information with subjective judgments from experts; Development of new learning algorithms; Consideration of different uncertainty theories, as general lower and upper probabilities, necessities and possibilities, belief and plausibility functions,...

References

1. S. Acid, L.M. de Campos, A. González, R. Molina, N. Pérez de la Blanca: Learning with CASTLE, in Symbolic and Quantitative Approaches to Uncertainty, Lecture Notes in Computer Science 548, R. Kruse, P. Siegel (Eds.), Springer Verlag (1991) 99–106
2. L.M. de Campos, M.T. Lamata, S. Moral: Logical connectives for combining fuzzy measures, in Methodologies for Intelligent Systems 3, Z.W. Ras, L. Saitta (Eds.), North-Holland, New York (1988) 11–18
3. L.M. de Campos, M.T. Lamata, S. Moral: The concept of conditional fuzzy measure, International Journal of Intelligent Systems 5 (1990) 237–246
4. J.E. Cano, S. Moral, J.F. Verdegay: Propagation of convex sets of probabilities in directed acyclic networks, Proceedings of the Fourth IPMU Conference (1992) 289–292
5. C.K. Chow, C.N. Liu: Approximating discrete probability distribution with dependence trees, IEEE Transactions on Information Theory 14 (1968) 462–467
6. G.F. Cooper, E. Herskovits: A Bayesian Method for the Induction of Probabilistic Networks from Data, Machine Learning 9 (1992) 309–347
7. H.E. Kyburg: Bayesian and non-bayesian evidential updating, Artificial Intelligence 31 (1987) 271–293
8. S.L. Lauritzen, D.J. Spiegelhalter: Local Computations with probabilities on graphical structures and their applications to expert systems, Journal of the Royal Statistical Society B-50 (1988) 157–224
9. J. Pearl: Probabilistic reasoning in intelligent systems: networks of plausible inference, Morgan and Kaufmann, San Mateo (1988)
10. G. Rebane, J. Pearl: The recovery of causal poly-trees from statistical data, in Uncertainty in Artificial Intelligence 3, L.N. Kanal, T.S. Levitt and J.F. Lemmer (Eds.), North-Holland (1989) 175–182
11. G. Shafer, P.P. Shenoy: Axioms for probability and belief function propagation, in Uncertainty in Artificial Intelligence 4, R.D. Shachter, T.S. Levitt, L.N. Kanal, J.F. Lemmer (Eds.), North-Holland, Amsterdam (1990) 169–198
12. P. Spirtes: Detecting causal relations in the presence of unmeasured variables, Uncertainty in Artificial Intelligence, Proc. of the Seventh Conference (1991) 392–397
13. B. Tessem: Interval representation on uncertainty in Artificial Intelligence, Ph. D. Thesis, Department of Informatics, University of Bergen, Norway (1989)

A Practical System for Defeasible Reasoning and Belief Revision[*]

Maria R. Cravo and João P. Martins

Instituto Superior Técnico
Av. Rovisco Pais
1000 Lisboa, Portugal
+351-1-841-7265
JMartins@interg.pt

1 Introduction

We present an implemented belief revision (henceforth BR) system, SNePSwD,[2] whose main features are the ability to perform nonmonotonic reasoning, and the capacity to revise its beliefs when necessary. Its reasoning is guided by a nonmonotonic logic, SWMC, which, besides allowing for defeasible inference, is appropriate to support an ATMS-like BR system. In what concerns the revision of beliefs, the system is based on a BR theory, which decides what changes should be made, e.g. which beliefs to discard to get rid of a contradiction. To efficiently propagate the consequences of a change, truth maintenance techniques are used.

An important point is the fact that each of the aspects we mentioned, the nonmonotonic logic, the BR theory, and the BR system, was not developed independently, but rather in an unified way. Thus, the logic itself determines the dependencies between propositions, which are essential to BR systems; the BR theory considers SWMC as the underlying logic, and is thus appropriate to guide the changes in the beliefs of a system whose reasoning is based on this logic; the system's reasoning is guided by SWMC, and its updates are based on the BR theory.

In terms of the established terminology, we can describe our system as a nonmonotonic ATMS, with reasoning and BR capabilities.

2 The underlying logic

To allow for the support of BR systems, the underlying logic, SWMC,[3] works with justified wffs. A *justified wff* is of the form $<A, \tau, \alpha, \gamma>$, where A is a wff, τ an origin tag, α an origin set, and γ a justification. The justified wff $<A, \tau, \alpha, \gamma>$ corresponds to a particular derivation of the wff A. The *origin tag* indicates

---

[*] This work was partially supported by Junta Nacional de Investigação Científica e Tecnológica (JNICT), under Grants 87-107, 90/167, and 1243/92.

[2] SNePSwD (*Semantic Network Processing System with Defaults*) is an extension of SNePS (Shapiro and Martins, 1990).

[3] From Shapiro, Wand, Martins, and Cravo.

how the justified wff was generated. It is an element of the set $\{hyp, asp, der\}$; *hyp* identifies hypotheses (non-derived or basic wffs), *asp* identifies assumptions, and *der* identifies derived wffs. The *origin set* indicates the dependencies of this justified wff on other wffs. It contains those hypotheses and assumptions that were used in that particular derivation of the wff. The *justification* indicates the wffs from which this justified wff was derived. It is is a set of wffs; these wffs are those that immediately originated the wff through the application of a rule of inference. Justifications are used by the BR system (see Section 4.4).

Hypotheses represent the available information, from which we want to draw conclusions. *Assumptions*, on the other hand, are used in the recording of dependencies, when we draw a defeasible conclusion by applying a default rule to a particular individual; they record the fact that the conclusion depends, among other things, on the *assumption* that the default rule is applicable to that individual.

2.1 Language and inference rules

SWMC (Cravo and Martins, 1991; Cravo, 1992) extends the language of FOL, $\mathcal{L}_{FOL}$, with: the set of *default rules*, $\mathcal{L}_D$, which are of the form $\triangledown(x)\, A(x) \rightarrow B(x)$, where $A(x) \in \mathcal{L}_{FOL}$, $B(x) \in \mathcal{L}_{FOL}$, and $\triangledown$ is called the *default quantifier*. For example, $\triangledown(x) Bird(x) \rightarrow Flies(x)$ is a default rule, whose intended meaning is *By default birds fly*, or *Typically birds fly*; the set of *assumptions*, $\mathcal{L}_A$, which are of the form $Applicable(D, c)$ where D is a default rule and c is an individual symbol. This wff is intended to represent the assumption that the default rule D is applicable to the individual c; the set of *exceptions*, $\mathcal{L}_E$, which are of the form $\forall(x)\, E(x) \rightarrow \neg Applicable(D, x)$ (where D is a default rule), meaning that E's are exceptions to the default rule D.

SWMC is a natural deduction system. It has two distinct sets of inference rules: (1) *standard rules*, which include a rule of hypothesis,[4] and basically two rules for each connective ($\wedge$, $\vee$, $\rightarrow$, $\neg$) and quantifier ($\forall$, $\exists$); and (2) *extended rules*, which deal with default rules. Due to space constraints, we only present one extended rule (the complete set of rules can be found in (Cravo, 1992)):

Default elimination. Let $D = \triangledown(x)\, A(x) \rightarrow B(x)$. From $<D, hyp, \{D\}, \{\}>$, and $<A(c), \tau, \alpha, \gamma>$ (where c is an individual symbol), we can infer the assumption $<Applicable(D, c), asp, \alpha', \gamma'>$, and $<B(c), der, \alpha', \gamma'>$, where $\alpha' = \{Applicable(D, c), D\} \cup \alpha$, and $\gamma' = \{Applicable(D, c), D, A(c)\}$.

Assumptions record the fact that when $B(c)$ is inferred from $\triangledown(x)\, A(x) \rightarrow B(x)$, and $A(c)$, the inferred wff depends not only on these two wffs, but also on the *assumption* that this default rule is applicable to the individual c.

Given a set of wffs β and a wff A, we say that A is *derivable* from β if, using the rules of inference of SWMC, it is possible to generate a justified wff of the form $<A, \tau, \alpha, \gamma>$, with $\alpha \subseteq \beta$.

---

[4] According to this rule, only wffs in $\mathcal{L}_{FOL} \cup \mathcal{L}_D \cup \mathcal{L}_E$ can be introduced as hypotheses.

2.2 Kinds of consequence

The notion of derivability in SWMC is not enough to capture the idea of consequence required in a nonmonotonic logic. Consequence is based on two concepts: context and belief space determined by a context. A *context* is any set of hypotheses. Given a consistent context, a *belief space* determined by this context is a consistent set of FOL wffs which are derivable from the hypotheses in the context, and eventually some assumptions. If we think of a context as representing the information available to an agent, a belief space defined by this context will correspond to an acceptable set of beliefs of the agent.

Determining the belief spaces defined by a context is not a single step process. It involves the construction of three intermediate sets of justified wffs: (1) the extended context; (2) the primitive cores; and (3) the cores.

A consistent context determines an *extended context*, a set of *justified wffs* whose origin tags are either *hyp* or *asp*: the hypotheses are all the hypotheses in the context, and the assumptions correspond to the assumptions which can consistently be raised from the default rules in the context. Since the extended context may contain mutually incompatible assumptions, the extended context is split into maximal consistent subsets, the *primitive cores* of the context. Each of these primitive cores will be a potential basis for constructing an acceptable set of beliefs. There are some situations in which some primitive cores cannot be considered acceptable and some of them have to be discarded (Cravo, 1992). The remaining are called the *cores* of the context, and each of them will define an acceptable set of beliefs or belief space: the *belief space* defined by a core is the set of all FOL wffs derivable from the hypotheses and assumptions in that core.

Having defined belief space we can now define the notion of consequence, between a context and a wff. When we say that a wff $A \in \mathcal{L}_{FOL}$ is a consequence of a set of hypotheses β, we may mean one of three things: 1) only the hypotheses in β were used in the derivation of A, i.e., A is derivable from β using classical logic; in this case we say that A is a *sound consequence* of β; 2) the wff A was derived using not only the hypotheses in β, but also possibly some assumptions, and A belongs to every belief space determined by β; in this case we say that A is a *plausible consequence* of β; 3) there is at least one belief space determined by β that contains A; in this case we say that A is a *conceivable consequence* of β. These notions correspond, respectively, to the intuitive statements: given β then A *must* follow; given β *there are reasons to suppose A*, and *no reasons against it*; given β, *there are reasons to suppose A, but there are also reasons against supposing A*.

We think that the distinction between the different kinds of consequence is very important: when faced with incomplete information we should be able to draw conclusions suggested by the default rules; however, in some situations, it is crucial to know whether a given conclusion is sound, plausible, or just conceivable. This is related to the skeptical/credulous distinction in nonmonotonic formalisms: in *skeptical approaches* only wffs that belong to every extension are considered as consequences—these correspond to sound and plausible consequences in SWMC; in *credulous approaches*, any wff that belongs to at least one extension is considered as a consequence of the theory—these correspond to conceivable consequences in SWMC. What other formalisms don't allow is the distinction between sound and plausible consequences, since they both belong to every extension of a theory. The recording of dependencies in SWMC allows for this distinction: sound consequences can be derived using only the hypotheses in the context, whereas plausible consequences also need one or more *assumptions* to be derived.

We will now briefly sketch the results of the comparison of our logic with CDL[5] (Brewka, 1991). In CDL, default rules are written just like in Default Logic. In our logic, the default $A(x) : B(x) / C(x)$ can be translated by the wffs: $\bigtriangledown(x)\ A(x) \rightarrow C(x)$, $\forall(x)\ \neg B(x) \rightarrow \neg Applicable(\bigtriangledown(x)\ A(x) \rightarrow C(x),\ x)$. The translation from SWMC to CDL is obvious. Given this translation, we prove (Cravo, 1992) that there is an exact correspondence between the extensions of a theory in CDL, and the sets of wffs derivable from the primitive cores of the corresponding context in SWMC. After his definition of extension, Brewka points out that it destroys part of the additional expressiveness of nonnormal defaults. To recover this expressiveness Brewka imposes an additional condition on extensions: he only considers as acceptable those extensions which are priority-preserving. Again, there is an "almost" exact correspondence between the priority-preserving extensions of a theory in CDL, and the sets of wffs derivable from the cores (i.e., the belief spaces) of the corresponding context in SWMC.

3 The belief revision theory

The revisions of belief performed by SNePSwD are guided by a BR theory presented in (Cravo, 1992). This theory uses a finite base for performing revisions, the current context, that corresponds to the basic beliefs of the system and act somewhat like a belief base in Nebel's sense (Nebel, 1990). However, our BR theory differs from other theories, e.g. (Gärdenfors, 1988; Nebel, 1990), in three aspects: (1) Since it is based on a nonmonotonic logic, the removal of a formula from a set of beliefs (belief space) may, in certain cases, be obtained either by the removal of hypotheses from the context or by the *addition* of hypotheses to the context. (2) It allows the specification of several partial orders between the hypotheses in the context as well as a partial order between the several partial orders. (3) The result of a revision may not be a unique set of beliefs but rather several equally acceptable sets.

The motivation behind points (2) and (3) is that, concerning the two best known BR theories (Gärdenfors, 1988; Nebel, 1990), we think, like (Doyle, 1991), that: "Both theories suffer from unnecessarily strong standards for correct revisions, and from very strong assumptions about what information is available to guide revisions. Specifically, the sense of 'rationality' postulated by these theories

---

[5] Cumulative Default Logic.

requires that rational revisions be unique (they do not permit equally acceptable revisions). They also require total orderings of all propositions, even though
most domains of knowledge in AI systems are too incomplete and ambiguous
to supply such complete orderings". Doyle adds that, in practice, the orderings available to guide revision consist of several partial orderings that may even
disagree between them.

When a change must be performed to a context β, the specified partial orders
(if any) are combined, yielding a single partial order, $\leq_\beta$. As usual, if it is
necessary to discard some hypotheses from β, the less valuable ones, according
to $\leq_\beta$, are chosen. Depending on the amount of information contained in $\leq_\beta$,
the result may be unique, or consist of several equally acceptable alternatives.

Although we do not describe here the technical details of our theory, we now
illustrate, through a small example, what is perhaps the most distinguishing
feature of our theory: it concerns the change of a context in such a way that
one of its consequences is no longer a consequence of the modified context,
when the consequence in question is not a sound one. Suppose that we know
that *typically birds fly, except for ostriches and penguins*, and that *Tweety is
a bird*. From this we may plausibly conclude that *Tweety flies*. Suppose now
that we have reasons to doubt that *Tweety flies*, although we are not sure
that it doesn't. In this situation, we will want to abandon the conclusion that
Tweety flies. Surely, the most natural way to achieve this is to believe that
Tweety is some kind of exception to the default rule, i.e., that it is either an
ostrich, or a penguin, or that it simply doesn't fly (which includes all possible exceptions). Surely too, we would not reject the information that *typically
birds fly* or that *Tweety is a bird*. The available information would be represented in SWMC by the context (for notational convenience the default ru-
le is represented by D) $\beta = \{\triangledown(x)\ Bird(x) \rightarrow Flies(x), \forall(x)\ Ostrich(x) \rightarrow
\neg Applicable(D, x), \forall(x)\ Penguin(x) \rightarrow \neg Applicable(D, x), Bird(Tweety)\}$. The
wff $Flies(Tweety)$ is a plausible consequence of β, because it needs the assumption $Applicable(D, Tweety)$ to be derived. So, to invalidate this derivation we
will add a wff to β. This wff must be such that the assumption can no longer be
raised in the new context, let's call it β'. Obviously, the addition of any of the
wffs $\neg Flies(Tweety)$, $Ostrich(Tweety)$, or $Penguin(Tweety)$ would do the job.
The wff $Flies(Tweety)$ is called the conclusion of $Applicable(D, Tweety)$. Formally, given an assumption $Applicable(\triangledown(x)\ A(x) \rightarrow B(x), c)$, its *conclusion* is
the wff $B(c)$. As for the wffs $Ostrich(Tweety)$, and $Penguin(Tweety)$ they correspond to the negations of the implicit assumptions of $Applicable(D, Tweety)$
in β. Formally, given any assumption $Applicable(D, c)$, and any context β, the
set of implicit assumptions of $Applicable(D, c)$ in β is the set $Implicit(D, c, \beta) =
\{\neg E(c) : \forall(x)\ E(x) \rightarrow \neg Applicable(D, x) \in \beta\}$. What our BR theory determines
is that to invalidate, in a context, a derivation containing an assumption, we add
to the context the disjunction of the negations of the following wffs: the conclusion of the assumption, and the implicit assumptions of the assumption. So, in
the case of the example, the new context would be $\beta' = \beta \cup \{\neg Flies(Tweety)
\lor Ostrich(Tweety) \lor Penguin(Tweety)\}$. This example shows that the way to

remove wffs that correspond to reasonable (but not sound) conclusions should be radically different from the way to remove sound conclusions, which is the only one considered in all other theories, because they all consider a monotonic underlying logic.

4 The belief revision system

We now describe some of the most interesting features of SNePSwD.

4.1 Resolving contradictions

SNePSwD considers, at any moment, a set of hypotheses, the *current context*, and performs reasoning in this context. One of the important roles of this system is the detection and removal of contradictions. The recording of dependencies defined by SWMC enables the distinction between two kinds of contradictions: apparent contradictions and real contradictions.

An *apparent contradiction* is one derived not only from hypotheses but also from some assumption(s). In this case, the way to "resolve" the contradiction is decided by the underlying logic: the current context does not change (its hypotheses alone are not inconsistent); the change occurs in the cores defined by the context, and the user of the system may not even be aware of this change.

A *real contradiction* is one derived only from hypotheses. When a real contradiction is derived in the current context, this context will typically be revised in order to get rid of the contradiction. This revision consists in the removal of one or more hypotheses, the culprits for the contradiction, from the current context. The hypotheses to be removed are determined by the underlying BR theory.

Regardless of whether the detected contradiction is an apparent one or a real one, a struture named KIS (Known Inconsistent Sets) is updated to reflect the fact that the set(s) of wffs from which the contradiction was derived is now known to be inconsistent.

4.2 Preferring belief spaces

The partial orders defined over the hypotheses of a context may also be used to determine a preferred belief space, when a context defines more than one belief space. In this case, besides the orders mentioned, another order, the *specificity order* is used to compute $\leq_\beta$. The specificity order is a partial order defined between default rules. Given two default rules, $D_1 = \nabla(x) \, A_1(x) \rightarrow B_1(x)$ and $D_2 = \nabla(x) \, A_2(x) \rightarrow B_2(x)$, belonging to a context β, we say that D_2 is more specific than D_1 in β, iff $\beta \vdash \forall(x) \, A_2(x) \rightarrow A_1(x)$ and $\beta \nvdash \forall(x) \, A_1(x) \rightarrow A_2(x)$. For example, the rule *By default penguins don't fly* is more specific than the rule *By default birds fly*, because all penguins are birds, and not all birds are penguins. In case of conflict between two default rules we should prefer to apply the more specific one. To determine whether there is a preferred belief space of a context β, the specificity order between the default rules of β is computed, and used, along with the other specified orders, to determine $\leq_\beta$ (the relative value of the specificity order in relation to the other orders can also be specified). The belief space (if any) which corresponds to the application of the more valuable default rules, according to $\leq_\beta$, is the preferred belief space.

4.3   Consistency in SNePSwD

In SWMC, the computation of the belief spaces defined by a context relies on the determination of the consistency of sets of wffs, a semi-decidable problem. For this reason, we cannot expect SNePSwD to always come up with the right answer concerning the consistency of a set of wffs. If we tried to obtain such perfection, we would get a system that, in some situations, would never come up with any answer at all. This doesn't mean that SNePSwD just jumps to conclusions suggested by default rules without any consistency check. Instead, SNePSwD performs a *restricted* consistency test. In particular, when SNePSwD applies a default rule $\bigtriangledown(x)\ A(x) \rightarrow B(x)$ to an individual c to conclude $B(c)$, it will also try to derive $\neg B(c)$ and $E_1(c)$, ..., $E_n(c)$, where E_1, ..., E_n are the known exceptions to the default rule, that is, for $1 \leq i \leq n$, $\forall(x)\ E_i(x) \rightarrow \neg Applicable(\bigtriangledown(x)\ A(x) \rightarrow B(x), x)$ is "known" by SNePSwD. If none of these derivations succeeds, SNePSwD will *assume* $B(c)$. Of course, one may say that, given this test, SNePSwD will sometimes assume "wrong" conclusions. But isn't this what defeasible reasoning is all about? We jump to conclusions which, in face of additional information or *after some more thinking*, may have to be abandoned. The important issue is that we keep in mind the status of these conclusions: they are just reasonable (plausible or conceivable, in SWMC's terminology) and when a contradiction is detected, they are the first ones to be abandoned. The dependency recording used by SNePSwD enables it to distinguish between reasonable conclusions and sound ones, and so it can recover from mistakes, as new information is obtained and/or new sets of wffs are discovered to be inconsistent.

4.4   The role of justifications

Justifications keep a record of the history of derivations. By inspecting the justifications we can reconstruct the sequence of inference steps that led to a particular derivation of a wff. SNePSwD uses justifications for two purposes: explanation and propagation of dependencies.

The justification of a justified wff whose wff is A, and whose origin set is contained in at least one of the cores of a given context β, provides an explanation for A in β: (1) if the justified wff corresponds to an hypothesis (its justification is the empty set), the explanation is simply "A by hypothesis"; (2) if the justified wff does not correspond to an hypothesis, and its justification is $\{J_1, \ldots, J_n\}$, the explanation is "A because J_1, ..., and J_n".

Besides the propagation of dependencies defined by the rules of inference of SWMC, SNePSwD performs another kind of dependency propagation, based on justifications. This propagation takes place when a new derivation is obtained for a wff A which has already been used to derive some other wff B. In these circumstances, a new justified wff with wff B is generated, which takes into account the new derivation for A.

5 Conclusion

We presented a computational system capable of defeasible reasoning, of revising its beliefs, and which uses truth maintenance techniques to maintain its set of beliefs.

An important point of our work is the fact that the nonmonotonic logic, the BR theory, and the BR system were not developed independently, but rather in an unified way. Thus, the logic itself determines the dependencies between propositions, which are essential to BR systems; the BR theory considers SWMC as the underlying logic, and is thus appropriate to guide the changes in the beliefs of a system whose reasoning is based on this logic; the system's reasoning is guided by SWMC, and its updates are based on the BR theory.

Although the underlying formalisms, i.e., the logic and the BR theory, were developed without any particular application in mind, we came to the conclusion that the resulting system can be successfully used in the solution on typical problems of AI, namely in the areas of diagnosis, inheritance, and counterfactual reasoning. This success comes from the combined use of the two formalisms as well as the truth maintenance techniques.

References

Brewka G.: Cumulative Default Logic: in defense of nonmonotonic inference rules. *Artificial Intelligence 50*, N.2, 183-205, 1991.

Cravo M.R.: *Raciocínio por Omissão e Revisão de Crenças: Dois Aspectos do Senso Comum*. PhD Thesis, Instituto Superior Técnico, Lisbon, Portugal, 1992.

Cravo M.R. and Martins J.P.: Being Aware of Assumptions. *Proc. Seventh Österreichische Artificial Intelligence Tagung*, Kaindl (ed), 137-146, Informatik-Fachberichte 287, Heidelberg, Germany: Springer-Verlag, 1991.

Doyle J.: Rational Belief Revision. *Proc. KR 91*, 163-174, Morgan Kaufmann Inc., San Mateo, CA, 1991.

Gärdenfors P.: *Knowledge in Flux: Modeling the Dynamics of Epistemic States*, The MIT Press, Cambridge, MA, 1988.

Nebel B.: *Reasoning and Revision in Hybrid Representation Systems*. Springer-Verlag, Heidelberg, Germany, 1990.

Shapiro S.C. e Martins J.P.: Recent Advances and Developments: The SNePS 2.1 Report. *Current Trends in SNePS - Semantic Network Processing System*, Kumar (ed), 1-13, Lecture Notes in Artificial Intelligence 437, Heidelberg, Germany: Springer-Verlag, 1990.

Influence of Granularity Level in Fuzzy Functional Dependencies[*]

J.C. Cubero[†], J.M. Medina, M.A. Vila

Dpto. Ciencias de la Computación e Inteligencia Artificial
Facultad de Ciencias. Universidad de Granada
Campus de Fuentenueva. 18071 Granada, Spain.
†carlos@robinson.ugr.es

Abstract. Relational Databases (R.D) can be considered the most widely used approach to Databases [5]. But in Classical R.D it is not possible to store or treat vague information.

When extending R.D to Fuzzy Relational Databases (F.R.D) it is needed more than a system capable of storing and treating fuzzy information in tables or relations: it must extend the notion that a relation represents the association between a set of key attributes and other set of attributes relationed with the former. The concept of *functional dependency* (f.d) is the key to understand and treat this problem.

In this paper we will present a refinement of the definition of f.f.d given in [6] attending to *granularity levels* imposed in the attributes. We justify this imposition from a semantic point of view.

1 Preliminaries

There are various extensions to the Relational model using Fuzzy Set Theory to model vagueness. A good survey can be found in [14]. We consider a general definition of Fuzzy Relational Database where a relation is a subset of $\times_{k=1}^{n} A_k$ with A_k the corresponding domain of discourse, and the values allowed in the tuples are numbers or scalars (elements of A_k), possibility distributions over the elements in A_k, etc (see [11, 15, 8]).

From now on, we will consider a set of attributes $\{A_h\}_{h=1...n}$ and an instance r of a relation scheme $REL(A_1, \ldots, A_n)$. For those attributes A, which admits a fuzzy treatment, let us suppose we have a **resemblance relation** R_A defined on D_A. This term is used to denote a reflexive and symmetric relation. In [2, 3] it is required in addition, transitivity (or pseudo transitivity) property to obtain equivalence classes. In [12] they work in a more general framework using partitions: but these impositions are too strong in real systems; so, their treatment and conclusions can hardly be applied to model real life worlds.

The existence of R_A is not really an imposition because it can be used $R_A(d, d') = \delta_{d,d'}$ when it is not wanted to establish any relation among the elements in D_A.

---

[*] Work partially supported by Research Project TIC 90-0690 M.E.C.

We consider, associated with each attribute A, several **levels of resemblance**: $\boldsymbol{\alpha}_A = \{\alpha_{i,A}\}_{i=1...h}$ (we will denote $\boldsymbol{\alpha}_A$ by α_A) and several **levels of precision** given by $\boldsymbol{\gamma}_A = \{\gamma_{j,A}\}_{j=1...h'}$ with $0 \leq \gamma_{j,A} \leq 1$ (we will denote $\boldsymbol{\gamma}_A$ by γ_A). We will work with normal fuzzy values; then we always must consider level one as level of precision: $\gamma_{1,A} = 1 \ \forall A$.

Now, we have resemblance and precision levels, and we must relate them. With each level of precision there must be associated a level of resemblance in the following sense:

$$\gamma_{j,A} \text{ is related to } \alpha_{\gamma_{j,A}} \text{ in such a way that } \gamma_{j,A} > \gamma_{j',A} \Rightarrow \alpha_{\gamma_{j,A}} \geq \alpha_{\gamma_{j',A}}$$

From now on, and for the sake of simplicity in the notation, we will assume $h = h'$, i.e., the same number of precision and resemblance levels for a given attribute.

2 Semantic Considerations Regarding F.F.D

2.1 What is a Fuzzy Function?

Let $A(t), B(t)$ a pair of fuzzy values for a tuple t and attributes A, B. We must translate the semantic imposition that $B(t)$ is determined by (related to) $A(t)$:

> $B(t)$ *is related to* $A(t)$ *means that: to each possible assignment 'a' of* $A(t)$ *-weighted with its membership degree- corresponds any possible assignment 'b' of* $B(t)$ *-weighted with its membership degree-* . In our approach, we graduate the weight given by the membership degree, through levels of precision.

If $B(t)$ is related to $A(t)$ and for instance $a \in \text{Kernel}(A(t))$, then the figure illustrates the fact that a is associated with any $B(t)$-value.

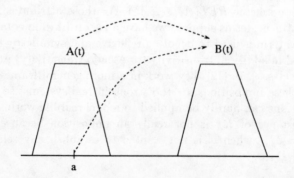

2.2 (α, β)-f.f.d

The natural fuzzy extension of functional dependency between two set of attributes X, Y is through the expression:

If $X(t_1)$ is X-resemblant to $X(t_2)$ then $Y(t_1)$ must be Y-resemblant to $Y(t_2)$

Attributes in X will be called **antecedent attributes** and **consequent attributes** for Y. Now, if $X = (A_k)_{k \in K}$ with A_k single attributes, the expression "$X(t_1)$ X-resemblant to $X(t_2)$" must be read as "Each $A_k(t_1)$ A_k-resemblant to $A_k(t_2)$".

In [6] we revised several approaches to *fuzzy functional dependencies* (f.f.d) [10, 9, 4]. Up to now, other approaches have appeared as [12] in the framework of Buckles and Petry [2] model. In [16] it is used the same definition that Raju and Majumdar [10] and introduces a special Join operator. The definition of f.f.d. given in [6] becomes:

Definition 1 *A relation r satisfies a $(\alpha, \beta) - $ ffd denoted by $X \xrightarrow{(\alpha, \beta)} Y$ with $X = (A_k)_{k \in K}$, $Y = (A_{k'})_{k' \in K'}$, $\alpha = (\alpha_{A_k})_{k \in K}$, $\beta = (\beta_{A_{k'}})_{k' \in K'}$, K, $K' \subseteq \{1 \ldots n\}$, if and only if:*

if $\{comp(A_k(t_1), A_k(t_2)) \geq \alpha_{A_k}\}_{k \in K}$ then $\{comp(A_{k'}(t_1), A_{k'}(t_2)) \geq \beta_{A_{k'}}\}_{k' \in K'}$

where *comp* is a compatibility measure between fuzzy sets. Now, we consider that each α_{A_k}, $\beta_{A_{k'}}$, is in fact, a vector of levels: $\alpha_{A_k} \equiv \{\alpha_{i,A_k}, i = 1 \ldots r\}$, $\beta_{A_{k'}} \equiv \{\beta_{j,A_{k'}}, j = 1 \ldots r'\}$

For the sake of simplicity, we will assume the same number of precision levels ($r = r'$) in each A_k $k = 1 \ldots n$: if it is not the case, then the expert must relate ones to others in the same way he proceed when relating resemblance levels and precision levels. So, and if we assume X, Y to be single attributes, and if there is no confusion, we will denote α_X, $\alpha_{i,X}$, α_Y, $\alpha_{i,Y}$ by $\alpha, \alpha_i, \beta, \beta_i$ respectively.

In order to define functional dependency between two (set of) attributes we have to *compare* two elements $A(t_1)$, $A(t_2)$ and $B(t_1)$, $B(t_2)$. We will treat single attributes first, and then we will faced with sets of attributes.

3   Granular f.f.d

3.1   Definition of Dependency

Case: $A(t_1)$, $B(t_1)$ Fuzzy Values and $A(t_2)$, $B(t_2)$ Crisp Let us consider an arbitrary assignment a in the kernel of $A(t_1)$ (level of precision equal to $\gamma_{A,1} = 1$). Then, applying the semantic interpretation of the previous section, a is in correspondence with any assignment b of $B(t_1)$. So, if $A(t_2)$ verifies $R_A(a, A(t_2)) \geq \alpha_1$ then, $B(t_2)$ must be $\beta_1 - $ resemblant to **all** the assignments in the $\gamma_{B,1} = 1$ cut of $B(t_1)$, i.e. the kernel of $B(t_1)$. In a similar manner if $A(t_2)$ is $\alpha_i -$resemblant with some $a \in (A(t_1))_{\gamma_i}$ then $B(t_2)$ must be $\beta_i -$resemblant to **all** the assignments in the $\gamma_{i,B}$ cut of $B(t_1)$.

With each attribute we must compute

$$comp^d{}_{\gamma_{i,A}}(A(t_1), A(t_2)) = \sup_{a \in (A(t_1))_{\gamma_{i,A}}} R_A(a, A(t_2))$$

$$comp^f{}_{\gamma_{i,B}}(B(t_1), B(t_2)) = \inf_{b \in (B(t_1))_{\gamma_{i,B}}} R_B(b, B(t_2))$$

so that we will say:

$$A(t_2) \simeq^d{}_{\gamma_{i,A}} A(t_1) \Leftrightarrow comp^d{}_{\gamma_{i,A}}(A(t_1), A(t_2)) \geq \alpha_i$$

$$B(t_2) \simeq^f{}_{\gamma_{i,B}} B(t_1) \Leftrightarrow comp^f{}_{\gamma_{i,B}}(B(t_1), B(t_2)) \geq \beta_i$$

Now, if $A(t_1)$ is a fuzzy value which contains for instance the crisp value $A(t_3)$ actually in the database, then it must be taking into account the information $A(t_3) \rightarrow B(t_3)$, so that it must be $B(t_2) \simeq_{\beta_i} B(t_3)$ too, although it were not $A(t_3) \simeq^d_{\alpha_i} A(t_2)$.

Case: $A(t_1), A(t_2), B(t_1), B(t_2)$ Fuzzy Values If we apply the same reasoning followed when one pair of values were crisp and the other fuzzy, we define now:

$$comp^d{}_{\gamma_{i,A}}(A(t_1), A(t_2)) = \sup_{a \in (A(t_1))_{\gamma_{i,A}}, a' \in (A(t_2))_{\gamma_{i,A}}} R_A(a, a')$$

$$comp^f{}_{\gamma_{i,B}}(B(t_1), B(t_2)) = \inf_{b \in (B(t_1))_{\gamma_{i,B}}, b' \in (B(t_2))_{\gamma_{i,B}}} R_B(b, b')$$

and we apply the same definition of f.f.d. of the previous case.

Now, if we have a set of antecedent attributes $X = (A_k)_{k \in K}$, we will say that $X(t_1)$ and $X(t_2)$ are resemblant at level $\gamma_{i,X}$ if:

$$X(t_1) \simeq^d{}_{\gamma_{i,X}} X(t_2) \Leftrightarrow A_k(t_1) \simeq^d{}_{\gamma_{i,A_k}} A_k(t_2) \quad \forall k \in K$$

We will say that they are not resemblant if:

$$X(t_1) \not\simeq^d X(t_2) \Leftrightarrow \exists i \in \{1 \ldots h\} \ A(t_1) \not\simeq^d{}_{\gamma_{i,A}} A(t_2)$$

and analogously for a set of consequent attributes (replacing $\simeq^d$ by $\simeq^f$).

The definition of dependency can be finally stated as:

Definition 2 *A relation r satisfies a* **Granular (α, β)–ffd**, *denoted by* $X \xrightarrow{(\alpha,\beta)} Y$ *if and only if every pair of tuples t_1, t_2 satisfy:*

For those $i \in \{1 \ldots h\}$ such that $X(t_1) \simeq^d{}_{\gamma_{i,X}} X(t_2)$ it must be :

$$Y(t) \simeq^f{}_{\gamma_{i,Y}} Y(t') \ \forall \ t, t' \text{ such that } X(t) \subseteq X(t_1) \ X(t') \subseteq X(t_2)$$

It can be shown, following [6], that this definition of dependency, verifies that Armstrong axioms are sound and complete; it is only needed the fact that if two fuzzy values are $\simeq^f$–resemblant, then they are $\simeq^d$–resemblant too, which is immediate to see, and taking $t = t_1$, $t' = t_2$.

3.2 Granularity Restriction in Data

Let now F be a fuzzy set on a domain of discourse D_A for an attribute A, where it is defined a resemblance relation R_A. We wonder if there must be any restriction for F if we want F to appear as a tuple value $A(t) = F$ in the Database. For the augmentation axiom to be true, it must be satisfied the particular case $A \xrightarrow{(\alpha,\beta)} A \ \forall \ A$. So, it must be $a \simeq_{\gamma_i}^J a$, whenever a is located twice into the database. This restriction becomes:

Restriction. *Let A be an attribute with levels of precision and resemblance given by $\gamma_{j,A}$ and $\alpha_{\gamma_{j,A}}$ respectively. Then $A(t)$ is a valid tuple value if and only if*

$$U(A(t)_{\gamma_{j,A}}) = \inf_{d,d' \in A(t)_{\gamma_{j,A}}} R_A(d,d') \geq \alpha_{\gamma_{j,A}}$$

This will be stated as "$A(t)$ satisfy the Granularity Level imposed in A".
This restriction states that the tuple attributes values can not be too fuzzy.

It is very important to note that when there **not** exists t' such that $X(t) \simeq_{\gamma_i}^d X(t')$ then, the granularity restriction is not necessary. In the classical crisp model, it is well known that there are too much problems with the null value when it is interpreted as "any value is a possible assignment" ("unknown"). It can appear as value of a consequent attribute $Y(t)$ **if** there is not in the database any tuple t' such that $X(t) = X(t')$. But if there exists such t', then "unknown" is not a valid assignment for $Y(t)$ if we want to maintain the dependency.

As said in [7] *"There is no fully satisfactory relational design theory as yet that includes null values"*. In fact, this statement is a particularization, when "null" is "unknown", of the following: *"There is not fully satisfactory relational (Classical) design theory as yet that includes fuzzy values"*. Our fuzzy extension of this restriction is that *"There is not fully satisfactory fuzzy relational design theory as yet that includes fuzzy values out from the granular restrictions"*. Of course, we must develop a design methodology to prove that there exists a fully satisfactory fuzzy relational design theory, but this is beyond the scope of this paper.

4 Concluding Remarks

We have treated a fundamental issue that have not been taken into account up now, that is the granularity level imposed in the attributes in the framework of Fuzzy Relational Databases. And it is of primary interest, because, as we have shown, *if our aim is to extend the Relational DataBase* **Model** *and not merely to build a Fuzzy Storing System, then we must impose granularity restrictions on the values that can appear in a tuple.* This imposition must be also taking into account, when defining fuzzy functional dependencies.

In order to complete the study of the influence of granularity restrictions in Fuzzy Relational Databases, it is necessary to treat the problem of redundancy and the definition of key attributes, as well as loss less decompositions for the Database Design. All of these issues will be treated in forthcoming works.

Remark. The authors are grateful to A. Kiss, J. Abad and O. Pons for their comments and discussions.

References

1. Beeri C., Fagin R., Howard J.H. (1977). *A Complete Axiomatization for Functional and Multivalued Dependencies*. ACM SIGMOD International Symposium on Management of Data pp 47-61
2. Buckles B.P., Petry F.E. (1982). *A Fuzzy Representation of Data for Relational Databases*. Fuzzy Sets and Systems, 7. pp 213-226
3. Buckles B.P., Petry F.E. (1984). *Extending the Fuzzy Database Fuzzy Numbers*. Information Sciences 34 pp 145-155
4. Chen G., Vandenbulcke J., Kerre E.E. (1991). *A Step Towards the Theory of Fuzzy Relational Database Design*. Proceedings on Computer, Management Science. IFSA'91. pp 44-47
5. Codd E.F. (1970). *A Relational Model of Data for Large Shared Data Banks*. Commun. ACM, 13, (6). pp 377-387
6. Cubero J.C., Vila M.A. *A New Definition of Fuzzy Functional Dependencies in Fuzzy Relational Databases* To appear in International Journal of Intelligent Systems.
7. Elmasri, R. Navathe, S.B. (1989). *Fundamentals of Database Systems*. The Benjamin/Cummings Publishing Co.
8. Medina J.M., Pons O., Vila M.A. (1993) *Gefred: A Generalized Model of Fuzzy Relational Databases* To appear in Infomation Sciences.
9. Prade H., Testemale C. (1987). *Representation of Soft Constraints and Fuzzy Attribute Values by Means of Possibility Distributions in Databases*. Analysis of Fuzzy Information. Vol II. Bezdek eds. CRC Press. pp 213-229.
10. Raju K., Majumdar A. (1988). *Fuzzy Functional Dependencies and Loss Less Join Decomposition on Fuzzy Relational Database Systems*. ACM Trans. on Database Systems, 13 (2) pp 129-166
11. Rundensteiner E.A., Hawkes L.W. Bandler W. (1989). *On Nearness Measures in Fuzzy Relational Data Models*. Journal of Approximate Reasoning, 3 pp 267-298
12. Shenoi S., Melton A., Fan L.T. (1992) *Functional Dependencies and Normal Forms in the Fuzzy Relational Database Model*. Information Sciences 60 pp 1-28
13. Ullman, J.D. *Principles of Database and Knowledge-Base Systems*. Vol I. Computer Science Press. 1988
14. Umano M., Fukami S. (1991). *Perspectives of Fuzzy Databases*. Japanese Journal of Fuzzy Theory and Systems, 3 (1) pp 75-91
15. Cubero J.C., Medina J.M., Pons O., Vila M.A. (1992). *A Logic Approach to Fuzzy Relational Databases*. To appear in International Journal of Intelligent Systems.
16. Weiyi L. (1992) *The Reduction of the Fuzzy Data Domain and Fuzzy Consistent Join*. Fuzzy Sets and Systems, 50 pp 89-96

A Logic for Reasoning about Safety in Decision Support Systems

S. K. Das[1] and J. Fox[2]

[1] Department of Computer Science
QMW, University of London
London E1 4NS
[2] Advanced Computation Laboratory
Imperial Cancer Research Fund
London WC2A 3PX

Abstract. Safety is increasingly recognised as an important property of a software system. The safety of a decision support system is a property that ensures that actions recommended by the system will have minimal undesirable consequences. The objective of this paper is to proposes a logical formalism for reasoning about the *external safety* of a decision support system. The proposed logical language makes provision for representing time, preferences, actions and also deontic and safety related operators such as "obligation", "safety" and "authorisation".

1 Introduction

A *decision support system* [3] is a computerised system which utilizes knowledge about a particular application area to help decision makers by recommending suitable actions. The *safety* of a decision support system is a property that ensures that actions recommended by the system will have minimal undesirable consequences. Undesirable consequences may result from recommendations which have arisen in any of the following situations: (Group I) hardware failure and human error (Group II) incorrect design/specification of the system and incorrect implementation or one that differs from the actual specification (Group III) inconsistency/redundancy/inaccuracy/incompleteness of the knowledge base, incorrect dynamic/static update of the knowledge base, lack of appropriate constraints imposed on the system, for example, *integrity constraints, safety constraints, liability and regulatory constraints*.

Ignoring the hardware failure and human error issues in Group I, for the moment, the so called *logical* or *internal safety* deals with Group II. An important part of internal safety has traditionally been maintained by a rigorous formal approach to design and implementation. Internal safety is always generic in nature and therefore does not need any particular attention for a particular application domain. *Proper* or *external safety* is concerned with Group III. Constraints in this group are collectively called *safety conditions* or *safety knowledge*. These safety conditions may be defined as properties which a knowledge base is required to satisfy, represented in some logical language. Safety conditions help in building consistent, complete and accurate knowledge bases and help to prevent incorrect updates.

The objective of this paper is to propose a logical formalism for reasoning about the external safety of a decision support system. Our approach is to extend the idea of integrity constraints in database systems [5]. Integrity constraints have been defined as properties which a database is required to satisfy; these properties are represented as closed first-order formulae. Thus, in this case, a database and its associated constraints are a uniform representation of the universe of discourse through a set of propositions and formulae. This kind of representation does not take into account a proper characterization of static and dynamic aspects of the universe of discourse among properties, events, processes.

Many applications of decision support systems involve reasoning with actions, events and time. In addition to these, deontic concepts of permission and obligation of actions and also preferences among actions come into the picture particularly when liability and regulatory aspects are taken into consideration. In view of this the logic $\mathcal{L}_{safe}$ enriches the propositional calculus by the introduction of a number of appropriately specialised modal operators. Formalisation through modal logic has the major advantage that its possible world semantics reflects the dynamic nature of the world. The generic nature of the logical theory of safety $\mathcal{L}_{safe}$ is intended to ensure its applicability irrespective of any particular application domain.

2 $\mathcal{L}_{safe}$ informally

The development of a logical theory of safety involves the description of a set of temporally qualified assertions outlining what is known about the universe of discourse in different periods of time and consequences of actions in different conditions. The description of the universe of discourse has two aspects: *static* and *dynamic*. The static aspect of the universe of discourse is described by *properties* (e.g., the patient has a cold) and dynamic aspects by *occurrences* (e.g., the patient is given an injection). For a detailed discussion of properties, occurrences, etc. readers are referred to [1]. An occurrence is either an event or a process. Some occurrences involve animate agents (i.e., decision makers) performing *actions*. We shall not consider the cases of occurrences where animate agents do not perform any actions. In light of this discussion, we consider the set of all propositional symbols sorted into properties and actions.

The description of the universe of discourse through a set of properties and occurrences represented in a certain logical theory is interpreted into a conceptual model which is an abstraction of the theory. A conceptual model corresponding to a universe of discourse consists of a set of possible worlds. Each possible world is a state of the conceptual model. Therefore each possible world is a possible state of the universe of discourse at a particular time interval. Some of these states will not be acceptable from the safety point of view. A set of safety conditions about the universe of discourse will be prevented from attaining these states and these safety conditions are expressed in formulae of the underlying logical theory.

The usefulness of time has already been mentioned above; it is considered to be interval oriented for example to deal with representation of the following safety related requirement in a protocol for cancer management: "It is obligatory that the patient undergoes chemotherapy within four weeks and preferably within two weeks after the initial biopsy has been completed". Our approach is like that of interval temporal logic in [1, 7] and discrete in nature. The temporal modal operators are the intervals $[t_1, t_2]$

where $t_1 \leq t_2$ and t_1, t_2 are integers. An operator $[t_1, t_2]$ governs the proposition ϕ as

$$[t_1, t_2]\phi$$

which says that if ϕ is a property, then ϕ is true during interval $[t_1, t_2]$ or if ϕ is an action then ϕ is taken sometime during $[t_1, t_2]$. If ϕ is an action and $[t_1, t_2]$ is the smallest interval over which that action is taken then $[t_1, t_2]\phi$ is written as $[t_1, t_2]!\phi$. An interval formula may be composed with another interval operator. If the modal operator $[t_3, t_4]$ is in the scope of the modal operator $[t_1, t_2]$ then $[t_3, t_4]$ has to be a subinterval of $[t_1, t_2]$. The specification of the interval $[t_3, t_4]$ can either be absolute or relative to $[t_1, t_2]$ taking t_1 as origin. For example, the relative specification $[3, 8][2, 4]\phi$ can be replaced by $[5, 7]\phi$. An interval of the form $[t, t]$ represents a time point and alternatively written as $[[t]]$. A temporal formula involving variable intervals such as $[t_1, t_2]$ and $[t, t + 2]$ represents a set of formulae. This set of formulae can be obtained by all possible valid substitutions to the t's.

Deontic logic [2] is a logic of norms and is well suited to specifying what actions are allowed in a universe of discourse. The deontic notion of obligation has been represented using one modal operator $< Oblg >$ applied on a proposition ϕ as

$$< Oblg > \phi$$

which says that if ϕ is a property then it is obligatory that ϕ or if ϕ is an action then it is obligatory to perform the action. There has been an analogy drawn between modal operator $\Box$ representing necessity and $< Oblg >$ introduced above, that is, interpreting $\Box$ in an obligatory sense to obtain $< Oblg >$. But not all obligatory sentences entail that those sentences currently hold but rather those sentences should somehow be brought about. In contrast, in classical modal logic, if a sentence p necessarily holds it means that p holds in every situation including the current one. This is characterised by the axiom $\Box p \rightarrow p$. However, $< Oblg > p \rightarrow p$ will not be an axiom of the system considered here. Note that the modal operator $[t_1, t_2]$ and $< Oblg >$ can govern any formulae rather than only propositions.

Recommending action is the central feature of a decision support system and therefore we shall be able to represent the sentences that are of the form "action α can be recommended", for example, "If the patient has operable bone cancer then protocol BO04 can be recommended". This is achieved by using the modal operator $< Reco >$ on actions such as

$$< Reco > \alpha$$

A recommended action is associated to two sets of safety conditions which are to be satisfied before it should be executed. The first set, called *safety preconditions*, have to be satisfied in the current state of the knowledge base and the second set, called *safety postconditions*, is expected to be satisfied in the state resulting from performing the action. For example, consider the sentence "If the patient is eligible for treatment under protocol BO03 and folinic acid rescue and prehydration schemes are instituted before chemotherapy and patient will be available for toxicity monitoring then the inclusion of high dose methotrexate in chemotherapy can be recommended". The safety precondition for the action (inclusion of high dose methotrexate in chemotherapy) is that the folinic acid rescue and prehydration schemes are instituted before chemotherapy. The safety postcondition is the availability of the patient for monitoring toxicity after the the action is carried out. Safety postconditions are verified by simulating the state obtained by performing the action. If the verification of safety preconditons and postconditions can be made fully, then a recommended action is considered as safe. Therefore, safeness implies recommendability. To represent the safeness property of an action, we introduce a modal operator < *Safe* > which governs an action as

$$< Safe > \alpha$$

This is interpreted as the action α is safe. If an action cannot be proved to be safe, that is, associated safety conditions are not verified fully and therefore the action may have undesirable consequences, then it can be authorised under special conditions. Authorisation is also useful for representing regulatory constraints, for example, "Authorisation from the patient or patient's guardian is necessary before operation". This constraint will force a decision maker to take appropriate action, that is, authorisation before prescribing to the patient. To represent the authorisation aspects of safety conditions another modal operator < *Auth* > is introduced and governs an action α as

$$< Auth > \alpha$$

is introduced which says that action α is authorised. In a decision making context, multiple choices of actions are usually offered to solve a particular problem. Consequently, the question of preferences among the actions will occur as is seen in the earlier example "It is obligatory ... preferably ...". The choice has to be made by taking into consideration the conditions or circumstances. The notion of preference [9] is introduced through the binary modal operator < *Pref* > which governs a tuple of modal atomic formulae as

$$< Pref > ([t_1, t_2]\alpha, [t_3, t_4]\beta)$$

and interpreted as action α during interval $[t_1, t_2]$ is preferred to action β during interval $[t_3, t_4]$. If an action α is always preferred to action β then it is simply written as < *Pref* > (α, β). The expression < *Pref* > $([t_1, t_2]\alpha, [t_3, t_4]\alpha)$ represents the fact that action α is preferred during $[t_1, t_2]$ than $[t_3, t_4]$.

Example: The example "It is obligatory ... chemotherapy ... after initial biopsy ..." cited earlier can be represented in $\mathcal{L}_{safe}$ as

$$[t_1, t_2]!InitialBiopsy \longrightarrow < Oblg > ((O_1 \vee O_2) \wedge \neg(O_1 \wedge O_2)) \wedge < Pref > (O_1, O_2)$$

where O_1 and O_2 represent the occurrences $[t_2, t_2 + 2]Chemotherapy$ and $[t_2, t_2 + 4]Chemotherapy$ respectively.

Example: Consider a robot working in an environment exposing objects to radiation and can execute actions such as *SwitchOff*, *SwitchOn*, etc. generated from a decision support system incorporated within it. For this particular application we construct the logic $\mathcal{L}_{safe}$ with these actions as well as properties such as *StateOn*, *StateOff*, etc. as propositional symbols. We introduce the special propositional symbol $\odot$ to represent a hazardous state of the knowledge base and the related equivalence $\neg\phi - \odot \equiv < Oblg > \phi$. Some of the proper axioms and safety conditions of the logic are as follows:

Rules

(R-1) If the switch is on and it is put off then it becomes off.

$$[[t_1]]StateOn \wedge [t_1, t_2]!SwitchOff - [t_2, \infty]StateOff$$

(R-2) If the switch is off and it is put on then it becomes on.

$$[[t_1]]StateOff \wedge [t_1, t_2]!SwitchOn - [t_2, \infty]StateOn$$

(R-3) Either switching on or switching off is itself an action at any time.

$$SwitchOff \vee SwitchOn - Switch$$

(R-4) If the object is not blocked then an action can be recommended at any time.

$$Nonblocked - < Reco > Switch$$

(R-5) The action to put the switch off is always safe (fail-safe action).

$$< Safe > SwitchOff$$

Integrity Constraints

(IC-1) Both switch on and off states cannot hold at any time.

$$StateOn \land StateOff \to \bot$$

(IC-2) The action to put the switch on (resp. off) cannot be recommended if the switch is already on (resp. off).

$$StateOn \land <Reco> SwitchOn \to \bot, \quad StateOff \land <Reco> SwitchOff \to \bot$$

(IC-3) The action to replace the object cannot be recommended if it is being exposed.

$$StateOn \land <Reco> Move \to \bot$$

Safety Constraints

(SC-1) Wait for at least three units of time if the object is found blocked; otherwise the system leads to a hazardous state.

$$[t_1, t_2]!Check \land [[t_2]]Blocked \to <Oblg> [t_2, t_2 + 3]!Wait$$

(SC-2) If more than five units of time is allowed to keep the switch at on state, then the system leads to a hazardous state: $[t_1, t_2]StateOn \land t_2 - t_1 > 5 \to \otimes$

(SC-3) If the object is blocked for nine units of time then it is obligatory that recommended switch action is authorised.

$$[[t]] <Reco> Switch \land [t - 9, t]Blocked \to <Oblg> [[t]] <Auth> Switch$$

3 Syntax, Semantics and Axioms

In this section we present very briefly the formal syntax, semantics, axioms schemes and soundness and completeness of $\mathcal{L}_{safe}$. The detail is left out of this version due to space limitations. The language of $\mathcal{L}_{safe}$ is the usual propositional logic extended with the modal operators introduced earlier. The set of propositions is divided into two non-intersecting subsets as properties and actions. A standard set of axiom schemes of propositional logic is considered first along with modus ponens. The system of *minimal deontic logic* [4] or *logic of obligation* $\mathcal{L}_o$ is obtained by adding the inference rule

$$\frac{\phi \to \psi}{<Oblg> \phi \to <Oblg> \psi}$$

and the axiom $\neg <Oblg> \bot$. Deontic necessity is evaluated with respect to every possible world. The logic is analyzed in terms of a model which has a structure $\mathcal{M}_o = <W, O, B>$ in which W is a set of possible worlds, B is a mapping from $Prop$ to subsets of W and O (obligation) is a mapping from W to a set of subsets of W, that is, $O(\omega)$ is a subset of W, for each world ω in W. This mapping O associates with each possible world ω the set $O(\omega)$ of propositions that is in some sense obligatory at ω, that is, $O : W \to \mathcal{P}(Prop)$. A proposition can be identified with a set of possible worlds in $\mathcal{M}_o$. Therefore, O becomes a function from W to $\mathcal{P}(\mathcal{P}(W))$, that is, $O : W \to \mathcal{P}(\mathcal{P}(W))$. A deontic proposition $<Oblg> \phi$ is evaluated in $\mathcal{M}_o$ as

$$\models_\omega^{\mathcal{M}_o} <Oblg> \phi \; iff \; \| \phi \|^{\mathcal{M}_o} \in O(\omega)$$

and satisfies the condition $\emptyset \notin O(\omega)$.

The logic $\mathcal{L}_{safe}$ is constructed from $\mathcal{L}_o$ by including the rest of the modal operators. Sentences containing temporal operators are evaluated with respect to pairs $<\omega, [t_1, t_2]>$ of worlds and time intervals. In other words, $\models_{<\omega,[t_1,t_2]>}^{\mathcal{M}_\alpha} \alpha$ means that α is true in ω in the interval $[t_1, t_2]$. The structure of the final model takes the form

$$\mathcal{M}_{safe} = <W, O, T, P, A, S, R>$$

where T (temporal) is a function which generalizes B and assigns meaning to primitive propositions by associating each primitive proposition ϕ with the combination of worlds and set of intervals when and where ϕ is true. Thus, $T : Prop \rightarrow \mathcal{P}(W \times I)$, where I = $\{[t_1, t_2]: t_1 \leq t_2\}$. The other mappings P (preference), A (authorisation), S (safety) and R (recommendation) are defined in a similar manner. Some of the other axioms and safety conditions which have been included in $\mathcal{L}_{safe}$ are given below:

$$[t_1, t_2]p \wedge t_1 \leq t_3 \wedge t_3 \leq t_4 \wedge t_4 \leq t_2 \rightarrow [t_3, t_4]p$$
$$[t_1, t_2]\alpha \wedge t_3 \leq t_1 \wedge t_1 \leq t_2 \wedge t_2 \leq t_4 \rightarrow [t_3, t_4]\alpha$$
$$\neg[t_1, t_2]\phi \leftrightarrow [t_1, t_2]\neg\phi$$
$$\neg[t_1, t_2](\phi \wedge \psi) \leftrightarrow \neg[t_1, t_2]\phi \wedge \neg[t_1, t_2]\psi$$
$$< Pref > (i\alpha, j\beta) \rightarrow \neg < Pref > (j\beta, i\alpha)$$
$$< Pref > (i\alpha, j\beta) \wedge < Pref > (j\beta, k\gamma) \rightarrow < Pref > (i\alpha, k\gamma)$$
$$< Safe > \alpha \rightarrow < Reco > \alpha$$

where p is a property, ϕ, ψ are formulae, α, β are actions and i, j, k are intervals.

4 Discussion

We shall compare $\mathcal{L}_{safe}$ with a few other theories although none of these has been developed to serve safety purposes exactly as $\mathcal{L}_{safe}$ does. The constraints expressed by logic L_{Deon} in [8] such as

$$\forall p, b(Person(p) \wedge Book(b) \Rightarrow [borrow(p, b)]\mathcal{O}(return(p, b)_{(\leq 30)}))$$

can be represented in first-order $\mathcal{L}_{safe}$ as

$$\forall x \forall y(Person(x) \wedge Book(y) \wedge [[t]]Borrow(x, y) \rightarrow < Oblg > [t, t + 30]Return(x, y))$$

The axioms of the theory of safety proposed in [6] such as

$$proposed(Act) \wedge possible(Act, New) \wedge unsafe(New) \rightarrow obligatory(authorise(Act))$$

can be rewritten in $\mathcal{L}_{safe}$ as

$$< Reco > Act \wedge \neg < Safe > Act \rightarrow < Oblg >< Auth > Act$$

Although, the current paper mainly deals with the technical concept and representation of safety, research on problems like a workable proof-procedure for $\mathcal{L}_{safe}$, simplification and validation of safety conditions for actions, etc. will be presented in subsequent papers.

References

1. J. F. Allen: Towards a general theory of action and time, North-Holland: Artificial Intelligence, 1984, Vol. 23, pp. 123-154
2. L. Aqvist: Deontic Logic, D. Reidel: Handbook of Philosophical Logic, Vol II, pp. 605-714
3. R. H. Bonczek, C. W. Holsapple and A. B. Whinston: Development in decision support systems, Academic Press, Inc.: Advances in Computers, 1984, Vol. 3, pp. 141-175
4. B. Chellas: Modal Logic, Cambridge University Press, 1980
5. S. K. Das: Deductive databases and logic programming, Addison-Wesley, 1992.
6. J. Fox: Engineering safety into expert systems, Direction in Safety-Critical Systems, Chapman and Hall, 1993
7. J. Y. Halpern and Y. Shoham: A propositional modal logic of time intervals, Journal of the Association for Computing Machinery, 1991, Vol. 38, No. 4, pp. 935-962
8. R. J. Wieringa, J. -J. Meyer, H. Weigand: Specifying dynamic and deontic integrity constraints, North-Holland: Data & Knowledge Engineering, 1989, Vol. 4, pp. 157-189
9. G. H. von Wright: The logic of preference, Edinburgh University Press, 1963

Acceptability of arguments as 'logical uncertainty'

Morten Elvang-Gøransson[1,2], Paul J. Krause[1] and John Fox[1]

[1] Advanced Computation Laboratory, Imperial Cancer Research Fund
London WC2A 3PX, UK
[2] Centre for Cognitive Informatics, University of Roskilde
DK-4000 Roskilde, Denmark

Abstract. We briefly discuss the argumentation-paradigm as a unifying framework for practical reasoning and then turn to the definition of a system of argumentation that induces a novel concept of logical uncertainty over conclusions drawn from inconsistent databases.

1 Introduction

A *system of argumentation* formalizes the notions of construction and use of arguments as a formal system, and makes explicit the difference between formal and practical reasoning. In formal reasoning all arguments are equally acceptable. This is not so in practical reasoning, where some arguments can be *more acceptable than* others. In this paper we focus on practical reasoning involving inconsistencies, but the *argumentation-paradigm* applies equally well to other kinds of practical reasoning [4, 7].

We describe how degrees of acceptability can be interpreted as a reflection of the *logical uncertainty* of arguments. A formal correspondence with possibility theory is established by showing that a 'naive' assignment of linguistic qualifiers to propositions, based on the maximal degree of acceptability of their supporting arguments, is in accordance with Dubois and Prade's axioms [2, 3] for possibility theory. This assignment is defined purely on the basis of patterns of argument. Those arguments which are the least open to defeat, given an inconsistent context, are the most certain. Arguments which are based on parts of the context that are themselves inconsistent are the least certain, i.e. the most vulnerable to defeat.

The idea of interpreting different degrees of acceptability as different degrees of logical uncertainty appears to be new. Other authors [1, 4, 8, 9] have suggested similar classifications of arguments (or their conclusions). However, they seem to focus more on the traditional credulous/sceptical distinction on consequence relations and do not give an explicit uncertainty interpretation.

2 The construction and use of arguments

Our basic position is that practical reasoning is a process of first constructing arguments, and then reaching a conclusion by picking the most acceptable argument. These two activities can (ideally) be seen as independent and sequential in time. The *construction of arguments* is in general based on a set of consequence relations. Arguments are formal derivations of an inference system, that are constructed using facts in some database as extra non-logical axioms. In general arguments are represented by two components: a conclusion and an explanation. The *conclusion* is the conclusion of the formal derivation. The *explanation* is an encoding of essential properties of the derivation. This can in extreme cases be either the complete proof tree or nothing at all. We will define a notion of *acceptability* whereby, depending on their form, such arguments can be judged more or less acceptable.

The *use of arguments* presupposes a notion of acceptability. This notion of acceptability is achieved by defining a hierarchy of classes of arguments, where each class reflects a certain degree of acceptability and the hierarchy itself reflects the ordering among these classes. Whether or not an argument has a certain degree of acceptability, depends on its ability to 'pay the price' of membership of the associated class. Acceptability criteria can be defined using properties such as consistency, defeat, relevance, chronological ignorance, closest worlds, most preferred model, specificity, epistemic entrenchment, etc.

Argumentation is the construction and use of arguments. A formal model of argumentation is a *system of argumentation*. Together with Dung [4], Lin and Shoham [7] and others we have observed that many systems for practical reasoning can be modelled as systems of argumentation.

It is in the context of this general view on practical reasoning as argumentation that the system we introduce below should be considered. This system of argumentation is an improved version of that presented in [5].

3   A simple system of argumentation

Arguments are constructed using natural deduction over a propositional database. Arguments are pairs (δ, p), where δ is the set of facts in the database from which the conclusion of the argument, p, is derived. Given a (possibly inconsistent) database, Δ, we have the following definitions.

Definition 1. If $\delta \subseteq \Delta$ is minimal such that $\delta \vdash p$, then (δ, p) is an *argument* from Δ. The argument (δ, p) from Δ is *grounded* on δ and is *supporting* p.

Definition 2. An argument (δ, p) is *consistent* if δ is consistent.

Definition 3. An argument (δ, p) is *tautological* if $\delta = \emptyset$.

Definition 4. Let (δ, p) and (γ, q) be arguments from Δ. The argument (γ, q) can be *defeated* in one of two ways. Firstly, (δ, p) *rebuts* (γ, q) if $p \leftrightarrow \neg q$. Secondly, (δ, p) *undercuts* (γ, q) if for some $r \in \gamma$, $p \leftrightarrow \neg r$.

We may now define a hierarchy of *acceptability classes* using these notions of defeat and argument.

Definition 5. Let Δ be any set of propositions defined over the language $\mathcal{L}$. Then the following classes reflect increasing degrees of acceptability:

$A_1(\Delta) = \{(\delta, p)|(\delta, p) \text{ is an argument from } \Delta\}$
$A_2(\Delta) = \{(\delta, p) \in A_1(\Delta)|(\delta, p) \text{ is a consistent argument from } \Delta\}$
$A_3(\Delta) = \{(\delta, p) \in A_2(\Delta)|\neg(\exists\delta')((\delta', \neg p) \in A_2(\Delta))\}$
$A_4(\Delta) = \{(\delta, p) \in A_3(\Delta)|(\forall q \in \delta)((\neg(\exists\delta')((\delta', \neg q) \in A_2(\Delta))))\}$
$A_5(\Delta) = \{(\delta, p) \in A_4(\Delta)|(\delta, p) \text{ is a tautological argument from } \Delta\}$

$A_3(\Delta)$ $(A_4(\Delta))$ is the class of arguments in $A_2(\Delta)$ $(A_3(\Delta))$ that are not rebutted (undercut) by some argument in $A_2(\Delta)$.

Proposition 6. $A_5(\Delta) \subseteq A_4(\Delta) \subseteq A_3(\Delta) \subseteq A_2(\Delta) \subseteq A_1(\Delta)$

Proposition 7 (Remark). $A_4(\Delta)$ *is equivalent to both of:*

- $\{(\delta, p) \in A_2(\Delta)|(\forall q \in \delta)((\neg(\exists\delta')((\delta', \neg q) \in A_2(\Delta))))\}$
- $\{(\delta, p) \in A_3(\Delta)|(\forall q \in \delta)((\exists\delta')((\delta', q) \in A_3(\Delta))))\}$

The relation *more acceptable than* between arguments is defined using the ordering that is induced by the set inclusion hierarchy of the acceptability classes.

Definition 8. Let (δ, p) and (γ, q) be arguments from Δ. Then the argument (δ, p) is more acceptable (w.r.t. Δ) than the argument (γ, q), iff for some i, $1 \le i \le 5$, $(\delta, p) \in A_i(\Delta)$ and $(\gamma, q) \notin A_i(\Delta)$. If p, q are conclusions in arguments from Δ, then we say that p is more acceptable than q if p has an argument that is more acceptable than any argument for q.

4 Logical uncertainty terms

In a recent paper [5] we suggested that the above hierarchy could be used to assign linguistic qualifiers of uncertainty to formulae. Essentially, we reproduce below this 'naive' assignment of uncertainty terms to propositions on the basis of their membership of acceptability classes. However, this presentation is simplified over that in [5], as the set of propositions that are members of each class is defined directly. We also add an extra class to include any well formed proposition in the language $\mathcal{L}$.

$$Cce(\Delta) = \{p|(\exists\delta)((\delta, p) \in A_5(\Delta))\}$$
$$Cco(\Delta) = \{p|(\exists\delta)((\delta, p) \in A_4(\Delta))\}$$
$$Cpr(\Delta) = \{p|(\exists\delta)((\delta, p) \in A_3(\Delta))\}$$
$$Cpl(\Delta) = \{p|(\exists\delta)((\delta, p) \in A_2(\Delta))\}$$
$$Csu(\Delta) = \{p|(\exists\delta)((\delta, p) \in A_1(\Delta))\}$$
$$Cop(\Delta) = \mathcal{L}$$

The postfixes denote: *ce*rtain, *co*nfirmed, *pr*obable, *pl*ausible, *su*pported, and *op*en, respectively. A *degree of acceptability* ordering is enforced over this class of consequence relations: $ce \succ co \succ pr \succ pl \succ su \succ op$.

Proposition 9.

- $Cce(\Delta) \subseteq Cco(\Delta) \subseteq Cpr(\Delta) \subseteq Cpl(\Delta) \subseteq Csu(\Delta) \subseteq Cop(\Delta)$
- *For any consistent* Δ: $Cco(\Delta) = Cpr(\Delta) = Cpl(\Delta) = Csu(\Delta)$
- *For any inconsistent* Δ: $Csu(\Delta) = Cop(\Delta)$

From these properties we can see that the acceptability hierarchy can 'run' in two different modes. In the case of consistent databases the terms *co*, *pr*, *pl* and *su* become equivalent in status, and we can only discriminate between formulae which are open, i.e. have no support, formulae which are supported by contingent data, and tautologies. In the case of inconsistent databases, support from the contradiction is propagated to all formulae in the language, and so the terms *su* and *op* coincide. However, the collapse of *co*, *pr*, *pl* and *su* is broken.

Proposition 10 (The closure property). *For any* x, $p \in Cx(\Delta)$ *and* $\vdash p \to q$ *imply* $q \in Cx(\Delta)$.

Throughout, we use x to syntactically stand for any of *ce*, *co*, *pr*, *pl*, *su* and *op*.

5 Discrete confidence measure

The acceptability ordering induces a candidate for a *discrete confidence measure*, which is the *confidence evaluation function* $g_\Delta : \mathcal{L} \to \{ce, co, pr, pl, su, op\}$:

$$g_\Delta(p) = max(\{x | p \in Cx(\Delta)\}),$$

where *max*, and also *min*, are defined for $(\{ce, co, pr, pl, su, op\}, \succ)$ with *ce* as the maximal element and *op* as the minimal element.

6 Statement of basic rationality criteria

We will now discuss to what extent our system of argumentation satisfies the axioms of possibility theory [2], as a weakened version of the basic axioms of probability measures. Dubois and Prade [2] consider these to be the weakest axioms that a general confidence evaluation function should satisfy to ensure a minimum of coherence.

Since any class of propositions, $Cx(\Delta)$, enjoys the closure property, it immediately follows that:

Proposition 11. *If* q *is derived from* p *and* $p \to q$ *using MP, then* $g_\Delta(p) \preceq g_\Delta(q)$.

In addition we have the following properties:

Proposition 12. $g_\Delta(\top) = ce$ *and* $g_\Delta(\bot) = \begin{cases} op & \text{iff } \Delta \text{ is consistent} \\ su & \text{iff } \Delta \text{ is inconsistent} \end{cases}$

These properties suggest the following amendment of the axioms of possibility theory.

$$(\text{Ax1}) \quad g_\Delta(\top) = ce$$
$$(\text{Ax2}) \quad g_\Delta(p) \preceq g_\Delta(q), \quad \text{if } \vdash p \to q$$
$$(\text{Ax3}) \quad g_\Delta(\bot) = \begin{cases} su, & \text{if } \Delta \text{ is inconsistent} \\ op, & \text{if } \Delta \text{ is consistent} \end{cases}$$

Regarding the third axiom, Ax3, the value op applies for consistent databases and the value su applies for inconsistent databases, cf. the discussion of 'modes' above.

Proposition 13.

– g_Δ satisfies Ax1–3 for any Δ.
– $max(g_\Delta(p), g_\Delta(q)) \preceq g_\Delta(p \vee q)$
– $g_\Delta(p \wedge q) \preceq min(g_\Delta(p), g_\Delta(q))$

The implication of Ax2 must be tautological in order to ensure that it is 'context' independent. Without this extra requirement, the assignment of propositions to acceptability classes would not satisfy Ax2. This is illustrated by the following example:

Example 1. Let $\Delta = \{p \wedge r, (p \to q) \wedge \neg r\}$. Here $p, p \to q$ are both probable (pr), but q is only supported (su). Thus $g_\Delta(p) \npreceq g_\Delta(q)$. This problem arises because we are trying to compare confidences which are derived from quite different contexts. The solution in this case is to combine information before it is applied. In the example, where we want to apply two different pieces of information, $p \to q$ and p, they must be combined before they can be applied. This is done by forming their conjunction, $p \wedge (p \to q)$. Since $(p \wedge (p \to q)) \to q$ is a tautology Ax2 applies to this case, and we have $g_\Delta(p \wedge (p \to q)) \preceq g_\Delta(q)$ (both are equal to su).

The example illustrates that the degree of uncertainty assigned to a proposition is strongly dependent on context – reflecting the fact that logics of uncertainty are not truth functional [3]. The following proposition explains how information can be combined and applied across the context-boundaries.

Proposition 14. $g_\Delta(p \wedge (p \to q)) \preceq g_\Delta(q)$ for any Δ.

It is easy to see that in the case where $g_\Delta(p \to q) = ce$, i.e. the implication is tautological, then this is equivalent to Ax2.

7 Summary and perspectives

Practical reasoning is seen as a two step process: the construction and the use of arguments. We call this view the argumentation paradigm and consider it to be a unifying framework for many practical reasoning systems. We have considered a simple system of argumentation, which proposes a novel approach to assigning qualifiers to propositions based on the acceptability of their supporting arguments in a specific context. We were able to elucidate a simple axiomatisation of the confidence evaluation represented by this qualifier assignment, and show that it is analogous to the axiom system satisfied by possibility theory. It appears that any acceptability hierarchy that has a linear ordering with a maximal and a minimal element, and which enjoys the closure property, can be assigned a similar set of linguistic terms to those we propose and that this assignment will satisfy properties similar to Ax1–3.

We think that the consequence relations induced by the acceptability classes might offer an interesting extension of the theory of belief revision [6]. Belief states could be revised at different degrees of uncertainty, and one might suggest the following set of operators as a first candidate for a refined set of such revision operators on a belief state Δ. Each operator is called 'the x-revision of Δ with p'.

$$\Delta \uparrow_x p = \{\Delta - \delta | p \in Cx(\{p\} \cup \Delta - \delta) \text{ and } \delta \subseteq \Delta \text{ is minimal}\}$$

This would allow some belief states to be classically inconsistent.

Acknowledgement We are thankful to Dr. Anthony Hunter, Dr. Nic Wilson and Simon Parsons for useful feed-back.

References

1. S. Benferhat, D. Dubois and H. Prade. Argumentative inference in uncertain and inconsistent knowledge bases. UAI'93. Pp. 411–419.
2. D. Dubois and H. Prade. Possibility Theory: An Approach to Computerised Processing of Uncertainty. Plenum Press, New York. 1988.
3. D. Dubois and H. Prade. An Introduction to Possibilistic and Fuzzy Logics. In: Non-Standard Logics for Automated Reasoning. Academic Press, London. 1988.
4. P.M. Dung. On the acceptability of arguments and its fundamental role in nonmonotonic reasoning, logic programming, and human's social and economic affairs. Accepted for IJCAI'93.
5. M. Elvang-Gøransson, J. Fox and P. Krause. Dialectic reasoning with inconsistent information. UAI'93. Pp. 114–121.
6. P. Gärdenfors. Knowledge in flux. MIT Press. 1988.
7. F. Lin and Y. Shoham. Argument systems: a uniform basis for nonmonotonic reasoning. KR'89. Pp. 245–255.
8. G. Pinkas and R.P. Loui. Reasoning from inconsistency: a taxonomy of principles for resolving conflict. KR'92. Pp. 709–719.
9. G. Wagner. Ex contradictione nihil sequitur. IJCAI'91. Pp. 538–543.

A Temporal Model Theory for Default Logic

Joeri Engelfriet
Jan Treur

Vrije Universiteit Amsterdam
Department of Mathematics and Computer Science
Artificial Intelligence Group
De Boelelaan 1081a, 1081 HV Amsterdam The Netherlands
email: joeri@cs.vu.nl, treur@cs.vu.nl

Abstract. By explicitly identifying the temporal aspect of a default rule as it is used in a reasoning process, it is argued that a natural semantic theory of Reiter's default logic is a temporal one. To be able to accommodate the lack of complete knowledge at any point in time, the temporal models should be partial models. A temporal partial logic is introduced, and it is shown that this logic can provide semantics for Reiter's default logic.

1 Introduction

Reasoning by default is an important ingredient in many reasoning patterns. One of the most well-known formalizations of this type of reasoning is Reiter's default logic (see [6], [1], [5]). Although a number of authors have defined semantics for this logic (e.g. [2], [4], [5], [10]), most of these approaches are complicated, ad hoc and have little intuitive justification or transparency.

Suppose we have an automated reasoning process which can reason using defaults. If at a certain point in time it wants to apply a default rule, it must be known that the justification of this rule remains consistent in the future of the reasoning process. Therefore the justifications of default rules introduce a temporal element in default reasoning. The reasoning process can be formalized by describing it as a sequence of *information states*, which are descriptions of the (partial) knowledge the process may have deduced up until a certain moment in time (see [7]). This justifies the use of a temporal partial logic to describe reasoning processes.

2 Temporal Partial Logic

As no substantial literature on the combination of temporal and partial logic is known to the authors, and the few approaches combining partial and modal logic as known (e.g., [8]) do not serve our purposes, we had to design our own temporal partial logic. In this section we introduce the temporal partial logic that we have defined to satisfy our requirements. We shall first describe partial (strong Kleene) logic. The language will consist of all classical propositional formulae of a certain signature Σ, an ordered sequence of atom names. By $\mathbf{At}(\Sigma)$ we denote the set of atoms of Σ and by $\mathbf{Lit}(\Sigma)$ the set of literals.

Definition 2.1 (partial model)
a) A *partial model* **M** of this signature is an assignment to each atom of Σ of a truth value $\mathbf{0}, \mathbf{1}$ or $\mathbf{u}$ standing for *false, true* and *undefined* respectively. If an atom

a is false in **M**, then the literal $\neg$ **a** is true in **M** and vice versa. If **a** is unknown, so is $\neg$ **a**.

b) The *ordering of truth values* is defined by $u \leq 0$, $u \leq 1$, $u \leq u$, $0 \leq 0$, $1 \leq 1$. We call the model **N** a *refinement* of the model **M**, denoted by **M** $\leq$ **N**, if for all atoms **a** it holds: **M(a)** $\leq$ **N(a)**.

c) For a set of formulae **K**, by **Lit(K)** we denote all literals in **K**. For any partial model **M** we define **Lit(M) = { L $\in$ Lit(Σ) | L is true in M }**. For any consistent set of literals **S** the unique partial model **N** with **Lit(N) = S** will be denoted by **< S >**.

d) If no atom has truth-value **u** in a model **M**, then **M** is called *complete*.

One can define the truth value of an arbitrary propositional formula in a partial model by induction on the structure of the formula, where we will use the Kleene definition for the connectives. By **M** $\models^+ \alpha$, **M** $\models^- \alpha$ and **M** $\models^u \alpha$ we will denote that α is true, false or undefined respectively. In the definition, only truth and falsity are defined; a formula is unknown if it is neither true nor false.

Definition 2.2 (interpretation of formulae in a partial model)
Let Σ be a signature, let **M** be a partial model for Σ.

a) For any propositional atom $p \in At(\Sigma)$:

$$M \models^+ p \qquad \Leftrightarrow \qquad M(p) = 1$$
$$M \models^- p \qquad \Leftrightarrow \qquad M(p) = 0$$

b) For any two propositional formulae φ and ψ:

(i) $M \models^+ \varphi \wedge \psi \qquad \Leftrightarrow \qquad M \models^+ \varphi$ and $M \models^+ \psi$

$\quad M \models^- \varphi \wedge \psi \qquad \Leftrightarrow \qquad M \models^- \varphi$ or $M \models^- \psi$

(ii) $M \models^+ \varphi \rightarrow \psi \qquad \Leftrightarrow \qquad M \models^- \varphi$ or $M \models^+ \psi$

$\quad M \models^- \varphi \rightarrow \psi \qquad \Leftrightarrow \qquad M \models^+ \varphi$ and $M \models^- \psi$

(iii) $M \models^+ \neg \varphi \qquad \Leftrightarrow \qquad M \models^- \varphi$

$\quad M \models^- \neg \varphi \qquad \Leftrightarrow \qquad M \models^+ \varphi$

We will now extend these models to partial temporal models, using $\mathbb{N}$ as a fixed time set.

Definition 2.3 (partial temporal model)
a) A *partial temporal model* **M** of signature Σ is a mapping $\mathbb{N} \times At(\Sigma) \rightarrow \{0, 1, u\}$. If $M(t, a) = 1$, 0 or u, we say that in **M**, at time point **t** the atom **a** is true, false or undefined respectively.

b) If **M** is a partial temporal model and $t \in \mathbb{N}$ is fixed, then the function M_t defined by $M_t(a) = M(t, a)$ is a partial model. We will sometimes use the notation $(M_t)_{t \in \mathbb{N}}$ where each M_t is a partial model as an equivalent description of a partial temporal model **M**.

c) As in the non-temporal case, we define the relation $\leq$ between partial temporal models as follows: **M** $\leq$ **N** if $M(t, a) \leq N(t, a)$ for all time points **t** and atoms **a**.

The language we will use is built up with the propositional atoms, connectives and three new operators: **C**, **F** and **G**. The operators **F** and **G** are temporal operators, where $F\alpha$ means that α will be true *sometimes* in the future and where $G\alpha$ means that α will be true *always* in the future. The formula $C\alpha$ means that α is *currently* true. We will use the notation $(M, t) \vDash^+ \alpha$, $(M, t) \vDash^- \alpha$ and $(M, t) \vDash^u \alpha$ to denote that the formula α is true, false and undefined respectively in model M at time point $t \in \mathbb{N}$. The semantics of the standard connectives are defined similarly to the non-temporal case with (M, t) as a model, instead of just M. The precise definition of the operators is as follows:

Definition 2.4 (semantics of operators)
Let a formula α, a partial temporal model M, and a time point $t \in \mathbb{N}$
be given, then:

a) $(M, t) \vDash^+ F\alpha \quad \Leftrightarrow \quad \exists s \in \mathbb{N} \; [s > t \; \& \; (M, s) \vDash^+ \alpha]$

     $(M, t) \vDash^- F\alpha \quad \Leftrightarrow \quad (M, s) \nvDash^+ F\alpha$

b) $(M, t) \vDash^+ G\alpha \quad \Leftrightarrow \quad \forall s \in \mathbb{N} \; [s > t \; \Rightarrow \; (M, s) \vDash^+ \alpha]$

     $(M, t) \vDash^- G\alpha \quad \Leftrightarrow \quad (M, t) \nvDash^+ G\alpha$

c) $(M, t) \vDash^+ C\alpha \quad \Leftrightarrow \quad (M, t) \vDash^+ \alpha$

     $(M, t) \vDash^- C\alpha \quad \Leftrightarrow \quad (M, t) \nvDash^+ C\alpha$

Note that if $C\alpha$ is false, then α is either false or undefined.

A set K of formulae, possibly containing operators, is said to hold in a partial temporal model M (or: M is a model of K), which will be written as $M \vDash^+ K$ if all formulae of K have truth-value true in M at all points in time. Furthermore, for any literal L, by $\sim L$ we mean p if $L = \neg p$ for some atom p, and we mean $\neg p$ if $L = p$ for some atom p.

What is most interesting about a reasoning process, are of course its final conclusions. To be able to talk about *final* conclusions, we have to assume that the reasoning is *conservative*, which means that once a fact is established, it will remain true in the future of the reasoning process. In that case a fact is a final conclusion of a process if it is established at any point in time.

Definition 2.5 (limit of a conservative model)
Let M be a partial temporal model. Then M is *conservative* if $M_t \leq M_s$ whenever $t \leq s$. The limit of M, denoted by $\lim M$, is the partial model with for all atoms p:

(i) $\lim M \vDash^+ p \quad \Leftrightarrow \quad \exists t \in \mathbb{N}: (M, t) \vDash^+ p$

(ii) $\lim M \vDash^- p \quad \Leftrightarrow \quad \exists t \in \mathbb{N}: (M, t) \vDash^- p$

Notice that p is undefined in $\lim M$ if and only if p is undefined in M for all $t \in \mathbb{N}$.

3 Translating Default Logic into Temporal Partial Logic

We will first give a brief overview of Reiter's default logic, restricted to a propositional language. A default rule is an expression of the form $(\alpha : \beta_1, .. , \beta_n) / \gamma$, where α, $\beta_1, .. , \beta_n$ and γ are propositional formulae. A *default theory* Δ is then a pair $< W, D >$ where W is a set of sentences (the *axioms* of Δ), and D a set of default rules. We will not give Reiter's original definition of an extension (see [1], [5], [6]), but a slight variation of a definition which in [6] has been shown to be equivalent to it.

Definition 3.1 (Reiter Extension)
Let $\Delta = <W, D>$ be a default theory of signature Σ, and let E be a consistent set of sentences for Σ. Then E is a Reiter extension of Δ if $E = \bigcup_{i=0}^{\infty} E_i$ where
$E_0 = Th(W)$, and for all $i \geq 0$
$$E_{i+1} = Th(E_i \cup \{ \omega \mid (\alpha : \beta_1, ... , \beta_n) / \omega \in D, \alpha \in E_i \text{ and }$$
$$\neg \beta_1 \notin E, ..., \neg \beta_n \notin E \})$$

If E is a Reiter extension, then throughout the paper by E_i we will denote the subsets of E as defined in this lemma. We will restrict the defaults to be *based on literals*, which means that all formulae in a default rule have to be literals. This is not an important hindrance, since if an arbitrary formula φ occurs in a default rule, one could extend the signature with a new atom F_φ, substitute this for φ and add a rule $\varphi \leftrightarrow F_\varphi$ to W. It can be shown that the adapted theory has extensions which are the same as the extensions of the original default theory if you omit from the former the formulae containing the new atom. The restriction is necessary to be able to describe the E_i with partial models.

Our intention is to establish a correspondence between the Reiter extensions of a default theory and partial temporal models which obey a number of rules. The correspondence we are aiming at will be such that the literals true in the temporal model at time t will be exactly those literals which are element of E_t and the literals in E will be those true in the limit model:
$$Lit(M_t) = Lit(E_t) \text{ and } Lit(lim \ M) = Lit(E).$$
We will investigate what requirements should be imposed on the partial temporal model M. Firstly, since the E_i are non-decreasing, our model should be conservative. If we define $C' = \{ C(L) \rightarrow G(L) \mid L \text{ a literal} \}$ it can be shown that a model M is conservative if and only if $M \vDash^+ C'$. Next we will try to see which rules will ensure in the model the effect of application of the default rules. To this end we have to look at how a default rule is used in our definition of an extension. The meaning of a default rule $(\alpha : \beta) / \gamma$ is that if $\alpha \in E_t$, and $\neg \beta \notin E$, then γ has to be in E_{t+1}, and consequently in E_s for all $s > t$. The requirement $\neg \beta \notin E$ is equivalent to $\neg \beta \notin E_i$ for all $i \in \mathbb{N}$, and as the sets E_i are non-decreasing, it is equivalent to $\neg \beta \notin E_i$ for all $i > t$. If we want to enforce a corresponding effect of the use of defaults in our model, we have to make sure that at all times, if α is currently true, and $\sim\beta$ is not true at any point in the future, then γ has to be true at all times in the future. This leads us to the rule:
$$C\alpha \wedge \neg F \sim\beta \rightarrow G\gamma$$
which has to be true in the model at all times. As the E_i are closed under logical entailment, a corresponding model will have to be semantically closed:

Definition 3.2 (semantically closed)
Let K be a set of propositional formulae, and let M be a partial temporal model. M is *consistent* with K if there exists a complete model of $Lit(M) \cup K$. The model M is called *semantically closed with respect to* K if for any literal L it holds: if $Lit(M) \cup K \vDash L$ then $M \vDash^+ L$, where $\vDash$ is the standard semantic consequence relation.

As we do not want any extra conclusions in the corresponding model than those which have to be drawn, we will take the minimal models with respect to $\leq$.

4 Correspondence Between Extensions and Temporal Models

We are now ready to formally define when a partial temporal model can play in a sense the role of a Reiter extension of a default theory. We shall from now on assume that the default rules in a default theory are based on literals.

Definition 4.1
Let $\Delta = <W, D>$ be a default theory of signature Σ. Define
$$C' = \{ C(L) \rightarrow G(L) \mid L \in Lit(\Sigma) \}$$
$$D' = \{ C\alpha \wedge \neg F\sim\beta_1 \wedge .... \wedge \neg F\sim\beta_n \rightarrow G\gamma \mid (\alpha : \beta_1, ..., \beta_n) / \gamma \in D \}$$
If a partial temporal model M of signature Σ satisfies the properties:
(i) $\quad M \models^+ C' \cup D'$
(ii) $\quad M$ is consistent with W and semantically closed with respect to W
then we call M a *temporal model of* the default theory Δ. If it is also a minimal model with respect to the refinement relation $\leq$ among the models which satisfy properties (i) and (ii), then M is called a *minimal temporal model of* the default theory Δ.

It turns out that these minimal temporal models correspond exactly to the Reiter extensions. There is one exception: if W is inconsistent, then there is always one (inconsistent) Reiter extension, whereas an inconsistent model does not exist.

Theorem 4.2
Let $\Delta = <W, D>$ be a default theory with D based on literals.
a) If M is a minimal temporal model of Δ, then $Th(Lit(lim\ M) \cup W)$ is a Reiter extension E of Δ. Moreover, $E_t = Th(Lit(M_t) \cup W)$ for all $t \in \mathbb{N}$.
b) If W is consistent and E a Reiter extension of Δ, then the partial temporal model M defined by $M = (< Lit(E_t) >)_{t \in \mathbb{N}}$ is a minimal temporal model of Δ with $Lit(lim\ M) = Lit(E)$.

5 Expressing Semantically Closedness by Temporal Axioms

Next we point out how to find a set of rules W', such that the models of this set are those which are semantically closed with respect to W. The method to construct such a theory W' is an adapted form of the method to construct rule-based knowledge bases satisfying a given functionality (see [9]). The semantically closedness restriction says that in a situation where certain literals true in a model M, together with W, can be used to infer another literal, this literal should be true in M. Now we can just rigorously describe each of these situations by a rule. So for each subset of literals F which can be used to infer a literal L using W, we make a rule expressing that if all literals in F are true, L should be true too. The case when F is empty (when a literal can be inferred from W alone) has to be taken care of separately:
$$W' = \{ C(L) \mid L \text{ literal}, W \models L \} \cup \{ C(con(F)) \rightarrow C(L) \mid L \text{ literal}, F \neq \emptyset \text{ a}$$
$$\text{finite set of literals with } F \cup W \models L \}$$
where the formula $con(F)$ is the conjunction of the elements of F. Now if we define $T_\Delta = W' \cup C' \cup D'$, then the temporal models of Δ are exactly the models of the theory T_Δ: we have a correspondence between the extensions of a default theory Δ and the minimal models of the associated temporal theory T_Δ.

6 Further Considerations and Conclusions

In other approaches to semantics for default logic (e.g. [2], [4], [10]) usually a preference relation on classes of models is defined. Maximal chains in these relations correspond in a sense to our partial temporal models, where our limit model plays the role of a minimal element of such a chain. The definition of these relations are often ad hoc, not intuitive and usually hide a process of default reasoning, which is made explicit in our models.

In this paper we have given a temporal interpretation to the notion of a justification in a default rule. This led us to a translation of a certain class of default theories into temporal theories, and to a one-to-one semantical correspondence between the Reiter extensions of such a default theory and the minimal partial models of its temporal translation. To this end we designed a temporal partial logic. This work enables one to use concepts from temporal logic to study default reasoning. Of course such a translation does not automatically imply that the problems of default logic will be solved at once. The temporal partial logic we designed may have its own complexity; the fact that we were able to embed a substantial fragment of default logic in it makes one expect that this logic is not a trivial one. Nevertheless, both this temporal partial logic, and its connection to default logic seem worth to be investigated further.

Acknowledgements
Wiebe van der Hoek and John-Jules Meyer have read an earlier version of this paper. This has led to a number of improvements. This work has been carried out in the context of the ESPRIT BRA project DRUMS II.

References

1. P. Besnard, An Introduction to Default Logic, Springer Verlag, 1989
2. P. Besnard, T. Schaub, Possible Worlds Semantics for Default Logics, to appear in Fundamenta Informaticae
3. J. Engelfriet, J. Treur, A Temporal Model Theory for Default Logic, Report, Vrije Universiteit Amsterdam, Department of Mathematics and Computer Science, 1993
4. D.W. Etherington, A Semantics for Default Logic, Proc. IJCAI-87. Also in: Reasoning with Incomplete Information, Morgan Kaufmann, 1988
5. W. Łukaszewicz, Non-monotonic reasoning: formalization of commonsense reasoning, Ellis Horwood, 1990
6. R. Reiter, A logic for default reasoning, Artificial Intelligence 13, 1980, pp. 81-132
7. Y.H. Tan, J. Treur, A bi-modular approach to nonmonotonic reasoning, In: De Glas, M., Gabbay, D. (eds.), Proc. World Congress on Fundamentals of Artificial Intelligence, WOCFAI-91, 1991, pp. 461-476. An adapted version will be published in Studia Logica.
8. E. Thijsse, Partial logic and knowledge representation, Ph.D. Thesis, Tilburg University, 1992
9. J. Treur, Completeness and definability in diagnostic expert systems, Proc. European Conf. on AI, ECAI-88, München, 1988, pp. 619-624.
10. F. Voorbraak, Preference-based semantics for nonmonotonic logics, to appear in Proc. IJCAI-93

Uncertainty in Constraint Satisfaction Problems: a Probabilistic Approach

Hélène Fargier - Jérôme Lang

Institut de Recherche en Informatique de Toulouse (I.R.I.T.) – C.N.R.S.
Université Paul Sabatier, 118 route de Narbonne
31062 Toulouse Cedex, France
email: {fargier, lang}@irit.fr

Abstract. We propose a framework for dealing with probabilistic uncertainty in constraint satisfaction problems, associating with each constraint the probability that it is a part of the real problem (the latter being only partially known). The probability degrees on the relevance of the constraints enable us to define, for each instanciation, the probability that it is a solution of the real problem. We briefly give a methodology for the search of the best solution (maximizing this probability).

1. Introduction.

Constraint Satisfaction Problems (CSP) consist generally in finding an assignment (or several, or all, etc.) of a set of variables which is compatible with a set of constraints. The classical CSP framework [9] [11] assumes that *the set of constraints is completely known from the beginning*, and that *no constraint can be relaxed*. Several attempts were made in order to give the CSP framework some forms of *flexibility* (see [1] for a survey). We distinguish namely between two different sources of flexibility, which must not be confused, although their treatment may sometimes seem analogous.

The latter point ("no constraint can be relaxed") leads to the definition of *preference-based problems*: the definition of the problem consists in set of constraints which should be all satisfied if possible, which is often not the case. For instance, consider a time-table problem where, besides the administrative constraints, each teacher specifies some wishes that are to be satisfied, if possible. Then, if the problem is overconstrained (i.e. it has no solution), it is "solved" by defining a preference ranking of the possible instanciations (according to some criteria depending on the constraints), which leads to the search of *preferred* solutions. For instance, a simple criterium [7] consists in preferring solutions satisfying the highest possible number of constraints; another type of approach [6] [14] consists in starting with a preference ordering on the constraints (given by the user), and then in preferring solutions minimizing the importance of the most important violated constraint.

The former point ("the set of constraints is completely known from the beginning") leads to define another kind of flexibility, that we call *incompleteness* (in the initial description of the problem): here, contrarily to preference-based problems where all initial constraints were definitely a part of the problem (their relaxation coming from the impossibility to satisfy them all), there is an ambiguity about the *relevance* of some constraints to the *real* problem (consider for example a robot moving in an ill-known environment, which knows that there could be an obstacle in point (x,y); or a robot knowing that there is an obstacle somewhere but which doesn't know exactly where). This is the kind of flexibility that we aim to handle in this paper.

To handle incomplete problems, two different kinds of approaches may be considered: *dynamical* approaches (when new constraints are added or retracted, a new solution is to be found, making the most useful use of the previous CSP; see for instance [4] or [17]); and *previsional* approaches: when we have a knowledge a priori about the real world (i.e. about the constraints which are likely to be added later on). This (uncertain) knowledge should be taken into account in order to give *cautious, robust* provisional solutions. This is what we aim to do in this paper, proposing namely a *probabilistic* modelling scheme. Intuitively, a probabilistic constraint satisfaction problem is a set of constraints, some of which are relevant to the real problem (i.e. they exist in the actual world, which is ill-known) with a complete certainty, and some of which do not, which means that they may or may not be relevant (with some probability) to the ill-known *real* problem. For example, in an agricultural planning problem [10], we have some probabilities a priori about the future weather, and some constraints appear only if it is dry, some others only if it is cold, etc.

After giving a formal definition of probabilistic CSPs, we propose the use of a Branch and Bound algorithm for the search of the *most probable* solution, which can be improved by the use of forward checking techniques and instantiation heuristics.

2. Probabilistic Constraint Satisfaction Problems

A *Constraint Satisfaction Problem* (CSP) is classically defined by a set of constraints $C = \{C_1,...,C_m\}$ restricting the possible values of a set $X=\{x_1,...,x_n\}$ of variables, each variable x_i ranging on a set of values D_i (generally finite). Each constraint C_i linking a set of variables $\{x_{i1},...,x_{ini}\}$ is classically described by an associated relation R_i: R_i is the subset of $D_{i1}\times...\times D_{ini}$ that specifies the tuples $(d_{i1},...,d_{ini})$ of values being compatible to each other according to C_i. The set $\{x_{i1},...,x_{ini}\}$ of variables involved in R_i will be denoted by $V(C_i)$. Let $s = (d_1,...,d_n) \in D_1\times...\times D_n$ be an *instantiation* of all variables; let $\mathcal{I} = D_1\times...\times D_n$ the set of all possible instantiations; s is a *solution* of C iff it satisfies all the constraints of C: $\forall\, C_i \in C$, $s{\downarrow}V(Ci) \in R_i$, where $s{\downarrow}V(Ci)$ denotes the projection of s on $V(C_i)$. If the set of solutions of C is empty, C is *inconsistent*. We define also $Sols(C_i) = \{s \in \mathcal{I}\ |\ s{\downarrow}V(Ci) \in R_i\}$ and $Sols(C) = \{s \in \mathcal{I}\ |\ s$ satisfies all the constraints of $C\}$.

When the set of constraints defining the real problem (denoted by P_{real}) is ill-known, i.e. when the relevance of some constraints is subject of uncertainty, a probability is assigned to the relevance of each constraint. More formally, a probabilistic CSP consists in a set of constraints $C = \{C_1,...,C_m\}$ and a set of probabilities p_i (one for each constraint of C): p_i is the probability that the constraint C_i is a constraint of the real problem P_{real}:

$$\Pr(C_i \in P_{real}) = p_i. \qquad\qquad \Pr(C_i \notin P_{real}) = 1 - p_i.$$

We assume that each p_i is > 0 (constraints being certainly not relevant are not significant at all) and that the relevance of two different constraints are two *independent* events, i.e. the probability that both C_i and C_j belong to P_{real} is

$$\Pr(C_i \in P_{real} \text{ and } C_j \in P_{real}) = \Pr(C_i \in P_{real}) \cdot \Pr(C_j \in P_{real}) = p_i \cdot p_j.$$

This assumption comes from the fact we consider each constraint as a piece of knowledge which should be relaxed independently of the others.

As an example, consider that a dinner is to be organised and that some guests are not sure whether they will come: Pr *(Mary comes)* = 0.7, Pr *(John comes)* = 0.5. The problem is to choose a wine (white or red) and a meal (beef, fish or turkey), knowing that Mary cannot drink white wine nor eat red meat and John, who is old-fashioned, drinks red wine with meat and white wine with fish or turkey. Moreover, the alcohol shop always has white wine, but may lack red wine (Pr (no red wine) = 0.6). The dispositions of Mary and John and the presence of red wine in the shop are independent on each other. This problem can be modelled as follows:

Variables: x_1 (wine) x_2 (meal)

Domains: D_1={white, red} D_2={beef, fish, turkey}

Constraints: C={C_1, C_2, C_3}

C_1: R_1 = {(white, turkey), (red, beef), (white, fish)} p_1=0.5 {John}

C_2: R_2 = {(white, turkey) (white, fish) (white, beef)} p_2=0.6 {shop}

C_3: R_3 = {(red, fish) (red, turkey)} p_3=0.7 {Mary}

3. The lattice of possible problems.

The set of possible constraints $\mathcal{C}$ defines a lattice of possible classical CSPs (see fig. 1), namely $2^{\mathcal{C}}$, in which only one problem is the real one P_{real} (i.e., the CSPs of $2^{\mathcal{C}}$ are mutually exclusive). The probabilities attached to the relevance of the constraints induce on $2^{\mathcal{C}}$ a probability distribution defined as follows: $P_j \in 2^{\mathcal{C}}$ is the *real* CSP if and only if each constraint of P_j is relevant and all other constraints (those in $\mathcal{C} - P_j$) do not, which gives, with the independence assumption:

$$pr(P_j) = pr(P_j = P_{real}) = \Pi \{p_i \mid C_i \in P_j\} . \Pi \{1 - p_i \mid C_i \in \mathcal{C} - P_j\}$$

In our example, Pr (P_{real} ={C_1, C_2}) = 0.5 * 0.6 * (1 - 0.7) = 0.09.

Some problems in this lattice may be inconsistent while some others are consistent. A consistent sub-CSP of $\mathcal{C}$ such that each of its strict superproblems is inconsistent is *maximal consistent* in $\mathcal{C}$. On our example, {C_1, C_2, C_3}, {C_1, C_3} and {C_2, C_3} are inconsistent: the two maximal consistent sub-CSPs are {C_1, C_2} and {C_3}.

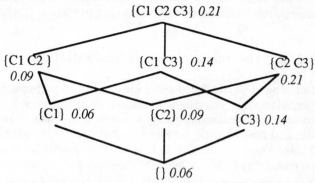

Figure 1: the lattice of sub-CSPs for the menu example

Trivially, a solution of a CSP is also a solution of all its sub-CSPs. If $\mathcal{C}$ is consistent, then $\mathcal{C}$ itself is obviously the only maximal consistent sub-CSP since in this case, all problems of $2^{\mathcal{C}}$ are consistent and so is the real problem. Otherwise, the real problem may be inconsistent; the probability that it is consistent is equal to $\Sigma \{ pr(P) \mid P \in 2^{\mathcal{C}}, P \text{ consistent} \}$.

Coming back to our example, since $\{\}, \{C_1\}, \{C_2\}, \{C_3\}, \{C_1,C_2\}$ are consistent and $\{C_1,C_3\}, \{C_2,C_3\}, \{C_1,C_2,C_3\}$ inconsistent, we have $Pr(P_{real}$ is consistent$)$ = $0.06 + 0.06 + 0.09 + 0.14 + 0.09 = 0.44$.

4. Probability attached an instanciation

Let $s \in \mathcal{I}$; if s satisfies all constraints in $\mathcal{C}$, then s is certainly a solution of P_{real}, whatever the latter is. Otherwise, it is a solution of P_{real} if and only if P_{real} does not contain any constraint violated by s. Let us note viol (s) (resp. sat (s)) the subset of $\mathcal{C}$ of constraints violated (resp. satisfied) by s. Clearly, viol (s) $\cup$ sat (s) = $\mathcal{C}$. The probability that s is a solution is (using the independence assumption) the probability that the constraints it violates are not relevant in P_{real}, i.e.:

$Pr(s \in Sols(P_{real})) = \prod \{ 1-p_i \mid C_i \in viol(s) \} = \Sigma \{ pr(P) \mid P \in 2^{\mathcal{C}}, s \in Sols(P) \}$.

In our example, $Pr((white, fish) \in Sols(P_{real})) = pr(\{\}) + pr(\{C_1\}) + pr(\{C_2\}) + pr(\{C_1,C_2\}) = 0.3$. Note that the events of two distinct instanciations being solutions of P_{real} are generally not independent (for instance (white, turkey) is a solution of P_{real} iff (white, fish) is).

Let s* be one of the instantiations maximizing the probability to be a solution of P_{real}. It can be proved that s* is solution of one of the maximal consistent sub-CSPs, say P* = sat (s*). It is also a solution of all sub-CSPs of P*, but does not satisfy any problem outside this sub-part of the lattice. Besides,

$$Pr(s^*) = Pr(P_{real} \subseteq P^*) \geq Pr(P_{real} = P^*)$$

It should be outlined that P* is not necessarily the most probable consistent problem in the lattice; it is not even one of its superproblems. In our example, the most probable instantiations are (white, turkey) and (white, fish). They correspond to P* = $\{C_1,C_2\}$, whereas the most probable problems are $\{C_1,C_2,C_3\}$ and $\{C_2,C_3\}$ (they are inconsistent) and the most probable consistent problem is $\{C_3\}$.

5. Searching for the most probable instantiation

A naive kind of request would be to solve only the most probable CSPs (using classical CSP techniques), or, since these problem may be inconsistent, to solve one of the most probable consistent problems. However these problems may have a very low probability, and besides their solutions do not necessarily have the highest probability to solve P_{real}. It seems more reasonable to search for an instantiation with a maximal probability to be a solution of P_{real}, i.e. a s* is such that

$Pr(s^* \in Sols(P_{real})) = Sup_{s \in \mathcal{I}} Pr(s \in Sols(P_{real})) = Sup_{s \in \mathcal{I}} \prod \{ 1-p_i \mid C_i \in viol(s) \}$.

If $\mathcal{C}$ is consistent, all solutions satisfying all constraints of $\mathcal{C}$ satisfy P_{real} (with probability 1), so they are obviously the best (i.e. most probable) instantiations.

Otherwise, we will obtain an instantiation satisfying one of the most probable maximal consistent sub-CSPs of $\mathcal{C}$ (as shown in Section 4). Hence, knowing one of best instantiations gives also one of the best maximal consistent sub-CSPs of $\mathcal{C}$.

Such an optimization problem can be solved using a classical tree-search algorithm, namely depth-first branch and bound. Variables are instanciated in a prescribed order, say $(x_1, ..., x_n)$. The root of the tree is the empty instantiation. Intermediate nodes denote partial instanciations. Leaves represent complete instanciations of $(x_1, ..., x_n)$, i.e. potential solutions. In a depth-first exploration of the tree, we keep track of the leaves $s = (u_1, ..., u_n)$ maximizing Pr $(s \in \text{Sols} (P_{real}))$.

It is possible to prune each branch leading necessarily to complete instanciations whose probability is not better than that of the best already evaluated instanciations. In other terms, it is useless to extend intermediary nodes $(u_1,...,u_k)$ such that Max $_s$ $\supset (u_1, ..., u_k)$ (Pr(s)) $\leq \alpha$, α being the current lower bound of the probability of the best instanciation. Threshold α may be initialized by 0 and updated when an instantiation $(u_1, ...,u_n)$ such as Pr $((u_1,...,u_n)) > \alpha$ is reached.

Computing Max $_{s \supset}(u_1, ..., u_k)$ Pr(s) is too costly, since it requires the computation of the probability of all complete extensions of $(u_1,...,u_k)$. So, we may practically compute an upper bound of it, called the *consistency* of the partial instantiation $(u_1,...,u_k)$, denoted by Cons$(u_1,...,u_k)$. It considers only the constraints C_i pertaining to the variables instanciated in $(u_1,...,u_k)$, i.e. such that $V(C_i) \subseteq \{x_1,...,x_k\}$: Cons$(u_1,...,u_k) = \prod \{1-p_j \mid C_j, V(C_j) \subseteq (x_1,...,x_k)$ and $C_j \in \text{viol}(u_1,...,u_k)\}$

This upper bound decreases when extending the nodes and becomes exact for complete instanciations. Moreover, it may be incrementally computed as the tree is explored downwards: Cons$(u_1,..,u_k,u_{k+1}) =$

Cons$(u_1,...,u_k).\prod \{1-p_j \mid C_j, \{x_{k+1}\} \subseteq V(Cj) \subseteq (x_1,...,x_{k+1})$ and $C_j \in \text{viol}(u_1,...,u_k)\}$.

When extending the current partial instantiation $(u_1,...,u_k)$ we first have to choose the next variable x_{k+1} to instantiate. For each of its possible values u_{k+1}, Cons$(u_1,...,u_k,u_{k+1})$ is computed: only the nodes such that Cons $(u_1,...,u_k,u_{k+1}) \geq \alpha$ are created. If there is no u_{k+1} satisfying this condition, then the algorithm backtracks. The search stops when no more node can be created. It is successful if a complete instance has been reached, and the best among those which have been reached is optimal.

Branch and bound is actually the extension in probabilistic CSP of the classical CSP standard search procedure (backtrack search). Making a step further, we propose to adapt to our framework well-known improvements of backtrack search for classical CSPs (see for instance [8]).

Indeed, heuristics may be used to enhance this tree search, namely on the order in which the variables are explored (vertical order) and, for each variable, on the order in which the values are explored (horizontal order). An obvious horizontal order is to choose first the values having the maximal consistency degree. As a vertical order, we will instantiate first the most constrained variable, i.e. the variable with the lowest number $n(x_i)$ of values that will be consistent with the current instantiation $(u_1,...,u_k)$ according to the constraint linking $(u_1,...,u_k)$ to x_i. Since some constraints are uncertain, the expected value n (x_i) is used:

$$E (n (x_i)) = \sum_{u_i \in D_i} \prod \{1-p_j \mid Cj, \{x_i\} \subseteq V(Cj) \subseteq \{x_1,...,x_k, x_i\} \text{ and } C_j \in \text{viol}(u_1,...,u_k)\}$$

Another way to enhance the efficiency of the search is to apply a "forward-checking" procedure when creating the node $(u_1,...,u_k)$: the idea to maintain, for each value u_h of each uninstantiated variable x_h, the consistency degree Cons $(u_1,.....,u_k, u_h)$. As soon as a new decision has been made $(x_k := u_k)$, it is propagated over all the variables x_j related to x_k:

Cons$(u_1,...,u_k,u_j)$ =

Cons$(u_1,...,u_{k-1},u_j).\prod\{1-p_j \mid Cj,V(Cj)\subseteq\{x_1,...,x_k,x_i\}$ and $Cj\in$ viol$(u_1,...,u_k, u_i)$ $\}$

If the propagation detects a x_h such as Max$_{u_h\in Dh}$ cons$(u_1,.....,u_h, u_j)\leq\alpha$, we know that there is no extension of $(u_1,.....,u_k)$ having a probability greater than α: the branch and bound procedure must backtrack. Hence, cuts in the search are discovered earlier than if using classical branch and bound. Moreover, it suits well the heuristic on vertical order, since the computation of $E(n(x_i))$ becomes obvious:

$$E(n(x_i)) = \sum \{Cons(u_1,.....,u_k,u_j) \mid u_i \in D_i\}$$

6. Related work

First, probabilistic CSPs can be given an interpretation in terms of Dempster-belief functions. Namely, stating that C_i is relevant with a probability p_i corresponds to the following mass assignment on the frame of discernment $\mathfrak{I} = D_1\times...\times D_n$ (set of all instanciations): m_i $(Sol(C_i)) = p_i$; m_i $(\mathfrak{I}) = 1-p_i$. This is actually very close to the recent approaches of Clarke and Gabbay [3] and Smets [16][1] who proposed logical frameworks dealing with *probability of provability* (where the masses p_i and $1-p_i$ are assigned respectively to a logical formula (or equivalently to the set of its models) φ_i and to classical tautology T (equivalently, the set of all classical interpretations). Then, finding a probability distribution on the lattice of possible CSPs corresponds to the combination of the n bodies of evidence $(\mathfrak{I}, m_i)$ (with $m_i(C_i) = p_i$ and m_i $(\mathfrak{I}) = 1-p_i)$ according to Dempster's rule (which is due to our independence assumption); namely, if P is a sub-CSP of $\mathfrak{C}$, pr (P) corresponds to m(Sols (P)) where $m = m_1 \oplus ... \oplus m_n$. Furthermore, the probability that s is a solution of the real problem corresponds to the contour function Pl $(\{s\})$. Note that *we do not renormalize* the result, which is justified by the fact that the real problem may be inconsistent, i.e. that it has no solutions (see [15] on this point); actually, $m(\emptyset)$ corresponds to the sum of the probabilities of the inconsistent sub-CSPs.

Note that the mentioned logical approaches [3] and [16] emphasize the probability of provability of a formula ψ (namely, Bel (ψ) w.r.t. the body of evidence resulting from the combination), whereas we are not concerned with deduction, but we are rather interested in computing the contour function (and more precisely in finding the instantiation maximizing it). Thus, the main difference between their approach and ours remains in the differences between the logical and the constraint-based points of view: a set of interpretations corresponds to a set of instanciations, but generally in logical formalisms the underlying assumption is that one and only one interpretation

---

[1] both approaches are based on Dempster's combination rule. Besides, Smets uses this approach to encode in Dempster-Shafer theory variable-strengths defaults rules.

represents the real world (though we may do not know which one) while in CSP there may be any number of real solutions.

Another possible connection is Pearl's distributed revision of composite beliefs ([12] Chapter 5), where the description of the system (i.e. the causal links between variables) correspond to constraints of probability 1 while the a priori probabilities of "failure" correspond to probabilistic constraints; the most probable explanation corresponds then clearly to the most probable instantiation. Note that Pearl's framework requires the structure of the graph link between variables to be a directed causal tree (whereas any kind of structure is allowed in the CSP formalism).

7. Conclusion

In this paper we extended the CSP framework to the case where the description of the problem contains uncertain constraints, namely by considering for each constraint the probability that it is a part of the ill-known real problem. We also proposed a method for searching the preferred instantiations (those being most probably solutions of the real problem). This algorithm and its enhancements (search heuristic, forward checking procedure) are inspirated by classical tools used in CSP resolution. It should be outlined that some known CSP techniques are already widely used in approximate reasoning. Namely, Dechter and Pearl's tree clustering [5] may be compared with Shafer and Shenoy's local computation in hypertree scheme [13] or Chatalic, Dubois and Prade's approach [2] of approximate reasoning based on the Dempster's rule of combination. This analogy suggests to study further the relationships between works done on the one side in approximate reasoning and combination of uncertain information, and, on the other side, in CSP algorithmics, in order to both provide the former domain with new efficient algorithms and allow the treatment of CSPs in presence of uncertainty.

An alternative to the search of the most probable solution would be the search of a *set* of instantiations which "covers" a large part of the lattice of possible CSPs, (i.e. s.t. there is a high probability for this set to contain a solution of the real problem). We are currently studying how sets of solutions can be practically computed.

The main limitation of our framework is our independence assumption between the events corresponding to the relevance of the constraints. A first improvement in this direction is suggested by Martin-Clouaire and Rellier [10], who propose to handle a set of families of constraints, with a probability distribution for each family, two distinct families being independent. However, extending our framework in such a way makes the search of the preferred solution(s) technically much harder.

More generally, incomplete CSPs should be replaced in the broader perspective of *flexible* CSPs, namely *preference-based* CSPs and *dynamic* CSPs. For the former, the close relationship between both problematics (incompleteness and preferences) has to be carefully studied (note that a probabilistic CSP can be formally considered as a preference-based CSP since the probabilities attached to the instantiations induce a preference relation). For the latter (dynamicity), a next step is to integrate the probabilistic handling of incompleteness (which can be considered as a *previsional* handling of dynamicity) to the (*reactive*) traditional handling of dynamicity in CSPs.

Acknowledgements
We would like to thank our collegues of the French research group "CSP flexibles" (the authors of [1]) for many helpful discussions.

References

1. Bel G., Bensana E., Berlandier P., David P., Fargier H., Gaspin C., Ghedira K., Janssen P., Jégou P., Kökeny T., Lang J., Lesaint D., Martin-Clouaire R., Neveu B., Rellier J.P., Schiex T., Trousse B., Verfaillie G., Vilarem M.C. (1992), Représentation et traitement pratique de la flexibilité dans les problèmes sous contraintes (in French), Actes des Journées du PRC-IA, Teknea, 369-428.
2. Chatalic P., Dubois D., Prade H. (1987) An Approach to Approximate Reasoning Based on the Dempster Rule of Combination. International Journal of Expert Systems 1 (1), 647-85.
3. Clarke M., Gabbay D. M. (1993) Probability of provability, manuscript.
4. Dechter A., Dechter R. (1988) Belief Maintenance in Dynamic Constraints Networks. Proc. AAAI 88, 37-42.
5. Dechter R., Pearl J. (1989) Tree clustering for constraint networks. Artificial Intelligence 38, 353-366.
6. Dubois D., Fargier H., Prade H. (1993), The calculus of fuzzy restrictions as a basis for flexible constraint satisfaction, Proc. 2nd IEEE Conf. on Fuzzy Sets, 1131-1136.
7. Freuder E.C., Wallace R.J. (1992), Partial Constraint Satisfaction, Artificial Intelligence, 58(1-3), 21-70.
8. Haralick R. M., Elliott G. L. (1980) Increasing Tree Search Efficiency for Constraint Satisfaction Problems, Artificial Intelligence 14, 263-313.
9. Mackworth A. K. (1977) Consistency in networks of relations. Artificial Intelligence 8, 99-118.
10. Martin-Clouaire R., Rellier J. P. (1993) personal communication. To appear in IJCAI Workshop on AI in Agriculture, Natural Resources and Environmental Sciences.
11. Montanari H. (1974) Networks of Constraints : Fundamental Properties and Application to Picture Processing. Information Science 7 , 1974, 95-132.
12. Pearl J. (1988), Probabilistic reasoning in intelligent systems: networks of plausible inference, Morgan Kaufman.
13. Shafer G., Shenoy P (1988) Local computation in hypertrees, Working paper N.201. School of Business, University of Kansas, 1988.
14. Schiex T. (1992) Possibilistic constraint satisfaction problems or how to handle soft constraints. Proc. 8th Conf. on Uncertainty in AI, 268-275.
15. Smets P. (1988), Belief Functions, in Non-Standard Logics for Automated Reasoning (P. Smets, A. Mamdani, D. Dubois, H. Prade eds.), Academic Press, 253-286.
16. Smets P. (1993) personal communication.
17. Van Hentenryck P. (1990) Incremental constraint satisfaction in logic programming. ICLP 90, 189-202.

Interference Logic = Conditional Logic + Frame Axiom

L. Fariñas del Cerro, A. Herzig

Applied Logic Group, I.R.I.T., Université Paul Sabatier
118 Route de Narbonne, 31062 Toulouse Cedex (France)
email: {farinas, herzig}@irit.fr

Abstract. We investigate the notion of interference between formulas as a basis for change operations. Such a notion permits us to enrich conditional logics with a frame axiom. This new logic allows us to solve in a natural way some of the problems appearing in the model based approach to change.

1 Introduction

Learning a new fact obliges us to modify the organisation of our knowledge. If we represent our knowledge by a theory (or knowledge base) KB, a new fact by a formula A (the change formula) and the operation of learning by an operator *, then what we are interested in is the outcome of the operation KB*A. More precisely, we want to compute what can be deduced from KB*A. (Thus we suppose here that changes, i.e. actions, updates, etc., can be described by their results, as suggested by von Wright and Segerberg.) We shall only treat here model-based approaches where the result of a change does not depend on the syntactical form of the formulas. We distinguish three aspects.
- The syntactical aspect: Clarify the relation between change and connectives.
- The semantical aspect: Reflect a change operation by operations on models.
- The practical (computational) aspect: Compute effectively what can be deduced from the changed knowledge base.

The ultimate goal is to give an axiomatics with a natural semantics for which a reasonable deduction method can be defined. We shall argue in the sequel that up to now, syntactical, semantical, and computational aspects have not been considered in an equilibrated way, and that in particular the latter has not been taken into account enough in the sense that a formula which does not interfere with the change formula should survive a change.

In this note we propose a new conditional logic which includes a frame axiom. We call this logic interference logic. First we review the foundational approaches to change and state our frame axiom which is based on the notion of interference (section 2). Then we give a precise definition of interference (section 3) and discuss its relationship with other concepts such as that of probabilistic independence (section 4). In section 5 we give a semantics and in section 6 an axiomatics for an independence logic. In section 7 we show how it can be used to reason about actions.

2 Revisions, Updates, and the Frame Problem

Most of the syntactical approaches up to now have concentrated on clarifying the relation between connectives and change. Most relevant in the discussion about the logical foundations of change have been the so-called AGM-postulates (Alchourrón et al. 1985, Gärdenfors 1988) - in fact an axiomatization (in the metalanguage) of the change operation - which are claimed by the authors to rule every rational belief revision operation. These postulates are meant to be a framework within which particular revision operations should fit. In particular in the case where the change is consistent with the knowledge base KB, the preservation postulate stipulates that the changed knowledge base results from just adding the formula representing the change.

Recently, there has been given evidence that when modelling a changing world (which is what we want e.g. in database updates and planning) this last postulate is not verified, and H. Katsuno and A. Mendelzon (1991) have proposed another type of change operations called updates. Roughly speaking, updates are the more general change operations in the sense that every (basic) revision operation is also an update operation.

Finding sets of postulates and giving semantics in terms of epistemic entrenchment orderings as done by Alchourrón, Gärdenfors and Makinson or Katsuno and Mendelzon sheds a new light on important problems in computer science such as database updates or planning, just as the work of Gabbay and Kraus, Lehmann and Maggidor did in the case of nonmonotonic reasoning. Nevertheless, from the practical point of view, we "cannot buy anything for that": Our aim is to find change operations which can be implemented in a reasonable manner, although it is clear that the theoretical complexity of change operations is generally very high (Eiter Gottlob 1992).

An important point we wish to make here is that all these approaches do not consider what in the artificial intelligence tradition has been called the *frame problem* : If a change formula A is inconsistent with the theory, the revision as well as the update postulates give us very little help.

Naively, what we would like is that at least every formula C which has "nothing to do" with the change formula A should not interfere with the change formula, and should be preserved under the change operation. This can be formulated as follows:

KB |- C iff KB*A |- C   if A and C do not interfere

We shall call that the *frame postulate*.

Now the main problem is to make precise what "interference" means.

As second point is that when we want to reason about change it is important to dispose of a language in which the change operation can be represented. An attractive choice is to define a *conditional logic* possessing an operator ">" where A>B means "Assuming A, B holds". From that a change operation can be defined via the *Ramsay Test*:

KB*A |- C iff KB |- A>C

Via the Ramsay Test, our frame postulate can be materialized as a particular axiom of the conditional logic under concern, that we call the *frame axiom*:

(FRAME)   C → A>C   *if A and C do not interfere*

Such an axiom has not been studied in the tradition of conditional logics. Here, it is central for us. In the next section we shall study the notion of interference in more detail.

3 Our Definition of Interference

In this section we want to give a formal account of interference in the context of reasoning about change. Our main hypothesis is that changes structure the set of elementary propositions in the sense that propositions are related to or interfere with a given change, if the truth value of the proposition may be modified by the change.

Let us illustrate our ideas with a traffic example. Let r and g respectively express the propositions "The traffic light is red" and "The traffic light is green". Now it seems quite intuitive to claim that r and g interfere. The reason is that there are situations where making r true makes g become false.[1] Hence we get the following informal definition of

---

[1] Note that this depends on the country under concern. In Great Britain, r and g do not interfere, because there is no possible (legal) change from a situation w to a situation w' such that ¬r and g were true in w and r and g in w' (nor any other combination making both change

interference:

> *Two formulas A and B interfere if there is a change (an action) which makes both formulas change their truth value at the same time.*

Formally we assume that interference is a primitive notion not derived from others. We suppose given a relation ~ on the set of formulas. A ~ B is read "A and B interfere". We suppose ~ to be a similarity, i.e. to be reflexive and symmetric. We give the following axiomatization of interference:

(reflexivity)   A ~ A
(symmetry)   if A ~ B then B ~ A
(negation)   if A ~ B then A ~ ¬B
(equivalence)   If A↔B and A ~ C then B ~ C

We remark that adding the (conjunction) rule: "if A ~ B then A ~ B∧C" to our list would be harmful: First, note that the (disjunction) rule "if A ~ B then A ~ B∨C" would follow from the rest: A ~ B entails A ~ ¬B by (negation). From that we can infer A ~ ¬B∧¬C by (conjunction), but there is no rule to get A ~ B∨C. Now let A and B be any formula. From A ~ A we infer A ~ A∧B by (conjunction). From that we infer A ~ (A∧B)∨(¬A∧B) by (disjunction). Now given that (A∧B)∨(¬A∧B) ↔ B, (equivalence) would trivialize interference, i.e. enable us to infer A ~ B for any A and B. It would be interesting to have a weaker form of conjunction which does not trivialize the notion, analogously to the discussion in (Gärdenfors 1978) in the frame of probabilistic independence.

4   Related Notions

We examine several other notions which are close to that of interference. Some of them permit to define it, and others are particular cases.

4.1 Interference Induced by Change

It is possible to write down the above informal definition of interference with our conditional operator:

> A and B interfere =
> <>(A∧B∧¬(¬A>B)) ∨ <>(A∧B∧¬(¬B>A))
> ∨ <>(¬A∧B∧¬(A>B)) ∨ <>(¬A∧B∧¬(¬B>¬A))
> ∨ <>(A∧¬B∧¬(¬A>¬B)) ∨ <>(A∧¬B∧¬(B>¬A))
> ∨ <>(¬A∧¬B∧¬(A>¬B)) ∨ <>(¬A∧¬B∧¬(B>¬A))

(We suppose the usual definitions of <> as A>true and [] as ¬<>¬A.) This would be an attractive way to speak about change as well as about interference through the same notion, viz. conditionals. Unfortunatey, the definitions are circular: In fact, our frame axiom involves interference on its turn. Writing it out we get

> C → A>C   if [](A∧C → ¬A>C) ∧ ... ∧ [](¬A∧C → A>C) ∧ ...

Supposing some basic conditional logic containing the so-called strong centering axiom (CS) A∧C → A>C (Lewis 1973) we can simplify the proviso and get equivalently

> C → A>C   if [](C → ¬A>C) ∧ ... ∧ [](C → A>C) ∧ ...

Hence the condition that we should require would be much too strong. Therefore we have preferred to consider interference as a primitive notion.

4.2 Interference as an Implicit Notion: Using Consistency

Another implicit notion of interference could be obtained through consistency: It is

---

at the same time): The traffic light always goes through yellow. As far as we know, r and g interfere in all other countries of the European Community.

tempting to formulate it as

> *A and B interfere iff A∧B or A∧¬B or ¬A∧B or ¬A∧¬B is in consistent*

Hence A and B interfere if there is a Boolean combination of them which is inconsistent. This a very weak notion, as demonstrated by the following counterexample: Let C be

$$p \wedge q \ . \vee . \ \neg p \wedge r$$

and let A be ¬q. As C and A do not interfere,

$$(p \wedge q) \vee (\neg p \wedge r) \ . \rightarrow . \ \neg q > ((p \wedge q) \vee (\neg p \wedge r))$$

would be a theorem. As we shall see lateron, this formula will not be valid in our semantics: Let w an interpretation such that w $\models$ p and w $\models$ q. (Hence w $\models$ C). Changing w by ¬q may lead to an interpretation w' such that w' $\models$ p. Hence w $\not\models$ C and w $\not\models$ C → A>C.

4.3 Interference as an Implicit Notion: Winslett's PMA

It is interesting to define interference using some implicit property on formulas. In fact, the most simple case is

> *A ~ B iff there is a propositional variable p common to A and B*

This is also a very economic way of specifying an interference relation: It is sufficient to give ~ only on the set of propositional variables. Axiomatically such a notion corresponds to adopt (reflexivity), (symmetry) and (negation), and to replace (equivalence) by two rules

> *(conjunction)*   *if A ~ B then A ~ B∧C*
> *(disjunction)*   *if A ~ B then A ~ B∨C*

The associated semantics is very close to Winslett's PMA (possible models approach, (Winslett 1990)). The above traffic light example shows already that it is not realistic to assume that different propositional variables have nothing to do with each other. For practical examples, the notion of a constraint (called "protected formula" in (Winslett 1990)) is employed to make the possible models approach work. In the case of our example, there should be a formula ¬(r∧g) stating a sort of mutual exclusion between "the traffic light is red" and "the traffic light is green".Then change should be made not only by the original change formula, but by a new change formula resulting from the conjunction of the original change formula and the constraints.

4.4 Interference as Dependency

Formally, the previous definition of interference is the same as in dependency logics (Epstein 1990, Fariñas Lugardon 1993). It is also (at least formally) related to the notion of a topic (Demolombe Jones 1992). In both of these, there is a set of topics T, and a mapping t associating to each propositional variable p a set of topics t(p). Now we can say that

> *A ~ B iff there are propositional variables p in A and q in B such that t(p)∩t(q) ≠ ∅*

In other words, A and B interfere if they are speaking about the same topic.

Although there is a formal analogy between these notions, it is not clear whether there is a deep relationship between them. E.g. in the switches example at the end of the paper we suppose that switches and light interfere, and that two switches do not interfere with each other, which is a quite strange requirement.

4.5 Interference as the Dual of Probabilistic Independence

We could have introduced in the place of interference the dual notion of independence, defined by A and B are independent iff A and B do not interfere. Hence

> *A ~ B iff P(A∧B) ≠ P(A)∗P(B)*

Indeed, Kolmogorov's axiomatisation of indepencence in probability theory (Kolmogorov 1956, cited in Fine 1973) is strictly stronger than the axiomatisation we have given in the previous section. Ours is strictly weaker in the sense we state no link between ~ and conjunction, whereas in (Fine 1973) a (quite complex) rule involving a relation of comparative probability is given. Nevertheless, this must be investigated further.

Note that if we adopt the interference definition for Winslett's possible models approach (see above) we get a much stronger axiomaitsation than Kolmogorov's in the sense that then ~ "passes through" classical conjunction and disjunction, contrarily to the independence relation in (Fine 1973).

4.6 Interference as Potential Causality

It is clear that interference has a lot to do with causality. We may formulate what we have in mind using a notion of *potential causality* as follows:

  A and B interfere iff A may cause B or B may cause A or ¬A may cause B or ...

Hence some "practical" formalization of causality would be highly welcome here. Unfortunately there seems to be no formal system around in the philosophical literature. Consequently we have restricted our discussion to just pointing out the link.

5 Semantics of Interference Logic IL(~)

In the sequel we present a new conditional logic that we call interference logic and that allows us to formalize changes. We suppose a language built from a set of propositional variables PVAR with the classical connectives plus a conditional operator $>$. In the formula $A>C$, A is called the *change formula*. For the time being we consider only formulas where every change formula is classical, i.e. there are no nested conditional operators. Let FOR be the set of such formulas.

As usual, semantics of conditional logics is given in terms of possible world models (Chellas 1975). Given an interference relation ~, a *model* relative to ~ is a triple

$$M^\sim = <W, f^\sim, m>$$

where W is a set of situations, $f^\sim$ is a selection function $f^\sim : 2^W \times W \to 2^W$ and m is a meaning function m: $W \to 2^{PVAR}$. We shall write $|A|_M$ for the extension of A in $M^\sim$, i.e. the set of situations in M at which A is true. The notion of satisfiability ($\models$) is defined as usual, in particular

$$M^\sim, w \models A>B \text{ iff for each } w' \text{ in } f^\sim(|A|_M, w), \ M^\sim, w' \models B$$

Then we add the following constraint to the classical normal conditional logic CK:

- if $w' \in f^\sim(|A|_M, w)$ and $p \in PVAR$ such that p does not interfere with A, then $p \in m(w)$ iff $p \in m(w')$

In other words, for every $p \in m(w) \div m(w')$ we have $p \sim A$, where $\div$ is symmetric difference.

Note that f is well-defined because classically equivalent updates lead to the same result: Suppose that p and q do not interfere, and that there are given two worlds w and w' such that $m(w) = \{p,q\}$ and $m(w') = \emptyset$. According to the constraint on f, neither do we have w' $\in f(w, \vdash \neg p\vdash)$, nor w' $\in f(w, \vdash \neg p \wedge (q \vee \neg q)\vdash)$, due to the rule (equivalence) in the axiomatics of interference.

This expresses that after the change by A, every propositional variable which does not interfere with A is preseved by the change, whereas for the rest of the propositional variables nothing is ensured. For example we ca say that after next French elections Eiffel tower will be at the same place, but money change rates might (but need not) change.

A interfering with A, it may seem a little bit puzzling that after change by A we are not sure about A. In fact, our operation is rather a "forget" (contraction, erasure) than an update operation. In the particular case of ~ being the identity relation, what we get is very close to Winslett's possible models approach. In (Fariñas Herzig 1993) there has been given an axiomatization and a proof procedure for the latter in terms of interference.

6 Axiomatics of Interference Logic IL(~)

The axiomatics of IL(~) is obtained by simply adding the (FRAME) axiom schema to the normal conditional logic CK (Chellas 1980):

    (RCEA)   *if $A \leftrightarrow B$ then $A > C \leftrightarrow B > C$*

    (RCK)   *if $B_1 \wedge ... \wedge B_n . \rightarrow C$ then $(A > B_1) \wedge ... \wedge (A > B_n) . \rightarrow A > C$*

    (FRAME) $C \rightarrow A > C$ *if   A and C do not interfere*

Note that (RCEA) ensures that change is syntax-independent.

7 Reasoning About Actions: Example

In this section we consider an example that present the power of our formalism. It shows in particular that it is more powerful than Winslett's possible models approach.

In general we use the following expresion to formalize change operations

$$KB \vdash_{IL(\sim)} A > ((A \wedge IC) \rightarrow C)$$

where KB is the knowledge base, A is the change formula, IC is a set of integrity contraints and C represents the result of the change.

Our example is from Lifschitz 1987. Let light mean "the light is on", up1 "switch 1 is up", and up2 "switch 2 is up". Let KB = {up1,up2,light}. There is a light controlled by two switches as follows:

up1   ¬up2

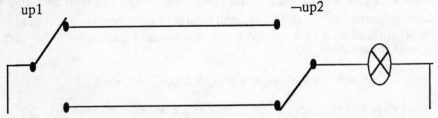

We consider here that switching is the only action which can be undertaken. Thus moving a switch can only change the truth value of light, and not that of the other switch. Hence up1 and up2 both only interfere with light, but not with the other switch. In other words, up1~light and up2~light. (Moreover, we have trivially up1~up1 and up2~up2.) The integrity contraints any situation should satisfy can be represented by the formula IC = light↔(up1↔up2).

Now switching the first switch means to update the knowledge base by ¬up1, and should lead to a state where up2 remains in its position and the light is off. Due to our interference notion, the only possible situations after updating the situation {up1,up2,light} by ¬up1 are {¬up1,up2,light} and {¬up1,up2,¬light}. Graphically we can represent the reasoning as follows:

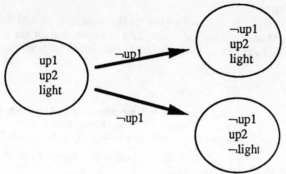

where the arrows represent the updates. Now it is the rôle of the integrity constraints to eliminate among these interpretations the non-intended ones, in our case {¬up1,¬up2,light}:

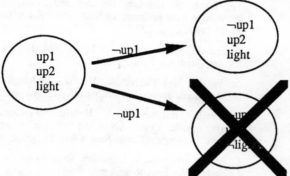

Hence after the update the only resulting situation is {¬up1,up2,¬light}. To sum it up, what we have shown is the following:

{up1,up2,light} $\models_{IL(\sim)}$ ¬up1 > ((¬up1∧(light↔(up1↔up2)))→(¬up1∧up2∧¬light))

The same reasoning can be done syntactically as well. Lifschitz's example is also a counterexample to a common way of employing integrity constraints. E.g. in (Winslett 1990) it is proposed to update the knowledge base by the conjunction of the change formula and the integrity constraints. For different reasons, such a formalization fails to produce the intended result in interference logic as well as in Winslett's possible models approach.

8   Conclusion

In this note we have given an axiomatics and a semantics for interference logic IL. IL is based on an interference relation between formulas which is reflexive and transitive and "passes through" negation and classical equivalence.

Such a notion of interference seems to us a promising tool to reason about change. We shall do further work on its relation with similar notions from various fields, such as the probabilistic notion of independence, the database notion of topics, and the philosophical notion of causality. We shall also work on the problem of automated deduction in IL. Via the Ramsay Test, such theorem proving methods for IL provide a means to mechanize change. For the interesting case where the propositional part of ~ is the identity relation, a theorem proving method via normal forming has been given in (Fariñas Herzig 1993).

Acknowledgements

We wish to thank Didier Dubois who gave us the reference to Kolmogorov's work, Nicolas Asher who challenged us with Lifschitz's example, and all our friends from the ESPRIT project MEDLAR (particularly Robert Demolombe) for comments and valuable discussions.

References

Alchourrón et al. 85	C. E. Alchourron, P. Gärdenfors and D. Makinson. On the Logic of Theory Change: Partial Meet Contractions and Revision Functions. J. Symb. Logic 50.2. pp 510-530, 1985.
Chellas 75	B.F. Chellas. Basic conditional logic. J. of Philos. Logic, 4, 1975, pp 133-53.
Demolombe Jones 1992	A logic for reasoning about "is about".Report, ONERA-CERT, Toulouse, 1992.
Eiter Gottlob 92	Th. Eiter, G. Gottlob, On the complexity of propositional knowledge base revision, updates, and counterfactuals. Journal of AI 57 (1992), pp. 227-270.
Epstein 90	R. Epstein, The semantics of Logic. Vol. 1: Propositional logics. Kluwer Academic Publishers, 1990.
Fariñas et al. 93	L. Fariñas del Cerro, A. Herzig, J. Lang. Ordering-based nonmonotonic reasoning. Journal of AI., to appear.
Fariñas Herzig 93	L. Fariñas del Cerro, A. Herzig. Revisions, updates and interference. In: Logic, Acion and Information, eds. A. Fuhrmann, H. Rott, DeGruyter (Berlin-New York). to appear in 1993.
Fariñas Lugardon 93	L. Fariñas del Cerro, V. Lugardon. Sequents for Dependence Logics. Logique et Analyse, to appear.
Fine 73	T. Fine, Theories of probability. Academic Press, 1973.
Gärdenfors 88	P. Gärdenfors. Knowlege in Flux. MIT Press, 1988.
Gärdenfors 78	P. Gärdenfors, On the Logic of Relevance. Synthese 37, 1978, pp 351-367.
Grahne 91	G. Grahne. Updates and Contrafactuals. Principles of Knowlege Representation and Reasoning. Morgan and Kaufmann, 1991.
Katsuno Mendelzon 91	H. Katsuno and A. O. Mendelzon. Propositional knowledge base revision and minimal change. J. of AI 52, 263-294, 1991.
Kolmogorov 56	A. Kolmogorov, Foundations of the Theory of Probability. Bronx, New York:Chelsea, 1956.
Léa Sombé 92	Léa Sombé, Révision de bases de connaissances. Actes des 4èmes Journées Nationales du PRC IA, Marseille, Oct. 1992. Teknea, Toulouse, 1992.
Lewis 73	D. K. Lewis. Counterfactuals. Blackwell, Oxford, 1973.
Lifschitz 87	V. Lifschitz, Formal Theories of Action. The Frame Problem in Artificial Intelligence: Proc. of the 1987 Workshop, Morgan Kaufmann, 1987
Winslett 90	M. Winslett. Updating Logical Databases. Cambridge Tracts in Theoretical Computer Science. Cambridge University Press 1990.

A Unifying Logical Framework for Reason Maintenance*

Detlef Fehrer

Max–Planck–Institut für Informatik
Im Stadtwald
D – 66123 Saarbrücken
Germany
e-mail: fehrer@mpi-sb.mpg.de

Abstract. We present a way to semantically describe reason maintenance systems, based on Gabbay's labelled deductive system idea. Our approach works for justification based as well as for assumption based methods, thus giving a *unifying* semantics to both of them. Instead of restricting ourselves to only propositional Horn clauses, we'll admit arbitrary logics, e.g. full first order language. This enables us to characterize systems as a whole, including both the reason maintenance component and the problem solver, nevertheless maintaining a separation between the basic logic and the part that describes the label propagation.

1 Introduction

Reason Maintenance Systems (RMS; originally called Truth Maintenance Systems in Doyle's paper ([Doy79])) perform the task of storing interdependences between items derived by some "problem solver", thus keeping track of what is currently believed by a system and in addition maintaining consistency. They are usually seen as a separate component interacting with the actual problem solver, whom it tells on demand which facts are believed and which are not, whereas the solver puts in items with their justifications or withdraws assumptions.

There exist a lot of implemented systems (cf. e.g. [Doy79], [dK86], [Goo87], [MS83], [MS88], [McA78], [Jun89]), that can be grouped with respect to two main criteria:

1. "Doyle-style" or *justification-based* systems ((J)TMS), which work in single contexts only and backtrack if consistency can't be preserved otherwise (e.g. [Doy79], [Goo87]), vs. *assumption-based* systems (ATMS), which maintain multiple contexts (e.g. [dK86], [MS83], [MS88], [Jun89]).
2. Systems that allow non-monotonic justifications (e.g. [Doy79], [Goo87], [Jun89]) as opposed to those that don't.

All of these systems have been described algorithmically. Later there have been numerous attempts to supply some of them with a semantics. Whereas

---

* This work has been supported by the Deutsche Forschungsgemeinschaft (DFG) under title Sonderforschungsbereich 314 Künstliche Intelligenz, project D2

some of the attempts don't fully describe the system in question (e.g. [XH91], [RDB89], [FH89]), this has successfully been done for de Kleer's (basic) ATMS in [FH90], while Doyle-style TMS has been related to logical programming and thus been supplied with some derivates of minimal model and stable model semantics ([Elk90], [Wit90], [GM90a][1]), as well as to autoepistemic logic ([Elk90], [JK90]). Not all of the given semantics are particularly intuitive, and most are very specialized and merely fitted to the system they are supposed to to characterize. It would be more satisfying, if it were possible to give a *unifying semantical framework* for Reason Maintenance, thus being able to describe all of those systems (and many more!), in order to make it easier to note the respective differences or to taylor new systems. A unifying framework has already been proposed by McDermott ([McD91]), and we will follow him in some respect, although he, too, describes it algorithmically.

Most authors point out, that a strict separation of the problem solver or "inference engine" and the component for Reason Maintenance were a good idea. Of course the possibility to modularize is appealing, for the inference mechanism could (at least theoretically) be replaced without the need of changing anything in the RMS. However, the RMS loses *much* of its potential power, if it isn't able to detect inconsistencies by itself, but has to be notified of contradictions, because it views the items it has to administer as *atomic*, i.e. has no insight into their internal structure nor their semantic contents! What even weighs more, a semantical characterization of the system as a whole depends on the interface between the two components, for the RMS can only deal with those interdependences which are explicitly given and the inference engine consequently should pass on *all the dependences it is capable of detecting*[2].

The labelled systems proposed here allow the system to detect everything the inference component could, and still maintain some kind of separation which eases the task of changing e.g. the inference rules. In the sequel we want to first propose a means to *semantically* describe a large class of RMS. Following we will give brief hints at how to describe some of the existent systems in our terminology.

2 Idea and basic approach

Recently Gabbay [Gab91] introduced the notion of a Labelled Deductive System. That is a deductive system whose underlying logic is extended by attaching labels to the formulae and allowing the inference rules to work not only on the formulae themselves, but also on these labels. Depending on the operations permitted on the labels the system as a whole represents a logic, which in general is different from the original one.

At first glance, this seems to be a purely syntactical matter. Indeed this is true, but in case the labels themselves consist of formulae of some logic and

---

[1] The latter article even deals with the dependency directed backtracking procedure.

[2] Which is not guaranteed in practice. Similar objections against the separation have been given e.g. in [MS88].

the operations on them are correct derivation steps with respect to some given semantics, it is possible to provide the "compound logic" with a genuine model theory.

We will use that approach to code the assumptions underlying a derived formula into the label part. The general idea is, that input formulae can be labelled with propositional atoms and derived formulae get the conjunction of their parents' labels. We can then account for multiple derivations by admitting disjunction within the labels. This is in fact the same as the labels in de Kleer's ATMS ([dK86]) which denote sets of *environments*, i.e. *sets of sets of assumptions*, and similar to the notion of "characteristic formula" in [FH90].

Whereas we choose full first-order predicate logic as basic logic, the labels are taken from propositional logic[3]. Within the scope of this paper we won't attach a meaning to negative literals, however. We nevertheless use the semantics of full propositional logic. We can do that, because we can guarantee that the "interesting" labels won't contain negative literals.

In the sequel we make use of the following notations: Labelled formulae are written as α:A, where α stands for the label and A for the unlabelled formula part. Given a labelled formula F, we refer to the label by $label(\text{F})$ and to the formula part by $formula(\text{F})$. If no confusion is possible, we'll simply speak of "formulae" when referring to labelled formulae. Let the labels $\perp$ and $\top$ stand for the false, respective true, formula. We further extend the functions $label$ and $formula$ to work on sets of formulae by defining

$$label(\Phi) := \bigwedge_{\phi \in \Phi} label(\phi) \quad \text{and} \quad formula(\Phi) := \bigcup_{\phi \in \Phi} \{formula(\phi)\}.$$

Definition 2.1 (positive label) *A label is called* positive *if its disjunctive normal form is either $\perp$ or $\top$ or consists solely of positive literals.*

Theorem 2.1 *The DNF of positive labels is* unique *up to the order of literals[4].*

In the following definition we freely use predicate and propositional logic (Tarskian) interpretations without defining them anew.

Definition 2.2 (logical consequence on labelled formulae) *Let Φ be a set of labelled formulae and α:F a single labelled formula. We say α:F follows (logically) from Φ (written as $\Phi \models \alpha$:F), iff $\exists \, \Psi_1, \ldots, \Psi_n \subseteq \Phi$, $n \geq 0$, with*

- $\forall \, \Psi_i : formula(\Psi_i) \models F$ *(wrt. predicate logic) and*
- $\alpha \Rightarrow \bigvee\limits_{i=1}^{n} label(\Psi_i)$ *(wrt. propositional logic).*

If there is no doubt as to what Φ we mean, we'll simply write $\models A$ instead of $\Phi \models A$[5].

---

[3] At least for the moment; we will dismiss that restriction in chapter 5.

[4] Note that $\top$ is an abbreviation of $A \vee \neg A$ for arbitrary A.

[5] According to this definition, $\perp$ and $\top$ correspond to $\{\}$ and $\{\{\}\}$ respectively, so that $\perp$:F holds for arbitrary F (derivable in no environment) and $\top$:A for every tautology A (derivable in the empty environment).

Definition 2.3 (basic and semi-basic sets, assumptions) *A set of labelled formulae is called* basic, *iff every label is atomic and no label occurs more than once. It is called* semi-basic, *if in addition the occurrence of arbitrary many formulae labelled* ⊤ *is allowed. The subset consisting of the formulae not labelled* ⊤ *is called* assumptions.

3 Maximal Labels, Nogoods and the ATMS

The approach above has the advantage that inconsistencies in the original set of formulae can be kept local in a way. So it is not the case that *anything* follows from an inconsistent database. E.g. $\{\alpha{:}A, \beta{:}\neg A, \gamma{:}C\}$ does imply $\alpha \wedge \beta \wedge \gamma{:}D$, but not $\beta{:}D$. In order to describe de Kleer's ATMS, for instance, we further have to introduce the notion of maximal labels.

Definition 3.1 (maximal label) *Let* Φ *be a semi-basic set of labelled formulae. We call the label* α *a* maximal label *for F (where F is an unlabelled formula), iff*

- $\Phi \models \alpha{:}F$ *and*
- *for all labels* β *with* $\Phi \models \beta{:}F$ $\beta \Rightarrow \alpha$ *holds.*

For this definition to make sense, we need the following theorem:

Theorem 3.1 (existence and uniqueness of maximal label) *Given an unlabelled formula F and a set of labelled formulae* Φ *there exists a label* α *(possibly* $\perp$*), such that* $\Phi \models \alpha{:}F$ *and* α *is maximal in the sense of definition 3.1. This* α *is unique up to logical equivalence. Moreover, if the given set of formulae is semi-basic,* α *is positive. We will denote the maximal label of a formula F by* maxlabel(F).

It is possible to include this maximality demand into the definition of logical consequence, which seems adequate, since current systems will produce states described by non-maximal labelled formulae only temporarily. We will, however, keep it separate, in order to be able to also characterize systems that proceed in an *incremental manner*. We will urgently need that when we concern systems whose label logic is no more decidable.

What will happen if the set of original formulae changes? As our labelled logic is *monotonic* (and it stays so even if we allow for non-monotonic justifications, as we soon will see), we don't have to dispose of anything derived so far, if we add new formulae, be it assumptions or not. Actually, this is one more reason to keep the maximality criterion separate, for maximality is not preserved, i.e. a definition of logical consequence including maximality would produce a non-monotonic logic.

Naturally we are not particularly interested in inconsistent contexts. We can restrict ourselves to consistent ones if we require the sets $\Psi_1, \ldots, \Psi_n$ in definition 2.2 to be consistent. For an inconsistent set is characterized by the fact that $\perp$

is derivable, we can alternatively add $\forall \Psi_i$: label$(\Psi_i) \not\Rightarrow$ maxlabel$(\bot)$ as a third point to definition 2.2. We will stick to the second alternative, because it opens the possibility of weakening the maxlabel part to other labels for $\bot$ or even replacing it by arbitrary other labels. So we define

Definition 3.2 (logical consequence respecting sets of labels) *Let Φ be a set of labelled formulae, $\alpha{:}F$ a single labelled formula, and Ω a set of labels (propositional formulae). We say $\alpha{:}F$ follows (logically) from Φ, respecting Ω, (written as $\Phi \downarrow \Omega \models \alpha{:}F$), iff $\exists \Psi_1, \ldots, \Psi_n \subseteq \Phi$, $n \geq 0$, with*

- $\forall \Psi_i$: *formula$(\Phi) \models F$ (wrt. predicate logic),*
- $\alpha \Rightarrow \bigvee_{i=1}^{n}$ *label(Ψ_i) and*
- $\forall \Psi_i$: *label$(\Psi_i) \not\Rightarrow \bigwedge_{\omega \in \Omega} \omega.$*

$\alpha{:}F$ *follows* consistently *from Φ, if $\Phi \downarrow \{maxlabel(\bot)\} \models \alpha{:}F$.*

In the RMS literature the term *nogood* has been coined. We will use it here, too, though with a slightly broader meaning.

Definition 3.3 (nogood[6]) *Any label α, for which $\models \alpha{:}\bot$ holds, is called a nogood.*

We are now in a position that allows us to describe de Kleer's ATMS in a straightforward manner. Paying attention to introduce new atoms for every "fresh" proposition, as the system has no knowledge of the internal structure, we represent justifications as $\top{:}A \wedge \ldots \wedge D \rightarrow F$ and assumptions as $\alpha{:}A$, where α is "fresh" and atomic. There is no difference between ordinary and nogood-justifications (these are simply justifications with $\bot$ on the right hand side of the implication). As can be seen easily, only Horn clauses occur in the description of an ATMS. The *maximal, consistent* labels of atomic formulae correspond to the labels computed by the ATMS.

4 Nonmonotonic Justifications and the TMS

When we look at justification-based systems, the introduction of non-monotonic justifications seems to complicate matters, whereas the restriction to merely one context appears simple, but the opposite turns out to be true. We make the implicit *assumption*, that every node is "out", if it can't be given a valid justification, explicit, by adding the formula $\alpha{:}\neg A$ for every node A with fresh α. Given a non-monotonic justification[7] F (SL (A B) (C D)), we simply translate to $\alpha \wedge \beta{:}A \wedge B \wedge \neg C \wedge \neg D \rightarrow F$, α and β being the labels assigned to $\neg C$ and

---

[6] Usual nogood definitions only admit nogoods (in our sense) containing no disjunctions.

[7] We don't deal with CP-justifications here.

¬D. We don't have to give any additional thought to dependency directed back-tracking, as we use full propositional logic and therefore get contrapositives for free (like in [GM90b]).

The *maximal, consistent* labels now show, whether A or ¬A can be given a valid justification or not. Because the TMS takes a global view, the labels have to be checked for some kind of compatibility. Unfortunately we can't get into closer details here.

5 Varying the Logics

The main advantage of our characterization lies in the fact, that we are free to change not only the basic logic, but also the logic of the labels. By changing the basic logic, we can dispose of the tight restrictions of existing systems, like sticking to Horn logic or propositional logics. The first extension has already been made by Reiter and de Kleer in [RdK87] and therefore taken into account in works like e.g. [Ino90]. Arguments for the admittance of full first order have been given in the introductory section, so we won't repeat them here.

There may be reasons to also change the labels' logic. E.g. it is often looked upon as positive, that justifications can be viewed as *directed*, explicitly excluding contrapositives. This certainly is a remarkable difference between RMS and various default logics and has been proposed as a cure to the so called anomalous extension problem (cf. eg. [Mor87], [Mor88]). We can cope with that by replacing the material implication in the second point of Definition 2.2 by a better suited implication. When doing this we of course have to pay attention to adapt normal forms etc., i.e. we have to switch the label logic. If we want a model theoretic semantics, we can get one, given a Hilbert axiomatization, as shown by Gabbay and Ohlbach in [GO92]. Similarly we can treat the relevance logic in the SNeBR system of Martins and Shapiro ([MS88]) and are thus able to provide the semantic characterization they have asked for in their article. Of course there are some interdependences between the label logic and the basic logic. But as long as the basic logic is monotonic, there won't be any problems, given the labels' logic is equivalent to or weaker than classical logic.

By taking full first-order labels we can even characterize various kinds of default or "typicality" logics (e.g. [Rei80], to name only the best known example). We could e.g. state $\top : \forall x \, \text{BIRD}(x) \land \neg \text{abnormal-bird}(x) \rightarrow \text{FLIES}(x)$, $\top : \text{BIRD}(\text{tweety})$, $\top : \neg \text{FLIES}(\text{tweety})$ and $\alpha(x) : \forall x \neg \text{abnormal-bird}(x)$, thus being able to correctly deduce $\alpha(tweety) : \text{FLIES}(\text{tweety})$ only with inconsistent label, whereas $\text{BIRD}(\text{hansi})$ and every further individual gets a consistent maxlabel.[8]

There are seemingly no restrictions to the choice of logic, so we hope we will also be able to catch extensions like e.g. [DLP90], which use possibilistic logic. Especially probabilistic and possibilistic logics may turn out to be very well-suited to an *incremental approach*.

---

[8] Actually that is more than usual default logics, for those let default schemata only stand for a collection of *ground instances*, whereas here arbitrary terms may appear within labels.

6 Conclusion and further work

We have succeeded in finding a unifying logical framework which allows us to describe and distinguish various approaches to reason maintenance semantically. In principle this description is straightforward, but the tedious work to really show adequacy has still to be done for some systems. Especially the choice of context in the TMS has to be worked upon. The possibility to really implement a system based on an incremental calculus using first order labels is the main goal to be pursued in the near future. Before this can be done, however, thorough studies on the admittance of proof strategies guaranteeing at least semi-decidability have to be undergone. This approach looks very promising for probabilistic and possibilistic reasoning, for the dispensation of maximality allows for *local propagation* (and therefore genuine logical inference rules).

References

[dK86]   Johan de Kleer. An Assumption–Based TMS. *Artificial Intelligence*, 28(1), pp. 127–162, 1986.

[DLP90]   Didier Dubois, Jérôme Lang, and Henri Prade. A Possibilistic Assumption-Based Truth Maintenance System with Uncertain Justifications, and its Application to Belief Revision. In J. P. Martins and M. Reinfrank, editors, *Truth Maintenance Systems*, volume 515 of *Lecture Notes in Artificial Intelligence*, pp. 87–106. Springer-Verlag, August 1990.

[Doy79]   Jon Doyle. A Truth Maintenance System. *Artificial Intelligence*, 12, pp. 231–272, 1979.

[Elk90]   Charles Elkan. A Rational Reconstruction of Nonmonotonic Truth Maintenance Systems. *Artificial Intelligence*, 43(2), pp. 219–234, 1990.

[FH89]   Yasushi Fujiwara and Shinichi Honiden. Relating the TMS to Autoepistemic Logic. In *IJCAI-89. Eleventh International Joint Conference on Artificial Intelligence*, volume 2, pp. 1199–1205, 1989.

[FH90]   Yasuchi Fujiwara and Shinichi Honiden. On logical foundations of the ATMS. In J. P. Martins and M. Reinfrank, editors, *Truth Maintenance Systems*, volume 515 of *Lecture Notes in Artificial Intelligence*, pp. 125–135. Springer-Verlag, August 1990.

[Gab91]   Dov Gabbay. Labelled Deductive Systems, Part I. CIS Bericht 90-22, Centrum für Informations- und Sprachverarbeitung, February 1991.

[GM90a]   Laura Giordano and Alberto Martelli. Generalized Stable Models, Truth Maintenance and Conflict Resolution. In David H. D. Warren and Peter Szeredi, editors, *Logic Programming. Proceedings of the Seventh International Conference*, Logic Programming Series, pp. 427–441, Cambridge, Massachusetts / London, England, 1990. MIT Press.

[GM90b]   Laura Giordano and Alberto Martelli. Truth Maintenance Systems and Belief Revision. In J. P. Martins and M. Reinfrank, editors, *Truth Maintenance Systems*, volume 515 of *Lecture Notes in Artificial Intelligence*, pp. 71–86. Springer-Verlag, August 1990.

[GO92]   Dov M. Gabbay and Hans Jürgen Ohlbach. From a Hilbert Calculus to its Model Theoretic Semantics. In Kryshna Broda, editor, *Proceedings of the*

4th UK Conference on Logic Programming, Workshops in Computing, pp. 218–252. Springer Verlag, 1992.

[Goo87] James. W. Goodwin. *A Theory and System for Non–Monotonic Reasoning.* Linköping studies in science and technology, dissertation no.165, Department of Computer and Information Science, Linköping University, S-581 83 Linköping, 1987.

[Ino90] Katsumi Inoue. An Abductive Procedure for the CMS/ATMS. In J. P. Martins and M. Reinfrank, editors, *Truth Maintenance Systems*, volume 515 of *Lecture Notes in Artificial Intelligence*, pp. 34–53. Springer-Verlag, August 1990.

[JK90] Ulrich Junker and Kurt Konolige. Computing the Extensions of Autoepistemic and Default Logics with a Truth Maintenance System. In *Proceedings of the 8th AAAI*, volume 1, pages 278–283, 1990.

[Jun89] Ulrich Junker. A Correct Non–Monotonic ATMS. In *Proc. of the IJCAI*, 1989.

[McA78] D. McAllester. A three valued truth maintenance system. AI Memo 473, AI lab, MIT Cambridge, 1978.

[McD91] Drew McDermott. A general framework for reason maintenance. *Artificial Intelligence*, 50(3), pp. 289–329, 1991.

[Mor87] P. H. Morris. Curing anomalous extensions. In *Proceedings of the AAAI-87*, pp. 437–442, Seattle, WA, 1987.

[Mor88] Paul H. Morris. The Anomalous Extension Problem in Default Reasoning. *Artificial Intelligence*, 35(2), pp. 383–399, 1988.

[MS83] João P. Martins and Stuart C. Shapiro. Reasoning in Multiple Belief Spaces. In *Proceedings of the IJCAI83*, pp. 370–373, 1983.

[MS88] João P. Martins and Stuart C. Shapiro. A Model for Belief Revision. *Artificial Intelligence*, 35, pp. 25–79, 1988.

[RDB89] Michael Reinfrank, Oskar Dressler, and Gerd Brewka. On the Relation Between Truth Maintenance and Autoepistemic Logic. In *IJCAI-89. Eleventh International Joint Conference on Artificial Intelligence*, volume 2, pp. 1206–1212, 1989.

[RdK87] Raymond Reiter and Johan de Kleer. Foundations of Assumption–Based Truth Maintenance Systems: Preliminary Report. In *Proceedings of the AAAI87*, pp. 183–188, Seattle, Washington, July 1987.

[Rei80] Raymond Reiter. A Logic for Default Reasoning. *Artificial Intelligence*, 13(1), pp. 81–132, 1980.

[Wit90] Cees Witteveen. A Skeptical Semantics for Truth Maintenance. In J. P. Martins and M. Reinfrank, editors, *Truth Maintenance Systems*, volume 515 of *Lecture Notes in Artificial Intelligence*, pp. 136–154. Springer-Verlag, August 1990.

[XH91] Wang Xianchang and Chen Huowang. On Semantics of TMS. In *IJCAI-91. 12th International Joint Conference on Artificial Intelligence*, volume 1, pp. 306–309, 1991.

Taxonomic Linear Theories

Christophe Fouqueré, Jacqueline Vauzeilles

LIPN-CNRS

Université Paris-Nord

93430 Villetaneuse

e-mail: {cf,jv}@lipn.univ-paris13.fr

Abstract. A *semantic network* is a structure for representing knowledge as a pattern of interconnected nodes and edges. This paper focuses on the *means* linear logic offers to represent these networks. In order to compare our inferences, we have chosen one nonmonotonic logic: default logic [9] serves as a reference. The main result proves the equivalence between linear logic and default logic in *taxonomic default theories*. We hope this will help to better understand the relations between nonmonotonicity and defeasible knowledge representation.

1 Introduction

A *semantic network* is a structure for representing knowledge as a pattern of interconnected nodes and edges. The nodes represent concepts or properties of a set of individuals whereas the edges represent relations between concepts. The network can be viewed as a hierarchy of concepts according to levels of generality. A more specific concept is said to *inherit* properties from its subsumers. The formalisation of human reasoning requires that some kinds of uncertain knowledge be represented in semantic networks as *default* edges: for example, we expect the concept of bird to be more specific than the concept of flying object, even if some species cannot fly. Generally speaking, we consider networks with *default* and *exception* edges, dealing respectively with defeasible and exceptional knowledge.

Nonmonotonic logics (see [2] for example) were developed in the last decade in order to represent defaults and exceptions in a logical way: the set of inferred grounded facts is the set of properties inherited by concepts. In this paper, we investigate the problem of formalising inheritance in semantic networks with default and exception links in a standard logic, namely linear logic ; this research was undertaken after a short paper by Girard [6]. In nonmonotonic logics, if T and S are two sets of formulae it is not necessarily true that the set of theorems of T∪S is included in the set of theorems of T; in other words, if A,B, C are three formulae, "C is provable from A", doesn't necessarily lead to "C is provable from A and B". Of course, linear logic is monotonic; however, its linear implication behaves non-monotonically with respect to the "times" connective so, although the sequent A ⊢ C is provable in linear logic the sequent A "times" B ⊢ C is not necessarily provable in linear logic. Linear logic is therefore able to formalise problems which have so far been handled using nonmonotonic logics.

In what follows, only semantic networks with default and exception links are considered. An exception is a direct inhibition of a concept: an exception link between A and B means that A is not a B (or A does not have the property B) whatever the number or kind of paths between A and B. Here is a very simple example to show graphically what we expect of such semantic networks.

Example: The two exceptions (dashed line with a double arrow) define an even cycle. It is known that even cycles may induce multiple extensions: let A be true. On the one hand one can infer B, C; on the other hand one can infer B', C'.

This example is described later using first linear logic and then default logic. In order to compare our inferences we have chosen one nonmonotonic logic, namely default logic [9] as a reference; even if it does not represent knowledge and natural inferences on them perfectly, default logic has been studied extensively and is certainly one of the simplest ways to express uncertain knowledge. The main result proves the equivalence between linear logic and default logic in these restricted theories. We hope this will help to better understand the relations between nonmonotonicity and defeasible knowledge representation.

Let us first define the taxonomic networks considered in this paper.

Definition 1: A TNE (Taxonomic Network with Exceptions) is defined as a triple $\mathbb{N}=<N, \rightarrow, \dashrightarrow>$ such that:

- N is a finite set of nodes
- $\rightarrow$, $\dashrightarrow$ are two functions that associate to each node of N a set of nodes of N with the following two constraints:
    - $<N, \rightarrow>$ is an oriented graph without cycles.
    - Let R be the set of roots of $<N, \rightarrow>$, then $R \cap \dashrightarrow(N) = \varnothing$.

2 Taxonomic Linear Theories

This section is devoted to the axiomatisation in linear logic of taxonomic networks, namely *taxonomic linear theories*. We start by showing that inferences correspond to a subset of provable sequents, *simple sequents*, and then go on to relate such proofs to *nets* via pseudo-nets. A pseudo-net is a finite graph composed of coloured vertices and of coloured oriented edges. Pseudo-nets constructed from standard proofs of simple sequents are called nets. It is proved that the main condition for a pseudo-net to be a net is that its orientation $\prec$ is an ordering.

The above problem will be formalised in the (intuitionistic) fragment of linear logic using the constant 1, the multiplicative connectives "times" ($\otimes$), and "linear implication" ($\multimap$), and the exponential connective "of course" (!); the reader will find axioms and rules of linear logic for this fragment in [5].[1] The properties of the multiplicative fragment of linear logic are essential in our representation: the

---

[1] Because of lack of space, the presentation of linear logic as well as proofs are not included here but can be found in [4].

properties of the constant "1" (which is a neutral element for the multiplicative conjunction "times") can be used to cancel information (we use $A \multimap 1$ to cancel A), while those of the exponential connective "!" can, using $!(A \multimap 1)$, cancel all occurrences of A.

The language L: A, B,..., A^+, B^+,..., A^-, B^-,... are atomic formulae. A^+ (resp. A^-)... are called *positive* (resp. *negative*) *signed* atomic formulae. A, B,... are called *unsigned* atomic formulae. The *literals* we consider are of the following forms: atomic formulae, $(A \multimap 1)$ with A atomic, $!(A \multimap 1)$ with A atomic. Atomic formulae and literals of the form $!(A \multimap 1)$ are *strict* literals. A *monomial* (resp. *signed*) is a linear product ($\otimes$) of strict literals (resp. *signed*); a monomial has *incompatible* literals if it contains two signed literals of the same variable with opposite signs (A^+ and A^-, or, B^+ and B^-,...).

Taxonomic linear theories in L: Now, we can explain how taxonomic networks with exceptions are represented in linear logic.

Definition 1: Let $\mathbb{N} = <N, \rightarrow, \dashrightarrow>$ be a taxonomic network with exceptions. We define a *taxonomic linear theory* $\mathbb{T}(\mathbb{N})$ as a set of *taxonomic proper axioms* (in L) on a set of propositional variables $V = N \cup \{A^+ / A \in N\} \cup \{A^- / A \in N\}$ as follows:

• $\mathbb{T}(\mathbb{N}) = \{ \Gamma(A) / A \in N \}$ such that

$$\Gamma(A) \equiv A \vdash A^+ \otimes B_1 \otimes ... \otimes B_m \otimes C_1^- \otimes !(C_1 \multimap 1) \otimes ... \otimes C_p^- \otimes !(C_p \multimap 1)$$

with $\rightarrow(A) = \{B_i / i \in [1,m]\}$, $\dashrightarrow(A) = \{C_j / j \in [1,p]\}$.

• A is a root of $<N, \rightarrow>$ iff A belongs to the set of prerequisites of simple sequents (see below).

• A sequent is *simple* iff it is of the following form: $A_1,...,A_r \vdash X$ where X is a signed monomial without incompatible literals and $A_1,...,A_r$ are the roots of $<N, \rightarrow>$. We say that $A_1,...,A_r$ are the *prerequisites* of the simple sequent $A_1,...,A_r \vdash X$.

Example (continued): $\mathbb{T} \equiv \{ A \vdash A^+ \otimes B \otimes B', \quad B \vdash B^+ \otimes B'^- \otimes !(B' \multimap 1) \otimes C,$
$B' \vdash B'^+ \otimes B^- \otimes !(B \multimap 1) \otimes C', \quad C \vdash C^+, \quad C' \vdash C'^+ \}$
The two provable simple sequents of $\mathbb{T}$ are:

$$A \vdash A^+ \otimes B^+ \otimes B'^- \otimes C^+ \quad \text{and} \quad A \vdash A^+ \otimes B^- \otimes B'^+ \otimes C'^+$$

Note that the following provable sequent of $\mathbb{T}$ has incompatible literals so is not a simple sequent: $A \vdash A^+ \otimes B^+ \otimes B'^- \otimes C^+ \otimes B^- \otimes B'^+ \otimes C'^+$.

Definition 2: A *standard* proof of a simple sequent is a proof (with only proper cuts) in which every left premiss of a !-l rule is an identity axiom, all $\otimes$-r, $\multimap$-l, !-l rules are used before cut-rules, each proper axiom occurring in the proof is a premiss of a cut-rule.

Lemma 1: If a simple sequent is provable, then it accepts a standard proof.

Quasi-simple sequents occur in the (standard) proofs of simple sequents. A sequent is *quasi-simple* iff it is of the following form: $C_1, ..., C_q, M_1, ..., M_r \vdash X$ where C_i are non-strict literals, M_i are monomials and X is a signed monomial without incompatible literals.

A quasi-simple sequent is *decomposed* iff each M_i is atomic. The notion of standard proof can obviously be extended to quasi-simple sequents.

Linear theories and nets

A proof contains many useless properties in its contexts. Girard has defined proof-structures [5] and then particular proof structures which are proof-nets and which correspond exactly to proofs in (some fragment of) linear logic. Similarly, we define *pseudo-nets* and associate a pseudo-net to any (standard) proof of a simple sequent of $\mathbb{T}$, which is said to be its *net*. The main criterion for a pseudo-net to be a net is that its vertices can be (partially) ordered. The notion of *pseudo-nets* and of *nets* in $\mathbb{T}$ are closely connected with the notions of pseudo-plans and plans used in [8] and we use the same terminology.

Definition 3: A *pseudo-net* (in $\mathbb{T}$) is a finite graph composed of coloured vertices and of coloured oriented edges as follows.

- Each *vertex* is labelled by a triple (A, p_A, n_A) A being an unsigned atomic formula A of $\mathbb{T}$, p_A and n_A being two integers. We say that A is the *name* of the vertex labelled by (A, p_A, n_A); in a pseudo-net there exists at most one vertex named A. Either the vertex (A, p_A, n_A) is white, n_A is null and the vertex is provided with the exits $x A_1, ..., x A_n$: in this case A is the antecedent of the axiom $A \vdash A^+ \otimes A_1 \otimes ... \otimes A_n \otimes !(B_1 \multimap 1) \otimes ... \otimes !(B_m \multimap 1)$ where each A_i is atomic and each B_j is atomic and unsigned. Or the vertex (A, p_A, n_A) is black, n_A is strictly positive and the vertex has no exit: in this case A^- occurs in a consequent of an axiom of $\mathbb{T}$.

- An *oriented* edge accepts an exit xO as its *origin* and a vertex named A as its *end*. An edge is given the colour *white* if $O \equiv A$ is an unsigned formula or the colour *black* if $O \equiv A^-$. An edge such that its origin is an exit xA of the vertex (B, p_B, n_B) has the *weight* p_B.

- The *number-of-white-edges* w_A (resp. *number-of-black-edges* b_A) of white (resp. black) edges whose end is the vertex named A is the sum of weights of white (resp. black) edges whose end is the vertex named A. We still have $w_A \leq p_A$ and $b_A \leq n_A$.

- The *entries of a pseudo-net* are the vertices (A, p_A, n_A) such that $w_A < p_A$.

- A pseudo-net has no *exit*: all the exits of a vertex are connected with another vertex.

The *orientation* of a pseudo-net is the transitive closure of the relation $\prec$ defined over the set of vertices by $(A, p_A, n_A) \prec (B, p_B, n_B)$ (or put simply $A \prec B$) iff there exists an exit xB of the vertex named A connected with the vertex named B.

Definition 4: To each subproof **D** of a standard proof of a simple sequent of $\mathbb{T}$ we associate a pseudo-net $\mathbb{D}$ in the following way.

• If **D** is an identity axiom, then $\mathbb{D}$ is empty.

• If **D** is obtained from **E** by application of a $\otimes$-l rule, a 1-l rule or a D-l rule then $\mathbb{D}$ is identical to $\mathbb{E}$.

• If **D** is obtained from $\mathbf{D}_1$ and $\mathbf{D}_2$ by application of a $\otimes$-r rule remark that $\mathbb{D}_1$ and $\mathbb{D}_2$ only have black vertices or are empty, then $\mathbb{D}$ is the "union" of $\mathbb{D}_1$ and $\mathbb{D}_2$ defined in the following way: if a vertex (A,p_A,n_A) belongs to $\mathbb{D}_2$ and not to $\mathbb{D}_1$ then add this vertex to $\mathbb{D}_1$ else if the vertex (A,p_A,n_A) belongs to $\mathbb{D}_1$ and the vertex (A,p'_A,n'_A) belongs to $\mathbb{D}_2$ then replace in $\mathbb{D}_1$ the vertex (A,p_A,n_A) by the vertex $(A,p_A+p'_A,n_A+n'_A)$.

• If **D** is obtained from **E** by application of a $\multimap$ -l rule on the formula $(A\multimap 1)$, then:
- if a (black) vertex labelled (A,p_A,n_A) belongs to $\mathbb{E}$, then $\mathbb{D}$ is the pseudo-net obtained from $\mathbb{E}$ by replacing the label (A,p_A,n_A) by (A,p_A+1,n_A+1);

- if no vertex labelled (A,p_A,n_A) belongs to $\mathbb{E}$, then $\mathbb{D}$ is the pseudo-net obtained from $\mathbb{E}$ by adding the black vertex $(A,1,1)$.

• If **D** is obtained from **E** by application of a W-l rule on the formula $!(A\multimap 1)$ then:
- if a (black) vertex labelled (A,p_A,n_A) belongs to $\mathbb{E}$, then $\mathbb{D}$ is the pseudo-net obtained from $\mathbb{E}$ by replacing the label (A,p_A,n_A) by (A,p_A,n_A+1);

- if no vertex labelled (A,p_A,n_A) belongs to $\mathbb{E}$, then $\mathbb{D}$ is the pseudo-net obtained from $\mathbb{E}$ by adding the black vertex $(A,0,1)$.

• If **D** is obtained from **E** by application of a C-l rule on the formula $!(A\multimap 1)$ then $\mathbb{D}$ is the pseudo-net obtained from $\mathbb{E}$ by replacing the label (A,p_A,n_A) by (A,p_A,n_A-1).

• If **D** is obtained by application of a cut-rule between the sequent $A \vdash A^+\otimes A_1\otimes \ldots\otimes A_n\otimes !(B_1\multimap 1)\otimes\ldots\otimes !(B_q\multimap 1)$ (each A_i being an atomic formula) and the conclusion sequent of the proof **E**, then:
- if a (white) vertex labelled $(A,p_A,0)$ belongs to $\mathbb{E}$, then $\mathbb{D}$ is the pseudo-net obtained from $\mathbb{E}$ by replacing the label $(A,p_A,0)$ by $(A,p_A+1,0)$;

- if no vertex labelled (A,p_A,n_A) belongs to $\mathbb{E}$, then $\mathbb{D}$ is the pseudo-net obtained from $\mathbb{E}$ by adding the white vertex $(A,1,0)$ and by linking each exit xA_j or xA_j^- to the vertex named A_j of $\mathbb{E}$.

Lemma 2: The above construction is correct: namely the graph that we have associated to a standard proof is a pseudo-net. Moreover, if **D** is the (standard) proof of the sequent $B_1,\ldots, B_p, !(C_1\multimap 1),\ldots, !(C_q\multimap 1) \vdash D_1^+\otimes\ldots\otimes D_t^+\otimes E_1^-\otimes\ldots\otimes E_s^-$ where B_i, C_j are unsigned literals, then the following conditions hold:

- Each D_i ($1 \leq i \leq t$) is the name of a white vertex of $\mathbb{D}$; if A is the name of a white vertex of $\mathbb{D}$, then A^+ occurs exactly p_A times among $D_1^+,...,D_t^+$.

- Each E_i ($1 \leq i \leq s$) is the name of a black vertex of $\mathbb{D}$; for each black vertex named A, A^- occurs exactly b_A times among $E_1^-,...,E_s^-$.

- Each B_i is an entry of $\mathbb{D}$; all the entries of $\mathbb{D}$ are among $B_1, ..., B_p$; each entry A of $\mathbb{D}$ occurs exactly $p_A - w_A$ times among $B_1, ..., B_p$.

- Each C_i is the name of a black vertex (C_i, p_{C_i}, n_{C_i}) of $\mathbb{D}$ such that $b_{C_i} < n_{C_i}$; for each black vertex named A such that $b_A < n_A$, $!(A \multimap 1)$ occurs exactly $n_A - b_A$ times among $!(C_1 \multimap 1),..., !(C_q \multimap 1)$.

Proof: by induction on a (standard) proof **D**.

Definition 5: A *net* is a pseudo-net constructed from a (standard) proof of a simple sequent $A_1,...,A_r \vdash D_1^+ \otimes ... \otimes D_p^+ \otimes E_1^- \otimes ... \otimes E_s^-$

Theorem 1: A pseudo-net is a net iff all entries are $A_1,...,A_r$, are white, for each black vertex (B_i, p_{B_i}, n_{B_i}) we have $b_{B_i} = n_{B_i}$ and if its orientation $\prec$ is an ordering.

Example (continued):

Here is the net associated to the proof (figure 1) of the simple sequent

$A \vdash A^+ \otimes B^+ \otimes B'^- \otimes C^+$

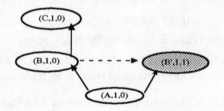

3 Exceptions in Default theory

3.1 Default Logic

Let us recall default propositional logic as introduced in [9] (see [2] for a complete presentation).

Definition 1: • A *default* is an expression of the following form: $\dfrac{\alpha : \beta}{\gamma}$, where α, β and γ are formulae of propositional logic. α is the *prerequisite*, β is the *justification*, γ is the *consequent*. A default theory is a pair (W,D), where W is a set of formulae of propositional logic, D is a set of defaults.

• A set of formulae $\mathfrak{E}$ is an *extension* of a default theory (W,D) iff $\Gamma(\mathfrak{E}) = \mathfrak{E}$, where $\Gamma(.)$ is defined in the following way. Let S be a set of formulae, $\Gamma(S)$ is the smallest set satisfying

(D_1) $W \subset \Gamma(S)$ $\qquad\qquad\qquad$ $(D_2)^2$ $Th(\Gamma(S)) = \Gamma(S)$

(D_3) If $\dfrac{\alpha : \beta}{\gamma} \in D$ and $\alpha \in \Gamma(S)$ and $\neg\beta \notin S$, then $\gamma \in \Gamma(S)$.

3.2 Taxonomic Default Theories

The formalisation of taxonomic networks in default logic was studied in [3].

Definition 1: Let $\mathbb{N} = <N, \to, \dashrightarrow>$ be a taxonomic network with exceptions. A taxonomic default theory $\mathbb{D}(\mathbb{N}) = (W(\mathbb{N}), D(\mathbb{N}))$ can be defined on a set of propositional variables V' as follows:

- $V' = N \cup \{E_A \, / \, A \in N\}$ $\qquad$ • $\dfrac{A : \neg E_B}{B} \in D(\mathbb{N})$ iff $\quad B \in \to(A)$

- $A \supset E_B \in W(\mathbb{N})$ iff $B \in \dashrightarrow(A)$ $\quad$ • $A \in W(\mathbb{N})$ iff $\quad A$ is a root of $<N, \to>$.

Example (continued): $D(\mathbb{N}) = \{\dfrac{A : \neg E_B}{B}, \dfrac{A : \neg E_B'}{B'}, \dfrac{B : \neg E_C}{C}, \dfrac{B' : \neg E_C'}{C'}\}$,

$W(\mathbb{N}) = \{A, B \supset E_B', B' \supset E_B\}$. The two extensions are $Th(\{A, B, C, E_B'\})$ and $Th(\{A, B', C', E_B\})$.

3.3 Taxonomic Linear Theories and Taxonomic Default Theories

If we have a taxonomic network with exceptions, the following theorem shows the exact correspondence between provable simple sequents of the associated taxonomic linear theory and the extensions of the associated taxonomic default theory.

Theorem1: Let $\mathbb{N} = <N, \Rightarrow, \to, \dashrightarrow>$ be a TNES, $\mathbb{T}(\mathbb{N})$ the associated taxonomic linear theory and $\mathbb{D}(\mathbb{N})$, the associated taxonomic default theory. Let $R = \{A_1, ..., A_r\}$ be the set of roots of $<N, \Rightarrow \cup \to>$; then there exists a simple sequent $A_1, ..., A_r \vdash$

$C_1^+ \otimes ... \otimes C_t^+ \otimes D_1^- \otimes ... \otimes D_s^-$ provable in $\mathbb{T}(\mathbb{N})$ iff there exists an extension $\mathcal{E}$ of $\mathbb{D}(\mathbb{N})$

such that $\forall i \in [1,t]$ $C_i \in \mathcal{E}$ and $\forall C \in N \cap \mathcal{E}$ $\exists i \in [1,t]$ such that $C = C_i$.

The proof is based on an equivalence between the set of axioms used in the proof of a simple sequent and the set of generator defaults of an extension (such sets of defaults exist (see [7])).

4 Conclusion

Paraphrasing Girard [6], we have therefore succeeded in finding an axiomatisation of taxonomical structures and reasoning with default and exception properties, without creating contradictions. Even if, in this paper, exceptions were interpreted as direct inhibitions of concepts, our work also concerns other kinds of interpretations, counter-exceptions and so on [4]. This work has to be viewed as a first step towards full interpretation of defaults and exceptions in linear logic, thus pursuing research in Artificial Intelligence using linear logic, namely research on planification.

---

[2]Let Γ be a set of formulae, $Th(\Gamma) \equiv \{F \, / \, \Gamma \vdash F\}$.

References

1. Ph. Besnard: An Introduction to Default Logic. Springer-Verlag (1989)

2. D.G. Bobrow (eds): Special Issue on Non Monotonic Logics, Artificial Intelligence, vol. 13 (1980)

3. C. Froidevaux, D. Kayser: Inheritance in Semantic Networks and Default Logic. In D. Smets, E. Mamdani, D. Dubois, H. Prade (eds).Non-Standard Logics for Automated Reasoning. London: Academic Press, 179-212 (1988)

4. C. Fouqueré, J. Vauzeilles: Taxonomic Linear Theories, LIPN Report, Université Paris-Nord (1993)

5. J.-Y. Girard: linear logic. Theoretical Computer Science 50, 1-102 (1987)

6. J.-Y. Girard: Logic and Exceptions: A Few Remarks. Journal of Logic and Computation 2, 111-118 (1992)

7. F. Lévy: Computing Extensions of Default Theories. In R. Kruse, P. Siegel (eds): Symbolic and Quantitative Approaches to Uncertainty. Lecture Notes in Computer Science 548. Berlin, 219-226 (1991)

8. M. Masseron: Generating Plans in linear logic II: A geometry of conjunctive actions. Theoretical Computer Science 113, (1993).

9. R. Reiter: A Logic for Default Reasoning. Artificial Intelligence 13, 81-132 (1980)

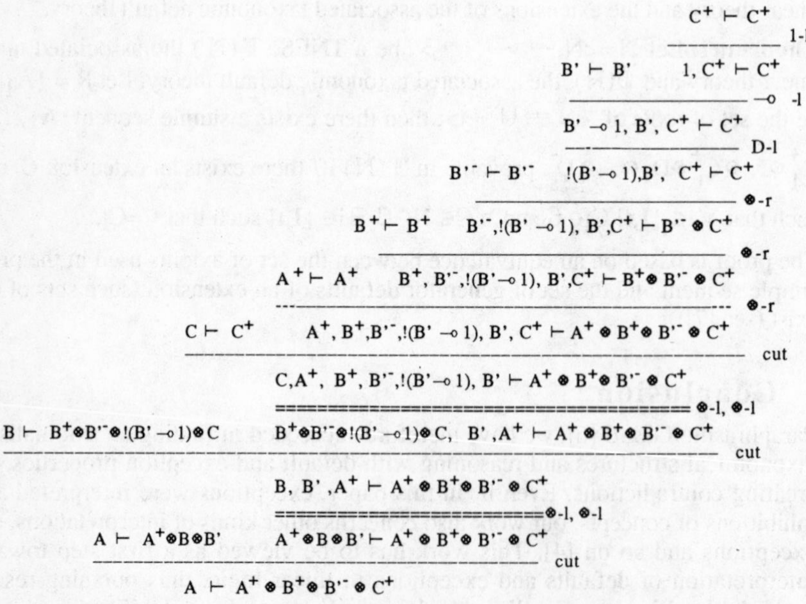

$$
\cfrac{
\cfrac{
\cfrac{
\cfrac{
\cfrac{
\cfrac{
\cfrac{
\cfrac{
C \vdash C^+ \qquad
\cfrac{
A^+ \vdash A^+ \qquad
\cfrac{
B^+ \vdash B^+ \qquad
\cfrac{
B'' \vdash B'' \qquad
\cfrac{
B' \vdash B' \qquad
\cfrac{
\cfrac{
}{C^+ \vdash C^+}\ \text{1-I}
}{1, C^+ \vdash C^+}
}{B' \multimap 1,\, B',\, C^+ \vdash C^+}\ \multimap\text{-I}
}{!(B' \multimap 1), B',\ C^+ \vdash C^+}\ \text{D-I}
}{B'', !(B' \multimap 1),\, B', C^+ \vdash B'' \otimes C^+}\ \otimes\text{-r}
}{B^+, B'', !(B' \multimap 1),\, B', C^+ \vdash B^+ \otimes B'' \otimes C^+}\ \otimes\text{-r}
}{A^+, B^+, B'', !(B' \multimap 1),\, B', C^+ \vdash A^+ \otimes B^+ \otimes B'' \otimes C^+}\ \otimes\text{-r}
}{C, A^+,\ B^+,\ B'', !(B' \multimap 1),\ B' \vdash A^+ \otimes B^+ \otimes B'' \otimes C^+}\ \text{cut}
$$

Fig. 1. Example (continued): a standard proof of the following simple sequent1. $A \vdash A^+ \otimes B^+ \otimes B'' \otimes C^+$

Making Inconsistency Respectable:
Part 2 - Meta-level handling of inconsistency

Dov Gabbay and Anthony Hunter

Department of Computing, Imperial College
180 Queen's Gate, London SW7 2BZ, UK

Abstract

Inconsistency in a database, when viewed purely logically, seem undesirable. Indeed the traditional approach to dealing with inconsistency in data is to employ means to restore consistency immediately. However, it is important to study the larger environment containing such databases, and the circumstances surrounding the inconsistency. We argue that within the larger environment, an inconsistency can be desirable, and useful, if we know appropriate actions to handle it. In some cases we may wish to remove the inconsistency, and in other cases we may wish to keep it. Moreover, we claim that inconsistencies only become meaningful when considered in the context of the larger environment, and in particular, of how they arise and are handled. In this paper we present a meta-level system that uses actions for handling inconsistent databases.

1 Introduction

In Part 1 (Gabbay and Hunter 1991), we presented the view that inconsistencies are not necessarily "bad", and that they can even be a useful as long as we can handle them appropriately. The traditional view of inconsistency is that it is local and relative to a database. However an inconsistency may have different meaning relative to the larger environment in which the database is used and with which it interacts.

We argue that dealing with inconsistencies is not necessarily done by restoring consistency but by supplying rules telling one how to act when the inconsistency arises. To illustrate our approach consider an airline booking system. It is normal practice for an airline to sell more tickets for a flight than there are seats on the flight. Even though this situation is inconsistent with the safety regulations, the airline will maintain the inconsistency until shortly before departure. The airline supports the inconsistency because it expects sufficient passengers not to show up at the airport, and therefore for the inconsistency to resolve itself. Furthermore, by maintaining the 'overbooking inconsistency' the airline can make more money. This is therefore an example of there being a cost-benefit in maintaining an inconsistency, and indeed of the inconsistency being desirable for the airline.

However, supporting this kind of inconsistency sometimes leads to difficult situations when, prior to departure, more people have checked in than expected. In this eventuality the airline staff are required to take some kind of action such as upgrading tourist class passengers to business class, or offering free tickets to passengers who are prepared to catch a later flight. In extreme situations they may even provide an extra aircraft. But despite the expense of some of these actions, they are rarely invoked, and therefore the 'overbooking inconsistency' is cost-effective overall.Furthermore, we are so used to the wider context of the airline inconsistency that some people might not even recognize it as an inconsistency.

Inconsistency handling in the booking system is an example of a general phenomenon found in database applications. Viewing the environment containing such databases, and the circumstances surrounding each inconsistency, indicates that we need to consider inconsistencies in terms of how and why they arise, and the actions that are performed on them. Indeed describing an inconsistency via the wider context of the database allows us to move away from the negative view of an inconsistency within a database. There are many other cases of database systems that can be described in a similar way to the booking system. For example, in a government tax database, inconsistencies in a taxpayers records are used to invoke inquiries into that taxpayer. Indeed from the perspective of the tax inspector, this is another application where inconsistencies are useful and desirable.

The problem we attempt to address here is the formalization of cases such as the booking system. Below, we consider some general requirements for the underlying languages. We provide a definition of a system for inconsistency handling, called the DA system, and we consider some of its positive and negative features.

2 Outline of a system for handling inconsistent data

To formalize inconsistency handling, we need to consider the object-language, and the action language. For example, for the booking system, we need an object-language for the declarative information about passengers, and flights, and we need an action language for representing the inconsistency handling undertaken. In effect, the action language connects the object-level inconsistencies to the larger environment in which the database operates.

For our action language, we need to be able to talk about the object-level inconsistency, and to be able to act on the inconsistency, either by invoking internal actions or external actions. Some of the key requirements can be summarized as follows: (1) Meta-language representation of object-level data and databases; (2) Facility to axiomatize object-level consequence relations; (3) State-based meta-languages for reasoning about the states of the data and databases; and (4) Separation of the object-level and meta-level semantics so that object level inconsistency does not force the meta-level to be inconsistent.

One possibility for our state-based meta-language would be some form of linear-time temporal logic, where we would allow quantification over formulae, and so specifiy how an object-level database should evolve over time. If a temporal logic specification is consistent, it is satisfiable by a class of models. So for example, for the temporal logic specification $\alpha \rightarrow \beta$, the class of models that can satisfy the specification can be defined by stating that for each $t \in \mathbb{N}$, in each model M on the linear structure $(\mathbb{N}, \geq)$, if $M \models \alpha$ at t, then $M \models \beta$ at t. In this way, we can view the meta-level handling of inconsistent object-level databases in terms of satisfying temporal logic specifications.

For our object-level we want to be able to reason with the same data using different consequence relations. For example, it may be desirable to switch from classical logic to paraconsistent, or relevance, or even non-monotonic logics. We also want to label object-level formulae to support handling. Such labelling may facilitate truth maintenance, or conflict resolution. To address these requirements of the object-level, we use the framework of the Labelled Deductive System (Gabbay 1991, 1993). In the Labelled Deductive System (LDS) languages are based on using labelled formulae, and defining proof rules in terms of both the formulae and the labels. In this way logical reasoning is naturally extended. A wide variety of non-standard logics have been considered in terms of LDS, including linear, resource, modal, and paraconsistent logics. The label can also be used to define new kinds of logic that are appropriate for certain applications. For example the family of prioritized logics are defined in terms of preferences expressed over labels, and can be used for non-monotonic reasoning (Hunter 1992). Another example, is the family of restricted access logics for inconsistent information, where data is labelled, and for certain combinations of data, access to proof rules is restricted, thereby avoiding trivialization from inconsistent data (Gabbay and Hunter 1993).

3 Syntax for the DA system

Below we provide a definition of a meta-level system, called the DA system, (the Data and Action system). We assume DA can be used as a meta-language for a variety of object-level languages including labelled languages. Object-level formulae are used as terms in the meta-level. This allows the meta-level to "talk" about object-level data. In this way we are connecting the object-level data to the meta-language via the naming of formulae as terms. The meta-level also has other terms that allow it to talk about things other than the object-level data.

The system is based on first-order linear temporal logic, with since and until. The rules of formation for the meta-level terms (ie the terms for DA) are defined as follows. Note that the language DA is not typed, and therefore the language makes no distinction between terms that are object-level formulae, and the other terms:

If X is an object-level variable then X is a meta-level variable

If X is a meta-level variable then X is a meta-level term

If s is an object-level logical, predicate or function symbol
then s is a meta-level function symbol

If f is a meta-level function, and $t_1, \ldots, t_n$ are meta-level terms
then $f(t_1, \ldots, t_n)$ is a meta-level term

The rules of formation for the meta-level formulae (ie the formulae of the DA system) are defined as usual from the sets of meta-level terms, meta-level predicate symbols, logical symbols and the temporal operators { LAST, NEXT, FUTURE, PAST, ALWAYS, . . }. For example, let Holds be a meta-level predicate symbol, let p, q be object-level predicate symbols, and let X, Y be variables, then the following is a formula,

$\forall X, Y ((\text{Holds}(p(X)) \land \text{Holds}(q(Y)) \rightarrow \text{Holds}(p(X) \land q(Y)))$

The proof theory is just the usual proof theory for first order linear temporal logic, with since and until, and includes first order classical proof theory. We do not present the axiomatization here, but but below we do provide a definition for the semantics. We need not commit ourselves further on the significance of time in this meta-language. However, we can use it for representing the real-time evolution of the database, or for the stepwise progress of actions on the database.

For some object-languages, the meta-language can be used to present an axiomatization of the consequence relations for the object-level. For example, we can consider an information system as a pair (Δ, Γ) where Γ is a an object-level database and Δ is a meta-level database that contains rules for acting on inconsistency in Γ. In this way, $\text{Holds}(\alpha)$ is a consequence of

Δ if and only if α is a consequence of Γ. Though in general, it is not always possible to provide a decidable axiomatization for the meta-level relation Holds, since some of the object-level languages we may be interested in are not decidable.

We have not discussed here issues of differentiating different sorts of terms. For example, if p(X) is an object-level formula, then it is likely that for purposes of inconsistency handling, we would wish to prohibit p(p(X)) as a term - since allowing such instatiations can lead to problems such as the liar paradox. Restrictions on such kinds of terms can be captured by adding appropriate axioms to the meta-level database. For more detailed discussion of issues pertaining to logic meta-languages, the reader is referred to Bowen (1982), Hill (1988), and Barringer (1991).

4 Semantics for the DA system

For this meta-language, we separate the proof theory and semantics for the object- language from the proof theory and semantics for the meta-level. We base the interpretation of DA on the natural numbers $(N, \geq)$ as the flow of time. An interpretation for the DA meta-language is a tuple $(D, N, \geq, h)$ where D is a non-empty domain, and h is a truth-assignment function. For this definition, the following conditions hold: (1) The set D is the Herbrand Universe generated from the terms of the meta-langauge; (2) If f is an n-place meta-level function then f is assigned to the mapping from $D^n \longrightarrow D$ as defined by $(\sigma_1, . . . , \sigma_n) \longrightarrow f(\sigma_1, . . . , \sigma_n)$; (3) If t is a ground meta-level term then t is assigned an object in D. The truth assignment function h is defined as follows:

For each m-place meta-level predicate symbol P and each $n \in N$,
then $h(n, P): N \times D^m \longrightarrow \{0,1\}$

If $P(t_1, . . . , t_n)$ is a ground meta-level atom and $n \in N$
then $h(n, P(t_1, . . . , t_n)) = h(n, P)(t_1, . . . , t_n)$

An interpretation as defined above is a model of α iff for all $n \in N$, $h(n, \alpha) = 1$. The truth assignment function h can be extended to any meta-level formulae α and β as follows:

$h(n, \alpha \wedge \beta) = 1$ iff $h(n, \alpha) = 1$ and $h(n, \beta) = 1$
$h(n, \alpha \rightarrow \beta) = 1$ iff $h(n, \alpha) = 0$ or $h(n, \beta) = 1$
$h(n, \neg\alpha) = 1$ iff $h(n, \alpha) = 0$
$h(n, U(\alpha, \beta)) = 1$ iff $\exists m(m > n$ and $h(m, \alpha) = 1)$ and $\forall k(n < k < m$ and $h(k, \beta) = 1)$
$h(n, S(\alpha, \beta)) = 1$ iff $\exists m(m < n$ and $h(m, \alpha) = 1)$ and $\forall k(m < k < n$ and $h(k, \beta) = 1)$
$h(n, \forall X.\alpha) = 1$ iff $\forall \beta \in D$, $h(n, \alpha[\beta/X]) = 1$

Note that the above definitions imply a rigid interpretation of variables. In other words, the binding of a variable is fixed over time. Below we define the semantics for some extra temporal operators that are definable using the US operators.

$h(n, NEXT \ \alpha) = 1$ iff $h(n + 1, \alpha) = 1$
$h(n, ALWAYS \ \alpha) = 1$ iff for all $i \in N$, $h(i, \alpha) = 1$

For these semantics we have just considered the language for the meta-level. The truth, or falsity, of a formula at the object-level does not necessarily affect the truth, or falsity, of formula at the meta-level. For example, an object-level database with the object-level formula House(red) false does not necessarily force the meta-level formula Holds(House(red)) also to be false. (Though appropriate axioms could be added to the meta-level database to form a direct connection between the object-level and the meta-level.)

Separating the semantics for the meta-level from the semantics of the object-level gives us increased flexibility in handling uncertain and inconsistent object-level data. For example, if we view our database from the meta-level, then as we can update or ammend our object-level database, and if that object-level database becomes inconsisitent it does not necessarily cause the meta-level database to become inconsistent. We discuss this further below. However, it is staightforward to write specifications in the meta-language that can act on any inconsistencies in the object-level. Furthermore, these specifications can be written so that if they are not met, then the meta-level also becomes inconsistent.

The definition of the Holds predicate does mean that all the object-level data and consequences are reflected upwards. In other words, via the Holds predicate, all the object-level data and consequences are represented at the meta-level, and so changing the object-level database will cause a change in the meta-level database. In contrast, the reflection downwards depends on the DA specification in the meta-level database. The actions specified by the DA axioms could directly affect the object-level - for example by truth maintenance - and hence constitute reflection downwards, or they may influence the outside world - and so not directly affect the object-level database.

5 Executing DA Specifications

In this section we illustrate how we can execute DA specifications, and in the next section we return to our case study.

The traditional view on temporal logics is of declarative statements about the world, or about possible worlds over time. These relate the truth of propositions in the past, in the present and in the future. An alternative view is to consider the logics in terms of a declarative past, and an imperative future, based on the intuition that a statement about the future can be imperative, initiating steps of action to ensure it becoming true.

More specifically, if we write DA specifications in the following form, where the antecedent refers to the past and present, and the consequent refers to the future, then we can execute such specifications so as to construct a model of the specification,

$$\text{ALWAYS}(\wedge_i \alpha_i \rightarrow \vee_j \beta_j)$$

Suppose then that we have a specification Δ in the form of a finite conjunction of such clauses such that each α_i and β_j is either a positive or negative literal. The executing agent tries to execute Δ in such a way as to build a model of Δ. It must make Δ true dynamically at each point in time. So at any time point, it will consider each such clause. If $\wedge_i \alpha_i$ is true then it must make the disjunction $\vee_j \beta_j$ true. The choosing of which β_j to make true (remember that β_j is a future formula) is a subtle (and not necessarily decidable) problem, and the agent will take into account several factors, such as commitment to make other clauses true, possible future deadlocks, and the environment at the time. Executable temporal logics that have been developed include USF (Gabbay 1989), MetateM (Barringer 1989), and MML (Barringer 1991).

6 Case Study: Airline booking system

In the introduction, we described an airline booking system that uses certain forms of inconsistency advantageously. Below we axiomatize interesting aspects of this system in the meta-language. For the object-level we assume the paraconsistent logic C_ω (da Costa 1974), though we will use an unlabelled version to ease exposition.

For the formalization of this problem we require the following object-level predicates, where P is the set of passengers, F is the flight, D is the date, and C is the set of 'checked- in' passsengers: Passengers(P, F, D); Overbooked(F, D); Checked-in(C, F, D), Commercial(F); and Legal(F). We also require the following object-level functions: size(P) which returns the number of elements in P; and capacity(F) returns the maximum number of passengers for the flight F. The following two axioms capture conditions under which Overbooked, or its negation, hold. The first holds when the number of passengers exceeds the capacity of the flight. The second axiom captures the specification that if the flight is a commercial flight, and that the flight is legal, then the relation Overbooked(F, D) is false.

Passengers(P, F, D) $\wedge$ Checked-in(C, F, D) $\wedge$ size(C) = X $\wedge$
$\quad$ capacity(F) = Y $\wedge$ (X > Y) $\rightarrow$ Overbooked(F, D)

Commercial(F) $\wedge$ Legal(F) $\rightarrow$ ¬Overbooked(F, D)

If the 'overbooked inconsistency' occurs prior to departure time, no action is specified. However, if it occurs at departure time, then below are specified three courses of action. The first is to upgrade the unplaced passengers. If that fails, then the second option is to offer bonus tickets and a later flight. Finally, if both the previous options fail, then arrange alternative travel. For this we require the following object-level relation, where P is the set of passengers, F is the flight, D is the date, and X is the set of passengers without seats: Unplaced-passengers(X, F, D), and the following meta-level relations, Offer-upgrade(X, F, D), Offer-bonus-tickets(X, F, D), and Arrange-alternative-travel(X, F, D).

ALWAYS($\forall$ X, F, D (Holds(Overbooked(F, D)) $\wedge$ Holds(¬Overbooked(F, D))
$\quad$ $\wedge$ Departure-time $\wedge$ Holds(Unplaced-passengers(X, F, D))
$\quad$ $\rightarrow$ NEXT(Offer-upgrade(X, F, D)))

ALWAYS($\forall$ X, F, D Holds(Overbooked(F, D)) $\wedge$ Holds(¬Overbooked(F, D))
$\quad$ $\wedge$ LAST Departure-time $\wedge$ Holds(Unplaced-passengers(X, F, D))
$\quad$ $\rightarrow$ NEXT(Offer-bonus-tickets(X, F, D)))

ALWAYS($\forall$ X, F, D Holds(Overbooked(F, D)) $\wedge$ Holds(¬Overbooked(F, D))
$\quad$ $\wedge$ LAST(LAST(Departure-time)) $\wedge$ Holds(Unplaced-passengers(X, F, D))
$\quad$ $\rightarrow$ NEXT(Arrange-alternative-travel(X, F, D)))

In this example, we can see how the object-level inconsistency is reflected upwards, via the Holds predicate, and how the meta-level actions are suggestions for the user to solve the inconsistency. The way this specification would be executed is that at departure time, if there is the inconsistency, then the antecedent of the first of these rules would hold, and the system would be forced to satisfy the specification by making the Offer-upgrade hold in the meta-level database. This would cause the Offer-upgrade suggestion to be made available to the user. If at the first time-point after this suggestion had been made, the inconsistency still held, then the antecedent of the second rule in the specification would hold, and this second rule would be executed. Finally, if at the second time-point after the departure time, the inconsistency still held, then the third rule would be executed. Finally, if at the third time-point the inconsistency still held, then the meta-language would have no further actions to handle the inconsistency. Note, in none of these rules is there a reflection downwards.

Obviously, we require a series of further axioms to fully describe the booking system. However, we have illustrated how the inconsistent object-level does not cause the meta- level to be inconsistent, and how appropriate external actions can be formalized.

7 Discussion

In this paper, we have illustrated how we can handle inconsistent databases in a formal way. We use a meta-language to specify how we act on an inconsistency, and this leads to a new perspective on inconsistency handling. We now need to use the formal language to further characterize the nature of inconsistency handling. In particular, we wish to identify axiom schemas that capture common features of inconsistency handling.

Since the DA system uses temporal logic, it is based on a well-developed theoretical basis. It is straightforward to show that the meta-level of the DA system inherits desirable properties of first-order US temporal logic such as a complete and sound proof theory, and of semi-decidability. Furthermore for some useful subsets of US temporal logic there are viable model building algorithms, such that if the meta-level specification is consistent then the algorithm is guaranteed to find a model of the specification (Barringer 1989).

Using this approach to handling uncertain and inconsistent data constitutes a fundamental move away from traditional views of database management. From this perspective of the DA language, we don't worry, per se, about the object-level databases. All we worry about is satisfying the specification for the meta-level language. In this way, we give up a requirement to make the object-level database consistent, and rather accept such situations as inevitable. We abstract away from the object-level, and shift the requirement of consistency to the level of the meta-level being consistent.

There have been a number of other approaches to addressing issues of inconsistency in data. There are the paraconsistent logics (for example da Costa 1974, Anderson and Belnap 1975), but these only localize inconsistency - they don't offer strategies for acting on inconsistency. In contrast, many approaches force consistency on data without consideration of the environment. Truth maintenance systems (de Kleer 1978, Doyle 1979), and belief revision theory (Gardenfors 1988) ensure consistency by rejecting formulae upon finding inconsistency. Similarly, Fagin et al (1983) proposed amending the database when finding inconsistency during updating. Even more restrictive is the use of integrity constraints in databases - which prohibit inconsistent data even entering the database.

However, recently, attempts have been made to accommodate inconsistent data in a database by taking account of the environment. For example, Balzer (1991) suggests "guards" on inconsistent data to minimize the negative ramifications, and then to warn the user of the inconsistency, and in Naqui and Rossi (1990) inconsistent data is allowed to enter the database, but the time that the data is entered is recorded, and newer the data takes precedence over the older data when resolving inconsistencies. We see our approach as generalizing these approaches. Though, of course, many of the details have not yet been addressed in our approach.

8 Acknowledgements

This work is currently being funded by UK SERC grant GR/G 29861, and by the CEC ESPRIT DRUMS 2 project. The first author is a SERC senior research fellow.

9 References

Anderson A and Belnap N (1975) Entailment, Princeton University Press

Balzer R (1991) Tolerating inconsistnecy, in proceedings of the 13th International Conference on Software Engineering, IEEE Press

Barringer H, Fisher M, Gabbay D, Gough G and Owens R (1989) MetateM: A framework for programming in temporal logic, in REX Workshop on Stepwise Refinement of Distributed Systems, LNCS 430, Springer Verlag

Barringer H, Fisher M, Gabbay D, and Hunter A (1991) Meta-reasoning in executable temporal logic, in Principles of Knowledge and Reasoning: Proceedings of the Second International Conference (KR91), Morgan Kaufmann

Bowen K and Kowalski R (1982) Amalgamating language and meta-language, in Clark K and Tarnlund S, Logic Programming, Academic Press

da Costa N C (1974) On the theory of inconsistent formal systems, Notre Dame Journal of Formal Logic, 15, 497-510

Doyle J (1979) A truth maintenance system, Artificial Intelligence, 12, 231 - 297

Fagin R, Ullman J and Vardi M (1983) On the semantics of updates in databases, in Proceedings of the Second Annual Association of Computing Machinery Symposium on Principles of Database Systems

Gabbay D (1989) Declarative past and imperative future: Executable temporal logic for intereactive systems, in Banieqbal B, Barringer H and Pneuli A, Proceedings of Colloquium on Temporal Logic in Specification, Lecture Notes in Computer Science, 398, Springer

Gabbay D (1991) Labelled deductive systems, Technical report, Centrum fur Informations und Sprachverarbeitung, Universitat Munchen

Gabbay D (1993) Labelled deductive systems: A position paper, in Proceedings of Logic Colloquium '90, Lecture Notes in Logic 1, Springer Verlag

Gabbay D and Hunter A (1991) Making inconsistency respectable: Part I, in Proceedings of Fundamentals of Artificial Intelligence Research '91, LNCS 535, Springer Verlag

Gabbay D and Hunter A (1993) Restricted access logics for inconsistent information, in Proceedings ESQARU'93, LNCS, Springer

Gardenfors P (1988) Knowledge in Flux, MIT Press

Hill P and Lloyd J (1988) Analysis of meta-programs, in Proceedings of the Workshop on Meta-programming in Logic Programming, University of Bristol

Hunter A (1992) A conceptualization of preferences in non-monotonic proof theory, in Pearce D and Wagner G, Logics in AI, Lecture Notes in Artificial Intelligence 633, Springer

de Kleer J (1978) An assumption-based TMS, Artificial Intelligence, 28, 127 - 162

Naqvi S and Rossi F (1990) Reasoning in inconsistent databases, in Debray S and Hermenegildo M, Logic Programming: Proceedings of the North American Conference, MIT Press

Restricted Access Logics for Inconsistent Information

Dov Gabbay and Anthony Hunter

Department of Computing, Imperial College
180, Queen's Gate, London, SW7 2BZ, UK

Abstract. For practical reasoning with classically inconsistent information, desiderata for an appropriate logic L could include (1) it is an extension of classical logic - in the sense that all classical tautologies are theorems of L, and (2) contradictions do not trivialize L - in the sense that ex falso quodlibet does not hold. Two ways of realizing the second desideratum, for any database that may be inconsistent, include (A) take weaker than classical proof rules, but use all the data, or (B) take all the classical proof rules, but restrict the access of the data to the proof rules. The problem with adopting option (A) is that desideratum (1) is then not realizable. In this paper, we pursue option (B) by adding extra conditions on the proof rules to stop certain subsets of the data using the classical proof rules. To facilitate the presentation, we use the approach of Labelled Deductive Systems - formulae are labelled, and proof rules defined to manipulate both the formulae and the labels. The extra conditions on the proof rules are then defined in terms of the labels. This gives us a class of logics, called restricted access logics, that meet the desiderata above.

1   Introduction

For practical reasoning, it is often difficult and inappropriate to maintain a consistent database. Unfortunately, this creates problems if we are to use a logic with such a database. For classical logic, the rule of reductio ad absurdum means that any conclusion can be drawn from the database. This renders the database useless and therefore classical logic is obviously unsatisfactory for this application. A possible solution is to weaken classical logic by dropping reductio ad absurdum. This gives a class of logics called paraconsistent logics such as C_ω (da Costa 1974). However, the weakening of the proof rules means that the connectives in the language do not behave in a classical fashion. For example (taken from Besnard 1991), disjunctive syllogism does not hold, $((\alpha \vee \beta) \wedge \neg\beta) \to \alpha$ whereas modus ponens does hold. So, for example, α does not follow from Database 1, whereas α does follow from Database 2.

$$\text{Database 1 is } \{(\alpha \vee \beta), \neg\beta\}$$

$$\text{Database 2 is } \{(\neg\beta \to \alpha), \neg\beta\}$$

There are many similar examples that could be confusing and counter-intuitive for users of such a practical reasoning system.

An alternative, which we explore in this paper, is to not weaken the classical proof rules, but rather to restrict the access of the data to the classical proof rules. The naive version of this is to only allow consistent subsets of the database to be used with the classical proof rules. This would allow intuitive manipulation of the data, but disallow the undesired application of Ex Falso Quodlibet (EFQ) on the inconsistent data.

In the following we define a new consequence relation that captures this reasoning, explore properties of this consequence relation, identify some of its drawbacks and finally, consider interesting variants. The overall objective is to identify logics that allow for the derivation of as many of the classical but non-trivial inferences as possible from inconsistent data. Obviously such inferences are weakly justified but we leave the selection of preferred subsets of these inferences to future work.

2   A logic of restricted access

To present restricted access logics, we use the approach of Labelled Deductive Systems (Gabbay 1991). We assume a set of logical symbols $\{\neg, \rightarrow, \vee, \wedge, \leftrightarrow\}$, a set of atoms $\{\alpha, \beta, \gamma, \cdots\}$, and form the set of formula $\{\alpha \vee \beta, \neg\alpha, \alpha \rightarrow \beta, \cdots\}$ in the usual way. We also assume the natural numbers N, so that if $i \subseteq \mathsf{N}$, and α is a formula, then i is a label, and i:α is a labelled formula. A database is a set of labelled formulae where each item is labelled with a unique singleton set. For the proof theory, we take the usual natural deduction classical proof rules and amend them to allow handling of labelled formulae. To support this, we define the function h as follows, where $\vdash$ denotes the classical consequence relation,

$$h(i) = 1 \text{ iff } \{\alpha \mid j \subseteq i \text{ and } j{:}\alpha \in \Delta\} \not\vdash \bot$$

Essentially $h(i) = 1$ if and only if the set of formulae from Δ that are used in the proof, as recorded by the label i, are consistent. Hence the h function is defined with respect to a database Δ. For our first restricted access logic, RAc, the proof rules, are defined as follows, where for $\rightarrow$I, RAA, and $\neg$I, each new assumption is labelled with the empty set. All the rules carry the labels of all the assumptions used in deriving each inference.

$$\wedge\text{I}\ \frac{i{:}\alpha, j{:}\beta,\ h(i\cup j)=1}{i\cup j{:}\alpha \wedge \beta} \qquad \wedge\text{E1}\ \frac{i{:}\alpha \wedge \beta,\ h(i)=1}{i{:}\alpha} \qquad \wedge\text{E2}\ \frac{i{:}\alpha \wedge \beta,\ h(i)=1}{i{:}\beta}$$

$$\rightarrow\text{I}\ \begin{array}{c} \emptyset{:}\alpha \\ \vdots \\ \underline{i{:}\beta,\ h(i)=1} \\ i{:}\alpha \rightarrow \beta \end{array} \qquad\qquad \rightarrow\text{E}\ \frac{i{:}\alpha,\ j{:}\alpha \rightarrow \beta,\ h(i\cup j)=1}{i\cup j{:}\beta}$$

$$\text{EFQ}\ \frac{i{:}\bot,\ h(i)=1}{i{:}\alpha} \qquad\qquad \text{RAA}\ \begin{array}{c} \emptyset{:}\neg\alpha \\ \vdots \\ \underline{i{:}\bot,\ h(i)=1} \\ i{:}\alpha \end{array}$$

$$\neg I \quad \begin{array}{c} \emptyset:\alpha \\ \vdots \\ \underline{i:\perp, \ h(i) = 1} \\ i:\neg\alpha \end{array} \qquad\qquad \neg E \frac{i:\alpha, \ j:\neg\alpha, \ h(i\cup j) = 1}{i\cup j:\perp}$$

In this way, the rules of EFQ, ¬I, and RAA are allowed to use a formula $i:\perp$ only if the inconsistency was not caused by inconsistent data from the database. In other words, inconsistency must result from the new assumptions labelled with the empty set in concert with the data from the database, or just from the new assumptions labelled with the empty set. We define the consequence relation $\vdash_c$ for RAc logic as follows, where we assume all items in Δ are uniquely labelled with singleton sets.

$$\Delta \vdash_c \alpha \text{ iff } \exists \text{ i such that there is a proof of } i{:}\alpha$$
$$\text{from } \Delta \text{ using the RAc proof rules}$$

Below, we give an example of an acceptable proof of $\neg\beta$ from the database $\Delta = \{\{1\} : \neg\alpha, \{2\} : \neg\alpha \rightarrow \neg\beta, \{3\} : \alpha\}$.

$$\frac{\{1\}{:}\neg\alpha, \{2\} : \neg\alpha \rightarrow \neg\beta, h(\{1,2\}) = 1}{\{1,2\} : \neg\beta}$$

We now give an example of an unacceptable proof of $\neg\beta$ from the database Δ. In this example, the condition $h(\{1,3\}) = 1$ does not hold.

$$\frac{\{1\}{:}\neg\alpha, \{3\}{:}\alpha \ \ h(\{1,3\}) \neq 1}{\{1,3\}{:}\perp, \ h(\{1,3\}) \neq 1}$$
$$\overline{\{1,3\}{:}\neg\beta}$$

As an example of proving a classical tautology using the RAc proof rules, consider $\neg\neg\alpha \rightarrow \alpha$,

$$\frac{\emptyset{:}\neg\neg\alpha \quad \emptyset{:}\neg\alpha \quad h(\emptyset) = 1}{\dfrac{\emptyset{:}\perp \quad h(\emptyset) = 1}{\dfrac{\emptyset{:}\alpha \quad h(\emptyset) = 1}{\emptyset{:}\neg\neg\alpha \rightarrow \alpha}}}$$

Since $h(\emptyset) = 1$, for any database Δ, it is straightforward to show the tautology with label $\emptyset$. To show this, first assume $\emptyset : \neg\neg\alpha$, and show $\emptyset : \alpha$. To do this, assume $\emptyset : \neg\alpha$. So these two assumptions give $\emptyset : \perp$, and hence $\emptyset : \alpha$. Effectively, we have a classical proof where all items are labelled with $\emptyset$.

These examples illustrate how the undesirable reasoning with EFQ is limited. We describe a consequence relation $\vdash_x$ as trivializable if and only if for all α, β, $\{\alpha, \neg\alpha\} \vdash_x \beta$. It is straightforward to show $\vdash_c$ is not trivializable. Furthermore, it is clear that if α is a classical tautology then $\vdash_c \alpha$ holds. It is also straightforward to show that the relation $\vdash_c$ is monotonic, and that it is reflexive for inconsistent inferences. Though it is not in general reflexive, as shown by the example, $\{\alpha \wedge \neg\alpha\} \not\vdash_c \alpha \wedge \neg\alpha$. Also, cut, as defined below, fails to hold in general,

$$\frac{\Delta \vdash_c \alpha \qquad \Delta \cup \{\alpha\} \vdash_c \beta}{\Delta \vdash_c \beta}$$

For a counterexample, consider the database $\{\{1\} : \delta, \{2\} : \neg\delta, \{3\} : \delta \to \alpha, \{4\} : \neg\delta \to (\alpha \to \beta)\}$. It is of interest to consider intuitionistic relevant logic (Tennant 1987) where disjunctive syllogism and or introduction hold, but cut fails.

For the following equivalence between RAc logic and classical logic, we define the map 'unlabel' from sets of labelled formulae to sets of (unlabelled) formulae,

$$\text{unlabel}(\Delta) = \{\alpha \mid i{:}\alpha \in \Delta\}$$

Result 1 *For all sets of labelled formulae Δ, and all formulae α, the following holds,*

$$\Delta \vdash_c \alpha \text{ iff } \exists \Gamma \subseteq \text{unlabel}(\Delta) \text{ such that } \Gamma \not\vdash \bot, \text{ and } \Gamma \vdash \alpha$$

This result shows that the $\vdash_c$ consequence relation is the existential consequence relation defined by Resher and Manor (1970).

However, RAc logic also limits deriving inferences such as $\alpha \wedge \neg\alpha$ that a user may need to obtain from $\{\{1\}{:}\alpha, \{2\}{:}\neg\alpha\}$. Hence, RAc logic is perhaps too constrained. The logic allows reasoning with consistent subsets of data but does not allow any reasoning with inconsistent subsets. In this way it is stronger than paraconsistent logics for consistent subsets but weaker than paraconsistent logics for inconsistent subsets. But since it seems reasonable to allow some form of paraconsistent reasoning with the inconsistent subsets we address this in the following section.

3 Further logics of restricted access

To address the restriction on reasoning with inconsistent subsets of data, we can increase the strength of our logic by defining paraconsistent proof rules to operate over inconsistent premises. For this we consider the C_ω paraconsistent logic (da Costa 1974), and its natural deduction presentation NC_ω (Raggio 1978). We amend the proof rules to incorporate a function g. Different definitions for g give us different RA logics.

$$p\wedge I \frac{i{:}\alpha, j{:}\beta, \ g(i{:}\alpha) = g(j{:}\beta) = 1}{i\cup j{:}\alpha \wedge \beta}$$

$$p\wedge E1 \frac{i{:}\alpha \wedge \beta, \ g(i{:}\alpha \wedge \beta) = 1}{i{:}\alpha} \qquad p\wedge E2 \frac{i{:}\alpha \wedge \beta, \ g(i{:}\alpha \wedge \beta) = 1}{i{:}\beta}$$

$$\emptyset{:}\alpha$$

$$p \to I \quad \frac{\begin{array}{c} \vdots \\ i{:}\beta,\ g(i{:}\beta)=1 \end{array}}{i{:}\alpha \to \beta} \qquad\qquad p \to E \ \frac{i{:}\alpha,\ j{:}\alpha \to \beta,\ g(i{:}\alpha)=g(i{:}\alpha \to \beta)=1}{i \cup j{:}\beta}$$

$$p \neg\neg E\ \frac{i{:}\ \neg\neg\alpha,\ g(i{:}\neg\neg\alpha)=1}{i{:}\ \alpha} \qquad\qquad \text{p-LEM}\ \frac{}{\emptyset\ :\ \alpha \vee \neg\alpha}$$

We define the consequence relation $\vdash_p$ for RAp logic as follows, where we assume all items in Δ are uniquely labelled with singleton sets.

$\Delta \vdash_p \alpha$ iff $\exists$ i such that there is a proof of i:α
from Δ using the RAp proof rules,
where for all j: β, g(j:β) = 1

Letting $g(j{:}\beta) = 1$ for all j: β, is essentially no restriction on the proof rules. We define the consequence relation $\vdash_{pc}$ for RApc logic as follows, where we assume all items in Δ are uniquely labelled with singleton sets of markers.

$$\Delta \vdash_{pc} \alpha \text{ iff } \Delta \vdash_c \alpha \text{ or } \Delta \vdash_p \alpha$$

This provides a weak merging of the RAc and RAp logics. Essentially, the logics "operate in parallel" without any inferences from the one logic being used by the other logic. We now consider a stronger merging of these logics, where inferences from one logic can be used by the other.

First consider a logic, RAm, where the consequence relation is the union of the RAc and the RAp proof rules as follows,

$\Delta \vdash_m \alpha$ iff $\exists$ i such that there is a proof of i:α
from Δ using the RAc and RAp proof rules
where g(j:β) = 1 iff (1) j:$\beta \in \Delta$
or (2) there is a proof of j: β from Δ
using the RAc proof rules and j $\neq \emptyset$.

For the definition of the function g, part(2) incorporates the condition j $\neq \emptyset$. This is to prohibit classical tautologies to be manipulated by the RAp proof rules. For example, for the database $\{\{1\}{:}\alpha \wedge \neg\alpha\}$, and the classical tautology $\emptyset{:}\alpha \wedge \neg\alpha \to \beta$, which can be derived by the RAc proof rules, we need to prohibit the application of $p \to$E.

Note for the definition of $\vdash_m$, we do not worry about RAp inferences being used by the RAc rules, since if the premises for the RAp inferences are inconsistent, then the RAc rules can not use the inferences, and if the premises for the RAp inference are consistent, then RAc rules derive the same inference.

Hence RAm uses the RAc proof rules to generate inferences from the consistent subsets $\Gamma_1, \cdots, \Gamma_n$ of Δ, and then from combinations of these inferences, uses the RAp proof rules to generate further inference, even though $\Gamma_1 \cup \cdots \cup \Gamma_n$ is not necessarily consistent.

Suprisingly, RAm is trivializable. As an example, consider the following database $\Delta = \{\{1\} : \alpha, \{2\} : \neg\alpha\}$. From the classically consistent subset $\{\{1\} : \alpha\}$, we can derive $\{1\} : \beta \rightarrow \alpha$, and then $\{1\} : \neg\alpha \rightarrow \neg\beta$, using the RAc rules. This inference can then be used together with $\{2\} : \neg\alpha$ by the RAp rule $\rightarrow$E to give $\neg\beta$. Hence even though neither RAp nor RAc are trivializable, the merging of them is. Essentially, these logics co-operate in re-introducing EFQ. RAc uses part of a minimally inconsistent subset of the data, to introduce trivial inferences into a implicational formula, and RAp uses the remainder of that inconsistent subset to eliminate the implication, and thereby allowing the trivialization.

To merge RAc and RAp logics without forming a trivializable logic, we need to restrict the RAc inferences that can be used by RAp logic. This restriction is captured by a new definition for the g function used in the RAp proof rules. For this we require the set of literals Φ, where if α is an atom, then $\{\alpha, \neg\alpha, \neg\neg\alpha, \neg\neg\neg\alpha, ...\} \subseteq \Phi$.

We now consider a new logic RAm2, where the consequence relation $\vdash_{m2}$ is defined as follows,

$$\Delta \vdash_{m2} \alpha \text{ iff } \exists \text{ i there is a proof of i:}\alpha$$
from Δ using the RAc and RAp proof rules
where $g(j:\beta) = 1$ iff (1) $j:\beta \in \Delta$
or (2) there is a proof of $j: \beta$ from Δ
using the RAc proof rules and $\beta \in \Phi$

This gives a stronger form of reasoning than RApc since classical consequences of (consistent parts of) the database, that are in Φ, can used by the paraconsistent relation. So for example from $\Delta = \{\{1\} : \alpha, \{2\}\neg\alpha, \{3\} : \neg\alpha \wedge (\neg\neg\alpha \rightarrow \beta)\}$, we can derive $\{1\} : \neg\neg\alpha$ by RAc, and therefore β by the RAp proof rules.

Result 2 *The consequence relation $\vdash_{m2}$ is not trivializable*

The definition of RAm2 is a cautious development on RApc. Only allowing literals from RAc reasoning to be used by the RAp reasoning is not the closest merging that we could make. For example we could allow more RAc inferences as data for the RAp proof theory. Indeed there is a large space of non-trivializable logics between RApc logic and classical logic. However, to delineate the boundary between trivializable logics and non-trivializable logics in this space, we need to further characterize the way that two logics can co-operate to bring about trivialization.

4 Properties of RA logics

We provide some results that inter-relate the different RA logics via their consequence closures. For any Δ, let $Cn(\Delta) = \{\alpha \mid \Delta \vdash \alpha\}$, and $Cx(\Delta) = \{\alpha \mid \Delta \vdash_x \alpha\}$, where $x \in \{ \text{p, c, pc, m, m2} \}$. We also require the function L, where if X is a set of labelled formulae, then $L(X) = \{ \text{i:}\alpha \mid \text{i:}\alpha \in X \text{ and } \alpha \in \Phi\}$.

Result 3 *For all sets of labelled formulae Δ, the following holds,*

$$Cpc(\Delta)=Cp(\Delta)\cup Cc(\Delta)$$
$$Cm(\Delta)=Cp(Cc(\Delta))=Cn(\Delta)$$
$$Cm2(\Delta)=Cp(L(Cc(\Delta))\cup \Delta)\cup Cc(\Delta))$$

Result 4 *For all sets of labelled formulae Δ, the following holds,*

If $\Delta \nvdash \bot$, then $Cp(\Delta) \subseteq Cc(\Delta)=Cpc(\Delta)=Cm2(\Delta)=Cm(\Delta)=Cn(\Delta)$

Result 5 *For all sets of labelled formulae Δ, the following holds,*

If $\Delta \vdash \bot$, then (i) $Cp(\Delta) \nsubseteq Cc(\Delta)$
and (ii) $Cc(\Delta) \nsubseteq Cp(\Delta)$
and (iii) $Cc(\Delta) \subseteq Cpc(\Delta) \subseteq Cm2(\Delta) \subseteq Cn(\Delta)$
and (iv) $Cp(\Delta) \subseteq Cpc(\Delta) \subseteq Cm2(\Delta) \subseteq Cn(\Delta)$

The results above also raise the question of whether there are other restricted access logics that allow even more inferences to be derived from inconsistent subset of the data. For example, from $\{\{1\} : \alpha \wedge \neg \alpha \wedge \beta, \{2\} : \neg\neg\beta \rightarrow \delta\}$, it can be argued that we should be able to derive β, and then $\neg\neg\beta$, to finally get δ. However, none of the RA logics defined in this paper support this. Nevertheless it is clear that we have a number of options in how we define the propagation of the labels, and of the nature of the consistency checks, in the proof theory. Furthermore, we could adopt an alternative paraconsistent logic such as PI^s (Batens 1980) or FR (Anderson 1975) to reason with the inconsistent subsets of the data.

5 Discussion

The RA logics as proposed here allow for the derivation of 'possible' conclusions to be drawn from a database. However, they do not solve many of the wider problems of handling inconsistent information - such as locating inconsistency, resolving inconsistency, or removing inconsistency. Nevertheless the RA logics do offer a non-trivializable logic that could be incorporated in a wider inconsistency system, such as proposed in Gabbay and Hunter (1991, 1992), and Finkelstein et al (1993), and hence form the basis of systems that could address locating, resolving and removing inconsistency.

One of the drawbacks of this approach is the decoupling of the notion of object-level implication, ie. $\rightarrow$, and from the notion of meta-level consequence as captured by the consequence relation. So for example, in these logics we have $\alpha \wedge \neg \alpha \rightarrow \beta$ as a tautology, but in none do we allow β as a consequence of $\alpha \wedge \neg \alpha$ being in the database. Another significant drawback is complexity. Though, this may be ameliorated by approximation techniques. For example checking whether a propositional formula entails a clause is computationally intractable, yet there is a polynomial approaximation that is based on two sequences of entailment relation (Cadoli 1991). The first sequence is sound and not complete, and the second sequence is complete but not sound. Both sequences converge to classical logic.

Finally, there is the relationship with truth maintenance systems that needs to be considered. Of particular interest is the version defined by Martins and Shapiro (1988) that is based on the relevance logic FR of Anderson and Belnap (1975).

6 Acknowledgements

This work has been partly supported by the ESPRIT BRA DRUMS2 project. The first author is SERC senior Research Fellow. Thanks for much helpful feedback are due to Morten Elvang.

7 References

Anderson A and Belnap N (1975) Entailment: The Logic of Relevance and Necessity, Princeton University Press

Besnard P (1991) Paraconsistent logic approach to knowledge representation, in de Glas M, and Gabbay D, Proceedings of the First World Conference on Fundamentals of Artificial Intelligence. Angkor

Batens D (1980) Paraconsistent extensional propositional logics, Logique et Analyse, 90-91, 195-234

Cadoli M and Schaerf M (1991) Approximate entailment, in Trends in Artificial Intelligence, Lecture Notes in Computer Science, 549, Springer

da Costa N C (1974) On the theory of inconsistent formal systems, Notre Dame Journal of Formal Logic, 15, 497 - 510

Finkelstein A, Gabbay D, Hunter A, Kramer J, and Nuseibeh B (1993) Inconsistency handling in multi-perspective specifications, in Proceedings of the Fourth European Software Engineering Conference, Lecture Notes in Computer Science, Springer

Gabbay D (1991) Labelled Deductive System, Technical Report, Centrum fur Informations und Sprachverarbeitung, Universitat Munchen

Gabbay D and Hunter A (1991) Making inconsistency respectable, Part 1, in Jorrand Ph. and Keleman J, Fundamentals of Artificial Intelligence Research, Lecture Notes in Artificial Intelligence, 535, Springer

Gabbay D and Hunter A (1992) Making inconsistency respectable, Part 2, in Proceedings of ECSQARU'93, Lecture Notes in Computer Science, Springer

Martins J and Shapiro S (1988) A model of belief revision, Artificial Intelligence, 35, 25 - 80

Raggio A (1978) in Arrunda A, da Costa N C, and Chuaqui R, Mathematical Logic, Proceedings of the First Brazilian Conference, Marcel Defabier

Resher N and Manor R (1970) On inference from inconsistent premises, Theory and Decision, 1, 179 - 219

Tennant N (1987) Natural deduction and sequent calculus for intuitionisitc relevant logic, Journal of Symbolic Logic, 52, 665-680

Translating Inaccessible Worlds Logic into Bimodal Logic *

Olivier Gasquet, Andreas Herzig

IRIT, Université Paul Sabatier - 118, route de Narbonne,
F-31062 Toulouse Cedex, France
E-mail: gasquet,herzig@irit.fr

Abstract. This paper addresses the problem of automated deduction for Humberstone's inaccessible worlds logic. We exhibit a sound and complete translation into a normal bimodal logic for which efficient proof methods have been devised in the last years. By the way, our translation provides a sound, complete and *finitary* axiomatization of Humberstone's inaccessible worlds logic.

1 Introduction

Humberstone (1983) has introduced a modal operator to speak about inaccessible worlds. Since then such a device has been studied in formal logic (Goranko, Passy 1989), (Goranko 1990). It has also been employed in the logics of knowledge and belief of Levesque et al. (1990), where the modal connective has been interpreted as "knowing only". Such logics validate $(\Box F \wedge \Box G) \rightarrow \Box(F \wedge G)$ and $(\Box F \wedge \Diamond G) \rightarrow \Diamond(F \wedge G)$, but neither $\Box true$ nor $\Box(F \wedge G) \rightarrow (\Box F \wedge \Box G)$.

Just as in the case of normal modal logics, one can generalize modal connectives by introducing parameters. What we obtain are multi-modal logics. Formally, a multi-modal language is built on a set of parameters whose elements are denoted by $a, b, c, \ldots$ E.g. $[a]p$ and $\neg[c]p \wedge [b]q$ are formulas. In an epistemic context, $[a]F$ can be read "agent a only knows F". For the sake of simplicity and readability, we restrict ourselves in the sequel to the mono-modal case. The extension to the multi-modal case is straightforward.

Possible world semantics for Humberstone's inaccessible worlds logic can be obtained through modifications of the truth conditions of standard possible worlds semantics. As for the latter, a *frame* is a couple (W, R), where W is a set of worlds, and $R : W \rightarrow 2^W$ is a mapping from W to subsets of W. A *model* consists of a frame and a meaning function m mapping possible worlds to subsets of the set of propositional variables. It is only the truth condition which differs from the standard one[2]:

---

* This work has been partially supported by the Esprit projects DRUMS II and MEDLAR II. Thanks to Philippe Balbiani, Luis Fariñas del Cerro, and Stephan Merz for their comments.

[2] All along this paper, $\models$ will denote the satisfiability relation in standard Kripke semantics. For inaccessible worlds semantics there will be an index $\models_{IW}$ which we shall omit if no confusion may arise.

- $M, w \models_{IW} \Box F$ iff for all v in $W(v \in R(w)$ **iff** $M, v \models_{IW} F)$

We suppose the usual notion of satisfiability and validity.[3]

In the next section, we briefly review the existing theorem proving methods for normal multi-modal logics . In Sect. 3, we translate logics with inaccessible worlds. The last section contains the proof.

2 The Basis: Theorem Proving for Normal Multi-Modal Logics

If we want to prove theorems of normal modal logics, the straightforward way is to use the relational translation into first-order logic.

In the last years there has been done a lot of work in order to improve that "naive" method. There have been devised several methods for logics such as K, D, KT4, or KT5. (The latter are better known as S4 and S5.) Among those, the most general and efficient approaches use a translation into First-Order Logic where particular theories mirror the particular features of the logic under concern. Thus, theorems e.g. of modal logic KT4 can be proven using monoid unification. Recently, the method has been extended to the multi-modal versions of these logics, where interaction axioms may occur: see (Ohlbach 1991, 1993), (Fariñas, Herzig 1993), (Gasquet 1993).

All these approaches focussed on normal modal logics. Here, we wish to concentrate on a weaker logic, and we shall show in the sequel that reasoning in that logic can be automatized by a translation into a normal multi-modal logic (which on its turn can be translated into First-Order Logic using the above methods).

3 The Translation

The idea of the translation is the following : The truth condition is equivalent to :

- $M, w \models_{IW} \Box F$ iff for all $v \in W$
  - if $v \in R(w)$ then $M, v \models_{IW} F$, **and**
  - if $v \in \bar{R}(w)$ then $M, v \models_{IW} \neg F$.

where $\bar{R}$ denote the complementary of R. What we do is to introduce two modal connectives, [1] to access R-successors, and [2] to access $\bar{R}$-successors. This leads to the following translation t from logic with inaccessible worlds into normal multi-modal logics defined as follows:

$t(p) = p$ if p is a propositional variable

---

[3] A formula F is *satisfiable in a frame* (W, R) if there is a world $w \in W$ and a meaning function m such that $((W, R), m), w \models_{IW} F$. F is *satisfiable in a class of frames* C if there is a frame of C wherein F is satisfiable. F is *true in a frame* (W, R) if for every world w and every meaning function m we have that $((W, R), m), w \models F$.

$$t(\Box F) = [1]t(F) \wedge [2]\neg t(F)$$

and homomorphic for the cases of the classical connectives. ([1] and [2] are arbitrary parameters.)

In order to get an exact translation, we must choose KT5[1∪2] as our target logic. [4]

Theorem 1. *F is valid in logic with inaccessible worlds iff $t(F)$ is valid in normal multi-modal logic $KT5[1 \cup 2]$.*

Proof. See next section.

Remark. Contrarily to what would be expected, our target logic is not required to satisfy that the accessibility relations for [1] and [2] have an empty intersection. In fact, it is sufficient to prove that KT5[1 ∪ 2] is characterized by the frames where: $R_1 \cup R_2$ is an equivalence relation **and** $R_1 \cap R_2 = \emptyset$. (This key lemma is given in the next section.)

Remark. The axiomatization given in (Humberstone 1983) is infinitary. On the contrary, our translation provides an indirect (because the modal connectives are not the original ones) but still modal axiomatization of this logic. Most of all, this axiomatization is finitary.

Example 1. The formula $\Box true$ is translated into $[1]true \wedge [2]\neg true$, which is not valid in KT5[1 ∪ 2]. Hence $\Box true$ is not valid in inaccessible worlds logic.

Example 2. The formula $\Box(p \wedge q) \to \Box p$ is translated into
$$[1](p \wedge q) \wedge [2]\neg(p \wedge q) \to [1]p \wedge [2]\neg p.$$
In KT5[1 ∪ 2], this formula is equivalent to the conjunction
$$(([1](p \wedge q) \wedge [2]\neg(p \wedge q)) \to [1]p) \wedge (([1](p \wedge q) \wedge [2]\neg(p \wedge q)) \to [2]\neg p).$$
Now the first one is valid in KT5[1 ∪ 2] (because of $[1](p \wedge q) \to [1]p$), but the second is not: Take a model consisting of a single world where p is true and q is false, and let it be accessible to itself through the relation R_2 associated to [2], but not through R_1.

Example 3. The formula $(\Box p \wedge \Box q) \to \Box(p \wedge q)$ is translated into
$$([1]p \wedge [2]\neg p \wedge [1]q \wedge [2]\neg q) \to [1](p \wedge q) \wedge [2]\neg(p \wedge q).$$
In KT5[1 ∪ 2], this formula is equivalent to the conjunction
$$(([1]p \wedge [2]\neg p \wedge [1]q \wedge [2]\neg q) \to [1](p \wedge q)) \wedge (([1]p \wedge [2]\neg p \wedge [1]q \wedge [2]\neg q) \to [2]\neg(p \wedge q)).$$
Now both the first one (because of $([1]p \wedge [1]q) \to [1](p \wedge q)$), and the second one (because of $[2]\neg p \to [2]\neg(p \wedge q)$), are valid in KT5[1 ∪ 2].

---

[4] By KT5[1 ∪ 2] we mean a normal multi-modal logic where both modal connectives [1] and [2] have the axioms of modal logic K, plus the axioms T and 5, stated for the modal operator [1 ∪ 2]. ($[1 \cup 2]F$ is an abreviation for $[1]F \wedge [2]F$.) In other words, KT5[1∪2] is axiomatized by some axiomatization of classical logic, necessitation rules for [1] and [2], plus the axioms $[1 \cup 2]F \to F$ and $\neg[1 \cup 2]F \to [1 \cup 2]\neg[1 \cup 2]F$. It is well-known that KT5[1∪2] is characterized by the class of Kripke frames (W, R_1, R_2) where $R_1 \cup R_2$ is an equivalence relation over W (see e.g. (Catach 1988)).

Example 4. The formula $(\Box p \wedge \Box q) \rightarrow (p \leftrightarrow q)$ is translated into

$\quad ([1]p \wedge [2]\neg p \wedge [1]q \wedge [2]\neg q) \rightarrow (p \leftrightarrow q)$.

In KT5[1 ∪ 2], the antecedens is equivalent to $([1](p \leftrightarrow q) \wedge [2](p \leftrightarrow q)$, and now

$\quad ([1](p \leftrightarrow q) \wedge [2](p \leftrightarrow q) \rightarrow (p \leftrightarrow q)$

is an instance of the T-axiom.

4 Proof

Lemma 2. *Let (W, R) be an inaccessible worlds frame wherein a formula F is satisfiable. Let $R_1 = R$ and $R_2 = W^2 \setminus R$. Then (W, R_1, R_2) is a frame for KT5[1 ∪ 2] wherein $t(F)$ is satisfiable.*

Proof. First note that the KT5[1 ∪ 2] axioms are true in (W, R_1, R_2) as $R_1 \cup R_2$ is an equivalence relation.

Let $M = (W, R, m)$, and $M' = (W, R_1, R_2, m)$, and suppose $M, w_0 \models_{IW} F$ for some $w_0 \in W$.

We prove that for every G and $w \in W$, $M, w \models_{IW} G$ iff $M', w \models t(G)$ by induction on the structure of G. The only non-trivial case is

- $M, w \models_{IW} \Box H$
- iff for all $v \in W$, $v \in R(w)$ iff $M, v \models_{IW} H$
- iff for all $v \in W$, $v \in R(w)$ iff $M', v \models t(H)$, by induction hypothesis
- iff for all v in W,
   - if $v \in R_1(w)$ then $M', v \models t(H)$ by construction of R_1, and
   - if $v \in R_2(w)$ then $M', v \models \neg t(H)$, by construction of R_2
- iff $M', w \models [1]t(H) \wedge [2]\neg t(H)$
- iff $M', w \models t(\Box H)$

Lemma 3. *KT5[1 ∪ 2] is characterized by the class of frames (W, R_1, R_2) where $R_1 \cup R_2$ is universal (i.e. $R_1 \cup R_2 = W^2$) and $R_1 \cap R_2 = \emptyset$.*

Proof. As the converse is trivial, we only have to prove that if F is KT5[1 ∪ 2]-satisfiable then it is also satisfiable in a frame (W, R_1, R_2) where $R_1 \cup R_2$ is an equivalence relation and $R_1 \cap R_2 = \emptyset$.

Suppose $(W, R_1, R_2, m), w_0 \models F$ for some $w_0 \in W$.

First, let W' be the connected part of W that contains w_0, i.e. the set of worlds that can be reached from w_0 via $R_1 \cup R_2$.

It is a well-known fact that (W', R_1, R_2, m) is still a model of KT5[1 ∪ 2][5], and $(W', R_1, R_2, m), w_0 \models F$.

Now, we build a new model which will simulate (W', R_1, R_2, m), but where the two relations will have an empty intersection.

Let V_1 and V_2 be two sets such that V_1, V_2 and W' are pairwise disjoint, and V_1

---

[5] In fact, only the restrictions of R_1 and R_2 should be considered, and we will assume these restrictions implicitly.

is isomorphic to W' via an isomorphism f_1, and V_2 is isomorphic to W' via an isomorphism f_2.

Let V denote $V_1 \cup V_2$, and R'_1 and R'_2 be defined as follows:

1. if $w \in (R_1 \cap R_2)(v)$ then for $i = 1, 2$
   - $f_i(w) \in R'_1(f_1(v))$, and
   - $f_i(w) \in R'_2(f_2(v))$
2. if $w \in R_1(v)$ only, then for $i, j = 1, 2$
   - $f_i(w) \in R'_1(f_j(v))$
3. if $w \in R_2(v)$ only, then for $i, j = 1, 2$
   - $f_i(w) \in R'_2(f_j(v))$

And, finally, let m' be defined by: $m'(f_i(w)) = m(w)$.
Then let $\varphi = f_1^{-1} \cup f_2^{-1}$.

φ is a pseudo-epimorphism from (V, R'_1, R'_2, m') onto (W', R_1, R_2, m) – (Hughes, Cresswell 1984). This ensures that F is satisfiable in (V, R'_1, R'_2, m'). Moreover, it can easily be shown that $R'_1 \cup R'_2$ is an equivalence relation over V, and even that it is equal to V^2, and that $R'_1 \cap R'_2 = \emptyset$. Hence, the lemma is proved.

Lemma 4. *Let (W, R_1, R_2) be a frame for KT5[1$\cup$2] wherein $t(F)$ is satisfiable. Then there is an inaccessible worlds frame wherein F is satisfiable.*

Proof. The proof is similar to that in (Humberstone 1983).
Suppose $M = (W, R_1, R_2, m)$, and $M, w_0 \models t(F)$ for some $w_0 \in W$. By the above lemma, we can suppose that $R_1 \cap R_2 = \emptyset$, and that $R_1 \cup R_2 = W^2$, i.e. R_2 is the complement of R_1. We prove that for every $w \in W$ and every formula $F, M, w \models t(F)$ iff $(W, R_1, m), w \models_{IW} F$ by induction on the structure of F. The only non-trivial case is:
$F = \Box G$, i.e. $t(F) = [1]t(G) \wedge [2]\neg t(G)$.

- From the left to right, suppose $M, w \models [1]t(G) \wedge [2]\neg t(G)$. If $v \in R_1$, as $M, w \models [1]t(G)$, we have that $M, v \models t(G)$, and by induction hypothesis, $M, v \models_{IW} G$. If $v \notin R_1$ then $v \in R_2$ (because $R_1 \cup R_2 = W^2$). As $M, w \models [2]\neg t(G)$, we have that $M, v \models \neg t(G)$, and by induction hypothesis, $M, v \models_{IW} \neg G$. Putting both together we get that $M, w \models_{IW} \Box G$.
- From the right to the left, suppose $M, w \models_{IW} \Box G$. Then v is in $R_1(w)$ iff $M, v \models_{IW} G$. By induction hypothesis, $v \in R_1(w)$ iff $M, v \models t(G)$. Hence $M, w \models [1]t(G)$. As $R_1 \cap R_2 = \emptyset$, we have that $M, w \models [2]\neg t(G)$. Putting both together we get that $M, w \models [1]t(G) \wedge [2]\neg t(G)$.

It is clear that this lemma cannot handle extensions of the basic inaccessible world logic e.g. with axiom D. The reason is that we cannot be sure that our construction of the inaccessible world model preserves the accessibility relation properties.

Now the theorem follows immediately from Lemmas 2 and 4.

5 Discussion and Conclusion

We have given a translation from Humberstone's modal logic of inaccessible worlds into a normal multi-modal logics. For the latter, now, standard translation methods exist.

It is well-known that for normal modal logics, if the accessibility relation property is a first-order condition then there is an exact translation into first-order logic. This holds as well in the case of Humberstone's logic of inaccessible worlds. Therefore, we should compare it with our translation:

E. g. the standard translation of $\Box p$ yields two clauses $\neg R(w_0, w) \vee p(w)$ and $R(w_0, w) \vee \neg p(w)$ (where w_0 is a constant and w is a variable). Our translation of $\Box p$ yields $[1]p \wedge [2]\neg p$ in a first step, and the functional translation into First-Order Logic yields two clauses $p(f)$ and $\neg p(g)$ where f is a variable of sort 1 and g is a variable of type 2. At first glance our translation looks much more elegant. But we must note that the equational theory corresponding to KT5$[1 \cup 2]$ is that of permutation groups for the least common supersort of 1 and 2. It would be interesting to find other target logics for which an exact translation exists and which are weaker than KT5$[1 \cup 2]$.

Independently from theorem proving issues, our translation permits to obtain an indirect but still modal axiomatization of Humberstone's inaccessible worlds logic, which moreover is finitary (contrarily to that of Humberstone 1983).

References

L. Catach, "Normal multimodal logics". Proc. Nat. Conf. on AI (AAAI 88), pp. 491-495, 1988.

Luis Fariñas del Cerro, Andreas Herzig, "Automated Deduction for Epistemic and Temporal Logics". Handbook of Logic in AI (eds D. Gabbay, A. Galton, C. Hogger), Oxford University Press, to appear.

Olivier Gasquet, "Deduction for Multimodal Logics". International Conference on Applied Logic (Logic at Work'93), Amsterdam, Holland, 1993.

Valentin Goranko, "Modal Definability in Enriched Languages". Notre Dame Journal of Formal Logic, vol. 31, 81-105, 1990.

Valentin Goranko, Solomon Passy, "Using the Universal Modality: Profits and Questions". Report, Sofia University, July 1989.

G. Hughes, M. J. Cresswell, "A companion to modal logic". Methuen & Co. Ltd, 1984.

I. Humberstone, "Inaccessible worlds". Notre Dame Journal of Formal Logic, vol. 24, 346-352, 1983.

H. Levesque, "All I know: A study in autoepistemic logic". J. of AI, 42: 263-309, 1990.

Andreas Nonnengart, "First-Order Modal Logic Theorem Proving and Functional Simulation", International Joint Conference on Artificial Intelligence, Chambéry, France, 1993.

Hans Jürgen Ohlbach, "Semantics-Based Translation Method for Modal Logics". J. of Logic and Computation, Vol. 1, 5, pp. 691-746, 1991.

Hans Jürgen Ohlbach, "Optimized Translation of Multi-Modal Logic into Predicate Logic". Proc. of Logic Programming and Automated Reasoning (LPAR), (ed. A. Voronkov), Springer Verlag, LNAI, 1993.

A New Approach to Semantic Aspects of Possibilistic Reasoning

Jörg Gebhardt   Rudolf Kruse

Department of Computer Science
University of Braunschweig
Bültenweg 74-75, D-38106 Braunschweig, Germany
Tel.: ..49.531.391.3283   FAX: ..49.531.391.5936
Email: gebhardt@ibr.cs.tu-bs.de

Abstract

The purpose of this paper is to develop a formal environment that provides well–founded semantics of possibilistic reasoning in knowledge–based systems. Representing the universe of discourse as a product space Ω which consists of the domains of a finite number of characterizing attributes, expert knowledge and also evidential knowledge are expected to be given by possibility distributions on subspaces of Ω.

Our numerical approach clarifies the semantic background for the representation, interpretation, and operative handling of possibility distributions that are viewed as information-compressed specifications of so-called valuated imperfect characteristics. Furthermore the concepts of correctness- and sufficiency-preservation show how to operate on possibility distributions and how to find an appropriate inference mechanism as well as a justified interpretation of possibilistic implication rules, where, postulating weak preconditions, the well–known Gödel relation is justified to be the right choice.

An implementation of the presented concepts to solve data fusion problems has been developed in cooperation with German Aerospace.

1   Introduction

In recent years the treatment of imperfect information has been perceived as one of the most important problems in the field of knowledge–based systems [Buchanan, Shortliffle 1984, Pearl 1988, Shafer, Pearl 1990, Kruse, Siegel 1991, Kruse et al. 1991b, Dubois, Prade 1992]. Throughout this paper, among the various formal settings proposed in different research directions, we restrict ourselves to the development of a suitable theoretical approach and an improved semantic background for possibilistic reasoning in a multidimensional space of hypotheses [Dubois, Prade 1991, Kruse et al. 1991a]. The considered universe of discourse is assumed to be a product space $\Omega = \Omega_1 \times \ldots \times \Omega_n$, defined by the domains Ω_i of underlying characteristic attributes A_i of interest. We investigate the meaning of inference mechanisms that are based on general *expert knowledge* (given by possibilistic implication rules) and state–dependent *evidential knowledge* (given by possibility distributions on subspaces of Ω).

Section 2 shows fundamental concepts of reasoning in product spaces, whereas section 3 gives a short introduction to our interpretation of possibilistic data [Gebhardt, Kruse 1993, Gebhardt et al. 1992]. Starting rather from a numerical than from a logical point of view, possibility distributions are considered here as *information-compressed* representations of so-called *valuated imperfect characteristics* which formally coincide, but semantically differ from random sets [Matheron 1975, Hestir et al. 1991]. In this connection the concepts of *correctness-* and *sufficiency-preservation* [Gebhardt et al. 1992] turn out to be essential for an appropriate handling of possibility distributions. The topic of section 4 is to apply them for obtaining a justified interpretation and handling of possibilistic implication rules. Postulating weak preconditions the *Gödel relation* proves to be the best choice for such an interpretation.

It should be emphasized that the methods of this paper, especially possibilistic inference referred to the Gödel relation, are realized in our interactive software tool POSSINFER. Some concluding remarks concerning the capabilities and limits of this software-tool will be mentioned in the last section.

2 Reasoning in Product Spaces

The aim of this paper is to clarify the semantic background of possibilistic reasoning in a multidimensional space of hypotheses from a numerical rather than from a logical point of view. In this section we introduce the formal environment in which crisp or imprecise knowledge is represented, neglecting at a first glance all aspects of uncertainty modelling that have to be involved in a later part of our investigations, when possibilistic inference will be discussed.

Starting point of our consideration is a finite set $\mathcal{A} = \{A_1, A_2, \ldots, A_n\}$ of *attributes* that characterize objects of a given object type. A state–dependent characterization $char(obj, state)$ of an object obj is given by a tuple $(a_1, a_2, \ldots, a_n)$ of *attribute values*, where a_i is taken from the domain $\Omega_i = Dom(A_i)$ attached to the attribute $A_i, i = 1, 2, \ldots, n$. Each subset $\mathcal{A}^*$ of $\mathcal{A}$ is determined by its identifying *index set* $I(\mathcal{A}^*) \overset{Df}{=} \{i \in \{1, 2, \ldots, n\} \mid A_i \in \mathcal{A}^*\}$. For all index sets $I, \emptyset \neq I \subseteq \{1, \ldots, n\}$, we define the families

$$\varphi_I : I \to \bigcup_{i \in I} \{\Omega_i\}, \quad (\forall i \in I)(\varphi_I(i) = \Omega_i)$$

and denote them by $(\Omega_i)_{i \in I}$. Furthermore let

$$\Omega^I \overset{Df}{=} \underset{i \in I}{\times} \Omega_i \overset{Df}{=} \{\varphi \mid \varphi : I \to \bigcup_{i \in I} \Omega_i \wedge (\forall i \in I)(\varphi(i) \in \Omega_i)\}$$

be the *product space* of the set system $(\Omega_i)_{i \in I}$. In the special case of $I \overset{Df}{=} I\!N_n \overset{Df}{=} \{1, 2, \ldots, n\}$ the product space $\Omega \overset{Df}{=} \Omega^{I\!N_n}$ is usually called the *universe of discourse* w.r.t. the underlying object type. For any non–empty index set I the subsets of Ω^I are called *characteristics*, since they may serve as characterizations of any relationships between the domains $\Omega_i, i \in I$. A characteristic $X_1 \subseteq \Omega^I$ is *correct* w.r.t. another characteristic $X_2 \subseteq \Omega^I$, if $X_2 \subseteq X_1$ is valid, which also means that X_2 is as least as *specific* as X_1. The goal of applying an inference mechanism in Ω is to obtain most specific correct characterizations w.r.t. an unknown characteristic S (e.g.: $S = \{char(obj, state)\}$), where all available influencing pieces of knowledge about S are, of course, assumed to be correct w.r.t. S.

The inference mechanism we intend to consider is based on *general knowledge* (i.e.: relationships between the domains $Dom(A_i)$, specified by a subset R of the *selection functions* φ the universe of discourse Ω consists of) and *evidential knowledge* (i.e.: imprecise observations of selected attribute values of $char(obj, state)$, specified by a characteristic $X_K \subseteq \Omega_K$, where K denotes the index set of all attributes that are accessed by the corresponding observation). If $R \subseteq \Omega$ and $X_K \subseteq \Omega_K$ are available, then the inference procedure is characterized by determining the set of all object states that coincide with R and X_K and are therefore possible candidates to be the (unknown) original value of $char(obj, state)$. To formalize the inference mechanism we need the notions of *cylindrical extension* and *projection* as well as the definition of the appropriate inference mappings.

Definition 1
Let $I, J \subseteq I\!N$ be nonempty sets of indices, where $I \subseteq J$.

(a) $\hat{\Pi}_I^J : 2^{\Omega^I} \to 2^{\Omega^J}$,

$\hat{\Pi}_I^J(\Phi) \overset{Df}{=} \{\psi \in \Omega^J \mid (\exists \varphi \in \Phi)(\forall i \in I)(\psi(i) = \varphi(i))\}$

is called the cylindrical extension *from Ω^I into Ω^J*.

(b) $\Pi_I^J : 2^{\Omega^J} \to 2^{\Omega^I}$,

$\Pi_I^J(\Psi) \overset{Df}{=} \{\phi \in \Omega^I \mid (\exists \psi \in \Psi)(\forall i \in I)(\psi(i) = \varphi(i))\}$

denotes the projection *from Ω^J onto Ω^I*.

Definition 2
Let $\emptyset \neq K \subseteq I\!N_n$ and $\emptyset \neq L \subseteq I\!N_n$. Then we define the inference mapping

$$\text{infer}_{K,L} : 2^\Omega \times 2^{\Omega^K} \to 2^{\Omega^L},$$

$$\text{infer}_{K,L}(R, X) \overset{Df}{=} \Pi_L^{I\!N_n}(R \cap \hat{\Pi}_K^{I\!N_n}(X)).$$

Let L be a nonempty set of selected indices. If R and $X \overset{Df}{=} \hat{\Pi}_K^{N_n}(X^K)$ assumed to be correct w.r.t. the unknown characteristic $S \overset{Df}{=} \{char(obj, state)\}$, then $infer_{K,L}(R, X^K)$ is correct w.r.t. $S^L \overset{Df}{=} \Pi_L^{N_n}(S)$ and the most specific characteristic that ensures the correctness w.r.t. S^L.

The frequently used linguistic form of a possibilistic implication rule is

$$R(K, L, \pi_A, \pi_B) : \underline{if} \ X \ \underline{is} \ \pi_A \ \underline{then} \ Y \ \underline{is} \ \pi_B,$$

where X and Y are variables taking their values on the set of all possibility functions (when normalized also called *possibility distributions*) on Ω^K and Ω^L, respectively, while $\pi_A : \Omega^K \to [0, 1]$ and $\pi_B : \Omega^L \to [0, 1]$ are themselves possibility functions.

In current research different approaches to the interpretation of possibilistic implication rules are recommended [Dubois, Prade 1992]. In the following we present a promising approach to the numerical view of possibilistic reasoning based on the reference paper [Gebhardt, Kruse 1993]. Obviously the interpretation of possibilistic implication rules and the investigation of the corresponding inference mechanism turns out to be much more complicated than the analogous considerations of imprecise implication rules, since at first we will have to incorporate uncertainty modelling (which will be supported by the concept of a *valuated imperfect characteristic*) as well as information compression aspects (which are connected with the induced concept of a possibility function), and then we finally will have to investigate how to represent a possibilistic implication rule $R(K, L, \pi_A, \pi_B)$ by a possibility function $\pi_R : \Omega \to [0, 1]$ that only depends on π_A and π_B. As a consequence the next section clarifies the origin of possibilistic data from our point of view (which delivers an interpretation of π_A and π_B), whereas section 4 is directed to the interpretation of possibilistic implication rules.

In this connection it should be mentioned that our interpretation of $R(K, L, \pi_A, \pi_B)$ reflects the development of a *constraint satisfaction mechanism*. Different approaches consist in investigating conditional possibilities $\pi_{A|B}$ and the underlying intuition of preference propagation [Dubois, Prade 1992].

3   On the Origin of Possibilistic Data

We now specify our intuitive view of imperfect knowledge and the origin of possibility functions. A mathematical heavy presentation occurs to be unavoidable, since we intend to provide a formal framework for the representation, interpretation, operative handling, and analysis of imperfect data. The clear semantics of the underlying concepts makes it feasible to compare well-known approaches to the modeling of imperfect knowledge as they are given in Bayes Theory, Shafer's Evidence Theory, and Possibility Theory [Gebhardt, Kruse 1993].

We only refer to some basic concepts, as far as they are relevant for handling possibilistic data and obtaining the important sufficiency-preservation theorem at the end of this section. We consider the case that the origin of imperfect data is due to situations, where the incompleteness of the available information does not support state-dependent specifications of objects by simply using their characterizing tuple of attribute values.

Three important kinds of imperfect knowledge to be investigated are imprecision, competition, and uncertainty. As an illustration we refer to the specification of so-called imperfect characteristics, which formalize imprecise, possibly contradicting and partially incorrect observations of attribute values with respect to a finite number of conflicting consideration contexts.

The integration of conflicting contexts is related to the phenomenon of *competition*, whereas *imprecision* shows that a specialization of the context-dependent characteristics attached to a imperfect characteristic is unjustified without having further information about the corresponding imperfectly specified object. These two types of partial ignorance can also be viewed as one possible origin of *vagueness*.

Uncertainty, on the other hand, is connected with the valuation of imperfect characteristics: When we have defined an imperfect characteristic to specify an imperfect observation of an inaccessible characteristic of an object's attribute in a given state, a decision maker should be enabled to quantify his or her degree of belief in this imperfect observation — either by objective measurement or by subjective valuation. Since we restrict ourselves to numerical, non-logical approaches to partial ignorance, the theory of measurement seems to be the adequate formal environment for the representation of uncertainty aspects.

Realizing the separation of imprecision, competition, and uncertainty, we define the concept of a valuated imperfect characteristic as follows:

Definition 3

Let D be a nonempty universe of discourse (domain) *and C a nonempty finite* set of contexts. *Furthermore let $\mathcal{M} = (C, 2^C, P_C)$ be a* (context) measure space.

$\Gamma_C(D) \overset{Df}{=} \{\gamma \mid \gamma : C \to 2^D\}$ *is defined to be the* set of all imperfect characteristics *of D w.r.t. C.*

Ignoring the contexts, $\Gamma(D) \overset{Df}{=} 2^D = \{A \mid A \subseteq D\}$ designates the set of all (imprecise) characteristics *of D.*

Involving the context measure space $\mathcal{M}$, each $\gamma \in \Gamma_C(D)$ is called valuated w.r.t. $\mathcal{M}$.

Obviously there are formal analogies, but semantic differences to the concept of a random set recommended by Matheron [Matheron 1975] and Nguyen [Hestir et al. 1991]. Considering the original idea of a random set, if $\gamma \in \Gamma_C(D)$, then for all $c \in C$, $\gamma(c)$ should be interpreted as an indivisible *set-valued datum* attached to an outcome c of an underlying random experiment which is formalized by a probability space $(C, 2^C, P_C)$.

Following a reasonable interpretation of Nguyen's approach, $\gamma(c)$ specifies the *set of single-valued data* which are possible in a context c, where $P_C(\{c\})$ quantifies the (objective or subjective) probability that c is the "true" context.

On the other hand, using γ as a valuated imperfect characteristic, $P_C(\{c\})$ reflects the weight with which the context c should be considered for delivering a *correct* specification of an original characteristic $Orig_\gamma \subseteq D$ (i.e.: $Orig_\gamma \subseteq \gamma(c)$), where $Orig_\gamma$ is an (inaccessible) state–dependent characterization of an object of interest.

Whenever $P_C(\{c\})$ stands for a correctness weight the interpretation of a valuated imperfect characteristic does not require that one of the available contexts is the "true" one which has to be selected.

The adequate choice of context measure spaces is an application–dependent problem. In practice incomplete information and the complexity of required operations will often advise us to avoid the detailed consideration of the underlying context measure spaces, but to use an *information compressed* specification of valuated imperfect characteristics, as done — from our point of view — in Possibility Theory [Dubois, Prade 1988] and Fuzzy Set Theory [Klir, Folger 1988, Dubois, Prade 1991]. Viewing a valuated imperfect characteristic $\gamma \in \Gamma_C(D)$ in a pure formal sense as a *generalized random set*, one promising way of coming to an information compressed representation of γ is the choice of the *one–point coverage* of γ, which we prefer — for semantic reasons — to be denoted as the *possibility function* of γ.

Definition 4

Let $\gamma \in \Gamma_C(D)$ be valuated w.r.t. $\mathcal{M} = (C, 2^C, P_C)$. Then,

$$\pi_\mathcal{M}[\gamma] : D \to I\!\!R_0^+, \quad \pi_\mathcal{M}[\gamma](d) \overset{Df}{=} P_C(\{c \in C \mid d \in \gamma(c)\})$$

is called the possibility function *of γ, where $I\!\!R_0^+ \overset{Df}{=} \{r \in I\!\!R \mid r \geq 0\}$.*

$POSS(D) \overset{Df}{=} \{\pi \mid \pi : D \to I\!\!R_0^+ \wedge |\pi(D)| \in I\!\!N\}$ *is defined to be the* set of all possibility functions *w.r.t. D. Furthermore let $POSS^+(D) \overset{Df}{=} POSS(D) \backslash \{0\}$.*

For $\pi \in POSS(D)$, $Repr(\pi) \overset{Df}{=} \{(\alpha, \pi_\alpha) \mid \alpha \in I\!\!R_0^+\}$ with the α-cuts $\pi_\alpha \overset{Df}{=} \{d \in D \mid \pi(d) \geq \alpha\}$ denotes the identifying set representation *of π. Let $\pi_1, \pi_2 \in POSS(D)$ and $\pi_1 < \pi_2$. Then π_1 is called* more specific *than π_2.*

If $\pi_\mathcal{M}[\gamma]$ is normalized, it may be interpreted as a possibility distribution in the sense of Possibility Theory [Dubois, Prade 1988], but there is even more behind $\pi_\mathcal{M}[\gamma]$ than only measuring possibility degrees. Whenever each context valuation $P_C(\{c\})$ is expected to be the presupposed *correctness weight* with which c delivers a *correct* imprecise characterization $\gamma(c)$ w.r.t. $Orig_\gamma$ (which means that $Orig_\gamma \subseteq \gamma(c)$), then, for all $\alpha \geq 0$, the α-cut $\pi_\mathcal{M}[\gamma]_\alpha$ is the most specific characteristic that is for sure correct w.r.t. $Orig_\gamma$, if the α-correctness of γ w.r.t. $Orig_\gamma$ is given (which means that the measure of all contexts $c \in C$ that are correct w.r.t. $Orig_\gamma$ equals α or is greater than α).

Definition 5

Let $\gamma \in \Gamma_C(D)$ be valuated w.r.t. $(C, 2^C, P_C)$ and $A, B \subseteq D$ two characteristics. Furthermore let $\alpha \geq 0$.

(a) B is correct w.r.t. A, iff $A \subseteq B$.

(b) γ is α-correct w.r.t. A, iff $P_C(\{c \in C \mid A \subseteq \gamma(c)\}) \geq \alpha$.

The choice of an appropriate correctness level α^* depends on the semantic environment in which $\gamma \in \Gamma_C(D)$ is used. If C is a set of outcomes of an underlying random experiment, then $P_C(\{c\})$ quantifies the probability of the outcome c.

In this case exactly one of the contexts contained in C is selected to be the "true" context, and P_C should be seen as a probability measure (i.e. $P_C(C) = 1$).

In a more general sense C is a set of contexts that represent distinguishable consideration points of view (e.g. experts, sensors). Then it is of course not always reasonable to talk about the existence of a single true context, but rather to interpret $P_C(\{c\})$ as the degree of success with which the context $c \in C$ has delivered correct imprecise characterizations $\gamma_i(c)$ w.r.t. a number of checkable representative imperfect observations $\gamma_i \in \Gamma_C(D)$ of original characteristics $Orig_{\gamma_i} \subseteq D, i = 1, \ldots, n$.

If we define

$$\alpha^{(i)} \overset{D\!f}{=} \max\{\alpha \mid Orig_{\gamma_i} \subseteq \pi_{\mathcal{M}}[\gamma_i]_\alpha\}, \; i = 1, \ldots, n, \text{ and}$$

$$\alpha_{\min} \overset{D\!f}{=} \min\{\alpha^{(i)} \mid i \in \{1, \ldots, n\}\},$$

$$\alpha_{\max} \overset{D\!f}{=} \max\{\alpha^{(i)} \mid i \in \{1, \ldots, n\}\},$$

then $\alpha^* \in [\alpha_{\min}, \alpha_{\max}]$ seems to be an acceptable choice for the postulation of the correctness degree of future imperfect characterizations $\gamma \in \Gamma_C(D)$ w.r.t. their (inaccessible) original $Orig_\gamma \subseteq D$. More specific values of α^* can be justified through tolerance intervals as well-known in the framework of mathematical statistics.

After the clarification of semantic aspects we now change over to the important question how to operate on possibility functions. Let $\gamma_i \in \Gamma_{C_i}(D_i)$ be valuated w.r.t. $\mathcal{M}_i = (C_i, 2^{C_i}, P_{C_i})$, $i = 1, \ldots, n$. Each γ_i is interpreted as a valuated α_i-correct specification of an imperfect observation of an inaccessible non-empty characteristic $A_i \subseteq D_i$. Furthermore let $f : \underset{i=1}{\overset{n}{\times}} \Gamma(D_i) \to \Gamma(D)$ be a function of imprecise characteristics. Suppose to have the task to determine the most specific characteristic in $\Gamma(D)$ which is correct w.r.t. $f(A_1, \ldots, A_n)$. This characteristic is called *sufficient* for f w.r.t. $(\gamma_1, \ldots, \gamma_n)$ and $(\alpha_1, \ldots, \alpha_n)$. We now formalize the notion of sufficiency and show how to evaluate sufficient characteristics.

Definition 6

Let $\gamma_i \in \Gamma_{C_i}(D_i)$, $i = 1, 2, \ldots, n$ be valuated w.r.t. $(C_i, 2^{C_i}, P_{C_i})$. Consider correctness-levels $\alpha_i > 0$, $i = 1, 2, \ldots, n$, a function $f : \underset{i=1}{\overset{n}{\times}} \Gamma(D_i) \to \Gamma(D)$, and a characteristic $F \in \Gamma(D)$.

(a) F is correct for f w.r.t. $(\gamma_1, \ldots, \gamma_n)$ and $(\alpha_1 \ldots, \alpha_n)$, iff

$$(\forall (A_1, \ldots, A_n) \in \underset{i=1}{\overset{n}{\times}} \Gamma(D_i))$$

$$((\forall i \in \{1, \ldots, n\})(\gamma_i \text{ is } \alpha_i - correct \text{ w.r.t. } A_i)$$

$$\Longrightarrow F \text{ is correct w.r.t. } f(A_1, \ldots, A_n));$$

(b) F is sufficient for f w.r.t. $(\gamma_1, \ldots, \gamma_n)$ and $(\alpha_1, \ldots, \alpha_n)$, iff F fulfils (a) and $(\forall F^* \subsetneq F)(F^*$ is not correct for f w.r.t. $(\gamma_1, \ldots, \gamma_n)$ and $(\alpha_1, \ldots, \alpha_n))$.

It turns out that under weak conditions there is an efficient computation of sufficient characteristics by application of the induced possibility functions $\pi_{\mathcal{M}_i}[\gamma_i]$, without explicitly referring to the underlying valuated imperfect characteristics and the context measure spaces $\mathcal{M}_i$.

Before coming to that result we state the following four definitions.

Definition 7

Let $D_1, D_2, \ldots D_n, D$ be universes of discourse and $f : \underset{i=1}{\overset{n}{\times}} \Gamma(D_i) \to \Gamma(D)$ a function.

(a) f is called correctness–preserving, *iff*
$f(A_1, \ldots, A_n) \subseteq f(B_1, \ldots, B_n)$ for all A_i, B_i with $A_i \subseteq B_i \subseteq D_i$, $i = 1, 2, \ldots, n$.

(b) f is called contradiction–preserving, *iff*

$$(\forall A_1, \ldots, A_n)((\exists i \in \{1, \ldots, n\})(A_i = \emptyset) \Longrightarrow f(A_1, \ldots, A_n) = \emptyset)$$

Definition 8
Let $D_1, \ldots, D_n, D$ be universes of discourse and $f : \underset{i=1}{\overset{n}{\times}} \Gamma(D_i) \to \Gamma(D)$ a contradiction–preserving
mapping. f is sufficiency–preserving, *iff*
$f(A_1 \cup B_1, \ldots, A_n \cup B_n) =$
$\bigcup \{f(C_1, \ldots, C_n) | (\forall j \in \{1, \ldots, n\})(C_j = A_j \vee C_j = B_j)\}$
  for all $A_i, B_i \in \Gamma(D_i), i = 1, 2, \ldots, n$.

Definition 9
Let $\pi \in POSS(D)$. π is correct (sufficient) for f w.r.t. $(\gamma_1, \ldots, \gamma_n)$, *iff*
$(\forall\ \alpha > 0)$ (π_α is correct (sufficient) for f w.r.t. $(\gamma_1, \ldots, \gamma_n)$ and $(\alpha, \ldots, \alpha)$).

Definition 10
Let $\pi_i \in POSS(D_i)$, $i = 1, \ldots, n$, and $f : \underset{i=1}{\overset{n}{\times}} \Gamma(D_i) \to \Gamma(D)$. The possibility function $f[\pi_1, \ldots, \pi_n]$:
$D \to I\!\!R_0^+$ which is determined by its identifying set representation
$Repr\ (f[\pi_1, \ldots, \pi_n]) \overset{\text{Df}}{=} \{(\alpha, f[\pi_1, \ldots, \pi_n]_\alpha) \mid \alpha \in I\!\!R_0^+\}$ with
$f[\pi_1, \ldots, \pi_n]_0 \overset{\text{Df}}{=} D$ and $(\forall\ \alpha > 0)$ $(f[\pi_1, \ldots, \pi_n]_\alpha = f((\pi_1)_\alpha, \ldots, (\pi_n)_\alpha))$
is called the image of $(\pi_1, \ldots, \pi_n)$ under f.

Theorem 1
Let $\mathcal{M}_i = (C_i, 2^{C_i}, P_{C_i})$, $|C_i| \geq 2$, $i = 1, \ldots, n$, be context measure spaces.
Additionally let $f : \underset{i=1}{\overset{n}{\times}} \Gamma(D_i) \to \Gamma(D)$ be a correctness– and contradiction–preserving mapping.
f is sufficiency–preserving, iff $(\forall\ (\gamma_1, \ldots, \gamma_n) \in \underset{i=1}{\overset{n}{\times}} \Gamma_{C_i}(D_i))$

$$(f\ [\pi_{\mathcal{M}_1}[\gamma_1], \ldots, \pi_{\mathcal{M}_n}[\gamma_n]]\ \text{sufficient for } f \text{ w.r.t. } (\gamma_1, \ldots, \gamma_n)).$$

The result is especially related to possibility functions, where $\alpha = \alpha_1 = \alpha_2 = \ldots = \alpha_n$, but an analogous theorem holds in the case when the levels α_i are chosen arbitrarily.
  Since the function *infer* (introduced in section 2) is sufficiency–preserving, this theorem can be applied to simplify the possibilistic inference mechanisms investigated in the following section.

4 Interpreting Possibilistic Implication Rules

Based on the information compression view of possibility functions and the results of the previous section we are in the position to motivate a well-founded mathematical interpretation of possibilistic inference. Let
$$R(K, L, \pi_A, \pi_B) : \underline{\text{if }} X \underline{\text{ is }} \pi_A \underline{\text{ then }} Y \underline{\text{ is }} \pi_B$$
be a possibilistic implication rule, where $X, \pi_A \in POSS^+(\Omega^K), Y, \pi_B \in POSS^+(\Omega^L), \emptyset \neq K \subseteq I\!\!N_n$,
$\emptyset \neq L \subseteq I\!\!N_n$, and $K \cap L = \emptyset$.

  To clarify the work that has to be done in this section, we first summarize what we expect to be the available information for the possibilistic inference mechanism, and what we intend to get as the result of applying the inference procedure.

  Again our starting point is the state–dependent description of an object of interest by an (imprecise) characteristic $S \subseteq \Omega^{I\!\!N_n}$. We assume that there exists general knowledge about the relationships between the domains $\Omega_i, i = 1, \ldots, n$, specified by a relation $R \subseteq \Omega$, and evidential knowledge about S, specified by a characteristic $X \subseteq \Omega^K$ and therefore restricted to those attributes that are identified by a chosen nonempty set $K \subseteq I\!N_n$. It is presupposed that R and X are reliable, which means that R is correct w.r.t. S and X is correct w.r.t. $S^K \stackrel{Df}{=} \Pi_K^{I\!N_n}(S)$. Hence, applying the inference mapping defined in section 2 we conclude that $infer_{K,L}(R,X)$ is the most specific characteristic that ensures correctness w.r.t. $S^L \stackrel{Df}{=} \Pi_L^{I\!N_n}(S)$, where $L \subseteq I\!N_n$ is the nonempty index set which identifies those attributes we are interested in. The situation becomes more difficult, when R and X are not directly accessible, but only imperfectly observed.

Let $\gamma_R \in \Gamma_C(\Omega)$ and $\gamma_X \in \Gamma_C(\Omega^K)$ be two imperfect characterizations of R and X, respectively, each of them valuated w.r.t. an appropriate context measure space $\mathcal{M} = (C, 2^C, P_C)$. As an example consider the different competing contexts contained in C as experts whose weights are quantified by the measure P_C. If we assume that neither γ_X nor γ_R is available, but only the information compressed representation of γ_X by its possibility function $\pi_X \stackrel{Df}{=} \pi_{\mathcal{M}}[\gamma_X]$, and a possibilistic implication rule $R(K, L, \pi_A, \pi_B)$, which has to be viewed as a partial specification of $\pi_{\mathcal{M}}[\gamma_R]$, then we reach the point where the possibilistic inference mechanism starts. The problems to be solved are the following:

- How should $R(K, L, \pi_A, \pi_B)$ be interpreted by a possibility function $\pi_R \in POSS^+(\Omega)$?

- Given π_R and π_X, which is the resulting possibility function $\pi_Y \in POSS^+(\Omega^L)$ that reflects the most specific possibilistic information on S^L?

The solution of these problems is referred to the interpretation of $R(K, L, \pi_A, \pi_B)$ as an implication rule that fulfills the following weak conditions:

(a) maximum specificity of conclusion π_B w.r.t. premise π_A,

(b) specialization of premise π_A does not affect the conclusion π_B,

(c) no information about the attributes that are not identified by the index set $K \cup L$.

We clarify the qualitative meaning of (a), (b), and (c) by formalization in terms of the previous section:
The idea behind (a) is that, whenever we know that $\pi_A = \pi_{\mathcal{M}}[\gamma_X]$, we expect to get π_B as the result of the inference procedure and as the most specific possibility function that may serve as a characterization of S^L without affecting correctness assumptions possibly made about γ_R w.r.t. R and γ_X w.r.t. X. In other words: We postulate that π_B is sufficient for $infer_{K,L}$ w.r.t. (γ_R, γ_X). Hence, the formulization of condition (a) is as follows:

$$(\forall \gamma_X \in \Gamma_C(\Omega^K))(\pi_{\mathcal{M}}[\gamma_X] = \pi_A \Longrightarrow \pi_B \text{ is sufficient for } infer_{K,L} \text{ w.r.t. } (\gamma_R, \gamma_X))$$

Since this condition is not easy to handle, we try to find an equivalent representation of it. Let $\pi \in POSS^+(\Omega^L)$ be the possibility function which is determined by its set representation $Repr(\pi) \stackrel{Df}{=} \{(\alpha, \pi_\alpha) \mid \alpha \geq 0\}$, where $\pi_0 \stackrel{Df}{=} \Omega^L$ and $\pi_\alpha \stackrel{Df}{=} infer_{K,L}(\pi_{\mathcal{M}}[\gamma_R]_\alpha, (\pi_A)_\alpha)$, $\alpha > 0$. Since it is easy to verify that $infer_{K,L}$ is sufficiency–preserving, application of theorem 1 yields

$$(\forall \gamma_X \in \Gamma_C(\Omega^K))(\pi_{\mathcal{M}}[\gamma_X] = \pi_A \Longrightarrow \pi \text{ is sufficient for } infer_{K,L} \text{ w.r.t. } (\gamma_R, \gamma_X)).$$

Hence, we derive the following equivalent formalization of condition (a):

(1a) $(\forall \alpha > 0)(infer_{K,L}(\pi_{\mathcal{M}}[\gamma_R]_\alpha, (\pi_A)_\alpha) = (\pi_B)_\alpha).$

The motivation for condition (b) refers to the fact that the possibilistic implication rule $R(K, L, \pi_A, \pi_B)$ gives no hint in which way π_B may be specialized, if $\pi_{\mathcal{M}}[\gamma_X]$ turns out to be more specific than π_A. All we know is that $\emptyset \neq \pi_{\mathcal{M}}[\gamma_X]_\alpha \subseteq (\pi_A)_\alpha$, $\alpha > 0$, implies

(1b) $(\forall \alpha > 0)(infer_{K,L}(\pi_{\mathcal{M}}[\gamma_R]_\alpha, \pi_{\mathcal{M}}[\gamma_X]_\alpha) \subseteq (\pi_B)_\alpha),$

since $infer_{K,L}$ is sufficiency–preserving and therefore even correctness–preserving. This means, whenever $\pi_{\mathcal{M}}[\gamma_X] \leq \pi_A$, π_B is at least correct for $infer_{K,L}$ w.r.t. (γ_R, γ_X), but not necessarily sufficient.

Combining (1a) and (1b) and considering the contradiction preserving property of $infer_{K,L}$, we obtain the following representation of (a) and (b):

$$(1) \quad (\forall \alpha > 0)(\forall A \subseteq \Omega^K)$$
$$(\emptyset \neq A \subseteq (\pi_A)_\alpha \vee A = (\pi_A)_\alpha = \emptyset \Longrightarrow infer_{K,L}(\pi_{\mathcal{M}}[\gamma_R]_\alpha, A) = (\pi_B)).$$

There is no need for an explanation of the trivial background of condition (c), which is formalized as follows:

$$(2) \quad (\forall c \in C)(\gamma_R(c) = \hat{\Pi}_{KUL}^{N_n}(\Pi_{KUL}^{N_n}(\gamma_R(c)))).$$

We are now prepared to find all possibility functions $\pi \in POSS(\Omega)$ induced by imperfect relations $\gamma_R \in \Gamma_C(\Omega)$ that agree with (1) and (2).

Theorem 2
Let $\pi_A \in POSS^+(\Omega^K), \pi_B \in POSS(\Omega^L), \emptyset \neq K \subseteq I\!\!N_n, \emptyset \neq L \subseteq I\!\!N_n, K \cap L = \emptyset.$

$$REL[\pi_A, \pi_B] \overset{DI}{=} \{\pi \in POSS(\Omega) \mid (\exists \mathcal{M})(\exists \gamma_R)$$
$$(\mathcal{M} = (C, 2^C, P_C) \text{ is context measure space } \wedge P_C(C) = 1$$
$$\wedge \gamma_R \in \Gamma_C(\Omega) \wedge \gamma_R \text{ fulfills } (1),(2) \wedge \pi = \pi_{\mathcal{M}}[\gamma_R])\}.$$

Then, for all $x \in \Omega^K, y \in \Omega^L, \omega \in \hat{\Pi}_K^{N_n}(\{x\}) \cap \hat{\Pi}_L^{N_n}(\{y\})$,

$$\min(REL[\pi_A, \pi_B])(\omega) = \min\{\pi_A(x), \pi_B(y)\},$$
$$\max(REL[\pi_A, \pi_B])(\omega) = \begin{cases} 1, & \text{if } \pi_A(x) \leq \pi_B(y), \\ \pi_B(y), & \text{if } \pi_A(x) > \pi_B(y). \end{cases}$$

$(REL[\pi_A, \pi_B], \leq)$ is a partially ordered set with a least and a greatest element. The greatest element is the *Gödel relation* (induced by π_A and π_B) which is also well-known in the field of multivalued logics. The Gödel relation $\varrho_{\text{Göd}}(\pi_A, \pi_B) \overset{DI}{=} \max(REL[\pi_A, \pi_B])$ is the only element of $REL[\pi_A, \pi_B]$ that shows the following property:
For all $\gamma_R \in \Gamma_C(\Omega)$ with $\pi_{\mathcal{M}}[\gamma_R] \in REL[\pi_A, \pi_B]$ we obtain

$$(\forall \alpha > 0)(\gamma_R \text{ is } \alpha\text{-correct w.r.t. } R \Longrightarrow \varrho_{\text{Göd}}(\pi_A, \pi_B) \text{ is } \alpha\text{-correct w.r.t. } R).$$

As the preservation of correctness properties is the fundamental aim of applying our model to approximate reasoning problems, the Gödel relation has turned out as the only reasonable interpretation of possibilistic implication rules, whenever the conditions (a), (b), and (c) are chosen to be accepted.
This interesting result suggests the conceptual incorporation of the Gödel relation into the design of possibilistic knowledge based systems, embedded in a mathematical well–founded and also semantic justified environment. In this connection it should be emphasized that it is quite simple to come to a sufficiency–preserving extension of $infer_{K,L}$ and an inference mapping with a larger number of parameters which admit the handling of conjunctive systems of possibilistic implication rules, where each of the rules is interpreted by its own Gödel relation.

5 Concluding Remarks

The main objective of this article is to present a consistent formal environment for well–founded reasoning with possibilistic data in a multidimensional space of hypotheses. Since realistic examples in this field tend to be rather complex in presentation, we have put main effort into the investigation of the underlying concepts. With the aim of handling data fusion problems, the considered approach, especially possibilistic inference referred to the Gödel relation, has been implemented in cooperation with German Aerospace on a SUN Workstation using the programming language C, the operating system UNIX, and the graphical surfaces X–Windows and OSF–Motif. To reduce time complexity and the amount of computer memory, the corresponding interactive tool POSSINFER assumes *qualitative knowledge* about existing dependencies to be encoded in terms of hypertrees. This allows to apply efficient local propagation algorithms as they are known from similar tools, like HUGIN, in the field of probabilistic reasoning [Lauritzen, Spiegelhalter 1988]. Possibility functions are stored in form of their identifying set representations. Further improvement of efficiency is reached by restriction to finite domains.

References

[Buchanan, Shortliffle 1984] B.G.Buchanan, E.H.Shortliffle: Rule–Based Expert Systems. Addison Wesley, Reading, Massachusetts (1984)

[Dubois, Prade 1988] D.Dubois, H.Prade: Possibility Theory, Plenum Press, New York (1988)

[Dubois, Prade 1991] D.Dubois, H.Prade: Fuzzy Sets in Approximate Reasoning, Part 1: Inference with Possibility Distributions, Fuzzy Sets and Systems 40, No.1 (1991), 143-202

[Dubois, Prade 1992] D.Dubois, H.Prade: Possibility Theory as a Basis for Preference Propagation in Automated Reasoning. Proc. FUZZIEEE'92, San Diego, 821-832 (1992)

[Gebhardt et al. 1992] J.Gebhardt, R.Kruse, D.Nauck: Information Compression in the Context Model. Proc. NAFIPS'92, Puerto Vallarta, Mexico, 1992

[Gebhardt, Kruse 1993] J.Gebhardt, R.Kruse: The Context Model — An Integrating View of Vagueness and Uncertainty, Int. Journal of Approximate Reasoning , (to appear)

[Hestir et al. 1991] K.Hestir, H.T.Nguyen, G.S.Rogers: A Random Set Formalism for Evidential Reasoning. In: I.R.Goodman, M.M.Gupta, H.T.Nguyen, G.S.Rogers (eds.): Conditional Logic in Expert Systems, Elsevier, North–Holland, 309-344 (1991)

[Klir, Folger 1988] G.J.Klir, T.A.Folger: Fuzzy Sets, Uncertainty, and Information, Prentice Hall, New York (1988)

[Kruse, Siegel 1991] R.Kruse, P.Siegel (eds.): Symbolic and Quantitaive Approaches to Uncertainty. Lecture Notes in Computer Science, Springer, Berlin (1991)

[Kruse et al. 1991a] R.Kruse, E.Schwecke, J.Heinsohn: Uncertainty and Vagueness in Knowledge Based Systems: Numerical Methods, Series Artificial Intelligence, Springer, Heidelberg (1991)

[Kruse et al. 1991b] R.Kruse, E.Schwecke, F.Klawonn: On a Tool for Reasoning with Mass Distributions. Proc. IJCAI'91, Sydney, 1190-1195 (1991)

[Lauritzen, Spiegelhalter 1988] S.L.Lauritzen, D.J.Spiegelhalter: Local Computation with Probabilities on Graphical Structures and their Application to Expert Systems. Journal of the Royal Statistical Society 50, 157-224 (1988)

[Matheron 1975] G.Matheron: Random Sets and Integral Geometry, Wiley, New York (1975)

[Pearl 1988] J.Pearl: Probabilistic Reasoning in Intelligent Systems, Networks of Plausible Inference, Morgan Kaufmann, New York (1988)

[Shafer, Pearl 1990] G.Shafer, J.Pearl: Readings in Uncertain Reasoning. Morgan Kaufmann, San Mateo, CA (1990)

PROBABILISTIC CONSISTENCY OF KNOWLEDGE BASES IN INFERENCE SYSTEMS

Angelo Gilio

Dipartimento di Metodi e Modelli Matematici,
Via A. Scarpa 10 - 00161 Roma, Italy.

Abstract. *We consider a probabilistic knowledge base represented by a conditional probability assessment on an arbitrary finite family of conditional events. Following the approach of de Finetti to conditional events, we use the concept of generalized atom to introduce a suitable matrix representing the truth values of the given conditional events. Moreover, we prove some theoretical results, by means of which using the linear programming technique a procedure to check the probabilistic consistency of the given knowledge base can be easily constructed. Finally, a simple example is examined.*

1 Introduction

In many applications of inference systems the probabilistic treatment of uncertainty, based on the technique of Bayesian networks, entails practical difficulties. In fact, due to the lack of information, often the assignment of a complete probability distribution is based on some arbitrary conditional independence assumptions.

An approach which needs to supply only as much probabilistic information as we have is that of de Finetti [1]. This methodology, in handling uncertainty, has the main advantage of allowing to assess numerical and/or qualitative probabilistic judgements on arbitrary families of conditional events. The approach of de Finetti to uncertainty treatment in expert systems has been examined in [2, 3, 4, 5, 6, 7, 8, 9, 10]. In this paper we consider a probabilistic knowledge base $(\mathscr{F},\mathscr{P})$, where $\mathscr{F} = \{E_1|H_1, E_2|H_2,...,E_n|H_n\}$ is a finite family of conditional events and $\mathscr{P} = (p_1, p_2,...,p_n)$ is a probability assessment on $\mathscr{F}$. In Section 2, based on the conditional events of $\mathscr{F}$, we determine a suitable partition of the certain event Ω. Then, using the concept of generalized atom introduced in [11], we define the matrix of truth values associated to $(\mathscr{F},\mathscr{P})$. In Section 3 some theorems on the consistency of the probabilistic knowledge base are proved. Then, based on the *linear programming* technique, an obvious procedure to check coherence of the given probability assessment can be used. Finally, in Section 4 a simple example is examined.

2 Generalized atoms and truth values matrix

A conditional event $E|H$ is looked upon as a three-valued entity taking one of the three values 1, 0, p (where p is a number between 0 and 1), according to whether it is true the event $E \cap H$, or $E^c \cap H$, or H^c, respectively. For a general discussion, see [12]. See also [13, 14, 15].

Let $\mathscr{F} = \{E_1|H_1, E_2|H_2, ..., E_n|H_n\}$ be a finite family of conditional events, and $\mathscr{P} = (p_1, p_2, ..., p_n)$ a probability assessment on $\mathscr{F}$, with $P(E_i|H_i) = p_i$. We denote by $(\mathscr{F}, \mathscr{P})$ the probabilistic knowledge base associated to $\mathscr{F}$ and $\mathscr{P}$.

For each subscript i, it is $E_i H_i \vee E_i^c H_i \vee H_i^c = \Omega$, so that developing the expression

$$\left[E_1 H_1 \vee E_1^c H_1 \vee H_1^c\right] \wedge \left[E_2 H_2 \vee E_2^c H_2 \vee H_2^c\right] \wedge ... \wedge \left[E_n H_n \vee E_n^c H_n \vee H_n^c\right]$$

we obtain a partition $\Pi = \{C_0, C_1, ..., C_m\}$ of Ω , the atoms C_h being all the (not impossible) logical products $A_1 A_2 ... A_n$, with $A_i \in \{E_i H_i, E_i^c H_i, H_i^c\}$. Denote by H_0 the event $H_1 \vee ... \vee H_n$ and by C_0 the atom $H_1^c H_2^c ... H_n^c = H_0^c$. Then, for each $h = 1, 2,$ ..., m, it is $C_h \subseteq H_0$, with $m \le 3^n - 1$. Note that, if $H_0 = \Omega$, then $C_0 = H_1^c H_2^c ... H_n^c = \oslash$ and $\Pi = \{C_1, C_2, ..., C_m\}$. To the atoms $C_1, C_2, ..., C_m$ we associate the generalized atoms $Q_1, Q_2, ..., Q_m$, defined as $Q_h = (q_{h1}, q_{h2}, ..., q_{hn})$, where

$$q_{hi} = \begin{cases} 1 & , \quad \text{if} \quad C_h \subseteq E_i H_i \\ 0 & , \quad \text{if} \quad C_h \subseteq E_i^c H_i \\ p_i & , \quad \text{if} \quad C_h \subseteq H_i^c \end{cases} \quad \begin{array}{l} i = 1, 2, ..., n \\ h = 1, 2, ..., m \end{array} .$$

The generalized atom Q_h is the vector of truth values assigned by C_h to the conditional events $E_1|H_1, ..., E_n|H_n$.

When $C_0 \ne \oslash$, besides the points Q_h, we must consider also the point $\mathscr{P}$, which represents the vector of truth values associated to the atom C_0 . We will also denote $\mathscr{P}$ by the symbol Q_0 . Then, given the probabilistic knowledge base $(\mathscr{F}, \mathscr{P})$, we can introduce the following matrix of truth values

$$\mathbb{Q} = \begin{bmatrix} \mathscr{P} \\ Q_1 \\ \vdots \\ Q_m \end{bmatrix} = \begin{bmatrix} p_1 & p_2 & \cdots & p_n \\ q_{11} & q_{12} & \cdots & q_{1n} \\ \cdots\cdots\cdots\cdots \\ q_{m1} & q_{m2} & \cdots & q_{mn} \end{bmatrix} .$$

We denote by J_0 the set $\{1, 2, ..., n\}$ and, given a subset $J \subseteq J_0$, by $Q_1^{(J)}, Q_2^{(J)}, ..., Q_{m_J}^{(J)}$ the generalized atoms relative to the probabilistic knowledge base $(\mathscr{F}_J, \mathscr{P}_J)$, where $\mathscr{F}_J$ is the subfamily $\{E_j|H_j : j \in J\} \subseteq \mathscr{F}$ and $\mathscr{P}_J$ is the subvector of $\mathscr{P}$ defined as $\mathscr{P}_J = (p_j : j \in J)$. Then, to $(\mathscr{F}_J, \mathscr{P}_J)$ we can associate a matrix of truth values $\mathbb{Q}_J$, with rows the vectors $\mathscr{P}_J, Q_1^{(J)}, ..., Q_{m_J}^{(J)}$. The matrix $\mathbb{Q}_J$ corresponds to the partition $\Pi_J = \left\{ C_0^{(J)}, C_1^{(J)}, ..., C_{m_J}^{(J)} \right\}$ obtained developing the expression $\underset{j \in J}{\wedge} \left[E_j H_j \vee E_j^c H_j \vee H_j^c \right]$, where the symbol $\wedge$ denotes the operation of logical product. We will also denote $\mathscr{P}_J$ by the symbol $Q_0^{(J)}$. Obviously, if $J = J_0$, then

$$(\mathscr{F}_J, \mathscr{P}_J) = (\mathscr{F}, \mathscr{P}) , \quad \Pi_J = \Pi , \quad \mathbb{Q}_J = \mathbb{Q} .$$

We denote by $\mathbf{3}_J$ the convex hull of the points $Q_1^{(J)}, Q_2^{(J)}, ...,$ $Q_{m_J}^{(J)}$. When $J = J_0$ we put $\mathbf{3}_J = \mathbf{3}$.

In Gilio (1990) the following results have been obtained:

(2.1) Theorem. If there exist m *positive* numbers $\lambda_1, ..., \lambda_m$, with $\sum_{h=1}^{m} \lambda_h = 1$, such that $\mathscr{P} = \sum_{h=1}^{m} \lambda_h Q_h$, then $\mathscr{P}$ is coherent.

(2.2) Theorem. The prevision point $\mathscr{P}$ is coherent *if and only if* $\mathscr{P}_J \in \mathbf{3}_J$ for every $J \subseteq J_0$.

3 Probabilistic consistency of the knowledge base

In this Section some results on the probabilistic consistency of the knowledge base $(\mathscr{F}, \mathscr{P})$ will be obtained.

We first examine some preliminary aspects. Two subsets I and J of the set J_0 determine two partitions

$$\Pi_I = \left\{ C_0^{(I)}, C_1^{(I)}, ..., C_{m_I}^{(I)} \right\} , \Pi_J = \left\{ C_0^{(J)}, C_1^{(J)}, ..., C_{m_J}^{(J)} \right\} .$$

Assuming I and J disjoint and denoting by T the set of pairs of subscripts (h,k) such that $C_h^{(I)} \wedge C_k^{(J)} \neq \varnothing$, h = 0, 1, ..., m_I, k = 0, 1, ..., m_J, to the subset $I \cup J$ there corresponds a partition $\Pi_{I \cup J} = \left\{ C_0^{(I \cup J)}, C_1^{(I \cup J)}, ..., C_{m_{I \cup J}}^{(I \cup J)} \right\}$, defined by $\Pi_{I \cup J} = \left\{ C_h^{(I)} \wedge C_k^{(J)} : (h,k) \in T \right\}$. Then, to the knowledge base $(\mathscr{F}_{I \cup J}, \mathscr{P}_{I \cup J})$ it is associated a matrix of truth values $\mathbb{Q}_{I \cup J}$, with rows all the vectors $\left[Q_h^{(I)}, Q_k^{(J)} \right]$ such that $(h,k) \in T$. Denote by \ the operation of *difference* between sets and, given $J \subseteq J_0$, by J^c the subset $J_0 \setminus J$. Then, choosing $I = J^c$, it follows $(\mathscr{F}_{I \cup J}, \mathscr{P}_{I \cup J}) = (\mathscr{F}, \mathscr{P})$ and $\mathbb{Q}_{I \cup J} = \mathbb{Q}$, so that, for every vector Q_t of the matrix $\mathbb{Q}$, there exists a pair (h_t, k_t) such that after a suitable permutation of subscripts it is

$$Q_t = \left[Q_{h_t}^{(J)}, Q_{k_t}^{(J^c)} \right] . \tag{1}$$

Then, denoting by the symbol $\cup$ the operation of logical sum and defining $H_J = \underset{j \in J}{\cup} H_j$, we have

(3.1) Theorem. Given a subset $J \subset J_0$, if there exist m non-

negative numbers λ_1, λ_2, ..., λ_m, with $\sum_{t=1}^{m} \lambda_t = 1$, such that

$\mathscr{P}_J = \sum_{t=1}^{m} \lambda_t Q_{h_t}^{(J)}$, then, if $\sum_{t\,:\,C_t \subseteq H_J} \lambda_t > 0$, it follows $\mathscr{P}_J \in \mathbf{\mathfrak{Z}}_J$.

Proof: Given a subset $J \subset J_0$, assume $\sum_{t\,:\,C_t \subseteq H_J} \lambda_t > 0$. For

every $k = 0,1,...,m_J$, defining $J_k = \{t \,:\, Q_{h_t}^{(J)} = Q_k^{(J)}\}$, we have

$$\sum_{t=1}^{m} \lambda_t Q_{h_t}^{(J)} = \sum_{k=0}^{m_J}\left[\sum_{t\in J_k}\lambda_t\right] Q_k^{(J)} = \left[\sum_{t\in J_0}\lambda_t\right]\mathscr{P}_J + \sum_{k=1}^{m_J}\left[\sum_{t\in J_k}\lambda_t\right] Q_k^{(J)} =$$

$$= w_0 \mathscr{P}_J + \sum_{k=1}^{m_J} w_k Q_k^{(J)} = \mathscr{P}_J \, ,$$

where, for each k, it is $w_k = \sum_{t\in J_k}\lambda_t$. Then, observing that

$$1 - w_0 = \sum_{k=1}^{m_J} w_k = \sum_{t\,:\,C_t \subseteq H_J} \lambda_t > 0$$

and defining $\lambda_k^{(J)} = w_k/(1 - w_0)$, we obtain $\mathscr{P}_J = \sum_{k=1}^{m_J} \lambda_k^{(J)} Q_k^{(J)}$,

with $\sum_{k=1}^{m_J}\lambda_k^{(J)} = 1$, that is $\mathscr{P}_J \in \mathbf{\mathfrak{Z}}_J$.

Given the assessment $\mathscr{P}$ on $\mathscr{F}$, assume that $\mathscr{P} \in \mathbf{\mathfrak{Z}}$ and denote
by $\mathscr{L}$ the set of vectors $\Lambda = (\lambda_1, \lambda_2, ..., \lambda_m)$, with $\sum_{t=1}^{m} \lambda_t = 1$
and $\lambda_t \geq 0$ for every t, such that $\mathscr{P} = \sum_{t=1}^{m} \lambda_t Q_t$. Then, introduce the subset I_0 of the set J_0 , defined as

$$I_0 = \{j \in J_0 \,:\, \sum_{t\,:\,C_t \subseteq H_j} \lambda_t = 0 \,,\, \forall \Lambda \in \mathscr{L}\} . \qquad (2)$$

We observe that, for each $j \in J_0$, the linear function

$$\phi_j(\Lambda) = \phi_j(\lambda_1, \lambda_2, ..., \lambda_m) = \sum_{t\,:\,C_t \subseteq H_j} \lambda_t \,,\quad \Lambda \in \mathscr{L} , \qquad (3)$$

is non-negative, so that the set I_0 can be determined by
solving the following linear programming problems

Max $\phi_j(\Lambda)$, subject to : $\Lambda \in \mathscr{L}$; $j = 1,2,...,n$.

Then, we construct I_0 applying the following rule

$$j \in I_0 \iff \text{Max } \phi_j(\Lambda) = 0 .$$

Note that, given a subset $J \subseteq J_0$, defining the function

$$\phi_J(\Lambda) = \sum_{t\,:\,C_t \subseteq H_J} \lambda_t \,,$$

for every $j \in J$, from $H_j \subseteq H_J$ it follows $\phi_j(\Lambda) \leq \phi_J(\Lambda)$.

Then, the following result is obtained.

(3.2) Theorem. If $\mathscr{P} \in \mathfrak{Z}$, then for every $J \subset J_0$ such that $J \backslash I_0 \neq \varnothing$ it is $\mathscr{P}_J \in \mathfrak{Z}_J$.

Proof: Assume $\mathscr{P} \in \mathfrak{Z}$ and $J \backslash I_0 \neq \varnothing$. After a suitable permutation of subscripts, we can write $\mathscr{P} = \left[\mathscr{P}_J , \mathscr{P}_{J^c} \right]$. Moreover, for every $(\lambda_1, \lambda_2, \ldots, \lambda_m) \in \mathscr{L}$, from (1) we have

$$\mathscr{P} = \sum_{t=1}^{m} \lambda_t Q_t = \sum_{t=1}^{m} \lambda_t \left[Q_{h_t}^{(J)}, Q_{k_t}^{(J^c)} \right] = \left(\sum_{t=1}^{m} \lambda_t Q_{h_t}^{(J)}, \sum_{t=1}^{m} \lambda_t Q_{k_t}^{(J^c)} \right),$$

so that $\mathscr{P}_J = \sum_{t=1}^{m} \lambda_t Q_{h_t}^{(J)}$. Since $J \backslash I_0 \neq \varnothing$, there exist $j \in J$ and $\varLambda \in \mathscr{L}$ such that $\phi_j(\varLambda) = \sum_{t : C_t \subseteq H_j} \lambda_t > 0$. Then,

$$\phi_j(\varLambda) = \sum_{t : C_t \subseteq H_J} \lambda_t \geq \sum_{t : C_t \subseteq H_j} \lambda_t > 0$$

and, from Theorem (3.1), it follows $\mathscr{P}_J \in \mathfrak{Z}_J$.

From Theorem (3.2) we have

(3.3) Theorem. The probability assessment $\mathscr{P}$ is coherent if and only if the following conditions are satisfied:
(i) $\mathscr{P} \in \mathfrak{Z}$; (ii) If $I_0 \neq \varnothing$, then $\mathscr{P}_{I_0}$ is coherent.

Proof: If $\mathscr{P}$ is coherent, then conditions (i) and (ii) obviously hold. Conversely, assume (i) and (ii) are satisfied. Since $\mathscr{P} \in \mathfrak{Z}$, the set $\mathscr{L}$ is not empty. Given a subset $J \subset J_0$, if $J \backslash I_0 \neq \varnothing$ then there exists $j \in J$ such that $\phi_j(\varLambda) > 0$ for some $\varLambda \in \mathscr{L}$, so that from Theorem (3.2) we have $\mathscr{P}_J \in \mathfrak{Z}_J$. Note that, if $I_0 = \varnothing$, then the condition $J \backslash I_0 \neq \varnothing$ is satisfied for every (not empty) subset J. On the other hand, assuming $I_0 \neq \varnothing$, if $J \subseteq I_0$, then from coherence of $\mathscr{P}_{I_0}$ it follows that $\mathscr{P}_J$ is coherent too, hence $\mathscr{P}_J \in \mathfrak{Z}_J$. Therefore, we have $\mathscr{P}_J \in \mathfrak{Z}_J$ for every $J \subseteq J_0$ and, from Theorem (2.2), the coherence of $\mathscr{P}$ follows.

From Theorem (3.3) we obtain

(3.4) Corollary. Given a coherent assessment $\mathscr{P}_J$ on $\mathscr{F}_J \subset \mathscr{F}$, denote by $\mathscr{P}$ an extension of $\mathscr{P}_J$ on $\mathscr{F}$. Then, if both the conditions $\mathscr{P} \in \mathfrak{Z}$ and $I_0 \subseteq J$ are satisfied, the assessment $\mathscr{P}$ is coherent.

Remark: Theorem (2.1) can be obtained as a Corollary from Theorem (3.3). In fact, if m positive numbers $\lambda_1, \lambda_2, \ldots, \lambda_m$, with $\sum_{t=1}^{m} \lambda_t = 1$, there exist such that $\mathscr{P} = \sum_{t=1}^{m} \lambda_t Q_t$, then it follows $\sum_{t : C_t \subseteq H_j} \lambda_t > 0$ for every $j \in J_0$, so that $I_0 = \varnothing$ and $\mathscr{P}$ is coherent.

Given a subset $J \subseteq J_0$, denote by $\mathscr{L}_J$ the set of non-negative vectors $\Lambda_J = (\lambda_1^{(J)}, \lambda_2^{(J)}, ..., \lambda_{m_J}^{(J)})$, with $\sum_{k=1}^{m_J} \lambda_k^{(J)} = 1$, such that $\mathscr{P}_J = \sum_{k=1}^{m_J} \lambda_k^{(J)} Q_k^{(J)}$. Assuming $\mathscr{P}_J \in \mathbf{3}_J$, i.e. $\mathscr{L}_J$ not empty, introduce the set I_J defined, analogously to I_0 in (2), as

$$I_J = \{j \in J : \sum_{k : C_k^{(J)} \subseteq H_j} \lambda_k^{(J)} = 0 , \forall \Lambda_J \in S_J\} . \qquad (4)$$

Obviously, $I_{J_0} = I_0$. Given a subset $J \subseteq J_0$, denote by $|J|$ the *cardinality* of J . From Theorem (3.3) we have

(3.5) Theorem. The conditional probability assessment $\mathscr{P}$ is coherent if and only if there exist k subsets $J_1, J_2, ..., J_k$, $k \leq n$, of the set J_0 , with $\varnothing \subseteq J_k \subset J_{k-1} \subset ... \subset J_1 \subset J_0$, such that the following conditions are satisfied:

(i) $\mathscr{P}_{J_h} \in \mathbf{3}_{J_h}$, i.e. $\mathscr{L}_{J_h} \neq \varnothing$, for each h = 0,1,...,k-1;

(i') If J_k is not empty, then $\mathscr{P}_{J_k} \in \mathbf{3}_{J_k}$;

(ii) $I_{J_h} = J_{h+1}$, h = 0,1,...,k-1, and $|I_{J_k}| \leq 1$.

Proof: Let $\mathscr{P} = (p_1, p_2, ..., p_n)$ a probability assessment on the family $\mathscr{F} = \{E_1|H_1, E_2|H_2, ..., E_n|H_n\}$. We obviously assume $0 \leq p_i \leq 1$ for every subscript i.

If $\mathscr{P}$ is coherent, then $\mathscr{P}_{J_0} = \mathscr{P} \in \mathbf{3} = \mathbf{3}_{J_0}$. If $|I_0| = 0$, the assertion is true, with k = 1 and $J_1 = \varnothing$. If $|I_0| = 1$, then the assertion is true, with k = 1 and $J_1 = I_0$. We observe that, denoting by j the integer such that $I_0 = \{j\}$, the condition $\mathscr{P}_{J_1} \in \mathbf{3}_{J_1}$ amounts to $0 \leq p_j \leq 1$.

If $|I_0| > 1$, using (4), we can introduce k subsets J_1, J_2, ..., J_k , defined as $J_1 = I_0 \subset J_0$, $J_2 = I_{J_1} \subset J_1$, ..., $J_k = I_{J_{k-1}} \subset J_{k-1}$, with $|I_k| \leq 1$, $k \leq n$. The coherence of $\mathscr{P}$ implies $\mathscr{P}_{J_h} \in \mathbf{3}_{J_h}$, h = 0,1,...,k-1, with $\mathscr{P}_{J_k} \in \mathbf{3}_{J_k}$ (if $J_k \neq \varnothing$), so that the assertion follows again.

Conversely, assume there exist $J_k \subset J_{k-1} \subset ... \subset J_1 \subset J_0$ such that the properties (i), (i') and (ii) are satisfied. It is $I_k = \varnothing$, or $I_k = \{j\}$ for some $j \in J_k$. If $I_k = \varnothing$, using Theorem (3.3), from the hypothesis $\mathscr{P}_{J_k} \in \mathbf{3}_{J_k}$ we have that $\mathscr{P}_{J_k}$ is coherent. If $I_k = \{j\}$, then $\mathscr{P}_{I_k} = (p_j)$ and its coherence amounts to $0 \leq p_j \leq 1$, so that we obtain again coherence of

$\mathscr{P}_{J_k}$. Using Theorem (3.3), from coherence of $\mathscr{P}_{J_k}$ and the hypotheses $\mathscr{P}_{J_{k-1}} \in \boldsymbol{3}_{J_{k-1}}$, $I_{J_{k-1}} = J_k$ it follows that $\mathscr{P}_{J_{k-1}}$ is coherent too. In the same way, iteratively applying Theorem (3.3), we obtain coherence of the assessments

$$\mathscr{P}_{J_h}, \quad h = k-2, k-3, ..., 1, 0 ,$$

so that $\mathscr{P} = \mathscr{P}_{J_0}$ is coherent and the assertion is proved.

Based on Theorem (3.5), a procedure to check coherence of a given conditional probability assessment $\mathscr{P}$ can be easily constructed. Within this procedure, the subsets $J_1, J_2, ..., J_k$, can be determined using the linear programming technique.

4 An application

To better illustrate some results of Section 3, let us consider a simple example of a probabilistic knowledge base $(\mathscr{F}, \mathscr{P})$, where $\mathscr{F} = \{E_1|H_1, E_2|H_2, E_3|H_3\}$, $\mathscr{P} = (p_1, p_2, p_3)$, such that $\Pi = \{C_0, C_1, C_2, C_3\}$, with $C_0 = H_1^c H_2^c H_3^c$ and $C_1 = E_1 H_1 E_2 H_2 E_3 H_3$, $C_2 = E_1^c H_1 E_2 H_2 E_3^c H_3$, $C_3 = H_1^c E_2^c H_2 E_3 H_3$.

Then $Q_0 = \mathscr{P}$ and

$$Q_1 = (1,1,1), \quad Q_2 = (0,1,0), \quad Q_3 = (p_1,0,0) .$$

It can be verified that $\mathscr{P} \in \boldsymbol{3}$ iff $p_3 = p_1 p_2$. Moreover, applying (2) and (3), with $\Lambda = (\lambda_1, \lambda_2, \lambda_3)$, we have

$$\phi_2(\Lambda) = \phi_3(\Lambda) = \lambda_1 + \lambda_2 + \lambda_3 = 1 > 0 , \quad \phi_1(\Lambda) = \lambda_1 + \lambda_2 ,$$

so that $I_0 \subseteq \{1\}$. Therefore, using Theorem (3.5) with $k = 1$, it follows that coherence of $\mathscr{P}$ amounts to the conditions $p_3 = p_1 p_2$ and $0 \le p_1, p_2, p_3 \le 1$.

We can distinguish two cases : a) $p_2 > 0$; b) $p_2 = 0$. Then, it can be verified that the system

$$p_i = \sum_{t=1}^{3} \lambda_t q_{ti}, \; i = 1,2,3; \quad \sum_{t=1}^{3} \lambda_t = 1 ; \quad \lambda_t \ge 0, \; t = 1,2,3,$$

representing condition $\mathscr{P} \in \boldsymbol{3}$, has in case a) the solution $\lambda_1 = p_1 p_2 > 0$, $\lambda_2 = p_2(1 - p_1)$, $\lambda_3 = 1 - p_2$, so that $I_0 = \varnothing$. In case b) the solution is $\lambda_1 = \lambda_2 = 0$, $\lambda_3 = 1$ and $I_0 = \{1\}$.

We observe that a model of the above example is given by any family $\mathscr{F} = \{E|F, F|H, E|H\}$ such that $E \subset F \subset H$.

In fact, as well known, in this case the coherence of $\mathscr{P}$ requires $P(E|H) = P(E|F)P(F|H)$.

References

1. B. De Finetti: Theory of probability. A.F.M. Smith and A. Machì (trs.), 2 Voll. New York: John Wiley 1974, 1975

2. A. Gilio, R. Scozzafava: Le probabilita' condizionate coerenti nei sistemi esperti. In: Atti Giornate di lavoro A.I.R.O. su "Ricerca Operativa e Intelligenza Artificiale". Pisa: Offset Grafica, 1988, pp. 317-330

3. G. Coletti, A. Gilio, R. Scozzafava: Coherent
    qualitative probability and uncertainty in Artificial
    Intelligence.In: C. N. Manikopoulos (ed.): Proc. of The
    8th Int. Congr. of Cybernetics and Systems 1. New York:
    The NJIT Press 1990, pp. 132-138

4. G. Coletti, A. Gilio, R. Scozzafava: Conditional events
    with vague information in expert systems. In: B. Bouchon-
    Meunier, R. R. Yager, L. A. Zadeh (eds.): Uncertainty in
    knowledge bases. Lecture Notes in Computer Science 521.
    Berlin: Springer - Verlag 1991, pp. 106-114

5. G. Coletti, A. Gilio, R. Scozzafava: Assessment of
    qualitative judgements for conditional events in expert
    systems. In: R. Kruse, P. Siegel (eds.): Symbolic and
    quantitative approaches to uncertainty. Lecture Notes in
    Computer Science 548. Berlin: Springer - Verlag 1991, pp.
    135-140

6. G. Coletti, A. Gilio, R. Scozzafava: Comparative
    probability for conditional events : a new look through
    coherence. Theory and Decision. (To appear)

7. G. Coletti: Comparative probabilities ruled coherence
    conditions and use in expert systems. Intern. Journal of
    General Systems. (To appear)

8. G. Coletti: Coherent numerical and ordinal probabilistic
    assessments. IEEE Transactions on Systems, Man, and
    Cybernetics. (To appear)

9. R. Scozzafava: Subjective probability versus belief
    functions in artificial intelligence. Intern. Journal of
    General Systems. (To appear)

10. A. Gilio, F. Spezzaferri: Knowledge integration for
    conditional probability assessments. In: D. Dubois, M.
    P. Wellman, B. D'Ambrosio, P. Smets (eds.): Uncertainty
    in Artificial Intelligence. San Mateo, California:
    Morgan Kaufmann Publishers 1992, pp. 98-103

11. A. Gilio: Criterio di penalizzazione e condizioni di
    coerenza nella valutazione soggettiva della probabilità.
    Bollettino della Unione Matematica Italiana (7) 4-B,
    645-660 (1990)

12. A. Gilio, R. Scozzafava: Conditional events in
    probability assessment and revision. IEEE Transactions
    on Systems, Man, and Cybernetics. (To appear)

13. P.G. Calabrese: Deduction and inference using conditional
    logic and probability. In: I.R. Goodman, M. M. Gupta, H.
    T. Nguyen, G. S. Rogers (eds.): Conditional Logic in
    Expert Systems. Amsterdam: North-Holland 1991, pp. 71-100

14. D. Dubois, H. Prade: Conditioning, non-monotonic logic
    and non-standard uncertainty models. In: I. R. Goodman,
    M. M. Gupta, H. T. Nguyen, G. S. Rogers (eds.):
    Conditional Logic in Expert Systems. Amsterdam: North -
    Holland 1991, pp. 115-158

15. I. R. Goodman, H. T. Nguyen, E. A. Walker: Conditional
    inference and logic for intelligent systems: a theory of
    measure-free conditioning. Amsterdam: North-Holland 1991

Weighting Independent Bodies of Evidence

Silviu Guiasu

Department of Mathematics and Statistics, York University
North York, Ontario, M3J 1P3, Canada

Abstract. The objective of this paper is to introduce a weighted combination of independent bodies of evidence which contains Hooper's, Dempster's, Bayes's, and Jeffrey's rules as special cases.

1 Introduction

A major problem in the logic of probable reasoning is the combination of evidence. Given independent bodies of evidence, a decision maker has to take all of them into account but the problem is how? Apparently, the only way of avoiding a rigid solution to this problem is to assign different weights to the available bodies of evidence by using any objective or subjective additional information about the reliability of this evidence. A physician, a judge, a researcher, use their past experience for weighting the evidence at hand before making up their minds about what conclusions to draw about the alternatives open to them. A detective tries to find out first of all how reliable the bodies of evidence are. The objective of this paper is to give a general mathematical rule of weighting independent bodies of evidence by using conditional credibilities about the reliability of this evidence. The well-known rules for combining evidence proposed by Hooper, Dempster, Bayes, and Jeffrey are obtained as special cases.

2 Weighting Bodies of Evidence

Let Z be a finite crisp (i.e. Cantor) set called *frame* or *universe*, and m_1 and m_2 two independent basic probability assignments on the class $\mathcal{P}(Z)$ of all subsets of Z. Thus,

$$m_i : \mathcal{P}(Z) \longrightarrow [0,1], \quad m_i(\emptyset) = 0, \quad \sum_{A \subseteq Z} m_i(A) = 1, \quad (i = 1, 2).$$

The basic probability assignments m_1 and m_2, as any other probability distributions from this paper, could be either objective (i.e. based on relative frequences from repeated past experiments) or subjective (i.e. reflecting personal credibilities). It is convenient to think of m_1 and m_2 as being associated with the bodies of evidence provided by two witnesses. Then, $m_i(A)$ is the degree of belief of the i-th witness that a specific element of Z, let us say the suspect in a criminal investigation, belongs to the subset A of the population Z, but not to any special subsubset of A. The corresponding belief and plausibility measures are

$$Bel_i(A) = \sum_{B \subseteq A} m_i(B), \qquad Pl_i(A) = \sum_{B \cap A \neq \emptyset} m_i(B), \qquad (i = 1, 2).$$

The direct (independent) product basic probability assignment is

$$m_1 \times m_2 : \mathcal{P}(Z) \times \mathcal{P}(Z) \longrightarrow [0, 1],$$

defined for $A \subseteq Z$ and $B \subseteq Z$ by $(m_1 \times m_2)(A, B) = m_1(A) m_2(B)$.

An essential problem is how to combine the basic probability assignments m_1 and m_2 induced by two independent bodies of evidence in order to get a new combined basic probability assignment m on $\mathcal{P}(Z)$? Intuitively, we are in the position of a judge who is provided with two bodies of evidence by two independent witnesses who may or may not be fully reliable. The judge may use her own credibility about the two witnesses, based on additional objective or subjective information about the reliability of their testimony, weighting the bodies of evidence correspondingly. Several specific ways of combining independent bodies of evidence have been proposed in literature. They will be obtained in section 4 as special cases of the general model discussed in this section.

Given a pair $\{A, B\}$ of focal sets of m_1 and m_2, respectively, which means that $m_1(A) > 0$ and $m_2(B) > 0$, let us denote by $\mathcal{B}(A, B)$ the class of subsets obtained by applying the logical operators $\cap$ *and*, $\cup$ *or*, and $^-$ *non* on A and B,

$$\mathcal{B}(A, B) = \{A, B, \bar{A}, \bar{B}, A \cup B, A \cup \bar{B}, \bar{A} \cup B, \bar{A} \cup \bar{B}, A \cap B, A \cap \bar{B}, \bar{A} \cap B, \bar{A} \cap \bar{B}, Z, \emptyset\}.$$

Denote by $\mathcal{F}_1$ and $\mathcal{F}_2$ the classes of focal sets of m_1 and m_2, respectively, i.e. the classes of subsets of Z referred to by the two witnesses in their testimony,

$$\mathcal{F}_1 = \{A; A \subseteq Z, m_1(A) > 0\}, \quad \mathcal{F}_2 = \{B; B \subseteq Z, m_2(B) > 0\}.$$

For each pair $A \in \mathcal{F}_1$ and $B \in \mathcal{F}_2$ of focal sets, let $\mathcal{G}(A, B) \subset \mathcal{P}(Z)$ be a class of distinct subsets of Z, representing the alternatives taken into account by the judge when the two witnesses focus on the subsets A and B, respectively. Two sets are distinct if they differ by at least one element. Often, $\mathcal{G}(A, B)$ is the class of distinct sets of $\mathcal{B}(A, B)$. Given the pair of focal sets $\{A, B\}$ of the two witnesses, the judge's *weight* of the alternatives corresponding to $\{A, B\}$ is a function $w(\cdot \mid A, B) : \mathcal{G}(A, B) \longrightarrow [0, \infty)$, where the number $w(D \mid A, B)$ may be interpreted as the weight given by the judge to the alternative $D \subseteq Z$ given the evidence $\{A, B\}$ provided by the two witnesses, respectively. The *weighted combined basic probability assignment* is then defined by

$$m(C) = \sum_{A \in \mathcal{F}_1, B \in \mathcal{F}_2} \sum_{D = C, D \in \mathcal{G}(A, B)} w(D \mid A, B) m_1(A) m_2(B), \qquad (1)$$

for all $C \in \mathcal{P}(Z)$. As m has to be a probability distribution on $\mathcal{P}(Z)$, the only restriction on the judge's weights of the available alternatives, besides being nonnegative, is to satisfy the equality

$$\sum_{C \in \mathcal{P}(Z)} \sum_{A \in \mathcal{F}_1, B \in \mathcal{F}_2} \sum_{D=C, D \in \mathcal{G}(A,B)} w(D \mid A, B) \, m_1(A) \, m_2(B) = 1.$$

As the two witnesses are not necessarily 100% reliable, when the pair of evidence $\{A, B\}$ is given, the judge still considers the alternatives induced by $\{A, B\}$, namely the distinct sets D from $\mathcal{B}(A, B)$, weighted by the credibilities $w(D \mid A, B)$. Thus, given the evidence $\{A, B\}$, a cautious judge that however trusts the two witnesses will give a positive weight only to the alternative $A \cup B$, i.e. $w(A \cup B \mid A, B) > 0$. A radical judge that however trusts both witnesses will give a positive weight only to the alternative $A \cap B$, i.e. $w(A \cap B \mid A, B) > 0$. A judge who does not fully trust the two witnesses will give a positive weight to Z too, i.e. $w(Z \mid A, B) > 0$, which means that all possibilities remain open in spite of the pair of evidence $\{A, B\}$. A judge who knows that the two witnesses are both notorious liars will prefer to give a positive weight to the negation of the evidence provided by them by taking $w(\bar{A} \cap \bar{B} \mid A, B) > 0$. Finally, a positive weight assigned to the empty set, i.e. $w(\emptyset \mid A, B) > 0$, would mean that in spite of the evidence $\{A, B\}$ provided by the two witnesses, the judge does not eliminate the possibility that the solution has to be looked for outside the given frame Z.

The combination rule (1) may be easily extended to the case when there are more than two independent bodies of evidence or when the bodies of evidence are not independent. In the last case, if the two bodies of evidence are dependent, the direct product basic probability assignment $m_1 \times m_2$ from (1) has to be replaced by the joint basic probability assignment $m_{1,2}$ defined on $\mathcal{P}(Z \times Z)$, where $m_{1,2}(A, B)$ is the probability that the two witnesses jointly focus on the subsets A and B of Z, respectively. In such a case, if m_1 and m_2 are the marginal basic probability assignments of $m_{1,2}$, then we can introduce the conditional basic probability assignment of a witness, given the choice of the other one. Thus, $m_{1,2}(A, B) = m_1(A) \, m_2(B \mid A) = m_1(A \mid B) \, m_2(B)$.

3 An Example

A criminal defendant has an alibi: somebody swears that the defendant was eating in his restaurant at the time of the crime. The witness has a good reputation so his testimony is seriously taken into account. But there is a strong body of circumstantial evidence attesting to the defendant's guilt; standing alone it would provide a degree of support (i.e. belief) of 9/10 for his guilt. What degrees of support does the combined evidence provide for the defendant's guilt and innocence? Denoting by $g = guilt$ and $i = innocence$, we have $Z = \{g, i\}$. The witness' testimony means $m_1(\{i\}) = 1$. The circumstantial evidence gives $m_2(\{g\}) = 9/10$ and $m_2(\{g, i\}) = 1/10$.

Case 1. The judge gives full credit to the witness' testimony:

$$w(\{i\} \mid \{i\}, \{g\}) = 1, \quad w(\{i\} \mid \{i\}, \{g, i\}) = 1,$$
$$w(\{g\} \mid \{i\}, \{g\}) = 0, \quad w(\{g\} \mid \{i\}, \{g, i\}) = 0,$$

and, according to (1), the corresponding weighted basic probability assignment is $m(\{i\}) = 1$, $m(\{g\}) = 0$.

Case 2. The judge has doubts about the witness' reliability as a result of some additional information about him:

$$w(\{i\} \mid \{i\}, \{g\}) = 1/10, \quad w(\{i\} \mid \{i\}, \{g, i\}) = 1/2,$$
$$w(\{g\} \mid \{i\}, \{g\}) = 9/10, \quad w(\{g\} \mid \{i\}, \{g, i\}) = 1/2,$$

in which case $m(\{i\}) = 0.14$, and $m(\{g\}) = 0.86$.

Case 3. The judge finds out that the witness is a good friend of the defendant and gives full credit to the circumstantial evidence:

$$w(\{i\} \mid \{i\}, \{g\}) = 0, \quad w(\{i\} \mid \{i\}, \{g, i\}) = 1/2,$$
$$w(\{g\} \mid \{i\}, \{g\}) = 1, \quad w(\{g\} \mid \{i\}, \{g, i\}) = 1/2,$$

in which case $m(\{i\}) = 0.05$, and $m(\{g\}) = 0.95$.

4 Special Cases

(a) Hooper's Rule. Assume that m_1 and m_2 have the same focal sets, namely $\mathcal{F}_1 = \mathcal{F}_2 = \{A, \bar{A}\}$ and let us take the only weights different from zero to be

$$w(A \mid A, A) = w(A \mid A, \bar{A}) = w(A \mid \bar{A}, A) = w(\bar{A} \mid \bar{A}, \bar{A}) = 1,$$

which means to give credit to A every time at least one witness points at A and to $\bar{A}$ only if both witnesses point at $\bar{A}$. The corresponding weighted combined basic probability assignment (1) becomes

$$m(A) = 1 - [1 - m_1(A)][1 - m_2(A)], \quad m(\bar{A}) = m_1(\bar{A}) \, m_2(\bar{A}).$$

According to [8], this rule for combining probabilities was used by G.Hooper in 1685. In fact, this is just the rule for calculating the reliability of a parallel system with independent components in operations research.

(b) Dempster's Rule. By taking the only weights different from zero to be $w(A \cap B \mid A, B) = c$, for all $A \in \mathcal{F}_1$, $B \in \mathcal{F}_2$ such that $A \cap B \neq \emptyset$, where the constant c is

$$c = \left[1 - \sum_{A \cap B = \emptyset} m_1(A) \, m_2(B) \right]^{-1},$$

equality (1) becomes Dempster's rule [3] of combining two independent bodies of evidence. According to [9], in the special case of a frame containing only two elements, this rule was used by J.H. Lambert in his Neues Organon published in 1764. Using Dempster's rule, the solution of the problem from Section 3 is:

$$w(\{i\} \cap \{g,i\} \mid \{i\}, \{g,i\}) = w(\{i\} \mid \{i\}, \{g,i\}) = [1 - (1)(9/10)]^{-1} = 10,$$
$$m(\{i\}) = 1, \quad m(\{g\}) = 0.$$

(c) Jeffrey's Rule. Let $Z = X \times Y$, where X and Y are two finite crisp sets. Let p_X be the *prior* probability distribution on X, $p_Y(\cdot \mid x)$ the *conditional prediction* probability distribution on Y given $x \in X$, p_Y the *prediction* probability distribution on Y, and q_Y the *actual* probability distribution on Y, where

$$p_Y(y) = \sum_{x \in X} p_Y(y \mid x) p_X(x).$$

Let m_1 and m_2 be two basic probability assignments on $\mathcal{P}(Z)$, such that

$$\mathcal{F}_1 = \{\{x\} \times Y; x \in X\} \quad \mathcal{F}_2 = \{X \times \{y\}; y \in Y\},$$
$$m_1(\{x\} \times Y) = p_X(x), \quad m_2(X \times \{y\}) = q_Y(y).$$

Case 1. Taking as weights the credibilities

$$w(\{x\} \times \{y\} \mid \{x\} \times Y, X \times \{y\}) = p_Y(y \mid x)/p_Y(y),$$

the corresponding basic probability assignment (1) becomes

$$m(\{x\} \times \{y\}) = \frac{p_X(x) \, p_Y(y \mid x)}{p_Y(y)} \, q_Y(y),$$

which is a probability distribution on $Z = X \times Y$, and its marginal probability distribution, namely

$$p_X(x \mid q_Y) = Bel(\{x\} \times Y) = \sum_{y \in Y} m(\{x\} \times \{y\})$$

gives Jeffrey's rule [7] for calculating the *posterior* probability distribution on X given the actual probability distribution q_Y,

$$p_X(x \mid q_Y) = \sum_{y \in Y} \frac{p_X(x) \, p_Y(y \mid x)}{p_Y(y)} \, q_Y(y). \tag{2}$$

A similar way of obtaining Jeffrey's rule, but using Bayes's rule for calculating the posterior probability distribution, was given in [6].

Case 2. Taking as weights the credibilities

$$w(\{x\} \times \{y\} \mid \{x\} \times Y, X \times \{y\}) = p_Y(y \mid x)/q_Y(y),$$

the corresponding basic probability assignment (1) becomes

$$m(\{x\} \times \{y\}) = p_Y(y \mid x) p_X(x),$$

which is just the joint probability distribution $p_{X,Y}$ induced on $X \times Y$ by the prior probability distribution p_X and the prediction conditional probability matrix $\{p_Y(y \mid x); x \in X, y \in Y\}$.

(d) **Bayes's Rule.** If the actual probability distribution on Y is degenerate,

$$q_Y(y) = \left\{ \begin{array}{l} 1, \text{ if } y = y_0; \\ 0, \text{ if } y \neq y_0, \end{array} \right.$$

then (2) becomes Bayes's rule [1] for calculating the posterior probabilities

$$p_X(x \mid y_0) = m(\{x\} \times \{y_0\}) = \frac{p_Y(y_0 \mid x) p_X(x)}{p_Y(y_0)}.$$

References

1. T.R.Bayes: An essay towards solving a problem in the doctrine of chances. Philosophical Transactions of the Royal Society in London 53, 370- 418 (1763)
2. B. Bouchon-Meunier: La logique floue. Paris: Presses Universitaires de France 1993
3. A.P. Dempster: Upper and lower probabilities induced by a multivalued mapping. Annals of Mathematical Statistics 38, 325-339 (1967)
4. D. Dubois, H. Prade: On the unicity of Dempster's rule of combination. International Journal of Intelligent Systems 1, 133-142 (1986)
5. S.Guiasu: A unitary treatment of several known measures of uncertainty induced by probability, possibility, fuzziness, plausibility, and belief. In: B.Bouchon-Meunier, L.Valverde, R.R.Yager (eds.): Uncertainty in intelligent systems. Amsterdam: Elsevier Science Publishing Co. 1993 (in press)
6. H.Ichihashi, H.Tanaka: Jeffrey-like rules of conditioning for the Dempster-Shafer theory of evidence. International Journal of Approximate Reasoning 3, 143-156 (1989)
7. R.C. Jeffrey: The logic of decision. New York: McGraw-Hill 1965
8. D.V. Lindley: The probability approach to the treatment of uncertainty in artificial intelligence and expert systems. Statistical Sciences 2, 17- 24 (1987)
9. G. Shafer: A mathematical theory of evidence. Princeton: Princeton University Press 1976
10. G. Shafer: Perspectives on the theory and practice of belief functions. International Journal of Approximate Reasoning 4, 323-362 (1990)

Default Logic: Orderings and Extensions

Mike Hopkins

Department of Computer Science,
Queen Mary and Westfield College,
University of London, UK.
leonardo@dcs.qmw.ac.uk

Abstract. An ordering on default rules is defined that formalises intuitive relationships between rules. Unlike Etherington's [Eth88] orderings on literals which were only used to guarantee the existence of a computable extension, ours are defined proof-theoretically and used as an integral part of an algorithm that efficiently calculates all extensions for several useful sub-classes of default logic. The algorithm represents a significant reduction in complexity over other existing methods, especially for large multi-domain examples where indepeneant partial extensions can be calculated for different groups of unrelated rules which can be combined to produce complete extensions. Also, by changing the definition of the orderings without altering the underlying algorithm, extensions can be calculated for variants of default logic that have been proposed since Reiter's original paper.

1 Introduction

Reiter's Default Logic [Rei80] has been the starting point for many proof-theoretic formulations of non-monotonic reasoning. Though logically intuitive, it has been variously criticised for being non-constructive, computationally intractable and generating too many (or too few) extensions, and many variants have been proposed.

This paper primarily addresses the problem of calculating extensions in Default Logic which, in general, is computationally intractable because of the requirement to check for consistency, and even the propositional case will be NP-hard in general. The algorithm we propose is based on computing logical relationships (or *orderings*) between default rules and we give explicit conditions for the calculation of extensions to be monotonic with respect to the application of rules; the method is most closely related to that of Levy [Lev91], whose theoretical approach we have found valuable, but our method appears to have the advantage for practical problems.

2 Exhaustive versus efficient calculation

We start by showing an inefficient method of calculating all extensions. We then show how it can be improved, introducing a large degree of determinism.

Given a default theory $\Delta = (D, W)$, with an extension $E_i = TH(W \cup CON(D'))$[1] for some $D' \subseteq D$. E_i can then be obtained by applying the default rules D' in some order after which, by the definition of an extension, no more rules will be applicable.

---

[1] $PRE(\delta)$, $JUS(\delta)$ and $CON(\delta)$ refer to the prerequisite, justification and consequent of the rule δ. Given a set of rules D then $CON(D)$ is the set of consequents of D.

Hence a method of calculating all extensions would be to apply the rules in every possible order[2] and then check the consistency of the justification for each rule used in producing each possible extension, discarding those where an inconsistency arises. A rule δ is *applicable* at each stage of the algorithm if $PRE(\delta)$ is provable and $JUS(\delta)$ is consistent with the current partial extension.

Example 1. $D = \left\{ \frac{a:b}{b}, \frac{a:\neg b}{\neg b}, \frac{a:c\neg b}{c}, \frac{xy}{y} \right\}$ and $W = \{a, x\}$: the above method would produce the following search tree where a path from the root to a leaf represents an extension. The branches that do not result in extensions have been removed for clarity.

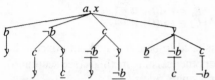

Despite this there is a large amount of duplication due to the different orders in which the rules can be applied. If the search proceeds from left to right in a breadth first manner then the horizontal lines show where we could improve efficiency by recognising the duplication.

To improve the efficiency, we see that $\frac{xy}{y}$ is not related to the other rules; the extensions of the theory could be produced by taking the union of the extensions produced the theories $\left(\left\{ \frac{xy}{y} \right\}, \{a, x\} \right)$ and $\left(\left\{ \frac{a:b}{b}, \frac{a:\neg b}{\neg b}, \frac{a:c\neg b}{c} \right\}, \{a, x\} \right)$. Also the two rules: $\frac{a:b}{b}$ and $\frac{a:\neg b}{\neg b}$ can each be applied but in doing so the other rule becomes inapplicable. The last rule $\frac{a:c\neg b}{c}$ is dependent on b not being in the extension and therefore this rule must be applied after $\frac{a:b}{b}$. Hence the rules can be grouped for application as follows, producing the improved tree:

1. $\frac{xy}{y}$
2. $\frac{a:b}{b}$ and $\frac{a:\neg b}{\neg b}$ where the only constraint on application is: 2 is before 3
3. $\frac{a:c\neg b}{c}$

We would therefore like to construct an algorithm that applies the rules in an order that maintains these constraints on application. The original complex search problem will be made deterministic provided there are no circularities.

3 Improving the Extension Calculation

We start by considering only finite propositional network theories[3] for which we define the following orderings: $\ll$, $\underset{\sim}{\ll}$ and $\diamond$ (pronounced *activate*, *disable* and *contradict* respectively)[4]: $\delta_1 \ll \delta_2$ if $W, CON(\delta_1) \vdash PRE(\delta_2)$, $\delta_1 \underset{\sim}{\ll} \delta_2$ if $W, CON(\delta_1) \vdash \neg EXCE(\delta_2)$ and $\delta_1 \diamond \delta_2$ if $W, CON(\delta_1) \vdash \neg CON(\delta_2)$

Ground orderings occur when $CON(\delta_1)$ is not required in the entailment; δ_1 is replaced by $\diamond$. An ordering, $\delta \ll \delta$, is ignored while $\delta \underset{\sim}{\ll} \delta$ is replaced by $\diamond \underset{\sim}{\ll} \delta$.

Given these definitions we first define what it means for a rule to be *applicable*:

Definition 1. δ is *applicable* w.r.t. to a theory if $\diamond \ll \delta$ and neither $\diamond \underset{\sim}{\ll} \delta$ nor $\diamond \diamond \delta$

To introduce determinism into the calculation of extensions we need to find the conditions under which the application of rules will be monotonic in the sense that

$$Ext(D_1 \cup D_2, W) = \left\{ E_2 \,\middle|\, \begin{array}{l} E_1 \in Ext(D_1, W) \\ E_2 \in Ext(D_2, E_1) \end{array} \right\}$$

---

[2] For simplicity we consider only propositional default logic where each rule is only used once. The application to rules containing free variables and no quantifiers is straightforward.

[3] A network theory is where W contains literals or disjunctions of the form $\alpha \vee \beta$ and D contains normal and semi-normal rules of the form $\frac{\alpha:\beta}{\beta}$ and $\frac{\alpha:\beta \wedge \gamma_1 \wedge \ldots \wedge \gamma_m}{\beta}$ where α, β and γ_i are literals.

[4] For a given network rule, δ, we have: $JUS(\delta) = CON(\delta) \wedge EXCE(\delta)$.

This can be shown to hold if D_1 is *potential* w.r.t. D_2:

Definition 2. D_1 is *potential* w.r.t. D_2 in a theory $(D_1 \cup D_2, W)$ if, for each $\delta \in D_1$, one of the following is true:

- $\diamond \ll \delta$ or if $\delta' \ll \delta$ then $\delta' \notin D_2$ **and** if $\delta' \underline{\ll} \delta$ or $\delta' \Leftrightarrow \delta$ then $\delta' \notin D_2$
- $\diamond \underline{\ll} \delta$ or $\diamond \Leftrightarrow \delta$
- not $\diamond \ll \delta$ **and** if $\delta' \ll \delta$ then $\delta' \notin D_1 \cup D_2$.

Hence D_1 is *potential* w.r.t. D_2 if there is no rule in D_2 that can change the applicability of a rule in D_1 w.r.t. W. If, given $(D_1 \cup D_2, W)$, D_1 and D_2 are potential w.r.t. each other:

$$Ext(D_1 \cup D_2, W) = \left\{ E_1 \cup E_2 \left| \begin{array}{l} E_1 \in Ext(D_1, W) \\ E_2 \in Ext(D_2, W) \end{array} \right. \right\}$$

If this holds then the two sets of subextensions need to be calculated only once. This produces a significant increase of efficiency over other existing methods (see section 6).

We also need the base cases. The first is for a single rule:

$$Ext(\{\delta\}, W) = \left\{ \begin{array}{ll} \{W \cup CON(\delta)\} & \text{if } app(\{\delta\}, W) \\ \{W\} & \text{otherwise} \end{array} \right.$$

where $app(D, W)$ is true when some rule in D is applicable w.r.t. W.

Unfortunately, this does not allow in general for rules that contradict each other. In the example in the previous section, only two rules contradicted each other and hence there were at most two extensions. We can guarantee this type of behaviour if we use a *restricted* form of default logic where W only contains literals. This means that the contradicting rules in D can be grouped into (D_1, D_2) tuples where every rule in D_1 has the same consequent which contradicts every rule in D_2. The extensions produced by the application of one of these tuples are given by:

$$Ext(D_1 \cup D_2, W) = \left\{ \begin{array}{ll} \{W \cup CON(D_1), W \cup CON(D_2)\} & \text{if } app(D_1, W) \text{ and } app(D_2, W) \\ \{W \cup CON(D_1)\} & \text{if } app(D_1, W) \text{ and not } app(D_2, W) \\ \{W \cup CON(D_2)\} & \text{if not } app(D_1, W) \text{ and } app(D_2, W) \\ \{W\} & \text{otherwise} \end{array} \right.$$

Further more we can guarantee the existence of a potential rule or tuple, and hence monotonicity and coherance for restricted theories, by insisting that the theory is ordered:

Definition 3. D is *ordered* if, for all $\delta \in D, \delta \not< \delta$ where $<$ is defined by:

- if $\delta' \ll \delta''$ or $\delta' \underline{\ll} \delta''$ then $\delta' < \delta''$
- if $\delta' < \delta''$ and $CON(\delta'') \vdash \neg CON(\delta''')$ then $\delta' < \delta'''$
- if $\delta' < \delta''$ and $\delta'' < \delta'''$ then $\delta' < \delta'''$

Unfortunately, if we generalise to unrestricted network theories we lose the ability to group contradicting rules into the above binary tuples and correspondingly we lose the binary enumeration of extensions on application of groups of contradicting rules:

Example 2. $W = \{a - \neg c, b - \neg c, b - \neg d\}$ and $D = \left\{ \delta_1 = \frac{:a}{a}, \delta_2 = \frac{:b}{b}, \delta_3 = \frac{:c}{c}, \delta_4 = \frac{:d}{d} \right\}$. This gives rise to the contradiction orderings: $\delta_1 \Leftrightarrow \delta_3$, $\delta_2 \Leftrightarrow \delta_3$ and $\delta_2 \Leftrightarrow \delta_4$. The theory has three extensions with generating defaults: $GD_1 = \{\delta_1, \delta_2\}$, $GD_2 = \{\delta_3, \delta_4\}$ and $GD_3 = \{\delta_1, \delta_4\}$

This example demonstrates that a group of contradicting rules can give rise to a large number of extensions. This is further complicated when not all the rules are initially applicable and when there are no minimal groups of contradicting rules that are potential.

The method used to overcome these problems is to treat the contradiction orderings as a constraint on the application of the rules. Given a set of potential rules, we find all the maximal sets of these rules such that no rule in each set contradicts another and for each rule outside the set there exists a rule in the set that it contradicts:

Definition 4. M_i is a *maximal non-contradicting subset* (*MNC* subset) of D if:
$$\forall \delta' \in M_i. \neg \exists \delta'' \in M_i. \delta' \diamond \delta'' \text{ and } \forall \delta' \in (D \backslash M_i). \exists \delta'' \in M_i. \delta' \diamond \delta''$$

Given an *MNC* subset for an ordered network theory, we can show that there will be at most one extension and hence, for n of these subsets, there are at most n extensions. As a corollary to this if, given one of these possible extensions, there exists a rule outside the associated subset that is applicable then this possible extension can be discarded and all the extensions for the theory will be included in the other possible extensions:

$$Ext(D, W) = \left\{ E \middle| D' \in MNC(D, W), E \in Ext(D', W), D'' = \left\{ \delta \middle| \begin{matrix} \delta' \in D' \backslash GD_E \\ \delta \in D \backslash D' \\ \delta \diamond \delta' \end{matrix} \right\}, \text{not } app(D'', E) \right\}$$

We need to allow for unordered theories when no potential rules can be found; we can use the method of Junker and Konolige [JK90] and Levy [Lev91] (for further comments see section 6), choosing any applicable rule. The calculation divides: (1) The rule is applied: if the justification is inconsistent with the solution then discard solution. (2) The rule is not applied: if the rule is applicable w.r.t. the solution then discard solution:

$$Ext(D, W) = \begin{cases} \left\{ E_1 \middle| \begin{matrix} E_1 \in Ext(D, W \cup CON(\delta)) \\ E_1 \not\vdash \neg JUS(\delta) \end{matrix} \right\} \bigcup \left\{ E_2 \middle| \begin{matrix} E_2 \in Ext(D, W) \\ E_2 \vdash \neg JUS(\delta) \end{matrix} \right\} & \text{if } \begin{matrix} app(\{\delta\}, W) \\ \text{for some } \delta \in D \end{matrix} \\ \{W\} & \text{otherwise} \end{cases}$$

The definitions above can be generalised to allow non-network semi-normal theories without altering the basic algorithm. We do this by allowing the antecedent of an ordering to be a list of rules: eg. $[\delta_1, \ldots, \delta_n] \ll \delta$ if $W, CONS(\delta_1), \ldots, CONS(\delta_n) \vdash PRE(\delta)$. The only definition that becomes slightly complicated is that of *potential*:

Definition 5. D_1 is *potential* w.r.t. D_2 if, for each $\delta \in D_1$, one of the following is true:

- $[] \ll \delta$ or if $[\delta_1, \ldots, \delta_n] \ll \delta$ then, for all $\delta' \in \{\delta_1, \ldots, \delta_n\}$, $\delta' \notin D_2$
  and if $[\delta_1, \ldots, \delta_n] \underset{\sim}{\ll} \delta$ or $[\delta_1, \ldots, \delta_n] \diamond \delta$ then, for all $\delta' \in \{\delta_1, \ldots, \delta_n\}$, $\delta' \notin D_2$
- $[] \underset{\sim}{\ll} \delta$ or $[] \diamond \delta$
- not $[] \ll \delta$ **and** if $[\delta_1, \ldots, \delta_n] \ll \delta$ then $\{\delta_1, \ldots, \delta_n\} \not\subseteq D_1 \cup D_2$.

To extend the system to non-normal rules, the *disable* ordering must be changed: $[\delta_1, \ldots, \delta_n] \underset{\sim}{\ll} \delta$ if $W, CONS(\delta_1), \ldots, CONS(\delta_n) \vdash \neg JUS(\delta)$. This increases the number of orderings and, when applying *MNC* subsets, more rules need to be checked to ensure that justifications are consistent in the final extensions (see [Hop90]). There have been proposals for systems that use non-normal rules (e.g. the taxonomic default theories of Froidevaux [Fro86]) but for most applications semi-normal rules are sufficient.

4 Considerations of complexity

Kautz and Selman [KS89] divide the complexity of extension calculation of into three parts, the inherent complexity of W, checking the consistency of the justifications of rules and the underlying complexity of the algorithm. Hence they consider theories where W is a conjunction of literals, analogous to restricted network theories, reducing the logical complexity to membership tests and, in effect, just leaving the extension calculation algorithm. Etherington's algorithm will, for a finite propositional disjunction-free theory (ordered by his definition), find an extension in time $O(n^2)$ (n rules). Given our orderings, an extension can be found in $O(n)$ for a restricted ordered semi-normal network theory. When calculating all extensions the worst case is when every rule contradicts another potentially producing $2^{n/2}$ extensions with $2^{n/2} + 2^{n/2} - 2$ rule applications. This is improved upon by including disable orderings, which help to reduce the number of extensions when used to disambiguate the theory, the incremental addition of facts to a system, which allows incremental calculation of extensions [Hop90], and the discovery of mutually potential groups of rules which significantly reduces the number of rule applications.

The calculation of orderings for unrestricted network theories is $O(n^2)$ (because the default rules introduce at most two literals) and can be generalised by allowing default rules of the form $\frac{\alpha_1 \wedge ... \wedge \alpha_n : (\beta_1 \vee \beta_2) \wedge (\gamma_{1,1} \vee ... \vee \gamma_{1m}) \wedge (\gamma_{2,1} \vee ...) \wedge ...}{\beta_1 \vee \beta_2}$ whilst still maintaining polynomial time.

Of particular importance are those rules with a number of conjuncts in the antecedent and correspondingly a number of disjuncts in the exception part of the rule. Any further generalisation to allow more than two disjuncts in sentences in W will potentially become combinatorially explosive.

The calculation of potential sets of rules can be done in polynomial time by finding the transitive closure of the combined activate and disable orderings between groups of contradicting rules. If a potential subsets contain circularities then as the calculation proceeds they may well disappear; it may well be productive to recalculate the potential subsets for these sets of rules during the extension calculation. In an incremental system they can be calculated incrementally as well.

5 Variants on Reiter's Default Logic

Variants of default logic have been suggested to overcome particular problems that arise from the Reiter's original definition. We can calculate the extensions by simply changing the definitions of the orderings on default rules and leaving the algorithm unchanged. Lukaszewicz [Luk88] gives a semi-monotonic, constructive logic where a rule can only be applied if it is both applicable and the addition of its consequent to the extension maintains the consistency of the justifications of all previously applied rules; this has the effect of removing the priority between rules. This effect can be introduced by replacing the *disable* ordering with: $[\delta_1, \ldots, \delta_n] \diamond \delta$ if $W, CONS(\delta_1), \ldots, CONS(\delta_n) \vdash JUS(\delta)$

Poole [Poo88] and Brewka [Bre90] extend this by making generating defaults justifications mutually consistent: $[\delta_1, \ldots, \delta_n] \diamond \delta$ if $W, JUS(\delta_1), \ldots, JUS(\delta_n) \vdash JUS(\delta)$

Brewka then suggests that there is a filtering of extensions to reintroduce the priorites between rules; this can be imitated by keeping the last definition but not using the change used for Lukaszewicz's variant. This reintroduces the possibility of incoherent theories.

6 Conclusion

Of Junker and Konolige's [JK90] and Levy's [Lev91] algorithms for calculating extensions, Levy's is the closest to that described here. He calculates the equivalent of two orderings instead of three by merging the disable and contradiction orderings. They also differ in that they have as antecedents, not only the rules whose antecedents entail the attributes of the ordering required, but also all the rules that represent the minimal universe that supports these entailments. In contrast the algorithm presented in this paper is such that only universes are built and hence this extra attribute of the orderings is not required. One obvious advantage is when there are multiple universes that can support a given ordering, which will result, in Levy's case, in multiple orderings being calculated.

The advantages of this algorithm over Levy's include grouping potential rules which easily facilitates systems where multiple extensions are disambiguated to reduce the number of extensions. The application of a potential group of rules guarantees that no other rules in the theory can invalidate the rules applied in the partial extensions and therefore the disambiguation can be performed without having to calculate the complete extensions of the theory. Also, when calculating all extensions, if at any time two mutually potential groups of rules can be found, significant saving can be achieved by applying the two groups independently, taking the cross-union of the partial extensions.

In addition to this, the nature of the orderings gives some insight into the complexity of the underlying algorithm, and isolates this from the complexity of deduction in the underlying logic that is involved in defining the orderings.

The calculation of extensions for variants of default logic can be achieved by redefining the orderings on rules and leaving the basic algorithm unchanged.

In [Hop90] we show how an implementation and generalisation of inferential distance can be obtained by using the information encapsulated in the orderings allowing us to reason about rules in an abstract way, formalising the intuitive relation between default rules. The notions of hierarchy, specificity and incompatibility correspond directly to the activate, disable and contradict ordering respectively.

References

[Bre90] G. Brewka. Cumulative default logic: In defense of nonmonotonic inference rules (draft). GMD, Postfach 1240, D5205 Sankt Augustin 1, Fed. Rep. of Germany, 1990.

[Eth88] D. W. Etherington. *Reasoning with Incomplete Information*. Pitman, London, 1988.

[Fro86] C. Froidevaux. Taxonomic default theories. In *ECAI*, pages 123–129, 1986.

[Hop90] M. S. Hopkins. *The Implementation of a Plausible Inference System*. PhD thesis, Queen Mary and Westfield, University of London, 1990.

[JK90] U. Junker and K. Konolige. Computing the extensions of autoepistemic and default logics with a tms. In *AAAI–90*, pages 278–283, 1990.

[KS89] H. A. Kautz and B. Selman. Hard problems for simple default logics. In *Proc. 1st Int. Conf. on Principle of Knowledge Representation and Reasoning*, pages 189–197, Toronto, 1989.

[Lev91] F. Levy. Computing extensions of default theories. In *European Conference on Symbolic and Quantitative Approaches to Uncertainty*, pages 219–226, Marseille, 1991. Springer-Verlag. Lecture Notes in Computer Science 548.

[Luk88] W. Lukaszewicz. Considerations on default logic - an alternative approach. *Computational Intelligence*, 4:1–16, 1988.

[Poo88] D. Poole. A logical framework for default reasoning. *Artificial Intelligence*, 36:27–47, 1988.

[Rei80] R. Reiter. A logic for default reasoning. *Artificial Intelligence*, 13:81–132, 1980.

Learning Causal Polytrees *

Juan F. Huete and Luis M. de Campos

Dpto. de Ciencias de la Computacion e I.A.
Universidad de Granada
18071 - Granada, Spain

Abstract. The essence of causality can be identified with a graphical structure representing relevance relationships between variables. In this paper the problem of infering causal relations from patterns of dependence is considered. We suppose that there exists a causal model, which is representable by a polytree structure and present an approach to the recovering problem. With this approach we can recover efficiently a polytree structure using marginal and conditional independence tests.

1 Introduction

The notion of causality is central to the understanding of human reasoning. Humans, usually, model empirical phenomena as cause-effect relationships.This concept of causality, permits us to deal with reasoning problems efficiently, separating the relevant from the superfluous. In this paper the problem of infering causal relations from patterns of dependence is considered. In our approach, we suppose that true cause-effect relationships are represented as connected directed acyclic graphs (dags) where each node represents a variable in the domain and the parents of that node correspond to its direct causes. This causal scheme is hidden, but in some way we can test relevance relationships between variables in the domain, trying to recover the causal scheme.Constructing a graph in this manner reflects conditional independence that humans feel exist among causes and effects.

The relevance or irrelevance between two variables is viewed as a test of dependence or independence between the variables. Different formalisms give rise to different definitions of relevance. Note that we don't use any specific formalism to encode the causal schema, so that any formalism could be used.

We can find many works related to the problem of recovering a causal scheme under probabilistic formalism, [1, 2, 9] . In some cases, the relevance relations are obtained from a set of data [5], by a distance measure among variables [4, 8] or directly from experts judgments [11] .

In the next section we introduce the previous concepts neccesary to define a causal scheme. In section 3 we present some concepts that permit us to develop an algorithm which recover a polytree structure, that is, a singly connected dag, that represents the model. In the last section, some conclusions are presented.

* This work has been supported by the European Economic Community under Project Esprit III b.r.a. 6156 (DRUMS II)

2   Causal schemes

The causal scheme could be considered as a Dependence Model [9], namely a rule that assigns truth values to the predicates " X *is independent of* Y *given* Z " , denoted by $I(X \mid Z \mid Y)$, where $X, Y,$ and Z are disjoint subsets of variables in the model. That is, we can test if a subset Z of elements takes part on a relation among the elements in X and those in Y.

We shall restrict our discussion to singly connected causal structures, therefore any pair of nodes is connected via no more than one trail. In that path, we can find a tail to tail node x, $(\alpha \leftarrow x \rightarrow \beta)$ or a tail to head node x, $(\alpha \rightarrow x \rightarrow \beta)$ representing the fact that α and β are dependent variables, but become independent variables given x. On the other hand a head to head node x could be found, $(\alpha \rightarrow x \leftarrow \beta)$, which represents that α and β are independent variables, but become dependent when x is known.

The previous ideas of dependence or independence between nodes in a graphical structure, will be extended with the following definition [6], called d-separation by Pearl [9]

Definition 1. *d-separation:*

1. Let Z be a set of nodes in a dag. A trail t is active by Z if (a) every head to head node with respect to t either is in Z or has a descendent in Z and (b) every other node along t is outside Z. Otherwise, the trail is said to be blocked by Z.
2. Let D be a causal network and X, Z and T three disjoint sets of nodes. Then, X and Y are said to be graphically independent given Z if there exists no active trail by Z between any node in X and any node in Y. Otherwise, X and Y are graphically dependent given Z.

Let M be a causal scheme, we say that a dag is an Independence map (I-map) if every d-separation in the graph implies an Independence in M. On the other hand, a causal network is called a Dependence Map (D-map) if every independence relation in the model, implies a d-separation in the dag. A dag is a *perfect* map of the dependency model if it is both an I-map and a D-map, in that case, we say that the dependence model M is *dag-isomorph*.

3   Recovering Polytrees Structures

To deal with the recovering problem, we only consider those causal schemes M, that can be represented by a simple dag, that is, a structure where between any two nodes, there exists only one path. Following Pearl's notation [9], we call such structures polytrees because they can be viewed as a collection of several causal trees fused together at the nodes where arrows converge head to head $(\rightarrow x \leftarrow)$.

For a node x, we will denote by Λ_x the set of nodes $y \in M$ such that x and y are dependent (marginally). In a polytree structure T, two variables x, y

are dependent (marginally dependent) if there is no head to head node in the unique path connecting them, otherwise they are marginally independent.

Let x be a variable in M, and y, z two variables in Λ_x. By making Conditional Independence test, we can stablish if y lies in the path conecting x and z.

To solve the recovering problem, initially, we consider an empty structure T. This structure reflects, at any moment, the skeleton that could be obtained if we only consider those nodes belonging to T. In each step, a new node will be included in the structure, and making conditional independence tests, the final position of this node in T is found. The next definition helps us in this process.

Definition 2. Let T be a causal structure, and let x be any variable in T. A Sheaf structure for x, denoted by Ψ_x, is the set of variables in the structure which are connected directly to x; therefore, a Sheaf structure will include the direct causes and the direct effects of x in T.

The next theorem permits us to detect whether the inclusion of a new variable in the structure T will affect a Sheaf structure for a node x in T.

Theorem 3. *Let M be a causal scheme, let x be any variable in M represented by a node in T, and Ψ_x be a Sheaf structure for x. Let z be a variable in M, but not in T and z belonging to Λ_x. After including z in T, Ψ_x will be modified if and only if one of the following conditions holds*

1. $I(x \mid z \mid y) = True$ in M for some $y \in \Psi_x$.
2. $I(x \mid y \mid z) = False$ in M, for all $y \in \Psi_x$.

If the previous theorem does not hold, then the node z does not belong to the Sheaf structure for x. The following theorem gives us a method which, directing the search through the partial structure, permits to detect those variables whose Sheaf structure must be modified.

Theorem 4. *In the same conditions of the previous theorem, if the conditions of this theorem do not hold, then there exists one and only one node $y \in \Psi_x$ such that $I(x \mid y \mid z) = True$ in M.*

Theorem 5. *The conditions in Theorem 3 and Theorem 4 are not satisfied simultaneously.*

Now, we will see graphically, how a Sheaf structure for a node x will be affected when we insert a new variable z, with $z \in \Lambda_x$, in the structure T. Suppose that for a node x in T, the figure 1.a) represent the Sheaf structure for x. Firstly, when theorem 3 holds we know that the Sheaf structure for the node x will be modified by the inclusion of z in T. In this case, if condition one is verified, the set of nodes belonging to Ψ_x is divided in two subsets, one which includes those nodes y_i, with $i = 1, \ldots, j$ where $I(x \mid z \mid y_i)$ is true, and the other which includes those nodes v_k, with $k = 1, \ldots, l$ where $I(x \mid z \mid v_k)$ is false. For any variable $y_i \in \Psi_x$ such that $I(x \mid z \mid y_i)$ holds, we must add two new edges, one between x and z and the other between z and y_i, and remove the edge between x and y_i. With these changes, z is now in Ψ_x and the nodes $y_i \notin \Psi_x$. This represents the fact that if z is known the variables x and y_i become independent, (see fig. 1b). If the condition two from Theorem 3 is verified, and condition one does not hold, add a new edge between x and z which reflects the knowledge that x and z are related variables (remember that z belong to Λ_x) and none of the nodes in Ψ_x affects this relation. (see fig. 2b)

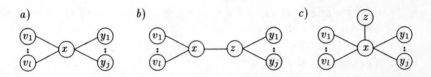

Fig. 1. a) Sheaf structure for x. b) Theorem 3.1 c) Theroem 3.2

When Theorem 4 holds, let $\Psi_x = \{v_1, \ldots, v_l, y\}$ and let y be the variable that makes true the relation $I(x \mid y \mid z)$. Then we know that y is in the path connecting x and z, and therefore our original problem can be solved by studying whether z belongs to the Sheaf structure for y (Ψ_y). (see fig. 2)

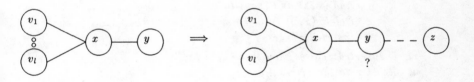

Fig. 2. Theorem4 holds

As we said, our algorithm starts with an empty structure T, and then a variable x is selected, finding those variables that are dependent with x, Λ_x. Then, we construct a structure T which includes x and the variables in Λ_x. In the following steps, select a new variable y from the structure T, find Λ_y, and for any $z \in \Lambda_y$ such that $z \notin T$ try to insert z in T. Note that, in the path between y and z, there are no head to head nodes; then, we could apply the previous theorems. Repeat this step until all the variables are in T.

The algorithm constructs a polytree structure representing a causal scheme in $O(n^2)$ steps, with n representing the number of variables in the scheme. Note that we only make marginal and first order conditional independence tests. With this algorithm, we can construct efficiently the skeleton of a polytree, but we do not mention how to recover the directionality of the arcs. We only could recover

Algorithm

1. *For each variable x in M Initialize Λ_x*
   Visited[x]=False ; Expand[x]=False
   For each variable y in M, such $x \neq y$
   If $I(x, y) =$ False Then Add y to Λ_x
2. *Select a node x from M, assign x to T; Expand[x]=True*
3. *While there exist non visited nodes in T*
   (a) *Select a non visited node x from T; Visited[x]= True*
   (b) *While there exist non expanded nodes in Λ_x, select a non expanded node z from Λ_x, new node to insert in T*
      i. *Expand[z]=True*
      ii. *Forward=True*
      iii. *Inserted=False*
      iv. *While Forward=True do*
         If all $y \in \Psi_x$ are tested
            Then Forward=False
            Else
               Select a new y in Ψ_x
               If $(x \mid y \mid z) =$ True
               Then $x = y$
      v. *For every y in Ψ_x do*
         If $(x \mid z \mid y) =$ True
            Add (x, z) and (z, y) to T
            Delete (x, y) from T
            Inserted=True
      vi. *If Inserted=False Then Add (x, z) to T*
      vii. *Reset x to the original value*

some oriented arcs, those where a head to head node is present, but we are free to choose the orientation of some set of nodes, those where a path $(x \leftarrow z \leftarrow y)$, $(x \leftarrow z \rightarrow y)$ or $(x \rightarrow z \rightarrow y)$ is present, as long as we do not introduce head to head patterns. These three orientations are indistinguishable, as they represent the same independence relationships. To recover the head to head orientation $(x \rightarrow z \leftarrow y)$ we could use the following test: " If two variables x and y are marginally independent and, given z, they become conditionally dependent, then the structure is oriented with a head to head arc".

4 Concluding Remarks

Learning algorithms, usually, need high order independence tests involving a great number of variables, such as $I(x \mid U - x, y \mid y)$, with U representing the set of variables in the causal scheme, and use a exponential number of independence relations. There are some algorithms [6, 7] which are polynomial in the number of independence verifications that recover simple structures. Chow and Liu [4] proposed a different approach to recover tree structures, in which a dependence measure among variables is used. The algorithm works under probabilistic formalism, recovering a tree structure in $O(n^2)$ steps and was extended by Rebane and Pearl [10] to recover polytrees. In this paper a learning algorithm which recover simple structures, in order $O(n^2)$, such as trees and polytrees, is given. The input to the algorithm can be obtained either from empirical data or from expert judgments. In future works we will try to extend the algorithm to structures where some kind of cycles are allowed, such as simple dags.

On the other hand, we are interested in learning causal structures from a dependence model where independence relationships are based on any formalism for uncertainty, as probability theory, Dempster-Shafer's theory, upper and lower probabilitites,...[3]. With these formalisms, testing for independence relationships may be expensive, so we are interested in doing only first order independence tests.

References

1. Acid S., Campos L.M. de, González A. Molina R., Pérez de la Blanca N.: Learning with CASTLE, in Symbolic and Quantitative approaches to Uncertainty. Lecture Notes in Computer Science **584**, R. Kruse R., Siegel P. (Eds). Springer Verlag,(1991) 99-106.
2. Acid S., Campos L.M. de, González A. Molina R., Pérez de la Blanca N.: CASTLE: A tool for bayesian learning. Proceedings of the ESPRIT 91 Conference, Commission of the European Communities, (1991) 363-377.
3. Campos L.M.de, Huete J.: Independence concepts in Upper and Lower probabilities. Proceedings of the Fourth IPMU Conference, (1992) 129-132.
4. Chow C.K., Liu C.N.: Approximating discrete probability distribution with dependence trees. IEEE Transactions on Information Theory **14**, (1968) 462-467.
5. Cooper G., Herskovits E.: A bayesian method for the induction of Probabilistic Networks from data. Machine Learning **9**, (1992) 309-347.
6. Geiger D., Paz A., Pearl J.: Learning causal trees from Dependence information. Proceedings of the Eighth National Conference on A.I. (1990) 770-776.
7. Geiger D., Paz A., Pearl J.: Learning Simple Causal Structures International Journal of Intelligent Systems, Vol **8**, (1993) 231-247.
8. Herskovits E., Cooper G.: KUTATO: An Entropy-Driven system for construction of probabilistic expert systems from Databases. Proceedings of the 6th Conference on Uncertainty in Artificial Intelligence, Cambridge MA. (1990) 54-62.
9. Pearl J.: Probabilistic Reasoning in intelligent systems: Networks of plausible inference. Morgan and Kaufman, San Mateo (1988).
10. Rebane G., Pearl J.: The recovery of causal poly-trees from statistical data, Uncertainty in Artificial Intelligence 3, Kanal L.N., Levitt T.S. and Lemmer J.F. Eds. North-Holland. (1989) 175-182.
11. Srinivas S., Russell S., Agogino A.: Automated construction of sparse Bayesian networks from unstructured probabilistic models and domain information. Uncertainty in Artificial Intelligence 5, Henrion M., Shachter R.D., Kanal L.N., Lemmer J.F. (Eds), North-Holland, Amsterdam. (1990) 295-308.

Symbolic Evidence, Arguments, Supports and Valuation Networks *)

Jürg Kohlas

Institute for Informatics, University of Fribourg
CH-1700 Fribourg (Switzerland)

Abstract. Starting from assumption-based propositional knowledge bases, symbolic evidence theory is developed. It is shown to be the qualitative equivalent of the well known numerical evidence theory (Dempster-Shafer theory). In particular it is shown how symbolic evidence fits into the framework of the axiomatic theory of valuation nets of Shenoy, Shafer (1990). This leads then to a local combination scheme for propagating symbolic arguments and supports similar to the methods of propagating probability or belief functions.

1. Assumption-Based Knowledge

Uncertain knowledge can be represented as logical formulas depending on certain assumptions representing uncertain propositions for which it is open wether they are true or not. Hypotheses can then be analyzed in terms of these assumptions, that is, it can be determined under which assumptions a hypothesis would be true. Those assumptions represent arguments or supports for the hypothesis, in the sense-that, if the assumptions are accepted, then the hypothesis must be true.

Let's illustrate this by a simple example describing an alarm system protecting against burglary. The following symbols represent propositions

a : the alarm is ringing
b : there is a burglary
e : an earthquake has occured
c : there is confirmation of an earthquake

In addition, a number of extra propositions, called **assumptions**, are introduced:

a_1 : the alarm system is functioning
a_2 : an extra cause for an alarm is present
a_6 : the earthquake sensor is sensitive.

---

*) *Research supported by grants No. 21-30186.90 and 21-32660.91 of the Swiss National Foundation for Research, Esprit Basic Research Activity Project DRUMSII (Defeasible Reasoning and Uncertainty Management)*

The following clauses describe the knowledge relating alarm, earthquake and burglary:

$$R_1 : \neg b \vee \neg a_1 \vee a \qquad R_2 : \neg e \vee \neg a_1 \vee a$$
$$R_3 : \neg a_2 \vee a \qquad\qquad R_4 : b \vee e \vee a_2 \vee \neg a$$
$$R_{13} : \neg e \vee \neg a_6 \vee c \qquad R_{14} : e \vee \neg c$$

R_1 for example states that if there is a burglary (b) and the alarm system is functioning (a_1), then there is an alarm (a). Suppose now that there is a simple clause a to be added as a further fact to this small knowledge base, stating that there is an alarm. Assuming that there is no extra cause for an alarm ($\neg a_2$), it follows from R_4 that there must be either a burglary or an earthquake ($b \vee e$). Suppose that the further fact, that there is no confirmation of an earthquake ($\neg c$) is given and assume that the earthquake sensor is sensitive (a_6), then it follows from R_{13} that there is no earthquake ($\neg e$) and hence finally that there must be a burglary. This conclusion is derived under the assumptions $\neg a_2$ and a_6.

This illustrates the kind of assumption based reasoning which is studied in this paper. Given a set of propositional symbols A, representing assumptions, a set of propositional symbols P and a set Σ of clauses over $A \cup P$ representing the available knowledge and facts, one may ask under which assumptions a hypothesis, represented by a propositional formula h, can be derived and thus proved to be true. All assumptions under which this is possible form the **support** of hypothesis h. If furthermore it is possible to weight the assumption with probabilities, the degree of support, that is, the reliability or the probability of provability of h can be computed (see Kohlas, Monney, 1993). This links assumption based truth maintenance (ATMS) to evidence theory (Dempster-Shafer theory), as is well known (Laskey, Lehner, 1989; Provan, 1990).

The probabilities of assumptions may however not be well known or not known altogether. Yet it would still be interesting to determine the supports of h in view of a qualitative, if not quantitative judgment of the likelihood of a hypothesis h. The development of this idea leads to a qualitative evidence theory instead of a numerical one. It will be shown here, that this qualitative evidence theory is entirely analogous to the well known numerical theory of evidence. The qualitative or symbolic support of hypotheses h correspond to the support (or belief) function and symbolic supports may be combined by a qualitative version of Dempster's rule. Indeed qualitative supports or arguments may be taken as valuations in the sense of valuation nets (Shenoy, Shafer, 1990) and thus propagated using local combinations.

The interest of this approach is twofold: First it leads to new computational approaches in assumption-based knowledge bases. The usual methods in this domain use resolution (see Kohlas, Monney, 1993). Although resolution is an efficient way of logical analysis making use of local combinations, the method fails to take into account the same kind of locality as propagation in valuation nets. Hence it is interesting to compare the two approaches. Also, once the symbolic supports are known, it is easy to compute degrees of support with varying probabilities of assumptions or to make sensitivity analysis relative to these probabilities. Second, this symbolic theory of evidence, although presented here in a finite setting of propositional logic, potentially could lead to a much more general axiomatic approach to evidence theory. This aspect however is yet to be explored.

2. Symbolic Knowledge, Arguments and Support

Before entering into the discussion of the basic model of knowledge considered in this paper, let's first summarize some elements of propositional logic as used in the sequel (for more details see for example Chang, Lee, 1973). If P is a set of propositional symbols, then $\mathcal{L}_P$ denotes the set of all well-formed propositional formulas using symbols from P, the propositional language over P. At the same time $B_P = \{0,1\}^{|P|}$ is the Boolean cube of all possible interpretations (assignments of truth values 0 or 1 to the propositional symbols) of formulas in $\mathcal{L}_P$. Note that if $Q \subseteq P$, then $\mathcal{L}_Q \subseteq \mathcal{L}_P$ and $B_P = B_Q \times B_{P-Q}$. If $h \in \mathcal{L}_P$, then $N(h) \subseteq B_P$ denotes the set of all interpretations for which h is true. If h is used as a statement (for example as part of a knowledge base), then this means that the possible common truth values of the propositions in P are restricted to the set $N(h)$. Two formulas h' and h'' are equivalent, written $h' = h''$, if they are true for exactly the same interpretations, that is, if $N(h') = N(h)$. Thus, every subset N in B_P determines a class of equivalent formulas h, such that $N(h) = N$ for any h of the class.

A formula f is a logical consequence of g, written $g \models f$, if $N(g) \subseteq N(f)$. A conjunction c of literals is called a prime implicant of f, if $c \models f$ and for no subconjunction $c' \subset c$ we have $c' \models f$. Any formula f is equivalent to the disjunction of its prime implicants, $f = \vee \{c : c \text{ is prime implicant for } f\}$. This latter formula is called the disjunctive normal form for f. It can be used to represent the equivalence class of f.

Now let A, P and Σ define an assumption-based knowledge base, where A is a set of propositional symbols called assumptions, P another disjoint set of propositional symbols and Σ a set $\{\xi_1, \xi_2, \ldots, \xi_m\}$ of clauses over $A + P$. Let $\xi = \xi_1 \wedge \xi_2 \ldots \wedge \xi_m$. We are interested in certain hypotheses h, expressed as well formed formulas in $\mathcal{L}_{P+A}$. What can we learn about the possible truth of h from Σ? If some assumptions can be assumed to be true, then h can possibly be deduced from Σ. So we may ask, under which assumptions h can be deduced from Σ. The more reasonable these assumptions, the more likely is the truth of h. This may be quantified by imposing probabilities on the assumptions and computing the probability that h can in fact be deduced from Σ (see Kohlas, Monney, 1993).

In view of these remarks consider **conjunctions** $a \in \mathcal{L}_A$ such that

$$(1) \quad a, \Sigma \models h.$$
$$(2) \quad a, \Sigma \not\models \circ \qquad\qquad (2.1)$$

(o denotes the falsity). Such conjunctions are called **support sets** of h relative to Σ (see also Reiter, DeKleer 1987). Conjunctions a, for which the system of clauses a, Σ is not satisfiable (for which condition (2) of (2.1) does not hold) are called **contradiction sets** relative to Σ, because they represent sets of assumptions which contradict the knowledge coded in Σ. Support sets a for h such that no subset is also a support set are called minimal support sets for h, similarly, contradiction sets a, such that no subset is still a contradiction set, are called minimal contradictions. The disjunctive formula

$$sp(h, \Sigma) = \vee \; \{a : a \text{ is a minimal support set of } h \text{ relative to } \Sigma\} \qquad (2.2)$$

is called the **support** of h relative to Σ and the disjunctive formula

$$sp(o, \Sigma) = \vee \; \{a : a \text{ is a minimal contradiction set relative to } \Sigma\} \qquad (2.3)$$

is called the **contradiction** relative to Σ.

We shall show that the support is analogous to numerical support (or belief) functions in evidence theory (Shafer, 1976). This leads then to a symbolic form of evidence theory; and if probabilities are imposed on the assumptions, it can be shown, that this symbolic evidence theory leads in fact to the usual numeric form of evidence theory. For the time being we fix Σ and omit reference to it in the formulas.

Define

$$pl(h) = \neg sp(\neg h). \qquad (2.4)$$

This represents the assumptions which do not permit to deduce $\neg h$, for which therefore h - even if not deducible - remains possible. Therefore $pl(h)$ is called the **possibility** of h (relative to Σ). It corresponds to the plausibility function of numerical evidence theory. Then we have

Theorem 2.1

(The proofs of the theorems are omitted here; they are given in the full paper (Kohlas, 1993) available from the author).

(1) Let $h_i, i = 1, \ldots, n; \; n \geq 1$ be formulas such that $h_i \models h$. Then

$$\wedge_{i=1}^{n} sp(h_i) = sp(\wedge_{i=1}^{n} h_i), \vee_{i=1}^{n} sp(h_i) \models sp(h) \qquad (2.5)$$

(2) Let $h_i, i = 1, \ldots, n; \; n \geq 1$ be formulas such that $h \models h_i$. Then

$$\vee_{i=1}^{n} pl(h_i) = pl(\vee_{i=1}^{n} h_i), pl(h) \models \wedge_{i=1}^{n} pl(h_i) \qquad (2.6)$$

This corresponds to the basic property of numerical support functions to be monotone Choquet capacities and for the numerical plausibility functions to be alternating Choquet capacities (Shafer, 1979).

Next, let Q be any finite set of propositional symbols (not necessarily contained in $A + P$) and define for any $h \in \mathcal{L}_Q$

$$m_Q(h) = sp(h) \wedge (\neg \vee \ \{sp(h') : h' \in \mathcal{L}_Q, h' \models h, h' \neq h\}. \tag{2.7}$$

This represents the assumptions which prove h, but nothing more precise than h within the language $\mathcal{L}_Q$; it corresponds to the basic probability assignment of numerical evidence theory. Therefore $m_Q(h)$ is called the **basic argument** for h relative to the language $\mathcal{L}_Q$ (and implicitly also relative to the knowledge base Σ, a reference we neglect for the moment, given that Σ is fixed). Note that $m_Q(h)$ may be $\circ$ for some h. The formulas h, for which $m_Q(h)$ is different from $\circ$ are called **focal** formulas. $m_Q(\circ) = sp(\circ)$ is the contradiction. The analogy to the basic probability assignment is underlined by the following two theorems:

Theorem 2.2

(1) If $h_1, h_2 \in \mathcal{L}_Q$, $h_1 \neq h_2$, then

$$m_Q(h_1) \wedge m_Q(h_2) = \circ. \tag{2.8}$$

(2)

$$\sum \{m_Q(h) : h \in \mathcal{L}_Q\} = T \tag{2.9}$$

(T denotes the tautology)

Note that the disjoint union is written as a sum (Σ).

Theorem 2.3 For any $h \in \mathcal{L}_Q$, $h \neq \circ$,

$$sp(h) = \sum \{m_Q(h') : h' \in \mathcal{L}_Q, h' \models h, h' \neq \circ\}. \tag{2.10}$$

$$pl(h) = \sum \{m_Q(h') : h' \in \mathcal{L}_Q, h' \wedge h \neq \circ\}. \tag{2.11}$$

(In theorems like this and the following ones, it is understood that the summation is taken over classes of equivalent formulas h').

Like in numerical evidence theory the support is the sum of the basic arguments which imply h and the possibility is the sum of the basic arguments which do not imply the negation of h or, equivalently, which do not contradict h. Note that we have defined m above in terms of sp. Here it is shown, how to obtain sp and pl from m. These transformations correspond to the Möbius transforms in numerical evidence theory. It is important to remark that m, sp and pl are equivalent representations and surrogates for the information contained in the assumption-based knowledge base Σ.

3. Projection and Extension

Suppose first that Q is a set of propositional symbols containing $A + P$. Then the next theorems shows that it is sufficient to know m_{A+P} in order to determine m_Q:

Theorem 3.1 If $Q \supseteq A+P$ and $h \in \mathcal{L}_{A+P}$, then $m_Q(h) = m_{A+P}(h)$. If $h \in \mathcal{L}_Q$, but $h \notin \mathcal{L}_{A+P}$, then $m_Q(h) = \mathrm{o}$.

This is called the **extension** theorem, it shows that the basic arguments are possibly non empty only for formulas from $\mathcal{L}_{A+P}$, but empty for statements (formulas) which can not be expressed (discerned) within $\mathcal{L}_{A+P}$. This theorem corresponds to the operation of vacuous extension defined in the numerical evidence theory (Shafer, 1976).

More interesting is the case of a $Q \subseteq A + P$. We have first to define the notion of projection of a formula in $\mathcal{L}_Q$ to $\mathcal{L}_{Q'}$, when $Q' \subseteq Q$. Any $h \in \mathcal{L}_Q$ can be expressed in disjunctive normal form. Its projection $proj'_Q(h)$ to $\mathcal{L}_{Q'}$ is obtained by eliminating all literals in the disjunctive normal form of h belonging to $Q - Q'$. Now, the next theorem tells how to pass from m_{A+P} to m_Q.

Theorem 3.2 If $Q \subseteq A + P$ and $h \in \mathcal{L}_Q$, then

$$m_Q(h) = \sum \{m_{A+P}(h') : h' \in \mathcal{L}_{A+P}, proj_Q(h') = h\}. \qquad (2.12)$$

This is called the **projection** or **marginalization** theorem. It will play an important role in the computational analysis of symbolic evidence theory in section 5.

4. Combining Knowledge

Up to now an assumption-based knowledge base A, P, Σ was fixed. But now we suppose that we dispose of two distinct assumption-based knowledge bases A_1, P_1, Σ_1 and A_2, P_2, Σ_2, which may by combined into a new assumption-based knowledge base $A = A_1 \cup A_2, P = P_1 \cup P_2, \Sigma = \Sigma_1 + \Sigma_2$. It will be interesting to see how basic arguments, supports and possibilities relative to the combined knowledge base can be obtained from basic arguments, supports and possibilities relative to the two factors constituting the combined base. In fact, these results will be used in section 5 in the inverse way, that is, it will be studied how a given assumption based knowledge base can be decomposed such that the basic arguments or supports or plausibilities can be determined relative to factor bases and then used to obtain the corresponding elements by combination.

The next theorem shows how to combine basic arguments:

Theorem 4.1 For any $h \in \mathcal{L}_{A+P}$

$$m_{A+P}(h, \Sigma) = \sum \{m_{A_1+P_1}(h_1, \Sigma_1) \wedge m_{A_2+P_2}(h_2, \Sigma_2)$$
$$: h_i \in \mathcal{L}_{A_i+P_i}, h_1 \wedge h_2 = h\}. \qquad (4.1)$$

This is a symbolic form of Dempster's rule. Note that this formula applies also to the determination of contradictions, that is to $m_{A+P}(\mathrm{o})$. By theorem 2.3, once m_{A+P} is known, the support and the possibility relative to the combined knowledge base can be derived. But there is also a direct way to obtain the support:

Theorem 4.2 For any $h \in \mathcal{L}_{A+P}$

$$sp(h, \Sigma) = \vee \{sp(h_1, \Sigma_1) \wedge sp(h_2, \Sigma_2) : h_i \in \mathcal{L}_{A_i+P_i}, h_1 \wedge h_2 \models h, h_1 \wedge h_2 \neq o\}.$$
(4.2)

5. Propagation of Basic Arguments and Valuations

Given an assumption-based knowledge base $A, P, \Sigma = \{\xi_1, \ldots, \xi_n\}$ the basic arguments relative to Σ can be computed iteratively using theorem 4.1 from $m(\cdot, \Sigma_i)$ and $m(\cdot, \{\xi_{i+1}\})$, where $\Sigma_i = \{\xi_1, \ldots, \xi_i\}$, for $i = 1, \ldots, n-1$. The basic arguments relative to $A + P$ for a single clause $x = \alpha_1 \vee \ldots \vee \alpha_r \vee \beta_1 \vee \ldots \vee \beta_s$, where the α_i are literals of assumptions and the β_j are literals of propositions out of P, is simple to determine: $\neg\alpha_1 \wedge \ldots \wedge \neg\alpha_r$ is the basic argument for the focal formula $(\neg\alpha_1 \wedge \ldots \wedge \neg\alpha_r) \wedge (\beta_1 \vee \ldots \vee \beta_s)$ and α_i is the basic argument for α_i itself and these are the only focal formulas. This way to compute the basic arguments is however in most cases too expensive. There are alternative methods based on resolution which permit to obtain supports relative to a knowledge base (Kohlas, Monney, 1993). All these methods however fail to take advantage of certain topological structures which may be inherent in an assumption-based knowledge base A, P, Σ.

In this section the approach of symbolic evidence theory will be placed into the framework of the abstract theory of valuation nets introduced by Shenoy, Shafer (1990). This theory allows for local combinations of basic arguments (or alternatively supports). And this locality of combination may reduce considerably the computational effort necessary to compute supports or possibilities for certain hypotheses. The following development follows Shenoy, Shafer (1990).

Let Q be any set of propositional symbols and $m_Q(h) \in \mathcal{L}_A$ for all $h \in \mathcal{L}_Q$ formulas defined over some set of assumptional symbols A such that the conditions of theorem 2.2 are satisfied:

$$(1)\ m_Q(h_1) \wedge m_Q(h_2) = o \text{ whenever } h_1 \neq h_2$$
$$(2)\ \sum \{m_Q(h) : h \in \mathcal{L}_Q\} = T.$$
(5.1)

Such a m_Q is called, in view of the axiomatic theory of Shenoy, Shafer (1990), a (symbolic) **valuation** of the set of propositional symbols Q. The valuation is called proper, if m_Q is different from o for at least one $h \neq o$. Given an assumption-based knowledge base A, P, Σ, then $m_Q(h, \Sigma)$ is such a valuation of Q according to theorem 2.2.

In extension of (2.12) and (4.1) we define the operations of marginalization (projection) and combination for valuations m_Q as follows: If $Q' \subseteq Q$, then for any $h \in \mathcal{L}_{Q'}$

$$m_{Q \downarrow Q'}(h) = \sum \{m_Q(h') : h' \in \mathcal{L}_Q, proj_{Q'}(h') = h\}$$
(5.2)

and $m_{Q \downarrow Q'}$ is a valuation of Q', called the **marginalization** of m_Q to Q'. If $Q' \not\subseteq Q$, then $m_{A \downarrow Q'}$ represents the extension of $m_{Q \downarrow Q \cap Q'}$ to Q', that is $m_{Q \downarrow Q'}(h) = m_{Q \downarrow Q \cap Q'}(h)$ for all $h \in \mathcal{L}_{Q \cap Q'}$ and $m_{Q \downarrow Q'}(h) = \circ$ for $h \in \mathcal{L}'_Q$ but not in $\mathcal{L}_{Q \cap Q'}$. Furthermore, for two valuations $m_{Q'}$ and $m_{Q''}$, define for any $h \in \mathcal{L}_{Q' \cup Q''}$

$$m_{Q'} \oplus m_{Q''}(h) = \sum \{m_{Q'}(h') \wedge m_{Q''}(h'') : h' \in \mathcal{L}_{Q'}, h'' \in \mathcal{L}_{Q''}, h' \wedge h'' = h\}.$$
(5.3)

where $m_{Q'} \oplus m_{Q''}$ is a valuation of $Q' \cup Q''$, called the **combination** of $m_{Q'}$ and $m_{Q''}$. The combination is called possible, if $m_{Q'} \oplus m_{Q''}$ is a proper valuation.

These operations enjoy the following basic properties:

Theorem 5.1
(1) Commutativity and associativity of combination: $m_R \oplus m_S = m_S \oplus m_R$, and $(m_R \oplus m_S) \oplus m_T = m_R \oplus (m_S \oplus m_T)$.
(2) Consonance of marginalization: If $R \subseteq S \subseteq T$, then $m_{T \downarrow R} = m_{(T \downarrow S) \downarrow R}$.
(3) Distributivity of marginalization over combination: $(m_R \oplus m_S)_{R \cup S \downarrow R} = m_R \oplus m_{S \downarrow R \cap S}$.

This theorem states that the axioms which Shenoy, Shafer (1990) impose on the valuations they consider in an abstract setting, are satisfied in this particular case. Symbolic evidence theory is thus an instance (a model) of the abstract theory of valuation nets.

If Q is any set of propositional symbols, and $\mathcal{H} = \{Q_i : i = 1, \dots, r\}$ a family of subsets of Q, then $\mathcal{H}$ is called a **hypergraph**; the elements of Q are called vertices of the hypergraph and the sets Q_i its hyperedges. Suppose b and t are distinct hyperedges in the hypergraph $\mathcal{H}$, $t \cap b \neq \emptyset$, and b contains every vertex of t that is contained in a hyperedge other than t, then t is called a **twig** of $\mathcal{H}$ and b a **branch** for t. If there is an ordering of the hyperedges of $\mathcal{H}$, say $Q_1, Q_2, \dots, Q_r$, such that Q_k is a twig in the hypergraph $\{Q_1, Q_2, \dots, Q_k\}$, then $\mathcal{H}$ is called a **hypertree** and the ordering of hyperedges a **hypertree construction sequence**.

If $\mathcal{H} = \{Q_i : i = 1, \dots, r\}$ is a hypergraph on Q, and m_Q and m_{Q_i}, $i = 1, 2, \dots, r$ valuations of the sets Q and Q_i, such that $m_Q = \oplus_{i=1}^r m_{Q_i}$, then we say that m_Q factorizes on $\mathcal{H}$. Consider the following theorem:

Theorem 5.2 (Shenoy, Shafer, 1990). Suppose $\mathcal{H}$ is a hypergraph on a set Q, m_H a valuation for each $H \in \mathcal{H}$, and $m_Q = \oplus \{m_H : H \in \mathcal{H}\}$ a factorization of m_Q on $\mathcal{H}$. If t is a twig in $\mathcal{H}$, b a branch for t, and $Q' = Q - \{t \cap b\}$ then

$$m_{Q \downarrow Q'} = (m_b \oplus m_{t \downarrow t \cap b}) \oplus (\oplus \{m_H : H \in \mathcal{H} - \{t, b\}\}).$$
(5.4)

This theorem shows that a twig can be eliminated in a hypergraph such that the marginal of the valuation relative to the remaining propositions factorizes on the remaining hypergraph. This result is especially interesting for hypertrees, because in this case a sequence of twigs can be eliminated in the reverse order of the hypertree construction sequence such that finally the marginal of m_Q relative to the last hyperedge in the sequence is obtained. This procedure uses only **local combinations** on the branches b corresponding to the twigs t (compare with (5.4)). Therefore, this may be an efficient procedure to compute the marginal of some factorized valuation.

Let us now apply these results to the computation of basic arguments relative to a given assumption-based knowledge base A, P, Σ. Let Q' be any set of propositional symbols, possibly containing also assumptions. In order to compute $m_{Q'}(\cdot, \Sigma)$ by the above procedure, a factorization of $m_Q(\cdot, \Sigma) = \oplus_{i=1}^r m_{Q_i}(\cdot, \Sigma_i)$ over some hypertree $\mathcal{H} = \{Q_1, \ldots, Q_r\}$ on Q has to be found, such that the Σ_i form a partition of Σ, $\cup_{i=1}^r Q_i = Q$ and $Q' \subseteq Q_1$. Then $m_{Q \downarrow Q_1}(\cdot, \Sigma) = m_{Q_1}(\cdot, \Sigma)$ can be found using local computations on the branches of the twigs of the hypertree only and finally $m_{Q'} = m_{(Q \downarrow Q_1) \downarrow Q'} = m_{Q_1 \downarrow Q'}$ can be obtained by marginalization from m_{Q_1}. The main question is then how to obtain such factorizations.

The general method is as follows: Consider any decomposition $\{\Sigma_i : i = 1, \ldots, r\}$ of Σ and let $A_i \subseteq A$ and $P_i \subseteq P$ denote the sets of assumptions and propositions appearing in the clauses of Σ_i. If $Q' \subseteq A_1 + P_1$ and $\mathcal{H} = \{A_i + P_i : i = 1, \ldots, r\}$ is a hypertree (in this case there is always a hypertree construction sequence starting with $A_1 + P_1$), then the factorization $m_{A+P}(\cdot, \Sigma) = \oplus_{i=1}^r m_{A_i + P_i}(\cdot, \Sigma_i)$ holds and the above method applies. If $\mathcal{H}$ is not a hypertree, then it may be possible to select sets $Q_j \supseteq A_i + P_i$, such that $\mathcal{H}' = \{Q_j : j = 1, \ldots, s\}$ is a hypertree. In this case, if $Q = \cup_{j=1}^s Q_j$ and $\Sigma_j' = \sum \{\Sigma_i : A_i + P_i \subseteq Q_j\}$, the factorization $m_Q(\cdot, \Sigma) = \oplus_{j=1}^s m_{Q_j}(\cdot, \Sigma_j')$ holds and the above procedure applies to this factorization. Note furthermore that $m_{Q_j}(\cdot, \Sigma_j') = \oplus \{m_{A_i + P_i}(\cdot, \Sigma_i) : A_i + P_i \subseteq Q_j\}$.

$\mathcal{H}'$ is called a covering hypertree of $\mathcal{H}$. Although $\{A+P\}$ is a trivial covering hypertree of $\mathcal{H}$, it is a difficult problem to find a good covering hypertree. This problem is discussed by Rose (1970), Bertele and Brioschi (1972), Tarjan and Yannakakis (1984), Kong (1986), Amborg et al (1987), Mellouli (1987), Zhang (1988) and Almond and Kong (1991).

A natural decomposition of Σ is the one with $\Sigma_i = \{\xi_i\}$ and one may look for covering hypertrees with respect to this decomposition. However there are sometimes other ways to obtain factorizations than the one just described. The following theorem may be useful for this purpose:

Theorem 5.3 Let A_1, P_1, Σ_1 and A_2, P_2, Σ_2 be two assumption-based knowledge bases and Q a set of propositional symbols such that $(A_1 + P_1) \cap (A_2 + P_2) \subseteq Q$. Let furthermore $m'_{A_1 + P_1}(\cdot) = m_{A_1 + P_1}(\cdot, \Sigma_1)$ and $m''_{A_2 + P_2}(\cdot) = m_{A_2 + P_2}(\cdot, \Sigma_2)$ and $m_Q(\cdot) = m_Q(\cdot, \Sigma)$. Then

$$m_Q = m_{A_1 + P_1' \downarrow Q \cap (A_1 + P_1)} \oplus m_{A_2 + P_2'' \downarrow Q \cap (A_2 + P_2)}. \tag{5.5}$$

This theorem says that, under certain conditions, basic arguments may be combined without fault on smaller sets than $(A_1 + P_1) \cup (A_2 + P_2)$ in order to obtain certain projections of the combined basic arguments. As an application suppose that there is a decomposition $\{\Sigma_i : i = 1, \ldots, r\}$ of Σ such that the A_i are mutually disjoint. Then $\cap_{i=1}^{r}(A_i + P_i) \subseteq P$ and hence according to theorem 5.3

$$m_P(\cdot, \Sigma) = \oplus_{i=1}^{r} m_{P_i}(\cdot, \Sigma_i) \qquad (5.6)$$

which is a factorization on the hypergraph $\{P_i : i = 1, \ldots, r\}$.

The following example serves to illustrate this approach: Consider the following system Σ of clauses (its is an extension of the example given in section 1, see also Kohlas, Monney, 1993):

$$
\begin{array}{ll}
R_1 : \ \neg b \vee \neg a_1 \vee a & R_8 : \ \neg a \vee a_4 \vee g \\
R_2 : \ \neg e \vee \neg a_1 \vee a & R_9 : \ \neg a_4 \vee \neg g \\
R_3 : \ \neg a_2 \vee a & R_{10} : \ a \vee \neg g \\
R_4 : \ b \vee e \vee a_2 \vee \neg a & R_{11} : \ \neg a \vee \neg a_5 \vee d \\
R_5 : \ \neg a \vee w & R_{12} : \ a_5 \vee \neg d \\
R_6 : \ \neg a_3 \vee w & R_{13} : \ \neg e \vee \neg a_6 \vee c \\
R_7 : \ a \vee a_3 \vee \neg w & R_{14} : \ e \vee \neg c
\end{array}
$$

Let's decompose Σ into the following groups of clauses: R1-R4, R5-R7, R8-R10, R11-R12 and R13-R14. Note first, that these groups of rules contain mutually disjoint sets of assumptions, such that the condition of the above discussed special case is fulfilled. Fig. 5.1 shows the hypergraph whose hyperedges are the sets of propositions P_i corresponding to these groups of clauses. It is easily seen, that this hypergraph is in fact a hypertree, for example with a hypertree construction sequence $\{\{a, b, \}, \{e, c\}, \{a, d\}, \{a, g\}, \{a, w\}\}$. Hence, if for example the basic arguments relative to $\{b\}$ are to be computed, then this hypertree construction sequence can be used for local combinations as described above.

In order to actually implement this procedure, the operations of marginalisation and combination must be coded. For this purpose a particular representation of the valuations m_Q as well as the formulas h of $\mathcal{L}_Q$ is needed. One possibility consists in representing m_Q and h by their disjunctive normal forms and the operations of marginalization and combination must be encoded in terms of this representation. It is not possible to enter here into a discussion of the details of these procedures.

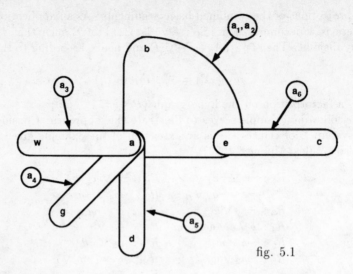

fig. 5.1

6. Conclusion

A method for obtaining basic arguments and therefore supports and possibilities relative to an assumption-based knowledge base is presented here. This method fits into the axiomatic theory of propagation of valuations in valuation nets developed by Shenoy, Shafer (1990). It is an alternative to resolution-based methods as described by Siegel (1987), Inoue (1991 and 1992) (see also Kohlas, Money, 1992). The relative merits of these two different approaches remain for the time being an open question. In general terms one may say that resolution methods are probably advantageous, if only one or a few hypotheses have to be judged, whereas the hypertree approach described here may be preferable, if many or all $h \in \mathcal{L}_Q$ for some Q or even for different Q must be judged simultaneously.

The result of these methods is the support or the possibility of a hypothesis. This allows a qualitative judgement of the credibility of the hypothesis. If one wants to weight the support quantitatively, then one may try to assess probabilities for the assumptions involved and then to compute the probabilities of the basic arguments $M_Q(h) = P(m_Q(h))$. Techniques for this computation can be found in the domain of reliability theory where similar problems have to be solved (see also Kohlas, Monney, 1992). It is easy to see, that $m_Q(h)$ is in fact a basic probability assignment in the sense of numerical evidence theory (Shafer, 1976) on the subsets $N(h)$ of the Boolean cube B_Q. The **degree of support** of a formula $h \in \mathcal{L}_Q$ is the conditional probability, that h can be deduced from Σ, given that the assumptions are not in contradiction with Σ. This is then in view of theorems 2.2 and 2.3

$$Sp(h) = P(sp(h)|\neg sp(\circ)) = \sum \{M_Q(h') : h' \models h, h' \neq \circ\}/(1 - M_Q(\circ)) \quad (6.1)$$

and, similarly, the **degree of plausibility** (or possibility)

$$Pl(h) = P(pl(h)|\neg sp(\circ)) = \sum \{M_Q(h') : h' \wedge h \neq \circ\}/(1 - M_Q(\circ)). \quad (6.2)$$

This corresponds to the definition of support and plausibility in evidence theory (see Shafer, 1976, and in particular also Dempster, 1967).

The advantage of combining and propagating symbolic arguments rather than basic probability assignments as is usually done (Shenoy, Shafer, 1990), resides in two points: First obtaining symbolic arguments may help to explain **why** a hypothesis is credible or not; because the explicit arguments are available. Secondly, once the symbolic basic arguments or supports are known, it is easy to perform **sensitivity analysis** on the probabilities assessed for the assumptions and furthermore to analyze the relative **importance** of the different assumptions for the judgement of the hypothesis.

References

ALMOND, R.; KONG, A. (1991): Optimality Issues in Constructing Markov Tree from Graphical Models. Res. Rep. A-3, Harvard Univ., Dept. of Stat.

ARNBORG, S.; CORNEIL, D.G.; PROSKUROWSKI, A. (1987): Complexity of Finding Embeddings in a k-Tree, *SIAM J. Algebraic and Discrete Methods*, **8**, 277-284.

BERTELE,U.; BRIOSCHI, F. (1972): *Nonserial Dynamic Programming.* Academic Press.

CHANG, C.L.; LEE, R.C.T. (1973): Symbolic and Mechanical Theorem Proving. Boston.

DEMPSTER, A. (1967): Upper and Lower Probabilities Induced by a Multivalued Mapping. *Annals Math. Stat.*, **38**, 325-339.

INOUE, K. (1991): Consequence-Finding Based on Ordered Resolution. Proc. IJCAI-91, 158-164.

INOUE, K. (1992): Linear Resolution for Consequence Finding. *Artificial Intelligence*, **56**, 301-353.

KOHLAS, J. (1991): The Reliability of Reasoning with Unreliable Arguments. *Annals of Operations Reseaarch*, **32**, 76-113.

KOHLAS, J. (1993): Symbolic Evidence, Arguments, Supports and Valuation Networks. *Institute for Informatics, University of Fribourg, Tech. Rep.*

KOHLAS, J.; MONNEY, P.A. (1993): Probabilistic Assumption-Based Reasoning. Inst. for Automation and Op. Res., University of Fribourg, Switzerland, Tech. Rep. No. 208.

KONG, A. (1986): Multivariate Belief Functions and Graphical Models. Doct. diss. Harvard Univ., Dept. of Stat.

LASKEY, K.B.; LEHNER, P.E. (1989): Assumptions, Beliefs and Probabilities. *Artificial Intelligence*, **41**, 65-77.

MELLOULI, K. (1987): On the Propagation of Beliefs in Networks Using the Dempster-Shafer Theory of Evidence. Doct. Diss., Univ. of Kansas, School of Business.

PROVAN, G.M. (1990): A Logic-Based Analysis of Dempster-Shafer Theory. *Int. J. Approximate Reasoning*, **4**, 451-495.

REITER. R., DE KLEER, J. (1987): Foundations of Assumption-Based Truth Maintenance Systems. Proc. Amer. Assoc. A.I., 183-188.

ROSE, D.J. (1970): Triangulated Graphs and the Elimination Process. *J. Math. Anal. and Appl.*, **32**, 597-609.

SHAFER, G. (1976 a): *A Mathematical Theory of Evidence*. Princeton University Press.

SHAFER, G. (1976 b): A Theory of Statistical Evidence. In: HARPER, HOOKER (eds.): Foundations of Probability Theory, Statistical Inference, and Statistical Theories of Science. Vol. II, Reidel, Dortrecht, 365-463.

SHAFER, G. (1979): Allocations of Probability. *Annals of Prob.*, **7**, 827-839.

SHENOY, P.P.; SHAFER, G. (1990): Axioms for Probability and Belief- Function Propagation. In: Shachter et al. (Eds.) (1990): *Uncertainty in Artificial Intelligence 4*, 575-610.

SIEGEL, P. (1987): Représentation et utilisation de la connaissance en calcul propositionnel. Ph. D. thesis, Univ. de Marseilles II.

TARJAN, R.E.; YANNAKAKIS, M. (1984): Simple Linear Time Algorithms to Test Chordality of Graphs, Test Acyclicity of Hypergraphs, and Selectively Reduce Acyclic Hypergraphs. *SIAM J. Computing*, **13**, 566-579.

ZHANG, L. (1988): Studies on Finding Hypertree Covers for Hypergraphs. Working Paper No. 198, Univ. of Kansas, School of Business.

A dynamic ordering relation for revision

KOHLER Arnaud
LIUP-MARSEILLE
Université de Provence UFR-MIM Case A
3, Place Victor Hugo
13331 MARSEILLE Cédex 3 FRANCE
Tél : 91 10 61 08
e-mail : kohler@gyptis.univ-mrs.fr

Abstract: one of the most frequently met problems in theory revision is the taking into account of the world history (the order of arrival of the information, for example) and links between knowledge (to what degree is a fact more important than another, for example ?). This paper proposes an algebraic approach to describe (or process) the changes of the world based on a dynamic partial order relation (representing preference) and to describe the models for some logical (deductive) systems. Though taking into account previous states (information is managed in priority following the order of arrival), we will see that the process avoids the necessity of keeping the complete world history.

This research is supported by the ESPRIT project DRUMS II and by the Ministère de la Recherche et de l'Espace, inter-PRC project : "Gestion de l'évolutif et de l'incertain dans une base de connaissances" (G.E.I.).

1 Introduction

Revision can be seen as any operation which turns a cognitive state **CSt** into a subsequent cognitive state **CSt'**. Two cases can be noted : *belief change* and *change world*, or *update*.

In this paper, we will be interested in the latter. Considering discrete time, during which information arrives at time t_1 (the first fact) t_2, t_3,.., t_n,.., our aim will be to manage the facts in priority according to their order of arrival. We will use a purely semantical knowledge representation, the *preferential models* ([BosSie85], [Sho88], [LehMag90]), and we shall suggest a process allowing the generation of an order relation on models with dynamic character (namely evolving with time). Although taking into account previous states, the process will avoid the necessity of keeping the complete world history.

In the first part, we will present an order relation on the models verifying the constraints that we have chosen. In the second part, we will use the academic example of "Tweety" to illustrate the formalism we propose.

2 A dynamic order relation for the preferential model

We consider a cognitive state **CSt** as a set of models with an order relation, describing knowledge at time t. We may neglect the order relation, and consider all models, or be interested in the prefered (minimal) models, and, more over, use a skeptical or credulus approach. We shall limit ourselves here to the minimal model approach.

We present here a dynamic order relation for preferential models. The idea is to create a temporal process allowing to manage the models according to the order of arrival of the facts. We will use for this the following partial order relation : let $(x_1, .., x_n)$ be a set formulas in order of arriving in time. For two models I and J, we note :

$$I \preceq_{(x_1,...,x_n)} J \text{ if } \exists i \, ((\forall k \geq i \, (J \vdash x_k \Rightarrow I \vdash x_k))$$

$$\text{and } (\exists j \geq i \, (I \vdash x_i \text{ and } (J \not\vdash x_i \text{ or } I \equiv J)))))^1$$

i.e. : I is smaller than J if a time t exists such that every formula arriving after t verified in J is verified in I and a formula exists which is verified in I but not in J, unless $I \equiv J$.

---

[1] We note in following $\preceq_{(x_1,...,x_n)}$: $\preceq$.

2.1 Definitions and notations

We will indicate in this section the definitions and notations necessary for the formalization of the process. We recall : a cognitif state **CSt** is a set of models with an order relation.

Definition 1 [LehMag90] *Let T be a theory. We say $A \in T$ is a* **prefered model** *of T iff $\neg \exists B \in T$ $(B \not\equiv A$ and $B \preceq A)$. A will be called the* **prefered model** *of T iff $\forall B \in T$ $(B \not\equiv A \Leftrightarrow A \preceq B)$.*

Definition 2 [LehMag90] *Let T be a theory. A order relation $\preceq$ on T will be called* **well-founded** *iff $\forall A \in T$:*

- *either A is a prefered model,*
- *or $\exists B \in T$ $(B \preceq A)$ and B is a prefered model.*

Definition 3 *Let T be a theory, and F a model of T. We define the following boolean function :*

$$P_{ref_T}(F) = \begin{cases} True & \text{if } F \text{ is a prefered model of } T \\ False & \text{otherwise} \end{cases}$$

To define the revision operations, we use a set of pairs $< \{Pre\}, \{Cons\} >$, with

- *Pre* : is either a set of formulas or a relation on the set of models which express the conditions **CSt** verified to apply the operation,

- *Cons* : is the new relation on the set of models if *Pre* is verified, permitting the passage of the cognitive state **CSt** to the state **CSt'**. The new ordering relation erases the former relation.

We shall introduce the follow abbrevations :

- $F \ll G$: $F \not\equiv G$ and F is directely inferior to G, i.e. :
  $F \not\equiv G$ and $F \preceq G$ and if $F \preceq H \preceq G$ then $F \equiv H$ or $G \equiv H$.

- $F \prec \succ G$: F and G are not ordered ($F \not\preceq G$ and $G \not\preceq F$).

- a composite operation is defined as follow : $< \{Pre.2\}, \{Cons.2\} >$ $\circ < \{Pre.1\}, \{Cons.1\} >$.

2.2   Formalism

To enable the revision of the state **CSt**, we need five operations. In this section, we present the formalization and the intuitive sense. In the rest of the section, x will be formula.

$(x \text{ prefered}) \bigcirc x : \; <\{I \ll M, M \ll N, I \not\ll N\} \, , \, \{M \prec\succ N\} > \circ$
$\qquad\qquad\qquad < \{I \vdash x, F \vdash \neg x\} \, , \, \{I \ll F\} >$

Considering a revision by fact x, the operation $\bigcirc x$ will reorder the models in a way such that in the prefered models only the facts consistent with the new information will hold. $\bigcirc x$ not being dynamic (it is not based on the previous state), this operation will only be used when the cognitive state **CSt** doesn't propose any prefered model (i.e. generally at time t_1 : the system records its first fact) or in the frame of belief change.

$(\text{extension by } x) \oplus x : \; <\{I \ll M, M \ll N, I \not\ll N\} \, , \, \{M \prec\succ N\} > \circ$
$\qquad\qquad\qquad < \{I \vdash x, F \vdash \neg x, P_{ref_{CSt}}(I)\} \, , \, \{I \ll F\} >$

This operation is equivalent to $\bigcirc x$, but the re-order affects just the prefered models. This particularity gives it a dynamic character, since it is an elaboration of the former order.

$(\text{retraction by } x) \oslash x : \; <\{I \vdash x, F \vdash \neg x, I \ll F\} \, , \, \{I \prec\succ F\} >$

All the order relations which favour a model containing x are erased. It is used only in the frame of belief revision.

$(x \text{ deleted}) \ominus x : \; <\{I \vdash x, F \vdash \neg x, I \ll F, P_{ref_{CSt}}(I)\} \, , \, \{I \prec\succ F\} >$

This operation is a retraction carried out only on the prefered models, this gives it a dynamic character for the same reasons as above.

$(\text{revision } x) \odot x : \; \ominus \neg x \oplus x$

Revision of a knowledge based on a fact x. $\odot x$ is obtained from Levy's identity.

Theorem   1 [KohSie93] $\preceq_{(x_1,\ldots,x_n)}$ *is a well-founded order relation.*

3   Examples

In our examples, $M_1 \ll M_2$ will be noted $M_2 \longrightarrow M_1$, and the prefered models will be underlined. We will not represent the reflexive relations. The following two examples will allow us to check the dynamic behaviour of the system. Indeed, they show that the order of arrival of facts is fundamental for the generation of the order of the models.

- Let XY, $\neg X\, Y$, $X\neg Y$ and $\neg X\neg Y$ be the models of the theory **CSt**. There is no relation between models at time t_0 (the models are all prefered models). We consider the following evolutions :

Diag.1 $(x_1 = \bigcirc X), (x_2 = \oplus Y), (x_3 = \oplus X \vee Y)(x_4 = \odot \neg Y)$

Diag.2 $(x'_1 = \bigcirc X), (x'_2 = \odot \neg Y)(x'_3 = \oplus Y), (x'_4 = \oplus X \vee Y)$

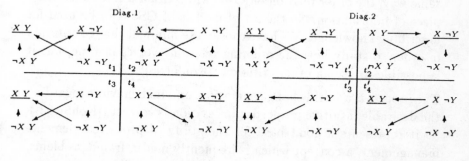

We see in the first example (diag.1) that the ordering relation evolves with time. The second example (diag.2) illustrates the importance of the order of arrival of the informations.

- In the example of Tweety, we use these propositions : "All birds fly" (denoted by a), "Penguin is a bird" (denoted by b), "Penguin does not fly" (denoted by c), "Tweety is a penguin" (denoted by p) and "Birds generally fly" (denoted by d). Considering the facts :

  - $\bigcirc a \odot b \odot c$: we obtain the prefered model abc.
  - $\odot p$: we obtain the prefered model $\neg abc$, i.e. : " All birds do not fly and Tweety is a penguin".
  - $\oplus a$: we obtain the prefered model $a\neg bc$, i.e. : "Tweety is a penguin and is not a bird".
  - $\oslash c$, we obtain the prefered models $ab\neg c$ and $a\neg bc$, i.e. : "Tweety is a penguin, and flies or penguin is not a bird".
  - $\odot b \wedge c$, we obtain the prefered model abc, i.e. : "Tweety is not a penguin".
  - $\odot d$, we obtain the prefered model $\neg abcd$, i.e. : "I do not know if Tweety is a penguin, but in the case it is, it is a bird which does not fly".

4 Conclusion - Perspectives

Considering **CSt** a set of models with an order relation, we have suggested a process which enables the generation of an order relation evolving in time on the possible patterns. It takes the order of arrival of facts into account, but the operation avoid to conserve the complete world history. Indeed, to move from a cognitive state **CSt** to a state **CSt'**, the process builds its choices on the **CSt** order relation, which contains a partial record of former events. In the same way, the order relation on **CSt'** will contain a trace of the new piece of information. So the set of models of **CSt'** can be used for describing knowledge. We have chosen the minimal change criterion in order to study how the ordering relation evolves in time, but it is possible to use an other criterion ([KohSie93]).

The process is a world change operation, and its behaviors regarding the desirable intuitive properties in revision is correct ([KohSie93]). So it represents a good base for the study of protected elements management, a concept which is frequently met in frame problems. We actually work on an extension of it.

5 BIBLIOGRAPHY

We thank Professor Morten Elvang for his relevant remarks about this article.

[BosSie85] Geneviève Bossu, Pierre Siegel, "Saturation, Nonmonotonic Reasoning and the Closed-World Assumption", Artificial Intelligence 25 (1985), pp 13-63.

[Sho88] Y. Shoham, "Reasoning About Change-Time and Causation from the Standpoint of Artificial Intelligence", The MIT Press, Cambridge, Mass.., 1988.

[LehMag90] Daniel Lehman, Menachem Magidor, "What does a conditional knowledge base entail ?", Departement of Computer Science, Hebrew University, Jerusalem 91904, Israel, June 1990.

[KohSie93] Arnaud Kohler, Pierre Siegel, "Ordering relation and revision", TR'93, LIUP-Marseille.

On Extensions of Marginals
for Decision-Making

Otakar Kříž

Institute of Information Theory and Automation
Academy of Sciences of the Czech Republic
Pod vodárenskou věží 4, 18208 Prague 8, Czech Republic
e-mail: kriz@cspgas11.bitnet

Abstract. An *extension of a set of marginals* (small-dimensional distributions) is a joint probability distribution that is a "good" representative of the knowledge (about the problem area) contained in the marginals . "Good" means with respect to the subsequent decision-making for which the extension is needed. In the context of probabilistic expert systems, constructing the extension from the marginals may be referred to as the *knowledge integration* [4], *reconstructability analysis* [9] or *marginal problem*. The paper surveys different types of known extensions and on the basis of underlying principles and considerations, new types of extensions – the *EEV-centroid* and the *weighted centroid* are suggested.

1. Introduction

Diagnostic expert systems are a special branch of decision support systems where the objects under investigation may be described with the help of a diagnosis variable η (taking its values in a finite set $\{d_i\}$ of diagnoses (hypotheses,classes)) and a set of symptom variables (attributes) $\xi_1, \xi_2, \ldots, \xi_n$ whose values are symptoms (evidences). Expert systems can be divided into two large groups: those which deal with *uncertainty* and those which don't. Expert systems with uncertainty can be further subdivided according to the way uncertainty is interpreted e.g. *probability, Dempster-Shafer theory, fuzzy set theory* or *possibility*.

In the sequel, the decision-making problem will be considered in the context of diagnostic expert systems with probabilistic background. Then, the most general model is an *all-explaining joint distribution* $P_{\eta\xi_1,\xi_2\ldots\xi_n}$. This is the knowledge base establishing all relations between the random variable η and symptom random variables $\xi_1, \xi_2 \ldots \xi_n$. This distribution is not available in detail (and if it were the case, we would not be able to store it in general) but we possess certain pieces of knowledge which may be interpreted as a set of marginals of this distribution or some relevant conditional probability or fragments of both.

In expert systems it is possible to distinguish two levels.

First, the unattainable goal is to reconstruct uniquely this theoretical unknown distribution $P^*_{\eta\xi_1\xi_2\ldots\xi_n}$ (that might have generated the data from which the marginals were estimated). But, it is always certain approximation $\hat{P}_{\eta\xi_1\xi_2\ldots\xi_n}$ only of this theoretical distribution $P^{\star}_{\eta\xi_1\xi_2\ldots\xi_n}$ what we get in the reconstruction process.

Second, having this approximation $\hat{P}_{\eta\xi_1\xi_2\ldots\xi_n}$ and knowing some facts (i.e. symptoms) about the object (e.g. a patient whose diagnosis we want to find out), we may calculate conditional probability of all diagnoses given the symptoms. Then, the diagnosis with the best ranking a posteriori probability is selected as the final decision.

But let us return to the first problem: What is the best approximation $\hat{P}_{\eta\xi_1\xi_2\ldots\xi_n}$ of the theoretical distribution $P^{\star}_{\eta\xi_1\xi_2\ldots\xi_n}$ when our general knowledge about the decision domain is just a finite set of *consistent* marginals ?

The widely accepted idea is to select such a representative $\hat{P}_{\eta\xi_1\xi_2\ldots\xi_n}$ (from the class $\mathcal{P}(\mathcal{K})$ of all joint distributions $P_{\eta\xi_1\xi_2\ldots\xi_n}$ consistent with a set $\mathcal{K} = \{P_{S_1}, P_{S_2}\ldots P_{S_k}\}$) whose entropy $H(\hat{P}_{\eta\xi_1\xi_2\ldots\xi_n})$ achieves the maximum value:

$$\hat{P}_{\eta\xi_1\xi_2\ldots\xi_n} = \underset{P\in\mathcal{P}(\mathcal{K})}{\mathrm{argmax}}\ H(P) \qquad \text{where}$$

$$H\left(P_{\eta\xi_1\xi_2\ldots\xi_{kn}}\right) = -\sum_{(d_i,x_1,\ldots x_n)} P_{\eta\xi_1\xi_2\ldots\xi_n}(d_i, x_1,\ldots x_n)\cdot\log P_{\eta\xi_1\xi_2\ldots\xi_n}(d_i, x_1,\ldots x_n)$$

Symbol S_i in P_{S_i} denotes the subset of random variables $\eta, \xi_1, \xi_2,\ldots\xi_n$ that are described by a given small-dimensional distribution P_{S_i} (which is a supposed marginal of the theoretical distribution $P^{\star}_{\eta\xi_1\xi_2\ldots\xi_n}$). When S_i is used as an upper index for a joint distribution P, the resulting symbol P^{S_i} stands for the marginal distribution of P.

The *maximal entropy extension* $\hat{P}_{\eta\xi_1\xi_2\ldots\xi_n}$ of the set of marginals $\mathcal{K} = \{P_{S_1}, P_{S_2}\ldots P_{S_k}\}$ can be obtained using *Iterative Proportional Fitting* procedure introduced by Stephan-Deming [3] that is based on subsequent computation of iterations:

$$P_i = P_{i-1}\frac{P_{S_j}}{P_{i-1}^{S_j}} \quad \text{where} \quad j = ((i-1)\bmod k) + 1 \quad \text{for iterating index} \quad i = 1, 2,\ldots$$

Certain shorthand was used in the formula. P_i – the next joint distribution in the generated sequence should be written as $(P_{\eta\xi_1\xi_2\ldots\xi_n}(d_l, x_1,\ldots x_n))_i$. Each next joint distribution P_i is obtained from the previous joint distribution P_{i-1} by multiplying it by a fraction where the numerator is the given P_{S_j} from $\mathcal{K}$ and the denominator is the reduction (marginalization) $P_{i-1}^{S_j}$ of P_{i-1} to the same set of variables S_j. This all is done in a cyclic way taking the given small - dimensional distributions P_{S_j} one by one from $\mathcal{K}$ and restarting again by P_{S_1} when P_{S_k} was used as the last "correction" factor. Naturally, the formula holds for all combinations $(d_l, x_1,\ldots x_n)$ of values of variables $\eta\xi_1\xi_2\ldots\xi_n$.

The maximal entropy extension is the limit of the sequence $P_0, P_1,\ldots$ if as the starting distribution P_0 is taken the uniform $(n+1)$-dimensional distribution and for special systems of sets of variables $\{S_1, S_2,\ldots S_k\}$ the sequence converges even in k steps.

Another type of possible extensions are the so called *centroids*. The notion is known from the *constrained mixture experiments* [7] where the aim is to find the center point of a region defined by a system of linear equations and inequalities of type

$$0 \le x_i \le 1 \quad (i = 1, 2, ...n); \qquad \sum_{i=1}^{n} x_i = 1. \tag{1}$$

Sometimes the lower and upper bounds are more specific

$$0 \le e_i \le x_i \le f_i \le 1 \quad (i = 1, 2, ...n); \tag{2}$$

or the convex polyhedron of feasible solutions $(x_1, x_2, \ldots, x_n)$ is defined by additional inequalities

$$b_j \le x_1 a_{j1} + x_2 a_{j2} + \cdots x_n a_{jn} \le c_j (j = 1, 2, ...m) \tag{3}$$

In fact, there exist two different definitions of centroids [11]

Averaged Extreme Vertices centroid (AEV) is the arithmetic mean of all extrem points of the polyhedron defined by the constraints.

Center Of Mass centroid (COM) is defined in accordance with the definition of the gravity center of a body in physics. It is more difficult to calculate COM than AEV-centroids as the exact method requires partioning of the polyhedron into mutually exclusive simplices, calculating their centroids and volumes and the final COM-centroid is the weighted (relative volume) average of centroids of all simplex regions [2],[11]. In general, AEV and COM centroids are not equal for the same convex polyhedron. Averaging in the case of linear centroids implies that we accept implicitly certain type of Euclidian metric for the space of joint distributions. (In case of the maximum entropy extensions a natural "distance" of distributions is Kullback-Leibler divergence.) In any case, both methods require computing of extreme vertices of the original polyhedron [7],[11],[14]. The basic idea is to inspect all the largest nonsingular submatrices of the matrix $A = \|a_{ij}\|$ whose rows are linear functionals (defining the constraining hyperplanes) and then testing nonnegativity of x_j.

In the context of looking for linear centroids of the class $\mathcal{P}(\mathcal{K})$ of joint distributions consistent with a set of marginals $\mathcal{K}$ the constraining conditions are more specific:

1. inequalities in (3) degenerate into a set of equations $\mathbf{Ax} = \mathbf{b}$ where $\mathbf{x} \in \langle 0, 1 \rangle^n$ and $\mathbf{b} \in \langle 0, 1 \rangle^m$

2. matrix $\mathbf{A}$ is of dimensionality $m \times n$ where even $m \ge n$ may hold but due to the linear dependence of the marginals the system $\mathbf{Ax} = \mathbf{b}$ is never overdetermined

3. coefficients a_{ij} of matrix $\mathbf{A}$ are integers 0 or 1

Barycenter of a family of distributions introduced by Perez [10] is a special type of extension where the representative of a set of marginals is looked for in other family of distribution as the "nearest" neighbour in sense of Kullback-Leibler divergence. More precisely, let $\mathcal{T}$ and $\mathcal{S}$ be subsets of a set $\mathcal{P}$ of all distributions and D is a measure of divergence of probability measures from $\mathcal{P}$. The D-barycenter of $\mathcal{S}$ taken in $\mathcal{T}$ is a probability measure $R_{D,\mathcal{S},\mathcal{T}}$ (if existing) satisfying

$$\sup_{P \in \mathcal{S}} D(R_{D,\mathcal{S},\mathcal{T}}, P) = \min_{R \in \mathcal{T}} \sup_{P \in \mathcal{S}} D(R, P)$$

2. Example

Let us illustrate possible differences of various extensions on a very simple example of two binary random variables. The theoretical distribution is denoted as $P^{\star}_{\eta\xi_1}$. The IPF algorithm converged in 2 iterations to the maximal entropical extension $P^{\triangle}_{\eta\xi_1}$. The AEV-centroid calculated from the extreme vertices is $P^{\diamond}_{\eta\xi_1}$. The COM-centroid has the same value. To have possibility of comparison, the product distribution $P^{\square}_{\eta\xi_1}$ corresponding to the independence of both variables η and ξ_1 is introduced as well. As it might be expected, it is identical with the maximal entropy extension $P^{\triangle}_{\eta\xi_1}$.

Knowledge base $\mathcal{K} = \{P^{\star}_{\eta}, P^{\star}_{\xi_1}\}$ is composed of only two marginals

$$P^{\star}_{\eta\xi_1} = \begin{array}{|c|c|}\hline \frac{1}{6} & \frac{7}{12} \\ \hline \frac{1}{6} & \frac{1}{12} \\ \hline \end{array} \quad \begin{array}{|c|}\hline \frac{3}{4} \\ \hline \frac{1}{4} \\ \hline \end{array}$$

$$P^{\star}_{\xi_1} = \begin{array}{|c|c|}\hline \frac{1}{3} & \frac{2}{3} \\ \hline \end{array} \quad P^{\star}_{\eta} \uparrow$$

$$H(P^{\star}_{\eta\xi_1}) = 1.61400$$
$$H(P^{\star}_{\xi_1}) = 0.91829$$
$$H(P^{\star}_{\eta}) = 0.81127$$

possible extensions of the marginals $P^{\star}_{\xi_1}$ and $P^{\star}_{\eta}$ are

$$P^{\triangle}_{\eta\xi_1} = \begin{array}{|c|c|}\hline \frac{1}{4} & \frac{1}{2} \\ \hline \frac{1}{12} & \frac{1}{6} \\ \hline \end{array} \qquad P^{\square}_{\eta\xi_1} = \begin{array}{|c|c|}\hline \frac{1}{4} & \frac{1}{2} \\ \hline \frac{1}{12} & \frac{1}{6} \\ \hline \end{array} \qquad P^{\diamond}_{\eta\xi_1} = \begin{array}{|c|c|}\hline \frac{5}{24} & \frac{13}{24} \\ \hline \frac{1}{8} & \frac{1}{8} \\ \hline \end{array}$$

and the corresponding entropies are

$$H(P^{\triangle}_{\eta\xi_1}) = 1.729573 \qquad H(P^{\square}_{\eta\xi_1}) = 1.729573 \qquad H(P^{\diamond}_{\eta\xi_1}) = 1.70058$$

The extremal distributions $P^{\frac{1}{12}}$ and $P^{\frac{1}{3}}$ (extreme vertices) and the general distribution P^{α} expressed with the help of parameter α are

$$P^{\frac{1}{12}}_{\eta\xi_1} = \begin{array}{|c|c|}\hline \frac{1}{12} & \frac{2}{3} \\ \hline \frac{1}{4} & 0 \\ \hline \end{array} \qquad P^{\frac{1}{3}}_{\eta\xi_1} = \begin{array}{|c|c|}\hline \frac{1}{3} & \frac{5}{12} \\ \hline 0 & \frac{1}{4} \\ \hline \end{array} \qquad P^{\alpha}_{\eta\xi_1} = \begin{array}{|c|c|}\hline \alpha & \frac{3}{4}-\alpha \\ \hline \frac{1}{3}-\alpha & \alpha-\frac{1}{12} \\ \hline \end{array}$$

and the corresponding entropies are

$$H(P^{\frac{1}{12}}_{\eta\xi_1}) = 1.18872 \qquad H(P^{\frac{1}{3}}_{\eta\xi_1}) = 1.55458$$

What is the impact of selecting different extensions on the final decision making? Let us suppose that the variable ξ_1 takes its values from the set $\{0,1\}$ and η from $\{d_1, d_2\}$. When we know that the value of the symptom variable ξ_1 is 0 for a patient, what should be his diagnosis?

First, let us suppose that the theoretical distribution is equal to the extreme distribution $P^{\frac{1}{3}}_{\eta\xi_1}$ with respective conditional probability $P^{\frac{1}{3}}_{\eta|\xi_1}$. Then, $P^{\frac{1}{3}}_{\eta|\xi_1}(d_1|0) = 1$ and therefore, as d_1 has the best ranking a posteriori probability, we may claim that the patient has the disease d_1.

Second, let $P^{\frac{1}{12}}_{\eta\xi_1}$ be the true theoretical distribution. Then,

$$P^{\frac{1}{12}}_{\eta|\xi_1}(d_1|0) = \frac{1}{4} \quad \text{and} \quad P^{\frac{1}{12}}_{\eta|\xi_1}(d_2|0) = \frac{3}{4}$$

and our decision should be the diagnosis d_2 (with probability of error 0.25).

3. Discussion of principles

The above mentioned example has illustrated both importance and weak points of the search for extensions. Selecting a represenative of a class of distributions is a sort of interpolation. The interpolation principles express some additional information to the knowledge contained in the marginals.

What is the quality (of the world described by a joint distribution) whose best numerical expression is maximizing entropy? Cheeseman [1] uses the term "the least commitment subject to the constraints. Any other choice would imply more information than was given in the problem." The maximum entropy method is sometimes called the least information method what is true due to the definition of information (present in a distribution with respect to another distribution) as the difference of the entropies of respective distributions. A little confusion may arise due to the fact that the notion of *information* is not always felt in this strict mathematical sense.

Expressed in other terms, maximal entropy corresponds to joint distributions whose "generating" random variables are (statistically) the most independent. One reason in favour of entropy principle (for others see e.g. [8]) may be that we always try to describe the decision making problem in attributes (symptom variables) that are, at least in our opinion, independent.

Therefore, the interpolation rule in case of the maximum entropy extension may be interpreted:

Select the distribution that is the most independent (from all those consistent with the marginals).

The interpolation principle in case of centroid extensions is different. The averaging (of extreme vertices) reveals the intention to find a point whose "distance" to all other points is the least possible one (in sense of certain metric). The approach supposes equal probability for all points from the polyhedron (i.e. the averaging integration uses the uniform a priori distribution on the space of all possible joint distributions from $\mathcal{P}(\mathcal{K})$). If this is the idea behind, the COM-centroid is the right choice. If we knew the background a priori distribution Q (of possible positions of the theoretical joint distribution P^*) differs from the uniform one (subjective Baysian approach), the averaging over the polyhedron would be performed using this distribution Q.

On the other hand, the AEV-centroids have not a good theoretical foundation (as they differ from COM-centroids in general).

It seems to be more reasonable to apply the minimax principle and knowing *all* extreme vertices to find the *two* most extreme vertices P^0 and P^1

$$\rho\left(P^0, P^1\right) = \max_{P, P' \in \mathcal{P}(\mathcal{K})} \rho\left(P, P'\right)$$

(either in the metric of the polyhedron or in a metric of the space of distributions) and to select the distribution from $\mathcal{P}(\mathcal{K})$ whose distance to both *Extreme Extreme vertices* (EEV) is the same and the minimal one.

$$\hat{P}_{\eta \xi_1 \xi_2 \dots \xi_n} = \operatorname*{argmin}_{P \in \mathcal{P}(\mathcal{K})} \max \left\{ \rho\left(P, P^0\right), \rho\left(P, P^1\right) \right\}$$

where ρ is a metric or divergence on distributions. This *EEV-centroid* protects against the worst case position of the theoretical $P^\star$. (All these considerations are valid if the metric ρ can be reasonably related to the decision error. More precisely, if we adapt our decision-making with respect to the extension $\hat{P}$ and the theoretical one is $P^\star$, the increase in decision errors should be monotonous function of $\rho(P^\star, \hat{P})$.)

Now, the extension problem seems to be directly connected with the principle we want to stick to and the subsequent selection of the extension is, at least theoretically, straightforward. Is there any other alternative?

4. Weighted extensions

The *extension problem* is just a subtask in a more global *decision-making problem*. We were given (as assumption) a set $\mathcal{K}$ of marginals P_{S_i}. We may summarize other assumptions and facts about the nature of the marginals:

- Marginals (small-dimensional distributions) are, in fact, obtainable only from a statistical material (data set describing symptoms and diagnoses of patients). No expert is usually able to tell off-hand (i.e. from his experience) consistent values of probabilities to say nothing of their precision.

- Having at our disposal the data set, we may calculate an estimate of the marginal for any set of variables S_i. Even more, the data itself can be transformed to an approximation $\hat{P}$ (of $P^\star$) which is the extension of all marginals computable from the data set.

- Why this $\hat{P}$ is not taken as a recommended extension of the given data set? The main reason is that there is never enough data to estimate all parameters defining P. The greater the cardinality of the marginal P_{S_i} (product of cardinalities of domains of variables in S_i), the more specific information for the decision-making but at the same time, the less reliable the estimate.

- In general extension problem, the fact is reflected very roughly in the way that the knowledge base $\mathcal{K}$ is composed only of marginals that exceed certain level of reliability. They have all the same weight (no ordering on $\mathcal{K}$) and on the other hand no other, less reliable, marginals are taken into consideration.

Let us define a reliability $\mathrm{rel}(P_{S_i})$ for each marginal P_{S_i} (from the knowledge base $\mathcal{K}$) e.g. to be inversely proportional to the number of "free" parameters in P_{S_i}. (Other possible definitions of reliability may be derived from confidence intervals.) Then, the weight $\mathrm{w}(P_{S_i})$ of P_{S_i} will be the reliability of P_{S_i} normalized with respect to all marginals in $\mathcal{K}$ and $P^w(\mathcal{K})$ is the *weighted extension* of $\mathcal{K}$

$$\mathrm{rel}(S_i) = \frac{1}{\prod_{j \in S_i} |\xi_j| - 1}, \qquad w(S_i) = \frac{\mathrm{rel}(S_i)}{\sum_{j \in \underline{\mathcal{K}}} \mathrm{rel}(S_j)}, \tag{4}$$

$$P^w(\mathcal{K}) = \sum_{i \in |\mathcal{K}|} \mathrm{w}(S_i) \left[P_{S_i} \prod_{j \in \{\eta, \xi_1, \dots \xi_n\} \setminus S_i} P_{\{j\}} \right], \tag{5}$$

where $\underline{\mathcal{K}} = \{S_1, S_2, \ldots S_k\}$, $|\,\mathcal{K}\,|$ denotes cardinality of set $\mathcal{K}$ and $|\,\xi_i\,|$ is the cardinality of the range of the random variable ξ_i. In other words, the extension $P^w(\mathcal{K})$ is obtained as a weighted sum of distributions in the brackets. These distributions are "constructed" as the product of some given P_{S_i} and of all one-dimensional marginal distributions $P_{\{j\}}$ for variables j not present in the set S_i.

The formula (5) may be interpreted in such a way that each of the generating distributions (expression in the brackets) "attracts" the resulting extension P^w with respective force $w(S_i)$ and P^w corresponds to the equilibrium of forces.

Returning to our example, each marginal P_η, P_{ξ_1} from $\mathcal{K}$ has reliability 1 and therefore the weights are both 0.5. The generating distributions will be in both cases the same – $P_\eta \cdot P_{\xi_1}$ and then the weighted extension $P^w_{\eta\xi_1}$ will be equal to the product extension – $P^\square_{\eta\xi_1}$.

If we added the theoretical distribution $P^\star_{\eta\xi_1}$ (supposing it is an estimate from the statistical data) to the $\mathcal{K}$, its reliability $\mathrm{rel}(P^\star_{\eta\xi_1})$ would be 0.33333. Then, the weights in this new knowledge base $\mathcal{K}' = \{P_\eta, P_{\xi_1}, P^\star_{\eta\xi_1}\}$ will be

$$\mathrm{w}(P_\eta) = \frac{3}{7} \qquad \mathrm{w}(P_{\xi_1}) = \frac{3}{7} \qquad \mathrm{w}(P^\star_{\eta\xi_1}) = \frac{1}{7}$$

and the resulting weighted extension will be

$$P^w_{\eta\xi_1} = \begin{array}{|cc|} \hline \frac{6}{7}\cdot\frac{1}{4}+\frac{1}{7}\cdot\frac{1}{6} & \frac{6}{7}\cdot\frac{1}{2}+\frac{1}{7}\cdot\frac{7}{12} \\ \frac{6}{7}\cdot\frac{1}{12}+\frac{1}{7}\cdot\frac{1}{6} & \frac{6}{7}\cdot\frac{1}{6}+\frac{1}{7}\cdot\frac{1}{12} \\ \hline \end{array} \qquad P^w_{\eta\xi_1} = \begin{array}{|cc|} \hline \frac{5}{21} & \frac{43}{84} \\ \frac{2}{21} & \frac{13}{84} \\ \hline \end{array}$$

Conclusion

Given certain statistical data and/or set of small-dimensional probabilistic distributions as the input knowledge about the problem area, it seems to be theoretically sound to try to reconstruct an all-explaining joint distribution from this partial knowledge. The decision-making adapted to this distribution (so-called Bayesian solution of the decision-making problem) is just selecting the diagnosis for which the conditional probability (recalculated from the joint distribution and supposing certain concrete evidence about the object) is the largest one.

The paper attracts the attention to the fact that there are several ways how to proceed from pieces of input knowledge (marginals) to the joint distribution even in the scope of probabilistic paradigm.

Each extension of marginals (i.e. representative of all joint distributions compatible with the input knowledge) may be justified with respect to some additional suppositions. Two new types of extensions are suggested to increase the quality of the decision-making but the "extension problem" seems to be still open, so far.

212

References

[1] P. Cheeseman: A method of computing generalized Bayesian probability values of expert systems. Proc. 6-th Joint Conf. on AI (IJCAI-83), Karlsruhe

[2] J. Cohen, T. Hickey: Two Algorithms for Determining Volumes of Convex Polyhedra, Journal of the Association for Computing Machinery 26, pp. 401 – 414.

[3] W.E. Deming, F.F. Stephan: On a least square adjustment of sampled frequency table when the expected marginal totals are known, Ann.Math.Stat. 11 (1940), pp. 427 – 444

[4] R. Jiroušek: A survey of methods used in probabilistic expert systems for knowledge integration. Knowledge based systems 3 (1990), 1, pp. 7 – 12.

[5] R. Jiroušek, O. Kříž: An expert system that accepts knowledge in form of statistical data. Compstat 88, Copenhagen

[6] S.L. Lauritzen, D. Spiegelhalter: Local computations with probabilities on graphical structures and their applications to expert systems, Journal of Royal Statistical Society Ser. B, 50 (1988) pp. 157 – 189

[7] R.A. Mc Lean, V.L. Anderson: Extreme Vertices Design of Mixture Experiments, Technometrics 8, pp. 447 – 454.

[8] E.T. Jaynes: On the rationale of maximum-entropy methods. Proc. of the IEEE 70 (1982), pp. 939 – 952.

[9] M. Pittarelli: Uncertainty and estimation in reconstructability analysis. International Journal of General Systems 18 (1982), pp. 1 – 58.

[10] A. Perez: The barycenter concept of a set of probability measures as a tool in statistical decision. Probability Theory and Mathematical Statistics,vol.2,VNU Science Press 1986 pp. 437-450.

[11] G.F. Piepel: Calculating Centroids in Constrained Mixture Experiments. Technometrics 25, No.3, pp. 279 – 283.

[12] R.D. Snee: Experimental Designs for Quadratic Models in Constrained Mixture Spaces. Technometrics 17, pp. 149 – 159.

[13] R.D. Snee: Experimental Designs for Mixture Systems with Multicomponent Constraints. Communications in Statistics A8, pp. 303 – 326.

[14] R.D. Snee, D.W. Marquardt: Extreme Vertices Designs for Linear Mixture Models. Technometrics 16, pp. 399 – 408.

On the Semantics of Negations

in Logic Programming

Els Laenens

Department of Computer Science
University of Antwerp (UIA)
Universiteitsplein 1, B2610 Wilrijk, Belgium

ABSTRACT

An extended logic program (ELP) is a logic program that allows for classical negation as well as for negation-as-failure. Previous proposals for ELP semantics can be divided into two classes. The first class avoids contradictions by means of an unnatural discrimination between positive literals and negative literals. In the second class, positive and negative literals have the same status, but contradictions may occur and therefor these semantics are not universally consistent (some programs have no consistent models). As both classes have their own specific shortcomings, we propose a new model-theoretic semantics for ELPs, called the pure semantics, based on the notions of unfounded set and assumption set. The pure semantics for ELPs resolves all contradictions while preserving the same status for positive and negative literals, thus overcoming the imperfections of previous semantics. This paper uses and extends the results obtained in[Lae92a] where a simplification and unification of the semantics for general logic programs (i.e. ELPs that don't contain classical negation) was proposed.

Topics: Theory of logic programming and deductive databases; Logic in computer science; Knowledge representation.

1. Introduction

A *general logic program* (GLPs)[Llo87a, Gel89a] (or seminegative program[Lae90a]) is a set of rules of the form

$$A_1 , .. , A_m , Not\ A_{m+1} , .. , Not\ A_n \ \rightarrow \ A$$

where $n \geq m \geq 0$, and each A_i is an atom.

As the rules of general logic programs may contain negation, they are more general than Horn clauses. General logic programs can only provide negative information implicitly through closed-world reasoning. Extended logic programs extend general logic programs by supporting also explicit negative information. An *extended logic program* (ELP) is a logic program that allows for classical negation (¬) as well as negation-as-failure (*Not*) [Gel89a, Kow90a, Prz90a], and is defined as a set of rules of the form

$$L_1 , \cdots , L_m , Not\ L_{m+1} , \cdots , Not\ L_n \rightarrow L_0$$

where $n \geq m \geq 0$, and each L_i is a literal, i.e. either A or $\neg A$ where A is an atom.

As pointed out in [Gel89a], some facts of common sense knowledge can be represented by logic programs more easily when classical negation is available. In McCarthy's example, a school bus may cross railway tracks under the condition that there is no approaching train. This fact cannot be expressed by the rule *Not train* $\rightarrow$ *cross* because this rule allows the bus to cross the tracks when there is no information about either the presence or the absence of a train - for instance, when the driver's vision is blocked. If, instead, classical negation is used, i.e. $\neg train \rightarrow cross$, then *cross* will only be true when the fact $\neg train$ is available. If this fact is absent, then the driver should wait, just as if there were a train in sight: *Not* $\neg train \rightarrow$ *wait*. For an excellent motivation of extended logic programs with many examples showing the use of classical negation in knowledge representation, we refer to [Gel89a].

We say that an *extended literal* is either a literal L or a negated literal *Not L*. So, for a given atom A, we have four types of extended literals: A, $\neg A$, *Not A* and *Not* $\neg A$. Note that not all *extended* literals can be derived explicitly through rule application, but all ordinary literals can. So the question arises as to how to deal with contradictions, e.g. what is the meaning of an ELP containing the following rules

$$\rightarrow p$$
$$\rightarrow \neg p$$

Previous proposals for ELP semantics can be divided into two classes.

- The approaches taken in[Lae90a, Kow90a] avoid contradictions by discriminating between positive literals and negative literals: rules with negated heads play the role of exceptions to rules with positive heads.

- In the answer set semantics[Gel89a] and the well-founded and 3-valued stable semantics[Prz90a] positive and negative literals have the same status, and contradictions may occur.

Both these approaches have their own specific shortcomings. The problem with the first approach is that it is based on an unnatural discrimination. Indeed, it is desirable to give the same status to all literals because in applications exceptions to positive and negative information are equally likely. The problem with the second approach is that its semantics is not universally consistent: some programs have no consistent models. For instance, the above example has only an inconsistent answer set[Gel89a] being the set of all literals (which contains both p and $\neg p$), and it has no well-founded or 3-

valued stable model [Prz90a]. We believe that, especially in the context of databases and knowledge representation in general, some (small) inconsistency in a program should not have the power to invalidate the entire program.

In this paper, our goal is to develop a semantics that overcomes these imperfections. The semantics of extended logic programs described below resolves all contradictions while preserving the same status for positive and negative literals. It is a natural extension of the results obtained in[Lae92a] where a simplification and unification of the semantics for *general* logic programs was proposed. Just as the pure semantics for GLPs, the pure semantics for ELPs is based on the notions of unfounded set[Gel88a] and assumption set [Lae90b, Lae90c, Gab91a, Lae92b].

We introduce the pure semantics in four steps in order to illustrate that it follows naturally from the intuitive meaning of negation-as-failure (*Not*) and classical negation ($\neg$). In section 2, we give an intuitive introduction to the pure semantics for logic programs. This results in a framework which we use in sections 3 and 4 for the formalization of the pure semantics for ELPs that contain only one kind of negation. In section 3, we discuss the pure semantics for general logic programs. In section 4, we introduce the pure semantics for ELPs that don't contain negation-as-failure. Finally, in section 5, the pure semantics for full ELPs is obtained by combining the results of sections 3 and 4. In section 6, we show that the new semantics meets our requirements (resolving all contradictions while preserving the same status for positive and negative literals), and consequently overcomes imperfections of previous proposals.

Notations: Given a rule r, $H(r)$ denotes the head of r and $B(r)$ denotes the set of all extended literals in the body of r. A term, atom, literal, extended literal, rule is *ground* if it is variable-free.

Given a logic program P, the Herbrand Universe of P (denoted H_P) is the set of all possible ground terms. The Herbrand Base of P (denoted B_P) is the set of all possible ground atoms whose predicate symbols occur in P and whose arguments are elements of H_P. A *ground instance* of a rule r in P is a rule obtained from r by replacing every variable X in r by $\phi(X)$, where ϕ is a mapping from the set of all variables occurring in P to H_P. The set of all ground instances of all rules in P is denoted by *ground*(P).

If S is a set of ground literals, then *Not* S denotes the set $\{$ *Not* $s \mid s \in S\}$, and if S is a set of ground atoms then $\neg S$ denotes the set $\{ \neg s \mid s \in S\}$.

Any subset of $B_P \cup \neg B_P$ is called an *interpretation* for P (there is no need to require that an interpretation be consistent as the definition of pure partial models ensures consistency). $\square$

2. Pure semantics

In this section, we give an intuitive introduction to the pure semantics for logic programming. This informal introduction will then serve as a general framework throughout this paper: we will formalize the pure semantics for different classes of logic programs in the next sections, showing that the pure semantics for ELPs follows naturally from the intuitive meaning of negation-as-failure (*Not*) and classical negation ($\neg$).

An interpretation reflects a meaning of a logic program - and is called a *model* - if it satisfies all rules of this program. Classically, this would amount to demanding that each rule is either non-applicable or applied. Those interpretations that are not models can be thought of as interpretations that are 'too poor', in the sense that they are not *deductively closed* (some rules are applicable but not applied). On the other hand however, models can still be 'too rich' since they may contain literals that cannot be actually inferred. It turns out that, in general, there are two categories of literals: the inferrable literals and the non-inferrable literals, called *assumptions*. An inferrable literal is a desired member of a model M since there is a good argument for its presence in M; assumptions are unwanted as members of models because they lack any motivation of this kind.

Consider P_1.

$$\rightarrow p$$
$$p \rightarrow q$$
$$a \rightarrow b$$

$I_1 = \{p\}$ and $I_2 = \varnothing$ are not deductively closed. $M_1 = \{p,q,a,b\}$ and $M_2 = \{p,q,b\}$ contain assumptions (a, b). $M_3 = \{p, q\}$ is both deductively closed and free from assumptions.

It is evident that we are only interested in **pure partial models**: interpretations that are deductively closed and free from assumptions at the same time.

Assume for a moment that - given an interpretation I for a logic program P - we can identify the set of all assumptions, denoted $A(I)$. Clearly, assumption-freeness translates to $I \cap A(I) = \varnothing$ which implies $I \subseteq \overline{A(I)}$ where $\overline{A(I)}$ is the complement of $A(I)$ in $B_P \cup \neg B_P$. But the definition of $A(I)$ indicates that $\overline{A(I)}$ contains only literals that are inferrable from I; so I is not deductively closed unless $\overline{A(I)} \subseteq I$. It follows that an interpretation I is a pure partial model iff its complement is the set of all assumptions, called the greatest assumption set.

Definition. Let P be an ELP and M an interpretation of P. M is a *pure partial model* of P iff its complement, $\overline{M} = (B_P \cup \neg B_P) - M$, is the greatest assumption set w.r.t. M, i.e. $\overline{M} = A(M)$. □

Obviously, this discussion lacks formality for we introduced $A(I)$ only in an informal way. Nevertheless, this informal discussion proves to be of great value in the process of assigning formal semantics to the different classes of logic programs. Indeed, given a class of logic programs, all we need to do in order to define its pure semantics is properly identify $A(I)$. We can state that the problem of assigning a formal semantics to the different classes of logic programs boils down to defining, for each class, the notion of greatest assumption set in a formal way.

3. Negation-as-failure (Not)

In order to concentrate on the meaning of negation-as-failure, the logic programs under consideration in this section are the ELPs that don't contain classical negation $(\neg)$. It follows from the definition of ELPs that these are precisely general logic programs (GLPs) in which case the head of a rule is always an atom. Thus pure partial models for GLPs are necessarily sets of atoms since other literals are clearly not inferrable. In other words, all literals that are not atoms are assumptions: $\neg B_p$ is part of every assumption set. In order to determine which atoms are in an assumption set, we need to specify when an atom is inferrable, i.e. when a rule is applicable. Applicability of a rule depends on the truth of its body and therefor in part on the semantics of $Not\ A_i$, i.e. on the semantics of negation-as-failure. At first sight, $Not\ A_i$ can be interpreted in two different ways: $Not\ A_i$ is true iff A_i is not true (that is false or undefined), or $Not\ A_i$ is true iff A_i is false. Since we aim at a universally consistent semantics, we are - as the next example illustrates - forced to exclude the first option.

Consider P_2:

$$Not\ p\ \rightarrow\ p$$

Using the first interpretation of Not , the rule is applicable iff p is false or undefined. Suppose that M is a pure partial model of P_2. There are two possibilities: p is in M and p is not in M. If p is in M, then p must be an assumption because the only rule $Not\ p\ \rightarrow\ p$ is not applicable. This clearly contradicts with M being a pure partial model. If on the other hand p is not in M, then p is either false or undefined. So the rule $Not\ p\ \rightarrow\ p$ is applicable and therefor M is not deductively closed which again contradicts with M being a pure partial model. It follows that, using the first interpretation of negation-as-failure, P_2 does not have a pure partial model.

Using the second interpretation, we will find that the empty set is a pure partial model of P_2 (see below).

We conclude that $Not\ A_i$ is true iff A_i is false. In order to formalize this, we need to characterize what it means for a literal to be 'false' w.r.t. a given interpretation. It was stated before that a pure partial model of a GLP is a set of atoms. This implies that pure partial models do not list atoms that are considered to be false (e.g. by including their negation). This is an important difference between all previous major GLP semantics (such as the well-founded semantics[Gel88a], the stable partial model semantics [Sac90a], the three-valued stable semantics[Prz90a]) and the pure semantics [Lae92a]: unlike the pure semantics, all other semantics put redundant information in their models. Indeed, all other semantics have the following feature in common: given an 'intended model' M, the set of negated atoms in M corresponds exactly with the greatest unfounded set[Gel88a] w.r.t. the set of atoms in M. In other words, the negated atoms do not add any information because they can be described in function of M's atoms. We believe that previous GLP semantics overestimate the role of negated atoms in their definition, which leads to a lot of confusion and complications especially when trying to incorporate classical negation besides negation-as-failure. A pure partial model lists explicitly all atoms that are true; all atoms that are false can be derived implicitly using the notion of greatest unfounded set as mentioned before.

Definition. Let P be a GLP and I an interpretation of P. $X \subseteq B_P \cup \neg B_P$ is an *unfounded set* of P w.r.t. I if for each $p \in X$ and for each $r \in ground(P)$ with $H(r) = p$ one of the following holds:

(U1) $B(r) \cap X \neq \emptyset$.

(U2) $B(r) \cap Not\ I \neq \emptyset$, i.e. r is *blocked* in I.

The *greatest unfounded set* of P w.r.t. I, denoted $U(I)$, is the union of all sets that are unfounded sets of P w.r.t. I. $U(I)$ is easily seen to be an unfounded set. $\square$

Intuitively, an unfounded set w.r.t. an interpretation I contains atoms that are known to be non-inferrable from I and from any extension of I. The greatest unfounded set w.r.t. I is exactly the set of all ground literals that are false w.r.t. I. The definition of rule applicability now follows immediately.

Definition. Let P be a GLP. Given an interpretation I of P and a rule r in $ground(P)$, we say that r is *applicable* in I iff $B(r) \subseteq I \cup Not\ U(I)$. $\square$

The next definition (which resembles the definition of unfounded sets) introduces assumption sets. Assumption sets differ from unfounded sets in that the atoms they contain are not inferrable from the interpretation at hand but might be inferrable from extensions of it. Unfounded sets contain ground atoms that are false; assumption sets contain ground atoms that are false or undefined. Hence every unfounded set is an assumption set. As an example, consider the logic program consisting of two rules $Not\ p \to q$ and $Not\ q \to p$; and let I be the empty set. The greatest unfounded set w.r.t. I is $\neg B_P$ whereas $\{p,q\}$ is an assumption set as neither p nor q is inferrable from I. Formally, this amounts to the following definition.

Definition. Let P be a GLP and let I be an interpretation of P. $X \subseteq B_P \cup \neg B_P$ is an *assumption set* of P w.r.t. I if for each p in X and for each rule r in $ground(P)$ with $H(r)=p$, one of the following holds:

(A1) $B(r) \cap X \neq \varnothing$.

(A2) $B(r) \cap Not\ I \neq \varnothing$.

(A3) $B(r) \not\subseteq I \cup Not\ U(I)$, i.e. r is *non-applicable* in I.

The *greatest assumption set* of P w.r.t. I, denoted $A(I)$, is the union of all sets that are assumption sets of P w.r.t. I. $A(I)$ is easily seen to be an assumption set.

I is said to be *assumption-free* iff $A(I) \cap I = \varnothing$. $\square$

As discussed in the previous section, this definition together with the definition of pure partial models formalizes the pure semantics for GLPs.

Consider P_3.

$$Not\ p \to q$$
$$Not\ q \to p$$

Let $M_1 = \varnothing$. Then $U(M_1) = \neg B_{P_3}$. $\overline{M_1} = B_{P_3} \cup \neg B_{P_3} = \{p, q, \neg p, \neg q\}$ is the greatest assumption set w.r.t. M_1 as no rule for p or q is applicable in M_1. Hence, M_1 is a pure partial model of P_3.

Let $M_2 = \{p\}$. Then $U(M_2) = \{q\} \cup \neg B_{P_3}$. So $\overline{M_2} = \{q\} \cup \neg B_{P_3}$ is the greatest unfounded set w.r.t. M_2, and since every unfounded set is an assumption set, we find that $\overline{M_2}$ is an assumption set. Moreover, $\{p,q\} \cup \neg B_{P_3}$ is not an assumption set as the rule $Not\ q \to p$ does not satisfy any of the conditions in the definition of assumption set: $Not\ q \to p$ is applicable in M_2, not blocked in M_2 and its body does not contain any 'assumptions'. So, $\overline{M_2}$ is the greatest assumption set w.r.t. M_2 which means that M_2 is a pure partial model of P_3. In much the same way, one can show that also $M_3=\{q\}$ is a pure partial model. And that's it; $M_4=\{p\,,\,q\}$ is not a pure partial model as the greatest assumption set w.r.t. M_4 is $M_4 \cup \neg B_{P_3}$.

Reconsider P_2.

$$Not\ p\ \rightarrow\ p$$

The empty set is the only pure partial model of P_2 since $B_{P_2} \cup \neg B_{P_2}=\{p\,,\,\neg p\}$ is an assumption set w.r.t. $\varnothing$ (*Not p* $\rightarrow$ *p* is non-applicable because $U(\varnothing)=\{\neg p\}$) and also w.r.t. $\{p\}$ (so $\{p\}$ is not assumption free and therefore it is not a pure partial model).

It was shown in[Lae92a] that the pure semantics for GLPs is universal in the sense that it captures the meaning of every GLP, that the pure partial models for GLPs are equivalent with the 3-valued stable models, that there is a unique minimal ($\subset$) pure partial model that is equivalent with the well-founded partial model, that the maximal pure partial models are equivalent with the stable partial models, and that the greatest lowerbound of all maximal pure partial models exists and is equivalent with the maximal deterministic model [Sac90a]. For a detailed discussion, we refer to [Lae91a,Lae92a]. We note that the semantics presented in this section are slightly different from those presented in [Lae92a]: in order to prepare for the semantics for ELPs we already incorporated $\neg B_P$ in the above definitions which obviously is of no use for GLPs as such.

4. Classical negation ($\neg$)

In this section, we focus on the semantics of classical negation. To this end, we consider logic programs that allow for classical negation but not for negation-as-failure. According to the definition of ELP, a *negative logic program (NLP)* is a set of rules of the form

$$L_1\,,\ \cdots\,,L_n\ \rightarrow\ L_0$$

where $n \geq 0$, and each L_i is a literal.

Note that not only atoms but also negated atoms are inferrable. A first consequence of this fact is that models must be sets of literals instead of sets of atoms as was the case in the previous section. Rule applicability is easy: given an NLP P, a rule r in $ground(P)$ is applicable in an interpretation I of P if all literals in its body are in I, i.e. $B(r) \subseteq I$. Another consequence is that the problem of contradictions shows up in this class of programs. As an example consider P_4.

$$\rightarrow\ p$$
$$\rightarrow\ \neg p$$

Both rules are applicable, but they clearly cannot be both applied in a consistent model.

For GLPs, a model for a logic program is an interpretation in which each rule is either applied or non-applicable. For NLPs, this classical notion of rule satisfaction is not enough as it cannot deal with a situation where competing rules (i.e. rules with complementary heads p and $\neg p$) are applicable. We therefore add that a rule is also satisfied if it has an applicable competing rule, and we say that it is 'defeated' by this competitor. A defeated rule should not be applied and is not to be used in the process of inferring literals. As unfounded sets contain literals that are known to be non-inferrable from the interpretation at hand and any extension of it, the definition of unfounded sets for NLPs is based on this idea of defeating.

Definition. Let P be an NLP and I an interpretation of P. $X \subseteq B_P \cup \neg B_P$ is an *unfounded set* of P w.r.t. I if for each $p \in X$ and for each $r \in ground(P)$ with $H(r)=p$ one of the following holds:

(U1) $B(r) \cap X \neq \varnothing$.

(U3) $\exists \hat{r} \in ground(P)$ with $H(\hat{r})=\neg p$ and $B(\hat{r}) \subseteq I$, i.e. r is *defeated* in I.

The *greatest unfounded set* of P w.r.t. I, denoted $U(I)$, is the union of all sets that are unfounded sets of P w.r.t. I. $U(I)$ is easily seen to be an unfounded set. $\square$

Because NLPs are free from negation-as-failure, there obviously is no equivalent for (U2).

As in the previous section, we weaken the notion of unfounded set in order to obtain assumption sets. Recall that assumption sets contain literals that are non-inferrable from the interpretation at hand but that might be inferrable from extensions of it. The definition of pure partial models, combined with the next definition of assumption set completes the pure semantics for NLPs.

Definition. Let P be an NLP and let I be an interpretation of P. $X \subseteq B_P \cup \neg B_P$ is an *assumption set* of P w.r.t. I if for each p in X and for each rule r in $ground(P)$ with $H(r)=p$, one of the following holds:

(A1) $B(r) \cap X \neq \varnothing$

(A3') $B(r) \not\subseteq I$, i.e. r is *non-applicable* in I

(A4) $\exists \hat{r} \in ground(P)$ with $H(\hat{r})=\neg p$ and $B(\hat{r}) \subseteq I$, i.e. r is *defeated* in I.

(A5) $\exists \hat{r} \in ground(P)$ with $H(\hat{r})=\neg p$ and $B(\hat{r}) \cap U(I)=\varnothing$, i.e. r is *defeasible* in I.

The *greatest assumption set* of P w.r.t. I, denoted $A(I)$, is the union of all sets that are assumption sets of P w.r.t. I. $A(I)$ is easily seen to be an assumption set.

I is said to be *assumption-free* iff $A(I) \cap I=\varnothing$. $\square$

Condition (A5), defeasibility, plays an important role in making the pure semantics universal. We illustrate this in the next example. Defeasibility essentially relaxes defeating: instead of demanding that a rule's competitor be applicable, we only require that its body not be "false", i.e. it is either true or undefined. Since the set of all literals that are false is exactly the greatest unfounded set (see previous section), this translates to the requirement that the intersection of the competitor's body and the greatest unfounded set be empty (i.e. (A5)).

Consider the following NLP which illustrates the necessity of condition (A5) in the definition of assumption set.

$$\to \neg p$$
$$\neg p \to p$$

Its only pure partial model is the empty set. Without condition (A5), this program would not have a pure partial model.

5. Extended logic programs

As mentioned before, an ELP is a logic program that incorporates both classical negation and negation-as-failure. It is important to note that there is no relationship between the two kinds of negation: negation-as-failure and classical negation are independent from one another; the semantics of one does not interfere with the semantics of the other. As a result, the semantics for ELPs are obtained by a rather straightforward merge of the semantics obtained in the previous sections. Only a few obvious modifications to the earlier conditions (U3), (A4) and (A5) are needed. Indeed, (U3') and (A4') are derived from (U3) and (A4) respectively by using the appropriate definition of rule applicability when also negation-as-failure is involved; similarly (A5') is obtained from (A5) by specifying the additional requirement that defeaters should not be blocked (i.e. $B(\hat{r}) \cap Not\ I = \varnothing$).

Definition. Let P be an ELP and I an interpretation of P. $X \subseteq B_P \cup \neg B_P$ is an *unfounded set* of P w.r.t. I if for each $p \in X$ and for each $r \in ground(P)$ with $H(r)=p$ one of the following holds:

(U1) $B(r) \cap X \neq \varnothing$.

(U2) $B(r) \cap Not\ I \neq \varnothing$, i.e. r is *blocked* in I

(U3') $\exists\ \hat{r} \in ground(P)$ with $H(\hat{r})=\neg p$ and $B(\hat{r}) \subseteq I \cup Not\ X$, i.e. r is *defeated* in I.

The *greatest unfounded set* of P w.r.t. I, denoted $U(I)$, is the union of all sets that are unfounded sets of P w.r.t. I. $U(I)$ is easily seen to be an unfounded set. $\square$

Definition. Let P be an ELP and let I be an interpretation of P. $X \subseteq B_P \cup \neg B_P$ is an *assumption set* of P w.r.t. I if for each p in X and for each rule r in $ground(P)$ with $H(r)=p$, one of the following holds:

(A1) $B(r) \cap X \neq \varnothing$

(A2) $B(r) \cap Not\ I \neq \varnothing$, i.e. r is *blocked* in I.

(A3) $B(r) \not\subseteq I \cup Not\ U(I)$, i.e. r is *non-applicable* in I

(A4') $\exists\ \hat{r} \in ground(P)$ with $H(\hat{r})=\neg p$ and $B(\hat{r}) \subseteq I \cup Not\ U(I)$, i.e. r is *defeated* in I.

(A5') $\exists\ \hat{r} \in ground(P)$ with $H(\hat{r})=\neg p$ and $B(\hat{r}) \cap (U(I) \cup Not\ I)=\varnothing$, i.e. r is *defeasible* in I.

The *greatest assumption set* of P w.r.t. I, denoted $A(I)$, is the union of all sets that are assumption sets of P w.r.t. I. $A(I)$ is easily seen to be an assumption set.

I is said to be *assumption-free* iff $A(I) \cap I = \varnothing$. $\square$

6. Some interesting features of the pure semantics

It is clear from the definitions above that the pure semantics preserves the same status for positive and negative literals, thus satisfying one of our initial requirements. We still need to show that the pure semantics is universally consistent in that it resolves all contradictions. This is the topic of this section, the theorems of which prove that every ELP has at least one pure partial model and that all pure partial models are consistent.

Theorem 1. *Every pure partial model of an ELP is consistent.*

Proof. Let M be a pure partial model for an ELP P and suppose that it is inconsistent, i.e. for some atom p both p and $\neg p$ are in M. By definition, neither p nor $\neg p$ are in $A(M)$. Hence there is a rule r in $ground(P)$ with $H(r)=p$ such that 1. $\forall \hat{r} \in ground(P)$ with $H(\hat{r})=\neg p, B(\hat{r}) \cap (U(M) \cup Not\ M) \neq \emptyset$. And there must also be a rule r' in $ground(P)$ with $H(r')=\neg p$ such that 2. $B(r') \cap A(M)=\emptyset$; and 3. $B(r') \cap Not\ M=\emptyset$. Obviously, 2 and 3 imply $B(r') \cap (A(M) \cup Not\ M)=\emptyset$ which contradicts with 1 since $U(M) \subseteq A(M)$. So we find that p and $\neg p$ cannot be both in M. $\square$

Lemma 1. *Let I and J be interpretations for an ELP P. If $I \subseteq J$, then $U(I) \subseteq U(J)$.*

Proof. We show that $U(I)$ is an unfounded set w.r.t. J. Let $p \in U(I)$. Then each rule r in $ground(P)$ with head p is either defeated or blocked in I, and thus also in J, or $B(r) \cap U(I) \neq \emptyset$. $\square$

Definition. Given an ELP P, the mapping W_P from interpretations to interpretations is defined as $W_P(I)=\{q \mid \exists$ rule r in $ground(P)$ with $H(r)=q$ such that r is applicable and non-defeasible in $I\}$.

Let α range over all countable ordinals. The sets I_α and I^∞, whose elements are literals in $B_P \cup \neg B_P$, are defined recursively by:

1. For limit ordinal α,

$$I_0=\emptyset$$

$$I_\alpha= \cup_{\beta < \alpha} I_\beta$$

2. For successor ordinal $k+1$,

$$I_{k+1}=W_P(I_k)$$

3. Finally,

$$I^\infty= \cup_\alpha I_\alpha$$

$\square$

Lemma 2. *The sequence I_α is monotonic.*

Proof. We first show that the transformation W_P is monotone. Let A and B be interpretations such that $A \subseteq B$. By Lemma 1, $U(A) \subseteq U(B)$. So every rule which is applicable in A is also applicable in B and every rule which is non-defeasible in A is also non-defeasible in B. Hence $W_P(A) \subseteq W_P(B)$, i.e. W_P is monotone.

The rest of the proof is by induction on α. For $\alpha=0$, the result is obvious. For $\alpha>0$, assume the lemma holds for $\beta < \alpha$. First let $\alpha=k+1$ be a successor ordinal. If $p \in I_k$, it follows from the above definitions that there is a smallest $\beta < k$ such that $p \in W_P(I_\beta)$. But W_P is monotonic, so it follows from the induction hypothesis that $p \in W_P(I_k)$, i.e. $p \in I_{k+1}$. Now let α be a limit ordinal. Then monotonicity follows immediately from the definition of I_α. $\square$

It follows from Tarski's fixpoint results[Tar55a] that I^∞ is the least fixed point of the operator W_P.

Lemma 3. *For any two ordinals α and β, if $W_P(I_\alpha) \cap U(I_\beta) \neq \emptyset$, then either $I_\alpha \cap U(I_\beta) \neq \emptyset$ or $I_\beta \cap U(I_\alpha) \neq \emptyset$.*

Proof. Assume $p \in W_P(I_\alpha) \cap U(I_\beta)$. $p \in U(I_\beta)$ means by definition that for each rule $r \in ground(P)$ with $H(r)=p$ either
(1) $B(r) \cap U(I_\beta) \neq \emptyset$ or
(2) $B(r) \cap Not\ I_\beta \neq \emptyset$ or
(3) $\exists\ \hat{r} \in ground(P)$ with $H(\hat{r})=\neg p$ such that $B(\hat{r}) \subseteq I_\beta \cup Not\ U(I_\beta)$.
By definition of W_P, $p \in W_P(I_\alpha)$ means
$\exists\ r \in ground(P)$ with $H(r)=p$ such that
(4) $B(r) \subseteq I_\alpha \cup Not\ U(I_\alpha)$ and
(5) $\forall\ \hat{r} \in ground(P)$ with $H(\hat{r})=\neg p, B(\hat{r}) \cap (U(I_\alpha) \cup Not\ I_\alpha) \neq \emptyset$.
In addition, it follows from the respective definitions that for any two subsets A and B of $B_P \cup \neg B_P$, $A \cap Not\ B=\emptyset$. In particular, $U(I_\beta) \cap Not\ U(I_\alpha)=\emptyset$, $I_\alpha \cap Not\ I_\beta=\emptyset$, $I_\beta \cap Not\ I_\alpha=\emptyset$ and $U(I_\alpha) \cap Not\ U(I_\beta)=\emptyset$. Using this, we conclude the following: (1) together with (4) yields $U(I_\beta) \cap I_\alpha \neq \emptyset$; (2) and (4) give $I_\beta \cap U(I_\alpha) \neq \emptyset$; and finally (3) and (5) gives $I_\beta \cap U(I_\alpha) \neq \emptyset$ or $I_\alpha \cap U(I_\beta) \neq \emptyset$. We find that either $I_\alpha \cap U(I_\beta) \neq \emptyset$ or $I_\beta \cap U(I_\alpha) \neq \emptyset$. $\square$

Lemma 4. *$I^\infty \cap U(I^\infty)=\emptyset$ for any ELP P.*

Proof. We prove by induction on α that $I_\alpha \cap U(I_\alpha)=\emptyset$. As $I_0=\emptyset$, the base case is obviously true. For $\alpha>0$ assume that the lemma is true for all $\beta < \alpha$.

(I) Let $\alpha=k+1$ be a successor ordinal. Assume that $I_\alpha \cap U(I_\alpha) \neq \emptyset$. Take the smallest possible $l \leq k$ for which there is a literal p such that $p \in I_{l+1} \cap U(I_{k+1})$ (l exists by Lemma 2). Then by Lemma 3, either $I_l \cap U(I_{k+1}) \neq \emptyset$ or $I_{k+1} \cap U(I_l) \neq \emptyset$. The former is clearly in contradiction with the definition of l. The latter is also false since it implies, using Lemma 2 and Lemma 1, that $I_{k+1} \cap U(I_k) \neq \emptyset$ which gives, by Lemma 3, $I_k \cap U(I_k) \neq \emptyset$. This is in contradiction with the induction hypothesis.

(II) Let α be a limit ordinal. Assume that there is a literal $p \in I_\alpha \cap U(I_\alpha)$. Take the least successor ordinal $k+1$ such that $p \in I_{k+1} \cap U(I_\alpha)$ (k exists by definition of I_α and Lemma 2). Lemma 3 then gives $I_k \cap U(I_\alpha) \neq \varnothing$ or $I_\alpha \cap U(I_k) \neq \varnothing$. But this is false since we can prove that $\forall\, k < \alpha$: (A) $I_\alpha \cap U(I_k) = \varnothing$ and (B) $I_k \cap U(I_\alpha) = \varnothing$. We first prove (A). Assume that $p \in I_\alpha \cap U(I_k)$ for some $k < \alpha$. Take the least successor ordinal $l+1$ such that $p \in I_{l+1} \cap U(I_k)$ (l exists by Lemma 2). Clearly $l+1 < \alpha$ (since α is a limit ordinal) and either $k \le l+1$ or $l+1 \le k$. Then, using Lemma 2, either $I_k \subseteq I_{l+1}$ or $I_{l+1} \subseteq I_k$. Thus, using Lemma 1, either $I_{l+1} \cap U(I_{l+1}) \neq \varnothing$ or $I_k \cap U(I_k) \neq \varnothing$. Both alternatives contradict with the induction hypothesis. This proves (A).

To prove (B), assume that for some $k < \alpha$, $I_k \cap U(I_\alpha) \neq \varnothing$. Take the smallest possible successor ordinal $l+1$ for which there is a literal p such that $p \in I_{l+1} \cap U(I_\alpha)$ (l exists by Lemma 2). Applying Lemma 3, we find that either $I_l \cap U(I_\alpha) \neq \varnothing$ or $I_\alpha \cap U(I_l) \neq \varnothing$. The former is in contradiction with the definition of l while the latter contradicts with part (A) of this proof (as $l < \alpha$). We find that our assumption was wrong, so (B) must be true. $\square$

Theorem 2. *Every ELP has at least one pure partial model, namely I^∞.*

Proof. Let P be an ELP. We show that I^∞ is a pure partial model for P, i.e. $\overline{I^\infty} = A(I^\infty)$. So we need to prove that $\overline{I^\infty} \subseteq A(I^\infty)$ and $I^\infty \cap A(I^\infty) = \varnothing$. The former follows immediately from the definitions of W_P and assumption set. To show the latter we first show that every defeated rule is also defeasible in I^∞ and every applicable rule is also non-blocked in I^∞. If r is defeated in I^∞ by $\hat{r}$ then $B(\hat{r}) \subseteq I^\infty \cup Not\, U(I^\infty)$ and using Lemma 4 we find $B(\hat{r}) \cap (U(I^\infty) \cup Not\, I^\infty) = \varnothing$, i.e. r is defeasible in I^∞. If r is applicable in I^∞ then $B(r) \subseteq I^\infty \cup Not\, U(I^\infty)$, and by Lemma 4, $B(r) \cap Not\, I^\infty = \varnothing$, i.e. r is non-blocked in I^∞. By the definition of W_P, only applicable (and thus non-blocked), non-defeasible (and thus non-defeated) rules can introduce elements in I^∞, and therefore, again by definition, I^∞ is assumption free, i.e. $I^\infty \cap A(I^\infty) = \varnothing$. $\square$

7. Conclusion

The pure semantics for extended logic programs is a universally consistent semantics that follows naturally from the intuitive meaning of the two kinds of negation that it supports: negation-as-failure and classical negation. We have shown that it is defined for *any* extended logic program and that it resolves all contradictions without unnatural discriminations, thus overcoming the shortcomings of previously proposed semantics, making it more useful for database applications and knowledge representation in general.

8. Acknowledgement

I am very grateful to Philippe Besnard for his stimulating and interesting comments and also to Dirk Vermeir for the many useful discussions. •

References

Gab91a.
> D. Gabbay, E. Laenens, and D. Vermeir, "Credulous vs. Sceptical Semantics for Ordered Logic Programs," in *Proceedings of the International Conference on Knowledge Representation (KR91)*, pp. 208-217, Morgan Kaufmann, 1991.

Gel88a.
> A. Van Gelder, K. Ross, and J. S. Schlipf, *The Well-Founded Semantics for General Logic Programs*, 1988. UCSC-CRL-88-16

Gel89a.
> M. Gelfond and V. Lifschitz, "Logic Programs with Classical Negation," *7th International Logic Programming Conference*, 1989.

Kow90a.
> R. Kowalski and F. Sadri, "Logic programs with exceptions," in *Proc. of the 7th International Logic Programming Conference*, pp. 579-597, MIT Press, 1990.

Lae90a.
> E. Laenens, D. Vermeir, and D. Sacca, "Extending logic programming," in *Proceedings of the SIGMOD conference*, pp. 184-193, 1990.

Lae90b.
> E. Laenens and D. Vermeir, "A Fixpoint Semantics of Ordered Logic," *Journal of Logic and Computation*, vol. 1, no. 2, pp. 159-185, 1990.

Lae90c.
> E. Laenens, "Foundations of Ordered Logic," *PhD Thesis, University of Antwerp (UIA)*, 1990.

Lae91a.
> E. Laenens, D. Vermeir, and C. Zaniolo, "Pure models for logic programs: a simplification and unification of logic programming semantics," *Technical report, 91-31*, 1991.

Lae92a.
> E. Laenens, D. Vermeir, and C. Zaniolo, "Logic programming semantics made easy," *Proceedings of the ICALP'92 conference*, pp. 499-508, 1992.

Lae92b.
> E. Laenens and D. Vermeir, "Assumption-free Semantics for Ordered Programs: On the Relationship between Well-Founded and Stable Partial Models," *Journal of Logic and Computation*, vol. 2, no. 2, pp. 133-172, 1992.

Llo87a.
> J. W. Lloyd, *Foundations of Logic Programming*, Springer Verlag, 1987.

Prz90a.
> T. Przymusinski, "Well-founded semantics coincides with three-valued stable semantics," *Fundamenta Informaticae*, vol. 13, pp. 445-463, IOS Press, 1990.

Sac90a.
> D. Sacca and C. Zaniolo, "Stable models and Non-determinism for logic

programs with negation," *Proc. ACM Symp. on Principles of Database Systems*, 1990.

Tar55a.

A. Tarski, "A Lattice Theoretical Fixpoint Theorem and its Application," *Pacific Journal of Mathematics*, no. 5, pp. 285-309, 1955.

Structure learning approaches in Causal Probabilistics Networks *

P. Larrañaga , Y. Yurramendi
Dept. of Computer Science and Artificial Intelligence
University of the Basque Country
649 p.k. E-20080 . Donostia-Spain
e-mail: ccplamup@si.ehu.es

July 15, 1993

Abstract

Causal Probabilistic Networks (CPN) , a method of reasoning using probabilities, has become popular over the last few years within the AI probability and uncertainty community. This paper begins with an introduction to this paradigm, followed by a presentation of some of the current approaches in the induction of the structure learning in CPN . The paper concludes with a concise presentation of alternative approaches to the problem, and the conclusions of this review.

1   Introduction

From a informal perspective CPN , they are Directed Acyclic Graphs (DAGs) , where the nodes are random variables, and the arcs specify the independence assumptions that must be hold between the random variables.To specify the probability distribution of a CPN, one must give the prior probabilities of all root nodes (nodes with no predecessors) and the conditional probabilities of all no root nodes, given all possible combinations of their direct predecessors. These numbers in conjunction with the DAG, specify the CPN completely.

In Pearl's words (Pearl 1993), some of the motivations of the growing of the CPN are the following:

1. The failure of rule-based systems to exhibit certain plausible patterns of reasoning is symptomatic of fundamental limitations.

*This work was supported by grant from the Gobierno Vasco - Departamento de Educación , Universidades e Investigación PGV 92-20

2. The consistent agreement between plausible reasoning and probability calculus, suggests that human intution invokes some crud form of probabilistic computation.

3. The computational difficulties that plagued earlier probabilistic systems could not be very fundamental and should be overcome by making the right choice of simplifying assumptions.

4. No reasoning can take place unless our knowledge embodies many (conditional) independence assumptions, and graphical forms are the only plausible way in which these assumptions could be represented.

5. If graphical knwoledge representation could be found, then it should be possible to use the links as message-passing channels.

2 Current approach in structure learning

2.1 Learning Causal Trees and Polytree

Chow and Liu (1968) developed a method that constructs a tree-structured Markov graph, from a database of discrete variables. If the data are being generated by an underlying distribution P that can be represented as a tree, then the Chow-Liu algorithm constructs a tree with a probability distribution that converges to P as the size of the database increases. If the data are not generated by a tree, then the algorithm constructs the tree that most closely approximates the underlying distribution P (in the sense of cross-entropy).

A polytree (singly connected network) is a belief network that constains at most one undirected path between any two nodes in the network. Rebane and Pearl (1989) used the Chow-Liu algorihm as the basis for an algorithm that recovers polytrees from a probability distribution. In determining the orientation of arcs, the Rebane-Pearl algorithm assumes the availability of a conditional-independence test.

Acid & De Campos & Gonzalez & Molina & Perez de la Blanca (1991) describe a learning algorithm implemented in CASTLE (CAusal STructures from inductive LEarning) more general that the former.

2.2 Learning structures in multiply connected networks

L. R. Andersen & J. H. Krebss & J. D. Andersen (1991) described a system called STENO including a model search for building the knowledge base, a shell for making the knowledge base available for users in consultation sessions, and a user interface. The knowledge base of the expert system is created by combining expert knowledge and a statistical model search in a model conversion scheme based on a theory developed by Lauritzen & Spiegelhalter, and using exact tests as suggested by Kreiner. The conversion sequence is as follows: A graphical model - a class of log-linear model that has the property that each member has a one-to-one correspondence to an undirected graph- is used for model search. Then the resulting graphical model is converted into a recursive model - model in which a certain orden is imposed on the variables- and into a Markov random field , that is used as a knowledge base for propagation of probabilities and inference.

Fung & Crawford (1990) have developped a system called CONSTRUCTOR that integrates techniques and concepts from probabilistic networks, artificial intelligence, and statistics in orden to induce Markov networks - undirected probabilistic networks - . The primary goal of CONSTRUCTOR is to find qualitative structure from data. CONSTRUCTOR finds structure by first, modelling each feature in a data set as a node in a Markov network and secondly, by finding the neighbours of each node in the network. In Markov networks, the neighbours of a node have the property of being the smallest set of nodes which shield the node from being affected by other nodes in the graph. This property is used in aheuristic search to identify each node's neighbours. The traditional $\mathcal{X}^2$ test for independence is used to test if a set of nodes shield another node. Cross-validation is used to estimate the quality of alternative approaches.

Malvestuto (1991) presents a heuristic procedure to approximate an $n-$ dimensional discrete probability distribution with a descomposable model of a given complexity. Without loss of generality, he shows that the search space can be restricted to a suitable subclass of descomposable models, whose members are called elementary models. The selected elementary model is constructed in an incremental manner according to a local-optimality criterium that consists in minimizing a suitable cost function.

E. Herskovits & G. Cooper (1990) constructs a system call KUTATO that constructs an initial CPN in which all the variables in the database are assumed to be marginally independent. The entropy of this belief network is calculated, and that arc is added that minimizes the entropy of the resulting CPN. Conditional probabilities for an arc are obtained directly from the database via symmetric Dirichlet probabilities.

Recently G.F. Cooper & E. Herskovits (1992) have developed a method to searches for a CPN structure that has a high posterior probability given the database, and outputs the structure and its probability. A CPN structure B_S is augmented by conditional probabilities B_P to form a CPN B. Thus, $B = (B_S, B_P)$ .Let D be a database of cases, Z be the set of variables represented by D , B_S one CPN structure containing exactly those variables that are in Z. Under four assumptions, Cooper & Herskovits got a formula for computing $P(B_{S_i}, D)$,and propose a heuristic-search-method for maximizing $P(B_S/D)$ that can be considered as a greedy-search method. The algorithm begins by making the assumption that a node has no parents , and then adds incrementally that parent whose addition most increases the probability of the resulting structure.

3 Alternative approach in structure learning

3.1 Genetics algorithms

Genetic algorithms (Goldberg 1989 , Michalewicz 1992)) are search algorithms based on the mechanics of natural selection and natural genetics. They combine survival of the fittest among string structures with a structured yet randomized information exchange to form a search algorithm which evolves to the optimum with probability 1. An pseudocodigo for an abstract genetic algorithm, can be as follows:

begin AGA
      Make initial population at random
      WHILE NOT stop DO
      BEGIN
      Select parents from the population
      Let the selected parents *Produce children*
      Mutate the children with a probability near zero
      Extend the population by adding the children to it
      Reduce the extended population to the original size
      END
      Output the optimum of the population.
end AGA

One alternative approach for structure learning of CPN based on Genetics algorithms, consists of applying a Genetic Algorithm (GA) to a population of individuals (structures of CPN), measuring the cost function by the formulae given by Cooper & Herkovits ,$P(B_S, D)$. The cardinality of the search space is given by Robinson formulae about the number, $f(n)$ - n number of nodes- , of possible structures of DAG with n nodes:

$$f(n) = \sum_{i=1}^{n}(-1)^{i+1}\binom{n}{i}2^{i(n-i)}f(n-i)$$

The number of individuals ni , that constitutes the initial population can be taken as a increasing function of $f(n)$. The topology or structures of the CPN can be represented by a connectivity matrix $C \in M(n,n)$ verifiying the DAG conditions. That is, we can consider the CPN structures as elements of the hypercub in $\mathcal{R}^{n^2}$.

3.2 Simulated Annealing (SA)

The algorithm known as Simulated Annealing (SA) Statistical Cooling, Stochastic Relaxation,.. (Aarts 1989) is based on the analogy between the physical annealing of solids - finding low energy states- and combinatorial optimisation problems.

We thought that SA can be used in conjunction with polytrees , using them as initial solutions for the SA algorithm.

3.3 Correspondence analysis

Another approach to the problem is based on correspondence analysis, a multivariate statistical technique based on space dimensionality reduction, that interpreting the factorial coordenates of the features attributes, permits to obtain the causality relations among the differents variables in the system.

4 Conclusions

After this brief revision of the approachs in the structure learning of CPN, we think that a realistic approach must be based on combining expert knowledge , statistical model search and artificial intelligence heuristic methods.

On the other hand , it is necessary to develop methods to measure the goodness of the approximations. For instance if the induction is being done from a database got by simulating a CPN, we must define a measure of distance between the initial CPN and the CPN obtained by the approach.

References

[1] Aarts E.H.L. , Korst J.H.M. (1989) *Simulated Annealing andf Boltzmann Machines* . Wiley , Chichester.

[2] Acid S.,De Campos L.M., Gonzalez A.,Molina R., Perez de la Blanca N.(1991) Learning with CASTLE , in Symbolic and Quantitative Approaches to Uncertainty. *Lectures Notes in Computer Science 548*R. Kruse, P. Siegel (Eds.). Springer Verlang 99-106.

[3] Andersen L.R., Jens H.K., Andersen D. (1991) Steno: an expert system for medical disgnosis based on graphical models and model search. *Journal of Applied Statistics* Vol 18, n 1, 139-153.

[4] Chow C.K., Liu C.N. (1968). Approximating discrete probability distributions with dependence trees.*IEEE Trans. on Info. Theory* IT-14, 462-467..

[5] Cooper G.F., Herskovits E.A. (1992) A Bayesian Method for the Induction of Probabilistic Networks from data. *Machine Learning* vol 9, 309-347.

[6] Fung R.M., Crawford S.L.(1990) Constructor:A system for the Induction of Probabilistic Models. *Proceedings of AAAI* 762-769

[7] Glymour C., Scheines R., Spirtes P., Kelly K. (1987) *Discovering Causal Structure.* New York: Academic Press.

[8] Goldberg D.E. (1989) *Genetic algorithms in search, optimization, machine learning.* Addison-Wesley.

[9] Herskovits E., Cooper G.(1990) Kutato:An Entropy-Driven System for Construction of probabilistic Expert Systems from Databases. *Knowledge Systems Laboratory.Medical Compuetr Science.Stanford University. Report KSL-90-22*

[10] Malvestuto F.M. (1991) Approximating discrete probability distributions with descomposable models.*IEEE Transactions on systems , man , and cybernetics* Vol. 21, No. 5, 1287-1294.

[11] Michalewicz Z. (1992) *Genetics Algorithms + Data Structures = Evolution Programs.* Springer-Verlang.

[12] Neapolitan R.E. (1990) *Probabilistic reasoning in Expert Systems. Theory and Algorithms.* John Wiley & Sons, Inc.

[13] Pearl J.(1988) *Probabilistic reasoning in intelligent systems* San Mateo CA: Morgan Kaufmann.

[14] Pearl J. (1993) Belief networks revisited .*Artificial Intelligence* 59. 49-56.

[15] Rebane G., Pearl J. (1989) The recovery of causal poly-trees from statistical data.*Uncertainty in Artificial Intelligence 3* 175-182.

Weak extensions for Default Theories
(extended abstract)

F. Lévy

LIPN
CNRS-URA 1507
University of Paris Nord
Avenue J.B. Clément
93430 Villetaneuse
France
E-mail : fl@lipn.univ-paris13.fr
Phone : (33)-1- 49 40 36 17

Abstract : We propose a notion of weak extension of a default theory, motivated by a kind of paraconsistent view of default reasoning, and which coincides with Reiter's extensions when they exist. When the default theory is inconsistent, in the sense that it has no extension, we determine defaults which are not involved in the inconsistency, preserving the possibility to draw some default conclusions. Moreover, any finite default theory has weak extensions, though the question remains open for infinite default theories. Weak extensions correspond to some consistent labelings of the defaults, according to a notion of consistency close to the standard one in the TMS, so computing weak extensions may adapt standard methods of the TMS. We also compare weak extensions to propositions based on a maximal consistent set of defaults, and show that maximal consistency generate far more extensions. Finally, we briefly sketch how our results can be extended to Autoepistemic Logic and to Logic Programming.

Default logic [Reiter 80] has the aim to formalize the use of typicality in common sense reasoning. Basically, a default is an inference rule which allows a particular deduction, but submits it to a consistency condition. This formalism is very appealing, since it is rather intuitive and modular. As most non monotonic logics, one default theory may allow to deduce several sets of beliefs, called extensions. Extensions are defined by a fixpoint technique, which expresses that every default deduction in the extension fits its consistency conditions.

Nevertheless, Reiter's definition has an undesirable consequence : default theories may happen to have no extension at all. As only normal default theories always have extensions, this has lead the community to focus on normal defaults.

Several works have addressed the lack of extensions issue. [Besnard 83] considers a transformation of general default theories into normal prerequisite-free ones. Most other approaches modify the way in which consistency conditions are aggregated when several defaults are considered. [Luka 85] suggests to inhibit a default rule when its conclusion contradicts the justification of an already triggered one, which replaces the fixpoint condition by a maximality condition. Other researchers have followed the same way, considering different notions of maximally consistent sets of formulas ([Poole 88], [Luka 88], [Brewka 89, 91], [Delgr & Jack 91], [Schaub 91]).

A review or a comparison of most of these approaches can be found in [Froi & Meng 92], [Moi 92] and [Schaub 92]

To allow any theory to have extensions, these suggestions nevertheless pay a price : the number of extensions in their new sense is generally greater than in Reiter's sense. Moreover, the faithfulness of these modifications to the intuitive meaning of a default (as long as it is consistent to believe its conclusion, believe it) is often debatable. We prefer to be as close as possible to this intuitive meaning, i.e. to consider that a default is triggered if its own justification is consistent, and to modify in a paraconsistent manner the way these conditions are aggregated : if an inconsistency arises, it involves only some culprits and not the whole theory, so the remaining defaults can still be consistently used.

We first recall Default Logic and some explanation of how default theories may happen to have no extension (1). We infer from that a new definition of extensions which delineates in these cases some limited ill-formed sets of defaults (those which are unstable), and allows typical reasoning with the remaining ones (2). We then consider implementation issues (3). A last part compares our definition with others in the domain of Default logic and in connected domains (4).

1 Extensions of standard default logic

1.1 Default logic

...

1.2 Theories which have no extensions

That extensions be fixpoints of the operator Γ has a well-known paradoxical consequence : if the operator Γ applied to the default theory ($\mathcal{W}$, $\mathcal{D}$) has no fixpoint, even the formulas of $\mathcal{W}$ are not believed. However, these formulas do not involve any default reasoning. A knowledge base involving a lot of defaults could easily happen not to have extensions. Let us take an example.

Example 1 : Suppose typical knowledge about various sorts of birds. Birds can generaly fly, except if their wings are too short. Penguins generaly have short wings, except those particular penguins which live in the Antartic. Birds which spend most of their activity swimming and fishing (for short : swimming birds) generaly live in the Antartic, except those which fly rather good too[1]. Suppose also the general knowledge that penguins and swimming birds are birds, and that Tweety is a penguin and a swimming bird. The corresponding default theory is :

$$(\partial_1(x)) \qquad \frac{\text{bird}(x) : \text{fly}(x) \wedge \neg\text{short-winged}(x)}{\text{fly}(x)}$$

$$(\partial_2(x)) \qquad \frac{\text{penguin}(x) : \text{short-winged}(x) \wedge \neg\text{antarctic-bird}(x)}{\text{short-winged}(x)}$$

$$(\partial_3(x)) \qquad \frac{\text{swimming-bird}(x) : \text{antarctic-bird}(x) \wedge \neg\text{fly}(x)}{\text{antarctic-bird}(x)}$$

$\{\text{penguin}(x) \Rightarrow \text{bird}(x), \text{swimming-bird}(x) \Rightarrow \text{bird}(x), \text{penguin}(\text{Tweety}),$
$\text{swimming-bird}(\text{Tweety})\}$.

This theory has no extension, so in standard default logic one can even not conclude that Tweety is a swimming bird, a penguin and hence a bird. In

---

[1] For the sake of simplicity, let us forget about the ducks and other birds which do not obey this rule...

Lukaszewicz approach as in Schaub's one, triggering any of these defaults inhibits the other two, and the theory has three extensions. Our solution will consider here that no default can be consistently triggered, but that at least the facts in $\mathcal{W}$ are preserved. More, if $\mathcal{D}$ has one more default, say that penguins live either in Arctic or in Antarctic, except if they are in a zoo :

$$(\partial_4(x)) \quad \frac{\text{penguin}(x) : \text{polar-living}(x) \wedge \neg\text{in-a-zoo}(x)}{\text{polar-living}(x)}$$

this default is not involved in the lack of extension, so it is preserved too (as it is in Lukasziewicz's and Shaub's version) and allows to infer that Tweety lives near the pole. •

2. Weak extensions

2.1 Weak fixpoints

Let us now recall some useful notions.
– A **default support** for a formula F is a set P of defaults such that there is at least one ordering $P = \{\partial_1, \ldots, \partial_n\}$ verifying for any i, $W \cup \{CONS(\partial_p) \mid p<i\} \vdash PRE(\partial_i)$, and $W \cup \{CONS(\partial_p) \mid p \leq n\} \vdash F$.
– S being a set of defaults and ∂ a default, ∂ is **grounded in S** if $PRE(\partial)$ has a default support included in S..
– A set S of defaults is **grounded** if any default ∂ of S is grounded in S.

If we return to the function Γ in the definition of extensions, it transforms any set E of formulas into a deductively closed set of formulas, and the set of defaults such that $PRE \in \Gamma(E)$ and $\neg JUSTIF \notin E$ is grounded. This induces a function Σ from sets of defaults into grounded sets of defaults : intuitively, $\Sigma(S)$ is the maximal grounded subset of those defaults which are not bloscked by $CONS(S)$, the set of consequents of S.

Definition 2 : Let $\Delta = (\mathcal{W}, \mathcal{D})$ be a default theory and S a subset of $\mathcal{D}$. $\Sigma(S)$ is the smallest subset of $\mathcal{D}$ which verifies the condition : for any default δ of $\mathcal{D}$, if ∂ is grounded in $\Sigma(S)$ and $\neg JUSTIF(\delta)$ is not in the deductive closure of $\mathcal{W} \cup CONS(S)$, then δ belongs to $\Sigma(S)$. •

It is easy to prove that Σ is a decreasing function of S, and that generating defaults for an extension are fixpoints of the function Σ..

If we consider the function Σ in Example 1, it has no fixpoint, but may loop through two cycles. As Tweety is the only ground term in the example, let us use ∂_i to abreviate $\partial_i(\text{Tweety})$; one cycle involves $\{\partial_4\}$ and $\{\partial_1, \partial_2, \partial_3, \partial_4\}$, the other one $\{\partial_1, \partial_4\}$, $\{\partial_1, \partial_2, \partial_4\}$, $\{\partial_2, \partial_4\}$, $\{\partial_2, \partial_3, \partial_4\}$, $\{\partial_3, \partial_4\}$, $\{\partial_3, \partial_1, \partial_4\}$. Note that ∂_4 is in each set of both cycles.

The remark has some generality. If a finite default theory has no extension, for any set S of defaults the sequence $\Sigma^n(S)$ enters for some value of n in a loop involving a finite number of sets. This set of sets is its own image under Σ, so it generalizes the notion of fixpoint of Σ. We give a definition which does not depend on the finiteness of the set of defaults, and ensures the existence of fixpoints :

Definition 3 : a weak fixpoint is a minimal set $\mathcal{F}$ of subsets of $\mathcal{D}$ such that :

$$\mathcal{F} = \{\Sigma(S) \mid S \in \mathcal{F}\}. •$$

Property 2 : any default theory has at least one weak fixpoint.

Proof (hint) : as Σ is decreasing, Σ^2 is monotonic, and has a least fix point. •

2.2 Weak extensions

A natural idea is that a weak fixpoint supports the defaults which are in every of its members. We call the defaults in every set of a weak fixpoint $\mathcal{F}$ the "generating defaults" of $\mathcal{F}$. To elaborate a definition of weak extensions, one must take two points into account :

– First the definition of weak fix points may apply to the function Γ as to Σ. The intuition underlying this conception is that typical reasoning may lead to oscillate between several sets of beliefs, and then to consider as faithful those which have revealed stable. But if one takes care of groundedness, one has to make a distinction between beliefs and default inferences : some beliefs may have a default support in each set of $\mathcal{F}$, but not the same in each, so they have none in the set of generating defaults. For the same reason, the intersection of all the sets in $\mathcal{F}$ may happen not to be grounded. In these cases, the theory built with $\mathcal{W}$ and the set of generating defaults of $\mathcal{F}$ would not support the beliefs or the inferences supported by each set of $\mathcal{F}$. Furthermore, the set of generating defaults of a weak fix point $\mathcal{F}$ may constitute a set of inferences which does not belong to $\mathcal{F}$, so it appears for the first time at this stage of the reasoning. As this new set should in turn be a starting point for some more oscillations, the faithfulness of its inferences is not in this case firmly established. We restrain in consequence the candidates to weak extension generation by requiring that the set of generating defaults belong to the weak fixpoint.

– The second point is a general requirement of every form of default reasoning : the extensions have to be as informative as possible. From this point of view, a weak fixpoint $\mathcal{F}$ determines three subsets of $\mathcal{D}$: generating defaults describe typical inferences which seem unproblematic, since they are in every set of $\mathcal{F}$; defaults in no set of $\mathcal{F}$ are also unproblematic, for the converse reason that they are never triggered ; the remaining ones represent unstable inferences being valid in some sets of $\mathcal{F}$ but not in all, so neither their acceptability nor their rejection is clearly established in $\mathcal{F}$. The informativeness can be considered through to different criteria : maximizing the set of generating defaults, or minimizing unstable ones. In our opinion, both are defensible choices. As every extension in the second sense is an extension in the first one, we take the minimization of unstable sets to be more informative, and we consider it in the paper.

We are now in position to define weak extensions and weak-extension generators :

Definition 4 : the **set of t-stable (resp : u-stable) defaults** of a weak fixpoint $\mathcal{F}$ of Σ is $\mathcal{D}_{\mathcal{F}} = (\bigcap_{S \in \mathcal{F}} S)$ (resp : $\mathcal{D} - (\bigcup_{S \in \mathcal{F}} S)$). Its set of **unstable** defaults is $(\bigcup_{S \in \mathcal{F}} S) - \mathcal{D}_{\mathcal{F}}$. $\mathcal{F}$ is **self-confirming** if $\mathcal{D}_{\mathcal{F}} \in \mathcal{F}$. •

T-stable (u-stable) stand here for stably triggered (unreached). The proof of property 2 exhibits a fixpoint L_p of Σ^2, such that $L_p \subseteq \Sigma(L_p)$. So either $\{L_p\}$, or $\{L_p, \Sigma(L_p)\}$ is a self-confirming weak fixpoint, and hence any default theory has at least one self-confirming weak fixpoint.

Definition 5 : a self-confirming weak fixpoint $\mathcal{F}$ of Σ is a **weak-extension generator** if its set of unstable defaults is minimal (in comparison with the sets of unstable defaults of other self-confirming weak fixpoints). The **weak extension** generated by $\mathcal{F}$ is the deductive closure E of $\mathcal{W} \cup CONS(\mathcal{D}_{\mathcal{F}})$. •

Weak extensions allow to cope with situations where Reiter's extentions don't work, and otherwise give the same extensions :

Theorem 1: If a default theory has extensions in Reiter's sense, its weak extensions are exactly Reiter's extensions.

Proof (hint) : every weak-extension generator has an empty set of unstable defaults.

We give now some examples of weak extensions :

Example 2 : $\partial_1 = \dfrac{\text{quaker} : \text{pacifist}}{\text{pacifist}}$, $\partial_2 = \dfrac{\text{republican} : \neg\text{pacifist}}{\neg\text{pacifist}}$, quaker, republican.

This theory is the simplest form of the classical "Nixon's diamond" : quakers are generally pacifists, republicans are generally not, Nixon is both quaker and republican. There are three self-confirming weak fixpoints $\{\{\partial_1\}\}$, $\{\{\partial_2\}\}$, $\{\{\partial_1, \partial_2\}$, $\phi\}$. The first two have the same set of unstable defaults ϕ and each generates one of Reiter's extension ; the third weak fixpoint has ∂_1 and ∂_2 unstable, so it is not minimal and does not generate a weak extension. •

Example 3 : Let us return once more to example 1. There are two weak fixpoints : $\mathcal{F}_1 = \{\{\partial_4\}, \{\partial_1, \partial_2, \partial_3, \partial_4\}\}$ and $\mathcal{F}_2 = \{\{\partial_1, \partial_4\}, \{\partial_1, \partial_2, \partial_4\}, \{\partial_2, \partial_4\}, \{\partial_2, \partial_3, \partial_4\}, \{\partial_3, \partial_4\}, \{\partial_3, \partial_1, \partial_4\}\}$. Both have the same sets of t-stable defaults $\{\partial_4\}$ and of unstable defaults $\{\partial_1, \partial_2, \partial_3\}$, but only $\mathcal{F}_1$ is self-confirming and yields a weak-extension generated by $\{\partial_4\}$. Note that fly(Tweety) $\vee$ short-winged(Tweety) $\vee$ antarctic-bird(Tweety) is believed in every set of $\mathcal{F}_2$, but is not supported by its t-stable defaults. A new theory built by adding a default with this formula as a prerequisite would have an ungrounded set of t-stable defaults.

Weak fixpoints may involve any number of sets of defaults, as they may be infinite. We give here a characterization of self confirming weak fixpoints which proves that they are much simpler, and which is the basis of the computational techniques presented in section 3.

Property 3 : The sets of t-stable defaults of self-confirming weak fixpoints are the fixpoints F of Σ^2 such that $F \subseteq \Sigma(F)$.

Note that there are fixpoints F of Σ^2 which are not the set of t-stable defaults of a self-confirming weak fixpoint. First if $F \subset \Sigma F)$, $\Sigma(F)$ is not t-stable. Second, F and $\Sigma(F)$ may happen not to be ordered by set inclusion. We give an example of that :

Example 4 : Let $\partial_1 = \dfrac{:a}{a}$, $\partial_2 = \dfrac{:\neg a}{\neg a}$, $\partial_3 = \dfrac{:b}{b}$, $\partial_4 = \dfrac{:\neg b}{\neg b}$.

$F_1 = \{\partial_1, \partial_2\}$ and $F_2 = \{\partial_3, \partial_4\}$ are fixpoints of Σ^2, and verify $\Sigma(F_1) = F_2$, $\Sigma(F_2) = F_1$. But $F_1 \cap F_2 = \phi$, so $\{F_1, F_2\}$ is not a self-confirming weak fixpoint. •

2.3 Properties of finite default theories

By a finite default theory, we mean a default theory with a finite set $\mathcal{D}$ of defaults. Finite default theories have interesting properties with regard to weak extensions. First, if the set of defaults is finite, it is easy to prove that there always exist a weak extension.

Theorem 2 : Every finite default theory has at least one weak extension.

Proof : since the sets of unstable defaults for weak fixpoints are finite, they always have at least one minimal element for set inclusion. This provides a weak extension generator •

We do not know at the time if this property extends to infinite default theories, since we do not know if there always exist a minimal set of unstable defaults. For finite default theories, unstable defaults can be more clearly shown to fit the intuitions underlying the notion of weak extension. We give here three properties which reinforce the arguments supporting the requirement of self confirmation :

– first, a self confirming weak fixpoint being given, taking as starting point for the iteration of Σ its t-stable defaults *plus* any set of unstable ones cannot change either the status of the t-stable defaults, or the status of u-stable ones.

Property 4 : Let $\mathcal{F}$ be a self confirming weak fixpoint of a finite default theory, and S a set of defaults such that $\mathcal{D}\mathcal{F} \subseteq S \subseteq \Sigma(\mathcal{D}\mathcal{F})$. Then, we have :

$$\forall n \quad \mathcal{D}\mathcal{F} \subseteq \Sigma^n(S) \subseteq \Sigma(\mathcal{D}\mathcal{F}).$$

– second, applying iteratively Σ from the set $\mathcal{D}\mathcal{F}$ of t-stable defaults of any weak fixpoint ends in the maximal t-stable set included in $\mathcal{D}\mathcal{F}$ and yielded by a self-confirming weak fixpoint

Property 5 : let $\mathcal{F}$ be any weak fixpoint. Then there is a n such that $G = \Sigma^{2n}(\mathcal{D}\mathcal{F})$ is a fixpoint of Σ^2. Moreover, any fixpoint of Σ^2 included in $\mathcal{D}\mathcal{F}$ is a subset of G.

– Third, for each self-confirming weak fixpoint $\mathcal{F}$, let the $\mathcal{F}$-reduced theory of $(\mathcal{W}, \mathcal{D})$ be $(\mathcal{W} \cup CONS(\mathcal{D}\mathcal{F}), \Sigma(\mathcal{D}\mathcal{F}) - \mathcal{D}\mathcal{F})$

Property 7 : $(\mathcal{W}, \mathcal{D})$ has no extension in Reiter's sense) iff none of its $\mathcal{F}$-reduced theories has extensions.

3. Computing weak extensions of finite default theories

To begin the computational issues, we consider first a labeling of defaults, and prove that the definition of self confirming weak fixpoints translates into a consistency condition on the labeling of defaults. In a second step, we indicate how this consistent labeling can be effectively obtained with the help of a Reason Maintenance System.

3.1 Consistent labelings

Our aim is to define for each self confirming weak fixpoint a labeling of defaults such that t-stable defaults are labeled in, u-stable ones are labeled out, and the remaining ones are unlabeled. We formulate now the consistency conditions that this labeling must satisfy.

Let us say, for the sake of brevity, that a default support is labeled in if all its defaults are labeled in, and that it is labeled out if at least one of its defaults is labeled out.

Definition 7 : a labeling is **consistent** if it verifies for any default ∂ :

– ∂ is labeled in iff PRE(∂) has a default support labeled in, and any default support of $\neg$JUSTIF(∂) is labeled out.

– ∂ is labeled out iff either all the default supports of PRE(∂) are labeled out, or at least one default support of $\neg$JUSTIF(∂) is labeled in •

Consistent labelings correspond exactly to self confirming weak fixpoints :

Theoreme 3 : If $\mathcal{F}$ is a self confirming weak fixpoint of $(\mathcal{W}, \mathcal{D})$, labeling its set $\mathcal{D}\mathcal{F}$ of t-stable defaults in and $\mathcal{D} - \Sigma(\mathcal{D}\mathcal{F})$ out (the remaining defaults being unlabeled) is a consistent labeling. Conversely, given a consistent labeling, let I (resp. O) be the set of defaults labeled in (resp. out). Then {I, $\mathcal{D}$ −O} is a self confirming weak fixpoint, and I is its set of t-stable defaults.

Note that consistent labelings do not take into account the minimality of unstable defaults and that it is possible for a consistent labeling to be an extension of another one. Consider for instance the example 3 : I = {∂_1} and O = {∂_2} is a consistent labeling, as is I = {∂_1, ∂_3} and O = {∂_2, ∂_4}. But weak extension generators correspond to some of the maximal consistent labelings.

3.2 Representing a default theory in a TMS

The computation of weak extensions may use the translation of default theories in a TMS proposed by [Junk & Kono 90]. A TMS is essentially a set of nodes representing formulas and linked by **TMS-justifications** of the form (in(M_1,...,M_p), out(NM_1,...,NM_q) → C), where the arrow indicates a directed propagation of labels on nodes.

[Junk & Kono 90] show that it is sufficient to represent in the nodes of the TMS the prerequisites, justifications and conclusions of the defaults. A default $\dfrac{A : B}{C}$ is translated by a TMS-justification (in(A), out(¬B) →C). All the formulas $C_1 \wedge \ldots \wedge C_n \Rightarrow F$ provable from $\mathcal{W}$, where the C_i are consequents of defaults and F is either a prerequisite, or a negated justification, are translated by monotonic TMS-justifications (in(C_1,...,C_n) → F). The paper indicates also how these justifications can be computed from the default theory.

3.3 Computing weak extensions

A consistent labeling of defaults is easily translated into a labeling of formulas in the TMS. We just have to extend the definition by stating that a formula is labeled in if and only if it has a default support labeled in, and out if and only if all its default supports are labeled out. As the labeling of a default is defined from the labeling of its prerequisite and of its conclusion, unfolding this definition yields the standard constraints on the labeling of the TMS.

The main difference is that a standard labeling is complete and consistent and thus represents extensions in Reiter's sense, while we require that a labeling be consistent but not necessarily complete. Building this labeling may use Goodwin-like techniques ([Goodwin 87]) : alternatively propagating the labels as far as possible, and then dynamically ordering strongly connected components and choosing in a least component a node which determines two possible continuations for the labeling process. Weak extensions are then represented by labelings with a minimal set of unlabeled formulas.

4. Comparisons

5. Conclusion

We have proposed a notion of weak extension of a default theory, motivated by a kind of paraconsistent view of default reasoning, such that at least any finite default theory has weak extensions. Our definition coincides with Reiter's one when there are Reiter's extensions, and otherwise determines defaults which are not involved in the inconsistency, preserving the possibility to draw some default conclusions. Weak extensions correspond to some consistent labelings of the defaults, according to a notion of consistency close to the standard one in the TMS, so computing weak extensions may adapt standard methods of the TMS. Finally, weak extensions generate far less extensions than propositions based on a maximal consistent set of formulas ; and the results can be extended to Autoepistemic Logic and to Logic Programming.

Bibliography

[Bara & Subr 90] C. R. Baral and V.S. Subrahmanian : "Stable and Extension Class Theory for Logic Programs and Default Logics" 3^d International Workshop on Nonmonotonic Reasoning, South Lake Tahoe, Cal, May and June 1990
[Besnard 83] P. Besnard : "Une procédure de décision en logique non monotone" Thesis, 1983 University of Rennes 1
[Brewka 89] G. Brewka : "Nonmonotonic Reasoning : From Theoretical Foundation Toward Efficient Computation" PHD Dissertation University of Hamburg
[Brewka 91] G. Brewka : "Cumulative Default Logic : in defense of nonmonotonic inference rules" Artificial Intelligence n° 50 1991 183–205
[Delgr & Jack 91] J. P. Delgrande and W. K. Jackson : "Default Logic Revisited" Proceedings KR 91 1991 118–127
[Ether 87] D. W. Etherington : "Formalizing Nonmonotonic Reasoning Systems" .Artificial Intelligence n° 31 1987
[Froi & Meng 92] C. Froidevaux, J. Mengin : "A Framework for Default Logics" LRI Research Report n°755 University of Paris Sud May 1992
[Goodwin 87] J. Goodwin : "A Theory and System for Non Monotonic Reasoning" Linköping studies in science and technology 165, 1987
[Junk & Kono 90] U. Junker, K. Konolige "Computing the Extensions of Autoepistemic and Default Logics with a Truth Maintenance System" AAAI 90,
[Luka 85] W. Lukaszewicz : "Two Results on Default Logic" Proceedings IJCAI 85 Los Angeles 1985 459–461
[Luka 88] W. Lukaszewicz: "Considerations on default logic — an alternative approach". Computational Intelligence n° 4 1988 1–16
[Moin 92] Y. Moinard : "Unifying varous approaches to Default Logic" Proceedings IPMU 92 Palma de Mallorca July 1992 61-64
[Moore 85] R.C. Moore : "Semantical Considerations on nonmonotonic Logic" Artificial Intelligence n°25 1985 75-94
[Poole 88] D. L. Poole : "A Logical Framework for Default Reasoning" ;Artificial Intelligence n° 36 1988 27-47
[Reiter 80] Raymond Reiter : "A Logic for Default Reasoning" Artificial Intelligence n° 13 avril 1980 81–132
[Schaub 91] T. Schaub : "Assertional Default Theories : a semantical View" Proceedings KR91 496-506
[Schaub 92] T. Schaub :"On constrained Default Theories" Proceedings ECAI 92 304-308

Recovering Incidence Functions

Weiru Liu   Alan Bundy   Dave Robertson

Dept. of AI, Univ. of Edinburgh, Edinburgh EH1 1HN

Abstract. In incidence calculus, inferences usually are made by calculating incidence sets and probabilities of formulae based on a given incidence function in an incidence calculus theory. However it is still the case that numerical values are assigned on some formulae directly without giving the incidence function. This paper discusses how to recover incidence functions in these cases. The result can be used to calculate mass functions from belief functions in the Dempster-Shafer theory of evidence (or DS theory) and define probability spaces from inner measures (or lower bounds) of probabilities on the relevant propositional language set.

1   Introduction

Incidence calculus [1, 3] as an alternative approach to dealing with uncertainty has a special feature *i.e.*, the indirect association of numerical uncertain assignment on formulae through a set of possible worlds. In this theory, uncertainties are associated with sets of possible worlds and these sets are, in turn, associated with some formulae. This gives incidence calculus the features of both symbolic and numerical reasoning methods. If we take incidence calculus as a symbolic inference technique, it has strong similarity with the ATMS [10]. If we use incidence calculus to make numerical uncertain inference, it can deal with cases for which Dempster-Shafer theory is adequate or inadequate to cope with [4, 9]. The crucial point in carrying out the above reasoning procedures relies on a special kind of function, called the incidence function. Without the existence of this function, many of the features in incidence calculus will be lost. However, in practice numerical values may be required to be assigned on some formulae directly without giving the corresponding incidence function. Therefore it is necessary both theoretically and practically to recover the incidence function in this circumstance. In [2, 3], a preliminary procedure has been described using the Monte Carlo method. This approach has further been developed in [12]. In this paper, we discuss this problem from a different perspective. An alternative approach to defining incidence functions from probability distributions is explored. The result gives a new way to check whether an numerical assignment on a set is a belief function and then calculate its mass functions when it is true in DS theory [13, 14] and to construct probability spaces from inner measures (or lower bounds) of probabilities on the relevant propositional language sets [5].

The paper is organized as follows. In section 2, a brief introduction to incidence calculus is given. The key features of incidence functions are discussed. Following this, an algorithm for calculating an incidence function based on numerical assignments is described in section 3. The application of the result to DS theory is introcuced in section 4. Section 5 contains a short conclusion.

2   Incidence Calculus

Incidence calculus is a logic for probabilistic reasoning. In incidence calculus, probabilities are not directly associated with formulae, rather sets of possible worlds are directly associated with formulae and probabilities (or lower and upper bounds of probabilities) of formulae are calculated from these sets.

2.1   Generalized Incidence Calculus

In generalized incidence calculus [8], a piece of evidence is described in a quintuple called an incidence calculus theory. An incidence calculus theory is normally in the form of $< W, \varrho, P, \mathcal{A}, i >$ where: W is a finite set of possible worlds. For all $w \in W$, $\varrho(w)$ is the probability of w and $wp(W) = 1$, where $wp(I) = \Sigma_{w \in I} \varrho(w)$. P is a finite set of propositions. At is the basic element set of P. If P is $\{p_1, ..., p_m\}$, then At is defined as for each $\phi \in At$, $\phi = \wedge p_i'$ (i=1, ..., m) where $p_i' = p_i$ or $p_i' = \neg p_i$, $\mathcal{L}(P)$ contains all elements produced from P using connectors $\wedge, \vee, \rightarrow, \neg$. $\mathcal{A}$ is a distinguished set of formulae in $\mathcal{L}(P)$ called the *axioms* of the theory. i is a function from the axioms $\mathcal{A}$ to 2^W, the set of subsets of W. $i(\phi)$ is to be thought of as the set of possible worlds in W in which ϕ is true, i.e. $i(\phi) = \{w \in W| \ w \models \phi\}$. $i(\phi)$ is called the *incidence* of ϕ. An incidence function i satisfies the conditions $i(\bot) = \{\}$ and $i(T) = W$.

Here $\bot$ stands for *False* and T means *True*. For any two formulae ϕ, ψ in $\mathcal{A}$, it is easy to prove that $i(\phi \wedge \psi) = i(\phi) \cap i(\psi)$ if $\phi \wedge \psi$ is in $\mathcal{A}$ based on the definition of i. If we use $\wedge(\mathcal{A})$ to denote the language set which contains $\mathcal{A}$ and all the possible conjunctions of its elements, then this function can be generated to any formula in this set by defining $i(\wedge \phi_j) = \cap_j i(\phi_j)$ if $\wedge_j \phi_j$ is not given initially. Therefore the set of axioms $\mathcal{A}$ can always be extended to a set in which the function i is closed under operator $\wedge$.

Since whenever we have a set of axioms $\mathcal{A}$ with a function i defined on it, where i suits the basic definition of incidences, this set of axioms can always be extended to another set which is closed under the operator $\wedge$ on i. In the following, we always assume that the set of axioms we name is already extended and is closed under $\wedge$, that is $\mathcal{A}$ is closed under $\wedge$. For any two elements in $\mathcal{A}$, we have

$$i(\phi_1 \wedge \phi_2) = i(\phi_1) \cap i(\phi_2) \tag{1}$$

In particular, if $i(\wedge_j \phi_j) = \{\}$ it doesn't matter whether this formula is in $\wedge(\mathcal{A})$ as this formula has no effect on further inferences. However if $\wedge_j \phi_j = \bot$, then $i(\wedge_j \phi_j) = \cap_j i(\phi_j)$ must be empty otherwise the information for constructing the function i is contradictory.

It is not usually possible to infer the incidences of all the formulae in $\mathcal{L}(P)$. What we can do is to define both the upper and lower bounds of the incidence using the functions i^* and i_* respectively. For all $\phi \in \mathcal{L}(P)$ these are defined as follows:

$$i^*(\phi) = W \setminus i_*(\neg\phi) \qquad i_*(\phi) = \bigcup_{\psi \rightarrow \phi = T} i(\psi) \tag{2}$$

where $\psi \rightarrow \phi = T$ iff $i(\psi \rightarrow \phi) = W$. For any $\phi \in \mathcal{A}$, we have $i_*(\phi) = i(\phi)$.

The lower bound represents the set of possible worlds in which ϕ is proved to be true and the upper bound represents the set of possible worlds in which $\neg\phi$ fails to be proved. Function $p_*(\phi) = wp(i_*(\phi))$ gives the degree of our belief in ϕ and function $p^*(\phi) = wp(i^*(\phi))$ represents the degree we fail to believe in $\neg\phi$. For a formula ϕ in $\mathcal{A}$, if $p_*(\phi) = p^*(\phi)$, then $p(\phi)$ is defined as $p_*(\phi)$ and is called the probability of this formula.

In the following, when we mention a lower bound of a probability distribution on $\mathcal{A}$, we always mean the function $p_*(*)$ calculated from the lower bound of incidence sets.

2.2   Basic Incidence Assignment

Definition *Basic incidence assignment*

Given a set of axioms $\mathcal{A}$, a function ii defined on $\mathcal{A}$ is called a basic incidence assignment if ii satisfies the following conditions:

$$ii(\phi) \cap ii(\psi) = \{\} \ \text{ where } \ \phi \neq \psi$$

$$ii(\bot) = \{\} \qquad ii(T) = \mathcal{W} \setminus \bigcup_j ii(\phi_j)$$

where $\mathcal{W}$ is a set of possible worlds.

The elements in $ii(\phi)$ make only ϕ true without making any of its superformulae true.

Proposition 1 *Given a set of axioms $\mathcal{A}$ with a basic incidence assignment ii, then the function i defined by equation (3) is an incidence function on $\mathcal{A}$.*

$$i(\phi) = \bigcup_{\phi_j \to \phi = T} ii(\phi_j) \qquad\qquad (3)$$

Proposition 2 *Given an incidence calculus theory $< \mathcal{W}, \varrho, P, \mathcal{A}, i >$, there exists a basic incidence assignment for the incidence function.*

PROOF This proof procedure is actually to construct a basic incidence assignment ii for the given incidence function.

The definition of i leads us to the conclusion that if $\psi \to \phi = T$ then $i(\psi) \subseteq i(\phi)$. As we assume that P is finite, then At, $\mathcal{L}(P)$ and $\mathcal{A}$ are all finite.

A subset $\mathcal{A}_0$ of $\mathcal{A}$ can be defined as $\mathcal{A}_0 = \{\psi_1, ..., \psi_n\}$ where $\mathcal{A}_0$ satisfies the condition that

$$\forall \psi_i \in \mathcal{A}_0, \forall \phi \in \mathcal{A}, \ if \ \phi \neq \psi_i \ then \ \phi \to \psi_i \neq T$$

Therefore, $\mathcal{A}_0$ contains the "smallest" formulae in $\mathcal{A}$ and $\mathcal{A}_0$ is not empty. In fact, we can get $\mathcal{A}_0$ using the following procedure. For a formula $\psi_i \in \mathcal{A}$, if $\exists \phi \in \mathcal{A}, \phi \neq \psi_i$ and $\phi \to \psi_i = T$, then we use ϕ to replace ψ_i and repeat the same procedure until we obtain a formula ϕ_j and we cannot find any formula which makes ϕ_j true, then ϕ_j will be in $\mathcal{A}_0$.

For any formula ϕ_i in $\mathcal{A} \setminus \mathcal{A}_0$, there are $\psi_{i1}, ..., \psi_{il} \in \mathcal{A}_0$ where $\psi_{ij} \to \phi_i = T$. So $i(\psi_{ij}) \subseteq i(\phi_i)$ and $(\bigcup_j i(\psi_{ij})) \subseteq i(\phi_i)$.

Algorithm A: From a function i, we can obtain another function ii using the following procedure:

Step 1: for every formula $\psi \in \mathcal{A}_0$, define $ii(\psi) = i(\psi)$.

Step 2: update $\mathcal{A}$ as $\mathcal{A} \setminus \mathcal{A}_0$.

Step 3: chose a formula ϕ_i in $\mathcal{A}$ which satisfies the requirement that there are $\psi_{i1}, ..., \psi_{il} \in \mathcal{A}_0$ where $\psi_{ij} \to \phi_i = T$ and for any $\phi_j \in \mathcal{A}$, if $\phi_j \neq \phi_i$, then $\phi_j \to \phi_i \neq T$. Define $ii(\phi_i) = i(\phi_i) \setminus \bigcup_j ii(\psi_{ij})$.

Step 4: delete ϕ_i from $\mathcal{A}$ and update $\mathcal{A}_0$ as $\mathcal{A}_0 \cup \{\phi_i\}$ when $ii(\phi_i) \neq \{\}$. If $\mathcal{A}$ is empty then terminate the procedure. Otherwise go to step 3.

Further defining $ii(T) = \mathcal{W} \setminus \cup_j ii(\phi_j)$, if $ii(T) \neq \{\}$ then $ii(T)$ represents only those possible worlds which make T true. This is also an alternative way to represent ignorance. That is, based on the current information we don't know which formula $ii(T)$ makes true except T. Adding T to $\mathcal{A}_0$, we get a function ii as $ii : \mathcal{A}_0 \to 2^{\mathcal{W}}$. Now we need to prove that ii is a basic incidence assignment. That is, we need to prove $ii(\phi_i) \cap ii(\phi_j) = \{\}$ where $\phi_i \neq \phi_j$. In [13], we have proved this result. So the equation $ii(\phi_i) \cap ii(\phi_j) = \{\}$ holds for any two distinct elements ϕ_i and ϕ_j in $\mathcal{A}_0$. As we also have $ii(T) = \mathcal{W} \setminus \cup_j ii(\phi_j)$ and $ii(\bot) = i(\bot) = \{\}$, ii is a basic incidence assignment.
QED

3 Recovering an Incidence Function from a Lower Bound of probabilities on a Set of Axioms

Given an incidence calculus theory, we can infer lower bounds of probabilities on formulae. However sometimes numerical assignments are given on some formulae directly without defining any incidence calculus theories. We are interested in how to build incidence calculus theories in these cases. The key part for an incidence calculus theory is to define its incidence function. In this section, we show a way to recover incidence functions in these circumstances.

When we know a proposition set P, its language set $L(P)$, a set of axioms $\mathcal{A}$ and an assignment of lower bound of probabilities on $\mathcal{A}$, our objective is to determine an incidence function i, a set of possible worlds $\mathcal{W}$ and the discrete probability distribution on $\mathcal{W}$ from which the corresponding probability distribution on $\mathcal{A}$ is produced. In order to achieve this goal, we will construct a function ii first and then form i.

For the set of axioms $\mathcal{A}$, we always assume that for $\phi_i, \phi_j \in \mathcal{A}$, $\phi_i \wedge \phi_j \in \mathcal{A}$ and $p(\phi_i \wedge \phi_j)$ is known. If it is not, we will assume that $p(\phi_i \wedge \phi_j) = 0$. When $\phi \to \phi_i = T$, $i(\phi) \subseteq i(\phi_i)$ and $p(\phi) \leq p(\phi_i)$.

In a similar way as we described in the above section, a special set $\mathcal{A}_0$ is constructible from $\mathcal{A}$ which satisfies the condition

$$\forall \phi \in \mathcal{A}_0, \forall \phi' \in \mathcal{A}, \phi' \rightarrow \phi \neq T, if\ \phi \neq \phi' \tag{4}$$

Assume that there are an incidence function i and a basic incidence assignment ii associated with this $\mathcal{A}$, then $w_1 = ii(\phi_i)$ and $w_2 = ii(\phi_j)$ must be two disjoint subsets of an unknown $\mathcal{W}$ because of the feature $ii(\phi_i) \cap ii(\phi_j) = \{\}$ when $\phi_i, \phi_j \in \mathcal{A}_0, \phi_i \neq \phi_j$. As it is required that the probability distribution on $\mathcal{W}$ should be discrete in incidence calculus, we treat w_1 and w_2 as two single elements in $\mathcal{W}$. The following procedure gives the algorithm for determining the incidence function i, its basic incidence assignment ii and the set of possible worlds with its probability distribution.

Algorithm B: Given $\mathcal{A}$ and a lower bound of probability distribution p_* on $\mathcal{A}$, determine a basic incidence assignment and an incidence function.

Step 1: Assume that $\mathcal{A}_0$ is a subset of $\mathcal{A}$ as defined above in (4). If there are l elements in $\mathcal{A}_0$, then l elements in $\mathcal{W}$ can be defined from $\mathcal{A}_0$ and define $\varrho(w_i) = p_*(\phi_i)$ for $i = 1, ..., l, \phi_i \in \mathcal{A}_0$. Further define $ii(\phi_i) = \{w_i\}$, $i(\phi_i) = \{w_i\}$ and $\mathcal{A}' := \mathcal{A} \setminus \mathcal{A}_0$.

Step 2: Chose a formula ψ from $\mathcal{A}'$ which satisfies the condition that $\forall \psi' \in \mathcal{A}'$, $\psi' \rightarrow \psi \neq T$ if $\psi' \neq \psi$.

For all $\phi_j \in \mathcal{A}_0$ repeat $p_*(\psi) := p_*(\psi) - p_*(\phi_j)$ when $\phi_j \rightarrow \psi = T$.

If $p_*(\psi) > 0$ then add an element w_{l+1} to $\mathcal{W}$ and define

$$ii(\psi) = \{w_{l+1}\} \qquad \varrho(w_{l+1}) = p_*(\psi) \qquad\qquad \mathcal{A}_0 := \mathcal{A}_0 \cup \{\psi\}$$
$$\mathcal{A} := \mathcal{A}' \setminus \{\psi\} \qquad i(\psi) = ii(\psi) \cup (\cup_{\phi_j \rightarrow \psi = T} ii(\phi_j)) \qquad l := l + 1$$

If $p_*(\psi) = 0$, define $ii(\psi) = \{\}$. If $p_*(\psi) < 0$, this assignment is not consistent, stop the procedure. Repeat this step until $\mathcal{A}'$ is empty.

Step 3: Finally if $\Sigma_j(p_*(\phi_j)) < 1$ then add an element w_{l+1} to $\mathcal{W}$ and then define $\varrho(w_{l+1}) = 1 - \Sigma_j p_*(\phi_j)$ and $ii(T) = \{w_{l+1}\}$.

Step 4: The resulting the set of possible worlds is $\mathcal{W} = \{w_1, w_2, ..., w_{l+1}\}$ and the probability distribution is $\varrho(w_i) = p_*(\phi_i)$ where $\phi_i \in \mathcal{A}_0$ and $\Sigma_i \varrho(w_i) = 1$. Two functions ii and i are defined as $ii(\phi_i) = \{w_i\}$ and $i(\phi) = \cup_{\phi_j \rightarrow \phi} ii(\phi_j)$, $\phi_j \in \mathcal{A}_0$. It is easy to prove that ii and i are a basic incidence assignment and an incidence function respectively. The corresponding incidence calculus theory is $< \mathcal{W}, \varrho, P, \mathcal{A}, i >$.

If there are n elements in $\mathcal{A}$ then there are at most $n+1$ elements in $\mathcal{W}$. This algorithm is entirely based on the result that $ii(\phi) \cap ii(\psi) = \{\}$. In algorithm B, for a formula ϕ, we keep deleting those portions in $p_*(\phi)$ which can be carried by its superformulae until we obtain the last bit which must be carried by ϕ itself. Then the last portion will only be contributed by its basic incidence set.

4 Extending the Result to DS Theory

One of the meaningful extensions of this algorithm is to calculate the mass function in DS theory when $\mathcal{A}$ is the whole language set $\mathcal{L}(P)$ and p_* is a belief function on it [13, 14] and, in particular, to recover the corresponding probability space when p_* is thought of as an inner measure (or a lower bound) on $\mathcal{A}$ in probability structures [5]. One may suspect that bel is usually defined on a frame of discernment[1] in DS theory rather on a set of formulae. We will briefly show how to build a belief function on a set of formulae here, more details can be found in [5]. Assume that we have a set of propositions P and its basic element set $\mathcal{A}t$. Because $\mathcal{A}t$ satisfies the definition of a frame of discernment, we can talk about a belief function on $\mathcal{A}t$. Further if we follow the one-to-one relationship between $2^{\mathcal{A}t}$ and $\mathcal{L}(P)$ as we have seen in section 2, then given a belief function bel on $\mathcal{A}t$, we can define a belief function on $\mathcal{L}(P)$ as $bel'(\phi) = bel(A_\phi)$ where $A_\phi \subseteq \mathcal{A}t$. Therefore we can also talk about a belief function on a language set $\mathcal{L}(P)$.

In DS theory, a function on a frame Θ is called a mass function, denoted as m if $\Sigma_A m(A) = 1$ where $A \subseteq \Theta$. The relationship between a belief function, denoted as bel, and its mass function is unique. They can be recovered from each other as follows.

$$bel(A) = \Sigma_{B \subseteq A} m(B)$$

$$m(A) = \Sigma_{B \subseteq A, B \neq \emptyset} (-1)^{a-b} bel(B)$$

where $a - b = | (A \wedge \neg B) |$ where $A, B \in L(P)$ [14]. $| A |$ stands for the element number in A.

In the following we show an alternative way to obtain a mass function from a belief function by means of incidence calculus. Assume that $\mathcal{A}$ is the whole language set $\mathcal{L}(P)$ and p_* is a belief function on $\mathcal{A}$, then p_* is also a lower bound of probability on $\mathcal{A}$ in incidence calculus as shown in [4, 9].

Algorithm C: Given a function bel on the set $\mathcal{L}(P) = \mathcal{A}$, determine whether bel is a belief function on this language set [2] and obtain its mass function m if it is.

Step 1: Delete all those elements in $\mathcal{A}$ in which $bel = 0$. Then as in algorithm B, define a subset $\mathcal{A}_0$ out of $\mathcal{A}$. For any $\phi \in \mathcal{A}_0$, define $m(\phi) = bel(\phi)$. Assume that there are l elements in $\mathcal{A}_0$. Define $\mathcal{A}' = \mathcal{A} \setminus \mathcal{A}_0$.

Step 2: Chose a formula ψ from $\mathcal{A}'$ which satisfies the condition that $\forall \psi' \in \mathcal{A}'$, $\psi' \rightarrow \psi \neq T$.

For all $\phi_j \in \mathcal{A}_0$ repeat $bel(\psi) := bel(\psi) - bel(\phi_j)$ when $\phi_j \rightarrow \psi = T$.

If $bel(\psi) > 0$, define: $\quad l := l + 1$

---

[1] A set is defined as a frame of discernment if this set contains mutually exclusive and exhaustive answers for a question.

[2] In fact, this language set can be any frame of discernment.

$$\mathcal{A}_0 := \mathcal{A}_0 \cup \{\psi\}$$
$$\mathcal{A}' := \mathcal{A}' \setminus \{\psi\}$$
$$m(\psi) := bel(\psi)$$

If $bel(\psi) = 0$ then ψ is not a focal element[3] of this belief function.

If $bel(\phi) < 0$ then this assignment is not a belief function, stop the procedure.

Repeat this step until $\mathcal{A}'$ is empty.

Step 3: All the elements in $\mathcal{A}_0$ will be the focal elements of this belief function and the function m defined in Step 2 is the corresponding mass function. It is easy tp prove that $\Sigma_A m(A) = 1$.

The algorithm tries to find the focal elements of a belief function one by one. Once all the focal elements are fixed and the uncertain values of these elements are defined, the corresponding mass function is known. The worst case of computational complexity of this algorithm is the same as the approach used in DS theory but it may be more efficient when the elements in $\mathcal{A}'$ are arranged in the decreasing sequence of their sizes. However the Fast Moebius Transform of Kennes and Smets remains faster than ours [6, 7]. The application of the algorithm to probability spaces is described in [11].

5 Summary

We have discussed an approach to defining an incidence function based on a probability measure in incidence calculus. The advantage of this approach is that its computational complexity is lower *i.e.* $o(|A|)$ comparing to the method discussed in [12]. The latter is exponential given the same set of axioms $\mathcal{A}$. The size of the set of possible worlds entirely depends on the size of $\mathcal{A}$. For example, if there are only two elements in $\mathcal{A}$, then we can define a set of possible worlds containing at most three elements. This is mainly because the probability distribution on the set of possible worlds must be discrete.

When we extend the result to DS theory and the probability space, we follow the known result that a lower bound in incidence calculus is equivalent to a belief function and a belief function is, in turn, equivalent to an inner measure in probability structures when these three theories concern the same problem space. Therefore the incidence assignment procedure can be not only used to define an incidence assignment but also used to construct an undefined probability space. In the latter case, a basis for an $\sigma-$algebra of a probability space is similar to a set of possible worlds except each subset in the basis usually contains more than one elements.

Acknowledgement

The authors are grateful for comments from Prof. P.Smets.

---

[3] When $m(A) > 0$, A is called a focal element of its belief function.

References

[1] Bundy,A., Incidence calculus: a mechanism for probability reasoning, *J. of Automated Reasoning.* 1, 263-283, 1985.

[2] Bundy,A., Correctness criteria of some algorithms for uncertain reasoning using incidence calculus., *J. of Automated reasoning.* 2 109-126., 1986.

[3] Bundy,A., Incidence Calculus, *The Encyclopedia of AI*, 663-668, 1992. It is also available as the Research paper No. 497 in the Dept. of Artificial Intelligence, Univ. of Edinburgh.

[4] Correa da Silva,F. and A.Bundy, On some equivalent relations between incidence calculus and Dempster-Shafer theory of evidence, *Proc. of sixth workshop of Uncertainty in Artificial Intelligence.* 378-383, 1990.

[5] Fagin,R. and J. Halpern, Uncertainty, belief and probability, Research Report of IBM, RJ 6191, 1989.

[6] Kennes,R. Computational aspects of the Moebius transform of a graph, *IEEE-SMC*, 22:201-223, 1991.

[7] Kennes,R. and Smets,Ph., Computational aspects of the Moebius Transform. *Proc. of the 6th Conf. on Uncertainty in AI* Eds. by P.Bonissone, M.Henrion, L.Kanal and J.Lemmer. Cambridge, MA. North Holland, 401-416, 1990a.

[8] Liu,W., Incidence calculus and generalized incidence calculus. Chapter 2 of a forthcoming PhD thesis. Dept. of AI, Univ. of Edinburgh, 1993.

[9] Liu,W. and A.Bundy, The combination of different pieces of evidence using incidence calculus, Research Paper 599, Dept. of Artificial Intelligence, Univ. of Edinburgh, 1992.

[10] Liu,W., A.Bundy and D.Robertson, On the relationship between incidence calculus and the ATMS, in this proceedings, 1993.

[11] Liu, W., A.Bundy and D.Robertson, Recovering incidence functions, forthcoming departmental research paper, 1993.

[12] McLean,R.G., *Testing and Extending the Incidence Calculus*, M.Sc. Dissertation, Dept. of Artificial Intelligence, Univ. of Edinburgh, 1992.

[13] Shafer,G., *A mathematical theory of evidence*, Princeton University Press. 1976.

[14] Smets,P., Belief functions, *Non-Standard Logics for Automated Reasoning*, (Smets, Mamdani, Dubois and Prade Eds.), 253-286, 1988.

On the Relations between Incidence Calculus and ATMS

Weiru Liu   Alan Bundy   Dave Robertson

Dept. of AI, Univ. of Edinburgh, Edinburgh EH1 1HN, UK

Abstract. This paper discusses the relationship between incidence calculus and the ATMS. It shows that managing labels for statements in an ATMS is similar to producing the incidence sets of these statements in incidence calculus. We will prove that a probabilistic ATMS can be implemented using incidence calculus. In this way, we can not only produce labels for all nodes in the system automatically, but also calculate the probability of any of such nodes in it. The reasoning results in incidence calculus can provide justifications for an ATMS automatically.

1 Introduction

The ATMS is a symbolic reasoning technique used in the artificial intelligence domain to deal with problems by providing dependent relations among statements during inference normally. This technique can only infer results with absolutely true or false. It lacks the ability to draw plausible conclusions such as that a conclusion is true with some degree of belief. However in many cases, pieces of information from a knowledge base provide assumptions and premises with uncertainties. It is necessary to let the ATMS have the ability to cope with uncertainty problems.

In order to overcome this problem, some research on the association of numerical uncertainties with ATMS has been carried out. In [8], De Kleer and Williams use probability theory to deal with such associated with assumptions. In [11, 15], the authors use possibilistic logic to handle this problem. In [11] both assumptions and justifications are associated with uncertainty measures. The uncertainty values associated with justifications are used to select the path for deriving a node. Only those pathes with strong supporting relations are used to infer the corresponding nodes. [15] continues the work carried out in [11] and extends it to deal with a military data fusion application. [5, 6, 14, 16, 19, 20] all use Dempster-Shafer theory of evidence to calculate beliefs in statements. Among them [16] studies a formal relation between DS theory and ATMS. It is proved in [16] that any belief network in DS theory can be translated into an ATMS structure. In such a system, the inference is performed based on ATMS techniques with a probability model on assumptions. One common limitation in all these extensions of the ATMS[1] is that the probabilities assigned to assumptions must be assumed probabilistically independent in order to calculate the degree of belief in a statement. In this paper, we continue this research and intend to provide a general basis for constructing a probabilistic ATMS. The uncertainty technique we have chosen is incidence calculus.

---

[1] Except the discussion in [11, 15] in which the topic was not discussed.

The main contributions of this paper are: We prove that incidence calculus and the ATMS are equivalent at both the symbolic reasoning level and numerical inference level if we associate proper probabilistic distributions on assumptions. We show that the integration of symbolic and numerical reasoning patterns are possible and incidence calculus itself is a typical example of this unification. The result of investigating the relationship between incidence calculus and ATMS can provide a theoretical basis for some results in [16]. We will show that incidence calculus can be used to provide justifications for nodes automatically without human involvement. Therefore a complete automatic ATMS system is constructible.

The paper is organized as follows. Section 2 introduces the basics of incidence calculus. In section 3 we introduce the ATMS notations and extend it by adding probabilities to assumptions. In section 4 we will explore how to manipulate labels of nodes and calculate degrees of belief in nodes in incidence calculus. In the concluding section, we summarize our results.

2 Incidence Calculus

Incidence calculus [1, 2] starts with two sets, the set P contains propositions and the set W consists of possible worlds with a probability distribution on them. For each element w of W, the probability on w, $\varrho(w)$, is known and $\Sigma \varrho(w) = 1$. From the set P, using logical operators $\wedge, \vee, \neg, \rightarrow$, a set of logical formulae are formed which is called the language set of P, denoted as $\mathcal{L}(P)$. The elements in the set W may make some formulae in $\mathcal{L}(P)$ true. For any $\phi \in \mathcal{L}(P)$, if every element in a subset W_1 of W makes ϕ true and W_1 is the maximal subset of this kind, then W_1 is represented as $i(\phi)$ in an incidence calculus theory and it is called the incidence set of ϕ. Therefore, the supporting set of a formula ϕ is $i(\phi)$ and its probability is $p(\phi) = wp(W_1)$ where $wp(W_1) = \Sigma_{w \in W_1} \varrho(w)$. It is assumed that $i(\bot) = \{\}$ and $i(T) = W$ where $\bot, T$ represent *false* and *true* respectively.

Definition 1: Incidence calculus theories: an incidence calculus theory is a quintuple $< W, \varrho, P, \mathcal{A}, i >$ where W is a set of possible worlds with a probability distribution ϱ, P is a set of propositions and $\mathcal{A}$ is a subset of $\mathcal{L}(P)$ which is called a set of axioms. The function i assigns an incidence set to every formula in $\mathcal{A}$. For any two formulae in $\mathcal{A}$, we have $i(\phi \wedge \psi) = i(\phi) \cap i(\psi)$.

Based on this definition, given two formulae $\phi, \psi \in \mathcal{A}$, we have $i(\phi) \subseteq i(\psi)$ if $\phi \rightarrow \psi = T$. For any other formula $\phi \in \mathcal{L}(P) \setminus \mathcal{A}$, it is possible to get the lower bound $i_*(\phi)$ of its incidence set as $i_*(\phi) = \bigcup_{\psi \rightarrow \phi = T} i(\psi)$ where $\psi \in \mathcal{A}$ and $\psi \rightarrow \phi = T$ iff $i(\psi \rightarrow \phi) = W$. The degree of our belief in a formula is defined as $p_*(\phi) = wp(i_*(\phi))$.

Definition 2: Semantic implication set and essential semantic implication set: for any formula $\phi \in L(P)$, if $\psi \rightarrow \phi = T$ then ϕ is said to be semantically implied by ψ, denoted as $\psi \models \phi$. Let $SI(\phi) = \{\psi \mid \psi \rightarrow \phi = T, \forall \psi \in \mathcal{A}\}$, set $SI(\phi)$ is called a semantical implication set of ϕ. Furthermore, let $ESI(\phi)$ be a subset of $SI(\phi)$ which satisfies the condition that a formula ψ is in $ESI(\phi)$

for any ψ' in $SI(\phi)$ $\psi \to \psi' \neq T$, then $ESI(\phi)$ is called an essential semantical implication set of ϕ. This is denoted as $ESI(\phi) \models \phi$.

Proposition 1 *If $SI(\phi)$ and $ESI(\phi)$ are a semantic implication set and an essential semantic implication set of ϕ, then the following equation holds: $i_*(\phi) = i_*(SI(\phi)) = i_*(ESI(\phi))$ where $i_*(SI(\phi)) = \bigcup_{\phi_j \in SI(\phi)} i(\phi_j)$.*

This proposition can be proved based on the definitions of lower bound of incidence set i_* and $SI(\phi)$ and $ESI(\phi)$ above. It will be proved later that the essential semantic implication set of a formula is exactly the same as the set of justifications of that formula in an ATMS.

When two incidence calculus theories are given on different sets of possible worlds and the two sets are probabilistically independent (or DS-Independent[2]), the combination can be performed using the Corollary 1 in [3]. Given that $< \mathcal{W}_1, \varrho_1, P, \mathcal{A}_1, i_1 >$ and $< \mathcal{W}_2, \varrho_2, P, \mathcal{A}_2, i_2 >$, applying Corollary 1 we get a combined theory $< \mathcal{W}_3, \varrho_3, P, \mathcal{A}_3, i_3 >$ where

$$\mathcal{W}_0 = \bigcup_{\phi \wedge \psi = \perp} i_1(\phi) \otimes i_2(\psi) \qquad \phi \in \mathcal{A}_1, \psi \in \mathcal{A}_2$$

$$\mathcal{W}_3 = \mathcal{W}_1 \otimes \mathcal{W}_2 \setminus \mathcal{W}_0$$

$$\varrho_3(w) = \varrho_3((w_{1i}, w_{2j})) = \frac{\varrho_1(w_{1i})\varrho_2(w_{2j})}{1 - \sum_{(w'_{1i}, w'_{2j}) \in \mathcal{W}_0} \varrho_1(w'_{1i})\varrho_2(w'_{2j})}$$

$$\mathcal{A}_3 = \{\varphi \mid \varphi = \phi \wedge \psi, where \phi \in \mathcal{A}_1, \psi \in \mathcal{A}_2, \varphi \neq \perp\}$$

$$i_3(\varphi) = \bigcup_{(\phi \wedge \psi \to \varphi) = T} (i_1(\phi) \otimes i_2(\psi)) \setminus \mathcal{W}_0 \qquad \phi \in \mathcal{A}_1, \psi \in \mathcal{A}_2$$

In general a pair (w_{1i}, w_{2j}) is an element of $\mathcal{W}_1 \otimes \mathcal{W}_2 \setminus \mathcal{W}_0$. It is required that T is automatically added into a set of axioms $\mathcal{A}$ if $\cup_{\phi \in A} i(\phi) \subset W$.

3 The ATMS

The truth maintenance system (TMS) [9] and later the ATMS [7] are both symbolic approaches to producing a set of statements in which we believe. The basic and central idea in such a system is that for each statement we believe in, a set of supporting statements (called labels or environments generally in the ATMS) is produced. A set of supporting statements is, in turn, obtained through a set of arguments attached to that statement (called justifications). In an ATMS, a justification of a statement (or called node) contains other statements

---

[2]See definition and explanation in [3]. In the analysis [3], two sets of possible worlds are probabilistically independent cannot guarantee they are DS-Independent when their original source is known. In the case that original source is the set product of these two sets, their probabilistic independence also implies their DS-Independence. In this paper, as we only consider the latter case, we will use term *probabilistically independent* to name the relations among two sets.

(or nodes) from which the current statement can be derived. Justifications are specified by the system designer. For instance, if we have two inference rules as: $r_1 : p \rightarrow q$ and $r_2 : q \rightarrow r$, then logically we can infer that $r_3 : p \rightarrow r$. In an ATMS, if r_1, r_2 and r_3 are represented by $node_1$, $node_2$ and $node_3$ respectively, then $node_3$ is derivable from the conjunction of $node_1$ and $node_2$ and we call (r_1, r_2) a justification of $node_3$. Normally a rule may have several justifications. Further more if r_1 and r_2 are valid under the conditions that A and B are true respectively, then rule r_3 is valid under the condition that $A \wedge B$ is true, denoted as $\{A, B\}$. $\{A\}, \{B\}$ and $\{A, B\}$ are called sets of supporting statements (or environments) of r_1, r_2 and r_3 respectively. A and B themselves are called assumptions. If we associate $node_3$ with the supporting statements such as $\{A, B\}$ and the dependent nodes such as $\{(r_1, r_2)\}$ then $node_3$ is generally in the form of $r_3 : p \rightarrow r, \{\{A, B\}...\}, \{(r_1, r_2)...\}$ when $node_3$ has more than one justification. The collection of all possible sets of supporting environments is called the label of a node. If we use $L(r_3)$ to denote the label of $node_3$, then $\{A, B\} \in L(r_3)$. If we assume that r_1, r_2 hold without requiring any dependent relation on other nodes, then $node_1$ and $node_2$ are represented as $r_1 : p \rightarrow q, \{\{A\}\}, \{()\}$ and $r_2 : q \rightarrow r, \{\{B\}\}, \{()\}$. Therefore, we can infer a label for any node as long as its justifications are known.

The advantage of this reasoning mechanism is that the dependent and supporting relations among nodes are explicitly specified, in particular, the supporting relations among assumptions and other nodes. This is obviously useful when we want to retrieve the reasoning path. It is also helpful for belief revision. The limitation of this reasoning pattern is that we cannot infer those statements which are probably true rather than absolutely true. However, if we attach numerical degrees of belief to the elements in the supporting set of a node, we may be able to infer a statement with a degree of belief. For example, if we know A is true with probability 0.8 and B is true with probability 0.7 and A and B are probabilistically independent, then the probability of $A \wedge B$ is true is 0.56. The belief in a node is considered as the probability of its label. So for $node_3$, our belief in it is 0.56.

Definition 3: Probabilistic assumption set:[3] a set $\{A, B, ..., C\}$, denoted as $S_{A,...,C}$, is called a probabilistic assumption set for assumptions $A, B, ..., C$ if the probabilities on $A, ..., C$ are given by a probability distribution p from a piece of evidence and $\Sigma_{D \in \{A,...,C\}} p(D) = 1$. The simplest probabilistic assumption set has two elements X and $\neg X$, denoted as $S_X = \{X, \neg X\}$. For any two assumptions in a set, it is assumed that $A_i \wedge A_j \Rightarrow \perp$ and $\vee A_j = T$ for $j = 1, ..., n$.

For two distinct probabilistic assumption sets S_A and S_B, the unified probabilistic assumption set set is defined as $S_{AB} = S_A \otimes S_B = \{(A_1, B_j) \mid A_i \in S_A, B_j \in S_B\}$ where $\otimes$ means set product and $p(A_i, B_j) = p_1(A_i) \times p_2(B_j)$. p_1 and p_2 are the probability distributions on S_A and S_B respectively.

Definition 4: Full extension of a label: assume that an environment of a node n is $\{A_1, A_2, ..., A_l\}$ where A_i are in different probabilistic assumption sets. Because $A_1 \wedge ... \wedge A_l \equiv A_1 \wedge ... \wedge A_l \wedge (\vee B_j \mid B_j \in S_B), A_1 \wedge ... \wedge A_n \rightarrow n$ and

---

[3] Similar definition is given in [16] called auxiliary hypothesis set.

$A_1 \wedge ... \wedge A_n \wedge (\vee_j B_j \mid B_j \in S_B) \rightarrow n$ (where S_B is a probabilistic assumption set which is different from S_{A_i}), $A_1 \wedge ... \wedge A_l \wedge (\vee B_j \mid B_j \in S_B)$ is called a full extension of the environment to S_B. If there are in total m assumptions in the ATMS, then the extension $A_1 \wedge ... \wedge (\vee B_i \mid B_i \in S_B) \wedge ... \wedge (\vee C_{m-l} \mid C_{m-l} \in S_C)$ is called the full extension of the environment to all assumptions, or simply called the full extension of the environment. Similarly if every environment in a label has been fully extended to all assumptions, then we call the result the full extension of the label, denoted as $FL(n)$.

4 Implementing an ATMS Using Incidence Calculus

Abstractly if we view the set of possible worlds in incidence calculus as the set of assumptions in an ATMS, and view the calculation of the incidence sets of formulae as the calculation of labels of nodes in the ATMS, then the two reasoning patterns are similar. As incidence calculus can draw a conclusion with a numerical degree of belief on it, incidence calculus actually possesses some features of both symbolic and numerical reasoning approaches. Therefore, incidence calculus can be used both as a theoretical basis for the implementation of a probabilistic ATMS by providing both labels and degrees of belief of statements and as an automatic reasoning model to provide justifications for an ATMS.

Now we will show how to manage assumptions in the ATMS in the way we manage sets of possible worlds in incidence calculus. Here we look at an example (from [16]).

Example 1 Assume that there are the following nodes in an ATMS:

assumed nodes: $n_1 :< b \rightarrow a, \{\{V\}\}, \{(V)\} >$ $\quad n_2 :< c \rightarrow a, \{\{W\}\}, \{(W)\} >$
$\qquad\qquad\quad n_3 :< d \rightarrow b, \{\{X\}\}, \{(X)\} >$ $\quad n_4 :< d \rightarrow c, \{\{Y\}\}, \{(Y)\} >$
$\qquad\qquad\quad n_5 :< e \rightarrow d, \{\{Z\}\}, \{(Z)\} >$
premise node: $\quad n_6 :< e, \{\{\}\}, \{()\} >$
derived nodes: $\quad n_7 :< d \rightarrow a, \{\{X, V\}, \{Y, W\}\}, \{(n_1, n_3), (n_2, n_4)\} >$
$\qquad\qquad\quad n_8 :< e \rightarrow a, \{\{Z, X, V\}, \{Z, Y, W\}\}, \{(n_7, n_5)\} >$
$\qquad\qquad\quad n_9 :< a, \{\{Z, X, V\}, \{Z, Y, W\}\}, \{(n_6, n_8)\} >$
assumption nodes: $\quad < X, \{\{X\}\}, \{(X)\} >, \quad < V, \{\{V\}\}, \{(V)\} >, \ ...$

The label of node a is $Bel(a) = Pr((Z \wedge X \wedge V) \vee (Z \wedge Y \wedge W))$. Given that probabilities on different assumptions are $p_1(V) = .7; p_2(W) = .8; p_3(X) = .6; p_4(Y) = .75; p_5(Z) = .8$, and they are probabilistically independent, the belief in a is $Bel(a) = 0.6144$ which is calculated based on $FL(a)$. A different calculation procedure can also be found in [16] which produces the same result.

Now let us see how his problem can be solved in incidence calculus theories. Suppose that we have the following six incidence calculus theories

$\qquad < S_V, \varrho_1, P, \{b \rightarrow a, T\}, i_1(b \rightarrow a) = \{V\}, i_1(T) = S_V >$
$\qquad < S_W, \varrho_2, P, \{c \rightarrow a, T\}, i_2(c \rightarrow a) = \{W\}, i_2(T) = S_W >$
$\qquad < S_X, \varrho_3, P, \{d \rightarrow b, T\}, i_3(d \rightarrow b) = \{X\}, i_3(T) = S_X >$

$$< S_Y, \varrho_4, P, \{d \to c, T\}, i_4(d \to c) = \{Y\}, i_4(T) = S_Y >$$
$$< S_Z, \varrho_5, P, \{e \to d, T\}, i_5(e \to d) = \{Z\}, i_5(T) = S_Z >$$
$$< S_E, \varrho_6(E) = 1, P, \{e\}, i_6(e) = S_E >$$

where $S_V = \{V, \neg V\}$, ..., $S_Z = \{Z, \neg Z\}$, and $S_E = \{E, \neg E\}$ are probabilistic assumption sets. If we assume that sets of $S_X, ..., S_Z, S_E$ are probabilistically independent, the combination of the first five theories produces an incidence calculus theory $< S_7, \varrho_7, P, \mathcal{A}_7, i_7 >$ in which the joint set is $S_7 = S_Z \otimes S_X \otimes S_V \otimes S_Y \otimes S_W$. Combining this theory with the sixth incidence calculus theory[4] we obtain $i(e \wedge \phi_1) = S_E Z X V S_Y S_W$, $i(e \wedge \phi_2) = S_E Z Y W S_X S_V$, $i(e \wedge \phi_1 \wedge \phi_2) = S_E Z X V Y W$, if we let $e \to d \wedge d \to b \wedge b \to a = \phi_1$ and $e \to d \wedge d \to c \wedge c \to a = \phi_2$. Because $e \wedge \phi_1 \to a$, $e \wedge \phi_2 \to a$ and $e \wedge \phi_1 \wedge \phi_2 \to a$, the following equation $i_*(a) = S_E Z X V S_Y S_W \cup S_E S_X S_V Z Y W$ holds. So $p_*(a) = wp(i_*(a)) = 0.6144$. Similarly we can also obtain $i_*(d \to a)$, $i_*(e \to a)$ as:

$$i_*(d \to a) = S_E S_Z X V S_Y S_W \cup S_E S_Z Y W S_X S_V$$
$$i_*(e \to a) = S_E Z X V S_Y S_W \cup S_E Z Y W S_X S_V$$

Therefore the following equations $i_*(d \to a) \equiv FL(d \to a)$, $i_*(e \to a) \equiv FL(e \to a)$ and $i_*(a) \equiv FL(a)$ hold. Here the symbol $\equiv$ is read as "equivalent to". An incidence set of a formula (or its lower bound) is equivalent to the full extension of the label of a node means that for any element in the incidence set there is one and only one conjunction part in $FL(*)$.

Theorem 1 *Given an ATMS, there exists a set of incidence calculus theories such that the reasoning result of the ATMS is equivalent to the result obtained from the combination of these theories. For any node d_i in an ATMS, $L(d_i) \backslash L(\perp)$ is equivalent to the incidence set of formulae d_i in incidence calculus.*

The proof is given in [17].

Example 2 Following the story in Example 1, suppose we are told later that f is also observed and there is a rule $f \to \neg c$ with degree .8 in the knowledge base. That is, three more nodes in the ATMS are used as shown below.

assumed node: $< f \to \neg c, \{\{U\}\}, \{(U)\} >$
premise node $< f, \{\{\}\}, \{()\} >$
assumption node $< U, \{\{U\}\}, \{(U)\} >$
and assumption sets $S_U = \{U, \neg U\}$, $S_F = \{F, \neg F\}$.
Here S_F is created to support premise node f.

In the ATMS, we can infer that one environment of node c is $\{E, Z, Y\}$ and one environment of node $\neg c$ is $\{F, U\}$. So the *nogood* environment is $\{E, X, Y, F, U\}$. The belief in node a needs to be recomputed in order to redistribute the weight of conflict on the other nodes. The revised belief in a is 0.366 given in [16].

Similar to Example 1, in incidence calculus two more incidence calculus theories are constructed from the assumed node and the premise node. Combining these two theories with the final one we obtained in Example 1, we have $W_0 = \{UZY\}$[5], $i_*(a) = \{ZXV \cup ZYW\} \backslash W_0$. Therefore $wp(\{UZY\}) = 0.48$ which

---

[4] The combination sequence does not affect the final result. Here in order to show the result explicitly, we take these two steps.

[5] In order to state the problem clearly, we use UZY instead of $UZY S_X S_W S_V S_E S_F$.

is the weight of conflict and $p'_*(a) = wp(\{ZXV \cup ZYW\}) \setminus \{UZY\}) = 0.366$ which is our belief in a. Both of these results are the same as those given in [16], but the calculation of belief in node a and the weight of conflict are based on incidence calculus theory.

5 Conclusions

Existing papers discuss the unification of an ATMS with numerical uncertain reasoning mechanisms [5, 6, 8, 11, 14, 15, 16, 19, 20]. The closest work to ours is described in [16]. In their paper the relations between the ATMS and the Dempster-Shafer theory of evidence is discussed. They claimed that the relation between the two theories is that the ATMS can be used to represent DS inference networks. More precisely, their result is that a set of belief functions can be equivalently translated into a corresponding ATMS system. In such systems the reasoning procedure is carried out as a normal ATMS together with performing the appropriate calculations of uncertainty values. However a formal proof of equivalence between the two theories is missing. We claim that incidence calculus, though closely related to DS theory [2, 3], also has strong similarities to the ATMS. These have allowed us to produce a proof of the equivalence between the two forms of inference.

The discussion in this paper tells us that incidence calculus itself is a unification of both symbolic and numerical approaches. It can therefore be regarded as a bridge between the two reasoning patterns. This result also gives theoretical support for research on the unification of the ATMS with numerical approaches. In incidence calculus structure, both symbolic supporting relations among statements and numerical calculation of degrees of belief in different statements are explicitly described. For a specific problem, incidence calculus can either be used as a support based symbolic reasoning system or be applied to deal with numerical uncertainties. This feature cannot be provided by pure symbolic or numerical approaches independently.

Another advantage of using incidence calculus to make inferences is that it doesn't require the problem solver to provide justifications. The whole reasoning procedure is performed automatically. The inference result can be used to produce the ATMS related justifications. The calculation of degrees of beliefs in nodes are based on the hypothesis that each assumption is in one auxiliary set and all these sets are probabilistically independent. Further work will consider the more general situation, that is, several assumptions are in one set as individual elements and there is a probability distribution on it.

References

[1] Bundy,A., Incidence calculus: A mechanism for probabilistic reasoning. *Journal of Automated Reasoning* 1:263-83, 1985.

[2] Bundy,A., Incidence calculus, *The Encyclopedia of AI.* 663-668, 1992.

[3] Bundy,A. and W. Liu, On Dempster's combination rule. Submitted to the Journal of Artificial Intelligence, 1993.

[4] Correa da Silva,F. and A.Bundy (1990) On some equivalent relations between incidence calculus and Dempster-Shafer theory of evidence. Proc. of sixth conference of uncertainty in artificial intelligence, pp.378-383.

[5] d'Ambrosio,B., A hybrid approach to reasoning under uncertainty, *Int. J. Approx. Reasoning* 2 (1988): 29-45.

[6] d'Ambrosio,B., Incremental Construction and Evaluation of Defeasible Probabilistic Models, *I.J.Approx. Reasoning* 4 (1990): 233-260.

[7] de Kleer,J., An assumption-based TMS. *Artificial Intelligence* 28 (1986) 127-162.

[8] de Kleer,J. and B.C.Williams, Diagnosing multiple faults, *Artificial Intelligence* 32 (1987) 97-130.

[9] Doyle,J., A truth maintenance system. *Artificial Intelligence* 12 (3): 231-72, 1979.

[10] Dubois,D., J.Lang and H.Prade, Handling uncertain knowledge in an ATMS using possibilistic logic, *ECAI-90 workshop on Truth Maintenance Systems*, (1990) Stockholm, Sweden.

[11] Falkenhainer, B., Towards a general purpose belief maintenance system, *Proc. 2nd workshop on Uncertainty in AI*. Philadelphia, 71-76, 1986.

[12] Fulvio Monai,F. and T.Chehire, Possibilistic Assumption based Truth Maintenance Systems, Validation in a Data Fusion Application, *Proc. of the eighth conference on uncertainty in artificial intelligence*. Stanford, 83-91, 1992.

[13] Laskey,K.B. and P.E.Lehner, Assumptions, Beliefs and Probabilities, *Artificial Intelligence* 41 (1989/90) 65-77.

[14] Liu,W. and A.Bundy, Constructing probabilistic ATMS using incidence calculus. Submitted, 1993.

[15] Pearl,J., *Probabilistic Reasoning in Intelligence Systems: networks of plausible inference*. Morgan Kaufmann Publishers, Inc., 1988.

[16] Proven,G.M., An analysis of ATMS-based techniques for computing Dempster-Shafer belief functions. *Proc. of the 11th International Joint Conf. on Artificial Intelligence*, p:1115-1120, 1989.

A Resolution Method for a Non Monotonic Multimodal Logic[1]

Christophe MATHIEU

L.I.U.P. Université de Provence CASE A
3 place Victor Hugo 13331 Marseille Cedex 3

✆: (33) 91 10 61 28   Fax: (33) 91 10 61 02
E-Mail: MATHIEU@gyptis.univ-mrs.fr

Abstract. In this paper we present a resolution method for a non monotonic multimodal logic: Hypothesis Theory. As we define a resolution method, we need modal formula to be in clausal normal form. But an important problem with modal logic is that there is no such simple normal form than in classical logic. So we propose an original clausal transformation for modal formulas. This translation avoids the exponential increase in size which may occur with another translation. Moreover, modal formulas and their translation entails the same formulas. This technique should increase the attractiveness of modal resolution based theorem provers for automated reasoning.

1   Introduction

Among all the non monotonic formalism such that Default logic [6], Autoepistemic logic [4], ... there is one which use a multimodal system based on the two modal system K and T: Hypothesis Theory [10], [8]. The interest of such theory for non monotonicity lies in these important properties. They are: first, the equivalence between syntactic and semantic definition (the logic is sound and complete), then the compactness result (therefore proof procedures exist) and the fact that every consistent hypothesis theory admits extensions, and lastly hypothesis theory gives a complete characterization of default logic as well as a simple criterion for the existence of extensions of a default theory [8].

To reason (automatically) with this formalism, we have to define a theorem prover. Many automated theorem prover are based on resolution [7], they deal with a given knowledge represented by a set of clauses that confers them a great simplicity and allows optimisations. But there is a lack of normal form theorems in modal logic. Then, among several automated deduction methods for multimodal logic given in the

---

[1] This work has been partially supported by the ESPRIT BRA (Basic Research Action) project DRUMS II (Defeasible Reasoning and Uncertainty Management Systems) Action 6156 of the European community and the french project PRC-GDR CNRS Gestion de l'évolutif et de l'incertain dans les bases de connaissances.

literature, some are based on translation into logic as classical logic or deterministic logic that possess normal form theorem [1].

To solve these problems, first we present a clause form translation for modal logic that converts any propositional modal formula f in a set C of what we called pseudo-clauses, featuring a linear ratio of lengths (5 if f doesn't contain modal operator chain i.e. the modal degree of f is equal to one). Secondly, we define the resolution method based on pseudo-clauses.

The basic idea of the translation, due to [11] and [5] (see also [9]), is to introduce new proposition P to refer to various sub-formulas A of the original formula. Then the assertion P→A can be added to the set of formulas (this technique is used in propositional calculus to cut a clause in two clauses of inferior length). This idea can be extended to modal logic: if the formula is $\Box$f (or $\Diamond$f), we add $\Box P \wedge \Box(P \rightarrow f)$ (or $\Diamond P \wedge \Box(P \rightarrow f)$) to the set of formulae where P is a new proposition, and $\Box$ ($\Diamond$) is the necessity (possible) operator of some modal logic. As the translation uses new propositions, the formula f and the set of modal pseudo-clauses C are equivalent on the language which contains only the propositions occurring in f. Particularly, the translation preserves the satisfiability or the unsatisfiability of the initial formula.

In the first part, we introduce the multimodal logic: hypothesis theory, in the second we present the modal pseudo-clausal translation, and finally, the resolution method for this logic.

2 Hypothesis Theory

2.1 The Modal Logic

The modal logic is defined as a *propositional multimodal system* with two modal operators L and [H]. L is the necessity operator of the standard modal system T that has a reflexive accessibility relation, and [H] is the one of the weakest standard modal system K. The only syntactical link between L and [H] is given by the logical interaction axiom: Lp → [H]p (It's impossible to hypothesise a fact whose negation is true). A hypothesis is defined by: Hp = ¬ [H]¬ p.

The *language* $\mathscr{L}$ of this system is an extension of propositional calculus language by the two modal operators L and [H]. Propositions and formulae are defined as usual (with the ∧ (and), ∨ (or), ¬ (not), →(implies) connectives), and if A is a formula then LA, [H]A and HA are formulae. The modal degree[2] of the formulas is equal to one.

We have two modal systems K and T, with an interaction axiom, also called inclusion axiom, Lp → [H]p. So the necessity operator [H] is weaker than L. Moreover, with the possible operator H (dual of [H]), we can have Hp and H¬p in the same consistent knowledge base. The resolution method will have to take into account these facts.

---

[2] The modal degree is the maximal number of modal operators fitting into each other of a formula f and can be define by: modal degree({}f)=Modal degree(f)+1 where {} is a modal operator $\Box$ or $\Diamond$.

For the semantic aspect, the hypothesis theory semantics is a multimodal Kripke semantics and the inclusion axiom is translated into $R_{[H]} \subset R_L$, if R_L and $R_{[H]}$ are the accessibility relations associated with L and [H] [8]. Truth functions, models and validity are defined as usual.

2.2 Hypothesis Theory

A Hypothesis Theory $\mathcal{H}$ is a set of formulae formulated in the language $\mathcal{L}$ containing additional formulae of the form Hp where p is any formula (Hp is a hypothesis).

Definition: A *Hypothesis Theory* $\mathcal{H}$ is given by $\mathcal{H} =$ (F, HY), where:
- F is a set of formulas
- HY is some set of hypotheses.

Hypothesis theory gives a complete characterization of default logic[3].

3 Modal Pseudo-Clausal Translation

Since our purpose is to present a proof procedure for hypothesis theory based on resolution, we need formulas to be in clausal form. So the first part of the procedure will consist in changing modal formulas to simplify the resolution method. The translation enables us to transform multimodal propositional formula into pseudo-clauses without exponential increase of lengths. Its interest is, first, that the translation should happen linearly (the ratio between the initial and final formula's length is linear), as the classical algorithm under conjunctive normal form is theoretically exponential. The typical propositional example is $(p_{11} \vee p_{12} \vee ... \vee p_{1n}) \wedge ... \wedge (p_{m1} \vee p_{m2} \vee ... \vee p_{mn})$ where the associated clausal form is a formula with n^m clauses of m literals. With our method, we obtain m+1 clauses of n+1 literals. Secondly, in normal modal logic $\Box (l_1 \vee l_2 \vee ... \vee l_n)$ and $\Box l_1 \vee \Box l_2 \vee ... \vee \Box l_n$, $\Diamond (l_1 \wedge l_2 \wedge ... \wedge l_n)$ and $\Diamond l_1 \wedge \Diamond l_2 \wedge ... \wedge \Diamond l_n$ are not equivalents. So it's impossible to exhibit the same normal form as in classical logic. With this translation, we obtain pseudo-literals that don't contain conjunction.

As our translation works for all modal systems, we represent in the following by $\Box_i$ and $\Diamond_i$, the necessity and the possible operators of a modal system i. To simplify the

---

[3] A default logic $\Delta = (D,W)$ is translated into a hypothesis theory (F,HY) with :
$LW = \{Lw \mid w \in W\}$, $LD = \{L\alpha \wedge H\beta \to L\gamma \mid \frac{\alpha : \beta}{\gamma} \in D\}$, $HY = \{H\beta \mid \beta \in JUST(D)\}$ and $F = LW \cup LD \cup \{Lp \to [H]p\}$. Extensions of F in HY are obtained by adding to F a subset HY' of HY such that F $\cup$ HY' is maximal consistent according to HY (maximal consistent according to HY means that if any other hypothesis of HY is added, the resulting theory is inconsistent). Non monotonicity comes from the fact that an extension is defined by adding hypotheses. Therefore, the addition of new formulae to F can prevent the addition of previously admissible hypotheses.

translation, we first put formulas into negative normal form; this can be done linearly and retaining the logical equivalence.

3.1 Negative Normal Form

Definition: A formula is in *negative normal form* if the $\neg$ connective occurs only in the literals and the $\rightarrow$ connective does not appear.

Theorem: *Any modal formula is equivalent to a formula in negative normal form with the same length.*

3.2 Pseudo-Clausal Translation

The result of the translation are pseudo-clauses.

Definition: A *pseudo-literal* is:
- a classical literal
- $\Diamond_i(l_j)$ where l_j is a classical literal
- $\Box_i(l_1 \vee l_2 \vee ... \vee l_n)$ where each l_j is a classical literal.

Definition: A *pseudo-clause* is a disjunction $pl_1...pl_n$, where each pl_j is a pseudo-literal.

Example: $\Box_i(B \vee C \vee F)$ or $\Diamond_i B$ are pseudo-literals, but not $\Box_i(A \wedge X)$ and $\Diamond_i(B \vee F)$.

Definition: Let $\mathcal{L}$ be a propositional multimodal language and $\mathcal{P}$ a set of propositions (non modal) that don't belong to $\mathcal{L}$. $\mathcal{L}\mathcal{P}$ is the language obtained by adding $\mathcal{P}$ to $\mathcal{L}$.

A formula f of $\mathcal{L}$ and a formula h of $\mathcal{L}\mathcal{P}$ are *$\mathcal{L}$-equivalent* ($\Leftrightarrow_{\mathcal{L}}$) iff for all formula k of $\mathcal{L}$: $\vDash f \rightarrow k$ if and only if $\vDash h \rightarrow k$ ($\vDash f$ means f is valid in all Kripke structures).

Theorem:

$$f \wedge g \qquad \Leftrightarrow_{\mathcal{L}} \qquad p \wedge (p \rightarrow f) \wedge (p \rightarrow g)$$
$$f \vee g \qquad \Leftrightarrow_{\mathcal{L}} \qquad p \wedge (p \rightarrow f \vee g)$$
$$\Box_i(f \Delta g) \qquad \Leftrightarrow_{\mathcal{L}} \qquad \Box_i(p \Delta g) \wedge \Box_i(p \rightarrow f) \text{ where } \Delta \text{ is } \vee \text{ or } \wedge$$
$$\Diamond_i(f \Delta g) \qquad \Leftrightarrow_{\mathcal{L}} \qquad \Diamond_i(p \Delta g) \wedge \Box_i(p \rightarrow f) \text{ where } \Delta \text{ is } \vee \text{ or } \wedge$$

$$\Box_i(f \wedge g) \qquad \Leftrightarrow_{\mathcal{L}} \qquad \Box_i(f) \wedge \Box_i(g)$$
$$\Diamond_i(f \vee g) \qquad \Leftrightarrow_{\mathcal{L}} \qquad \Diamond_i(f) \vee \Diamond_i(g)$$

(The two last equivalencies are classical modal equivalencies)

Proof: See [3]

Example: The formula $\Box_i((A \wedge B) \vee (C \wedge D) \vee (E \wedge F))$ is translate into the set of clauses:

$\Box_i(P_1 \vee P_2 \vee P_3)$	$\Box_i(P_1 \rightarrow A)$	$\Box_i(P_2 \rightarrow C)$	$\Box_i(P_3 \rightarrow E)$
	$\Box_i(P_1 \rightarrow B)$	$\Box_i(P_2 \rightarrow D)$	$\Box_i(P_3 \rightarrow F)$

With three steps as the following: $\square_i(P_1 \vee (C \wedge D) \vee (E \wedge F)) \wedge \square_i(P_1 \to A \wedge B)$
$\square_i(P_1 \vee (C \wedge D) \vee (E \wedge F)) \wedge \square_i(P_1 \to A) \wedge \square_i(P_1 \to B)$

But a recursive and anarchic use of the theorem would not permit the achievement of a set of modal pseudo-clause without exponential increase of the ratio of the lengths. To make this ratio linear, we must replace only the elementary sub formulas (the non splittable formulas) of the formula.

3.3 A Linear Translation in Modal Logic

Definition : A *non splittable formula* is a conjunction or a disjunction of pseudo-literals.

Example: In the formula $\square_i((A \wedge B) \vee (C \wedge D) \vee (E \wedge F))$ there are three non splittable formulas: $(A \wedge B)$, $(C \wedge D)$ and $(E \wedge F)$.

The translation algorithm has been implemented in Prolog II in case of formulas have a modal degree equal to one.

Property: *Any propositional modal formula f can be translated in a set of modal pseudo-clauses C such that the ratio of the lengths of f and C is at most 5.*

Proof: In the modal case, if we decrease the length of the formula by one unit, we must add at most two clauses of a total length 6. This maximal difference correspond to the translation of the formula $\square_i(a_1 \wedge a_2)$ into $\square_i P \wedge \square_i(P \to a_1) \wedge \square_i(P \to a_2)$. After the translation, the remaining formula has a length at most equal to L-1, if L is the length of the initial formula. We obtain a ratio of length at most equal to 5. ∎

4. Resolution Method

To make some automated reasoning, we need to check the validity of a formula. As formulas are in modal pseudo-clausal form, we now describe a resolution method for the Hypothesis theory formulas which is an extension of the classical resolution.

The resolution method is defined by resolution and factorization rules. We represent by $l\ C_1$ the pseudo-clause $a_1 \vee \ldots \vee a_n \vee l \vee a'_1 \vee \ldots \vee a'_m$, and by D_i a disjunction of pseudo-literals. RES(l_1,l_2) $C_1\ C_2$ is the resolvante of two pseudo-clauses $l_1\ C_1$ and $l_2\ C_2$, and FUS (l_1,l_2) C the factorization of two pseudo-literals in the clause $l_1\ l_2\ C$. ⊥ will represent the empty clause. The rules are defined for the K and T systems. We note $\square_K$, $\lozenge_K$ and $\square_T$, $\lozenge_T$ the modal operators of the K and T systems.

4.1 The Resolution Rule is : $\dfrac{l_1\ C_1 \qquad l_2\ C_2}{\text{RES}(l_1,l_2)\ C_1\ C_2}$ where RES is defined by :

Classical Rules
- RES$(l,\neg l)$ $\Rightarrow$ ⊥
- RES$(l\ D_1, l'\ D_2)$ $\Rightarrow$ $D_1\ D_2$ if RES(l,l') $\Rightarrow$ ⊥

Modal Rules for K
- Simplification rule : $\Diamond_K \bot \;\Rightarrow\; \bot$
- $\text{RES}(\Box_K D_1, \Box_K D_2) \;\Rightarrow\; \Box_K[\text{RES}(D_1, D_2)]$
- $\text{RES}(\Box_K D_1, \Diamond_K D_2) \;\Rightarrow\; \Diamond_K[\text{RES}(D_1, D_2)]$

Modal Rules for T
- Modal Rules for K
- Simplification rule : $\Box_T \bot \;\Rightarrow\; \bot$
- $\text{RES}(\Box_T D_1, D_2) \;\Rightarrow\; \text{RES}(D_1, D_2)$

Interaction Rules (if the interaction axiom is $\Box_T p \rightarrow \Box_K p$)
- $\text{RES}(\Box_T D_1, \Box_K D_2) \;\Rightarrow\; \Box_K[\text{RES}(D_1, D_2)]$
- $\text{RES}(\Box_T D_1, \Diamond_K D_2) \;\Rightarrow\; \Diamond_K[\text{RES}(D_1, D_2)]$

4.2 The Factorization Rule is : $\dfrac{l_1 \; l_2 \; C}{\text{FUS}(l_1, l_2) \; C}$ where FUS is defined by :

- FUS (l,l) $\;\Rightarrow\; l$
- FUS $(\Box_T l, l)$ $\;\Rightarrow\; l$
- FUS $(l\,D_1, l'\,D_2)$ $\;\Rightarrow\;$ FUS (l, l') FUS (D_1, D_2)
- FUS $(\Box_K D_1 \Box_K D_2)$ $\;\Rightarrow\; \Box_K$ FUS (D_1, D_2)
- FUS $(\Diamond_K D_1, \Diamond_K D_2)$ $\;\Rightarrow\; \Diamond_K$ FUS (D_1, D_2)
- FUS $(\Box_T D_1, \Box_T D_2)$ $\;\Rightarrow\; \Box_T$ FUS (D_1, D_2)
- FUS $(\Diamond_T D_1, \Diamond_T D_2)$ $\;\Rightarrow\; \Diamond_T$ FUS (D_1, D_2)
- FUS $(\Box_T D_1, \Diamond_T D_2)$ $\;\Rightarrow\; \Diamond_T$ FUS (D_1, D_2)
- FUS $(\Box_T D_1, \Box_K D_2)$ $\;\Rightarrow\; \Box_K$ FUS (D_1, D_2)

  (if the interaction axiom is $\Box_T p \rightarrow \Box_K p$)

Theorem: *The resolution method for the hypothesis theory is sound and complete.*

Proof : See [3].

5 Conclusion

We present a resolution method for a non monotonic modal logic. This method is based on a translation of formulas into clausal form. This translation permits to obtain from a propositional modal formula f, a set of modal clauses whose length depends only linearly on the length of f. The set of clauses is $\mathcal{L}$-equivalent with the initial formula i.e. equivalent on the $\mathcal{L}$ language. This result is more general in the sense that it can be used not only to check the satisfiability of a set of formulas but also to produce formula with consequence finding algorithm. It appears that this translation should significantly increase the use of resolution based theorem provers for modal logic.

Such a translation can be generalized to modal formulas with modal degree greater than 1. The definition of a pseudo-literal is changing into a recursive one:

Definition: A *pseudo-literal* is:
- a classical literal
- $\Diamond_i(l_1 \vee l_2 \vee \ldots \vee l_n)$ where each l_j is a pseudo-literal
- $\Box_i(l_1 \vee l_2 \vee \ldots \vee l_n)$ where each l_j is a pseudo-literal

Example: $\Box_i(B \vee \Diamond_i B \vee F)$ or $\Diamond_i(B \vee \Diamond_i(B \vee \Box_i F))$ are pseudo-literals.
The translation theorem is:

Theorem : *If $F = u\,G\,v$ is a multimodal formula in negative normal form of a multimodal language $\mathcal{L}$, u and v are sequence of symbols of $\mathcal{L}$. If G is a sub-formula of F and P a proposition that doesn't belong to $\mathcal{L}$ $F = u\,G\,v$ is translate into ${}^tF = u\,P\,v \wedge \Box_i{}^n(P \rightarrow G)$ where n is the number of modal operators governing G such that F and ${}^tF$ are $\mathcal{L}$-equivalents.*

The linear property becomes:

Property: *Any propositional modal formula f can be translated in a set of modal pseudo-clauses C such that the ratio of the lengths of f and C is at most $2n+3$, where n is the modal degree of f.*

This complete translation can be found in [3].

References

1. L. Fariñas Del Cerro, A. Herzig: Modal Deduction with Applications in Epistemic and Temporal Logics. 5th draft, to appear in : Handbook of Logic in Artificial Intelligence edited by Dov Gabbay and Chris Hogger, Oxford University Press (1991)

2. Léa Sombé (Besnard P., Cordier M-O., Dubois D., Farinas del Cerro L., Froidevaux C., Moinard Y., Prade H., Schwind C., Siegel P.): Reasoning under Incomplete Information in Artificial Intelligence, John Wiley (1990)

3. C. Mathieu: Une procédure de preuve pour une logique modale non monotone, Thèse de doctorat informatique de l'université de Provence, Marseille, (1993)

4. R. Moore: Autoepistemic Logic, Non-Standard Logics for Automated Reasoning (P. Smets, A. Mandani, D. Dubois, H. Prade Eds.) Academic Press, London, pp 105-136, (1988)

5. D. A. Plaisted and S. Greenbaum: A Structure-Preserving Clause Form Translation, Journal of Symbolic Computation, 2, pp 293-304, (1986)

6. R. Reiter: A Logic for Default Reasoning, Artificial intelligence 13, pp 81-132, (1980)

7. J. A. Robinson: A Machine Oriented Logic Based on the Resolution Principle, JACM, Vol 12 n°1, pp 23-41, (1965)

8. C. Schwind and P. Siegel: Hypothesis Theory for Nonmonotonic Reasoning, Workshop on Non Standard Queries and Answers, Toulouse, (1991)

9. P. Siegel: Représentation et utilisation de la connaissance en calcul propositionnel, Thèse de Doctorat d'état en Informatique, Université d'Aix-Marseille II, (1987)

10. P. Siegel: A Modal Logic for Nonmonotonic Reasoning, Workshop DRUMS, Marseille, (1990)

11. G.S. Tseitin: On the Complexity of Derivations in Propositionnal Calculus, Studies In Constructive Mathematics And Mathematical Logic Part II, (1968) and Automation Of Reasoning 2: Classical Papers On Computational Logic pp 466-483 Siekmann Wrightson eds (1983)

A Default Logic Based on Epistemic States[1]

(extended abstract)[†]

J.-J. Ch. Meyer [#]
W. van der Hoek

Utrecht University
Department of Computer Science
P.O. Box 80089, 3508 TB Utrecht
The Netherlands
e-mail: jj@cs.ruu.nl, wiebe@cs.ruu.nl

Abstract. We indicate how default logic can be based on epistemic logic, and particularly how we may employ Halpern & Moses' minimal epistemic states for this purpose. In the context of default reasoning Halpern & Moses' entailment based on honest formulas is used to infer what is considered epistemically possible. These epistemic possibilities can be used in defaults in a way that is similar to the representation in AEL, but in which the nonmonotonicity appears at a different place: at the inference of ignorance rather than at the jumping to conclusions. In this way we obtain a simple and natural non-monotonic logic for default reasoning that is cumulative, almost by design. We give a model-theoretical characterization of the non-monotonic entailment associated with this logic in terms of S5-like models.

1 Introduction

Default logic (DL), auto-epistemic logic (AEL) and other approaches to nonmonotonic reasoning suffer from a technical complexity that is not in line with naive common-sense reasoning. They employ fixed-point constructions and higher-order logic in order to define the belief sets that one likes to associate with some base set of knowledge.

In [MH1,2] we introduced a logic S5P that is—like AEL—a *modal* logic, but that—*un*like AEL—does not involve any fixed points or higher-order formulas. S5P contains a certainty and possibility operator. Furthermore, the logic has a modality to indicate that some assertion holds by default. This gave some desirable properties with respect to e.g. transitivity and contraposition, which troubled AEL. Also reasoning by cases is supported by this logic in contrast with e.g. Reiter's DL. Some problem remained, however, in motivating the origin of the certainty, and even more importantly, the possibility of making an assertion in a particular situation. Here we solve this by considering Halpern & Moses' minimal states of knowledge. Thus we

---

[1] This research is partially supported by the Free University at Amsterdam and project DRUMS which is funded by a grant from the Commission of the European Communities under the ESPRIT III-Program, Basic Research Project 6156.
[†] Proofs are omitted: they can be found in the full paper [HM3].
[#] Also affiliated with the University of Nijmegen.

obtain a simple and natural nonmonotonic logic for default reasoning. This logic is cumulative in the sense of Kraus, Lehmann & Magidor [KLM], almost trivially.

2 Epistemic Logic

We introduce a language of *epistemic formulas* (Cf. [Hi, HM2]). Let $\mathbf{P}$ be a set of propositional constants; $\mathbf{P} = \{p_n \mid n \in \mathbb{N}\}$ or $\mathbf{P} = \{p_0,...,p_{n-1}\}$ for some $n \geq 1$. The set $\mathcal{L}(\mathbf{P})$ of epistemic formulas $\varphi, \psi,...$ is the smallest set containing $\mathbf{P} \cup \{\bot\}$ closed under infix placing of connectives from $\{\wedge, \vee, \supset, \equiv\}$ and prefix placing of the operators $\neg$, K and M. Here $K\varphi$ is read as: φ is known, and $M\varphi$ as φ is considered (epistemically) possible. Formulas without modal operators are *objective* formulas.

Epistemic formulas are interpreted by means of S5-Kripke models ([Kr)). An *S5-Kripke model* $\mathbb{M}$ is a tuple $\langle S, \pi, \wp \rangle$ where S is a set of *states*, $\pi: S \rightarrow (\mathbf{P} \rightarrow \{\mathfrak{t}, \mathfrak{f}\})$ is a truth assignment per state, and $\wp = S \times S$. We denote the class of all S5-Kripke models by $\mathcal{S5}$. A *world* w is a pair $(\mathbb{M}, s)$ with $\mathbb{M} \in \mathcal{S5}$ and $s \in S$. The class of worlds is denoted by $\mathcal{S5}^+$. As, in an S5-model, $\wp$ can be inferred from S, we also write $\langle S, \pi \rangle$. Moroever, we identify states with their truth assignments. For $\mathbb{M}_1 = \langle S_1, \pi_1 \rangle$ and $\mathbb{M}_2 = \langle S_2, \pi_2 \rangle$, we define $\mathbb{M}_1 \cup \mathbb{M}_2 = \langle S_1 \cup S_2, \pi_1 \cup \pi_2 \rangle$, where $(\pi_1 \cup \pi_2)(s) = \pi_1(s)$ if $s \in S_1$, and $= \pi_2(s)$, if $s \in S_2$ (note that in case $s \in S_1 \cap S_2$, there is no conflict.). Moreover, $\mathbb{M}_1 \subseteq \mathbb{M}_2$ iff $S_1 \subseteq S_2$. We define $(\mathbb{M}, s) \vDash \varphi$ by induction on φ, where the modal cases are:

- $(\mathbb{M}, s) \vDash K\varphi \Leftrightarrow (\mathbb{M}, t) \vDash \varphi$ for all t with $(s, t) \in \wp$, i.e., all $t \in S$;
- $(\mathbb{M}, s) \vDash M\varphi \Leftrightarrow (\mathbb{M}, t) \vDash \varphi$ for some t with $(s, t) \in \wp$, i.e., some $t \in S$.

Formula φ is *valid in a model* $\mathbb{M}$ if for all $s \in S$: $(\mathbb{M}, s) \vDash \varphi$. Notation: $\mathbb{M} \vDash \varphi$; φ is *valid*, notation $\vDash \varphi$, if $\mathbb{M} \vDash \varphi$ for all $\mathbb{M} \in \mathcal{S5}$; φ is *satisfiable* if there is some $w \in \mathcal{S5}^+$ with $w \vDash \varphi$. We recall the system **S5**, having the axioms: (A1) All propositional tautologies; (A2) $(K\varphi \wedge K(\varphi \rightarrow \psi)) \rightarrow K\psi$; (A3) $K\varphi \rightarrow \varphi$; (A4) $K\varphi \rightarrow KK\varphi$; (A5) $\neg K\varphi \rightarrow K\neg K\varphi$, and derivation rules Modus Ponens and Generalisation ($\varphi / K\varphi$). As is well-known, **S5** is a sound and complete axiomatisation of validity in $\mathcal{S5}$.

3 Halpern & Moses' Minimal Epistemic States

In [HM] Halpern and Moses proposed an elegant characterisation of an epistemic state, i.e. a state of knowledge of an agent, characterising exactly those facts she knows. We discuss some ingredients; Proposition 3.1 can be found in [Mo]; Proposition 3.2 up to and including Theorem 3.5 are from [HM]. First we introduce the notion of a stable set which represents the knowledge of a rational introspective agent.

A set Φ of epistemic formulas is *stable* if it satisfies the following: (St 1) all instances of propositional tautologies are in Φ; (St 2) $\varphi \in \Phi$ and $\varphi \supset \psi \in \Phi \Rightarrow \psi \in$

Φ; (St 3) $\varphi \in \Phi \Leftrightarrow K\varphi \in \Phi$; (St 4) $\varphi \notin \Phi \Leftrightarrow \neg K\varphi \in \Phi$; (St 5) Φ is propositional consistent, meaning that from Φ one cannot derive $\bot$ by using Propositional Logic (A1, R1) only.

PROPOSITION 3.1. *A stable set of epistemic formulas is uniquely determined by the objective formulas it contains .*∎

PROPOSITION 3.2. *Let Φ, Φ' be stable sets of epistemic formulas such that $\Phi \subseteq \Phi'$. Then $\Phi = \Phi'$.* ∎

If we write $\mathrm{Prop}(\Phi)$ for the set containing exactly Φ's objective formulas, Proposition 3.1 says that a stable set Φ of formulas is uniquely determined by $\mathrm{Prop}(\Phi)$. We now represent the epistemic state of "only knowing φ" by the stable set $\Sigma \ni \varphi$ for which $\mathrm{Prop}(\Sigma)$ is minimal (with respect to $\subseteq$). Such a Σ is not defined for every formule φ; φ is called *honest$_S$* if there is a stable set Σ^φ containing φ such that for all stable sets $\Sigma \ni \varphi$ it holds that $\mathrm{Prop}(\Sigma^\varphi) \subseteq \mathrm{Prop}(\Sigma)$. From [HM] we know that $Kp_1 \vee Kp_2$ is not honest$_S$. Semantically, for any $\mathbb{M} \in S5$, let $K(\mathbb{M})$ be the set of facts known in $\mathbb{M}$: $K(\mathbb{M}) = \{\varphi \mid \mathbb{M} \vDash \varphi\}$. Then $K(\mathbb{M})$ is a stable set.

PROPOSITION 3.3. (i) *Let $\mathbb{M}_1$, $\mathbb{M}_2$ be S5-models such that $\mathbb{M}_1 \subseteq \mathbb{M}_2$. Now, although $K(\mathbb{M}_1) \supseteq K(\mathbb{M}_2)$ does not need to hold, we do have $\mathrm{Prop}(K(\mathbb{M}_1)) \supseteq \mathrm{Prop}(K(\mathbb{M}_2))$.*
(ii) *For any S5-models $\mathbb{M}_1$, $\mathbb{M}_2$ it holds that $\mathrm{Prop}(K(\mathbb{M}_1 \cup \mathbb{M}_2)) = \mathrm{Prop}(K(\mathbb{M}_1)) \cap \mathrm{Prop}(K(\mathbb{M}_2))$ and $\mathrm{Prop}(K(\mathbb{M}_1 \cap \mathbb{M}_2)) \supseteq \mathrm{Prop}(K(\mathbb{M}_1)) \cup \mathrm{Prop}(K(\mathbb{M}_2))$.* ∎

PROPOSITION 3.4. *Every stable set Σ of epistemic formulas determines an S5 Kripke model $\mathbb{M}_\Sigma$ for which it holds that $\Sigma = K(\mathbb{M}_\Sigma)$. Moreover, if $\mathbf{P}$ is a finite set, then $\mathbb{M}_\Sigma$ is the unique S5-Kripke model with this property.* ∎

The model associated with the state of knowledge of an agent "only knowing φ" is now given by the union of all S5-models $\mathbb{M} = \langle S, \pi \rangle$ in which it holds that $K\varphi$: $\mathbb{M}_\varphi = \bigcup \{\mathbb{M} \mid \mathbb{M} \vDash K\varphi\}$. However, not always $\mathbb{M}_\varphi \vDash K\varphi$ holds! We define: φ is *honest$_M$* $\Leftrightarrow \varphi \in K(\mathbb{M}_\varphi)$. We now have that the two notions of honesty coincide:

THEOREM 3.5 *For any formula φ we have:*
(i) φ is *honest$_S$* $\Leftrightarrow \varphi$ is *honest$_M$*
(ii) φ is *honest$_S$* $\Rightarrow K(\mathbb{M}_\varphi) = \Sigma^\varphi$. ∎

Although honesty is not preserved by disjunction, it *is* preserved by conjunction, under the following restriction: Two honest formulas φ and ψ are *mutually h-consistent* if $\mathrm{Prop}(\Sigma^\varphi) \cup \mathrm{Prop}(\Sigma^\psi)$ is (propositionally) consistent.

PROPOSITION 3.6. *Let φ and ψ be two honest formulas. Then: φ and ψ are mutually h-consistent if* $\mathbb{M}_\varphi \cap \mathbb{M}_\psi \neq \emptyset$. ∎

PROPOSITION 3.7. *If φ and ψ are honest, and such that φ and ψ are mutually h-consistent, then $\varphi \wedge \psi$ is honest.* ∎

Now we define an entailment relation $\vdash$ for an honest φ, as follows: $\varphi \vdash \psi \;\Leftrightarrow\; \psi \in \Sigma^\varphi$. In the sequel when writing $\varphi \vdash \psi$, we assume φ being honest. We have $\varphi \vdash \varphi$, since $\varphi \in \Sigma^\varphi$. Also, if p and q are distinct atoms, we have that e.g. $p \vdash Kp$; $p \vdash \neg Kq$; $p \vdash K(p \vee q)$; $p \vee q \vdash \neg Kp \wedge \neg Kq$; $p \wedge q \vdash Kp \wedge Kq$.

COROLLARY (of Theorem 3.5(ii)) 3.8. $\varphi \vdash \psi \;\Leftrightarrow\; \mathbb{M}_\varphi \vDash K\psi \;(\Leftrightarrow\; \mathbb{M}_\varphi \vDash \psi)$. ∎

This gives a semantical characterisation of $\vdash$. In general, honesty is not preserved by $\vdash$: we have $p \vdash Kp$, and hence $p \vdash Kp \vee Kq$, of which the conclusion is not honest, whereas p *is* honest.

PROPOSITION 3.9. *Let φ be honest. Then $\varphi \vdash \psi$ implies that $\varphi \wedge \psi$ is honest.* ∎

EXAMPLE. $p \vdash \neg Kq$, and $p \wedge q \vdash Kq$, but *not* $p \wedge q \vdash \neg Kq$. ∎

From the example we learn that $\vdash$ is nonmonotonic. For a finite set of formulas Γ we define $\Gamma \vdash \varphi$ iff $\Gamma^* \vdash \varphi$ (i.e. $\varphi \in \Sigma^{\Gamma^*}$), where Γ^* is the conjunction of the formulas in Γ.

4 Epistemic Default Logic (EDL)

The statement that normally birds fly is represented in Reiter's DL ([Rei, Lu]) by a statement 'b : f / f', expressing that if we consider a bird, and *it is consistent to assume* that it can fly, then we assume that it can. In this inference a rather dangerous jump is made from 'consistent to assume f' to 'f' itself. We avoid this jump by using a special modality to indicate that this assertion f is practically believed, but by no means certain. For this, in [MH1,2] we introduced a P-modality.

Now, however, we concentrate on the statement "it is consistent to assume". In Reiter's DL this is interpreted as being consistent with the resulting belief set ("extension"). Since in Reiter's DL we cannot distinguish between real facts and assumptions on the basis of a default, this results in the need for some fixed-point construction. On the other hand, if one *does* make a distinction between (certain) facts and (default) assumptions, the need for such a construction disappears, and we may use a simple modal semantics (Cf. [MH1,2]). The certainty and possibility operators refer to the possible epistemic alternatives in the model, without dependency on the assertions that are assumed (by default) as in DL and AEL. The question remained, however, how these alternatives collected in the model, (representing the knowledge available to the agent), come about. In [MH1,2] we hinted at a process in which one starts with some base knowledge and during which certain information is added. For the change in certain knowledge from one state of knowledge to another we use dynamic logic in [MH1,2]. Since in [MH1,2] we always include in our reasoning the assumption that an assertion is possible, and never make jumps, the approach there was entirely monotonic. One may view it as a logic of expectations, given certain possibilities.

In this paper we explain how the certainties and possibilities mentioned above are obtained. By doing this we turn the approach into a truly nonmonotonic one. But we emphasize that we still keep an important difference with AEL and DL. In our approach we retain the P-modality to indicate that an assertion is made by default. Thus we still make no jumps in this sense. Instead, we infer from a base set of knowledge the assertions that are not known, and hence which possibilities remain. Notably the approach of section 3 yields a theory for doing just this, to derive ignorance from knowledge given! What the approach amounts to is minimisation of the objective knowledge given a set of base facts. This approach is nonmonotonic. But the nonmonotonicity appears at a different place: in the determination of what one knows and what not, rather than jumping to conclusions with respect to some default. Halpern & Moses' theory as such does not treat defaults at all. It was devised to reason about the knowledge and ignorance of processes in a distributed computer system. But, as shown in Shoham's book ([Sh2]) it is a typical example of nonmonotonic reasoning by means of a preference criterion.

In the sequel we combine our earlier approach to reason with preferences with Halpern & Moses' entailment for epistemic states to obtain an adequate logic for default reasoning. The language $\mathbf{L_{EDL}}$ is defined in a way similar to $\mathcal{L}(\mathbf{P})$, but now the modal operators are in $\{K, M, P_i \mid (i = 1,...,n)\}$. Informally, $P_i\varphi$ is read as "φ is preferred / a practical belief (within frame of reference i)". As we shall see below, a frame of reference refers to a subset of the set of *a priori* possible worlds that together constitute a body of preferred belief. We need multiple P-modalities, since we may have to distinguish multiple frames of reference, in (more or less) the same way as in Reiter's DL one may have multiple 'extensions'. Our P_i is close to the PA (possible assumption) of [TT] and the D (default) operator of [Do].

We refer to formulas in $\mathbf{L_{EDL}}$ as *EDL-formulas*. They are interpreted by Kripke-structures of the form $(S, \pi, S_1,..., S_n, \wp, \wp_1,..., \wp_n)$, where S, π and $\wp$ are as before, and $S_i \subseteq S$ are sets of preferred worlds; $\wp_i = S \times S_i \subseteq \wp$. $\mathcal{S5P}$ denotes the collection of such Kripke-structures. The interpretation of the K- and M-modalities are as before, and for the P-modalities we define:

- $(\mathbb{M},s) \models P_i\varphi$ iff $(\mathbb{M},t) \models \varphi$ for all $t \in S_i$. (I.e., $P_i\varphi$ is true if φ is a practical belief within frame S_i.)

We say that a model $\mathbb{M} = (S, \pi, S_1,..., S_n, \wp, \wp_1,..., \wp_n) \in S5P$ *extends* a model $\mathbb{M}' = (S', \pi', \wp') \in S5$, if $S = S'$, $\pi = \pi'$ and $\wp = \wp'$. $\mathbb{M}'$ is then called the $S5$-reduction of $\mathbb{M}$. We axiomatise (the theory of) $S5P$ as follows (cf. [MH1,2]): take the **S5** system for the modality K (and M) and use **K45** for the P-modalities, together with the axioms (A6) $K\varphi \supset P_i\varphi$ ('certain' implies 'preferred' in any frame), (A7) $KP_i\varphi \equiv P_i\varphi$, (A8) $\neg P_i\bot \supset (P_iP_j\varphi \equiv P_j\varphi)$, (A9) $\neg P_i\bot \supset (P_iK\varphi \equiv K\varphi)$. (A7) through (A9) guarantee that we have no non-trivial nested modalities. We call the resulting system **S5P**. In the sequel we will write $\Gamma \vdash_{S5P} \varphi$ or $\varphi \in Th_{S5P}(\Gamma)$ to indicate that φ is an **S5P**-consequence of Γ. We mean this in the more liberal sense: it is possible to derive φ from the assertions in Γ by means of the axioms and rules of the system **S5P**, *including the necessitation rule*. (So, in effect we consider the assertions in Γ as additional axioms: $\Gamma \vdash_{S5P} \varphi$ iff $\vdash_{S5P \cup \Gamma} \varphi$.) Completeness of **S5P** w.r.t. $S5P$ is established in a standard way.

In $\mathbf{L_{EDL}}$ we express a defaults $\varphi : \psi / \chi$ as $\varphi \wedge M\psi \supset P\chi$. Here φ, ψ and χ are objective formulas. The reading of such a formula is "if φ is true and ψ is possible, then χ is a default belief". Multiple defaults $\{ \varphi_i : \psi_i / \chi_i \}_i$ are represented by formulas $\varphi_i \wedge M\psi_i \supset P_i\chi_i$, where φ_i, ψ_i and χ_i are again objective formulas. In [MH1,2] we showed that employing the logic **S5P** for default reasoning, we do not encounter the problems with contraposition and transitivity that are present in other modal approaches such as AEL. Now we define a default theory Θ as a pair (W, Δ), where W is a finite set of objective formulas describing (necessary) facts about the world, and Δ is a finite set of defaults $\{\varphi_i \wedge M\psi_i \supset P_{f(i)}\chi_i \mid i = 1, ...,n\}$ where f: $\{1, ..., n\} \to \{1, ..., n\}$. The sets W and Δ are considered as sets of axioms, and we may apply necessitation to the formulas in them. Given $\Theta = (W, \Delta)$, we define the $\vdash_\Delta$ as follows. Suppose that φ is honest and φ and W^* are mutually h-consistent. Thus $\Sigma^{\varphi \wedge W^*}$ is well-defined. Then: $\varphi \vdash_\Theta \psi \Leftrightarrow_{def} \psi \in Th_{S5P}(\Sigma^{\varphi \wedge W^*} \cup \Delta)$.

EXAMPLE (Tweety). Consider $\Theta = (W, \Delta)$ with $W = \{p \supset \neg f\}$ and $\Delta = \{b \wedge Mf \supset Pf\}$, representing that penguins do not fly, and that by default birds fly. Now consider the following inferences (To stress the application of Δ we denote such a step by $\vdash_\Delta$.): (i). $b \vdash b \wedge \neg K\neg f \vdash_{S5P} b \wedge Mf \vdash_\Delta Pf$, i.e., $b \vdash_\Theta Pf$, meaning that from the mere fact that Tweety is a bird, we conclude that Tweety is assumed to fly; which must be contrasted to the inference: (ii). $b \wedge p \vdash Kp \vdash_{S5P} K\neg f \vdash_{S5P} \neg Mf \nvdash_\Delta Pf$, i.e, **not** $b \wedge p \vdash_\Theta Pf$, meaning that in case Tweety is a penguin, we cannot infer that Tweety is assumed to fly (instead, we derived to know that Tweety does not fly). ∎

THEOREM 4.1. *Consider a default theory* $\Theta = (W, \Delta)$, *where* Δ *is finite, and let* $\varphi \in$ $\mathcal{L}(P)$ *(thus not containing P-modalities) be an honest formula such that* φ *and* W^* *are mutually h-consistent. Then we have that:*

$$\varphi \vdash_\Theta \psi \;\Leftrightarrow\; \mathbb{M} \models K\Delta^* \supset \psi \text{ for all } \mathbb{M} \in S5P \text{ such that } K(\mathbb{M}_{\varphi \wedge W^*}) \subseteq K(\mathbb{M}).$$

Moreover, if **P** *is finite, we have:*

$$\varphi \vdash_\Theta \psi \;\Leftrightarrow\; \mathbb{M} \models K\Delta^* \supset \psi \text{ for all } \mathbb{M} \in S5P \text{ extending } \mathbb{M}_{\varphi \wedge W^*} \in S5. \;\blacksquare$$

The significance of the semantical characterization of $\vdash_\Theta$ in 4.1 is most easily seen if the number of primitive propositions is finite. Then it states that in order to check whether $\varphi \vdash_\Theta \psi$ holds, we first consider the model $\mathbb{M}_{\varphi \wedge W^*}$ that is determined by the honest formula $\varphi \wedge W^*$ describing the premise that we have (φ) together with the background information about the world (W^*). Then we consider all $S5P$-models $\mathbb{M}$ that have $\mathbb{M}_{\varphi \wedge W^*}$ as a reduction, and check whether imposing the defaults on them— i.e., letting them satisfy the *global* condition $K\Delta^*$—implies the consequence ψ.

5 Cumulativity

In [Ga, Ma, KLM] some yard-sticks for examining nonmonotonic logics in the form of meta-properties are provided. One of the criteria mentioned is *cumulativity*. We show that EDL satisfies cumulativity, thus establishing a desirable property for a logic dealing with default reasoning[2].

We shall concentrate on the notion of (finistic) cumulativity as defined in [KLM]: An entailment relation $\vdash$ is called *cumulative* iff the following conditions hold: (Γ's denote finite sets of formulas; $\models$ means propositional validity.) (i) $\Gamma \vdash \varphi$, for every $\varphi \in \Gamma$ (reflexivity); (ii) If $\models \Gamma_1^* \equiv \Gamma_2^*$ and $\Gamma_1 \vdash \varphi$ then $\Gamma_2 \vdash \varphi$ (left logical equivalence); (iii) If $\models \varphi \supset \psi$ and $\Gamma \vdash \varphi$ then $\Gamma \vdash \psi$ (right weakening); (iv) If $\Gamma \cup \{\varphi\} \vdash \psi$ and $\Gamma \vdash \varphi$, then $\Gamma \vdash \psi$ (cut); (v) If $\Gamma \vdash \varphi$ and $\Gamma \vdash \psi$ then $\Gamma \cup \{\varphi\} \vdash$ ψ (cautious monotonicity).

When showing that $\vdash_\Theta$ is cumulative, it has to be understood that it is only meaningful to consider $\Gamma \vdash_\Theta \varphi$ when Γ^* is an honest epistemic formula, and thus does not contain P-modalities.

THEOREM 5.1. *For any default theory* $\Theta = (W, \Delta)$, *the entailment relation* $\vdash_\Theta$ *is cumulative.* $\blacksquare$

To some extent this result is a direct consequence of the design of our logic. In particular, our approach forbids the use of default beliefs of the form $P\psi$ as premises

---

[2]Also Brewka ([Br]) has proposed a cumulative default logic, but as he starts out with Reiter's logic, mending cumulativity results in a substantially more complicated logic than ours. In the full paper we also discuss other, similar approaches.

of the entailment relation $\vdash_\Theta$. (These premises must be honest epistemic formulas, so without P-modalities.) This implies that, for instance, the property of cautious monotonicity (if $\Gamma \vdash \varphi$ and $\Gamma \vdash \psi$ then $\Gamma \cup \{\varphi\} \vdash \psi$) may only involve formulas φ that do not contain P-operators, and this case is easy to prove (see above). Speaking philosophically, this is an important restriction, meaning essentially that default beliefs do not (or, rather, are not allowed to) influence the epistemic state with respect to (certain) knowledge and epistemic possibilities. We claim that this is intuitively right, and we designed the logic in this way on purpose. Quite another (technical) matter, which we do not pursue in this paper, is whether the cumulativity result can be extended somehow to a notion of default entailment where also default beliefs (involving P-modalities) can be used as premises. This might be a topic for further research. We do not see the need for such a complication at this moment, since we can treat (at least a large part of) default reasoning without it.

6 Conclusion

In this paper we proposed a default logic based on a theory of epistemic states and an entailment associated with this. Although this entailment relation is nonmonotonic, this is not due to the infamous "jumping to conclusions" as in other DL's like Reiter's. On the contrary, we distinguish facts from assertions that are assumed by default. The nonmonotonicity arises from the way we reason about epistemic states. We obtain an inference mechanism that may conclude from a set of premises that something is (as yet) unknown, which is clearly nonmonotonic. In retrospect we conclude that by disentangling the nature of nonmonotonicity in other DL's, one obtains a logic that is well-behaved in the sense that it is cumulative. Essentially, cumulativity is maintained by the use of special P-modalities to distinguish default beliefs from certain facts: default beliefs do not change the epistemic state with respect to certain knowledge and epistemic possibilities. We also believe that—in comparison with approaches that employ preferential entailment after Shoham [Sh1,2]—in our approach it is exhibited in a clear-cut manner where preferences play a role in default reasoning. In our opinion the most important place is that where it is determined what is known and what is not. Then, on the basis of the outcome of this, default rules may be applied in a monotonic manner, after which it may be necessary again to put a preference order on the outcomes of this, which we believe is very domain- and even user-dependent.

References

[Br]   G. Brewka, Nonmonotonic Reasoning: Logical Foundations of Commonsense, Cambridge University Press, Cambridge, 1991.
[Do]   P. Doherty, NM3 - A Three-Valued Cumulative Non-Monotonic Formalism, in: Logics in AI, (J. van Eijck, ed.), LNCS 478, Springer, Berlin, 1991, pp. 196-211.

273

[Ga]   D.M. Gabbay, Theoretical Foundations for Non-Monotonic Reasoning in Expert Systems, in: K.R. Apt (ed.), Proc. NATO Advanced Study Institute on Logics and Models of Concurrent Systems, Springer, Berlin, 1985, pp. 439-457.

[Hi]   J. Hintikka, Knowledge and Belief, Cornell University Press, Ithaca (N.Y.), 1962.

[HM]   J.Y. Halpern & Y.O. Moses, Towards a Theory of Knowledge and Ignorance, Proc. Workshop on Non-Monotonic Reasoning, AAAI, 1984.

[Kr]   S. Kripke, Semantic Analysis of Modal Logic, Zeitschrift für Mathematische Logik und Grundlagen der Mathematik 9, 1963, pp. 67-96.

[KLM]   S. Kraus, D. Lehmann & M. Magidor, Nonmonotonic Reasoning, Preferential Models and Cumulative Logics, Artificial Intelligence 44, 1990, pp. 167-207.

[Lu]   W. Lukaszewicz, Non-Monotonic Reasoning (Formalisation of Commonsense Reasoning), Ellis Horwood, New York, 1990.

[Ma]   D. Makinson, General Theory of Cumulative Inference, in: M. Reinfrank, J. de Kleer, M. Ginsberg & E. Sandewall (eds.), Proceedings Non-Monotonic Reasoning, 2nd Int. Workshop, LNCS 346, Springer, Berlin, 1989, pp. 1-18.

[MH1]   J.-J.Ch. Meyer & W. van der Hoek, Non-Monotonic Reasoning by Monotonic Means, in J. van Eijck (ed.), Logics in AI (Proc. JELIA '90), LNCS 478, Springer, 1991, pp. 399-411.

[MH2]   J.-J.Ch. Meyer & W. van der Hoek, A Modal Logic for Nonmonotonic Reasoning, in: W. van der Hoek, J.-J. Ch. Meyer, Y.H. Tan & C. Witteveen (eds.), Non-Monotonic Reasoning and Partial Semantics, Ellis Horwood, Chichester, 1992, pp. 37-77.

[MH3]   J.-J.Ch. Meyer & W. van der Hoek, A Cumulative Default Logic Based on Epistemic States, Techn. Report Free University IR-288, Amsterdam (1992).

[Mo]   R.C. Moore, Semantical Considerations on Nonmonotonic Logic, Artificial Intelligence 25, 1985, pp. 75-94.

[Rei]   R. Reiter, A Logic for Default Reasoning, Artificial Intelligence 13, 1980, pp. 81-132.

[Sh1]   Y. Shoham, A Semantical Approach to Nonmonotonic Logics, in: Readings in Nonmonotonic Reasoning (M.L. Ginsberg, ed.), Morgan Kaufmann, Los Altos, 1987, pp. 227-250.

[Sh2]   Y. Shoham, Reasoning about Change, MIT Press, Cambridge, Massachusetts, 1988.

[TT]   Y.-H. Tan & J. Treur, A Bi-Modular Approach to Non-Monotonic Reasoning, in: Proc. WOCFAI'91 (M. DeGlas & D. Gabbay, eds.), Paris, 1991, pp. 461-475.

A Formal Language for Convex Sets of Probabilities*

Serafín Moral

Departamento de Ciencias de la Computación e I.A.
Universidad de Granada, 18071 - Granada - Spain
e-mail: smc@robinson.ugr.es

Abstract. In this paper, a new language for convex sets of probabilities operators is presented. Its main advantage is that it allows a more direct representation of initial pieces of information without transforming them in more complex representations. The language includes logical operators and numerical values. It will allow, in some cases, a reduction of the complexity of the calculations associated to convex sets of probabilities.

1 Introduction

Convex sets of probabilities have been used as a model for unknown or partially known probabilities [2, 5, 6, 7, 8, 12, 13, 14]. The basic idea is that if for a variable X taking values on a finite set U we do not have the exact values of probabilities, we may have a convex set of probability distributions. For example, the complete ignorance is represented by the set of all the probability distributions on U.

Essentially, all the models working with convex sets of probabilities are based on the same principle:

> 'To extend an operator from Probability Theory to Convex Sets of Probabilities, repeat the operator for all the probabilities of the convex set.
> If the result is not a convex set, then take the convex hull'

This principle has been applied to the following three basic operations:

a) To combine an 'a priori' convex set with a conditional convex set to produce a bidimensional convex set.
b) To marginalize a bidimensional convex set on one of its components.
c) To calculate the conditional convex set given the observation of a set, $A \subseteq U$.

The resulting operations, in the case of a) and b) have been always the same. However, in the case of conditioning, different interpretations of the above principle have given rise to different generalizations of conditioning for convex sets.

Here we shall consider the calculus with convex sets developed in [3], which is based on the conditioning given in [9].

---

* This work has been supported by the DGICYT under proyect PS89/152

We consider convex sets with a finite set of extreme probabilities. This makes possible the calculations with convex sets: we have to carry out the operations for a finite set of points. This assumption is also justified by the elicitation procedure considered by Walley [14], in which a generalization of bayesian betting behaviour gives rise to convex sets of probabilities with a finite set of extreme points.

The main problem of this methodology, is the high complexity of working with convex sets. On one hand, we have the combination of an 'a priori' convex set and a conditional information. This operation is carried out by pointwise multiplication of the extreme points. If one of the sets has n_1 extreme points, and the other n_2, then by combination we obtain $n_1 \times n_2$ points. In that way, each time we perform a combination operation, the number of points may grow on a combinatorial way.

Some of the resulting $n_1 \times n_2$ points may be non-extreme. However, to remove the non-extreme points we have to apply a convex hull algorithm which has an associated cost. In concrete the Gift Wrapping algorithm [10] has a complexity of order $O(n^{[d/2]} \log(n))$, where d is the dimension of the space, that is the number of cases of the set to which this algorithm is applied, and $[d/2]$ is the integer division. Then, for high dimensions the algorithm to remove non extreme points may be inefficient.

Other aspect that increases the complexity of working with convex sets is that we may give a very simple specification of a problem which determines a very high number of extreme points. Consider, for example, a finite set $U = \{u_1, \ldots, u_n\}$, and a mass assignment, m, defined on it [5, 11], that is, a mapping, $m : 2^U \to [0, 1]$, verifying the following properties:

1. $m(\emptyset) = 0$ 2. $\sum_{A \subseteq U} m(A) = 1$

According to Dempster [5] this defines a convex set of probabilities. The extreme points of it can be calculated on the following way:

– For each permutation σ on $\{1, \ldots, n\}$, consider the probability p_σ, given by

$$p_\sigma(u) = \sum_{\sigma(i)=Min\{\sigma(j)|u_j \in A\}} m(A)$$

– The set of extreme points of the associated convex set is

$$\{p_\sigma \mid \sigma \text{ is a permutation on } \{1, \ldots, n\} \}$$

Though some of these probabilities may be identical for two different permutations, the number of extreme points can be of order $n!$, which is intractable.

The aim of this paper is to develop a formal language allowing a more versatile handling of convex sets of probabilities. In particular, it will allow to work directly with mass assignment representations without transforming them to convex sets.

The paper is organized as follows: In the second section we consider some technical operations with convex sets. In the third section, we study the model of calculating with convex sets of probabilities introduced in [3]. In the forth section we introduce the formal language giving a representation theorem for it. Finally, in the fifth section, we consider the conclussions.

2 Operations with Convex Sets

In this section we fix the notation and define the operations with convex sets that will be used in the following sections. This section is mainly technical and does not assume that points are probabilities.

The following notation will be used. We shall consider that sets $U_i, i = 1, \ldots, n$, are all finite,

- If $I \subseteq \{1, \ldots, n\}$, then $U_I = \prod_{i \in I} U_i$

- If $u \in U_J$ and $I \subseteq J$, then $u^{\downarrow I}$ or $u^{\downarrow \prod_{i \in I} U_i}$ will denote the element $v \in \prod_{i \in I} U_i$, such that, $v^i = u^i, \forall i \in I$. That is, the point obtained from u, by dropping the extra coordinates: those not in I.

- If h is a mapping, $h : U_J \longrightarrow [0,1]$, and $I \subseteq J$, then the mapping, $\overline{h} : \prod_{i \in I} U_i \longrightarrow [0,1]$, defined by

$$\overline{h}(v) = \sum_{u^{\downarrow I} = v} h(u)$$

will be denoted as $h^{\downarrow I}$ or $h^{\downarrow \prod_{i \in I} U_i}$.

- If h_1, h_2 are mappings, $h_1 : U_I \longrightarrow [0,1]$, $h_2 : U_J \longrightarrow [0,1]$, then the mapping $h' : \prod_{i \in I \cup J} U_i \longrightarrow [0,1]$ defined by

$$h'(v) = h_1(v^{\downarrow I}).h_2(v^{\downarrow J})$$

will be denoted as $h_1.h_2$.

For convex sets of mappings (sometimes also called points) defined on sets $U_I, I \subseteq \{1, \ldots, n\}$, we give the following two definitions, which will we the basis to express the calculations with convex sets of probalities.

- If H_1, H_2 are convex sets of mappings defined on U_I, U_J, repectively, then

$$H_1 \otimes H_2 = CH\{h_1.h_2 \mid h_1 \in H_1, h_2 \in H_2\}$$

where CH denotes the convex hull. It is important to notice that, it is enough to carry out the combination operator for the extreme points of H_1 and H_2. That is, if $Ext(H)$ denotes the set of extreme points of convex set H, then we have

$$H_1 \otimes H_2 = CH\{h_1.h_2 \mid h_1 \in Ext(H_1), h_2 \in Ext(H_2)\}$$

- If H is a convex set of mappings defined on U_I and $J \subseteq I$, then

$$H^{\downarrow J} = CH\{h^{\downarrow J} \mid h \in H\}$$

$H^{\downarrow J}$ will be also denoted by $H^{\downarrow \prod_{j \in J} U_j}$. As above it is enough to carry out the operation for the extreme points of the convex set.

3 Calculus with Convex Sets of Probabilities

In this section we describe a model for the calculation with convex sets of probabilities. Assume that we have a population Ω and a variable X defined on Ω and taking its values on a finite set $U = \{u_1, ..., u_n\}$. If the knowledge about the frequencies with which X takes its values on U is not exact, we may have a set H^X of possible probability distributions.

We shall consider that H^X is always a convex set with a finite set of extreme points $p_1, ..., p_k$. In case H^X is not convex, we shall always consider its convex hull [2]: $\mathrm{CH}(H^X) = \{\sum_i \alpha_i.p_i \mid p_i \in H^X, \alpha \in [0,1], \sum_i \alpha_i = 1\}$. Reasons for this transformation may be found in [2, 14].

In Probability Theory, when we have two or more variables, the most usual way of expressing our knowledge about them is not by giving a global probability distribution for all of them, but by means of several pieces of information, from which it is possible to build a global distribution.

For example, in the simplest case, we have two variables X and Y taking values on finite sets U and V respectively. To express our knowledge about these variables, we may give a marginal probabity distribution about X, p^X, and a probability distribution about Y given X, $p^{Y|X}$. From these two pieces of information, we may buid a global probability for (X, Y), $p^{X,Y}$, given by: $p^{X,Y} = p^X.p^{Y|X}$

In our approach, in which the knowledge about probabilities is not so exact, a conditional information will be a convex set, $H^{Y|X}$, of mappings, $h : U \times V \longrightarrow [0, 1]$, verifying

$$\sum_{v \in V} h(u, v) = 1, \forall u \in U$$

and with a finite set of extreme points, $\mathrm{Ext}(H^{Y|X}) = \{h_1, \ldots, h_l\}$.

This is more general than assuming that a conditional piece of information is a convex set of probabilities for every possible value of X, that is, for every element $u \in U$, [3].

If we have a convex set H^X for variable X with extreme points $\{p_1, \ldots, p_k\}$ and a conditional piece of information, $H^{Y|X}$, with extreme points $\{h_1, \ldots, h_l\}$, then we shall define a global information about the pair of variables (X, Y), as the convex set, $H^{X,Y}$, of probability distributions on $U \times V$ given by:

$$H^{X,Y} = H^X \otimes H^{Y|X} = \mathrm{CH}\{p_1.h_1, .., p_1.h_l, p_2.h_1, .., p_2.h_l, \ldots, p_k.h_1, .., p_k.h_l\}$$

In the following, we describe the process of obtaining marginal information for a variable from some piece of information relating a wider set of variables. If we have a global convex set $H^{X,Y}$ with extreme points $\{h_1, \ldots, h_n\}$ of possible bidimensional probabilities for variables (X, Y), then we define the marginal convex sets, H^X and H^Y, for variables X and Y, as follows:

$$H^X = (H^{X,Y})^{\downarrow U} = \mathrm{CH}\{h_1^{\downarrow U}, \ldots, h_n^{\downarrow U}\}$$

$$H^Y = (H^{X,Y})^{\downarrow V} = \mathrm{CH}\{h_1^{\downarrow V}, \ldots, h_n^{\downarrow V}\}$$

Finally, we consider the problem of conditioning. Assume a convex set for variable X: $H^X = \mathrm{CH}\{p_1, \ldots, p_n\}$ and that we have observed 'X *belongs to* A', then the result of conditioning is the convex set, $H^X|A$, generated by points $\{p_1.l_A, \ldots, p_n.l_A\}$ where l_A is the likelihood associated with set A ($l_A(u) = 1, if\ u \in A; l_A(u) = 0$, otherwise). That is $H^X|A = H^X \otimes \{l_A\}$

It is important to remark that $H^X|A$ is a convex set of differently normalized functions. If we call $r_i = \sum_{u \in U} p_i(u).l_A(u) = P_i(A)$, then by calculating $(p_i.l_A)/r_i$ we get the conditional probability distribution $p_i(.|A)$. The set $H' = \{p(.|A) \mid p \in H\}$ was proposed by Dempster, [5], as the set of conditioning, and has been widely used. However, this set produces very large intervals, the reason being that, by normalizing each probability, we loose the information provided by values r_i.

The assignation of probability intervals to $H^X|A$ has been studied in [9, 8]. The resulting intervals are, in general, smaller that the ones obtainded with H'.

4   The Language

Assume a finite set, U, the set of expressions associated with convex sets of probabilities on U is defined according to the following rules,

1. If $u \in U$, **u** is an expression. It has associated a convex set with an only probability distribution: the probability, p_u, degenerated on u.
2. **N** is an expression. It denotes the contradiction, that this the convex set containing the mapping: $\delta(u) = 0, \quad \forall u \in U$
3. If $\mathbf{E_1}$ and $\mathbf{E_2}$ are expressions, representing the convex sets H_1 and H_2, respectively, then $(\mathbf{E_1} + \mathbf{E_2})$ is an expression representing the convex set, $H = \{h_1 + h_2 \mid h_1 \in H_1, h_2 \in H_2\}$.
4. If $\mathbf{E_1}$ and $\mathbf{E_2}$ are expressions, representing the convex sets H_1 and H_2, respectively, then $(\mathbf{E_1} \vee \mathbf{E_2})$ is an expression representing the convex set, $H = CH\{h \mid (h \in H_1) \vee (h \in H_2)\}$.
5. If $\mathbf{E}$ is an expression representing the convex set H, and α is a real number ($\alpha \geq 0$), then $(\alpha\mathbf{E})$ is an expression representing the convex set $\alpha H = \{\alpha h \mid h \in H\}$.

With these rules we have defined the set of expressions defined on a finite set U, and how to associate a convex set to a given expression. If $\mathbf{E}$ is an expression, $C(\mathbf{E})$ will denote the convex set associated to it. $\mathcal{E}_U$ will be the set of expression defined on set U.

An expression is said to be simple if does not contain the $\vee$ operator.

We shall assume that there is an equality relationship defined on $\mathcal{E}_U$ and verifying the following axioms.

A1 *Commutative.*- $\forall \mathbf{E_1}, \mathbf{E_2} \in \mathcal{E}_U, \quad \mathbf{E_1} \vee \mathbf{E_2} = \mathbf{E_2} \vee \mathbf{E_1}, \quad \mathbf{E_1} + \mathbf{E_2} = \mathbf{E_2} + \mathbf{E_1}$
A2 *Associative.*- $\forall \mathbf{E_1}, \mathbf{E_2}, \mathbf{E_3} \in \mathcal{E}_U,$

$$(\mathbf{E_1} \vee \mathbf{E_2}) \vee \mathbf{E_3} = \mathbf{E_1} \vee (\mathbf{E_2} \vee \mathbf{E_3}), \quad (\mathbf{E_1} + \mathbf{E_2}) + \mathbf{E_3} = \mathbf{E_1} + (\mathbf{E_2} + \mathbf{E_3})$$

A3 *Idempotent.-* $\forall \mathbf{E} \in \mathcal{E}_U, \quad \mathbf{E} \vee \mathbf{E} = \mathbf{E}$

A4 *Distributive of* $+$ *with respect to* $\vee$.- $\forall \mathbf{E_1}, \mathbf{E_2}, \mathbf{E_3} \in \mathcal{E}_U,$

$$\mathbf{E_1} + (\mathbf{E_2} \vee \mathbf{E_3}) = (\mathbf{E_1} + \mathbf{E_2}) \vee (\mathbf{E_1} + \mathbf{E_3})$$

A5 *Distributive with respect to with respect to the addition of real numbers.-*
$\forall \mathbf{E} \in \mathcal{E}_U, \forall \alpha_1, \alpha_2 \geq 0, \quad (\alpha_1 + \alpha_2)\mathbf{E} = \alpha_1 \mathbf{E} + \alpha_2 \mathbf{E}$

A6 *Distributive of the combination by a real number with respect to* $+$ *and* $\vee$.-
$\forall \mathbf{E_1}, \mathbf{E_2} \in \mathcal{E}_U, \forall \alpha \geq 0,$

$$\alpha(\mathbf{E_1} \vee \mathbf{E_2}) = \alpha \mathbf{E_1} \vee \alpha \mathbf{E_2}, \qquad \alpha(\mathbf{E_1} + \mathbf{E_2}) = \alpha \mathbf{E_1} + \alpha \mathbf{E_2}$$

A7 *Associative with respect to the multiplication of real numbers.-* $\forall \alpha, \beta \geq 0, \mathbf{E} \in$
$\mathcal{E}_U, \quad \alpha(\beta \mathbf{E}) = (\alpha\beta)\mathbf{E}$

A8 *Neutral Element.-* $\forall \mathbf{E} \in \mathcal{E}_U, \quad 1\mathbf{E} = \mathbf{E}, \quad \mathbf{N} + \mathbf{E} = \mathbf{E}$

A9 *Convex Combination.-* $\forall \mathbf{E_1}, \mathbf{E_2}, \mathbf{E_3} \in \mathcal{E}_U,$ if $\exists \alpha \geq 0,$ such that,
$\mathbf{E_3} = \alpha \mathbf{E_1} + (1 - \alpha)\mathbf{E_2},$ then $\mathbf{E_1} \vee \mathbf{E_2} \vee \mathbf{E_3} = \mathbf{E_1} \vee \mathbf{E_2}.$

With these axioms, we can show the following representation theorem.

Theorem 1. *If* $\mathbf{E_1}, \mathbf{E_2} \in \mathcal{E}_U,$ *it can be deduced that* $\mathbf{E_1} = \mathbf{E_2}$ *if and only if*
$C(\mathbf{E_1}) = C(\mathbf{E_2}).$

Now, to use the expressions to calculate with convex sets of probabilities, we have to define the operations of combination and marginalization. We assume that $U = U_1 \times \cdots \times U_n,$ $I, J \subseteq \{1, \ldots, n\}.$

Definition 2. *If* $\mathbf{E_1} \in \mathcal{E}_{U_I}, \mathbf{E_2} \in \mathcal{E}_{U_J},$ *the combination of* $\mathbf{E_1}$ *and* $\mathbf{E_2}$ *is an expression,* $\mathbf{E_1} \otimes \mathbf{E_2} \in \mathcal{E}_{U_{I \cup J}}$ *defined by the following rules*

- If $u_1 \in U_I, u_2 \in U_J,$ then
$$\mathbf{u_1} \otimes \mathbf{u_2} = \mathbf{N}, \qquad \text{if } u_1^{\downarrow I \cap J} \neq u_2^{\downarrow I \cap J}$$

$$\mathbf{u_1} \otimes \mathbf{u_2} = \mathbf{u}, \qquad \text{if } u_1^{\downarrow I \cap J} = u_2^{\downarrow I \cap J}$$

where $u \in U_{I \cup J}$ is given by $u^{\downarrow I} = u_1, u^{\downarrow J} = u_2.$
- $\forall \mathbf{E_1}, \mathbf{E_2} \in \mathcal{E}_{U_I}, \mathbf{E_3} \in \mathcal{E}_{U_J}, \quad (\mathbf{E_1} \vee \mathbf{E_2}) \otimes \mathbf{E_3} = (\mathbf{E_1} \otimes \mathbf{E_3}) \vee (\mathbf{E_2} \otimes \mathbf{E_3})$
- $\forall \mathbf{E_1} \in \mathcal{E}_{U_I}, \mathbf{E_2} \in \mathcal{E}_{U_J}, \alpha \geq 0, \quad (\alpha \mathbf{E_1}) \otimes \mathbf{E_2} = \alpha(\mathbf{E_1} \otimes \mathbf{E_2})$
- $\forall \mathbf{E_1}, \mathbf{E_2} \in \mathcal{E}_{U_I}, \mathbf{E_3} \in \mathcal{E}_{U_J},$ if $\mathbf{E_3}$ is simple then

$$(\mathbf{E_1} + \mathbf{E_2}) \otimes \mathbf{E_3} = (\mathbf{E_1} \otimes \mathbf{E_3}) + (\mathbf{E_2} \otimes \mathbf{E_3})$$

- $\forall \mathbf{E_1} \in \mathcal{E}_{U_I}, \mathbf{E_2} \in \mathcal{E}_{U_J}, \quad \mathbf{E_1} \otimes \mathbf{E_2} = \mathbf{E_2} \otimes \mathbf{E_1}$

Definition 3. *If* $\mathbf{E_1} \in \mathcal{E}_{U_I},$ *and* $J \subseteq I,$ *then the marginalization of* $\mathbf{E_1}$ *to* $U_J,$ *is an expression,* $(\mathbf{E_1})^{\downarrow J} \in \mathcal{E}_{U_J},$ *given by the following rules*

- If $u_1 \in U_I,$ and $u_1^{\downarrow J} = u_2,$ then $(\mathbf{u_1})^{\downarrow J} = \mathbf{u_2}$
- $\forall \mathbf{E_1}, \mathbf{E_2} \in \mathcal{E}_{U_I}, \quad (\mathbf{E_1} \vee \mathbf{E_2})^{\downarrow I} = \mathbf{E_1}^{\downarrow I} \vee \mathbf{E_2}^{\downarrow I}$

- $\forall \mathbf{E_1} \in \mathcal{E}_{U_I}, \alpha \geq 0, \quad (\alpha \mathbf{E_1})^{\downarrow \mathbf{J}} = \alpha(\mathbf{E}_1^{\downarrow \mathbf{J}})$
- $\forall \mathbf{E_1}, \mathbf{E_2} \in \mathcal{E}_{U_I}, \quad (\mathbf{E_1} + \mathbf{E_2})^{\downarrow \mathbf{I}} = \mathbf{E}_1^{\downarrow \mathbf{I}} + \mathbf{E}_2^{\downarrow \mathbf{I}}$

Finally we show the correspondence of these aperations with the analogous ones defined for convex sets.

Theorem 4. *If* $\mathbf{E_1}, \mathbf{E_2}$ *are expressions then*

$$C(\mathbf{E_1} \otimes \mathbf{E_2}) = C(\mathbf{E_1}) \otimes C(\mathbf{E_2}), \quad C(\mathbf{E}_1^{\downarrow \mathbf{J}}) = C(\mathbf{E_1})^{\downarrow J}$$

Example 1. Let us assume two variables, X and Y, taking values on sets $U = \{u_1, u_2\}$, and $V = \{v_1, v_2, v_3, v_4\}$, respectively. Let us consider that we do not know anything about how X takes its values, which is represented by the expression on U: $\mathbf{E_1} = \mathbf{u_1} \vee \mathbf{u_2}$, and that the conditional information for Y given X is given by the expression:

$$\mathbf{E_2} = (0.3((\mathbf{u_1}, \mathbf{v_1}) \vee (\mathbf{u_1}, \mathbf{v_2})) + 0.7((\mathbf{u_1}, \mathbf{v_2}) \vee (\mathbf{u_1}, \mathbf{v_3}) \vee (\mathbf{u_1}, \mathbf{v_4}))$$
$$+ 0.5((\mathbf{u_2}, \mathbf{v_1}) \vee (\mathbf{u_2}, \mathbf{v_3})) + 0.5((\mathbf{u_2}, \mathbf{v_2}) \vee (\mathbf{u_2}, \mathbf{v_3}))$$

The combination of $\mathbf{E_1}$ and $\mathbf{E_2}$ gives rise to a bidimensional expression about (X, Y), and it is given by

$$\mathbf{E_1} \otimes \mathbf{E_2} = [(0.3((\mathbf{u_1}, \mathbf{v_1}) \vee (\mathbf{u_1}, \mathbf{v_2})) + 0.7((\mathbf{u_1}, \mathbf{v_2}) \vee (\mathbf{u_1}, \mathbf{v_3}) \vee (\mathbf{u_1}, \mathbf{v_4})))]$$
$$\vee [0.5((\mathbf{u_2}, \mathbf{v_1}) \vee (\mathbf{u_2}, \mathbf{v_3})) + 0.5((\mathbf{u_2}, \mathbf{v_2}) \vee (\mathbf{u_2}, \mathbf{v_3}))]$$

In these conditions, let us assume that we observe that the value of Y is in the set $\{v_1, v_2\}$. This fact is represented by the expression: $\mathbf{E_3} = \mathbf{v_1} + \mathbf{v_2}$

The combination of $\mathbf{E_1} \otimes \mathbf{E_2}$ with $\mathbf{E_3}$ represents the conditional bidimensional information, and it is given by

$$(\mathbf{E_1} \otimes \mathbf{E_2}) \otimes \mathbf{E_3} = [(0.3((\mathbf{u_1}, \mathbf{v_1}) \vee (\mathbf{u_1}, \mathbf{v_2})) + 0.7((\mathbf{u_1}, \mathbf{v_2}) \vee \mathbf{N}))]$$
$$\vee [0.5((\mathbf{u_2}, \mathbf{v_1}) \vee \mathbf{N} + 0.5((\mathbf{u_2}, \mathbf{v_2}) \vee \mathbf{N})]$$

The marginalization on U will provide the conditional information on U, given the observation $Y \in \{v_1, v_2\}$, which is given by the expression

$$(0.3\mathbf{u_1} + 0.7(\mathbf{u_1} \vee \mathbf{N})) \vee (0.5(\mathbf{u_2} \vee \mathbf{N}) + 0.5(\mathbf{u_2} \vee \mathbf{N})) = \mathbf{u_1} \vee 0.3\mathbf{u_1} \vee \mathbf{u_2} \vee \mathbf{N}$$

In the caculation of this conditional information, we have avoided the calculation of all the extreme points of E_2 (there are 24 extreme points). This would have been necessary in a direct application of convex sets calculation procedures.

5 Conclusions

We have presented a formal language for convex sets of probabilities, which may help to reduce the complexity of the calculations. It may be interesting by itself, becuase it can help us to understand the model of calculus with imprecise probabilities, that was given in [3] and that we have presented in section 3.

One of the main problems of the language is that on the definition of combination $(\mathbf{E_1} + \mathbf{E_2}) \otimes \mathbf{E_3}$ is not, in general, equal to $(\mathbf{E_1} \otimes \mathbf{E_3}) + (\mathbf{E_2} \otimes \mathbf{E_3})$.

281

It is only true when $\mathbf{E_3}$ is a simple expression. This implies that if we want to perform $\mathbf{E} \otimes \mathbf{E'}$ and none of the expressions, $\mathbf{E}$ or $\mathbf{E'}$, is simple, then we have to transform one of them putting it as an or-combination of simple expressions. This fact posses a difficulty to the calculation with formal expressions.

Our posterior work will consider the use of this formal language in the propagation algorithms for convex sets of probabilities given in [3, 1].

References

1. Cano J.E., M. Delgado, S. Moral (1993) An axiomatic system for the propagation of uncertainty in directed acyclic networks. *International Journal of Approximate Reasoning* 8, 253-280.
2. Cano J.E., S. Moral, J.F. Verdegay-López (1991) Combination of Upper and Lower Probabilities. In: *Uncertainty in Artificial Intelligence. Proceedings of the 7th Conference* (B.D'Ambrosio, P. Smets, P.P. Bonissone, eds.) Morgan & Kaufmann (San Mateo) 61-68.
3. Cano J.E., S. Moral, J.F. Verdegay-López (1992) Propagation of convex sets of probabilities in directed acyclic networks. Proceedings of the IPMU'93 Conference, Mallorca, 289-292.
4. Choquet G. (1953/54) Theorie of capacities. *Ann. Inst. Fourier* 5, 131-292.
5. Dempster A.P. (1967) Upper and lower probabilities induced by a multivalued mapping. *Annals of Mathematical Statistics* 38, 325-339.
6. Levi I. (1980) *The Enterprise of Knowledge.* MIT Press.
7. Levi I. (1985) Imprecision and indeterminacy in probability judgement *Philosophy of Science* 52, 390-409.
8. Moral S. (1992) Calculating uncertainty intervals from conditional convex sets of probabilities. In: *Uncertainty in Artificial Intelligence. Proceedings of the 8th Conference* (D. Dubois, M.P. Wellman, B.D'Ambrosio, P. Smets, eds.) Morgan & Kaufmann, San Mateo, 199-206.
9. Moral S., L.M. de Campos (1991) Updating uncertain information. In: Uncertainty in Knowledge Bases (B. Bouchon-Meunier, R.R. Yager, L.A. Zadeh,eds.) Springer Verlag, Lectures Notes in Computer Science N. 521, Berlin, 58-67. .
10. Preparata F.P., M.I. Shamos (1985) *Computational Geometry. An Introduction.* Springer Verlag, New York.
11. Shafer G. (1976) *A Mathematical Theory of Evidence.* Princeton University Press, Princeton.
12. Snow P. (1991) Improved posterior probability estimates from prior and conditional linear constraint systems. *IEEE SMC* 21, 464-469.
13. Stirling W., D. Morrel (1991) Convex bayes decision theory. *IEEE SMC* 21, 163-183.
14. Walley P. (1991) *Statistical Reasoning with Imprecise Probabilities.* Chapman and Hall, London.

A LATTICE-THEORETIC ANALYSIS OF ATMS PROBLEM SOLVING

Teow-Hin Ngair[1] and *Gregory Provan*[2]

[1] Institute of Systems Science, National University of Singapore
Kent Ridge, S(0511), Republic of Singapore
[2] Computer and Information Science Department, University of Pennsylvania
Philadelphia PA, 19104-6389, USA

Abstract. This paper presents a lattice-theoretic formalization of the
ATMS which allows us to define the semantics of the ATMS, the ATMS
labeling operation, as well as focusing algorithms for the ATMS. These focusing algorithms are integrated cleanly within the proposed framework
by assigning a real-valued cost to the lattice boundary sets, and allow
performance improvements even for cases where there is little domain-
dependent knowledge. The resulting BF-ATMS algorithm explores a search
space of size polynomial in the number of assumptions, even for problems which are proven to have labels of size exponential in the number
of assumptions. Empirical testing indicates significant speedups over the
standard ATMS for such problems, while retaining the multiple-context
capability of an ATMS, the important properties of consistency, minimality, soundness, as well as the property of bounded completeness.

1 INTRODUCTION

The Assumption-Based Truth Maintenance System (ATMS) is a useful and powerful general problem-solving tool which has been widely used within AI. The
range of applications include qualitative physics [12], visual interpretation [2, 20],
nonmonotonic reasoning and diagnosis [7, 9]. The ATMS allows search to be simultaneously conducted on multiple contexts, where each context defines a set
of assumptions about the problem domain. However, this flexibility comes at
the cost of a high overhead due to storing many (and sometimes exponentially
many) sets of such assumptions. Controlling the problem solver does not allevi-
ate the poor performance on many tasks, such as diagnostic reasoning, as it is
the ATMS's generation of an enormous number of labels which is often the cause
of inefficiency [21]. Moreover, it is not always necessary to compute all labels for
some domains, such as diagnosis. Various methods have been proposed to focus
the ATMS on certain subsets of the search space (*e.g.* [8, 11, 13]), but none have
been both general and effective.

This paper presents a lattice-theoretic formalization of assumption-based reasoning, developing an implementation-independent description of the semantics
of the ATMS [4], the ATMS labeling operation, as well as ATMS focusing algorithms. The uniqueness of this formalization is that it directly addresses the
operations which account for the efficiency and underlying basis of the ATMS:

assumption-set operations on the boundary between consistent and inconsistent assumption sets in the assumption-set lattice. A second unique aspect of this formalization is that it integrates an analysis of the semantics of the ATMS and the ATMS label operation with an approximation algorithm (or focusing algorithm) for the ATMS. This approximation algorithm is necessary since the ATMS solves an NP-hard task [21, 23]. In particular, by introducing a simple partial-ordering onto variables (via a real-valued cost function, which can be a probability measure, integer-valued weight, etc.), completeness guarantees are traded off for a "bounded" completeness property (for the labels assigned to variables). This focusing algorithm is integrated cleanly within the proposed framework (producing a mixed symbolic/numeric system), and allows significant performance improvements even for cases where there is little domain-dependent knowledge. This contrasts with other focusing algorithms such as [6, 5, 8, 13, 11, 3], which lack a similar formal understanding, require relatively more domain knowledge or are strictly less general or less efficient.

2 ATMS FORMALIZATION

First, let us review a formal lattice-theoretic description of the ATMS. What has been lacking in most previous formalizations, a semantics for ATMS operations like label computation, is described here in a uniform, implementation-independent framework. The following description and definitions of the ATMS are adapted from [15, 17]: An ATMS is specified by a set Q of propositional atoms, a set $\mathcal{F}$ of input formulas constructed from Q, a distinguished element $\bot \in Q$ denoting falsity and a set $\mathcal{A} \subseteq Q$ of propositional atoms, called the *assumptions*. Usually, one refers to a subset of $\mathcal{A}$ as an *environment* and the set of all environments as the environment lattice, *i.e.* the power set lattice for $\mathcal{A}$. In addition, some propositional atoms are identified as *premises*, which are always considered to be true. In the basic ATMS, only Horn clauses are allowed in $\mathcal{F}$, while in the extended ATMS, disjunctions of assumptions are also allowed. In this paper, we will only be concerned with the basic ATMS.

For each propositional atom X appearing in Q, an ATMS is required to compute the following set of environments [22]:

$$\{p \subseteq \mathcal{A} \mid \bar{p} \vee X \text{ is a prime implicate}^3 \text{of } \mathcal{F}\}, \tag{1}$$

where p is interpreted as a conjunction of literals and $\bar{p}$ is the negation of p. An ATMS *label*, denoted by L_X, is a set of environments associated with each propositional atom X appearing in Q. An ATMS algorithm is supposed to manipulate the labels so that when it terminates, each label will have the correct values as stipulated by equation (1). The following defines the operations that can be used to manipulate the labels in an ATMS:

Definition: Given two labels A and B, we say that A is *subsumed* by B, written as $A \preceq B$, if for every environment $p \in A$, there exists environment $p' \in B$ such

---

³ Including the tautological implicates.

that $p' \subseteq p$. The operations *meet*, *join* and *difference* of A and B are defined as: $A \wedge B = \mathcal{MAX}(\{p_1 \cup p_2 \mid p_1 \in A, p_2 \in B\})$; $A \vee B = \mathcal{MAX}(A \cup B)$; $A - B = \{p \in A \mid \not\exists p' \in B \text{ s.t. } p' \subseteq p\}$, where $\mathcal{MAX}$ is the function which returns the maximal elements under the $\preceq$ ordering. $\square$

Semantics: The semantics of the ATMS can be characterized by specifying that, if $X \not\equiv \bot$, and $\mathcal{F} \cup p$ denotes $\mathcal{F} \cup \{\Rightarrow x \mid x \in p\}$, the output ($L_X$'s) of the ATMS,[4] must satisfy $L_\bot = \mathcal{MAX}(\{p \subseteq \mathcal{A} \mid \mathcal{F} \cup p \text{ is inconsistent}\})$, and $L_X = \mathcal{MAX}(\{p \subseteq \mathcal{A} \mid \mathcal{F} \cup p \text{ is consistent, and } \mathcal{F} \cup p \models X\})$.

Algorithm: We characterize the fundamental step in a basic ATMS algorithm as follows: For any justification $\psi (\equiv X_1, \ldots, X_n \Rightarrow Y) \in \mathcal{F}$, we say that ψ is *applicable* in the ATMS if in the current state of the ATMS, we have $L_{X_1} \wedge \cdots \wedge L_{X_n} \not\preceq L_Y$; Furthermore, the *application* of an applicable ψ is the modification of L_Y to $L_Y \vee (L_{X_1} \wedge \cdots \wedge L_{X_n})$; and if $Y \equiv \bot$, we perform the additional step of removing the new inconsistent environments from every $X \not\equiv \bot$: $L_X \leftarrow L_X - L_\bot$.

Intuitively, a justification is said to be applicable if some environments are already known to entail every antecedent node but are not yet included in the label of the consequence node. The application of the justification is then a rectification of this problem. Furthermore, if the consequence node represents the inconsistency, then the newly added inconsistent environments are removed from every other node so as to reduce duplicity. A *basic ATMS algorithm* repeatedly finds an applicable justification and applies it.[5] The above algorithm has been shown [15] to converge with the results as specified in equation (1).

3   COST FUNCTIONS

It is known that the ATMS solves an NP-hard problem [23, 21], and intractability has been observed in practice (e.g. [20]). In response, a variety of approximation techniques have been proposed [8, 13, 11, 3].

Definition: A *cost function* $\varrho : 2^{\mathcal{A}} \to \mathbb{R}$ assigns a real-valued cost to any set of assumptions. ϱ induces a total ordering $\leq$ onto assumption sets. A cost function ϱ is said to satisfy the *monotonicity criterion* if $A \subseteq B \Rightarrow \varrho(A) \leq \varrho(B)$.

ATMS labels naturally observe the monotonicity criterion, since label minimality is determined by set inclusion. Assigning a cost ordering on assumption sets allows search to be focused on the least-cost environments. In any such search, it is desirable to maintain the important ATMS label properties, which were defined in [4]: For every propositional atom X the ATMS is said to have the property: **Soundness:** if for all $p \in L_X$, $\mathcal{F} \cup p \models X$; **Consistency:** if every $p \in L_X$ is consistent, *i.e.* $\mathcal{F} \cup p \not\models \bot$; **Minimality:** if for all $p \in L_X$, there exists no $p' \subseteq \mathcal{A}$ such that $p' \subseteq p$ and $\mathcal{F} \cup p' \models X$; **Completeness:** if for all p such that $\mathcal{F} \cup p \models X$, there exists $p' \in L_X$ such that $p' \subseteq p$.

---

[4] The semantics of the input to the ATMS are discussed in the full paper.
[5] The initialization of nodes labels in the ATMS is ignored here for simplicity.

Of these, it is most important to maintain soundness, consistency and minimality. If completeness is sacrificed, "approximate" solutions can be computed; even so, it is desirable to maintain admissibility (an optimal solution will be found if it exists). One such approximation is to maintain a "bounded" completeness in the solutions computed, in which environments with costs lower than a given bound are guaranteed to be generated. The BF-ATMS algorithm described in the next section is an efficient method for computing such approximate solutions. We assume monotonicity holds for the rest of the paper.

Two broad classes of cost function, probabilistic and integer-valued, can be defined. These two classes of cost function, and their application to the ATMS, are discussed in the full paper [18]. The next section discusses the incorporation of the ATMS with integer-valued cost functions, and the application of such cost functions to examples (in which the monotonicity criterion is satisfied).

4 ATMS FOCUSED SEARCH ALGORITHM

Consider each application of a justification $(X_1, \ldots, X_n \Rightarrow Y)$ in the basic ATMS algorithm. First, we need to check condition A, i.e. $L_{X_1} \wedge \cdots \wedge L_{X_n} \not\preceq L_Y \vee L_\perp$, where $L_X \wedge L_Y = \mathcal{MAX}(\{p_x \cup p_y \mid p_x \in L_X, p_y \in L_Y\})$, and $\mathcal{MAX}$ performs the subsumption checking and returns the maximal environments (minimal subsets) in the set. If condition A is found to be true, the ATMS algorithm proceeds to update the label of Y to $L_Y \vee (L_{X_1} \wedge \cdots \wedge L_{X_n})$ [and $-L_\perp$ if $Y \not\equiv \perp$], where $L_X \vee L_Y = \mathcal{MAX}(L_X \cup L_Y)$. In each of the $\wedge$ operations, an environment in the first set is unioned with an environment in the second set to produce a new environment. Hence, by the monotonicity criterion of a cost function and the abstract definition of the basic ATMS algorithm, it is clear that:

Lemma 1. *In each step of the basic ATMS algorithm, the cost of every newly generated environment is always larger than or equal to the costs of the environments which generate it.*

The above lemma is of great significance if we wish to set a cost upper-bound on the environments generated by the ATMS. It tells us that we will never block the generation of a desirable environment due to the elimination of environments which exceed the upper bound. Therefore, we may immediately disregard, during each step of the basic ATMS algorithm, many of the environments that would otherwise be generated by the standard ATMS algorithm and incur heavy (probably exponential) computational cost later. Consequently, the *bounded basic ATMS* algorithm defined below is guaranteed to generate all and only the correct environments with costs lower or equal to a given cost bound, and at the same time, achieve greatly reduced run time.

Definition: A *Bounded Basic ATMS* algorithm is the basic ATMS algorithm modified to accept a cost bound $\mathcal{B}$, a cost function ϱ, and with the $\wedge$ operation changed to: $L_X \wedge L_Y = \mathcal{MAX}(\{p_x \cup p_y \mid p_x \in L_X, p_y \in L_Y \text{ and } \varrho(p) \leq \mathcal{B}\})$.

In the following, we outline a breadth-first like search strategy for finding the minimum cost environments for any node Y in a basic ATMS using the bounded basic ATMS algorithm.

Procedure BF-ATMS (Y)
1. set the bound to be the lowest possible, *i.e.* the empty environment cost;
2. introduce all assumptions with cost lower or equal to the current bound;
3. run the bounded basic ATMS algorithm with the current cost bound;
4. if an environment appears in the label of Y, stop and report the result;
5. increase the bound to the next higher cost, goto step 2.

Note that the BF-ATMS algorithm generates each valid environment in a breadth-first fashion, *i.e.* it will generate all correct environments with lower costs before it generates the environments with next higher cost. In particular, the environments with minimum cost will always be generated first. Note that the environments generated during each run of the basic ATMS algorithm are cached and need not be generated again when the cost bound is increased. Also, note that the run-time of this algorithm is exponential in the cost bound. Again, we would like to point out that the improved efficiency of the BF-ATMS algorithm is largely due to the ability of the basic ATMS algorithm (while remaining correct) to ignore environments over the cost bound in each of its execution steps and hence, to prevent them from incurring heavy costs in all later computation. Also, the compactness of the label representation helps to eliminate many representational and computational redundancies (see [4]) which is why the BF-ATMS algorithm is superior to a simple generate-and-test breadth-first search algorithm. In terms of the four desirable properties defined in Section 3, a characterization of the BF-ATMS algorithm is the following:

Proposition 2. *At the termination of each loop in the BF-ATMS algorithm, the labels generated will satisfy the sound, consistent and minimal properties of an ATMS. Furthermore, the labels also enjoy the "bounded" completeness property which means that they contain every environment (consistent or inconsistent) with cost lower or equal to a given bound.*

To see the efficiency on an example which produces exponential behavior, consider the following set $\mathcal{J}$ of justifications: $A_i \Rightarrow B_i$ $i \in [1, n]$ and $b_{2*k-1}^j, b_{2*k}^j \Rightarrow b_k^{j+1}$ $k \in [1, n/2^j], j \in [1, \log n]$. where $b_i^1 \equiv B_i$ and all other b's are non-assumptions. Note that the length of each justification is 3 and the number of justifications is $2 * n - 1 = O(n)$. However, it is not hard to see that the label of $b_1^{\log n}$ is $\{\{X_1, \ldots, X_n\} \mid X_i \equiv A_i \text{ or } X_i \equiv B_i, 1 \le i \le n\}$, which is $O(2^n)$ in size. The above result establishes an exponential lower bound for the complexity of any ATMS algorithm that is complete. On the other hand, the NP-hardness of the ATMS task does not tell us exactly what factors affect the complexity.

As another example, let us consider a circuit inspired by the pathological example in $\mathcal{J}$, as shown in figure 1. In this problem, the output of the circuit (0) does not correspond to the expected output (1). Using conflict and kernel definitions from [7], one can deduce from this observation that the collection of conflicts is $\{\{\text{AB}(X_1), \ldots, \text{AB}(X_n), \text{AB}(C_1), \ldots, \text{AB}(C_n), \text{AB}(D)\} \mid X_i \equiv$

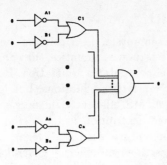

Fig. 1. A circuit with an exponential number of conflicts

A_i or $X_i \equiv B_i$} which is exponential in size. However, the set of kernel diagnoses is $\{\{\text{AB}(A_i), \text{AB}(B_i)\} \mid 1 \leq i \leq n\} \cup \{\{\text{AB}(C_i)\} \mid 1 \leq i \leq n\} \cup \{\text{AB}(D)\}$ which is linear in size. Therefore, to generate kernel diagnoses by using an ATMS to compute all conflicts [7] is bound to be inefficient.

We shall use the example from clause set $\mathcal{J}$ with $n = 16$ to illustrate some of the complexity issues regarding the BF-ATMS algorithm. Initially, we used the number of assumptions in an environment as its cost and obtained the empirical results shown in Table 1. The BF-ATMS algorithm can generate the ATMS labels

Cost bound	Total labels size	Time (seconds)
0	0	0.00
1	48	0.02
2	80	0.08
4	144	0.26
8	656	15.0
16	66192	> one hour[6]

Table 1. Example run of BF-ATMS with various bounds

in an incremental fashion and terminates rather rapidly for a low cost bound. However, the simple cost function is not very helpful in finding the minimum cost environments for all the nodes efficiently in our example, because the cost of every environment in the node b_1^5 is 16. But we can solve this problem by changing the cost function to indicate the preference of choosing assumptions of type A instead of type B. In particular, we can assign to each assumption the cost of 1 if it is of the form A_i, otherwise, the cost of 100. The sum of assumption costs is then used as the cost of an environment. With this modified cost function, the BF-ATMS can compute a minimum cost environment for every node in less than 0.2 second. The same (inefficient) cost function can also help generate an even parity and several odd parity 20-bit strings in about 0.5 second and 3 seconds respectively. In conclusion, the selection of a good (but not necessary the best) cost function for the given problem is essential for efficiently deriving the desirable solutions. Costs functions which guarantee polynomial performance in the ATMS are discussed in [18].

---

[6] The system ran out of memory after about 100 minutes of CPU-time.

5 RELATED WORK

Our formalization allows a semantical description of the ATMS and its label operations. In contrast, the best-known semantics, that proposed in [22], formalizes the labels, but not the label-computation operation. Benanev et al. [1] describe the ATMS as solving Boolean-lattice equations, but ignore the algorithms responsible for making the ATMS efficient. Ginsberg's bilattice formalism [14] uses a relatively complicated description just to demonstrate that the removal of nogoods in the label representation is indeed legal.

In addition, we have described an efficient general focusing method for the ATMS. With a similar goal, some researchers have described other techniques for focusing the ATMS label updating process to avoid generating unwanted environments [8, 13, 11, 3]. In addition, our approach is related to, but different from, the simple application of heuristic search techniques [19] to the ATMS. Due to space limitations, a full discussion of the differences between this work and each of these papers is omitted, and can be found in [18]. In summary, note that the incorporation of backtracking into an ATMS [8] can be considered as a particular instance of a BF-ATMS where a special cost function is imposed on the literals in the task-specific control disjunctions. The *focusing* of the ATMS on only small assumption sets at any one time and fixing of an upper bound on the length of environments [13, 11] introduces an *ad hoc* and unwieldy control structure in the problem solver itself in comparison with the BF-ATMS algorithm.

6 CONCLUSIONS

This paper has described the application of a lattice-theoretic formalization to the ATMS which allows precise descriptions of the ATMS semantics and efficient approximation-algorithms. In particular, introducing a general notion of cost functions to the design of a new ATMS focusing algorithm which focuses the label generation process to help the ATMS attain the efficiency of a traditional single-context TMS [10, 16]. At the same time, it retains the multiple-context capability of an ATMS and the important properties of an ATMS like consistency, minimality, and soundness, in addition to the property of bounded completeness. An implementation of BF-ATMS demonstrates that the BF-ATMS algorithm quickly solves some problems proven to have labels which are of size exponential in the number of assumptions. Moreover, the generality of the cost-function approach as well as the usefulness of the BF-ATMS algorithm are demonstrated by their applications to consistency-based diagnosis [18]. Dramatic efficiency improvements are also obtained in this domain.

References

1. D. Benanev, A.L. Brown, and D.E. Gaucas. An Algebraic Foundation for Truth Maintenance. In *Proc. IJCAI*, pages 973–980, 1987.

2. R.M. Bodington, G.D. Sullivan, and K.D. Baker. Experiments on the Use of the ATMS to Label Features for Object Recognition. In *Proc. of ECCV-90*, pages 542–551, 1990.

3. John W. Collins and Dennis DeCoste. CATMS: An ATMS Which Avoids Label Explosions. In *Proc. of AAAI-91*, pages 281–287, 1991.

4. Johan de Kleer. An assumption-based TMS. *Artificial Intelligence*, 28:127–162, 1986.

5. Johan de Kleer. Focusing on probable diagnoses. *Proc. of AAAI-91*, pages 842–848, 1991.

6. Johan de Kleer. Optimizing Focusing Model-Based Diagnoses. *Proc. of Third Diagnosis Workshop*, pages 26–29, 1992.

7. Johan de Kleer, Alan K. Mackworth, and Raymond Reiter. Characterizing diagnoses. *Proc. of AAAI-90*, pages 324–330, 1990.

8. Johan de Kleer and Brian C. Williams. Back to backtracking: Controlling the ATMS. *Proc. of AAAI-87*, pages 910–917, 1987.

9. Johan de Kleer and Brian C. Williams. Diagnosing multiple faults. *Artificial Intelligence*, 32:97–130, 1987.

10. Jon Doyle. A truth maintenance system. *Artificial Intelligence*, 12:231–272, 1979.

11. O. Dressler and A. Farquar. Putting the Problem Solver Back in the Driver's Seat: Contextual Control of the ATMS. In *Second AAAI Workshop on Model-Based Reasoning*, pages 106–112, 1990.

12. Kenneth D. Forbus. The qualitative process engine. In Daniel S. Weld and Johan de Kleer, editors, *Readings in Qualitative Reasoning About Physical Systems*, pages 220–235. Morgan Kaufmann, 1990.

13. Kenneth D. Forbus and Johan de Kleer. Focusing the ATMS. *Proc. of AAAI-88*, pages 193–198, 1988.

14. M. Ginsberg. Multivalued Logics: A Uniform Approach to Reasoning in Artificial Intelligence. *Computational Intelligence*, pages 265–316, 1988.

15. Carl A. Gunter, Teow-Hin Ngair, Prakash Panangaden, and Devika Subramanian. The common order-theoretic structure of version spaces and ATMS's. Technical Report MS-CIS-90-86, University of Pennsylvania, 1990.

16. D. McAllester. A Widely Used Truth Maintenance System. Unpublished, 1985.

17. Teow-Hin Ngair. Convex spaces: An order-theoretic structure for problem solving. Technical Report MIS-CS-92-60, CIS Department, University of Pennsylvania, 1992.

18. Teow-Hin Ngair and Gregory Provan. Focusing ATMS for Problem-Solving: A Formal Approach. Technical Report MS-CIS-92-61, University of Pennsylvania, 1992.

19. J. Pearl. *Heuristics*. Addison-Wesley, Reading, Mass., 1984.

20. G. Provan. *Complexity Analysis of Truth Maintenance Systems, with Application to High Level Vision*. PhD thesis, Faculty of Mathematics, University of Oxford, 1990.

21. G. Provan. The Computational Complexity of Multiple-Context Truth Maintenance Systems. In *Proc. of ECAI-90*, pages 522–527, 1990.

22. R. Reiter and J. de Kleer. Foundations of Assumption-based Truth Maintenance Systems: Preliminary Report. In *Proc. of AAAI-87*, pages 183–188, 1987.

23. B. Selman and H. Levesque. Abductive and Default Reasoning: A Computational Core. In *Proc. AAAI*, pages 343–348, 1990.

Examples of Causal Probabilistic Expert Systems

Masoud Noormohammadian and Ulrich G. Oppel

Mathematisches Institut der Ludwig-Maximilians-Universität München
Theresienstr. 39, D 80333 München, Germany

Causal probabilistic networks are designed to describe biological, medical, social, economical, and technical systems which are subject to randomness and uncertainty. A causal probabilistic network (CPN) is a directed graph $G := (V, \mathcal{E})$ and a family of Markov kernels $(\mathcal{P}_v: v \in V)$. The nodes v of the graph represent random variables X_v describing subsystems. The links connecting the nodes represent cause-effect relations which are quantified by conditional probabilities of events of the state space of a child node v given the states of the state spaces of the parent nodes u; e.g. see (8) and (13). These conditional probabilities are represented by the given Markov kernels $\mathcal{P}_v: S_{Pa(v)} \times \mathfrak{S}_v \to [0,1]$ with $((x_u: u \in Pa(v)), B) \to \mathcal{P}_v(x_u: u \in Pa(v); B)$ where $(S_W, \mathfrak{S}_W)$ is the product of the state spaces $(S_u, \mathfrak{S}_u)$ of the nodes $u \in W \subset V$.

If the directed graph is acyclic and finite, the family of Markov kernels determines a probability measure $\mathbb{P}$ on the product of the state spaces of all nodes; this probability measure $\mathbb{P}: \mathfrak{S}_V \to [0,1]$ is obtained by some ancestral ordering of the nodes (which is an enumeration of the nodes such that no descendent is enumerated before one of its ancestors) and the Markov composition of the given Markov kernels (which is an iterative application of Fubini's theorem). This construction of $\mathbb{P}$ is independent of the chosen ancestral ordering. $\mathbb{P}$ is uniquely determined as a directed Markov field with the given Markov kernels as conditional probabilities; e.g. see (10). The Markov composition is continuous with respect to all kinds of topologies, e.g. for the topology of uniform convergence, the topology of pointwise convergence, and (if the states spaces are polish and the Markov kernels are Feller kernels which fulfil some uniform tightness condition) the weak convergence.; see (7).

If the directed graph is cyclic, such a probability measure $\mathbb{P}$, representing the common distribution of all nodes, must not exist ("transient" case, some state space is infinite) or exists, but is not unique ("recurrent" and "nonergodic" case, e.g. all state spaces are finite).

However, some systems are described by a CPN with a cyclic graph. Often such a CPN C with a cyclic graph $G := (V, \mathcal{E})$ may be transformed by "cutting apart" and "unrolling" into a finite or infinite sequence $(C_n: n \in N)$ of repetitions of an acyclic CPN. The result of such transforming is a CPN C_{ac} with the graph $G_{ac} := (V_{ac}, \mathcal{E}_{ac})$ with $V_{ac} := \bigcup_{n \in N} V_n$ and $V_n := V$. One possible way to define $\mathcal{E}_{ac}$ is to define the edges not within V according to $\mathcal{E}$, but between V_n and V_{n+1}

according to $\mathcal{E}$. Accordingly, the Markov kernels $\mathcal{P}_v$ are transformed into Markov kernels $\mathcal{P}_v^{(n+1)}$ for $v \in V_{n+1}$. $\mathcal{P}_v^{(1)}$ for $v \in V_1$ is a degenerate Markov kernel (i.e. probability measure, $v \in V_1$ has no parents in G_{ac}); it may be chosen arbitrarily. This new CPN C_{ac} is acyclic.

Such a CPN C_{ac} may be considered as a Markov chain: the state space of this Markov chain consists of the common state space $(S_V, \mathfrak{S}_V)$ of the original CPN C; its transition probability is the "common" Markov kernel $\mathcal{P}$ which is determined by the family of Markov kernels of the original CPN C, but now considered as transition probabilities from the state spaces of the parents of a node v considered as nodes in the CPN C_n to the state space of this node as a node in C_{n+1}. The starting distribution μ: $\mathfrak{S}_{V_i} \to [0,1]$ of this Markov chain may be chosen arbitrarily. It is well known that μ and $\mathcal{P}$ define a probability measure $\mathbb{P}^\mu$: $\mathfrak{S}_V^N \to [0,1]$ which is a Markov chain with the state space $(S_V, \mathfrak{S}_V)$. If μ is the product of the family of probability measures $(\mathcal{P}_v^{(1)}: v \in V_1)$, then $\mathbb{P}^\mu$ is the directed Markov field which is determined by the CPN C_{ac}. (This is because of the chosen specific form of the graph G_{ac}. Here the nodes of the set of nodes V_1 are all "independent". To construct an acyclic CPN from a cyclic CPN, we could also proceed in a different way.)

A system which may be modeled as a sequence of repetitions of a CPN usually has some asymptotic stationarity or periodicity properties. This follows from the fact that it may be considered as a Markov chain as we showed above. Such properties may be used to correct or to adapt the Markov kernels. A general method to describe a complex system more efficiently, more flexibly, and more realistically is to transform a compartmental model of such a system into a sequence of repetitions of a CPN. Some metabolic processes are described by such compartmental models. They are characterized by a cyclic graph and a system of differential equations. In (12) a general method is introduced to transform such a system into a sequence of acyclic CPNs. This method is based on the solution of the system of differential equations and a stochastification procedure. The result of such transforming is a more realistic model of the metabolic process which may be simulated and adapted to new evidence very easily using the shell HUGIN. In contrary to that, the adaption of the deterministic process of the compartmental model to new evidence is not possible in general; this a consequence of the uniquenes of the solution of an initial value problem for a system of differential equations according to the Picard-Lindelöf theorem. Furthermore, such a stochastified description of a metabolic process easily may be modified by adding additional nodes for additional effects to the CPN. The stochastification of such a model and its enlargement may be controlled and eventually adapted to general knowledge about the system by considering asymptotic periodicity and stationarity properties of the Markov chain which is associated to the constructed sequence of CPNs.

Sometimes a system may be modeled by a sequence of CPNs which is starting with a CPN representing only general knowledge about similar systems. As time goes by, more and more information about the specific system is collected which may be used to adapt the Markov kernels of the CPNs step by step to those of the given specific system. The adaption may be achieved by properly designed estimators of the Markov kernels or by introducing new evidence. This may be done using the shell HUGIN.

We shall present examples of expert systems which are based on single CPNs and on sequences of adapted and controlled CPNs and which are constructed and operated using the shell HUGIN. They are applied to risk analysis in genetics, diagnosis of the stock market, claims reserving, evaluation of multisensor systems, and diagnosis and prognosis of metabolic processes.

GENRISK, an expert system for genetic risk analysis:

Genetics seem to be well suited for the application of classical probability theory and CPNs. We shall introduce the causal probabilistic expert system GENRISK as an example of a very simple, but powerful medical expert system. The structure of the graph of the CPN is given in a very natural way by the genealogical tree. The conditional probabilities describing the stochastic relations from node to node may be obtained from the rules of genetics. The probability distributions of the nodes without ancestors (in the graph which is describing only a limited part of the genealogical tree) may be obtained from the Hardy - Weinberg law or some of its generalizations. These probability distributions are the stationary Hardy - Weinberg distributions. They and the parameters of the Markov kernels can be obtained for the population under examination from statistical data which is usually easily accesible; for details see (11) and (5).

GENRISK is designed for diagnosis, simulation, and prediction of genetic deseases such as the cystic pancreas fibrosis (mucoviszidosis; presumably only one defective gene) and the Alzheimer desease (at least two defective genes). We shall demonstrate how to insert new knowledge and how to propagate this knowledge within the system.

AKTALYST, an expertsystem for stock market analysis:

In capital market analysis we have to investigate very complex situations. A large number of different models may be constructed without a justified preference to a specific modeling approach. Only the consideration of a large variety of models (respectively indicators) and an experience-based examination of their applicability may give us a hint upon the appearance of decision relevant stock market phenomenas. The diagnostic abilities of these models, wether they are described in terms of causal dependency frameworks (representing qualitative knowledge) or derived from mathematical models (permitting numerical applications), have continously to be verified by experience. Hence, an expert, working with information and money on the capital market, has to look for an inference scheme which provides both a mechanism to handle numerical assessments and a possibility to test the validity of models based on causal dependency frameworks.

Combining the conceptual framework of CPNs with methods of statistical inference, Matthias Barth provided such an inference scheme for a specific mid- and shorttime period stock market analysis in close cooperation with the financial analyst of a German health insurance company; see (1) and (2). The basic inference scheme of his expert system AKTALYST was provided by the shell HUGIN which allows both to test alternative models (respectively indicators) and to collect relevant information to evaluate an experience-based aggregate rating of the current condition of the stock market.

Using a given set of indicators (30-days-momentum of the return of emissions (5 years), 10-days-momentum of it, 20-days- average of it; 20-days-average of the return of the US emissions (10 years), 20-days-average of the 3-month-interest rate, 10-days-average of the 3-month-interest rate, short range oszillator, advance-decline indicator, put-call ratio, trend-volume indicator, 30-days-DAX-momentum), the problem was to predict situations (buy, hold, sell) by a method applied by the financial analyst (weighted averages of ratings derived from the indicators) and by a method based on a CPN. These predictions were compared with the a posteriori evaluations by the financial analyst. The initialization of the network was based on the German index DAX in the period from April 89 to December 89; afterwards the network was updated daily. The correlation of the outcome of the financial analyst's method to the a posteriori evaluation was calculated for the period from January 1990 to December 1991: it was 0.452 (which is not bad). The correlation of the predictions of AKTALYST to the a posteriori evaluation was 0.499.

IBNR, an expert system for claims reserving:

The causal probabilistic expert system IBNR is based on ideas of Ch. Hachemeister (4) for estimation of and reservation for (incurred but not reported) claims which is an important issue for reinsurance companies. Claims reserving is an exercise in estimation of certain parameters conditional on the accumulated information about the claims concerned. The general idea of Hachemeister is that a particular set of claim statuses is chosen such that, at any given moment, a given claim must have one of those statuses. It is assumed that here exists a probability of transition to any other particular status. Indeed, these transition probabilities can be obtained from the worksheets for the individual claims (runoff tables of estimations, reservations, and payments). Hence, the process of claims reserving may be modeled as a CPN. Using the shell HUGIN, not only estimates of expected global claim sizes will be possible, but also estimates of individual claim sizes and of their distribution will be possible. The expert system IBNR has been initialized with data of a German reinsurance company. The Markov kernels of its CPN is updated using weighted memory. A more detailed discussion of this procedure and first evaluations will be presented.

MULTISENS, an expert system for a traffic guidance system:

The causal probabilistic expert system MULTISENS is a prototype of an expert system for the automatic evaluation of a multisensor system. Using stochastic cause-effect relations, with such an expert system it is possible to reduce uncertainty about the evaluation of some sensors by introducing evidence from other sensors. In a traffic guidance system, which is about to be developed by the DLR (German Space Research Establishment) and a Bavarian motor company, a LIDAR (light detection and ranging, LASER RADAR) is used to detect obstacles and to determine visibility. The visibility is obtained from the LIDAR signals for different fields of view using additional knowledge from other sensors and the inference system of the expert system.

In dense aerosols (e.g. spray, radiative fog, advective fog) the LIDAR return signal contains not only parts which are due to single scattering, but which are also due to multiple scattering of the photons of the emitted collimated LASER beam. From different fields of view the relation of the single scattering to the multiple scattering part of the return signal may be obtained. From this relation and the type of the atmospheric scatterers the visibility may be determined. Without knowing the type of the scatterers (e.g. spray, radiative fog, advective fog) this is not possible. Hence, it is necessary to obtain from other sensors (e.g. headlights on or off, fog lamp on or off, rear fog-light on or off, wipers on or off, temperature, height above sea level, relative humidity, day time, season) additional knowledge about the type of scatterers. Indeed, based on such indicators the expert system MULTISENS allows to obtain sufficient information to decide which type of scatterers should be the basis for the evaluation of the visibility from the LIDAR signal. For details see (9).

DIAB1, an expert system for the glucose-insulin metabolism:

Metabolic processes are immensely involved since they are comprising the anatomy of the organs, the physiology of the organ functions and transport processes, and long chains of numerous cycles of linked biochemical reactions. Hence, any model of a metabolic process is an extreme simplification which has to be done to be able to study such a process at all. The Bolie model for the glucose-insulin interactions is such an oversimplified, but well established two compartment model for the glucose-insulin metabolism. It has the following system of linear mass balance equations:

$$dq_1/dt\ (t) = - p_1\ q_1(t) - p_2\ q_2(t) + \varphi(t)$$
$$dq_2/dt\ (t) = - p_3\ q_2(t) + p_4\ q_1(t)$$

with initial values $q_1(0) = 0$ and $q_2(0) = 0$,

where q_1 and q_2 are the deviations of the glucose and insulin concentration from their fasting levels, respectively, φ is an impulsive or continuous supply of glucose, and $p_1, ... , p_4$ are individual constants; for details see (3) and (4). According to the principles described above, this compartmental model was transformed into a sequence of acyclic CPNs, enlarged with additional nodes for the glucose supply, and constructed with the shell HUGIN; for details see (12). Such a causal probabilistic expert system may be used as a basis for the construction of a more realistic and therefore a necessarily more complex CPN for simulation, diagnosis, and prognosis of the glucose-insulin metabolism.

References:

(1) Barth, M.: Aktienmarktanalyse mit kausal-probabilistischen Expertensystemen. Diplomarbeit: Fachbereich Mathematik, L-M-Universität München, 1992.

(2) Barth, M.: AKTALYST, ein kausal-probabilistisches Expertensystem zur Wertpapieranalyse. Münchner Blätter zur Versicherungsmathematik. Heft 20. Juni 1993.

(3) Bolie, V.W.: Coefficients of normal blood glucose regulation. J. Appl. Physiol. 16 (1979), 783-788.

(4) Carson, E.R.; Cobelli, C.: Finkelstein, L.: The Mathematical Modeling of Metabolic and Endocrine Systems. Model Formulation, Identification, and Validation. J. Wiley and Sons: New York, 1983.

(5) Gruseck, S.: Risikoanalyse in der Genetik mit kausal-probabilistischen Expertensystemen. Diplomarbeit: Fachbereich Mathematik, L-M-Universität München, 1993.

(6) Hachemeister, C.A.: A stochastic model for loss reserving. Transactions of the 21st International Congress of Actuaries, 1 (1980), 185-194.

(7) Matthes, R.; Oppel, U.G.: Convergence of causal probabilistic networks. In: Bouchon-Meunier, B.; Valverde, L.; Yager, R.R. (ed.): Intelligent Systems with Uncertainty. Elsevier: to appear 1993.

(8) Lauritzen, S.L.; Spiegelhalter, D.: Local Computations with Probabilities on Graphical Structures and Their Application to Expert Systems. J. Roy. Stat. Soc. B, 50 (2) (1988), 157-224.

(9) Noormohammadian, M.; Oppel, U.G.; Starkov, A.: Expertensysteme zur Datenanalyse technischer und ökologischer Multisensorsysteme. In: Werner, Ch.; Tacke, M.; Günther, K.; Klein, V.; Weber, K.; Woods, P.; Weitcamp, C.; Kunz, J. (ed.): LASER in der Umweltmeßtechnik. Springer: to appear 1993.

(10) Oppel, U.G.: Every complex system can be determined by a causal probabilistic network without cycles and every such network determines a Markov field. In: Kruse, R.; Siegel, P.: Symbolic and Quantitative Approaches to Uncertainty. Springer: Berlin, 1991.

(11) Oppel, U.G.; Moser, W.: Kausal-probabilistische Netze zur Konstruktion medizinischer Expertensysteme für Diagnose, Simulation und Prognose. Biometrie und Informatik in Medizin und Biologie 23 (1992), 84-93.

(12) Oppel, U.G.; Hierle, A.: Janke, L.; Moser, W.: Transformation of compartmental models into sequences of causal probabilistic networks. Proceedings of AIME'93, 4th Conference on Artificial Intelligence in Medicine Europe, Munich, October 3-6, 1993.

(13) Pearl, J.: Probabilistic Reasoning in Intelligent Systems: Networks of Plausible Inference. Morgan Kaufmann: San Matteo, 1988.

A mixed approach of revision in propositional calculus

Odile PAPINI[1]* and Antoine RAUZY[2]

[1] G.I.A. Université d'Aix-Marseille II,163 avenue de Luminy, 13288 Marseille cédex 9 FRANCE, Tel: 91 26 93 12. Fax: 91 26 92 75, e-mail: papini@gia.univ-mrs.fr
[2] La.B.R.I. CNRS Université de Bordeaux I, 351 cours de la liberation, 33405 Talence cédex FRANCE, Tel: 56 84 60 83. Fax: 56 84 66 69, e-mail: rauzy@petrel.greco-prog.fr

Abstract. In this paper, we focus on minimal change in the revision of knowledge bases represented by propositional formulas. We first present a quick survey of semantic and syntactic approaches of revision, we then propose a mixed approach of revision which uses both semantic and syntactic means.

1 Introduction

When a new item of information is added to a knowledge base, inconsistency can result. Revision means modifying the knowledge base, in order to maintain consistency, to keep new information, and to remove the least possible previous information items. C.Alchourron, P.Gärdenfors and D.Makinson [1] [4] formulated postulates which express the properties that a knowledge set *(that is, a deductively closed set of formulas)* has to satisfy, after information has been added. $K * \mu$ denotes the knowledge set K revised by a formula μ.

These postulates do not make it possible however to define an effective revision function which calculates, from the initial knowledge base, the state of the base after the addition of more information.

In [11] a complete revision function when the added formula is represented by a propositional clause which satisfies the first six Gärdenfors postulates, and which is able to calculate the state of the knowledge base after the addition of information, was proposed. This function involves the intersection between minimal inconsistent subsets. According to whether or not this intersection is reduced to the added clause, two different algorithms stemming from the semantic evaluation refutation method [5] [9] were described. It was focused on keeping consistency in the knowledge base. Changing minimally the knowledge base meant removing a minimal number of clauses. In the case where revision function might give several results, the choice was left to the user.

After a quick survey of semantic and syntactic approaches and their respective critiques, we propose a revision function that stems from the one previously presented. This function in detecting the causes of inconsistencies uses semantic means, and in revising minimally uses both semantic and syntactic means.

---

* I should like to thank C.Schwind for helpful discussions and for her support.

2 A quick survey of different revision approaches

2.1 Semantic approaches

These approaches also called model-based approaches, have been surveyed by Katsuno and Mendelzon [6] [12] . The knowledge base K is represented by a propositional formula ψ such that $K = \{\phi, \psi \vdash \phi\}$. The knowledge base revision by a formula μ consists of finding the model of μ which is the closest possible to a model of the knowledge base ψ . This operation is denoted $\psi \circ \mu$, Katsuno and Mendelzon establish a correspondence between $K * \mu$ and $\psi \circ \mu$. The principle of minimal change for revision takes the form of finding a model of the added formula closest to a model of the initial knowledge base, the principle of minimal change leads to the definition of orders between interpretations.

Dalal [3] uses the number of propositional variables on which two interpretations differ as a measure of the "distance" between them. The chosen model of μ is such that the Hamming distance between this model and the model of ψ is minimal.

Bordiga [2] concentrates on sets of propositional variables on which a model of ψ and a model of μ differ. $Diff(I, J)$ denotes the sets of propositional variables on which the two interpretations I and J differ. $Diff(I, \mu)$ denotes the collection of $Diff(I, J)$ where J is a model of μ. J a model of μ is chosen if there is some model I of ψ such that $Diff(I, J)$ is a minimal element of $Diff(I, \mu)$.

Winslett [13] proposes a revision operation which coincides with Bordiga's one in the case where $\psi \circ \mu$ is inconsistent, however when ψ is consistent with μ she defines the revision in the same way as in the inconsistent case.

These semantic approaches are of interest from a theoretical point of view, particularly because of the fact that the Gärdenfors postulates are reformulated, however these approaches may be subject to criticism on several points.

Concerning the knowledge representation, the knowledge base K is represented by a formula ψ, and is defined by the set of formulas that can be deduced from ψ. However the new knowledge base $\psi \circ \mu$ is not precisely defined, we only have a model of it, and it is not possible to describe the revised knowledge base.

On the other hand, these approaches stem from the principle of irrelevance of syntax, in fact the revision operation has to be independent of the syntax of the knowledge base. Not everybody agrees with this principle essentially for two reasons. Firstly, some knowledge bases can describe situations where some formulas can't be removed, for example physical laws, so syntax has to be taken into account. Secondly, two equivalent knowledge bases can be revised in different ways, as shown in the example proposed by Hansson and cited by Gärdenfors.

Example 1. Suppose we are standing in the street where there are two fast food restaurants a and b. We meet somebody eating french fried potatoes, we conclude that at least one of the fast food restaurant is open, $\psi_0 = \{a \vee b\}$. Moreover seeing from a distance that the restaurant a has its lights on, we suppose that a is open, $\psi_1 = \{a \vee b, a\}$. Upon reaching the fast food restaurant a, we find that it is closed for remodeling, $\psi_2 = \{a \vee b, \neg a\}$. We deduce that the fast food b restaurant is open. In contrast, suppose that we had not met anyone eating french fried potatoes, seeing from a distance that the fast food restaurant a has its lights on, we suppose that a is open, $\psi'_1 = \{a\}$. Upon reaching the restaurant a, we find that it is closed for remodeling, $\psi'_2 = \{\emptyset\}$. We deduce that no fast food restaurant is open. ψ_1 and ψ'_1 are logically equivalent, but $\psi_1 \circ \{\neg a\}$ and $\psi'_1 \circ \{\neg a\}$ are different.

In fact, Katsuno and Mendelzon don't respect the principle of irrelevance of syntax, in order to solve the integrity constraints problem, they define a new revision operation where they isolate the formulas that representent the integrity constraints, denoted IC, from the rest of the knowledge base, as follows: $\psi \circ^{IC} \mu = \psi \circ (\mu \wedge IC)$.

Concerning the principle of the minimality of revision, the previously mentioned authors define an order or a distance between the models. For example in the Dalal's method, when several models of μ are found where the distance to a model of ψ is minimal, the revised base $\psi \circ \mu$ is the set of formulas that agree with these models. Can we consider, in this case that the principle of minimality of revision is verified?

Example 2. Consider the following knowledge base $\psi = (a \vee b) \wedge (\neg a \vee b)$ and the added formula is $\mu = (\neg b \vee a) \wedge \neg b$. The models of ψ are $I_1 = (1,1)$ and $I_2 = (0,1)$, the models of μ are $J_1 = (1,0)$ and $J_2 = (0,0)$. $d(I_1, J_1) = 1$ and $d(I_2, J_2) = 1$. According to Dalal the revised knowledge base $\psi \circ \mu$ is the set of formulas for which the models are J_1 and J_2. $form(J_1, J_2)$ denotes the corresponding set of formulas, if $form(I_1, I_2)$ denotes the set of formulas corresponding to ψ, $form(J_1, J_2) \cap form(I_1, I_2) = \emptyset$

2.2 Syntactic approaches

These approaches also called syntax-based approaches, can be interpreted as assigning higher relevance to explicitly represented formulas.

Nebel [7] [12] first proposed a revision operation for finite knowledge bases drawing inspiration from the revision operation for deductively closed theories proposed by Gärdenfors. This revision operation is defined from the contraction operation, via the Levi identity. $K * x = CONS(K - \neg x \cup \{x\})$ where $CONS(F)$ denotes the set of formulas deducible from F. The contraction operation needs maximal consistent subsets of formulas not implying a formula y, denoted $K \downarrow y$, and a selection function S.

The contraction operation is then defined as follows:
$K - y = \cap S(K \downarrow y)$ *if* $y \notin CONS(\emptyset)$.
$K - y = K$ *otherwise.*

The Nebel's revision operation called simple base revision is defined selecting maximal subsets not implying a given sentence, then taking the intersection of the consequences of these subsets:

$$K \oplus x = (\bigcap_{Y \in (K \downarrow \neg x)} CONS(Y)) + x.$$

The operation $\oplus$ considers all formulas in the knowledge base as equally relevant. In most applications, however, it is necessary to distinguish between the relevance of formulas. For this purpose he [8] partitions the knowledge base into disjointed priority classes $K_i, i \geq 1$ and defines the prioritized removal of x, written $Z \Downarrow x$ such that formulas in K_i have higher priority than those in K_j iff $i < j$:

The prioritized base revision operation is defined by:

$$K \oplus^p x = CONS((\bigvee(Z \Downarrow \neg x)) \wedge x)$$

It is worthy of note that this approach takes into account the relevance of syntax, however it raises some questions.

The revision operation defined by Nebel uses contraction, via Levi identity. Does it not seem more efficient to directly define a revision operation?

The prioritized base revision gives more relevance to the initial knowledge base than to the added set of formulas. Does it not seem interesting to also take into account the added set of formulas?

Several formulas of the knowledge base may have the same priority, what happens in this case?

3   A mixed approach of revision

A mixed approach means that in detecting inconsistencies we use semantic means and in minimally revising we use both semantic and syntactic means.

3.1   definitions

In what follows, the items contained in the knowledge base are expressed in propositional calculus. K denotes the knowledge base represented by a finite consistent set of formulas. A denotes a finite consistent set of formulas not included in K. F denotes $K \cup A$ and we suppose F inconsistent.

Definition 1. *We call vocabulary the set of propositional variables that appear in a given set of formulas. Let X be a set of formulas, V_X denotes the vocabulary of X*

In the following we use the classical definitions of interpretation, model and counter-model. $\mathcal{J}$ denotes the set of all the interpretations of F on the vocabulary V_F. $\mathcal{M}_A$ denotes the set of interpretations of $\mathcal{J}$ that satisfy A. Since A is consistent $\mathcal{M}_A$ is not a empty set.

Definition 2. *Let I be belonging to $\mathcal{M}_A$. The removed set associated with I is defined as the set $R_I = \{f : \forall f \in K, I[f] = 0, I[A] = 1\}$. In other words a removed set is the set of non-satisfied formulas by an interpretation of $\mathcal{M}_A$.*

Remark. If R_I is a removed set of F then $F - R_I$ is consistent.

Proposition 3. *The mapping that associates to each I in $\mathcal{M}_A$ the removed set R_I is surjective.*

3.2   Counter-models construction

Our revision strategy consists of determining a removed set to take out from the knowledge base in order to restore consistency. To do that we construct some interpretations of F that are extended models of A and that are extended counter-models of K. The surjectivity of the mapping previously defined ensures the determination of all the removed sets.

Example 3. Consider the following knowledge base $F = K \cup A$ where $K = \{a \vee b, \neg a \vee b\}$ and $A = \{a \vee \neg b, \neg b\}$. K and A are consistent sets of formulas. The interpretations constructed as previously seen are $I_1 = (1, 0)$ and $I_2 = (0, 0)$. The removed set $R_{I_1} = \{\neg a \vee b\}$ corresponds to the interpretation I_1 and the removed set $R_{I_2} = \{a \vee b\}$ corresponds to the interpretation I_2.

In what follows V_K denotes the vocabulary of K and V_A denotes the vocabulary of A.

Proposition 4. $V_K \cap V_A \neq \emptyset$.

This Proposition shows that the propositional variables which cause the inconsistency of $K \cup A$, belong to $V_K \cap V_A$. In order to determine all the removed sets, we construct the set of interpretations of F which are extended models of A on V_F.

Remark. According to a computing point of view, if we have a beginning of interpretations on $V_K \cap V_A$, in order to determine the removed sets it is sufficient that there exists a complement of these interpretations on V_K / V_A

Proposition 5. *Let $\mathcal{J}_K$ be the set of the restrictions of the interpretations of $\mathcal{M}_A$ on V_K. The construction of $\mathcal{J}_K$ makes it possible to determine all the removed sets of F.*

Remark. Only choosing in $\mathcal{J}_K$ the interpretations which restrictions on V_K / V_A are models of K allows the construction of models of A "rather close" to the models of K. The adopted measure of the closeness is here the Hamming distance. This remark provides a semantic criterion for minimal change.

Example 4. Consider the following knowledge base $F = K \cup A$. $K = \{a, a \vee b, \neg a \vee b, \neg a \vee c, \neg b \vee a\}$ $A = \{\neg b \vee \neg c, \neg b \vee c, d \vee e\}$. $V_K = \{a, b, c\}$, $V_A = \{b, c, d, e\}$ and $V_K \cap V_A = \{b, c\}$. On $V_K \cap V_A$ the restrictions of the models of A are $M_{A_1} = (0, 1)$ and $M_{A_2} = (0, 0)$. On V_A / V_K we choose $M_{A_3} = (1, 1)$ as the restriction of the model of A. As $V_K / V_A = \{a\}$, the variable a can be assigned either to the value 1 or to the value 0. So the interpretations are $I_1 = (1, 0, 1, 1, 1)$, $I_2 = (1, 0, 0, 1, 1)$, $I_3 = (0, 0, 1, 1, 1)$ and $I_4 = (0, 0, 0, 1, 1)$ with $R_{I_1} = \{\neg a \vee b\}$, $R_{I_2} = \{\neg a \vee b, \neg a \vee c\}$, $R_{I_3} = \{a, a \vee b\}$, $R_{I_4} = R_{I_3}$ the corresponding removed sets.
Using the previous remark, as $M_K = (1, 1, 1)$ is the only model of K on V_K, we only choose to assign the value 1 to the variable a, and the only interpretations are $I_1 = (1, 0, 1, 1, 1)$ and $I_2 = (1, 0, 0, 1, 1)$ with $R_{I_1} = \{\neg a \vee b\}$ and $R_{I_2} = \{\neg a \vee b, \neg a \vee c\}$ the corresponding removed sets.

3.3 Definition of an order between removed sets

(From now on, we consider the set of clauses corresponding to propositional formulas)

As seen in the previous examples, even if taking into account the semantic criterion, the construction of counter-models may give several removed sets. Our purpose is to determine the "best" one to remove from the knowledge base in order to maintain consistency. This "best" one is the removed set that allows us to remove the "least possible previous information". The meaning of the "least possible information" depends on the assumed point of view. Our point of view is defining a total order between interpretations and thus on the removed sets from the syntax. We argue that the revision operation has to depend firstly on the added clauses of A, since new information seems to be more relevant than the old information, and thereafter on the initial knowledge base K. Therefore our revision operation has to verify the three following criteria:

1 *keeping in the knowledge base, the clauses which contain literals not appearing in the clauses of A.* The $K \cup A$ inconsistency is not directly dependent of these clauses .

2 *keeping in the knowledge base, the clauses which contain literals appearing in the clauses of A.* By the revision definition, the clauses of A have to be kept in the knowledge base; As much as possible, it seems reasonable to keep the clauses of K which contain literals appearing in the clauses of A .

3 *removing from the knowledge base, the clauses which contain the opposites of literals appearing in the clauses of A.* By the revision definition, the clauses of A have to be kept in the knowledge base; As much as possible, it seems reasonable to remove clauses of K which contain the opposites of literals appearing in clauses of A . The $K \cup A$ inconsistency is directly dependent of these clauses .

For each set of added clauses A, we choose three integers α, β, γ, such that $\alpha \gg \beta \gg \gamma$. We define a total order between the removed sets assigning to each removed set R_i an integer called weight and denoted w_i. Computing the weight of the removed set is done assigning to each literal l_j appearing in R_i, an integer q_j as follows:

If $l_j \notin V_A$ then $q_j = \alpha$

If $l_j \in V_A$ then

    If l_j appears in one clause of A then $q_j = \beta$

    If $\neg l_j$ appears in one clause of A then $q_j = \gamma$

Therefore the weight of a removed set R_i is defined by $w_i = \sum_j q_j$, this weighting allows us to define a total order between interpretations, thus between removed sets, revising is performed removing from the knowledge base the removed set of minimal weight.

$K * A = (K \cup A) - R_m$ where $w_m = min(w_i)$, denotes the revised knowledge base.

Example 5. In example 3, the weight of $R_{I_1} = \{\neg a \vee b\}$ is $w_1 = 2\gamma$, the weight of $R_{I_2} = \{a \vee b\}$ is $w_2 = \beta + \gamma$, revision is performed only removing R_{I_1}. Let $M_1(1,1)$ and $M_2(0,1)$ be the models of K, $d(M_1, I_1) = 1$ and $d(M_2, I_2) = 1$ *(where d is the Hamming distance)*. With Dalal's revision operation, neither $a \vee b$ nor $\neg a \vee b$ belongs to $form(I_1, I_2)$.

In example 4, the weight of $R_{I_1} = \{\neg a \vee b\}$ is $w_1 = \beta + \gamma$, the weight of $R_{I_2} = \{\neg a \vee b, \neg a \vee c\}$ is $w_2 = 2(\beta + \alpha)$, the weight of $R_{I_3} = \{a, a \vee b\}$ is $w_3 = 2\alpha + \gamma$, revision is performed only removing R_{I_1}. With Dalal's revision operation the same result is obtained.

Remark. Literals l_j and $\neg l_j$ may appear in a set of clauses A. When $l_j \in V_K \cap V_A$, two weighting are constructed, one according to l_j denoted w_{l_j} and the other according to $\neg l_j$ denoted $w_{\neg l_j}$. Revision is performed removing the removed set corresponding to the minimal weight $w_m = min(w_{l_j}, w_{\neg l_j})$.

Remark. In the case where a minimal weight cannot be determined, the choice is left to the user. Generally these are symmetric problems where extra-logic properties have to be taken into account.

Remark. To solve the problem of integrity constaints, we isolate the clauses IC representing the integrity constraints, and $K * (A \cup IC) = (K \cup (A \cup IC)) - R_m$ denotes the revised knowledge base.

Proposition 6. *The revised knowlegde base defined by $K * A = (K \cup A) - R_m$ where $w_m = min(w_i)$ verifies the first five Gärdenfors postulates.*

Remark. This revision strategy is a syntax-based approach and depends on the added clauses , thus $(G6)$, $(G7)$ and $(G8)$ are not verified. If the set of added formulas is reduced to one clause $(G6)$ is verified.

3.4 implementation

In order to determine the "best" removed set, we compute some interpretations according to consequences of proposition 4 and 5 and remark in 3.2. We construct a binary decision tree corresponding to the semantic evaluation [5] [9] were all the literals belonging to $V_K \cap V_A$ are selected. A leaf of the tree is reached when all the clauses are either satisfied or not. Each leaf of the tree is labelled by a set of non-satisfied clauses which is a removed set [11], and the weighting is then computed according to 3.3.

4   Conclusion

This revision approach is a mixed one. It uses an efficient refutation procedure like semantic evaluation to compute some extented models of A, it uses semantic means to reduce the number of these models, and it uses syntactic means to take advantage of the relevance of the added formula in order to satisfy the principle of minimal change.

References

1. C. Alchourron, P. Gärdenfors, D. Makinson. On the logic of theory change: Partial meet functions for contraction and revision. *Journal of Symbolic Logic 50:510-530*, 1985.
2. A. Bordiga. Language features for flexible handling of exceptions in information systems. *ACM Trans. Database Syst.* ,(10):563-603, 1985.
3. M. Dalal. Investigations into a theory of knowledge base revision. *Proceedings of the Seventh National Conference on Artificial Intelligence*, :475-479, 1988.
4. P. Gärdenfors. Knowledge in flux: modelling the dynamics of epistemic states. *MIT Press*, 1988.
5. S. Jeannicot, L. Oxusoff, A. Rauzy. Evaluation sémantique en calcul propositionnel: une propriété de coupure pour rendre efficace la procédure de Davis et Putnam. *Revue d'Intelligence Artificielle* ,(2):1 41-60, 1988.
6. H. Katsuno, A. Mendelzon. Propositional knowledge base revision and minimal change. *Artificial Intelligence* ,(52):263-294, 1991.
7. B. Nebel. A knowledge level analysis of belief revision. *Proceedings of the 1st International Conference on Principles of Knowledge Representation and Reasoning,R.J. Brachman,H.J. Levesque, and R. Reiter editors.Toronto. Ontario.* ,:301-311, 1989.
8. B. Nebel. Belief revision and default reasoning: syntax-based approaches. *Proceedings of Knowledge Representation* ,:30 417-427, 1991.
9. L. Oxusoff, A. Rauzy. Evaluation sémantique en calcul propositionnel. *Thèse de doctorat. GIA Université d'Aix-Marseille II. Luminy,*1989.
10. O. Papini. Revision in propositional calculus. *Proceedings of ECSQAU 91. Lectures Notes in Computer Sciences.R.Kruse P.Siegel Eds. Springer Verlag* ,(548):272-276, 1991.
11. O. Papini. A complete revision function in propositional calculus. *Proceedings of ECAI 92. B.Neumann Ed. J.Wiley & sons,*339-343, 1992.
12. Lea Sombe. Revision de bases de connaissances. *Actes des 4emes journes nationales du PRC-GDR IA. Marseille,*207-235, 1992.
13. M. Winslett. Reasoning about action using a possible models approach. *Proceedings of the Seventh National Conference on Artificial Intelligence*, :89-93, 1988.

Integrating Uncertainty Handling Formalisms in Distributed Artificial Intelligence

Simon Parsons[1][2] and Alessandro Saffiotti[3]

[1] Advanced Computation Laboratory, Imperial Cancer Research Fund,
P.O. Box 123, Lincoln's Inn Fields, London WC2A 3PX, United Kingdom.
[2] Department of Electronic Engineering, Queen Mary and Westfield College,
Mile End Road, London E1 4NS.
[3] IRIDIA, Université Libre de Bruxelles, 50 Av Rooseveldt, CP 194/6
B-1050 Bruxelles, Belgium

Abstract. In distributed artificial intelligence systems it is important that the constituent intelligent systems communicate. This may be a problem if the systems use different methods to represent uncertain information. This paper presents a method that enables systems that use different uncertainty handling formalisms to qualitatively integrate their uncertain information, and argues that this makes it possible for distributed intelligent systems to achieve tasks that would otherwise be beyond them.

1 Introduction

Distributed artificial intelligence (DAI) is that part of the field of artificial intelligence that deals with problem solving distributed amongst a number of intelligent systems. Thus DAI combines the power of artificial intelligence techniques with the advantages of distributed systems such as robustness and the ability to combine existing systems together in new configurations. One particular advantage of distributed artificial intelligence is the ability to take several existing systems and couple them together [2] perhaps with some new systems, into a community of agents that can tackle problems that are beyond the scope of any individual system. Thus a number of medical expert systems, each specialising in a particular area, can be used together to solve problems that are insoluble by any one system on its own [1].

When building distributed communities of agents, communication between the agents is very important. In order for agents to be able to communicate, they either need to use the same knowledge representation method, or have a means of translating between the methods used by different agents. This is especially true if the various agents are capable of handling uncertainty [11]. If different agents have different means of handling uncertainty, then one agent that, say, uses possibility theory to represent its uncertainty will not be able to understand the results of another agent that employs belief functions unless the agents have a means of translating from one formalism to another.

2 An Example of a Multi-agent System

As an example of the problems that different formalisms can pose consider the following hypothetical situation. We have a community of medical agents which between them have access to a body of medical knowledge similar to that of the Oxford System of Medicine [5]. This knowledge can be summarised in a network, a fragment of which is shown in Figure 1. This fragment encodes the medical information that joint trauma (T) leads to loose knee bodies (K), and that these and arthritis (A) cause pain (P). The incidence of arthritis is influenced by dislocation (D) of the joint in question and by the patient suffering from Sjorgen's syndrome (S). Sjorgen's syndrome affects the incidence of vasculitis (V), and vasculitis leads to vasculitic lesions (L). Consider further that none of the agents

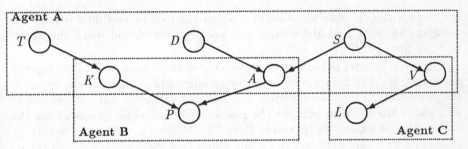

Fig. 1. Medical knowledge about arthritis and associated conditions

has knowledge of the complete network, since, like the modular systems of [1], each is a specialist in a narrow area. In Figure 1, agent A has knowledge of the associations between diseases and their causes; agent B is a specialist in pain; and agent C's main competence is with lesions. Notice that some nodes are shared between different agents: these constitute the communication channels between them. Suppose now that the agents use different methods for representing the uncertainty inherent in the medical knowledge. Thus the strengths of the influences known to agent A are given as probabilities, reflecting the fact that there is good statistical data relating the various complaints. Agent B represents strengths as possibilities [4], with values based on the physical possibility of one condition influencing another. Finally, the dependencies used by agent C are quantified by subjective values of belief strength, expressed using belief functions [9]. All of these numerical values are given in Table 1. The lack of conditional belief values other than those given is a result of ignorance about the incidence of pain under these circumstances. It is important to notice that the heterogeneity in the way uncertainty is represented across different agents is not an oddity of the system, but a consequence of the fact that uncertainty may be present in many different forms, and each form should be represented by the formalism that is most suitable for the job [8].

Given the information distributed among the agents, it should be possible for the community to reason from what is known about joint trauma and Sjor-

Table 1. Conditional values for the medical example

$p(k \mid t)$	$= 0.6$	$p(v \mid s)$	$= 0.1$
$p(k \mid \neg t)$	$= 0.2$	$p(v \mid \neg s)$	$= 0.3$
$p(a \mid d, s)$	$= 0.9$	$p(a \mid \neg d, s)$	$= 0.6$
$p(a \mid d, \neg s)$	$= 0.6$	$p(a \mid \neg d, \neg s)$	$= 0.4$
$bel(p \mid k, a)$	$= 0.9$	$bel(p \mid k, \neg a)$	$= 0.7$
$bel(p \mid \neg k, a)$	$= 0.7$	$bel(p \mid k \cup \neg k, a)$	$= 0.6$
$bel(p \mid k, a \cup \neg a)$	$= 0.7$	$bel(\neg p \mid \neg k, \neg a)$	$= 0.5$
$bel(\neg p \mid \neg k, a \cup \neg a)$	$= 0.4$		
$\Pi(l \mid v)$	$= 1$	$\Pi(l \mid \neg v)$	$= 1$
$\Pi(\neg l \mid v)$	$= 0.1$	$\Pi(\neg l \mid \neg v)$	$= 0.1$

gen's syndrome to establish something about the pain or vasculitic lesions. For instance, knowing that the patient has joint trauma should make the agents increase their belief in her suffering pain.

However, in order to perform deduction across the boundaries of their individual knowledge, the agents need to exchange information. Agent A can calculate the probability of loose knee bodies, arthritis and vasculitis, but nothing can be said about the belief in pain, or the possibility of vasculitic lesions unless this information is passed on to agents B and C. Moreover, unless the agents exchange information, nothing can be said about how these quantities will change when it is established, for instance, that the patient in question is suffering from Sjorgen's syndrome. Because all the information is represented using different formalisms, it is not possible for the multi-agent system to make these sort of cross-deductions in a direct way; in order for the overall system to perform reasoning we need some kind of integration between the different formalisms.

Two solutions are commonly employed in the DAI literature. The first one is to provide each agent with the ability to translate knowledge (and uncertainty) expressed in its own language into the language of any agent it needs to communicate with, and *vice-versa*. The complexity of this solution quickly becomes prohibitive as the number of agents grows. Moreover, translating from one formalism to another is not always feasible, and may introduce arbitrary assumptions (e.g., assumptions of equiprobability).

The second solution is to develop a common knowledge representation language, or *interlingua*, and require all inter-agent communications to use this interlingua [2]. Although this solution is in general less expensive than the previous one, its cost can still be very high, and developing an interlingua that is powerful enough to subsume each of the individual languages may be unfeasible. An alternative approach is to adopt an interlingua that is weak enough to be subsumed by all of the agents' languages. In the remainder of this paper we outline a technique of this kind that may be used to integrate different uncertainty representation formalisms, and discuss it in the context of the example given above. Space restrictions unfortunately limit the discussion, but more detail may be found in [6] and proofs of all results may be found in [7].

3 Integrating the Formalisms

Our approach to integrate different uncertainty handling formalisms is grounded on the notion of *degrading*: given a representation of uncertainty, we degrade its information content to a level that can be shared between all the different formalisms; this degraded information is then communicated between agents. We represent degraded uncertainty as qualitative changes: given knowledge of conditional probabilities, possibilities and beliefs relating a set of hypotheses, we focus on how the probabilities, possibilities and beliefs will change when we have new evidence. More precisely, we use the conditional values to establish the qualitative values of the derivatives that relate the probabilities, possibilities and beliefs, that is to establish whether the derivatives are positive [+], negative [−] or zero [0]. The derivatives tell us how changes in value move through a network. This method of integration is fully described elsewhere [6, 7]

Consider three variables A, B, and C related such that if $p(A)$ increases, $p(B)$ decreases, and if $bel(B)$ increases, $bel(C)$ increases. In other words, $\left[\frac{\partial p(B)}{\partial p(A)}\right] = [-]$ and $\left[\frac{\partial bel(C)}{\partial bel(B)}\right] = [+]$. These derivatives allow us to propagate changes in value from node to node so that given $\Delta p(A)$ we can establish $\Delta p(B)$, and if we know $\Delta bel(B)$ we can establish $\Delta bel(C)$. If we accept the following *monotonicity assumption*:

> If the value of a hypothesis in one formalism increases, the value of the same hypothesis in any other formalism does not decrease,

then we can use the qualitative changes to integrate different formalisms as follows. If we have $\Delta p(A) = [+]$ then $\Delta p(B) = [-]$. Now, from $\Delta p(B) = [-]$, we know that $\Delta bel(B) = [-]$ or $[0]$, and so we can establish that $bel(C) = [-]$ or $[0]$. Other translations may be carried out in exactly the same manner.

So to come back to our example, the agent that deals with probabilistic knowledge knows that $\Delta p(s) = [+]$, $\Delta p(t) = [0]$ and $\Delta p(d) = [0]$ since the only change that it knows about is that the patient is now observed to be suffering from Sjorgen's syndrome. Since a change of [0] can never become a change of [+] or [−] [6] it can ignore the latter changes, and using the fact that $p(x)+p(\neg x) = 1$ for all x it knows that $\Delta p(\neg s) = [-]$. Now, Theorems 3.1 and 5.1 from [7] establish the qualitative derivatives that link V and A to S from the values of Table 1. These results are that:

$$\left[\frac{\partial p(v)}{\partial p(s)}\right] = [-], \left[\frac{\partial p(v)}{\partial p(\neg s)}\right] = [+], \left[\frac{\partial p(a)}{\partial p(s)}\right] = [+], \text{and } \left[\frac{\partial p(a)}{\partial p(\neg s)}\right] = [-],$$

so that $\Delta p(a) = [+]$, and $\Delta p(v) = [-]$ from which it is possible to deduce that $\Delta p(\neg a) = [-]$ and $\Delta p(\neg v) = [+]$. These results may then be passed to the agents that deal with possibilities and beliefs. Using the monotonicity assumption these agents know that if the probability of a hypothesis increases then both the possibility of that hypothesis and the belief in it do not decrease. Similarly if the probability decreases then the possibility and belief do not increase. Thus the agent that handles beliefs knows that $\Delta bel(a) = [+]$ or $[0]$, $\Delta bel(\neg a) = [-]$ or $[0]$ while the agent that deals with possibilities knows that $\Delta \Pi(v) = [-]$ or $[0]$ and $\Delta \Pi(\neg v) = [+]$ or $[0]$. Now, Theorem 5.3 in [7], when applied to the values in Table 1. gives:

$$\left[\frac{\partial bel(p)}{\partial bel(a)}\right] = [+], \left[\frac{\partial bel(p)}{\partial bel(\neg a)}\right] = [0], \left[\frac{\partial bel(\neg p)}{\partial bel(a)}\right] = [-], \text{and} \left[\frac{\partial bel(\neg p)}{\partial bel(\neg a)}\right] = [+],$$

Thus the agent that deals with beliefs can tell that $\Delta bel(p) = [+]$ or $[0]$ and $\Delta bel(\neg p) = [-]$ or $[0]$. Since the agent that deals with possibility is initially ignorant about the possibility of vasculitis, we have $\Pi(v) = \Pi(\neg v) = 1$, and Theorem 3.2 in [7] gives:

$$\left[\frac{\partial \Pi(l)}{\partial \Pi(v)}\right] = [0], \left[\frac{\partial \Pi(l)}{\partial \Pi(\neg v)}\right] = [0], \left[\frac{\partial \Pi(\neg l)}{\partial \Pi(v)}\right] = [0], \text{and} \left[\frac{\partial \Pi(\neg l)}{\partial \Pi(\neg v)}\right] = [0],$$

with the result that $\Delta \Pi(v) = \Delta \Pi(\neg v) = [0]$. Thus the result of the new evidence about the patient's suffering from Sjorgen's syndrome is that belief in the patient's pain may increase, while the possibility of the patient having vasculitic lesions is unaffected. Notice that the achievement of this conclusion has required the integration of the knowledge available to different agents, and would otherwise have been beyond the system. As discussed in [6] it is also possible to integrate while performing diagnostic reasoning from observations about P and L to learn something about $p(t)$ and $p(s)$

4 Discussion

We have outlined a scheme for integrating uncertainty handling formalisms, in the setting of distributed artificial intelligence, as a means of enabling communication between intelligent agents. The integration is qualitative and is based upon the analysis of the relationships between variables in probability, possibility and evidence theories, and what we have called the monotonicity assumption. Two important issues arise from this integration: the validity of the monotonicity assumption, and the usefulness of the qualitative results.

There are several informal arguments that may be made in favour of the monotonicity assumption (as well as more formal ones — see [6]). Firstly, this assumption seems to be intuitively acceptable as a principle of coherence. Similar principles have been proposed for the relation between probability and possibility [10], and between subjective and objective probability [3]. Secondly, and perhaps more importantly, this seems to be the weakest assumption that allows some form of integration. In fact, relaxing this assumption would eliminate any constraint between values of belief in different formalism, and render any communication content free, and strengthening it would lead to the introduction of spurious information in certain cases.

As for the usefulness of the qualitative results, it is clear that the kind of qualitative integration introduced above is extremely weak, and will never produce as accurate results as a complete numerical integration because the method

suffers from the usual problems of qualitative reasoning. The qualitative integration can only say that a value increases, decreases or does not change, and
so cannot distinguish an increase of 0.01 from an increase of 0.99. Furthermore,
the combination of an increase and decrease in value of a single variable due to
two pieces of evidence will always give [?] indicating that it is impossible to say
what the overall change is.

However, despite these disadvantages, qualitative integration is worthwhile. It
provides information that could not otherwise be obtained, allowing co-operation
between intelligent systems that would otherwise be impossible. Furthermore,
the kind of qualitative indications provided by the system are easy to understand
and so can be extremely helpful in assisting human decision makers, for instance
in analyzing the possible consequences of a therapeutic treatment. Finally, it
is possible to improve the precision of the results generated by the qualitative
integration, by combining qualitative and quantitative information. In particular
it is possible to use interval analysis to handle the bounds on the values of
probability, possibility and belief values after integration [6].

Acknowledgements: the work described in this paper was partly supported
by a grant from ESPRIT Basic Research Action 3085, DRUMS.

References

1. Agustí-Cullell, J., Esteva, F., García, P., Godó, L., Sierra, C. Combining Multiple-
valued logics in modular expert systems, *Proceedings of the 7th Conference on Uncertainty in Artificial Intelligence*, (1991).
2. Avouris, N. M. and Gasser, L. (eds.) *Distributed Artificial Intelligence; Theory and
Praxis*, Kluwer Academic Press, (1992).
3. De Finetti, B. Sul significato soggettivo della probabilità, *Fundamenta Mathematica*
17 (1931) 298–329.
4. Dubois, D. and Prade, H. Possibility Theory: An Approach to Computerized Processing of Uncertainty, Plenum Press, New York, (1988).
5. Glowinski, A. O'Neil, M., Fox, J. Design of a generic information system and its
application to Primary Care, *Proceedings of the European Conference on Artificial
Intelligence in Medicine*, (1989).
6. Parsons, S. Qualitative methods for reasoning under uncertainty, PhD. Thesis, Department of Electronic Engineering, Queen Mary and Westfield College, (1993)
7. Parsons, S. and Mamdani, E. H. On reasoning in networks with qualitative uncertainty, *Proceedings of the 9th Conference on Uncertainty in Artificial Intelligence*,
(1993).
8. Saffiotti, A. An AI view of the treatment of uncertainty, *The Knowledge Engineering
Review*, **2**(2) (1987) 75–97.
9. Shafer, G. *A mathematical theory of evidence*, Princeton University Press, (1976).
10. Zadeh, L. A. Fuzzy sets as the basis for a theory of possibility, *Fuzzy sets and
systems*, **1** (1978) 1–28.
11. Zhang, C. Cooperation under uncertainty in distributed expert systems, *Artificial
Intelligence*, **56** (1992) 21–69.

Variations of constrained default logic

Torsten Schaub

IRISA
Campus de Beaulieu
F-35042 Rennes Cedex

Abstract. Recently a variant of Reiter's default logic, called constrained default logic, has been developed in order to overcome certain short-comings of the original approach. In this paper, we introduce a very simple but powerful extension of constrained default logic, called pre-constrained default logic. We demonstrate that adding certain pre-constraints to default theories results in very expressive systems: Apart from representing heuristic control information, pre-constraints provide simple mechanisms for dealing with default lemmas and for incorporating priorities. Finally, we describe how pre-constrained default logic is related to other well-known approaches.

1 Default logics

Constrained default logic, or ConDL, has been introduced in [8, 2] in order to overcome several technical and counterintuitive shortcomings of Reiter's original default logic [7], DL say. As a result, ConDL possesses several desirable properties. For instance, ConDL guarantees the existence of extensions (ie. sets of default conclusions), ConDL is semi-monotonic, which is indispensable for reasonable proof procedures, and it commits to assumptions, ie. it rejects conclusions based on contradictory consistency assumptions.

Now, let us fathom out the technical reason for these improvements: In default logics, knowledge is represented by *default theories* (D, W), which consist of a set of *facts* W and a set of defaults D. A default is of the form $\frac{\alpha : \beta}{\gamma}$; it applies if its *prerequisite* α is provable from the extension and its *justification* β is consistent in a certain way. A set of conclusions sanctioned by a given set of defaults is called an *extension*.

In DL, informally, an extension E of a default theory (D, W) is the smallest deductively closed set of (closed) formulas[1] containing W such that for any $\frac{\alpha : \beta}{\gamma} \in D$, if $\alpha \in E$ and $\neg\beta \notin E$ then $\gamma \in E$. As mentioned above, this definition leads to several difficulties. As argued in [1, 9, 2], these difficulties are mainly caused by DL's poor treatment of implicit consistency assumptions.

Consider a variant of the so-called "broken arms" example [6]: By default a robot's arms, a_1 and a_2 say, are usable, $U(x)$, unless they are broken, $B(x)$:

$$D = \left\{ \frac{: U(a_1) \wedge \neg B(a_1)}{U(a_1)}, \frac{: U(a_2) \wedge \neg B(a_2)}{U(a_2)} \right\}$$

Suppose a technician tells you that (at least) one of Roby's arms is broken but she cannot remember which: $W = \{B(a_1) \vee B(a_2)\}$.

---

[1] We refer to sentences as formulas instead of closed formulas.

In DL, we get one extension containing $U(a_1) \wedge U(a_2)$. Thus, the preceding theory directs us to conclude that both arms are usable, even though one of them is known to be broken. From a technical point of view, the difficulty is that in DL justifications need only be individually consistent with an extension. This results in conclusions based on contradictory consistency assumptions [6].

Among others, this phenomenon is addressed in ConDL. The basic idea is to distinguish between an extension and its underlying constraints given by the justifications of all applying defaults. Informally, a so-called constrained extension (E, C) of a default theory (D, W) is the pair of smallest deductively closed sets of formulas containing W such that for any $\frac{\alpha : \beta}{\gamma} \in D$, if $\alpha \in E$ and $\neg(\beta \wedge \gamma) \notin C$ then $\gamma \in E$ and $\beta \wedge \gamma \in C$. The constraints C consist of the extension E along with all justifications of all applying defaults. This enforces the joint consistency of the justifications of the applying defaults with an extension at hand.

Indeed, ConDL yields two constrained extensions in the previous example: One containing $U(a_1)$ constrained by $\neg B(a_1)$ and $B(a_2)$ and another one containing $U(a_2)$ constrained by $\neg B(a_2)$ and $B(a_1)$. In both cases the inapplicable default is blocked since its justification is inconsistent with the given constraints.

The example shows how constraints avoid the usage of incompatible justifications. However, the constraints are accumulated dynamically while forming an extension. In particular, there are yet no means of controlling this process. Also, more freedom would be desirable: One might only be interested in certain scenarios while suppressing others. This is addressed in Section 2 in a straightforward way by supplementing each default theory with certain pre-constraints. Despite its simplicity, this approach offers several opportunities: Apart from focussing on certain scenarios, it provides a simple approach for handling default lemmas. In addition, it allows for characterizing Theorist [5] in an arguably simpler way than other proposals. Also, we obtain an exact correspondence to a variant of DL due to Brewka [1], as shown in Section 3. Finally, we show in Section 4 that the approach offers an elegant way of incorporating priorities into default logics and show how this variation is related to the preferred subtheory approach [1].

2 Pre-constrained default logic

We introduce a very simple yet powerful extension of ConDL, called *pre-constrained default logic* or PreConDL. The basic idea is to supplement the constraints found in a constrained extension with some kind of *pre-constraints*. The purpose of pre-constraints is to direct the reasoning process by enforcing their consistency. In other words, the context of reasoning becomes predetermined and therefore dominated by some given consistency requirements.

A *pre-constrained default theory* (D, W, C_P) consists of a set of formulas W, a set of defaults D, and a set of formulas C_P representing the pre-constraints. In order to ensure that pre-constraints do not introduce any inconsistencies, we require that $W \cup C_P$ being inconsistent implies W being inconsistent.

Definition 2.1 *Let* (D, W, C_P) *be a pre-constrained default theory and let* E *and* C *be sets of formulas. Define* $E_0 = W$ *and* $C_0 = W \cup C_P$ *and for* $i \geq 0$

$$E_{i+1} = \mathit{Th}(E_i) \cup \left\{ \ \gamma \ \mid \frac{\alpha : \beta}{\gamma} \in D, \alpha \in E_i, C \cup \{\beta\} \cup \{\gamma\} \not\vdash \bot \right\}$$
$$C_{i+1} = \mathit{Th}(C_i) \cup \left\{ \beta \wedge \gamma \mid \frac{\alpha : \beta}{\gamma} \in D, \alpha \in E_i, C \cup \{\beta\} \cup \{\gamma\} \not\vdash \bot \right\}$$

(E, C) *is a pre-constrained extension of* (D, W) *iff* $(E, C) = (\bigcup_{i=0}^{\infty} E_i, \bigcup_{i=0}^{\infty} C_i)$.

Observe that the pre-constraints C_P enter merely the constraints C and not the extension E. Thus, pre-constraints direct the reasoning process without actually becoming a part of it. Notice furthermore that adding pre-constraints never increases the number of applying defaults.

The step from ConDL to PreConDL is so small that all of the properties of ConDL carry over to its pre-constrained counterpart. This extremely tight relationship becomes even more apparent by the fact that pre-constrained extensions can be computed in ConDL. The idea is to shift the information given by the pre-constraints to the justifications of the defaults:

Theorem 2.1 *Let* (D, W, C_P) *be a pre-constrained default theory and let*

$$D' = \left\{ \frac{\alpha : \beta \wedge \widehat{C}_P}{\gamma} \ \middle| \ \frac{\alpha : \beta}{\gamma} \in D \right\} \cup \left\{ \frac{: \widehat{C}_P}{\top} \right\},$$

where $\widehat{C}_P$ *is the conjunction of all formulas contained in a finite set of pre-constraints* C_P. *Let* E *and* C *be sets of formulas. Then,* (E, C) *is a pre-constrained extension of* (D, W, C_P) *iff* (E, C) *is a constrained extension of* (D', W).

The purpose of the synthetic default $\frac{: \widehat{C}_P}{\top}$ (where $\top$ is any tautology) is to add the pre-constraints C_P to the resulting constraints C if no other default applies.

The use of pre-constraints allows for many interesting enhancements of the original approach. First of all, notice that pre-constraints usually reduce the number of extensions. This is similar to the use of constraints in Theorist [5], in the sense of providing means to suppress undesirable extensions. Consider our previous example. Suppose now that experience shows that a_1 is very reliable, so that we want to focus on scenarios in which a_1 is not broken (without actually asserting this heuristic information within the facts). This can be achieved by adding $\neg B(a_1)$ to the pre-constraints, which results in the following pre-constrained default theory:

$$\left(\left\{ \frac{: U(a_1) \wedge \neg B(a_1)}{U(a_1)}, \frac{: U(a_2) \wedge \neg B(a_2)}{U(a_2)} \right\}, \{B(a_1) \vee B(a_2)\}, \{\neg B(a_1)\} \right)$$

We obtain only one pre-constrained extension asserting $U(a_1)$ constrained by $\neg B(a_1)$ and $B(a_2)$; this corresponds to the first constrained extension obtained previously. Note that adding a default $\frac{: \neg B(a_1)}{\neg B(a_1)}$, saying that usually a_1 is not broken, would not eliminate the second constrained extension obtained above.

A more sophisticated way of incorporating heuristic control information can be achieved by naming defaults with certain applicability predicates [1], followed by an axiomatization of this control information using pre-constraints. Consider the statements "students are typically adults", "adults are typically employed", and "students are typically not employed" along with the corresponding default theory: $\left(\left\{ \frac{S : A}{A}, \frac{A : E}{E}, \frac{S : \neg E}{\neg E} \right\}, \{S\} \right)$. Since default logics cannot deal with specificity, this theory gives two extensions, $\mathit{Th}(\{A, \neg E, S\})$ and $\mathit{Th}(\{A, E, S\})$.

Brewka [1] would address this problem by supplementing each justification of a default with an applicability proposition, say A_1, A_2, and A_3, along with an additional fact, $S \rightarrow \neg A_2$, saying that the second default should not apply for students. However, this axiom should not appear in the facts since it is pure control information concerned with applicability. Now, this can be avoided in PreConDL by adding the aforementioned axiom to the pre-constraints and introducing Brewka's applicability propositions:

$$\left(\left\{ \frac{S : A \wedge A_1}{A}, \frac{A : E \wedge A_2}{E}, \frac{S : \neg E \wedge A_3}{\neg E} \right\}, \{S\}, \{S \rightarrow \neg A_2\} \right)$$

This default theory yields the more specific extension $Th(\{A, \neg E, S\})$ constrained by $S \rightarrow \neg A_2$, among others. In this way, we can adopt Brewka's method without mixing up world knowledge with control knowledge.

Also, PreConDL offers a simple solution for handling default lemmas. As shown in [4][2], adding a default conclusion to the facts of a default theory may change the set of derivable conclusions. This prevents us from turning default conclusions into default lemmas for reducing computational efforts. As shown in [1], this failure stems from the inability to account for the consistency assumptions underlying a default conclusion whenever we are adding it to the facts. In PreConDL, this shortcoming can be addressed by additionally taking the consistency assumptions underlying a conclusion and adding them to the pre-constraints. This way, pre-constraints serve as a means to accumulate the consistency assumptions underlying any lemmatized default conclusion. Thus, turning a default conclusion into a default lemma is performed by adding the actual lemma to the facts, and its underlying consistency assumptions to the pre-constraints.

Let us see what happens while lemmatizing a default conclusion according to the above recipe. The pre-constrained default theory [4] $\left(\left\{ \frac{:A}{A}, \frac{A \vee B : \neg A}{\neg A} \right\}, \emptyset, \emptyset \right)$ has one extension: $Th(\{A\})$. Lemmatizing the default conclusion $A \vee B$ by simply adding $A \vee B$ to the facts results in an additional extension $Th(\{\neg A, B\})$ since the second default becomes applicable. Accordingly, we have changed the set of derivable conclusions. However, lemmatizing $A \vee B$ as described above yields a pre-constrained default theory, whose facts contain the default lemma $A \vee B$ and whose pre-constraints contain the consistency assumptions made while deriving it. These are given by the justification A of the default $\frac{:A}{A}$. This yields

$$\left(\left\{ \frac{:A}{A}, \frac{A \vee B : \neg A}{\neg A} \right\}, \{A \vee B\}, \{A\} \right)$$

which has the same extension and no others. Even though the prerequisite of the default $\frac{A \vee B : \neg A}{\neg A}$ is now derivable, its justification is inconsistent with the pre-constraints. So, this default is blocked and does not produce a second extension.

In order to lemmatize a default conclusion α in general, we have to take α, a minimal set of defaults D_α used for deriving α, and then we add α to the facts and add the justifications and consequents of the defaults in D_α to the pre-constraints. This approach does neither produce any new nor modify any previous extensions.

---

[2] We shall not deal with the formal property of cumulativity, which causes this failure.

This solution offers the following advantages. First, the approach simply deals with first-order formulas and thus avoids extra-logical formalisms as lemma default rules (cf. [9]), or an extended language as cumulative default logic [1], CumDL say. Second, the use of pre-constraints eliminates extensions which are inconsistent with the default lemma or even its underlying assumptions. However, we encounter the same drawback as found in CumDL [1]: We obtain an inconsistent system whenever we are faced with new facts contradicting formerly lemmatized conclusions or their underlying assumptions.

3 Relationships to other approaches

The idea of constraining nonmonotonic theories is quite similar to Theorist [5]. There, defaults are usually named; constraints refer to these names in order to direct the reasoning process. Formally, a *Theorist system* is a triple $(\mathcal{F}, \Delta, \mathcal{C})$ of sets of formulas, where $\mathcal{F}$ represents *facts*, Δ represents *defaults*, and $\mathcal{C}$ is a set of *constraints*.[3] In this approach, any default may be assumed as long as it is consistent with the facts and the constraints. Accordingly, a set of formulas E is a *Theorist extension* iff $E = Th(\mathcal{F} \cup \Delta')$ for a maximal $\Delta' \subseteq \Delta$ such that $\mathcal{F} \cup \Delta' \cup \mathcal{C}$ is consistent.

As an example, consider the following Theorist system, (T) say, in which the "actual defaults" $A \to C$ and $B \to \neg C$ are named by $n_{A \to C}$ and $n_{B \to \neg C}$:

$$\left(\left\{ \begin{array}{l} A, B, \\ n_{A \to C} \to (A \to C), \\ n_{B \to \neg C} \to (B \to \neg C) \end{array} \right\}, \left\{ \begin{array}{l} n_{A \to C}, \\ n_{B \to \neg C} \end{array} \right\}, \{ C \to \neg n_{B \to \neg C} \} \right)$$

We obtain two Theorist extensions from (T): One contains $n_{A \to C}$ and C, and the other one contains $n_{B \to \neg C}$ and $\neg C$.

Now, we turn to the relationship between Theorist and DL: Poole [5] has shown that Theorist systems of the form $(\mathcal{F}, \Delta, \emptyset)$ correspond to default theories of the form $(\{ \frac{:\gamma}{\gamma} \mid \gamma \in \Delta \}, \mathcal{F})$ and vice versa. The interesting case is, however, Theorist with constraints. Independently, [1] and [3] have shown that Theorist systems of the form $(\mathcal{F}, \Delta, \mathcal{C})$ correspond to default theories of the form $(\{ \frac{:\gamma \wedge \widehat{C}}{\gamma} \mid \gamma \in \Delta \}, \mathcal{F})$ and vice versa, where $\widehat{C}$ is the conjunction of all formulas in $\mathcal{C}$.

Interestingly, there are three ways of establishing correspondences between Theorist systems with constraints and restricted default theories in (Pre)ConDL. First of all, notice that the above equivalences carry over to ConDL. The next default theory shows the translation of the Theorist system (T) into a prerequisite-free default theory, as described in [1, 3]:

$$\left(\left\{ \begin{array}{l} \frac{:n_{A \to C} \wedge (C \to \neg n_{B \to \neg C})}{n_{A \to C}}, \\ \frac{:n_{B \to \neg C} \wedge (\widehat{C} \to \neg n_{B \to \neg C})}{n_{B \to \neg C}} \end{array} \right\}, \left\{ \begin{array}{l} A, B, \\ n_{A \to C} \to (A \to C), \\ n_{B \to \neg C} \to (B \to \neg C) \end{array} \right\} \right)$$

Clearly, we obtain the same two extensions from this default theory. However, this translation introduces a tremendous amount of redundancy since the constraints of the Theorist system are copied to each justification of each default.

---

[3] In what follows, we expect $\mathcal{C}$ to be consistent with $\mathcal{F}$.

Fortunately, there is a more compact representation in PreConDL: Theorist systems with constraints turn out to be equivalent to prerequisite-free normal default theories in PreConDL in the following sense:

Theorem 3.1 *Let W, E, C, C_P and Δ be sets of formulas and let $D = \{\frac{:\beta}{\beta} \mid \beta \in \Delta\}$. Then, (E, C) is a pre-constrained extension of (D, W, C_P) iff E is a Theorist extension of (W, Δ, C_P).*

Then, the Theorist system (T) yields the pre-constrained default theory

$$\left(\left\{ \begin{array}{c} \frac{:n_{A \to C}}{n_{A \to C}}, \\ \frac{:n_{B \to \neg C}}{n_{B \to \neg C}} \end{array} \right\}, \left\{ \begin{array}{c} A, B, \\ n_{A \to C} \to (A \to C), \\ n_{B \to \neg C} \to (B \to \neg C) \end{array} \right\}, \{C \to \neg n_{B \to \neg C}\} \right)$$

along with the above extensions. We observe that this transformation into PreConDL is closer to the Theorist system (T) than the one into "usual" (Con)DL. As in Theorist, the constraints are kept separately from the defaults by means of pre-constraints. This seems to be preferable to the approach taken in [1, 3], where the constraints are duplicated in order to become a part of the justifications of the defaults. Consequently, PreConDL seems to be better suited for capturing Theorist then ordinary (Con)DL.

A third translation between ConDL and Theorist has been proposed in [2]. However, this translation is not fully bidirectional: It is restricted to certain Theorist systems since it aims at eliminating names, like $n_{B \to \neg C}$, found in Theorist.

Another closely related approach is CumDL [1] where assertions, ie. formulas labeled with the justifications and consequents of applied defaults (eg. $\langle \alpha, \{\alpha_1, \ldots, \alpha_n\} \rangle$), are used. An assertional default theory is a pair (D, W), where D is a set of defaults and W is a set of assertions. Informally, an assertional extension of (D, W) is the smallest set of assertions $\mathcal{E}$ being deductively closed under an extended[4] theory operator $\widehat{Th}$ and containing W such that for any $\frac{\alpha : \beta}{\gamma} \in D$, if $\langle \alpha, Supp(\alpha) \rangle \in \mathcal{E}$ and $Form(\mathcal{E}) \cup Supp(\mathcal{E}) \cup \{\beta, \gamma\} \nvdash \perp$ then $\langle \gamma, Supp(\alpha) \cup \{\beta, \gamma\} \rangle \in \mathcal{E}$.

A relationship between ConDL and CumDL was stated in [9] for assertional default theories (D, W) having non-supported facts, ie. $Supp(W) = \emptyset$. An even closer relationship is given between PreConDL and CumDL for supported facts:

Theorem 3.2 *Let (D, W, C_P) be a pre-constrained default theory and (D, W) an assertional default theory such that $W = Form(W)$ and $C_P = Supp(W)$. Then, if (E, C) is a pre-constrained extension of (D, W, C_P) then there is an assertional extension $\mathcal{E}$ of (D, W) such that $E = Form(\mathcal{E})$ and $C = Th(Form(\mathcal{E}) \cup Supp(\mathcal{E}))$; and, if $\mathcal{E}$ is an assertional extension of (D, W) then $(Form(\mathcal{E}), Th(Form(\mathcal{E}) \cup Supp(\mathcal{E})))$ is a pre-constrained extension of (D, W, C_P).*

As in the case of Theorist, it appears that PreConDL is better suited to account for a related approach, here CumDL, then ordinary ConDL.

---

[4] Let $Form(\xi)$ be the asserted formula and $Supp(\xi)$ the support of an assertion ξ: if $\xi_1, \ldots, \xi_n \in \widehat{Th}(\mathcal{S})$ and $Form(\xi_1), \ldots, Form(\xi_n) \vdash \alpha$ then $\langle \alpha, \cup_{i=1}^{n} Supp(\xi_i) \rangle \in \widehat{Th}(\mathcal{S})$.

4 Prioritized constrained default logic

Usually, priorities reduce the number of solutions and often lead to more plausible results. So far, there was no way to incorporate priorities into ConDL. This gap is addressed below by building on PreConDL: A *prioritized default theory* $(\tilde{D}, W)$ consists of a set of formulas W and a *sequence* of finite sets of defaults $\tilde{D} = \langle D_0, \ldots, D_m \rangle$ representing a hierarchy of sets of defaults. The defaults in a layer D_i are meant to have a higher priority than those in a layer D_j provided that $j > i$. Where $GD_D^{(E,C)} = \{ \frac{\alpha \,:\, \beta}{\gamma} \in D \mid \alpha \in E, \neg(\beta \wedge \gamma) \notin C \}$ and *Justif* and *Conseq* give the justifications and consequents of a set of defaults, a *prioritized constrained extension* is defined as follows.

Definition 4.1 *Let* $(\langle D_0, \ldots, D_m \rangle, W)$ *be a prioritized default theory and let* E *and* C *be sets of formulas. Define* (E_0, C_0) *to be a constrained extension of* (D_0, W) *and for* $i \geq 0$ (E_{i+1}, C_{i+1}) *to be a pre-constrained extension of*

$$\left(\bigcup_{j=0}^{i+1} D_j, W \cup Conseq\left(GD_{\cup_{j=0}^{i} D_j}^{(E_i, C_i)} \right), Justif\left(GD_{\cup_{j=0}^{i} D_j}^{(E_i, C_i)} \right) \right)$$

(E, C) *is a prioritized constrained extension of* $(\langle D_0, \ldots, D_m \rangle, W)$ *iff* $(E, C) = (\bigcup_{i=0}^{m} E_i, \bigcup_{i=0}^{m} C_i)$.

Notice that each "layer" admits several extensions which themselves may produce multiple extensions. Observe also that by semi-monotonicity every prioritized constrained extension is also a constrained extension but not vice versa:

Theorem 4.1 *Let* $(\tilde{D}, W)$ *be a prioritized default theory such that* $\tilde{D} = \langle D_0, \ldots, D_m \rangle$ *and let* E *and* C *be sets of formulas. If* (E, C) *is a prioritized constrained extension of* $(\tilde{D}, W)$, *then* (E, C) *is a constrained extension of the default theory* $(D_1 \cup \ldots \cup D_m, W)$.

Note that this theorem does not hold for a prioritized variant of DL proposed in [1], since DL does not enjoy semi-monotonicity. Another interesting point in Definition 4.1 is that a default in D_i may contribute to all partial constrained extensions (E_j, C_j) where $j > i$. Again, this is different from [1], where the application of defaults whose prerequisite is derived in a "higher" layer is impossible.

In order to illustrate our approach briefly, let us reconsider the "broken arms" example: A more elegant way of expressing the fact that the robot arm a_1 is more reliable than a_2 is to give the first default priority over the second one:

$$\left(\left\langle \left\{ \frac{:U(a_1) \wedge \neg B(a_1)}{U(a_1)} \right\}, \left\{ \frac{:U(a_2) \wedge \neg B(a_2)}{U(a_2)} \right\} \right\rangle, \{ B(a_1) \vee B(a_2) \} \right)$$

In a first step, we consider the default theory $(\{ \frac{:U(a_1) \wedge \neg B(a_1)}{U(a_1)} \}, \{ B(a_1) \vee B(a_2) \})$ yielding a single constrained extension containing $U(a_1)$ constrained by $\neg B(a_1)$ and $B(a_2)$. In a second step, we get the same conclusions from

$$\left(\left\{ \frac{:U(a_1) \wedge \neg B(a_1)}{U(a_1)}, \frac{:U(a_2) \wedge \neg B(a_2)}{U(a_2)} \right\}, \{ B(a_1) \vee B(a_2), U(a_1) \}, \{ U(a_1) \wedge \neg B(a_1) \} \right)$$

since the second default is blocked by the pre-contraints accumulated so far.

Our approach is similar to Brewka's preferred subtheories [1] in introducing a hierarchy which serves as a total order on sets of defaults. In fact, it subsumes the approach taken by preferred subtheories: Given a sequence of sets of formulas $\tilde{T} = \langle T_0, \ldots, T_m \rangle$, then $S = \bigcup_{i=0}^{m} S_i$ is a preferred subtheory of $\tilde{T}$ iff $\bigcup_{i=0}^{j} S_i$ is a maximal consistent subset of $\bigcup_{i=0}^{j} T_i$ for all $j \in \{0, \ldots, m\}$. Then, we obtain the following result:[5]

Theorem 4.2 *Let* $\tilde{T} = \langle T_0, \ldots, T_m \rangle$ *be a sequence of finite sets of formulas and* $\tilde{D} = \langle D_0, \ldots, D_m \rangle$ *a sequence of sets of defaults such that* $D_i = \{ \frac{:\beta}{\beta} \mid \beta \in T_i \}$ *for all* $i \in \{1, \ldots, m\}$. *Let* E *be a set of formulas. Then,* (E, E) *is a prioritized constrained extension of* $(\tilde{D}, \emptyset)$ *iff* E *is a preferred subtheory of* $\tilde{T}$.

5 Conclusion

We have presented an extremely simple but powerful extension of ConDL: Pre-ConDL accounts for situations in which we want to restrict our reasoning to certain contexts by enforcing reasoning under certain consistency assumptions. We have argued in favor of pre-constraints as a means of controlling the inference process in ConDL. This approach has led to several enhancements of the original approach: Apart from the incorporation of heuristic control information, the approach provides a simple way of handling default lemmas and allows for an elegant way of incorporating priorities into ConDL. Moreover, PreConDL yields more precise relationships to other approaches, like Theorist and CumDL, than obtainable in the original approach. Also, we have shown how these relationships extend to prioritized ConDL and Brewka's preferred subtheory approach.

Acknowledgements

This work was inspired by valuable discussions with G. Brewka and U. Junker. Thanks are also due to A. Rothschild for comments on an earlier draft. This research was supported by the *CEC* within *HCM* under grant ERB4001GT922433.

References

1. G. Brewka. *Nonmonotonic Reasoning: Logical Foundations of Commonsense.* Cambridge University, 1991.
2. J. Delgrande, K. Jackson, T. Schaub. Alternative approaches to default logic. Submitted, June 1992.
3. J. Dix. On cumulativity in default logic and its relation to Poole's approach. In B. Neumann, ed., *Proc. of ECAI'92*, 289-293. Wiley, 1992.
4. D. Makinson. General theory of cumulative inference. In M. Reinfrank et al., eds., *Proc. 2nd NMR Workshop*, 1-18. Springer, 1989.
5. D. Poole. A logical framework for default reasoning. *Artificial Intelligence*, 36:27-47, 1988.
6. D. Poole. What the lottery paradox tells us about default reasoning. In R. Brachman et al., eds., *Proc. of KR'89*, 333-340. Morgan Kaufmann, 1989.
7. R. Reiter. A logic for default reasoning. *Artificial Intelligence*, 13(1-2):81-132, 1980.
8. T. Schaub. On commitment and cumulativity in default logics. In R. Kruse, ed., *Proc. of ECSQAU'91*, 304-309. Springer, 1991.
9. T. Schaub. On constrained default theories. In B. Neumann, ed., *Proc. of ECAI'92*, 304-308. Wiley, 1992.

---

[5] A similar correspondence has been established in [1] between preferred subtheories and the prioritized version of DL proposed in [1].

Information Sets in Decision Theory

Prakash P. Shenoy

School of Business, University of Kansas
Summerfield Hall, Lawrence, KS 66045-2003, USA.
pshenoy@ukanvm.cc.ukans.edu

Abstract. Information sets were first defined by von Neumann and Morgenstern in 1944 in the context of extensive form games. In this paper, we examine the use of information sets for representing Bayesian decision problems. We call a decision tree with information sets a game tree. We also describe a roll-back procedure for solving game trees using local computation.

1 Introduction

Information sets were defined first by von Neumann and Morgenstern [1944] in the context of extensive form games. In 1953, Kuhn proposed a more general definition of extensive form games. Extensive form games were extensively studied in the 1950s and had a strong influence on the decision tree technique for representing and solving decision problems proposed by Raiffa and Schlaifer [1961]. Since a decision problem can be viewed as a game in which there is only one player, the use of information sets in decision theory is natural.

We call a decision tree with information sets *a game tree*. Although there are many features in common between game trees and decision trees, there is a key difference in how information constraints are encoded. In decision trees, information constraints are encoded by the sequencing of the decision and chance nodes in the directed tree. Thus if the true value of a chance variable R is known at the time a value of a decision variable T is chosen, then node R must precede node T in the decision tree. The converse is also true. If the true value of a chance variable R is not known at the time a value of a decision variable T is chosen, then node R must follow node T in the decision tree. In game trees, information constraints are encoded partially by sequencing of chance and decision nodes, and partially by information sets. Thus, as in decision trees, if the true value of a chance variable R is known at the time a value of a decision variable T is chosen, then node R must precede node T in the game tree. The converse is not true. If the true value of a chance variable R is not known at the time a value of a decision variable T is chosen, then node R does not have to follow node T in the game tree. We could have R precede T and use information sets instead to encode the lack of knowledge of R when a value of T has to be chosen.

The added flexibility of game trees in sequencing decision and chance nodes has two important consequences. First, in game trees, we could use the sequence of variables to represent time or causation instead of information. In decision trees, the sequence of nodes must represent information and nothing else. Thus, for example, if variable D (disease, present or not) is the cause of variable S (symptom, exhibited or not), and the decision maker has to make a decision T (to treat or not) after observing the true value of S (but not D), then in a decision tree, the sequence must be STD. In a game tree, however, we could, for example, choose sequence DST which represents time (disease comes first, symptom next, and treatment last).

Second, assuming we have a causal probability model for the chance variables in a decision problem, if we choose to sequence the chance variables to represent causation, then there is no need for Bayesian revision of probabilities for representing a problem as a game tree. The need for Bayesian revision of probabilities in decision tree representation is a major drawback from the viewpoint of artificial intelligence for two important reasons. First, since representation is typically done by humans, and solution by machine, the representation technique should facilitate representation of a problem. Ideally, no preprocessing should be required before we can represent a problem in machine solvable form. Decision trees violate this maxim whereas game trees do not. Second, the Bayesian revision of probabilities required in decision trees can be computationally intractable if the number of chance variables is large. Elsewhere we have shown that most of the computation involved in Bayesian revision of probabilities is unnecessary for solving the problem [Shenoy 1993a].

An outline of this paper is as follows. In Section 2, we describe the oil wildcatter's problem [Raiffa 1967]. This is a small problem involving Bayesian revision of probabilities. We describe the traditional decision tree representation and solution of this problem. In Section 3, we describe a game tree representation and illustrate it using the oil wildcatter's problem. Finally in Section 4, we describe a roll-back method for solving game trees using local computation. Shenoy [1993b] compares game trees to decision trees, influence diagrams, and valuation networks.

2 The Oil Wildcatter's Problem

The oil wildcatter's problem is reproduced with minor modifications from Raiffa [1968]. An oil wildcatter must decide either to drill (d) or not to drill (~d). He is uncertain whether the hole is dry (dr), wet (we) or soaking (so). Table I shows his monetary payoffs and his subjective probabilities of the various states. The cost of drilling is $70,000. The net return associated with the d-we pair is $50,000 that is interpreted as a return of $120,000 less the $70,000 cost of drilling. Similarly the $200,000 associated with the d-so pair is a net return (a return of $270,000 less the $70,000 cost of drilling).

At a cost of $10,000, the wildcatter could take seismic soundings that will help determine the geological structure at the site. The soundings will disclose whether the terrain below has no structure (ns)—that's bad, or open structure (os)—that's so-so, or closed structure (cs)—that's really hopeful. The experts have provided us with Table II that shows the probabilities of seismic test results conditional on the amount of oil.

Figures 1 and 2 show a decision tree representation and solution of this problem. Notice that even before we can completely specify the decision tree, we have to compute the conditional probabilities required by the decision tree (since they are not given in the statement of the problem). This is done in Figure 1. In Figure 1, the probability tree on the left computes the joint probabilities, and the probability tree on the right computes the marginals of test results and the conditional probabilities of amount of oil given test results.

Figure 2 shows the solution of the oil wildcatter's problem using the roll-back procedure. The optimal strategy is to do a seismic test; not drill if seismic test reveals no structure, and drill if the seismic test reveals either open or closed structure. The expected profit associated with this strategy is $22,500.

Table I. The Payoff Matrix for the Oil Wildcatter's Problem

	Wildcatter's profit, $ (π)		Act Drill (d)	Not drill (~d)	Probability of state
State	Dry	(dr)	−70,000	0	0.500
	Wet	(we)	50,000	0	0.300
	Soaking	(so)	200,000	0	0.200

Table II. Probabilities of Seismic Test Results Conditional on the Amount of Oil

P(R I O)			Seismic Test Results (R) No structure (ns)	Open structure (os)	Closed structure (cs)
Amount of Oil (O)	Dry	(dr)	0.600	0.300	0.100
	Wet	(we)	0.300	0.400	0.300
	Soaking	(so)	0.100	0.400	0.500

Figure 1. The preprocessing of probabilities in the oil wildcatter's problem.

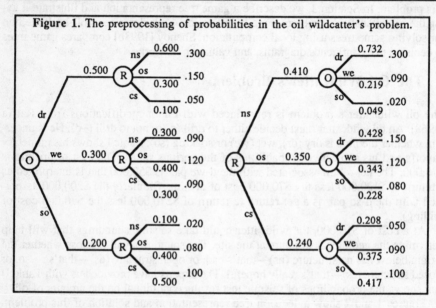

3 Game Tree Representation

In this section, we sketch a game tree representation of a decision problem (see Shenoy [1993b] for details). We use Kuhn's [1953] definition of an extensive form game appropriately modified. In particular, we assume only one player, and we assume perfect recall.

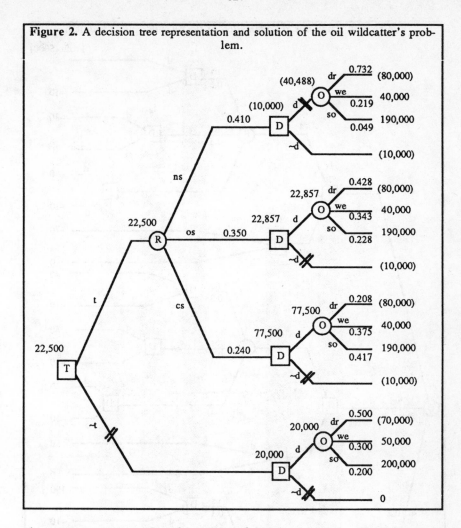

Figure 2. A decision tree representation and solution of the oil wildcatter's problem.

A game tree representation of a decision problem consists of a rooted tree, a utility function on the leaves of the rooted tree, a probability distribution on the edges emanating from a chance node for each chance node, and information sets satisfying some regularity conditions [Kuhn 1953, Hart 1992].

Figure 3 shows a game tree representation of the oil wildcatter's problem. Notice that in the game tree, random variable O (amount of oil) comes before R (test results). Also the decision nodes are partitioned into 5 information sets, I_1, ..., I_5. I_1, for example, encodes the fact that the oil wildcatter does not know the amount of oil at the time he decides whether to conduct a seismic test (t) or not (~t). I_2 encodes the fact that the oil wildcatter knows the decision made at node T (no seismic test, i.e., ~t), but not the amount of oil. At I_3, I_4, and I_5, the oil wildcatter knows the decision at node T (conduct a seismic test, i.e., t), and the test result, but not the amount of oil. Notice that no preprocessing is required to represent the problem as a game tree.

322

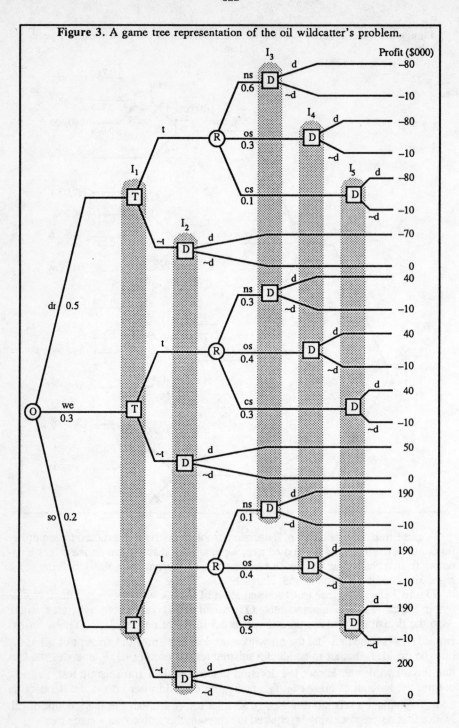

Figure 3. A game tree representation of the oil wildcatter's problem.

4 Game Tree Solution

In this section, we sketch a method for solving a decision problem using local computation starting from its game tree representation (see [Shenoy 1993b] for details).

If each information set is a singleton, then we solve the game tree using the backward recursion method of dynamic programming [Zermelo 1913, Kuhn 1953]. This technique is also called "roll-back procedure" in decision tree literature. A decision tree can be thought of as a game tree in which each information set is a singleton subset.

The backward recursion method of dynamic programming can be generalized to include non-singleton information sets. We start from the neighbors of payoff nodes and go toward the root until the entire tree has been pruned. The rule for pruning chance nodes is exactly the same as in the roll-back procedure of decision trees. The rule for pruning decision nodes is slightly different from the roll-back procedure of decision trees.

Pruning Decision Nodes. The rule for pruning decision nodes in singleton information sets is exactly the same as in decision tree.

Suppose we have a non-singleton information set such that the edges leading out of the decision nodes end at payoff nodes. First, we compute the conditional probability distribution on the decision nodes of the information set conditioned on the event that we have reached the information set (the details of this step are explained in the following paragraph). Second, for each value of the decision variable associated with the information set, we compute the expected payoff using the payoffs at the end of corresponding edges and using the conditional distribution computed in the first step. Third, we identify a value of the decision variable (and the corresponding edges of each decision node) associated with the maximum expected payoff. Fourth, we prune each decision node by replacing the corresponding subtree by a payoff node whose payoff is equal to the payoff at the end of its edge identified in step 3. We call this technique (for pruning decision nodes in an information set) pruning by *maximization of conditional expectation*. Pruning by maximization of conditional expectation generalizes the method of pruning a singleton information set by maximization.

Computing the conditional distribution for an information set is easy. For each decision node in the information set, we simply multiply all probabilities on the edges in the path from the root to the decision node. If the path involves acts, then we assume the probabilities of such edges to be 1. This gives an unconditional distribution on the nodes in the information set. The sum of these probabilities gives us the probability of reaching the information set assuming prior decisions that allow us to get there. To compute the conditional distribution, we normalize this unconditional distribution by dividing by the sum of the probabilities. As we will see, from a computational perspective, the normalization step is unnecessary and can be dispensed with. It is only required for semantical reasons.

We will illustrate pruning decision nodes by conditional expectation for the game tree representation of the oil wildcatter's problem. Consider information set I_5. Notice that all three decision nodes in I_5 have edges leading to payoff nodes. The unconditional distribution for the three nodes in I_5 (from top to bottom) is given by the probability vector $(0.5*0.1, 0.3*0.3, 0.2*0.5) = (0.05, 0.09, 0.10)$. The sum of these probabilities is 0.24. The conditional distribution is given by $(\frac{0.05}{0.24}, \frac{0.09}{0.24}, \frac{0.10}{0.24}) = (0.208, 0.375, 0.417)$. Thus for $D = d$, the expected payoff is $(0.208 *\!-\!80) + (0.375*40) + (0.417*190) = 77.5$, and for $D = \sim\!d$, the expected payoff is $(0.208 *\!-\!10) + (0.375*\!-\!10) + (0.417*\!-\!10) = -10$. Since $77.5 > -10$, we identify edge $D = d$ with each node in I_5.

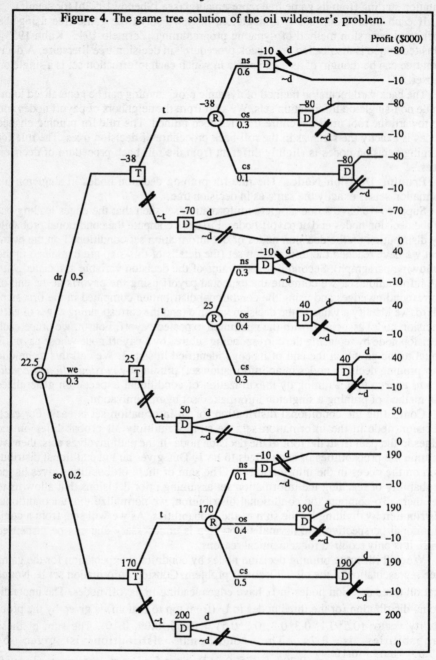

Figure 4. The game tree solution of the oil wildcatter's problem.

Notice that for the purposes of pruning decision nodes in an information set, there is no need to normalize the unconditional distribution. We can compute the "expected payoff" using the unconditional probability distribution since the same normalization constant (that is always positive) can be factored out of all expected values being compared. Thus, solving game trees involves no divisions.

A comment on computing the unconditional probability distribution of an information set. If we have a game tree with many variables, then computing the conditional distribution as described above can be computationally intensive. However, note that we can simplify the computation as follows. If the paths from the root to the decision nodes in an information set share a common sub-path, then the probabilities on the common sub-path can be ignored in computing the conditional distribution. This is because these probabilities get canceled in the normalization process. Furthermore, if the paths from the root to the decision nodes include edges having the same probability, then again, we can ignore these probabilities for the same reason as above. Thus to a limited extent, we can exploit conditional independencies in the joint probability distribution.

Figure 4 shows the result after we prune the entire game tree. The optimal strategy and its expected profit is exactly the same as in the case of the decision tree solution reported in Section 2.

Acknowledgments

This work is based upon work supported in part by the National Science Foundation under Grant No. SES-9213558. I am grateful to referees S. Dittmer and U. G. Oppel for their comments on an earlier draft.

References

Hart, S. (1992), "Games in extensive and strategic forms," in R. J. Aumann and S. Hart (eds.), *Handbook of Game Theory with Economic Applications*, 1, 19–40, North-Holland, Amsterdam.

Kuhn, H. W. (1953), "Extensive games and the problem of information," in H. W. Kuhn and A. W. Tucker (eds.), *Contributions to the Theory of Games*, 2, 193-216, Princeton University Press, Princeton, NJ.

Raiffa, H. and R. O. Schlaifer (1961), *Applied Statistical Decision Theory*, Harvard Business School, Cambridge, MA.

Raiffa, H. (1967), *Decision Analysis: Introductory Lectures on Choices Under Uncertainty*, Addison-Wesley, Reading, MA.

Shenoy, P. P. (1993a), "A comparison of graphical techniques for decision analysis," *European Journal of Operational Research*, in press.

Shenoy, P. P. (1993b), "Game trees for decision analysis," Working Paper No. 239, School of Business, University of Kansas, Lawrence, KS.

von Neumann, J. and O. Morgenstern (1944), *Theory of Games and Economic Behavior*, 1st edition (2nd edition 1947, 3rd edition 1953), Princeton University Press, Princeton, NJ.

Zermelo, E. (1913), "Uber eine anwendung der mengenlehre auf die theorie des schachspiels," *Proceedings of the Fifth International Congress of Mathematics*, Cambridge, U.K., 2, 501-504.

The Preferential Semantics of A Multi-Modal Nonmonotonic Logic*

Hua Shu

Dept. of Computer Science and Business Administration

University of Karlskrona/Ronneby

S-372 25 Ronneby, Sweden

Abstract: In this paper, we present a preferential semantics of a multi-modal nonmonotonic logic. By distinguishing different levels of nonmonotonicity exhibited by modal nonmonotonic logics, we argue that the previously constructed modal non-monotonic logics (e.g. McDermott's nonmonotonic logic and Moore's autoepistemic logic) are mostly concerned with a level of nonmonotonicity that is dependent on the underlying modal systems. There is, however, another level of nonmonotonicity that is by itself independent on the underlying modal system. Modal logics constructed to exhibit the latter level of nonmonotonicity are dependent on the conventions imposed at the level of meta-language.

1 Introduction

In constructing logics for applications involving commonsense reasoning, we find modal nonmonotonic logics particularly useful. It is shown that most of the well-known nonmonotonic logics can be defined with a similar nonmonotonic mechanism by varying the underlying modal systems [4, 8, 3].

In this paper, we argue that, since the strength of modal logic is its expressiveness of different levels of (non-)monotonicity, it makes little sense to discuss modal nonmonotonic logics without mentioning what kind of nonmonotonicity is concerned. For example, the issue of the dependence of modal nonmonotonic logics on the underlying modal systems [3] is not equally relevant to modal non-monotonic logics based on conventions imposed at the level of meta-language.

In the following sections, we first discuss the distinction between level-I and level-III nonmonotonicity and review the well-known nonmonotonic logics with respect to the distinction. Then we present a multi-modal logic with a preferential semantics that is intended to exhibit level-III nonmonotonicity. It occurs to us that this class of modal logics is paid relatively less attention in the literature.

*The financial support of this work is provided by the Blekinge Research Foundation.

2 Modal Frames

We assume a first-order language, augmented with modal operators M_i ($1 \leq i \leq m$). A formula with (resp. without) modal operator is called a modal (resp. base) formula. A *modal frame* of a m-modal logic is a tuple

$$\mu = \langle \mathcal{W}, R_1, ..., R_m, w_0, \mathcal{O} \rangle$$

where $\mathcal{W}$ is a set of possible worlds, $R_1, ..., R_m \subseteq W \times \mathcal{W}$ are the *accessibility relations*, w_0 is a member of W denoting the actual world, and $\mathcal{O}$ is the object domain. We assume that every possible world $w \in \mathcal{W}$ is a first-order interpretation. This seemingly different way of interpreting the modal language is essentially the same as the standard interpretation of a modal language where possible worlds are constants through which certain facts are indexed. The only difference is that possible worlds here are meta-level constructs rather than meta-level constants, and the interpretation function is hidden behind the possible-world constructs. A base formula α is true at a world w in the modal frame μ, denoted $\langle \mu, w \rangle \models \alpha$, if and only if the interpretation w is a first-order model of the formula. The *truth set* of a base formula α, denoted $\|\alpha\|^\mu$, is the set of first-order models of α in a modal frame μ, i.e. $\|\alpha\|^\mu = \{w \in \mathcal{W} \mid \langle \mu, w \rangle \models \alpha\}$. Let

$$F_i^n(\mu, w) = \{w' \mid wR_i^n w', R_i \in \mu\} \ (n \geq 1)$$

denote the set of possible worlds in μ accessible from w through the relation R_i^n, called the R_i^n-*descendant set* of w in μ. Then for a base formula α,

$$\langle \mu, w \rangle \models M_i^n \alpha \text{ if and only if } F_i^n(\mu, w) \subseteq \|\alpha\|^\mu$$

If a formula ϕ is true at every possible world w in the model μ, then ϕ is true in the modal model μ, denoted $\mu \models \phi$. μ is a *modal model* of ϕ. The set of modal models of a formula ϕ is denoted with $Mmod(\phi)$. If $Mmod(\alpha) \subseteq Mmod(\beta)$, then α is said to entail β, denoted $\alpha \models \beta$.

3 Level-I Nonmonotonicity

With modal logic, it is possible to exhibit the property of (non-)monotonicity at the level of possible world in the modal frames (called *Level-I (non-)monotonicity*). In a modal language, object constant symbols, which always represent the same individuals, are distinguished from 0-place function symbols, which may denote different individuals in different possible worlds. One form of level-I monotonicity is described by:

$$\langle \mu, w \rangle \models \alpha \text{ only if } \langle \mu, w \rangle \models M_i \alpha \tag{1}$$

Violating such a rule leads to level-I nonmonotonicity.

The above-mentioned property (1) of monotonicity can be enforced with the schema T ($M_i \alpha \Rightarrow \alpha$, where $\Rightarrow$ is used to denote logical implication), possibly in addition to other schemas. Consequently, the corresponding property of level-I nonmonotonicity can be implemented by introducing inference rules that violate these schemas. Generally speaking,

Proposition 1 *The property of level-I nonmonotonicity is implemented by introducing inference rules that reject certain schemas that enforces the property of monotonicity.*

Examples: McDermott's nonmonotonic logic (NML) is constructed by introducing inference rules that reject the schemas T, B, 4 and 5 [1], while accepting the schemas K and D. Autoepistemic logic, on the other hand, is constructed by introducing inference rules that violate the schemas T and B, while accepting the schemas K, D, 4 and 5 (refer Theorem 2.2 in [3]). This is why autoepistemic logic coincides with McDermott's NML when the latter has the underlying modal system K45 [8]; with 4 and 5 enforced by the underlying modal system, the inference rules of NML in practice reject only T and B.

Based on Proposition 1, we can understand better the condition under which a level-I nonmonotonic logic collapses into a monotonic one:

Proposition 2 *Any modal logic which exhibits level-I nonmonotonicity collapses into a monotonic one when the underlying modal system enforces the schemas that are violated by the introduced inference rules.*

Examples: McDermott's NML collapses into a monotonic one when the underlying modal system is S5 [5]. The reason is that in S5, all the violated schemas in NML, i.e. T, B, 4 and 5, are satisfied and the inference rules that violate the schemas never have a chance to be applied. Similarly, it is reckoned that autoepistemic logic collapses into a monotonic one when the underlying modal system is either KTB or S5 because those are the systems that enforce the schemas T and B.

4 Level-II and level-III Nonmonotonicity

Among the well-known nonmonotonic formalisms, Reiter's default logic is an exception; it is not intended to exhibit level-I nonmonotonicity. Not surprisingly, searching for a modal counterpart of the default logic turned out to be a difficult undertaking [2]. The default logic is an example of nonmonotonic logics beyond level-I nonmonotonic ones.

Above level-I monotonicity, there are two additional levels [1]. *Level-II monotonicity* is at the level of object language which may be described as:

$$\alpha \Rightarrow \beta \models \alpha \wedge \gamma \Rightarrow \beta.$$

---

[1] The schemas are named according to [2]. The schema B is $\alpha \Rightarrow M_i \neg M_i \neg \alpha$.

[2] There is a restricted modal translation of the default logic that is proved to be faithfully described with the underlying modal system N (the system with only the rule of necessitation, without any schema for handling modalities) [4].

In addition, *level-III monotonicity* is at the level of meta-language, which can be described with the following rule:

$$\alpha \models \beta \text{ only if } \alpha, \gamma \models \beta.$$

Logics that violates this rule exhibits level-III nonmonotonicity. In this paper, we are only concerned with level-III nonmonotonicity.

A well-known convention of nonmonotonic reasoning that is beyond the scope of level-I nonmonotonicity is *chronological minimization of change*, used in constructing temporal logics [7]. This convention can be formalized as the meta-level criterion for a logic that exhibits level-III nonmonotonicity.

Level-III monotonicity, being imposed at the meta-level, is by itself independent on the underlying modal system. Although it can be argued that any modal system with the schema T would not be appropriate for constructing level-I nonmonotonic logics, because the logics might collapse into a monotonic one, we can feel free to use such a modal system to construct level-III modal nonmonotonic logics.

5   Characterizing the Theorems of the Logic

In the rest of this paper, a level-III nonmonotonic logic is described. We start with the notion of a *preference theory*. Similar to the notion of reliability theory given in [6], a preference theory is a pair $\langle \Sigma, \prec \rangle$, where Σ is a set of sentences in a modal language, and $\prec$ is a partial relation between the sentences in Σ. The relation $\prec$ is an important element of the theory because it encodes the meta-level, subjective criteria of preference.

All the sentences in Σ have the form $\varphi \Rightarrow \psi$, where both φ and ψ are conjunctions of formulas in the modal language. The modalities involved in ψ are said to be *logically dependent* on the modality involved in φ. This way, the modalities can be partially or totally ordered. A *dependency enumeration of the modalities* $M_1, ..., M_m$ is a total ordering of the modalities such that if $i < j$, then M_j is possibly dependent on M_i, but not visa versa.

If the left-hand side of a sentence is justified by a theorem set, then the sentence is *applicable* in the theorem set. The *application* of such a sentence to a theorem set D_i is to add to the set D_i the right-hand side of the sentence. To resolve the conflict between sentences, it is assumed that if $\varphi \Rightarrow \psi_1$ and $\varphi \Rightarrow \psi_2$ are two applicable sentences in a theorem set D_i, then $\psi_1 \prec \psi_2$ or $\psi_2 \prec \psi_1$. The following definition characterizes the set of theorems of a given preference theory.

Definition 1 *Let $\langle \Sigma, \prec \rangle$ be a preference theory and $M_1, M_2, ..., M_m$ be a dependency enumeration of the modalities. Assume that the underlying modal system is S. Consider the following inductive construction of a set of theorems, where the consequence closure is based on the provability in the modal logic S:*

1). D_0 is the consequence closure of all the base tautologies φ and the negations of all the other base formulas;

2). D_{i+1} $(i \geq 0)$ is the consequence closure of the set which is D_i plus the result of applying all the sentences in Σ whose right-hand side involves the modality M_{i+1}. In case there are multiple applicable sentences, the one whose right-hand side is most preferred (minimal) w.r.t $\prec$ is chosen (by assumption, such a sentence always exists). All the formulas of the form $M_{i+1}\varphi$ which are not in the consequence closure are made false.

The set of theorems D of the given preference theory is D_∞.

6 The Semantics of the Multi-Modal Nonmonotonic Logic

In this section, we give a preferential semantics of the multi-modal logic defined. The essence of the preferential semantics is the preference relation $\ll$ between modal frames.

Definition 2 *Let μ and μ' be two modal frames, and*

$$En(\mu) = \{\varphi \mid \varphi \in \Sigma \text{ and } \mu \models \varphi\}$$

be the set of sentences satisfied by the modal frame μ. The model μ is said to be preferable to the model μ' with respect to a relation $\prec$, denoted $\mu \ll_\prec \mu'$, if and only if there is a partition of the accessibility relations $\Delta = (\mathcal{R}_=, \mathcal{R}_\prec, \mathcal{R}.)$ such that the following conditions are satisfied:

1). for any modality R_k in $\mathcal{R}_=$, $\mu \models M_k\varphi$ iff $\mu' \models M_k\varphi$ (φ is a base formula);

2). either $(En(\mu') - En(\mu))$ is empty, or for $M_i\varphi \in (En(\mu') - En(\mu))$, there is $M_j\psi \in (En(\mu) - En(\mu'))$ such that the modalities R_i and R_j are in $\mathcal{R}_\prec$, and $M_j\psi \prec M_i\varphi$ holds;

3). $\mathcal{R}.$ consists of modalities they are allowed to vary.

$\mu \in Mmod_{\ll_\prec}(\Sigma)$ iff there is no modal model μ' of Σ such that $\mu' \ll_\prec \mu$. Now, we can give the following theorem which guarantees the soundness and the completeness of the logic:

Theorem 1 *Let $\langle \Sigma, \prec \rangle$ be a preference theory and $\mathcal{A}(\langle \Sigma, \prec \rangle)$ contain all the sets of theorems of the given preference theory constructed according to Definition 1, each set corresponding to a possible dependency enumerations of the modalities. Then:*

$$Mmod_{\ll_\prec}(\Sigma) = \bigcup_{D \in \mathcal{A}(\langle \Sigma, \prec \rangle)} Mmod(D)$$

Proof sketch: Assume that there is some model μ' which is different from a model $\mu \in Mmod_{\ll_\prec}(\Sigma)$ in a sentence of the form $M_i\varphi$. μ and μ' agree on all the other sentences with modalities M_k, where $k < i$. We need to prove that μ' cannot be a member of $Mmod_{\ll_\prec}(\Sigma)$. There are two possible cases:

Case 1: $\mu \models M_i\varphi$ and $\mu' \not\models M_i\varphi$. By the construction procedure, there must exist a sentence $\varphi' \Rightarrow M_i\varphi$ in Σ, such that $\mu \models \varphi'$. Since μ and μ' agree on all the sentence involving modalities M_k, where $k < i$, it must be the case that

$\mu' \models \varphi'$ as well. Since $\mu' \not\models M_i\varphi$, it must be the case that there is another sentence $\varphi' \Rightarrow M_j\psi$ such that $M_j\psi \prec M_i\varphi$. But this means that there are two conflicting sentences applied for μ, which contradicts the rule of the construction procedure. Thus $(En(\mu) - En(\mu'))$ is empty.

Case 2: $\mu' \models M_i\varphi$ and $\mu \not\models M_i\varphi$. This, together with the conclusion of the first case, implies that $\mu' \ll_\prec \mu$ (Definition 2), meaning that μ cannot be a member of $Mmod_{\ll_\prec}(\Sigma)$, which contradicts the assumption.

7 Conclusions

This work is intended to broaden the view of modal nonmonotonic logics by emphasizing the distinction between different classes of such logics. The logic presented here is inspired by the modal nonmonotonic logics constructed to formalize the convention of chronological minimization of change in commonsense temporal reasoning [7]. It is intended to show that the preference relation between modal frames, being the essence of the preferential semantics, is crucially dependent on the meta-level, subjective criterion of preference, rather than the underlying modal system.

References

[1] J.V. Benthem. Partiality and nonmonotonicity in classical logic. CSLI Report CSLI-84-12, Center for the study of language and information, Stanford, 1984.

[2] B.F. Chellas. *Modal Logic: an Introduction.* Cambridge University Press, 1980.

[3] W. Marek, G. F. Shvarts, and M. Truszczynski. Modal nonmonotonic logics: ranges, characterization, computation. In *International Conference on Principles of Knowledge Representation and Reasoning*, pages 395–404, 1991.

[4] W. Marek and M. Truszczynski. Modal logic for default reasoning. In *Annals of Mathematics and Artificial Intelligence*, volume 1, pages 275–302, 1990.

[5] D. McDermott. Nonmonotonic logic II. *Journal of ACM*, 29:33–57, 1982.

[6] N. Roos. A logic for reasoning with inconsistent knowledge. *Artificial Intelligence*, 57(1):69–104, 1992.

[7] Yoav Shoham. *Reasoning about Change.* MIT Press, 1988.

[8] G.F. Shvarts. Autoepistemic modal logics. In *The Conference on Theoretical Aspects of Reasoning About Knowledge 1990*, pages 97–109. Morgan Kaufmann Publishers, Inc., 1990.

Probability of Deductibility and Belief Functions

Philippe SMETS[1]
IRIDIA, Université Libre de Bruxelles
50 av. F. Roosevelt, CP194/6. B-1050 Brussels, Belgium.

Abstracts: We present an interpretation of Dempster-Shafer theory based on the probability of deductibility. We present two forms of revision (conditioning) that lead to the geometrical rule of conditioning and to Dempster rule of conditioning, respectively.

1. Introduction.

Dempster-Shafer theory has received much attention recently in AI, both in favorable and unfavorable ways (see the special issues of the Intern. J. Approx. Reasoning, vol. 4, 1990 and vol. 6, 1992). Most criticisms are based on confusion that result from an inappropriate mixing of several interpretations of the theory. No specific interpretation is 'better' than any other, each fits a specific domain. Ruspini (1986) and Pearl (1988) have considered logical foundations of the model based on the concepts of the probability of a modal proposition (knowing) or of the probability of provability. We analyze in detail the probability of deductibility interpretation and show how the conditioning rules can be derived. We present the concept of the probability of the deductibility of some propositions. We show the relation of these particular probability functions with the belief functions. Finally we study two conditioning processes that correspond to the geometrical rule of conditioning and to the unnormalized (Dempster) rule of conditioning, respectively. This paper focuses essentially on Dempster-Shafer theory, its relation to the Transferable Belief Model is analyzed in the conclusions. The case where probabilities are derived, and the conditioning by adding new hypothesis are studied in the full report (Smets, 1993b)

2. Probability of Deductibility.

Pearl (1988) presents the 'probability of provability' interpretation of Dempster-Shafer theory. Ruspini (1986) studied a similar problem by using the modal approach, considering the 'probability of knowing'. The probability of deductibility fits essentially with the same ideas. Conceptually, it is not different from the original Dempsterian approach (Dempster 1967) but it provides a nice framework. It can be described as follows.

---

[1] This work has been partially funded by the CEC-ESPRIT III Basic Research Project 6156 (DRUMS II), and the Communauté Française de Belgique, ARC 92/97-160 (BELON).

Let $\mathcal{H}$ be a finite Boolean algebra of propositions. These propositions are called the hypothesis. Let $\mathcal{L}$ be another finite Boolean algebra of propositions. We assume that for every hypothesis $H \in \mathcal{H}$ there is a set $\mathbb{L}(H) = \{L_i: L_i \in \mathcal{L}, i=1, 2..r\}$ of propositions L_i deductible under H. Let $M(H) = L_1 \& L_2...\& L_r$ be the conjunction of all these propositions in $\mathbb{L}(H)$. $M(H) \in \mathcal{L}$ as $\mathcal{L}$ is a Boolean algebra. M is a function from $\mathcal{H}$ to $\mathcal{L}$ and $M(H)$ is the most specific proposition in $\mathcal{L}$ that can be deduced from H.

So: $\forall H \in \mathcal{H}, \exists M(H) \in \mathcal{L}$ such that $H \vdash L$ for every $L \in \mathcal{L}$ such that $M(H) \vdash L$.

In particular $M(\perp) = \perp$, as $\perp \vdash L$ and $\perp \vdash \neg L$ for any $L \in \mathcal{L}$, so $M(\perp) = L \& \neg L = \perp$.

The **deductibility relation** $\vdash$ is very general. It must only satisfy the following requirements:

        If $H \vdash L$ then $H \vdash L \vee L'$ (right weakening)

        If $H \vdash L$ and $H \vdash L'$ then $H \vdash L \& L'$ (and)

In particular, $\vdash$ does not satisfy:

        If $H \vdash L \vee L'$ then $H \vdash L$ or $H \vdash L'$

The impact of this requiring will be studied in section 4.

Suppose there is a **probability measure** $P_{\mathcal{H}}: 2^{\mathcal{H}} \to [0,1]$ on $2^{\mathcal{H}}$ and let $p_{\mathcal{H}}: \mathcal{H} \to [0,1]$ be the related probability function on $\mathcal{H}$ with $p_{\mathcal{H}}(H) = P_{\mathcal{H}}(\{H\})$ for every $H \in \mathcal{H}$. Note that $\mathcal{H}$ is already an algebra, usually the power set of some set. As $\perp \in H$, $p_{\mathcal{H}}(\perp)$ may be positive[2].

Given the function $M : \mathcal{H} \to \mathcal{L}$, we can define on $\mathcal{L}$ the probability that $L \in \mathcal{L}$ is deductible and $\neg L$ is not deductible. It is denoted by $P_{\mathcal{L}}(\mapsto L)$. We use the symbol $\mapsto$ in $P_{\mathcal{L}}$ to enhance the fact that those H that would also prove $\neg L$ are eliminated. $P_{\mathcal{L}}(\mapsto L)$ is the probability that an hypothesis selected randomly in $\mathcal{H}$ (according to the probability measure $P_{\mathcal{H}}$) proves L and does not prove $\neg L$ (thus eliminating the hypothesis equivalent to the contradiction and denoted $\perp$)

$$P_{\mathcal{L}}(\mapsto L) =_{def} P_{\mathcal{H}}(\{H : H \in \mathcal{H}, H \vdash L, H \nvdash \neg L\}) = \sum_{H: H \vdash L, H \nvdash \neg L} p_{\mathcal{H}}(H)$$

Example 1: (This didactic example will be studied throughout the paper). To illustrate the meaning of the various components of the model, let the propositions:

    R   = 'It rains'
    W   = 'It is windy'
    C   = 'Paul spend the evening with Carol'
    J   = 'Paul spend the evening with John'

---

[2] In Smets (1992a) a similar problem is analyzed, i.e., belief functions where $m(\emptyset)$ might be positive.

Let $\mathscr{H}$ = P({R, ¬R} x {W, ¬W}) where P denotes the power set and x denotes the Cartesian product. Let $\mathscr{L}$ = P({C, ¬C} x {J, ¬J}) . Let T denotes the tautology.

$H_i \in \mathscr{H}$		$p\mathscr{H}$	$M(H_i) \in \mathscr{L}$	
H_1	T	.10	L_1	J
H_2	R	.15	L_2	¬C&J
H_3	W	.18	L_3	C
H_4	R&W	.24	L_4	C&¬J
H_5	R&¬W	.30	L_5	¬C∨¬J
H_6	R&¬R	.03	L_6	⊥

Table 1: Elements of $\mathscr{H}$, $\mathscr{L}$ and the probability distribution $p\mathscr{H}$ on $\mathscr{H}$.

Table 1 presents a set of hypothesis (H_1 to H_6), their M values (L_1 to L_6) and the probability distribution $p\mathscr{H}$. The origin of such data could be that I am trying to guess with whom Paul will spend his evening (an element of $\mathscr{L}$), and Paul's intentions depends on the information Paul will have about the weather (an element of $\mathscr{H}$).

1) there are 6 weather reports (H_i : i=1, ..6) available about tonight weather (H_i),

2) Paul will obtain only one of them and the probability that Paul obtains report H_i is $p\mathscr{H}(H_i)$, and

3) the M values are the most specific information I know about Paul's intentions ($M(H_i)$) according to what he knows about the weather (H_i).

In particular H_6 is a report that says 'R and ¬R' (i.e. ⊥). In that case, every proposition in L is deductible, in particular J and ¬J, hence $M(\perp) = \perp$.

Then for instance:

$P\mathscr{L}(\mapsto T) = p\mathscr{H}(H_1) + p\mathscr{H}(H_2) + p\mathscr{H}(H_3) + p\mathscr{H}(H_4) + p\mathscr{H}(H_5) = .97$

$P\mathscr{L}(\mapsto J) = p\mathscr{H}(H_1) + p\mathscr{H}(H_2) = .25$

$P\mathscr{L}(\mapsto ¬J) = p\mathscr{H}(H_4) = .24$

$P\mathscr{L}(\mapsto C\&J) = 0.00$

$P\mathscr{L}(\mapsto ¬C\&J) = p\mathscr{H}(H_2) = 0.15.$

So one have, among others,

$P\mathscr{L}(\mapsto T) = .987 < 1.00$

$P\mathscr{L}(\mapsto J) = .25 < 1 - P\mathscr{L}(\mapsto ¬J) = 1 - .24 = .76$

and $\quad P\mathscr{L}(\mapsto J) = .25 > P\mathscr{L}(\mapsto C\&J) + P\mathscr{L}(\mapsto ¬C\&J) = 0.00 + 0.15$

Those inequalities are typical of the unnormalized belief functions and indeed $P\mathscr{L}(\mapsto L)$ considers as a function of L happens to be a belief function on $\mathscr{L}$ as shown now. $\quad\nabla$

Let bel : $\mathscr{L} \to [0,1]$ be the (unnormalized) **belief function**[3] on $\mathscr{L}$ induced by a given basic belief assignment m on $\mathscr{L}$. By definition bel(L) is the sum of the basic belief masses m(X) given to the propositions X in $\mathscr{L}$ that imply L without implying $\neg$L (thus excluding $\bot$):

$$bel(L) = \sum_{X:X \in \mathscr{L}, X \vdash L, X \nvdash \neg L} m(X)$$

It can be shown that $P_\mathscr{G}(\mapsto L)$, $L \in \mathscr{L}$ is equal to the belief function $bel_\mathscr{G}$ on $\mathscr{L}$ induced by the basic belief assignment $m_\mathscr{G}: \mathscr{L} \to [0,1]$ with:

$$m_\mathscr{G}(L) \quad = \sum_{H:M(H)=L} p_\mathscr{H}(H)$$

and $m_\mathscr{G}(L) = 0$ if the sum is taken over an empty set.

One has:

$$P_\mathscr{G}(\mapsto L) = \sum_{H:H \vdash L, H \nvdash \neg L} p_\mathscr{H}(H) = \sum_{H:M(H) \vdash L, M(H) \nvdash \neg L} p_\mathscr{H}(H)$$

$$= \sum_{L_i \in \mathscr{L}: L_i \vdash L, L_i \nvdash \neg L} \sum_{H:M(H)=L_i} p_\mathscr{H}(H) = \sum_{L_i \vdash L, L_i \nvdash \neg L} m_\mathscr{G}(L_i)$$

So: $P_\mathscr{G}(\mapsto L) = bel_\mathscr{G}(L)$.

Similarly the plausibility function $pl_\mathscr{G}$ is :

$$pl_\mathscr{G}(L) = bel_\mathscr{G}(T) - bel_\mathscr{G}(\neg L) = \sum_{X \& L \neq \bot} m_\mathscr{G}(X)$$

where T is the maximal element of $\mathscr{L}$. It can be shown that:

$$pl_\mathscr{G}(L) = \sum_{H:M(H) \& L \neq \bot} p_\mathscr{H}(H)$$

Example 2: Given the data of table 1, table 2 presents the belief and plausibility values for several propositions of $\mathscr{L}$. ∇

---

[3] bel is an unnormalized belief function as we do not require m($\bot$)=0 (Smets 1988, 1992a).

	bel$\mathscr{L}$	pl$\mathscr{L}$
C & J	.00	.28
¬C & J	.15	.55
J	.25	.73
C ∨ ¬J	.42	.82
¬C ∨ ¬J	.69	.97
¬J	.24	.72
⊤	.97	.97

Table 2: Belief and plausibility values for several propositions of $\mathscr{L}$.

This model for the probability of deductibility is not different from Dempster's model (Dempster 1967) and Shafer's translator model (Shafer and Tversky 1985, Dubois et al. 1991). Both models consider an X domain (the translator-source domain) endowed with a probability measure, an Y domain (the message-data domain) and a one-to-many mapping from X to Y. The $\mathscr{H}$ space corresponds to the X domain, the $\mathscr{L}$ to the Y, the M mapping to the one-to-many mapping, and P$\mathscr{H}$ to the probability on the X domain.

We proceed by considering two revision processes that correspond to some data-conditioning and some source-conditioning, i.e., conditioning on an information relative to the data or to the source (Kruse and Gebhardt, 1993).

The **data-conditioning** fits to the scenario where we learn that a particular proposition L* of $\mathscr{L}$ is true. In that case, the hypothesis H that was proving all the propositions in $\mathscr{L}$ proved by M(H) now proves all propositions in $\mathscr{L}$ proved by M(H)&L*. The basic belief assignment m$\mathscr{L}$ is revised into m$\mathscr{L}$* with:

$$m\mathscr{L}^*(L) = \sum_{H:M(H)\&L^*=L} p\mathscr{H}(H)$$

As for all L∈$\mathscr{L}$ such that L⊢L*, one has L&L*≡L. Then the revised plausibility pl$\mathscr{L}$* on $\mathscr{L}$ for those L⊢L* is:

$$pl\mathscr{L}^*(L) = \sum_{X:X\&L\neq\perp} m\mathscr{L}^*(X) = \sum_{X:X\&L\neq\perp} \sum_{H:M(H)\&L^*=X} p\mathscr{H}(H)$$

$$= \sum_{H:M(H)\&L\&L^*\neq\perp} p\mathscr{H}(H) = pl\mathscr{L}(L)$$

In general, for all L∈$\mathscr{L}$, L≠⊥,

$$pl\mathscr{L}^*(L) = pl\mathscr{L}^*(L\&L^*) = pl\mathscr{L}(L\&L^*).$$

and
$$bel\mathscr{L}^*(L) = pl\mathscr{L}^*(\top) - pl\mathscr{L}^*(\neg L) = pl\mathscr{L}(L^*) - pl\mathscr{L}(\neg L\&L^*) =$$
$$= bel\mathscr{L}(\top) - bel\mathscr{L}(\neg L^*) - bel\mathscr{L}(\top) + bel\mathscr{L}(L\vee\neg L^*)$$

$$= \mathrm{bel}_{\mathscr{G}}(L \vee \neg L^*) - \mathrm{bel}_{\mathscr{G}}(\neg L^*).$$

These relations for $\mathrm{bel}_{\mathscr{G}}^*$ and $\mathrm{pl}_{\mathscr{G}}^*$ correspond to the **unnormalized rule of conditioning** (Smets 1993a) Normalization is achieved by further conditioning on L being not equivalent to a contradiction. After normalization, the resulting relation is Dempster's rule of conditioning.

Example 3: Suppose we learn that John spent the evening with Paul. What can we say about Carol. So $L^* = J$. Table 3 present the result of the revision of the data of table 2 by this information. The data are obtained by replacing the L_i by L_i &J in table 1. ▽

	$\mathrm{bel}_{\mathscr{G}}^*$	$\mathrm{pl}_{\mathscr{G}}^*$
C & J	.18	.28
¬C & J	.45	.55
J	.73	.73

Table 3: Belief and plausibility values for several propositions of $\mathscr{L}$ after data-conditioning on $L^* = J$.

The **source-conditioning** fits to the scenario. Given $L^{**} \in \mathscr{L}$, we consider only on those hypothesis H that prove L^{**} (without proving $\neg L^{**}$) and ask what is then the probability that L is deductible, for all $L \in \mathscr{L}$ that prove L^{**}. This revision corresponds to the impact of the information 'H proves L^{**}', or equivalently 'L^{**} is deductible'. Therefore we restrict our attention to those $H \in \mathscr{H}$ such that $H \vdash L^{**}$, $H \nvdash \neg L^{**}$.

Let $L \vdash L^{**}$. So $L \& L^{**} = L$. Let $P_{\mathscr{G}}^{**}(\vdash L)$ be the probability that L is deductible by one of those hypothesis that prove L^{**} without proving $\neg L^{**}$. It is:

$$
\begin{aligned}
\mathrm{bel}_{\mathscr{G}}^{**}(L) &= P_{\mathscr{H}}(\{H: H \vdash L, H \nvdash \neg L\} \mid H \vdash L^{**}, H \nvdash \neg L^{**}) = \\
&= \frac{P_{\mathscr{H}}(\{H: H \vdash L \& L^{**}, H \nvdash \neg(L \& L^{**})\})}{P_{\mathscr{H}}(\{H: H \vdash L^{**}, H \nvdash \neg L^{**})\}} \\
&= \frac{P_{\mathscr{H}}(\{H: H \vdash L, H \nvdash \neg L\})}{P_{\mathscr{H}}(\{H: H \vdash L^{**}, H \nvdash \neg L^{**}\})} \\
&= \frac{\mathrm{bel}_{\mathscr{G}}(L \& L^{**})}{\mathrm{bel}_{\mathscr{G}}(L^{**})}
\end{aligned}
$$

This relation is known as the **geometrical rule of conditioning** (Shafer 1976b, Suppes and Zanotti, 1977).

Example 4: Suppose we learn that H proves $L^{**} = J$, i.e., we learn that the source was in fact such that it should prove that John would spend the evening with Paul, or equivalently that it was inn fact necessary that John spend the evening with Paul (not that John just did it). Only H_1 and H_2 remain relevant and :

$$\mathrm{bel}_{\mathscr{L}}^{**}(\neg C) = \frac{.15}{.10 + .15} = .60$$

$$\mathrm{bel}_{\mathscr{L}}^{**}(C) = .00$$

$$\mathrm{bel}_{\mathscr{L}}^{**}(C \vee \neg C) = 1.00. \qquad\qquad \nabla$$

Suppose there is a partition Π of $\mathscr{L}$ such that M(H) is an element of Π for all H with $p_{\mathscr{H}}(H) > 0$. In that case $\mathrm{bel}_{\mathscr{L}}$ becomes an additive measure on 2^{Π} (a probability measure if it were normalized). When all belief functions are normalized, the whole model collapses into a classical probability model and both revision cases degenerate into the classical Bayes' rule of conditioning.

The source-conditioning results can be also obtained by conditioning the probability measure $p_{\mathscr{H}}$ on $\mathscr{H}$ by the event $H \in H^{**} =_{\mathrm{def}} \{H' : M(H') \& L^{**} \neq \bot\}$. The initial probability measure $p_{\mathscr{H}}$ is updated into the new probability function $p_{\mathscr{H}}^{**}$ by:

$$p_{\mathscr{H}}^{**}(H) = \frac{p_{\mathscr{H}}(H)}{\displaystyle\sum_{H':M(H')\&L^*\neq\bot} p_{\mathscr{H}}(H')} \qquad \text{for H such that } M(H)\&L^*\neq\bot.$$

and $\qquad p_{\mathscr{H}}^{**}(H) = 0 \qquad\qquad\qquad$ for H such that $M(H)\&L^*=\bot$.

Then for $L \in L^{**}$, $\mathrm{bel}_{\mathscr{L}}^{**}(L) = P_{\mathscr{L}}^{**}(\mapsto L)$ where $P_{\mathscr{L}}^{**}(\mapsto L)$ is computed directly from $p_{\mathscr{H}}^{**}(H)$:

$$P_{\mathscr{L}}(\mapsto L) = \sum_{H:H \vdash L, H \nvdash \neg L} p_{\mathscr{H}}^{**}(H) =_{\mathrm{def}} P_{\mathscr{H}}^{**}(\{H : H \in H^{**}, H \vdash L, H \nvdash \neg L\})$$

It might be worth reconsidering the conditioning events. In the first case (data conditioning), we revise our belief on the information 'L* is true'. In the second case (the source conditioning), we revise our beliefs on the fact 'L** is deducible from the hypothesis in $\mathscr{H}$. The first case seems the most natural form of conditioning, what does not mean it always applies. The second form is the one encountered more naturally in the random set approach of belief function (Nguyen 1978, Smets 1991a, 1991b). It is also the one encountered by applying Bayes' rule of conditioning blindly. If one writes:

$$\mathrm{bel}(A|B) = P(\mapsto A | \mapsto B),$$

then it becomes very tempting to write:

$$P(\mapsto A | \mapsto B) = \frac{P(\mapsto A \ \& \ \mapsto B)}{P(\mapsto B)} = \frac{P(\mapsto A \& B)}{P(\mapsto B)}$$

in which case,

$$\mathrm{bel}(A|B) = \frac{\mathrm{bel}(A \& B)}{\mathrm{bel}(B)}.$$

The adequate choice between the two rules is straightforward when the conditioning event is well understood. The real problem resides in not applying blindly Bayes' rule as the geometrical rule would automatically result, even when Dempster's rule would be the adequate rule.

3. Conclusions.

We have presented in detail the probability of deductibility interpretation of Dempster-Shafer theory. We have derived the revision rules that can be described under that interpretation. Both Dempster's rule of conditioning and the geometric rule of conditioning are obtained.

This derivation based on the probability of deductibility covers the cases considered by Dempster-Shafer theory (Dempster 1967), but not all those considered by the transferable belief model where the probability measure on a hypothesis space is not necessarily assumed.

Dempster-Shafer theory has been criticized by the Bayesians as inappropriate: they claim that the conditioning by Dempster's rule of conditioning is inadequate. A strict Bayesian will claim the existence of a probability measure $P_{\mathcal{H} \times \mathcal{L}}$ on the product space $\mathcal{H} \times \mathcal{L}$ that represents the agent's belief on that space[4]. They ask for the application of Bayes' rule of conditioning on $P_{\mathcal{H} \times \mathcal{L}}$, and the marginalization of the result on L. Of course, the available information consists only on the marginalization of $P_{\mathcal{H} \times \mathcal{L}}$ on $\mathcal{H}$. The conditioning process cannot be achieved in general by lack of appropriate information. Only upper and lower conditional probabilities can be computed (Fagin and Halpern, 1990, Jaffray, 1992). Bayesians conclude that Dempster's rule of conditioning is inappropriate (Levi, 1983) what is exact once their preliminary assumption (the probability measure on $\mathcal{H} \times \mathcal{L}$ that represents the agent's belief on that space) is accepted.

To get out of the Bayesian criticisms, it is sufficient to reject the probability measure on the product space $\mathcal{H} \times \mathcal{L}$ i.e. to reject the Bayesian dogma that there exists a probability measure on ANY and EVERY space. Not assuming a probability measure on $\mathcal{H} \times \mathcal{L}$ that represents the agent's belief is what is achieved explicitly in the Hints' model of Kohlas (1990) (and implicitly in Dempster-Shafer theory). In the transferable belief model we even go further by not requiring the existence of any hypothesis space $\mathcal{H}$ and considering ONLY the $\mathcal{L}$ space by itself, cutting therefore all links with Dempster-Shafer model.

---

[4] Of course, mathematically, one can always construct many probability measures on $\mathcal{H} \times \mathcal{L}$. The question is: does one of these probability measures represents an agent's belief or not. Bayesians claim yes.

In the transferable belief model, we consider only the basic belief assignment m_L and its related belief function bel_L and plausibility function $pl_\mathscr{L}$. No concept of some $\mathscr{H}$ space endowed with a probability measure is needed. The meaning of $m_\mathscr{L}(L)$ for $L\in\mathscr{L}$ is such that $m_\mathscr{L}(L)$ is the part of belief allocated to L and that could be allocated to any proposition L' that proves L if further information justifies such transfer. Dempster's rule of conditioning is directly introduced as it is part of the overall description of the transferable belief model. The geometrical rule is derived if one ask for the proportion of the beliefs that support $L\in\mathscr{L}$ given they support $L^{**}\in\mathscr{L}$. Both rules have also been derived axiomatically in Smets (1992b) while looking for quantitative representations of credibility in general.

References.

DEMPSTER A.P. (1967) Upper and lower probabilities induced by a multplevalued mapping. Ann. Math. Statistics 38:325-339.

DUBOIS D., GARBOLINO P., KYBURG H.E., PRADE H. and SMETS Ph. (1991) Quantified Uncertainty. J. Applied Non-Classical Logics 1:105-197.

JAFFRAY J.Y. (1992) Bayesian Updating and belief functions. IEEE Trans. SMC, 22:1144-1152.

KOHLAS J. and MONNEY P. A. (1990) Modeling and reasoning with hints. Technical Report. Inst. Automation and OR. Univ. Fribourg.

KRUSE R. and GEBHARDT J. (1993) Updating mechanisms for imprecise data. DRUMS II workshop on Belief Change. Duboie D. and Prade H. Eds., IRIT, Univ. Paul Sabatier, Toulouse, pg. 8-22.

EARL J. (1988) Probabilistic reasoning in intelligent systems: networks of plausible inference. Morgan Kaufmann Pub. San Mateo, Ca, USA.

RUSPINI E.H. (1986) The logical foundations of evidential reasoning. Technical note 408, SRI International, Menlo Park, Ca.

SHAFER G. (1976a) A mathematical theory of evidence. Princeton Univ. Press. Princeton, NJ.

SHAFER G. (1976b) A theory of statistical evidence. in Foundations of probability theory, statistical inference, and statistical theories of science. Harper and Hooker ed. Reidel, Doordrecht-Holland.

SHAFER G. and TVERSKY A. (1985) Laages and designs for probability. Cognitive Sc. 9:309-339.

SMETS P. (1988) Belief functions. in SMETS Ph, MAMDANI A., DUBOIS D. and PRADE H. eds. Non standard logics for automated reasoning. Academic Press, London p 253-286.

SMETS P. (1991a) About updating. in D'Ambrosio B., Smets P., and Bonissone P.P. eds, Uncertainty in AI 91, Morgan Kaufmann, San Mateo, Ca, USA, 1991, 378-385.

SMETS P. (1992b) An axiomatic justifiaction for the use of belief function to quantify beliefs. IRIDIA-TR- 92-11. To appear in IJCAI-93.

SMETS P. (1993a) Belief functions: the disjunctive rule of combination and the generalized Bayesian theorem. Int. J. Approximate Reasoning.

SMETS P. (1993b) Probability od deducibility and belief functions. IRIDIA-TR-93-5/2

SMETS P. and KENNES R. (1990) The transferable belief model. Technical Report: IRIDIA-TR-90-14.

Formal Properties of Conditional Independence in Different Calculi of AI[1]

Milan Studený

Institute of Information Theory and Automation
Academy of Sciences of Czech Republic
Pod vodárenskou věží 4, 18208 Prague 8, Czech Republic
e-mail: studeny@cspgas11.bitnet

Abstract. In this paper formal properties of CI in different frameworks are studied. The first part is devoted to the comparison of three different frameworks for study CI: probability theory, theory of relational databases and Spohn's theory of ordinal conditional functions. Although CI–models arising in these frameworks are very similar (they satisfy semigraphoid axioms) we give examples showing that their formal properties still differ (each other). On the other hand, we find that (within each of these frameworks) there exists no finite complete axiomatic characterization of CI–models by finding an infinite set of sound inference rules (the same in all three frameworks). In the second part further frameworks for CI are discussed: Dempster–Shafer theory, possibility theory and (general) Shenoy's theory of valuation–based systems.

1 Introduction

The concept of *conditional independence* (CI) seems to attract attention of researches in last two decades. The properties of CI were studied in several branches of AI, let us mention some of them :

- probabilistic reasoning

- theory of relational databases

- theory of ordinal conditional functions

- theory of belief functions

- possibility theory.

The reason is evident – the knowledge concerning independence (resp. dependence) can simplify many reasoning tasks. Here, we give a short survey of current state.

So far, the most advanced results concerning properties of CI were achieved in the probabilistic framework. The concept of stochastic CI has been studied in probability theory and modern statistics for many years (see [2, 11]). Its importance for the theory of probabilistic ES consists in the fact that any CI–statement can be interpreted

---

[1]This research was supported by the internal grant n.275105 of the Academy of Sciences of Czech Republic "Conditional independence properties in uncertainty processing".

as certain qualitative relationship among symptoms. This brings the possibility of finding the adequate structural model of such ES. This role of CI was discerned and highlighted by the group around J. Pearl [6] (A.Paz, D.Geiger, T.Verma) but many other researchers dealt more or less explicitly with this concept.

Nevertheless, an analogy of the concept of CI was studied (even earlier) is the theory of relational databases [7]. The counterpart of CI in that theory is the concept of *embedded multivalued dependency* (EMVD). Note that an equivalent concept of *qualitative conditional independence* also appeared in ES theory [8].

Another framework in which the concept of CI appeared, is Spohn's theory of *ordinal conditional functions* [12]. This theory, motivated from philosophical point of view, gives a tool for a mathematical description of the dynamic handling of deterministic epistemology, in this sense it constitutes a counterpart of the probabilistic description of epistemic state. As soon as the concept of CI for ordinal conditional functions was introduced, researchers began to study its properties [4], especially for the special class of natural conditional functions (NCF) called "disbelief function" in [9] or "ranking function" in [3].

One of the most popular approaches to dealing with uncertainty in ES is Dempster–Shafer's theory of belief functions. The concept of CI for variables on which belief functions are defined (i.e. the parallel with concepts of CI studied in probability theory and in the theory of NCFs) was introduced lately by Shenoy [10]. Another definition of (unconditional) independence (also for variables) appeared in [1].

Further framework in which CI can be studied is Zadeh's *possibility theory*. This theory was formulated in the end of seventies as certain model of qualitative description of subjective judgements. Lately, Shenoy introduced the concept of CI also in this field. The above mentioned Shenoy's work [10] gives certain unifying point of view on different calculi dealing with CI. He introduced very abstract concept of *valuation–based system* (VBS) and defined CI for VBSs.

2 Basic Definitions

All above mentioned frameworks for study CI have some common setting. Throughout the paper a collection of nonempty finite sets $\{X_i ; \ i \in N\}$ is supposed to be given. The index set N is also nonempty and finite. Whenever $\emptyset \neq A \subset N$ the symbol X_A denotes the cartesian product $\prod_{i \in A} X_i$. Power set of a set S will be denoted by $exp\,S$.

The symbol $T(N)$ is reserved for the collection of triplets $\langle A, B, C \rangle$ of pairwise disjoint subsets of N where $A \neq \emptyset \neq B$. Following Pearl [6] we call every subset of $T(N)$ *dependency model over* N. A dependency model is called *semigraphoid* iff it is closed under following four inference rules (called axioms by many authors):

$$\langle A, B, C \rangle \rightarrow \langle B, A, C \rangle \qquad\qquad\qquad symmetry$$
$$\langle A, B \cup C, D \rangle \rightarrow \langle A, C, D \rangle \qquad\qquad decomposition$$
$$\langle A, B \cup C, D \rangle \rightarrow \langle A, B, C \cup D \rangle \qquad\qquad weak\ union$$
$$[\langle A, C, D \rangle \,\&\, \langle A, B, C \cup D \rangle] \rightarrow \langle A, B \cup C, D \rangle \qquad contraction.$$

Now, we show how dependency models arise in probability theory, the theory of relational databases and the theory of conditional functions.

DEFINITION 1 (CI–models in probability theory)
Probability measure over N is specified by a nonnegative real function
$P : X_N \rightarrow \langle 0, \infty \rangle$ such that $\sum \{P(a); a \in X_N\} = 1$. The formula
$P(A) = \sum \{P(a); a \in A\}$ whenever $A \subset X_N$
defines an additive set function (on $exp\, X_N$) i.e. *probability measure over N*. Whenever
$\emptyset \neq S \subsetneq N$ and P is a probability measure over N, then its *marginal measure on S* is
a probability measure P^S over S defined as follows:
$P^S(A) = P(A \times X_{N \setminus S})$ for $A \subset X_S$.
Moreover, we put $P^N \equiv P$.
Having a probability measure P over N and a triplet $\langle A, B, C \rangle \in T(N)$ we say that
A is conditionally independent of B given C in P and write $A \perp B|C(P)$ iff
$\forall a \in X_A \quad b \in X_B \quad c \in X_C \qquad P^{A \cup B \cup C}(abc) \cdot P^C(c) = P^{A \cup C}(ac) \cdot P^{B \cup C}(bc)$
(take $P^{\emptyset}(\cdot) = 1$). The dependency model $\{\langle A, B, C \rangle \in T(N); A \perp B|C(P)\}$ is then
called the *CI–model induced by P*.

The concept of CI in the theory of relational databases is known as embedded
multivalued dependency :

DEFINITION 2 (CI–models in the theory of relational databases)
Database relation over N is a nonempty subset of X_N. Having a database relation
$\emptyset \neq R \subset X_N$ and $\emptyset \neq S \subsetneq N$ the *marginal relation* R^S is a database relation over S
defined as follows:
$s \in R^S \Leftrightarrow [(s,t) \in R$ for some $t \in X_{N \setminus s}]$ whenever $s \in X_S$.
Of course, $R^N \equiv R$.
Having a database relation R over N and $\langle A, B, C \rangle \in T(N)$ write $A \perp B|C(R)$ iff
$\forall a \in X_A \quad b \in X_B \quad c \in X_C \quad (a,c) \in R^{A \cup C}$ & $(b,c) \in R^{B \cup C} \Rightarrow (a,b,c) \in R^{A \cup B \cup C}$.
The dependency model $\{\langle A, B, C \rangle \in T(N); A \perp B|C(R)\}$ is then called the *CI–model
induced by R*.

Finally, we define the concept of CI for a special class of ordinal conditional functions, namely so-called natural conditional functions (according to Hunter [4]).

DEFINITION 3 (CI–models in the theory of ordinal conditional functions)
Natural conditional function over N is specified by a nonnegative integer function
$\kappa : X_N \rightarrow \{0, 1, 2, \ldots\}$ satisfying $min\, \{\kappa(a); a \in X_N\} = 0$. The formula
$\kappa(A) = min\, \{\kappa(a); a \in A\}$ whenever $\emptyset \neq A \subset X_N$
then defines a set function on $(exp\, X_N) \setminus \{\emptyset\}$ called the *natural conditional function
(NCF) over N*. If moreover $\emptyset \neq S \subsetneq N$, then its *marginal NCF* is an NCF over S
defined as follows:
$\kappa^S(A) = \kappa(A \times X_{N \setminus S})$ for $A \subset X_S$.
Moreover, $\kappa^N \equiv \kappa$.
Having an NCF κ over N and a triplet $\langle A, B, C \rangle \in T(N)$ write $A \perp B|C(\kappa)$ iff
$\forall a \in X_A \quad b \in X_B \quad c \in X_C \qquad \kappa^{A \cup B \cup C}(abc) + \kappa^C(c) = \kappa^{A \cup C}(ac) + \kappa^{B \cup C}(bc)$
(take $\kappa^{\emptyset}(\cdot) = 0$). The dependency model $\{\langle A, B, C \rangle \in T(N); \quad A \perp B|C(\kappa)\}$ is
called the *CI–model induced by κ*.

3 Comparison

Having introduced the class of CI–models for some specific framework we may ask which inference rules (or axioms) of the form :
$$[\langle A_1, B_1, C_1\rangle \ \& \ \ldots \ \& \ \langle A_n, B_n, C_n\rangle] \rightarrow \langle A_{n+1}, B_{n+1}, C_{n+1}\rangle$$
are *sound* in this particular framework i.e. whether for every instance ♦ of the framework (i.e. probability measure resp. database relation resp. NCF) it holds :
if $[A_1 \perp B_1 | C_1(\blacklozenge) \ \& \ \ldots \ \& \ A_n \perp B_n | C_n(\blacklozenge)]$ then $A_{n+1} \perp B_{n+1} | C_{n+1}(\blacklozenge)$.

Moreover, we may ask whether there exists a finite *axiomatic characterization* of CI–models i.e. a finite collection of such inference rules characterizing CI–models (for the particular framework) as dependency models satisfying that finite collection of inference rules. Such characterization (even for subclasses of CI–models) would have great importance for reasoning task within the particular framework.

Thus, the classes of CI–models arising in 3 above mentioned frameworks can be compared : we may ask which inference rules are sound in each of the frameworks, whether they differ and whether there exist finite axiomatic characterizations.

At the first sight (according to basic results) the classes of CI-models are very alike: CI-models from all three areas are semigraphoids (for the probabilistic case see [11], for database relations [7], for NCFs [4]). Nevertheless, the classes are indeed different as the following examples show.

EXAMPLE 1   The following inference rule
$$[\langle A, B, C \cup D\rangle \ \& \ \langle C, D, A\rangle \ \& \ \langle C, D, B\rangle \ \& \ \langle A, B, \emptyset\rangle] \longrightarrow \langle C, D, \emptyset\rangle$$
is sound in probabilistic framework but not in the framework of relational databases and ordinal conditional functions. The probabilistic soundness can be proved using some tools of information theory, for details see [14]. To show that it is not sound for relational databases it suffices to give an example of a database relation R such that the *antecedents* are satisfied i.e. $A \perp B | C \cup D(R), \ldots, A \perp B | \emptyset(R)$ but the *consequent* is not valid i.e. $\neg[C \perp D | \emptyset(R)]$. To this end we simply take $X_A = \{a, a'\}$, $X_B = \{b, b'\}$, $X_C = \{c, c'\}$, $X_D = \{d, d'\}$ and define R on $X_A \times X_B \times X_C \times X_D$ by the following table (the bullet in a box $[ab, cd]$ means that $(abcd) \in R$).

R	ab	ab'	a'b	a'b'
cd	•	•	•	•
cd'	•			
c'd				•
c'd'				

Similarly we can refute the soundness of this inference rule for NCFs. Take the same sets $X_A, \ldots, X_D$ and define an NCF κ by the following table (the number in a box $[ab, cd]$ is the value $\kappa(abcd)$):

κ	ab	ab'	a'b	a'b'
cd	0	1	1	2
cd'	1	1	1	1
c'd	0	0	0	0
c'd'	2	1	1	0

Note that another example that this inference rule fails in the case of NCFs was already given by Spohn [13].

EXAMPLE 2   The following inference rule
$$[\langle A, B, C \cup D\rangle \,\&\, \langle C, D, A\rangle \,\&\, \langle C, D, B\rangle] \longrightarrow \langle C, D, A \cup B\rangle$$
is sound in the framework of relational databases but fails for probabilistic measures and NCFs. Its soundness is easy to see:

Suppose $(a, b, c) \in R^{A \cup B \cup C}$ and $(a, b, d) \in R^{A \cup B \cup D}$. As $(a, c) \in R^{A \cup C}$ and $(a, d) \in R^{A \cup D}$ by $C \perp D | A(R)$ derive $(a, c, d) \in R^{A \cup C \cup D}$. Similarly by $C \perp D | B(R)$ get $(b, c, d) \in R^{B \cup C \cup D}$ and hence using $A \perp B | C \cup D(R)$ finally get $(a, b, c, d) \in R^{A \cup B \cup C \cup D}$.

To refute the probabilistic soundness take X_A, X_B, X_C, X_D from Example 1 and define on $X_A \times X_B \times X_C \times X_D$ the probability measure P as follows (the value in the box $[ab, cd]$ is $P(abcd)$):

P	ab	ab'	$a'b$	$a'b'$
cd	0.2	0	0	0
cd'	0.2	0	0	0
$c'd$	0.2	0	0	0
$c'd'$	0.1	0.1	0.1	0.1

The counterexample refuting soundness for NCFs was already given in Example 1.

EXAMPLE 3   The following inference rule
$$[\langle A, B, C \cup D\rangle \,\&\, \langle A, C, B \cup D\rangle] \longrightarrow \langle A, B \cup C, D\rangle$$
well–known as *intersection* [6] is sound in the framework of ordinal conditional functions but fails for probabilistic measures and database relations. Its soundness was shown in [12] or [4]. To refute the probabilistic soundness put $D = \emptyset$, take $X_A = \{a, a'\}$, $X_B = \{b, b'\}$, $X_C = \{c, c'\}$ and define on $X_A \times X_B \times X_C$ a probability measure P as follows:

P	bc	bc'	$b'c$	$b'c'$
a	0.5	0	0	0
a'	0	0	0	0.5

The counterexample for relational databases can be obtained easily :
simply take the support $R = \{x \in X_N;\ P(x) > 0\}$.

Note that the intersection inference rule holds also for strictly positive probability measures. Also further 3 inference rules sound for NCFs (see [13]) hold for strictly positive probability measures.

On the other hand, in all three above mentioned frameworks the following inference rules are sound ($n \geq 3$):
$$[\langle A, B_1, B_2\rangle \,\&\, \ldots \,\&\, \langle A, B_j, B_{j+1}\rangle \,\&\, \ldots \,\&\, \langle A, B_{n-1}, B_n\rangle \,\&\, \langle A, B_n, B_1\rangle] \longrightarrow \langle A, B_2, B_1\rangle$$
Moreover, as every proper subset of the collection of antecedents is a CI–model (in all 3 frameworks) this sequence of inference rules can be used to show that for each $n \geq 3$ and every hypothetic complete system $\mathcal{S}$ of sound inference rules there exists an inference rule in $\mathcal{S}$ with at least n antecedents. These results are proved for the probabilistic framework in [15], for relational databases in [7] and for NCFs in [16].

THEOREM   For each of the three above mentioned frameworks there exist no finite complete axiomatic characterization of CI–models.

4   Discussion

Let us mention further frameworks for CI which in some sense comprehend the frameworks above – namely possibility theory and Dempster–Shafer theory. The definitions below originate from Shenoy's work [10] where the concept of CI is defined for arbitrary framework satisfying certain general system of axioms for so–called *valuation–based systems*. The main result of that work says that every CI–model arising in such a framework is a semigraphoid.

DEFINITION 4 (CI–models in possibility theory)
Possibility function over N is specified by a real function $\pi : X_N \to \langle 0, 1 \rangle$ such that $max\,\{\pi(a);\ a \in X_N\} = 1$. The formula
$$\pi(A) = max\,\{\pi(a);\ a \in A\} \qquad \text{whenever} \quad \emptyset \neq A \subset X_N$$
defines a set function on $(exp\,X_N) \setminus \{\emptyset\}$ called *possibility function over N*. Whenever $\emptyset \neq S \subsetneq N$ its *marginal function on S* is a possibility function over S defined as follows:
$$\pi^S(A) = \pi(A \times X_{N \setminus S}) \qquad \text{for} \quad \emptyset \neq A \subset X_S\,.$$
Of course, $\pi^N \equiv \pi$.
Having a possibility function π over N and $\langle A, B, C \rangle \in T(N)$ write $A \perp B | C(\pi)$ iff
$$\forall \quad a \in X_A \quad b \in X_B \quad c \in X_C \quad \pi^{A \cup B \cup C}(abc) \cdot \pi^C(c) = \pi^{AC}(ac) \cdot \pi^{BC}(bc)\,.$$
For empty C put $\pi^\emptyset(c) = 1$. The dependency model $\{\langle A, B, C \rangle \in T(N); A \perp B | C(\pi)\}$ is called the *CI–model induced by π*.

This framework in fact involves frameworks for relational databases and NCFs. Indeed, we can assign the following possibility function to each database relation $R \subset X_N$:
$$\pi_R(A) = \begin{cases} 1 & \text{in case } A = R \\ 0 & \text{otherwise.} \end{cases}$$
It makes no problem to verify that the CI–model induced by R coincides with the CI–model induced by π_R. Similarly, to every NCF κ over N we can assign the possibility function π_κ as follows :
$$\pi_\kappa(A) = e^{-\kappa(A)} \qquad \text{whenever} \quad \emptyset \neq A \subset X_N.$$
This definition ensures that the CI–model induced by κ is identical with the CI–model induced by π_κ. Thus, the class of possibilistic CI–models includes strictly both database CI–models and CI–models arising in NCF theory (the inclusion is proper by Examples 2 and 3).

Shenoy in [10] defines CI also in the framework of Dempster–Shafer theory. This definition specialized to the unconditional case coincides with the concept of independence for evidence measures from [1].

DEFINITION 5 (CI–models in Dempster–Shafer theory)
Basic probability assignment (BPA) over N is specified by a real function
$\mathbf{m} : exp\,X_N \to \langle 0, \infty)$ such that $\sum \{\mathbf{m}(A); A \subset X_N\} = 1$ and $\mathbf{m}(\emptyset) = 0$.
The sets $A \subset X_N$ satisfying $\mathbf{m}(A) > 0$ are called *focal elements*. The formula
$Com_\mathbf{m}(A) = \sum \{\mathbf{m}(B); A \subset B\} \qquad \text{whenever} \quad A \subset X_N$
defines so–called *commonality function* which corresponds uniquely to the BPA (i.e.

there exist an inverse formula). Whenever $\emptyset \neq S \subsetneq N$ and $\mathbf{m}$ is a BPA over N, then its *marginal BPA over S* is defined as follows :
$$\mathbf{m}^S(A) = \sum \{ \mathbf{m}(\mathsf{B}), \quad \mathsf{B} \subset X_N \quad \mathsf{B}^S = A \} \qquad \text{for} \quad A \subset X_S$$
(the projection B^S was introduced in the second definition). Moreover, $\mathbf{m}^N \equiv \mathbf{m}$. Having a BPA $\mathbf{m}$ over N and a triplet $\langle A, B, C \rangle \in T(N)$ write $A \perp B | C(\mathbf{m})$ iff
$$\forall \mathsf{E} \subset X_{A \cup B \cup C} \quad Com_{\mathbf{m}^{A \cup B \cup C}}(\mathsf{E}) \cdot Com_{\mathbf{m}^C}(\mathsf{E}^C) = Com_{\mathbf{m}^{A \cup C}}(\mathsf{E}^{A \cup C}) \cdot Com_{\mathbf{m}^{B \cup C}}(\mathsf{E}^{B \cup C})$$
(take $Com_{\mathbf{m}^\emptyset}(\cdot) = 1$). The dependency model $\{ \langle A, B, C \rangle \in T(N); A \perp B | C(\mathbf{m}) \}$ is called the *CI–model induced by $\mathbf{m}$*.

Note that the presented definition of CI is in fact one of the equivalent definitions from [10] (use Lemma 3.1(v) there); the definition can be reformulated in terms of BPAs but it would be too complicated. Only important fact is that in case $A \perp B | C(\mathbf{m})$ the focal elements of $\mathbf{m}^{A \cup B \cup C}$ have the form
$$\mathsf{F} * \mathsf{G} = \{(a, b, c); (a, c) \in \mathsf{F} \quad (b, c) \in \mathsf{G}\} \text{ for } \mathsf{F} \subset X_{A \cup C} \text{ and } \mathsf{G} \subset X_{B \cup C} \text{ with } \mathsf{F}^C = \mathsf{G}^C.$$
The above defined class of CI–models involves both database and probabilistic CI–models. Every database relation $\mathsf{R} \subset X_N$ can be identified with a BPA :
$$\mathbf{m}_{\mathsf{R}}(A) = \begin{cases} 1 & \text{in case } A = \mathsf{R} \\ 0 & \text{otherwise} \end{cases}$$
in such a way that the corresponding CI–models coincide. Similarly, every probability measure P over N defines a BPA $\mathbf{m}_P$ as follows :
$$\mathbf{m}_P(A) = \begin{cases} P(x) & \text{whenever } A = \{x\} \text{ for } x \in X_N \\ 0 & \text{otherwise.} \end{cases}$$
Of course, the CI–model induced by P is the CI–model induced by $\mathbf{m}_P$. Thus, using Examples 1 and 2 we can derive that the presented class of CI–models for BPAs has probabilistic and database CI–models as proper subsets.

Nevertheless, the presented definition does not seem to us to be suitable in the framework of Dempster–Shafer theory. We have two objection.

Firstly, this CI is not "consistent with marginalization". This means that it may happen that for a couple of BPA's $\mathbf{m}_1$ over $A \cup C$ and $\mathbf{m}_2$ over $B \cup C$ which are consonant (i.e. $\mathbf{m}_1^C = \mathbf{m}_2^C$) there exists no BPA $\mathbf{m}$ over $A \cup B \cup C$ such that $\mathbf{m}^{A \cup C} = \mathbf{m}_1$, $\mathbf{m}^{B \cup C} = \mathbf{m}_2$ and $A \perp B | C(\mathbf{m})$. In all other mentioned frameworks such "conditional product" exists and it is uniquely determined.

Secondly, Dempster–Shafer theory was intended to embed both possibility functions and probability measures (see [5]). Concretely, every possibility function π over N is identified with a BPA $\mathbf{m}_\pi$ whose collection of focal elements is a nest i.e.
$$\forall A, B \subset X_N \text{ with } \mathbf{m}_\pi(A), \mathbf{m}_\pi(B) > 0 \text{ either } A \subset B \text{ or } B \subset A$$
by means of the relation $\pi(x) = \sum \{\mathbf{m}_\pi(B); x \in B\}$ (for details see [5]). Therefore the concept of CI for BPAs should generalize CI for possibility functions. Nevertheless, this is not true even in the unconditional case. The reason is clear: if we consider two possibilistic BPA's with two focal elements then their product has as focal elements cartesian products of "marginal" focal elements – but this class is not a nest i.e. the product does not represent possibilistic BPA.

We think that the concept CI in Dempster-Shafer theory should comprehend both probabilistic and possibilistic CI and be "consistent with marginalization". However, so far we don't find an adequate definition of CI within this framework.

References

1. L.M. de Campos, J.F. Huete: Independence concepts in upper and lower probabilities. In: Proceedings of IPMU'92 (inter. conf. on Information Processing and Management of Uncertainty in knowledge–based systems, Mallorca, July 6–10, 1992), 129-132

2. A.P. Dawid: Conditional independence in statistical theory. Journal of the Royal Statistical Society B 41, 1–31 (1979)

3. M. Goldszmidt, J. Pearl: Rank–based systems: a simple approach to belief revision, belief update, and reasoning about evidence and actions. In: Proceedings of the 3rd International Conference on Principles of Knowledge Representation and Reasoning, Cambridge, MA, October 1992, 661-672

4. D. Hunter: Graphoids and natural conditional functions. International Journal of Approximate Reasoning 5, 489–504 (1991)

5. G.J. Klir, T.A.Folger: Fuzzy Sets, Uncertainty and Information. Prentice Hall. Englewood Cliffs, N.J. 1988

6. J. Pearl: Probabilistic Reasoning in Intelligent Systems: Networks of Plausible Inference. Morgan Kaufman. San Mateo, California 1988

7. Y. Sagiv, S.F. Walecka: Subset dependencies and completeness result for a subclass of embedded multivalued dependencies. Journal of the Association for Computing Machinery 29, 103–117 (1982)

8. G. Shafer, P.P. Shenoy, K. Mellouli: Propagating belief functions in qualitative Markov trees. International Journal of Approximate Reasoning 1, 349–400 (1987)

9. P.P. Shenoy: On Spohn's rule for revision of beliefs. International Journal of Approximate Reasoning 5, 149–181 (1991)

10. P.P. Shenoy: Conditional independence in valuation–based systems. School of Business working paper n. 236, University of Kansas, Lawrence 1992, submitted to Annals of Statistics

11. W. Spohn: Stochastic independence, causal independence and shieldability. Journal of Philosophical Logic 9, 73–99 (1980)

12. W. Spohn: Ordinal conditional functions: a dynamic theory of epistemic states. In: W.L. Harper, B. Skyrms (eds.): Causation in Decision, Belief Change, and Statistics, vol. II . Kluwer Academic Publishers. Dordrecht 1988, 105–134

13. W. Spohn: On the properties of conditional independence. to appear in P. Humphreys (eds.): Patrick Suppes - Mathematical Philosopher. Synthese 1993

14. M. Studený: Multiinformation and the problem of characterization of conditional independence relations. Problems of Control and Information Theory 18, 3–16 (1989)

15. M.Studený: Conditional independence relations have no finite complete characterization. In: Transactions of 11-th Prague Conference on Information Theory, Statistical Decision Functions and Random Processes vol.B . Academia. Prague 1992, 377-396

16. M. Studený: Conditional independence and natural conditional functions. submitted to International Journal of Approximate Reasoning

A Proof Theory for Constructive Default Logic*

Yao-Hua Tan

Erasmus University Rotterdam, Department of Computer Science,
P.O. Box 1738, 3000 DR Rotterdam, The Netherlands, tan@cs.few.eur.nl

Free University Amsterdam, Department of Mathematics and Computer Science,
De Boelelaan 1081a, 1081 HV Amsterdam, The Netherlands, tan@cs.vu.nl

Abstract. In earlier papers we developed a constructive version of Reiter's default logic; *Constructive Default Logic* (*CDL*) which is a default logic in which the fixed-point definition of extensions is replaced by a constructive definition. Constructive extensions have a computational advantage over Reiter's extensions. Reiter's default logic lacks a default proof theory for non-normal default rules, which was already observed by Reiter himself to be a weakness of his logic. In this paper we show that CDL does have a default proof theory.

1 Introduction

One of the sources of the complexity problems in default logic is its non-constructive character. In [4] Reiter defines extensions in default logic by a fixed-point definition, which is not constructive. In recent years it was observed by several researchers that the complexity problem of default logic can be heuristically improved by making the default reasoning process more constructive (for an extensive discussion of this point see e.g. [1]). We have developed a constructive version of Reiter's default logic. *Constructive Default Logic* (*CDL*) is a default logic in which the fixed-point definition of extensions is replaced by a constructive definition. Constructive extensions have a computational advantage over Reiter extensions. A detailed discussion about the heuristic advantages of constructive default logic in comparison to Reiter's default logic can be found in [7]. Apart from being non-constructive it is well-known that Reiter's default logic lacks a default proof theory for non-normal default rules, which was already observed by Reiter himself to be a weakness of his logic. In this paper we will show that CDL does have a default proof theory.

2 Constructive Default Logic

Constructive default logic is default logic in which the normal fixed-point extensions of Reiter are replaced by so-called constructive extensions. Research on constructive default logic was reported earlier in [5], [6] and [7]. Constructive extensions are parameterized by a selection function that controls the generation process of the constructive extension. Default logic is a classical logic extended with so-called default rules (see [4], or [1]). We write *default rules* as $(\alpha : \beta_1,...,\beta_n / \omega)$, where α, β_i and ω are logical formulas. The formula α is called the *prerequisite*, β_i the *justifications* and ω the *conclusion* of the default rule. A default rule is called *normal* if the justification is equivalent to the conclusion, i.e. if it is of the form $(\alpha : \beta / \beta)$. A *default theory* $\Delta = <W, D>$ consists of a set of logical formulas W and a set of default rules D. Let $Th(S)$ denote the deductive closure in a logic L of a set S

* This research was partially supported by ESPRIT III BRA Project No. 6156 DRUMS II.

of L-formulas. To distinguish Reiter's extensions from our constructive extensions, we will call the first R-extensions. Reiter defines in [4] the R-extension as follows.

Definition 2.1 A set of sentences E is an *R-extension* of the default theory $\Delta = <W, D>$, if $E = \bigcup_{i=0}^{\infty} E_i$, where each layer E_i is defined as follows:

for $i = 0$; $E_0 = W$,

for $i \geq 0$; $E_{i+1} = Th(E_i) \cup \{\omega \mid (\alpha : \beta_1,..., \beta_n / \omega) \in D, \alpha \in E_i, \text{ and } \neg\beta_1,..., \neg\beta_n \notin E\}$.

Note that this definition is a fixed-point definition, which in principle is not constructive. In the definition of the layer E_{i+1} it is required that the formulas $\neg\beta_1,..., \neg\beta_n$ are not contained in E. Hence, the definition of each layer E_{i+1} depends on the *final outcome E*. A selection function, which will be denoted by σ, selects a subset of default conclusions from the set of all default conclusions that can be derived at a certain layer. Indices i from an index set I are added to indicate that the selection is made at the i-th reasoning step. Let L be a logic and let U be a set of well-formed formulas of L. Let $P(U)$ denote the set of all subsets $V \subseteq U$, and let I be an index set. The function $\sigma : I \times P(U) \to P(U)$ is called a *selection function* if for every subset V of U and every index i holds that $\sigma(i, V) \subseteq V$. Let D be a set of defaults. The *set of consequences* of D, denoted as $Cons(D)$ is defined by $Cons(D) = \{\omega \mid (\alpha : \beta_1,..., \beta_n / \omega) \in D\}$. Suppose $\Delta = <W, D>$ is a default theory and $\sigma : I \times P(U) \to P(U)$ is a selection function. We call σ a *selection function related to* Δ if $U = Cons(D)$. The set of selection functions related to Δ is denoted by $Sel(\Delta)$. In this paper the index set I will always be the set of natural numbers, with the usual ordering. Instead of $\sigma(i, V)$ we will also write simply $\sigma_i(V)$. We will say that a selection function is an *identity* selection function if for all $V \subseteq Cons(D)$ and for all i holds $\sigma_i(V) = V$. And we will say that a selection is an *empty* selection function if for all $V \subseteq Cons(D)$ and for all i holds $\sigma_i(V) = \emptyset$. Next we define the notion of a σ-constructive extension. This is a constructive extension of which the construction is controlled by a selection function σ.

Definition 2.2 Let $\Delta = <W, D>$ be a default theory and σ be a selection function related to Δ. A set of sentences C^σ is called the σ-*constructive extension* of the default theory Δ, if $C^\sigma = \bigcup_{i=0}^{\infty} C^\sigma_i$

for $i = 0$; $C^\sigma_0 = W$,

for $i \geq 0$; $C^\sigma_{i+1} = Th(C^\sigma_i) \cup \sigma_{i+1}(Cons(D^\sigma_{i+1}))$,

where $D^\sigma_{i+1} = \{(\alpha : \beta_1,..., \beta_n / \omega) \in D \mid \alpha \in C^\sigma_i, \text{ and } \neg\beta_1,...,\neg\beta_n \notin Th(C^\sigma_i)\}$.

We will call default logic based on σ-constructive extensions *Constructive Default Logic* (*CDL*). In the sequel we will refer to Reiter's default logic with R-extensions as *DL*. If it is clear from the context, we will usually omit the σ prefix, and simply call it constructive extension. For a given default theory $\Delta = <W, D>$ there is a collection of such σ-constructive extensions, parameterized by selection functions $\sigma \in Sel(\Delta)$. Let $\Delta = <W, D>$ be a default theory and suppose σ is a selection function related to Δ. A default rule $(\alpha : \beta_1,..., \beta_n / \omega) \in D$ is called *applicable* at stage i if $(\alpha : \beta_1,..., \beta_n / \omega) \in D^\sigma_i$. We say that a default $(\alpha : \beta_1,..., \beta_n / \omega) \in D$ *is used in principle* by σ at stage i if it is applicable and $\omega \in \sigma_i(Cons(D^\sigma_i))$. In this case we also say that the formula ω *is selected* by σ at stage i. Selection functions are useful for the following reasons. Consider the following example.

Example 2.3 Let $\Delta = <W, D>$ be a default theory with $W = \emptyset$ and $D = \{(:p / p),$

$(: \neg p / \neg p)\}$. Consider the identity selection function σ, i.e. $\sigma_i(V) = V$ for all i and subsets $V \subseteq Cons(D)$, then σ generates the constructive extension $C^\sigma = Th(\{p, \neg p\})$, which is inconsistent. This is due to the fact that both defaults in D can be applied and are selected by σ at stage C^σ_1 in the construction of C^σ, i.e. $\sigma_1(Cons(D^\sigma_1)) = \{p, \neg p\}$.

From this example follows immediately that a constructive extension C^σ of a default theory $\Delta = \langle W, D \rangle$ can be *inconsistent*, although W is *consistent*. This observation clearly distinguishes CDL from DL, because Reiter proved that every R-extension of a default theory $\Delta = \langle W, D \rangle$ is inconsistent if and only if W is inconsistent (see Corollary 2.2 in [4]). From Example 2.3 also follows immediately that DL and CDL are not equivalent for normal defaults. This distinguishes CDL from every alternative default logic proposed in the literature, because all the alternative default logics I know of are equivalent to DL with respect to normal default rules (for an extensive survey of alternative default logics see [1]). We can impose constraints on the selection functions in order to prevent inconsistencies between default conclusions. Let $\Delta = \langle W, D \rangle$ be a default theory, and let σ be a selection function related to Δ. We say that σ satisfies the *C-constraint* if for all i and every $V \subseteq Cons(D)$ we have that $W \cup \sigma_i(V)$ is consistent. This C-constraint solves the inconsistency in Example 2.3, because the identity selection function σ selects $\sigma_1(D^\sigma_0) = \{p, \neg p\}$, hence it does not satisfy the C-constraint. In addition to inconsistent default conclusions there is another phenomenon which is typical for constructive extensions. Consider the following example.

Example 2.4 Let $\Delta = \langle W, D \rangle$ be a default theory with $W = \{q \rightarrow \neg p\}$ and $D = \{(: p / q)\}$. Consider the identity selection function σ, i.e. for all i and $V \subseteq Cons(D)$ we have $\sigma_i(V) = V$, then σ generates the constructive extension $C^\sigma = Th(\{q, \neg p\})$. This is counterintuitive, because the justification p of the default rule $(: p / q)$ is violated by the conclusion of the implication $q \rightarrow \neg p$.

What happens in this example is that the default rule defeats its own justification indirectly. First the default can be applied at a certain stage, but at a later stage the conclusion of this default leads to a violation of the justification of this default rule. Also this problem can be solved by imposing a constraint, the so-called non-self-defeating constraint, on selection functions. A default $(\alpha : \beta_1,...,\beta_n / \omega) \in D$ that in principle is used at stage i by a selection function σ is called *defeated* by σ, if there is some $j \geq i$ such that $\neg \beta_k \in Th(C^\sigma_j)$ for some k with $1 \leq k \leq n$. We call σ *self-defeating* if there is some stage i and some formula ω that is selected by σ at i such that all defaults $(\alpha : \beta_1,..., \beta_n / \omega) \in D^\sigma_i$ with consequence ω are defeated by σ. If σ is not self-defeating, then we say that σ is *non-self-defeating (NSD)*, or that it satisfies the NSD-constraint, or simply that it is NSD. We can prove that if a selection function satisfies the NSD-constraint, then it satisfies the C-constraint (for the proof see [6].) The σ-constructive extensions are in some respects more intuitive than R-extensions. Lukaszewicz observed in [3] that R-extensions sometimes yield counter-intuitive results. This can be illustrated with the following example.

Example 2.5 Let Δ be the default theory with $W = \varnothing$ and $D = \{(: p / q), (: \neg q / s)\}$. The support for the conclusion q is as weak as the support for the conclusion s. In the first case the formula $\neg p$ should not be in the extension, and in the second case the formula $\neg q$. Since W is empty, one expects that Δ has two extensions; one that contains q, and another one that contains s (or one extension that contains both conclusions). However, Δ has only one R-extension, namely $E = Th(\{q\})$, which lacks s.

The application of the first default blocks the application of the second default, because the justification of the second default is violated by the conclusion of the first one.

With σ-constructive extensions these counter-intuitive results can be avoided. Consider two selection functions σ and σ', of which the first one never selects the formula q, whereas the second is the identity function that selects everything i.e. $\sigma'(V) = V$ for all V. It is clear that $C^\sigma = Th(\{s\})$, because the application of $(: \neg q / s)$ is no longer blocked by $(: p / q)$, because the conclusion q is not selected by σ. In addition there is also a σ-constructive extension of Δ, $C^{\sigma'} = E = Th(\{q\})$, which contains the conclusion q.

3 A Proof Theory for Constructive Default Logic

A proof theory for default logic is defined as follows. Let $Pre(D)$ denote the set of prerequisites of the default rules in D, and $Jus(D)$ the set of justifications of default rules in D. We use the definition of Guerreiro, Cassanova and Hemerly given in [4], which is related to the definition of default proof theory given by Lukaszewicz in [3].

Definition 3.1 Let $\Delta = <W, D>$ be a default theory and φ a sentence. A finite sequence $< D_0, ..., D_k >$ of finite subsets of D is a *default proof* of φ from Δ iff

1. $W \cup Cons(D_k) \vdash \varphi$,
2. For $1 \leq i \leq k$, $W \cup Cons(D_{i-1}) \vdash Pre(D_i)$,
3. $D_0 = \varnothing$,
4. If W is consistent, then for each $\beta \in \bigcup_{i=0}^{k} Jus(D_i)$ holds

$$W \cup \bigcup_{i=0}^{k} Cons(D_i) \cup \{\beta\} \text{ is consistent.}$$

First we define soundness and completeness of a default proof theory in the general case. Let S refer to the notion of extension as it is defined in a particular default logic. For example, S refers to R-extensions in Reiter's default logic, and to constructive extensions in constructive default logic. We say that a default proof theory is *sound* if for every formula φ and every $< D_0, ..., D_k >$ which is a default proof of φ from Δ, there is an extension S of Δ such that $\varphi \in S$. And a default proof theory is *correct* if for every formula φ and for every extension S of Δ such that $\varphi \in S$, there is a $< D_0, ..., D_k >$ which is a default proof of φ from Δ. Reiter observed already in [4] that his default logic only has a sound and complete default proof theory for the normal defaults, but not for non-normal ones. It can easily be illustrated why Reiter's default logic is not sound with respect to the default proof theory as defined in Definition 3.1. Consider the two default theories $\Delta = <\varnothing, \{(: p / q), (: \neg q / s)\} >$ and $\Delta' = <\varnothing, \{(: \neg q / s)\} >$. Now one can easily check that the sequence $< D_0, D_1 >$ with $D_0 = \varnothing$ and $D_1 = \{(: \neg q / s)\}$ is a default proof of the formula s from Δ as well as Δ'. However, Δ has only one R-extension, and that one does not contain the formula s. In the following theorems it is shown that constructive default logic has a default proof theory. First we state two propositions that are used in the proofs of the main theorems. The proofs of these propositions are omitted, but can be found in [6].

Proposition 3.2 Let C^σ be a constructive extension for the default theory $\Delta = <W, D>$, then for each stage i with $i \geq 1$ holds $C^\sigma i \subseteq Th(W \cup \bigcup_{j=0}^{i} \sigma_j(Cons(D^\sigma_j)))$,

Proposition 3.3 Let C^σ be a constructive extension for the default theory $\Delta = \langle W, D \rangle$, then $C^\sigma = Th(W \cup \bigcup_{i=0}^{\infty} \sigma_i(Cons(D^\sigma_i)))$,

We can only prove completeness with respect to a subclass of constructive extensions; namely the extensions that are NSD. This restriction is needed for the following reason. Consider again Example 2.4. In this example there was a default theory Δ with $W = \{q \rightarrow \neg p\}$ and $D = \{(:p/q)\}$. This Δ has a constructive extension $C^\sigma = Th(\{q, \neg p\})$ of which the selection function σ is not NSD. One can easily verify that the only way to derive the formula q with a default proof from Δ is with a sequence $\langle B_0, ..., B_k \rangle$ such that $(:p/q) \in B_k$. However, with respect to this sequence we have that $W \cup \bigcup_{i=0}^{k} Cons(B_i) \cup \{p\}$ is inconsistent, hence it violates condition (4) of the definition of a default proof, and therefore this sequence is not a default proof.

Theorem 3.4 (NSD-completeness of default proof theory w.r.t. CDL)
Let C^σ be a constructive extension of a default theory $\Delta = \langle W, D \rangle$ with D a finite set of defaults. If a formula φ is contained in C^σ and the selection function σ is NSD, then there is a default proof of φ from Δ.

Proof. Let the formula φ be contained in a constructive extension C^σ of a default theory $\Delta = \langle W, D \rangle$ with a selection function σ that is NSD. Let D^σ_i be the set of defaults that are derivable at stage i in the construction of C^σ, i.e. for $i > 0$ we define $D^\sigma_i = \{(\alpha : \beta_1, ..., \beta_n / \omega) \in D \mid \alpha \in C^\sigma_{i-1}, \text{ and } \neg \beta_1, ..., \neg \beta_n \notin Th(C^\sigma_{i-1})\}$. And let SD^σ_i denote the set of applicable default from D^σ_i of which the conclusions are selected by σ_i, i.e. $SD^\sigma_i = \{(\alpha : \beta_1, ..., \beta_n / \omega) \in D^\sigma_i \mid \omega \in \sigma_i(Cons(D^\sigma_i))\}$. Let C^σ_k be the first stage in C^σ that contains φ. If $k = 0$, then $\varphi \in C^\sigma_0 = W$, and one can easily verify that the sequence $\langle B_0 \rangle$ with $B_0 = \varnothing$ is a default proof of φ from Δ. If $k > 0$, then define each set B_i in the finite sequence $\langle B_0, ..., B_k \rangle$ as follows $B_0 = \varnothing$ and $B_i = \bigcup_{j=0}^{i} SD^\sigma_j$, for $1 \leq i \leq k$. It is obvious that $\langle B_0, ..., B_k \rangle$ is a finite sequence of finite subsets, because the set of defaults D is finite. We have to prove that this sequence is a default proof. We check the four conditions of Definition 3.1.

(1) First we have to prove that $W \cup Cons(B_k) \vdash \varphi$. Since we have that $\varphi \in C^\sigma_k$ with $k \geq 1$ it follows by Proposition 3.2 that $\varphi \in Th(W \cup \bigcup_{j=0}^{k} \sigma_j(Cons(D^\sigma_j)))$. Since $\bigcup_{j=0}^{k} \sigma_j(Cons(D^\sigma_j)) = \bigcup_{j=0}^{k} Cons(SD^\sigma_j) = Cons(\bigcup_{j=0}^{k} SD^\sigma_j) = Cons(B_k)$, it follows that $\varphi \in Th(W \cup Cons(B_k))$, and hence $W \cup Cons(B_k) \vdash \varphi$.

(2) Next we have to prove that for each i with $1 \leq i \leq k$ holds $W \cup Cons(B_{i-1}) \vdash Pre(B_i)$. Let $\alpha \in Pre(B_i)$, then there is a default $(\alpha : \beta_1, ..., \beta_n / \omega) \in B_i$. Since, $B_i = \bigcup_{j=0}^{i} SD^\sigma_j$ there is an m with $0 \leq m \leq i$ such that $(\alpha : \beta_1, ..., \beta_n / \omega) \in SD^\sigma_m$, and hence we have $\alpha \in C^\sigma_{m-1}$. Consequently, by Proposition 3.2 it follows that $\alpha \in Th(W \cup \bigcup_{j=0}^{m-1} \sigma_j(Cons(D^\sigma_j)))$. Since $m \leq i$, it follows that $\alpha \in Th(W \cup \bigcup_{j=0}^{i-1} \sigma_j(Cons(D^\sigma_j)))$.
Since, $\bigcup_{j=0}^{i-1} \sigma_j(Cons(D^\sigma_j)) = \bigcup_{j=0}^{i-1} Cons(SD^\sigma_j) = Cons(\bigcup_{j=0}^{i-1} SD^\sigma_j) = Cons(B_{i-1})$, it follows that $\alpha \in Th(W \cup Cons(B_{i-1}))$, and hence $W \cup Cons(B_{i-1}) \vdash \alpha$.
(3) $B_0 = \varnothing$ follows by definition.

(4) We have to show that if W is consistent, then for each $\beta \in \overset{k}{\underset{i=0}{\cup}} Jus(B_i)$ holds $W \cup \overset{k}{\underset{i=0}{\cup}} Cons(B_i) \cup \{\beta\}$ is consistent. Assume that W is consistent and for a certain $\beta' \in \overset{k}{\underset{i=0}{\cup}} Jus(B_i)$ the set $W \cup \overset{k}{\underset{i=0}{\cup}} Cons(B_i) \cup \{\beta'\}$ is inconsistent. Note that $\overset{k}{\underset{i=0}{\cup}} B_i = B_k$, hence it follows that $\overset{k}{\underset{i=0}{\cup}} Jus(B_i) = Jus(\overset{k}{\underset{i=0}{\cup}} B_i) = Jus(B_k)$. Let SD^σ_j be the first stage in B_k in which a default is applicable with the justification β' of which the conclusion is selected by σ_j. Since this default is applicable in SD^σ_j, it follows that $\neg \beta' \notin Th(C^\sigma_{j-1})$. But this implies that $\neg \beta'$ must have been derived at a later stage C^σ_m with $j \leq m \leq k$, which contradicts the assumption that the selection function σ is NSD. ∎

Theorem 3.5   (NSD-soundness of default proof theory w.r.t. CDL)
If there is a default proof of φ from $\Delta = <W, D>$, then there is a constructive extension C^σ of Δ with a selection function σ such that $\varphi \in C^\sigma$.

Proof. Suppose φ has a default proof from $\Delta = <W, D>$, then there is a finite sequence $<B_0,..., B_k>$ of finite subsets B_i of D such that it is a default proof of φ from Δ. We use this sequence to generate a constructive extension C^σ of Δ that contains the formula φ in the following way. Now define the selection function σ that is used to generate C^σ as follows;

$\sigma_{2n}(Cons(D^\sigma_{2n})) = Cons(B_n)$, for $0 \leq n \leq k$,
$\sigma_{2n+1}(Cons(D^\sigma_{2n+1})) = \varnothing$, for $0 \leq n \leq k$,
$\sigma_n(Cons(D^\sigma_{2n+1})) = \varnothing$, for $n > 2k$,

and for any V and any i such that $V \neq Cons(D^\sigma_i)$, we have $\sigma_i(V) = \varnothing$.

If we can prove that σ is a selection function, then it follows immediately from the definition of σ that C^σ is a constructive extension for Δ such that $\varphi \in C^\sigma$. So, what remains to be proven is that this σ is a selection function.

Due to the definition given above it is trivially true that σ is a function. To prove that σ also satisfies the requirement of a selection function we have to prove that for all stages i in the construction of C^σ holds $\sigma_i(Cons(D^\sigma_i)) \subseteq Cons(D^\sigma_i)$. Note that this trivially holds for every stage i with an empty selection; i.e. for $i = 2n+1$ with $1 \leq n \leq k$, and for $i > 2k$. Hence, we only have to prove $Cons(B_i) \subseteq Cons(D^\sigma_{2i})$, for $0 \leq i \leq k$.

Note that by definition $B_0 = \varnothing$. Suppose $\omega \in Cons(B_i)$ with $1 \leq i \leq k$, then there is a default $\partial = (\alpha : \beta_1,...,\beta_n / \omega) \in B_i$, and therefore we also have (1) $(\alpha : \beta_1,..., \beta_n / \omega) \in D$. Since, $<B_0,..., B_k>$ is a default proof it follows that for any i with $1 \leq i \leq k$ holds $W \cup Cons(B_{i-1}) \vdash Pre(B_i)$, and consequently it follows in particular that $W \cup Cons(B_{i-1}) \vdash \alpha$. Hence, by definition of σ it also follows that $W \cup \sigma_{2(i-1)}(Cons(D^\sigma_{2(i-1)})) \vdash \alpha$, and thus we have $\alpha \in Th(C^\sigma_{2(i-1)})$, and hence it follows that (2) $\alpha \in C^\sigma_{2i-1}$. By definition of default proof it follows that each $\beta \in \overset{k}{\underset{i=0}{\cup}} Jus(B_i)$ is consistent with $W \cup \overset{k}{\underset{i=0}{\cup}} Cons(B_i)$. Hence, this implies that (3) each $\beta \in \overset{2k}{\underset{i=0}{\cup}} Jus(SD^\sigma_i)$ is consistent with $W \cup \overset{2k}{\underset{i=0}{\cup}} Cons(SD^\sigma_i)$. Since we know from Proposition 3.3 that $C^\sigma = Th(W \cup \overset{\infty}{\underset{i=0}{\cup}} \sigma_i(Cons(D^\sigma_i)))$, we also know that $C^\sigma = Th(W \cup \overset{2k}{\underset{i=0}{\cup}} \sigma_i(Cons(D^\sigma_i)))$, because after stage $2k$ no new default conclusions are selected by σ. Since $\overset{2k}{\underset{i=0}{\cup}} \sigma_i(Cons(D^\sigma_i)) = \overset{2k}{\underset{i=0}{\cup}} Cons(SD^\sigma_i)$, it follows from (3) that for all justifications $\beta_1,...,\beta_n$ from the default rule ∂ we have $\neg \beta_1,...,\neg \beta_n \notin C^\sigma$, and hence also (4) $\neg \beta_1,...,\neg \beta_n \notin Th(C^\sigma_{2i-1})$. From (1), (2) and (4) it follows that $\partial \in D^\sigma_{2i}$, and therefore its conclusion ω is contained in $Cons(D^\sigma_{2i})$. Consequently, σ is a selection function.

355

Suppose that σ is not NSD, i.e. σ is self-defeating. Hence, there is a stage i and a formula ω that is selected by σ at stage i such that for every applicable default rule $(\alpha : \beta_1,...,\beta_n / \omega) \in D^\sigma_i$ with conclusion ω there is some later stage $j > i$ such that $\neg \beta_m \in Th(C^\sigma_j)$ with $1 \le m \le n$. This implies that $\neg \beta_m \in C^\sigma$, hence by Proposition 3.3 it also follows that $\neg \beta_m \in Th(W \cup \bigcup_{i=0}^{\infty} \sigma_i(Cons(D^\sigma_i)))$. Since every selection of σ after stage $2k$ is empty, it follows that we have

$$Th(W \cup \bigcup_{i=0}^{\infty} \sigma_i(Cons(D^\sigma_i))) = Th(W \cup \bigcup_{i=0}^{2k} \sigma_i(Cons(D^\sigma_i))),$$

and hence $\neg \beta_m \in Th(W \cup \bigcup_{i=0}^{2k} \sigma_i(Cons(D^\sigma_i)))$. Since, $\bigcup_{i=0}^{2k} \sigma_i(Cons(D^\sigma_i)) = \bigcup_{i=0}^{k} Cons(B_i)$, it follows that $W \cup \bigcup_{i=0}^{k} Cons(B_i) \cup \{\beta_m\}$ is inconsistent, which contradicts the assumption that the sequence $< B_0,..., B_k >$ satisfies condition (4) of the definition of a default proof. ∎

References

1. C. Froidevaux and J. Mengin, *A framework for comparing default logics*, Tech. Report LRI, Universite Paris Sud, 1992. (extended abstract appeared in *Proceedings of the JELIA 92*, Berlin, 1992.)

2. R.A. Gueirrero, M.A. Cassanova and A.S. Hemerly, Contributions to a proof theory for generic defaults, *Proc. ECAI 90*, 1990.

3. W. Lukaszewicz, Considerations on default logic - An alternative approach, *Computational Intelligence*, 4:1-16, 1988.

4. R. Reiter, A logic for default reasoning, *Artificial Intelligence* 13, pp. 81-132.

5. Y.H. Tan, BMS - A meta-level approach to non-monotonic reasoning, in: W. Van der Hoek, J.-J. Ch. Meyer, Y.H. Tan and C. Witteveen (eds.), *Non-Monotonic Reasoning and Partial Semantics*, Series in Artificial Intelligence, Ellis Horwood Publishers, 1992.

6. Y.H. Tan, *A proof theory for constructive default logic*, Tech. Report, Dept. of Computer Science, Erasmus University Rotterdam, Rotterdam, May 1993.

7. Y.H. Tan, J. Treur, Constructive default logic and the control of defeasible reasoning, In: B. Neumann (ed.), *Proc. of the European Conference on Artificial Intelligence, ECAI '92*, John Wiley and Sons, 1992, pp. 299-303.

Plausible Inference for Default Conditionals

Emil Weydert

Max-Planck-Institute for Computer Science, Im Stadtwald, D-66123 Saarbrücken, Germany

emil@mpi-sb.mpg.de

1 Introduction

Since the eighties, there have been lots of proposals about how to formalize defeasible reasoning. Among them, conditional logical approaches have become increasingly popular. Here, defaults are mostly interpreted as abstract encodings of objective normality relationships. That is, "*if* A, *then by default* B" is taken to mean "*if* A, *then normally* B". One of the main strengths of this account is that defaults are no longer regarded as procedural - no special rule-like character, like in default logic - or ethereal - no implicit encoding, like in circumscription - entities, but they get truth conditions and become fully integrated into a propositional logical context. Using a conditional framework is also conceptually rather appealing. Being expressive and straightforward, it greatly simplifies the formalization of default knowledge. In particular, we do no longer need an explicit encoding of specificity-preference[1]. This and the existence of solid semantic foundations, partly based on a fruitful pre-AI research tradition in philosophical logic, guarantee transparency and make conditional logics an appropriate tool for knowledge engineering.

The second half of the eighties saw the beginning and convergence of several lines of research committed to some conditional viewpoint [e.g., Gab 85, Del 88, Sho 87, Mak 89, 93, KLM 90, LM 92, Bou 90, 92, Wey 91, 93]. From these investigations emerged a certain consensus about the appropriate rules or axioms for flat (= non-nested) default conditionals, notably those given by **CT4D-** (Boutilier) or **R$^+$ (HRC°)** (Weydert), including in particular the principles found in Lehmann's preferential or rational logic. So, concerning the monotonic logic for flat normal implication, we are fixed. But of course, we also have to look for a corresponding reasonable nonmonotonic entailment relation $\approx$ extending $\vdash$, the monotonic one, and describing the plausible consequences of possibly infinite premise sets (e.g. the *defeasible modus ponens (rule)*: {A, A => B} $\approx$ B, but {A, A => B} $\not\vdash$ B). In particular, it should allow us to implement plausible guessing strategies meeting our practical needs but too shaky to incorporate into a monotonic background logic (e.g. *defeasible chaining* : {A, A => A', A' => B} $\approx$ B, for sufficiently independent A, A', B). A rather rudimentary but often implicitly adopted approach has been to consider only finite knowledge bases **KB** = **KB**[*fact*]$\cup$**KB**[*default*], where **KB**[*fact*] = {A_0, ..., A_n} is a set of default-free statements and **KB**[*default*] contains only positive conditionals, and to stipulate **KB** $\approx$ B iff **KB** $\vdash$ (A_0& ... &A_n => B). But in general, this will not even give us defeasible chaining, forcing us to look for more sophisticated approaches.

In this paper[2], we shall therefore consider defeasible inference relations, defined for arbitrary sets of boolean combinations of non-modal facts and defaults, on top of a monotonic core logic for default conditionals. First, we shall present a semantics and a proof theory for *flat hyperrational conditional logic*, a strong logic for normal implication[3]. Then, we are going to formulate our basic *regular-inference*-conditions for nonmonotonic entailment relations extending the monotonic core inference and claiming to provide an appropriate interpretation for our default conditional. Next, we shall construct a preferential semantic framework describing the class of *pre-hyperentailment relations*, which turn out to satisfy our standard regularity requirements. This approach will then be exemplified and specified by *elementary hyperentailment*, a powerful and transparent semantic-based plausible inference relation implementing the idea of assuming maximal normality in a very general way and correctly solving many old and new benchmark problems. Last but not least, we shall discuss the strengths and limits of our proposal and take a look at competing accounts.

---

[1] The standard example is : "*Tweety is a bird, Tweety is a penguin, by default birds can fly, by default penguins cannot fly, every penguin is a bird*" should defeasibly entail "*Tweety can't fly*".

[2] Thanks to Jürgen Dix, Hans Kamp and Sven Lorenz, who helped to make this paper a more intelligible one.

[3] For nested normal implication, the reader is invited to consult [Wey 93].

2 Monotonic entailment

Statements or rules like "*if* A, *then by default* B" appear to be true or reasonable just when assertions like "A *normally / plausibly implies* B" do. Such instances of normal implication may best be interpreted as telling us that w.r.t. some normality ranking of possible worlds, the most normal or typical alternatives verifying A also satisfy B[4]. By using total instead of partial normality orders, i.e. committing ourselves to some unique "real" ordering, we implicitly take a quasi-realist viewpoint. Consequently, whatever the exact formal realization, we shall see defaults here as statements about a somewhat idealized (possible) world model, which have definite truth-conditions. In [Wey 93], we have proposed a possible world semantics for *nested* default conditionals, whose flat version generalizes ranked model structures [Mak 93]. It will provide the semantic framework for our present object-level analysis of default conditionals.

Definition 2.1 Let L be a language closed under the usual propositional connectives. $\underline{N} = (N, 1M, \models, \leq)$ is called an *actualized ranked model structure (ARS)* w.r.t. L *iff* **1.** 1M is a set of worlds (1M : *universe*), **2.** $\models$ is a classical satisfaction relation on 1M x L (i.e. usual handling of the connectives), **3.** $\leq$ is a total pre-order on 1M ($\leq$: *normality ordering*)[5], **4.** $N \in$ 1M (N : *actual world*).

This is mainly a Kripke structure where the valuation has been replaced by an abstract satisfaction relation. For meta-level considerations, we are also going to use *preferential model structures*, where the actual world is missing and $\leq$ only needs to be a pre-order.

In this paper, we are only concerned with flat default conditionals. So, given a classical language L, i.e. closed under $\neg$, &, $\vee$, $\rightarrow$, $\leftrightarrow$, we take as our default language $L°(\Rightarrow)$, i.e. the smallest set extending L which is closed under the usual propositional connectives and contains A $\Rightarrow$ B for all A, B in L. Its semantics is given below.

Definition 2.2 Let $\underline{N} = (N, 1M, \models, \leq)$ be an actualized ranked model structure w.r.t. L and let $L°(\Rightarrow) \supseteq \Sigma \cup \{A\}$. ARS-*satisfaction* $\Vert=$ on $L°(\Rightarrow)$ is then inductively defined by (1) $\underline{N} \Vert= A$ iff $N \models A$ for connective-free A in L, (2) as usual for the classical connectives, (3) $\underline{N} \Vert= A \Rightarrow B$ iff $\forall M \models A \exists M' \Vert= A$ (M'$\leq$ M and $\forall N' \leq M'$ N'$\Vert= A \rightarrow B$))[6]. The Tarskian ARS-*consequence* $\Vert-$ is given by $\Sigma \Vert- A$ iff every $\Vert=$-model of Σ is also a $\Vert-$model of A.

Thus, a default conditional A $\Rightarrow$ B will be verified just when there are no A-worlds at all or when we can find a non-empty initial segment of A-worlds satisfying B. This limit evaluation procedure, which has also been used by Boutilier, appears to be the most natural way to proceed and permits us to get rid of artificial ordering restrictions like smoothness or stopperedness. As might have been expected from the intuitions behind our semantic construction, our default conditional is very well-behaved and can be characterized as follows.

Theorem 2.1 Let $\vdash$ be the *flat hyperrational conditional logic on* $L°(\Rightarrow)$, i.e. the smallest derivability notion $\vdash$ on $L°(\Rightarrow)$ verifying **HRC°** : the propositional tautologies, the modus ponens rule for material implication and **R 1 - R 8**, where **R 1** : $P \Rightarrow P$ (*Reflexivity*), **R 2** : $P \Rightarrow R \leftrightarrow Q \Rightarrow R$, if $\vdash P \leftrightarrow Q$ (*Left Equivalence*), **R 3** : $P \Rightarrow Q \rightarrow P \Rightarrow R$, if $\vdash Q \rightarrow R$ (*Right Weakening*), **R 4** : $(P \Rightarrow Q \& P \Rightarrow R) \rightarrow P \Rightarrow Q\&R$ (*And*), **R 5** : $(P \Rightarrow R \& Q \Rightarrow R) \rightarrow P \vee Q \Rightarrow R$ (*Or*), **R 6** : $(P \Rightarrow Q \& P \Rightarrow R) \rightarrow P\&Q \Rightarrow R$ (*Cautious Monotony*), **R 7** : $(P \Rightarrow R \& \neg(P \Rightarrow \neg Q)) \rightarrow P\&Q \Rightarrow R$ (*Rational Monotony*), **R 8** : $P \Rightarrow F \rightarrow \neg P$ (*Correctness for* $\Rightarrow$). Furthermore, let $\Vert-$ be the ARS-inference on $L°(\Rightarrow)$. Then we have for $L°(\Rightarrow) \supseteq \Sigma \cup \{P\}$, $\Sigma \Vert- P$ iff $\Sigma \vdash P$.

R 1 - 7 correspond to the (boolean) object-level version of Lehmann's rationality postulates for plausible reasoning and to Lewis' system V [Lewis 73]. $N(P) = \neg P \Rightarrow F$ is best interpreted as "$\neg P$ *is necessary*". **R 8** then corresponds to the *flat veridicality*-axiom for neces-

---

[4]Another, closely related possibility is a qualitative probabilistic interpretation, reading "A$\Rightarrow$B" as "A&$\neg$B is qualitatively smaller / of negligible weight compared to A&B" [Wey 91].
[5] For historical reasons, we shall read "x $\leq$ x' " as "x is at least as normal / plausible as x' ".
[6] This condition is also applicable to model structures carrying arbitrary pre-orders.

sity. Further discussion can be found in [Wey 93]. As far as default conditionals of depth one are concerned, our list of postulates seems to be conceptually exhaustive.

Given all these results, we can say that the monotonic logic for flat default conditionals encoding normal implication is fairly well understood. On the other hand, the exploration of nonmonotonic consequence relations for default conditionals has just begun.

3 Nonmonotonic entailment

Up to now, we have only looked at strict, i.e. monotonic, syntactically or semantically founded consequence relations for default conditionals. We have not yet explicitly considered what should be the essence of every account of defeasible reasoning, namely one or several nonmonotonic entailment relations extending monotonic inference and telling us which plausible consequences can be drawn from a given, possibly infinitary set of facts and defaults representing actual and generic world knowledge. To a certain extent, we can think of such defeasible inference relations as sets of meta-level defaults allowing infinitely many premises and, as part of the logical framework, being fixed once and for ever. We shall use them to implement more speculative but intuitively appealing plausible guessing strategies (e.g. default chaining, as an uncontroversial instance), necessary for practical purposes but too powerful to be encoded within a monotonic conditional framework.

Given a language $L°(\Rightarrow)$ as before, $\vdash$ will be the (monotonic) **HRC°**-inference and $\approx$ be a plausible consequence relation on $L°(\Rightarrow)$. Because of our quasi-realist view of object-level defaults, which are expected to encode normal relationships in the real world, contrary to a common practice, we shall put together facts and defaults in the premise set. First of all, we are going to propose several fundamental principles for plausible entailment relations concerned with **HRC°** default conditionals. Let $bcc_{L°(\Rightarrow)}$ be the set of boolean combinations of conditionals from $L°(\Rightarrow)$ and Cn be the **HRC°**-closure. Also, for $L°(\Rightarrow) \supseteq X, Y, \{P, Q, R\}$, let X^π / P^π be the set / formula obtained from X / P by replacing every propositional variable v by $\pi(v) = \neg^{\pi_1(v)} \pi_2(v)$, where $\pi_1(v) \in \{0, 1\}$ ($\neg^0 = \neg\neg, \neg^1 = \neg$) and π_2 is a permutation of variables from $L°(\Rightarrow)$ (π is called a *signed-variable-permutation* or *s.v.p.*).

Definition 3.1 $\approx$ is called a *regular inference relation* on $L°(\Rightarrow)$ w.r.t. $\vdash$ *iff* $\{X \mid L°(\Rightarrow) \supseteq X\} \times L°(\Rightarrow) \supseteq \approx$ and $\approx$ satisfies **P1 - P6** :

P1. $X \vdash P$ implies $X \approx P$ *(Supraclassicality)*

P2. $X \approx R$ implies $(X \approx P$ iff $X \cup \{R\} \approx P)$ *(Cumulativity)*

P3. $X \approx P$, $Y \approx P$ implies $Cn(X) \cap Cn(Y) \approx P$ *(Distributivity)*

P4. For $P, Q \in L$, $bcc_{L°(\Rightarrow)} \supseteq X$: **1.** $X \cup \{P\} \approx Q$ implies $X \approx P \Rightarrow Q$
   (Defeasible Deduction)   **2.** $X \cup \{\neg N(\neg P)\} \approx P \Rightarrow Q$ implies $X \cup \{P\} \approx Q$

P5. $X \approx F$ implies $X \vdash F$ *(Consistency Preservation)*

P6. $X \approx P$ iff $X^\pi \approx P^\pi$, for every s.v.p. π *(Invariance)*

A plausible inference relation should extend the monotonic background logic (**P1**), support a cautious form of monotony (**P2**, "only if"), allow the use of lemmata (**P2**, "if") and validate reasoning by cases (**P3**). Note that **P1 - P3** encode a semi-finitary version of Lehmann's *preferentiality*. Object- and meta-level should be linked by a deduction principle appropriate for a nonmonotonic setting and backing the default character of our conditional (**P4**). The condition $bcc_{L°(\Rightarrow)} \supseteq X$ in **P4** is necessary to allow a correct handling of specificity[7]. In **P4.2**, $\neg N(\neg P)$ takes into account nasty interactions between P and X. If possible, strict and defeasible inference should rely on the same inconsistency notion, which calls for a consistency preservation principle (**P5**). Last but not least, we should insist on invariance under renaming of variables (**P6**). Another conditio sine qua non is the defeasible modus ponens rule, which will guarantee that our object-level default conditional means and does what it is expected to mean and do, linking it in a natural way to our nonmonotonic inference relation. The strict modus ponens rule $\{A, A \Rightarrow B\} \vdash B$, of course, will be absolutely unacceptable, unless we are in a limiting context where $\vdash A \rightarrow B$. In fact, the defeasible form already follows from **P4**, which gives us even more, because supraclassicality yields

---

[7] Otherwise, we could deduce, for instance, $\{Bird(a), Penguin (a), Bird(a) \Rightarrow Canfly(a), Penguin(a) \& Bird(a) \Rightarrow \neg Canfly(a)\} \approx Canfly(a)$ from the (by supraclassicality) valid pattern $\{Bird(a), Penguin(a), Bird(a) \Rightarrow Canfly(a), Penguin(a) \& Bird(a) \Rightarrow \neg Canfly(a), \neg N(\neg Bird(a))\} \approx Bird(a) \Rightarrow Canfly(a)$.

$\{A \Rightarrow B, \neg N(\neg P)\} \cup X \models A \Rightarrow B$:

GDMP-rule : $\{A, A \Rightarrow B\} \cup X \models B$, if $bcc_{L^\circ(\Rightarrow)} \supseteq X$ and $A, B \in L$.

Note that this principle stands for a certain independence of facts and defaults, which brings us closer to the mainstream convention of fact-default separation.

What we need to find next are suitable ways for defining regular consequence relations by semantic means. Defeasible entailment relations are intended to express plausible inference patterns, which should reflect preferences among actualized ranked model structures based on some notion of inherent normality. For instance, an ARS with lots of exceptional (= not maximally normal) worlds might be inherently less normal than another one whose worlds are concentrated in the non-exceptional part. This would justify defeasible relationships like $\emptyset \models \neg(T \Rightarrow R)$ for $|/- R$ (because ARSs with non-exceptional $\neg R$-worlds would be preferred). However, there may be different, a priori equally plausible ways to evaluate the relative normality of ARSs. Also, our intuitions may fail to support clear-cut decisions, forcing us to deal with non-total normality pre-orders at the meta-level. Therefore, we shall interpret defeasible inference relations by special second-order *preferential* model structures comparing normality-hierarchies, which will be evaluated in a suitable way. We shall call them *hyperstructures*.

W.l.o.g. let L be a classical propositional language with atoms P_i ($i \in I \neq \emptyset$), whose models can be identified with elements of $2^I = \{f \mid f : I \to \{0, 1\}\}$. A corresponding classical satisfaction relation $\models$ is defined for $N \in 2^I$ and $i \in I$ by $N \models P_i$ iff $N(i) = 1$. Furthermore, let $TP^-(2^I)$ be the set of all total pre-orders $\leq$ included in $2^I \times 2^I$ (but, not necessarily with dom($\leq$) = 2^I) which have minima[8]. Then, $ARS^-(2^I) = \{(N, \text{dom}(\leq), \models, \leq) \mid \leq \in TP^-(2^I), N \in \text{dom}(\leq))\}$[9] is a representative set of actualized ranked model structures w.r.t. L, i.e. every **HRC°**-consistent $L^\circ(\Rightarrow)$-theory has a model in $ARS^-(2^I)$. In the following, our actualized ranked model structures will always be elements of $ARS^-(2^I)$.

So, our task now will be to encode suitable meta normality concepts by pre-orders $\ll$ on $TP^-(2^I)$, which will determine those preferential structures to be used as hyperstructures. The interpretation mode for our "meta-conditionals" w.r.t. this framework, however, will be different from the standard procedure and will depend on considerations about the role of the actual world position. We want to impose two general constraints upon $\ll$. First of all, we require that the total pre-order $2^I \times 2^I$ - i.e. no exceptional worlds - should be the (unique) $\ll$-smallest element. This reflects the common view that in the absence of any information, we should assume every possible alternative to be equally normal or plausible. Secondly, $\ll$ should be invariant under renaming and polarity-changes of variables, i.e. structured permutations of 2^I s.t. $(n_i \mid i \in I) \longmapsto (p_i(n_{f(i)}) \mid i \in I)$, where f / p_i are bijections on $I / \{0, 1\}$. We shall refer to pre-orders on $TP^-(2^I)$ satisfying these prerequisites as *hyperorderings*. The relation $\ll^\#$ on $ARS^-(2^I)$, defined by $(N', \text{dom}(\leq'), \models, \leq') \ll^\# (N, \text{dom}(\leq), \models, \leq)$ iff $\leq' \ll \leq$, will then be called the *extended hyperordering* associated with $\ll$.

Definition 3.1 lH is called a *hyperstructure* for L *iff* there is a hyperordering $\ll$ on $TP^-(2^I)$ s.t. lH = $(TP^-(2^I), \ll)$.

To understand what is going on, we may consider a hyperordering for a language with a single propositional variable A. Let $|I| = 1$ and $\{-a, a\} = \{Ix\{0\}, Ix\{1\}\} = 2^I$ be the set of all possible worlds, with $-a \models \neg A$ and $a \models A$. Then the *elementary hyperordering* $\ll$ (cf. 4) for this language is given by the following relationships : $\{(-a,-a)\} \gg \{(-a,-a), (-a,a), (a,a)\} \gg \{(-a,-a), (-a,a), (a,-a), (a,a)\} \ll \{(a,a), (a,-a), (-a,-a)\} \ll \{(a,a)\}$.

Every hyperstructure lH will now provide a possibly very rudimentary defeasible entailment relation $\models_{lH}$ for $L^\circ(\Rightarrow)$, called the lH-*entailment* or a *pre-hyperentailment* relation. The evaluation strategy characterizing the nonmonotonic semantics of $\models_{lH}$ is based on a two-stage procedure which adequately handles the interactions between the total pre-order and the actual world positions, i.e. between global and local normality, by looking first at the former. Σ lH-*entails* B just holds when every $ARS^-(2^I)$-model of Σ can be $\ll^\#$-minorized by a $\ll^\#$-downcone whose elements share the property that their most normal actual-world-variants supporting Σ are also verifying B.

---

[8] For technical purposes, to avoid artificial complications, we restrict ourselves w.l.o.g. to total pre-orders with non-empty bottom-levels, enforcing the existence of maximally normal worlds.

[9] For the sake of notational simplicity, we write "$\models$" but mean "$\models \cap \text{dom}(\leq) \times L$".

Definition 3.2 Let $lH = (TP^-(2^I), \ll)$ be a hyperstructure for L, $L^°(\Rightarrow) \supseteq \Sigma \cup \{B\}$. Then, $\Sigma \; lH\text{-}entails$ B, written $\Sigma \models_{lH} B$, iff

$\forall \; \underline{N} \in ARS^-(2^I)$ with $\underline{N} \; \| = \Sigma \quad \exists \; \underline{N}'' \in ARS^-(2^I)$ with $N'' \| = \Sigma$, $\underline{N}'' \ll^\# \underline{N}$

$\forall \; \underline{N}' = (N', \text{dom}(\leq'), \models, \leq') \in ARS^-(2^I)$ with $\underline{N}' \| = \Sigma$, $\underline{N}' \ll^\# \underline{N}''$

$\exists \; N^° \in \text{dom}(\leq')$ with $(N^°, \text{dom}(\leq'), \models, \leq') \| = \Sigma$

$\forall \; N^{°'} \in \text{dom}(\leq')$ with $N^{°'} \leq' N^°$, we have $(N^{°'}, \text{dom}(\leq'), \models, \leq') \| = B$.

We can show that pre-hyperentailment relations satisfy all the desirable properties **P1 - P6**.

Theorem 3.1 If lH is as above, then $\models_{lH}$ is a regular inference relation on $L^°(\Rightarrow)$ w.r.t. $\vdash$.

The class of pre-hyperentailment relations represents a promising starting point for the development of powerful plausible entailment strategies, but it is too large to provide a reasonable inference tool by itself. So, we can prove for each hyperstructure lH that $\emptyset \models_{lH} \neg(T \Rightarrow P)$ if $\nvdash P$, but unfortunately, principles well known from nonmonotonic inheritance, like defeasible chaining, are not always validated. Therefore, we have to look for appropriate specific hyperstructures, implementing more sophisticated entailment paradigms.

4 Elementary hyperentailment

The main role of the hyperstructure approach to defeasible reasoning is to provide an integrated general framework for default conditionals and corresponding nonmonotonic entailment relations, appropriately linking object and meta-level defaults and enforcing several plausible and practical rationality postulates. But whereas our basic principles have been implemented rather well, really speculative inference is hardly served by the constraints for pre-hyperentailment relations. Consider for instance irrelevance reasoning, which is exemplified by the pattern $B \Rightarrow F \models_{lH} B\&G \Rightarrow F$ (*defeasible monotony*), for independent atoms B, G, F. Setting B : Bird(*George*), G : Green(*George*) and F : Fly(*George*), we want to conclude from "*George is a bird normally implies that he flies*" in the absence of other information that "*George is a green bird normally implies that he flies*". Unfortunately, this reasoning scheme fails for most hyperstructures (e.g. if $\ll$ is maximal, i.e. if $\ll = (\{2^I x2^I\} x TP^-(2^I)) \cup (TP^-(2^I) \setminus \{2^I x2^I\})^2)$. So, we have to find natural conditions for hyperorderings helping us to get the obvious patterns right without adopting an ad hoc strategy.

In the following, we are going to present *elementary hyperentailment*, a simple but very natural and powerful approach, whose beginnings can be traced back to [Wey 91a], where a preliminary version was discussed in a somewhat different formal context. The basic ideas are : **1.** Assuming everything to be as normal as possible, without considering additional structural / dependency / syntactic information. In particular, when comparing two normality orderings, always prefer that one whose worlds are most concentrated at the bottom. **2.** Deciding about preferences as soon as possible, i.e. at the least exceptional level, which means adopting a lexicographic strategy. **3.** Working within the hyperstructure framework. These principles are implemented by what we call *elementary hyperstructures*.

First, we need some more definitions. For every $\leq \in TP^-(2^I)$ and $x \in \text{dom}(\leq)$, set $S_\leq[x] = \{x' \mid x \leq x'\} \cup (2^I \setminus \text{dom}(\leq))$, which is the set of all worlds being at most as $\leq$-normal as x or not in $\leq$'s universe. Then $\mathbf{ch}[\leq] = \{S_\leq[x] \mid x \in \text{dom}(\leq)\} \cup \{2^I \setminus \text{dom}(\leq)\}$ is linearly ordered by inclusion and gives us a linear hierarchy on 2^I with max. 2^I (= $S_\leq[x]$ for $\leq$-minimal x) and min. $2^I \setminus \text{dom}(\leq)$. We shall call $\mathbf{ch}[\leq]$ the *characteristic sequence* of $\leq$ because we can reconstruct the initial total pre-order from it. An intuitively appealing way to compare the inherent normality of two total pre-orders $\leq$ and $\leq'$ from $TP^-(2^I)$ would be to look at the elements of $\mathbf{ch}[\leq]$ and $\mathbf{ch}[\leq']$ one by one, beginning at the top, and to see which one makes a smaller amount of worlds exceptional at the first level where a divergence occurs (e.g. if $2^I \supset S' \supset S \supset \emptyset$, $\mathbf{ch}[\leq] = \{2^I, S', \emptyset\}$ and $\mathbf{ch}[\leq'] = \{2^I, S\}$, then $\leq'$ would be preferred, despite the fact that the universe of $\leq$ is larger than that of $\leq'$). Such a lexicographic procedure would make the exceptionality structure below that level irrelevant.

However, because our hierarchies don't have to be well-founded, this strategy doesn't always work. Consider for instance two normality orderings $\leq$ and $\leq'$ with $\mathbf{ch}[\leq] = \{2^I\} \cup \{S_{-1/n} \mid n \in \mathbf{Nat} \setminus \{0,1\}\} \cup \{S_{1/n} \mid n \in \mathbf{Nat} \setminus \{0\}\} \cup \{S_n \mid n \in \mathbf{Nat} \setminus \{0\}\} \cup \{2^I \setminus \text{dom}(\leq)\}$ and

$\mathbf{ch}[\leq'] = \{2^I\} \cup \{S_{-1/n} \mid n \in \mathbf{Nat}\setminus\{0,1\}\} \cup \{S_{1/2n} \mid n \in \mathbf{Nat}\setminus\{0\}\} \cup \{S_{2n} \mid n \in \mathbf{Nat}\setminus\{0\}\} \cup \{2^I \setminus \mathrm{dom}(\leq')\}$, where we assume $2^I \supset S_i \supset S_{i'} \supset 2^I \setminus \mathrm{dom}(\leq)$, $2^I \setminus \mathrm{dom}(\leq')$ for $i <_r i'$[10]. Then, it is not obvious which class S_i in $\mathbf{ch}[\leq']$ should be compared to, say S_3, in $\mathbf{ch}[\leq]$. Because absolute scales are missing, any stipulations about the relative positions of classes in the non-well-founded part of two characteristic sequences would be purely arbitrary.

So, may be, we should simply ignore the subdivisions of the non-well-founded chunk and consider only its union. That is, from any characteristic sequence $\mathbf{ch}[\leq]$ we are going to derive a well-founded sequence $\mathbf{wf}[\leq]$ summarizing the features of $\leq$ relevant for implementing our basic inherent normality comparison strategy.

If $\mathbf{ch'}[\leq]$ is the maximal $\supset$-well-founded upper part of $\mathbf{ch}[\leq]$, then we set $\mathbf{wf}[\leq] = \mathbf{ch'}[\leq] \cup \{\cup(\mathbf{ch}[\leq] \setminus \mathbf{ch'}[\leq])\}$. Furthermore, let $\mathbf{es}[\leq] = (\mathbf{wf}[\leq](\alpha) \mid 0 <_{ord} \alpha <_{ord} \max(\omega, |2^I|^+))$[11] $= (\mathbf{wf}[\leq](1), \mathbf{wf}[\leq](2), ..., \mathbf{wf}[\leq](\alpha), ...)$ be an ordinal enumeration of $\mathbf{wf}[\leq]$, where $\mathbf{wf}[\leq](\alpha)$ is the αth-largest element of $\mathbf{wf}[\leq]$ if it exists, and $\mathbf{wf}[\leq](\alpha) = \cup(\mathbf{ch}[\leq] \setminus \mathbf{ch'}[\leq])$ otherwise. We call $\mathbf{es}[\leq]$ the *elementary sequence* of $\leq$. In the previous example, for instance, $\mathbf{wf}[\leq] = \{2^I, S_{-1/2}, ..., S_{-1/n}, ..., \cup\{S_{1/n} \mid n \in \mathbf{Nat}\setminus\{0\}\}\}$, which gives us $\mathbf{wf}[\leq](1) = 2^I$, $\mathbf{wf}[\leq](n) = S_{-1/n}$ ($n \in \mathbf{Nat}\setminus\{0, 1\}$), $\mathbf{wf}[\leq](\omega) = \mathbf{wf}[\leq](\omega+1) = ... = \cup\{S_{1/n} \mid n \in \mathbf{Nat}\setminus\{0\}\}$. Representing sets by formulas, the elementary sequences associated with $\leq \in TP^-(\{-a, a\})$ (cf. below Def. 3.1) are : $\mathbf{es}[\{(-a,-a)\}] = (\mathbf{T}, A^*)$, $\mathbf{es}[\{(a,a)\}] = (\mathbf{T}, \neg A^*)$, $\mathbf{es}[\{(-a,-a), (-a,a), (a,a)\}] = (\mathbf{T}, A, F^*)$, $\mathbf{es}[\{(a,a), (a,-a), (-a,-a)\}] = (\mathbf{T}, \neg A, F^*)$, $\mathbf{es}[\{(-a,-a), (-a,a), (a,-a), (a,a)\}] = (\mathbf{T}, F^*)$[12]. Elementary sequences will now be used to define hyperorderings on $TP^-(2^I)$ fitting our ideas about inherent normality comparisons.

Definition 4.1 Let $<<_0$ be the binary relation on $TP^-(2^I)$ defined by $\leq <<_0 \leq'$ iff there is a smallest α with $\mathbf{wf}[\leq](\alpha) \neq \mathbf{wf}[\leq'](\alpha)$ and α satisfies $\mathbf{wf}[\leq'](\alpha) \supset \mathbf{wf}[\leq](\alpha)$. Then $\underline{<<}_0 = <<_0 \cup id_{TP^-(2^I)}$ is called the *elementary hyperordering* on $TP^-(2^I)$.

Obviously, $\underline{<<}_0$ is a partial order on $TP^-(2^I)$. Since $\mathbf{es}[2^I \times 2^I] = (\mathbf{wf}[2^I \times 2^I](\alpha) \mid 0 <_{ord} \alpha <_{ord} |2^I|^+) = (2^I, \emptyset, \emptyset, ...)$, but $\mathbf{es}[\leq] \neq (2^I, \emptyset, \emptyset, ...)$ for $\leq \neq 2^I \times 2^I$, $2^I \times 2^I$ will be the $\underline{<<}_0$-smallest element of $TP^-(2^I)$. It is also easy to see that $\underline{<<}_0$ only depends on inclusion-relationships between components of elementary sequences, which are conserved under structured 2^I-permutations (cf. above). Hence, $\underline{<<}_0$ is a hyperordering.

Theorem 4.1 $IH0(2^I) = (TP^-(2^I), \underline{<<}_0)$ is a hyperstructure for L.

The nonmonotonic entailment relation $\models_{IH0(2^I)}$ on $L^\circ(\Rightarrow)$ induced by $IH0(2^I)$ is called *elementary hyperentailment* or $IH0$-*entailment* for L. It is important to note that elementary hyperentailment is a purely semantic concept. Once the language has been fixed, it doesn't depend in any way on syntactic or extralogical information. In particular, it is even invariant under arbitrary permutations of the relevant universe 2^I, going beyond the basic stipulations of our framework. $IH0$-entailment is also a very powerful speculative inference notion. It is difficult to find a stronger and equally transparent nonmonotonic entailment strategy without giving up the semantic perspective, the qualitative approach or the purely conditional logical context. We shall illustrate its inferential power by some popular examples. In the following, A, B, ... will be logically independent formulas in L, the premise set parentheses $\{, \}$ will be omitted and $\models$ will stand for $\models_{IH0(2^I)}$. For each example, we shall indicate (representing sets by formulas) the elementary sequence of the $\underline{<<}_0$-smallest $TP^-(2^I)$-element[13] among those associated with ARSs satisfying the premises. Because of our defeasible deduction principle **P4**, we always have for P, R $\in$ L : $\{P, some\ boolean\ combinations\ of\ conditionals\} \models R$ iff $\{some\ boolean\ combinations\ of\ conditionals, \neg \mathbf{N}(\neg P)\} \models P \Rightarrow R$. Using **P4** and the supraclassicality of $\models$, resp. the $\underline{<<}_0$-bottom-position of $2^I \times 2^I$, we can immediately verify three standard desiderata for nonmonotonic

---

[10] $<_r$ is the usual real number ordering.

[11] $<_{ord}$ is the usual ordinal number ordering. The cardinal number of a given set S is the minimal ordinal number whose set of $<_{ord}$-predecessors has the same cardinality as S. $|2^I|$ is the cardinal number of 2^I, $|2^I|^+$ is the successor cardinal of $|2^I|$. ω is the first and $\omega+1$ the second infinite ordinal number. An account of infinitary ordinal and cardinal number theory can be found in any good book on set theory.

[12] In this context, "A* " always denotes a constant A-sequence.

[13] In our examples, this can be done. But the existence of a $\underline{<<}_0$-smallest element is not always guaranteed because $\underline{<<}_0$ is neither total nor well-founded.

entailment relations on $L^\circ(\Rightarrow)$ which are valid for arbitrary pre-hyperentailment relations :

Defeasible modus ponens (rule) : $H, H \Rightarrow F \mathrel{\vert\approx} F$ $(\mathbf{T}, H\&\neg F, F^*)$

Specificity : $S, S \Rightarrow A, S \Rightarrow \neg R, A \Rightarrow R \mathrel{\vert\approx} \neg R$ $(\mathbf{T}, S\vee(A\&\neg R), S\&(\neg A\vee R), F^*)$

Global homogeneity : $\mathbf{T} \mathrel{\vert\approx} \neg(S \Rightarrow R)$ $(\mathbf{T}, F^*)$

Note that global homogeneity nicely reflects our minimal commitment strategy. Other popular defeasible inference patterns whose realization really depends on $lH0(2^I)$ are

Defeasible monotony : $B \Rightarrow W \mathrel{\vert\approx} B\&A \Rightarrow W$ $(\mathbf{T}, B\&\neg W, F^*)$

Defeasible contraposition : $S \Rightarrow Q \mathrel{\vert\approx} \neg Q \Rightarrow \neg S$ $(\mathbf{T}, S\&\neg Q, F^*)$

Defeasible chaining : $S, S \Rightarrow H, H \Rightarrow P \mathrel{\vert\approx} P$ $(\mathbf{T}, S\&\neg H \vee H\&\neg P, F^*)$

The validity of defeasible chaining, for instance, follows from the fact that making only S&¬H- and H&¬P-worlds (equally) exceptional is just enough to satisfy the premises. In particular, S&¬P-worlds will become exceptional, whereas S&P&H-worlds (whose existence is guaranteed by the logical independence assumption) can stay among the most normal ones, which, together with our definitions, gives us the conclusion. Further interesting and adequately handled benchmark problems are the following ones.

Weak big birds hammer (WBBH) : $(\mathbf{T}, \ B\&(\neg F\vee\neg S), \ B\&\neg S\&F^*)$
$B \Rightarrow F\&S, \ N((B\&(\neg F\vee\neg S)) \rightarrow \neg F) \mathrel{\vert\not\approx} B\&\neg F \Rightarrow S$

This non-inference is rather obvious given that the premises make $B(\&\neg F)\&\neg S$ an unspecified sub-proposition of B&¬F. If it is exceptional, it is because of B&¬F.

Big birds hammer (BBH) : $(\mathbf{T}, \ B\&(\neg F\vee\neg S), \ B\&\neg S\&F, \ F^*)$
$B \Rightarrow F\&S, \ B\&(\neg F\vee\neg S) \Rightarrow \neg F \mathrel{\vert\not\approx} B\&\neg F \Rightarrow S$

Here, the situation is more confusing. But the second entailment failure derives its justification from the very plausible assumption that replacing defaults by hard implications within a positive conditional knowledge base, e.g. switching from **BBH** to **WBBH**, should not reduce the set of defaults plausibly entailed. In fact, having absolutely no evidence (e.g. hidden in disjunctive conditional expressions) for B&¬F $\Rightarrow$ S, we may think about strengthening them to ... $\mathrel{\vert\approx} \neg(B\&\neg F \Rightarrow S)$, which is validated by $lH0$-entailment.

Theorem 4.2 If $X \cup \{P\}$ contains only conjunctions of possibly negated conditionals and X is consistent as well as finite, then we have $X \mathrel{\vert\not\approx}_{lH0(2^I)} P$ iff $X \mathrel{\vert\approx}_{lH0(2^I)} \neg P$.

A drawback of elementary hyperentailment, however, is its inability to deal with reasoning patterns involving implicit independence assumptions.

¬Defeasible exceptional monotony : $(\mathbf{T}, (S\&\neg G)\vee(S\&\neg B), F^*)$
$S \Rightarrow G, S \Rightarrow B \mathrel{\vert\not\approx} S\&\neg G \Rightarrow B$

Even if S, B, G are distinct propositional variables, defeasible exceptional monotony will fail. This failure is linked to $\mathrel{\vert\approx}_{lH0(2^I)}$'s far-reaching syntax-independency w.r.t. the chosen language. There is also a more general result marking the limits for any reasonable attempt to deal with examples like these. Let's call an entailment relation on $L^\circ(\Rightarrow)$ *abusive* if there is an $A \in L$ s.t. $\mathrel{\vert\!/}\text{-}A$ and $\mathbf{T} \Rightarrow A \mathrel{\vert\approx} N(A)$ (i.e. *"normally"* A defeasibly entails *"necessarily"* A"). So, abusing really means locally trivializing normality.

Theorem 4.3 Every pre-hyperentailment relation $\mathrel{\vert\approx}_{lH}$ on $L^\circ(\Rightarrow)$ which verifies defeasible exceptional monotony and whose hyperstructure lH is invariant under arbitrary permutations of the full universe 2^I, is abusive.

Nevertheless, by its power, its transparency and its simple, natural semantic foundations, elementary hyperentailment continues to be a particularly valuable plausible reasoning tool.

5 Comparisons

In the literature, we find several closing-up procedures for sets of conditional expressions. In general, the corresponding formalisms are less expressive and structurally less coherent than lH-entailment relations. **1.** Elementary hyperentailment shares some basic ideas with Lehmann's *rational closure* [LM 92], which is based on a somewhat more cumbersome comparison criterion and has two main drawbacks. First of all, the basic language is too weak, allowing only isolated positive conditionals but no mixed knowledge bases containing boolean combinations of contingent and modal information. Secondly, there is no integrated framework linking in a suitable way nonmonotonic inference and the object-level default conditional. Nevertheless, rational closure agrees with 1H0-entailment for finite positive conditional premise sets. **2.** Pearl's Z-1-*entailment* is equivalent to rational closure [GoP 91]. **3.** Geffner's *conditional entailment* [GeP 92] is formulated as an assumption-based default theory generating priorities by itself. In addition to the standard examples it also verifies defeasible exceptional monotony. But it fails to give the expected answer in the big birds hammer example. Its main weaknesses are the heterogeneous framework, the weak language and in particular the absence of a reasonable conditional logic at the object-level, which causes a strong, uncontrolled influence of syntax. Within this less expressive context, it still fails to be cumulative. **4.** *Maximum entropy entailment* [GMP 90] is concerned with maximizing property independence based on an entropy measure. But our previous remarks apply here as well. **5.** Lehmann has recently proposed a new framework [Leh 92] mixing ideas from *default logic and rational closure*. His theory provides for many examples the intuitively correct answers (exceptional monotony and beyond), but it doesn't get the big birds hammer right. Unfortunately, the framework is also strongly presentation-dependent and not very expressive. A further handicap is the non-cumulative entailment relation. **6.** *Commonsense entailment* [AM 91] is a more expressive (first-order) formal framework primarily designed to deal with the complexities of generics. They get the basic patterns right (e.g. specificity, defeasible modus ponens rule, chaining), but exceptional monotony is missing and their defeasible inference relation is only cumulative. Some further disadvantages are the huge, not so transparent entailment machinery, the weak object-level conditional and lacking links between object- and meta-level. In particular, they don't have any kind of defeasible deduction principle.

References

[AM 91] N. Asher, M. Morreau. Commonsense entailment: a modal theory of nonmonotonic reasoning. In *Proceedings of the 12th IJCAI*. Morgan Kaufmann.
[Bou 90] C. Boutilier. Conditional logics of normality as modal systems. In *Proceedings of AAAI 90*. Boston, MA, 1990.
[Bou 92] C. Boutilier. *Conditional logics fordefault reasoning and belief revision*. Ph.D.thesis, technical report 92-1, Dpt. of Computer Science, University of British Columbia.
[Del 88] J. Delgrande. An approach to default reasoning based on a first-order conditional logic: a revised report. *AI*, 36:63-90.
[Gab 85] D. Gabbay. Theoretical foundations for nonmonotonic reasoning in expert systems. In *Logics and models of concurrent systems*, ed. K.R. Apt. Berlin, Springer.
[GMP 90] M. Goldszmidt, P. Morris, J. Pearl. A maximum entropy approach to nonmonotonic reasoning. In *Proceedings of AAAI 90*. Boston, MA, 1990.
[GoP 91] M.Goldszmidt, J. Pearl. On the relation between rational closure and system Z. In *The Third International Workshop on Nonmonotonic Reasoning*, South Lake Tahoe.
[GeP 92] H. Geffner, J. Pearl. Conditional entailment : bridging two approaches to default reasoning. *Artificial Intelligence*, 53: 209 - 244, 1992.
[KLM 90] S. Kraus, D. Lehmann, M. Magidor. Nonmonotonic reasoning preferential models and cumulative logics. *Artificial Intelligence*, 44: 167-207, 1990.
[LM 92] D. Lehmann, M. Magidor. What does a conditional knowledge base entail ? *Artificial Intelligence*, 55: 1 - 60, 1992.
[Leh 92] D. Lehmann. Another perspective on default reasoning. Technical report TR 92-12, Department of Computer Science, Hebrew University, Jerusalem.
[Lew 73] D.K. Lewis. *Counterfactuals*. Harvard University Press.
[Mak 89] D. Makinson. General theory of cumulative inference. In *Proc. of the 2nd international workshop on nonmonotonic reasoning*, eds. M. Reinfrank et al. Berlin, Springer.
[Mak 93] D. Makinson. General patterns in nonmonotonic reasoning. In *Handbook of Logic in Artificial intelligence and Logic Programming (vol II)*, eds. D.Gabbay, C. Hogger. Oxford University Press.
[Sho 87] Y. Shoham. A semantical approach to non-monotonic logics. In *Proceedings of the Symposium on Logics in Computer Science*, 275-279, Ithaca, N.Y..
[Wey 91] E. Weydert. Qualitative magnitude reasoning. Towards a new syntax and semantics for default reasoning. In *Nonmonotonic and Inductive Logics*, eds. Dix, Jantke, Schmitt. Springer-Verlag.
[Wey 91a] E. Weydert. Elementary Hyperentailment. Nonmonotonic reasoning about defaults. In *Proceedings of the ECSQAU 91*, eds. Kruse, Siegel. Springer-Verlag.
[Wey 93] E. Weydert. Hyperrational conditionals. In *Proceedings of the European Workshop on Theoretical Foundations of Knowledge representation and Reasoning, ECAI 92*, eds. Lakemeyer, Nebel. Springer.

Decision-Making with Belief Functions and Pignistic Probabilities

Nic Wilson

Department of Computer Science
Queen Mary and Westfield College
Mile End Rd., London E1 4NS, UK

Abstract The paper discusses the different approaches to decision-making using Belief Functions. In particular, I describe Philippe Smets' method of decision-making, which transforms a Belief Function into a single probability function, the pignistic probability function. This transformation is sensitive to the choice of frame of discernment, which is often, to a large extent, arbitrary. It thus seems natural to consider all refinements of a frame of discernment and their associated pignistic probability functions and decisions. The main result of the paper is that this is equivalent to the standard approach.

1 Introduction

When using Belief Functions in Dempster-Shafer theory, the standard way of making a decision is by considering the set $\mathcal{P}$ all Bayesian probability functions that dominate the Belief Function, and considering lower and upper expected utility with respect to this family. Philippe Smets suggests an alternative method for decision-making using Belief Functions; from Bel over frame Θ, using his 'Generalized Principle of Insufficient Reason' he generates a single probability function P, called the pignistic probability function associated with Bel; he treats this a Bayesian probability function, and considers expected utility with respect to P.

A major problem with the Bayesian theory is that Bayesian beliefs cannot be satisfactorily elicited when the agent is ignorant about some of the propositions of interest. In the extreme case where the agent is completely ignorant about all the propositions of interest the Principle of Insufficient Reason is employed to generate the Bayesian beliefs. (For less extreme cases a generalisation, the Maximum Entropy method is sometimes used to generate Bayesian beliefs). However the probability function we arrive at depends crucially on the frame of discernment used to represent the problem. This is unsatisfactory since we always have a great deal of freedom in the choice of frame, for example, we can refine the frame in an arbitrary way. In some simple situations there is a clearly natural choice of frame (e.g. when considering the outcome of a throw of a die); very often, though, there is no such 'canonical frame', and so an arbitrary choice must be made, thus leading to (at least to some extent) arbitrary Bayesian beliefs (I discuss these issues at greater length in [Wilson, 92a]).

An important advantage of Dempster-Shafer Theory (and other theories, such as Lower Probability [Walley, 91] and Possibility Theory [Dubois and Prade, 88]) over the Bayesian theory is that the choice of frame is not such a crucial issue, and we can refine a frame without essentially changing the Belief Function. With his Generalized

Principle of Insufficient Reason, Smets appears to throw away this advantage, since the pignistic probability produced depends on the choice of frame (and when the belief is vacuous reduces to the Principle of Insufficient Reason), thus leading to (at least some extent) arbitrary probability functions and hence arbitrary decisions.

A possible way to remedy this might be to consider the set $\mathcal{P}^R$ of pignistic probabilities with respect to all possible frames for expressing the problem. However, it is hard to specify this in general, but we can at least consider the set $\mathcal{P}^S$ of pignistic probability functions with respect to all refinements of the original frame.

The main result of this paper is that if we do this, and consider lower and upper expected utility with respect to $\mathcal{P}^S$, then we get the same results as if we consider lower and upper expected utility with respect to $\mathcal{P}$. (Since $\mathcal{P}^S \subseteq \mathcal{P}^R$ this means that we will also get the same results if we consider lower and upper expected utility with respect to $\mathcal{P}^R$). Thus this pignistic probability approach to decision-making leads to the same decisions as the more standard approach.

In section 2, I discuss Bayesian decision theory and a generalisation which allows sets of Bayesian probability functions. In section 3, Belief Functions are defined, and the relationship with sets of Bayesian probability functions is discussed. Section 4 calculates upper and lower expected utility with respect to a Belief Function. Section 5 shows that a pignistic probability approach to decision-making, when one considers pignistic probabilities for all refinements of the frame, leads to the same decisions as the standard approach.

Some of these results appeared in [Wilson, 91b, 92b]. The proofs can be found in [Wilson, 92b] or the longer version of the paper.

2 Bayesian Decision Theory

In Bayesian decision theory, when making a decision one must list the possible choices (which we assume to be finite). For each choice the set of possible outcomes Θ must be listed (where these outcomes are mutually exclusive and exhaustive; we also only consider finite Θ). The Bayesian probability function P over Θ of the agent must be elicited, together with a utility function U on Θ. Loosely speaking, the agent considers that the chance that outcome x occurs is $P(x)$, and that if x does occur, then she will gain $U(x)$ units of utility.

For each choice the expected value of utility U with respect to P is calculated, which will be written as $P \cdot U$; (this is considering P and U as vectors of length $|\Theta|$ and performing a 'dot' product). Thus $P \cdot U = \sum_{x \in \Theta} P(x)U(x)$.

The agent then makes a choice which has maximum expected utility.

This framework can be criticised in many ways. For example, there are very serious problems with the concept of a linear scale of utility, into which we can convert all gains or losses. However, in this paper I will ignore the problems with utility, and assume a utility function U on Θ.

Bayesian probability as a representation of subjective degrees of belief has also been much criticised (see [Walley, 91] for recent, thorough criticism). An obvious generalisation (which answers many of the criticisms) is to allow a family $\mathcal{P}$ of Bayesian probability functions. It is natural then to consider lower expected utility $E_*[U]$ defined to be $\inf_{P \in \mathcal{P}} P \cdot U$, and upper expected utility $E^*[U] = \sup_{P \in \mathcal{P}} P \cdot U$.

This may give a uniquely attractive decision—when the lower expected utility of one choice is greater than the upper expected utility of any other. Perhaps more typically, there will be no uniquely attractive decision; then, for example, we might consider choices which maximised lower expected utility.

3 Belief Functions and Lower Probability

A function $m : 2^\Theta \to [0,1]$ is said to be a mass function over Θ if $m(\emptyset) = 0$ and $\sum_{X \subseteq \Theta} m(X) = 1$ [Shafer, 76]. A function $\text{Bel} : 2^\Theta \to [0,1]$ is said to be a Belief Function over Θ if there exists a mass function m over Θ with for all $X \subseteq \Theta$, $\text{Bel}(X) = \sum_{Y \subseteq X} m(Y)$. Associated with every mass function is a unique Belief Function, and associated with every Belief Function is a unique mass function.

For Belief Function Bel over Θ, the set of compatible measures $\mathcal{P}$ of Bel is defined to be the set of probability functions P over Θ such that P dominates Bel, i.e., for all $X \subseteq \Theta$, $P(X) \geq \text{Bel}(X)$ [Dempster, 67]. $\mathcal{P}$ is a convex set. Incidentally, if P dominates Bel then Pl dominates P, where Pl is the plausibility function associated with Bel, defined in [Shafer, 76]. It is also easy to show that Bel is the lower envelope of $\mathcal{P}$ and Pl is the upper envelope, i.e., for $X \subseteq \Theta$, $\text{Bel}(X) = \inf\{P(X) : P \in \mathcal{P}\}$, and $\text{Pl}(X) = \sup\{P(X) : P \in \mathcal{P}\}$.

Belief Functions have been suggested as a representation of certain convex sets of probability functions, so that e.g., Bel is a representation of $\mathcal{P}$, see, for example, [Fagin and Halpern, 89; Wasserman, 90; Jaffray, 92]. Obviously, then $\mathcal{P}$ has a clear interpretation.

In Dempster-Shafer theory, the connection between Belief Functions and sets of Bayesian probability functions is slightly more controversial (see e.g., [Shafer, 90]). However, Dempster intended that the set of compatible probability functions be used in decision-making (see also [Dempster and Kong, 87]). Shafer, at least to some extent, goes along with this, in that he suggests in [Shafer, 81, page 22] that Belief Functions may be used for betting (and hence decision-making), by using lower expectation. (Although his approach does not explicitly deal with $\mathcal{P}$, it leads, as he points out, to the same values of upper and lower expected utility.) The consequences of this approach are explored in the next section.

Philippe Smets, however, has suggested a different approach. This is explored in section 5.

4 Upper and Lower Expected Utility for Belief Functions

Bel is a Belief Function over Θ, with associated mass function m. $\mathcal{P}$ is the set of compatible probability functions. U is the utility function.

Definition 4.1

A function π will be called an *order* (on Θ) if it is a bijection from Θ to $\{1, \ldots, |\Theta|\}$. For every order π we shall define a member of $\mathcal{P}$, P_π. (The P_πs turn out to be the extremal points of $\mathcal{P}$ [Dempster, 67, p329].)

Definition 4.2

For every order π on Θ, define probability function P_π on Θ by

$$\text{for } x \in \Theta, \quad P_\pi(x) = \sum_{B:\max(\pi(B))=\pi(x)} m(B),$$

where $\max(\pi(B))$ means $\max_{y \in B} \pi(y)$. P_π is formed by distributing the masses among the elements of Θ in a particular way—$m(B)$ is allocated to the $x \in B$ with the largest value of π. P_π is a probability function since it is non-negative and $\sum_{x \in \Theta} P_\pi(x) = \text{Bel}(\Theta) = 1$. Furthermore $P_\pi \in \mathcal{P}$ since for any $Y \subseteq \Theta$,

$$P_\pi(Y) = \sum_{B:\max(\pi(B)) \in \pi(Y)} m(B) \geq \sum_{B \subseteq Y} m(B) = \text{Bel}(Y).$$

For $X \subseteq \Theta$ an order π_U will be defined such that P_{π_U} is the member of $\mathcal{P}$ which minimises the expected utility $P \cdot U$. π_U gives lower values to elements with higher utility U.

Definition 4.3

Let π_U be an order satisfying
  if $x, y \in X$ and $U(x) > U(y)$ then $\pi_U(x) < \pi_U(y)$.
Clearly such a π_U exists, but is not necessarily unique if, for example, $U(x) = U(y)$ for some different $x, y \in \Theta$. This is not important, and for convenience it will be assumed that a particular order π_U has been picked that satisfies these properties.

Proposition 4.4

$P_{\pi_U} \cdot U \leq P \cdot U$ for all $P \in \mathcal{P}$. Furthermore, the lower expected utility of U with respect to $\mathcal{P}$, $E_*[U]$, is equal to $P_{\pi_U} \cdot U$.

Note that the last part follows immediately from the first part since $P_{\pi_U} \in \mathcal{P}$.

This proposition follows from [Dempster, 67 p329]. A more detailed proof is also given in the longer version of this paper.

In fact, the upper and lower expected utilities can be expressed in a neat way.

Proposition 4.5

$$E_*[U] = \sum_{B \subseteq \Theta} m(B) U_*(B)$$

$$\text{and} \quad E^*[U] = \sum_{B \subseteq \Theta} m(B) U^*(B)$$

where $U_*(B) = \min_{y \in B} U(y)$ and $U^*(B) = \max_{y \in B} U(y)$; (c.f. [Shafer, 81, equation (8)]).

This result means that the standard Monte-Carlo algorithm [Wilson, 89, 91a] for calculating combined Dempster-Shafer belief (when a number of Belief Functions are combined using Dempster's rule) can be adapted to computationally efficiently calculate upper and lower expected utilities from the composite Belief Functions. We perform a large number of trials; for each trial, we use the method of the standard algorithm to pick subset B with chance $m(B)$; the value of the trial is then defined to be $U_*(B)$. To estimate lower expected utility, we average the value of these trials.

5 Pignistic Probabilities

Smets considers that uncertainty should be expressed by a Belief Function, but when it comes to making a decision, Bayesian decision theory should be used: utilities should be elicited, and the Belief Function should be reduced to a Bayesian probability function, known as the pignistic probability function, by a procedure called the Generalized Insufficient Reason Principle [Smets, 89, 90; Smets and Kennes, 89].

Definition 5.1

The *pignistic probability* P associated with Bel is defined by

$$\text{for } Y \subseteq \Theta, \quad P(Y) = \sum_{B \subseteq \Theta} m(B) \frac{|B \cap Y|}{|B|}.$$

P is produced by distributing each mass $m(B)$ equally over the elements of B; it is easily seen to be an additive probability function over Θ.

Smets suggests that P should be used in conjunction with utilities for decision-making: the expectation of utility is taken with respect to P.

It could be argued that any transformation from a Belief Function to a probability must involve some arbitrary choices. The Generalized Insufficient Reason Principle reduces to the notorious Principle of Insufficient Reason when Bel is the vacuous Belief Function, with $m(\Theta) = 1$. In other situations it is also dependent on the frame chosen to express the problem. It seems that one of the motivations of the development of Dempster-Shafer Theory was to avoid such a dubious principle, and its dependence on the choice of frame. The intention of Shafer in [Shafer, 76] seems to be that the frame should be sufficient to represent the problem, but apart from that the choice is essentially arbitrary. This means that any refinement of the frame will do equally well. Smets' theory no longer has this property.

Refinement of a frame means splitting some of the possibilities into a number of other possibilities. Let $\omega : \Theta \mapsto 2^\Phi$ be a finite refining of Θ where the frame Φ is the refinement of Θ, so that $\omega(x) \cap \omega(y) = \emptyset \iff x \neq y$ and $\omega(\Theta) \equiv \bigcup_{x \in \Theta} \omega(x) = \Phi$. [Shafer, 76, p115]. The interpretation of ω is as follows: for $x \in \Theta$, $\omega(x)$ is intended to denote the same proposition as x (so x is true if and only if $\omega(x)$ is true). If $|\omega(x)| > 1$ then ω splits x into more than one possibility.

ω induces from Bel a Belief Function Bel_ω over Φ with mass function m_ω defined by $m_\omega(\omega(B)) = m(B)$ for all $B \subseteq \Theta$. Bel_ω is essentially the same Belief Function as Bel, but just translated into a different language. Let P_ω^Φ be the pignistic probability associated with Bel_ω. P_ω^Φ induces through ω a probability function P_ω on Θ: for $x \in \Theta$, $P_\omega(x) = P_\omega^\Phi(\omega(x))$.

5.2 Example

Let $\Theta = \{x, y\}$, $\Phi = \{a, b, c\}$ and refining ω be given by $\omega(x) = \{a\}$ and $\omega(y) = \{b, c\}$. x and a therefore denote the same proposition (and so a is a relabelling of x). y denotes the same proposition as $\{b, c\}$, so the refining splits possibility y into two possibilities b and c. Define mass function m by $\text{m}(\Theta) = 0.6$ and $\text{m}(\{y\}) = 0.4$, and let Bel be the associated Belief Function. The pignistic probability function P associated with Bel is given by $P(\{x\}) = 0.3$ and $P(\{y\}) = 0.7$.

Mass function m_ω is given by $\text{m}_\omega(\Phi) = 0.6$ and $\text{m}_\omega(\{b, c\}) = 0.4$. Pignistic probability function P_ω^Φ is given by $P_\omega^\Phi(\{a\}) = 0.2$, $P_\omega^\Phi(\{b\}) = 0.4$ and $P_\omega^\Phi(\{c\}) = 0.4$. Note that the pignistic probabilities of equivalent propositions are not equal, e.g., $P(\{x\}) \neq P_\omega^\Phi(\{a\})$. P_ω gives the values of P_ω^Φ back on the original frame Θ; $P_\omega(x) = 0.2$, $P_\omega(y) = P_\omega^\Phi(\{b, c\}) = 0.8$. The values of expected utility will generally also be different. For example if utility function U is defined by $U(x) = 3$, $U(y) = -1$, then expected utility with respect to P is equal to 0.2, and expected utility with respect to P_ω is equal to -0.2.

Often the choice of frame Θ is arbitrary, refinement Φ being just as appropriate a frame, and Bel_ω giving the same information as Bel. In this case there seems no reason to prefer P over any P_ω. This leads to the following definition.

Definition 5.3

$\mathcal{P}^S$, the set of pignistic transforms of Bel is defined to be $\{P_\omega \ : \ \omega$ is a refining of $\Theta\}$. It can easily be shown that $\mathcal{P}^S$ is a subset of $\mathcal{P}$, the set of probability functions on Θ that dominate Bel, and also that $\text{Bel}(X) = \inf_{P \in \mathcal{P}^S} P(X)$, so that even taking a pignistic probability approach leads to Bel being the lower bound for a family of probability functions.

Definition 5.4

For $\lambda : \Theta \mapsto \mathbb{N}$, extend λ to 2^Θ by setting $\lambda(\emptyset) = 0$ and, for $Y \subseteq \Theta$, $\lambda(Y) = \sum_{y \in Y} \lambda(y)$; P^λ is defined by

$$P^\lambda(Y) = \sum_{B \subseteq \Theta} \text{m}(B) \frac{\lambda(Y \cap B)}{\lambda(B)}.$$

The following result follows easily from the observation that $P^\lambda = P_\omega$ when for all x, $\lambda(x) = |\omega(x)|$.

Proposition 5.5

$\mathcal{P}^S = \{P^\lambda \mid \lambda : \Theta \mapsto \mathbb{N}\}$.

Proposition 5.6

Let $\overline{\mathcal{P}^S}$ denote the topological closure (i.e. closure under limits) of $\mathcal{P}^S$ (viewed as a subset of $\mathbb{R}^{|\Theta|}$). Given utility function U on Θ, define $u : \mathcal{P} \to \mathbb{R}$ by $u(P) = P \cdot U$.

Then, for all orders π on Θ, $\overline{\mathcal{P}^S} \ni P_\pi$, and $\overline{u(\mathcal{P}^S)} \ni u(P_\pi)$. (See section 4. for the definitions of an order π, and P_π associated with Bel).

Theorem 5.7

Let E_* and E^* be lower and upper expectation (respectively) over $\mathcal{P}$, and let E_*^S and E_S^* be lower and upper expectation (respectively) over $\mathcal{P}^S$.
Then $E_*^S = E_*$ and $E_S^* = E^*$.
Therefore lower and upper expected utilities (and so decisions) are unaffected by using the set of pignistic transforms of a Belief Function rather than the set of all compatible probability functions of the Belief Function.

Proof

Let U be a utility function. Since $\mathcal{P}^S \subseteq \mathcal{P}$, $E_*^S(U) \geq E_*(U)$.
By proposition 4.4, and using u defined in 5.6,

$$E_*(U) = P_{\pi_U} \cdot U = u(P_{\pi_U})$$
$$\geq \inf\left(\overline{u(\mathcal{P}^S)}\right) \quad \text{since } u(P_{\pi_U}) \in \overline{u(\mathcal{P}^S)} \text{ by proposition 5.6.}$$

Therefore $E_*(U) \geq \inf(u(\mathcal{P}^S)) = E_*^S(U)$, using the fact that for $X \subseteq \mathbb{R}$, the infimum of the closure of X, $\inf\overline{X}$ is equal to $\inf X$. Therefore $E_*^S = E_*$. The proof for upper expectations is similar.

Dempster [67] also shows that the convex closure of $\{P_\pi : \pi \text{ is an order}\}$ is $\mathcal{P}$, which shows that the convex closure of $\overline{\mathcal{P}^S}$ is $\mathcal{P}$. In other words $\mathcal{P}$ is the closure of $\mathcal{P}^S$ under limits and mixtures (it does not matter which order these are done in).

6 Discussion

These results show that Smets' approach to decision-making is closer to the standard approach than is immediately apparent. However, Smets' approach does have some advantages; in situations where there does seem to be a natural choice of frame and we have to make a decision then it might be argued that the pignistic probability function P is a sensible choice to make from $\mathcal{P}$ for calculating expected utility. Similarly if one felt that a set of frames were the most natural we might consider just those associated pignistic probability functions, thus narrowing down the decision options.

Acknowledgements This work was supported by the ESPRIT basic research action DRUMS (3085), and a SERC postdoctoral research fellowship. Thanks to Philippe Smets and Mike Clarke for many useful and enjoyable discussions.

References

Dempster, A. P., 67, Upper and Lower Probabilities Induced by a Multi-valued Mapping. *Annals of Mathematical Statistics* 38: 325-39.

Dempster, A. P., and Kong, A., 87, in discussion of G. Shafer, Probability Judgment in Artificial Intelligence and Expert Systems (with discussion) *Statistical Science*, 2, No.1, 3-44.

Dubois, D. and Prade, H., 88, Possibility Theory: An Approach to Computerized Processing and Uncertainty, Plenum Press, New York.

Fagin R., and Halpern, J. Y., 89, Uncertainty, Belief and Probability, *Proc., International Joint Conference on AI* (IJCAI-89), 1161-1167.

Jaffray, J-Y, 92, Bayesian Updating and Belief Functions, *IEEE Trans. SMC*, 22: 1144–1152.

Shafer, G., 76, *A Mathematical Theory of Evidence*, Princeton University Press, Princeton, NJ.

Shafer, G., 81, Constructive Probability, *Synthese*, 48: 1-60.

Shafer, G., 90, Perspectives on the Theory and Practice of Belief Functions, *International Journal of Approximate Reasoning* 4: 323-362.

Smets, Ph. 89, Constructing the Pignistic Probability Function in a Context of Uncertainty, in *Proc. 5th Conference on Uncertainty in Artificial Intelligence*, Windsor.

Smets, Ph. 90, Decisions and Belief Functions, *TIMS-ORSA 90*, also research report TR/IRIDIA/90-10, IRIDIA, Université Libre de Bruxelles, 50 av. F. Roosevelt, CP194/6, 1050 Bruxelles, Belgique.

Smets, Ph., and Kennes, R., 89, The Transferable Belief Model: Comparison with Bayesian Models, research report TR/IRIDIA/89-1, IRIDIA, Université Libre de Bruxelles, 50 av. F. Roosevelt, CP194/6, 1050 Bruxelles, Belgique.

Walley, P., 91, *Statistical Reasoning with Imprecise Probabilities*, Chapman and Hall, London.

Wasserman, L. A., 90, Prior Envelopes Based on Belief Functions, *Annals of Statistics* 18, No.1: 454-464.

Wilson, Nic, 89, Justification, Computational Efficiency and Generalisation of the Dempster-Shafer Theory, Research Report no. 15, June 1989, Dept. of Computing and Mathematical Sciences, Oxford Polytechnic., to appear in *Artificial Intelligence*.

Wilson, Nic, 91a, A Monte-Carlo Algorithm for Dempster-Shafer Belief, *Proc. 7th Conference on Uncertainty in Artificial Intelligence*, B. D'Ambrosio, P. Smets and P. Bonissone (eds.), Morgan Kaufmann, 414-417.

Wilson, Nic, 91b, The Representation of Prior Knowledge in a Dempster-Shafer Approach, *Proceedings of the DRUMS workshop on Integration of Uncertainty Formalisms*, Blanes, Spain, June 1991; also Research Report, Department of Computer Science, Queen Mary and Westfield College, University of London, E1 4NS.

Wilson, Nic, 92a, How Much Do You Believe?, *International Journal of Approximate Reasoning*, 6, No. 3, 345-366.

Wilson, Nic, 92b, Some Theoretical Aspects of the Dempster-Shafer Theory, PhD thesis, Oxford Polytechnic, May 1992.

Default Logic and Dempster-Shafer Theory

Nic Wilson

Department of Computer Science
Queen Mary and Westfield College
Mile End Rd., London E1 4NS, UK

Abstract A new version of Reiter's Default Logic is developed which has a number of advantages: it is computationally much simpler and has some more intuitive properties, such as cumulativity. Furthermore, it is shown that this Default Logic is a limiting case of a Dempster-Shafer framework, thereby demonstrating a strong connection between two apparently very different approaches to reasoning with uncertainty, and opening up the possibility of mixing default and numerical rules within the same framework.

1 Introduction

Reiter's Default Logic is an apparently intuitive way of formalising default rules and inferences from them; Dempster-Shafer theory is a popular numerical formalism for reasoning about uncertainty. The primary aim of this paper is to demonstrate a strong connection between these two very different approaches to reasoning with uncertainty, showing how a default logic can be viewed as a limit of a Dempster-Shafer framework. However, this work has some other important consequences. In order to capture the full expressiveness of default logic, the Dempster-Shafer framework is extended, thus allowing it to be applied to other logics apart from a finite propositional calculus. It also turns out that the version of default logic achieved in this way has a number of important advantages over the standard version and other suggested modifications of it (see [Wilson, 93] for details); for example, it is computationally much simpler, and obeys natural cumulativity properties which the standard version does not. It can also be expressed very simply in terms of a monotonic logic on an extended language, thus avoiding awkward fixed-point definitions. This approach to default logic can be extended easily so that it can represent orderings, indicating preferences or dominance information between default rules.

Section 2 reformulates Reiter's Default Logic in terms of inference rules and redefines extensions, so that they have more desirable properties than Reiter's extensions, hence producing a new default logic; section 3 shows how a class of logics can be constructed from the sources of evidence Dempster-Shafer framework, defining a B-extension to be a set of closed wffs whose belief can be simultaneously made to tend to 1, by appropriate choice of the reliabilities of the sources; section 4 shows how the default logics defined in section 2 can be generated from the sources of evidences construction given in section 3.

Some related results appeared in [Wilson, 90a, 90b, 93]; proofs are given in [Wilson, 92, 93].

2 Default Logic

One type of uncertain rule is a default rule—in the absence of information indicating that the circumstances are exceptional, the rule is fired, though the consequence of the rule may later have to be retracted, if it's discovered that circumstances are in fact exceptional.

Reiter's Default Logic [Reiter, 80; Besnard, 89] is a logic for reasoning with default rules. A default rule $a : b / c$ is intended to represent the rule 'If we know a then deduce c, as long as b is consistent'. a is known as the pre-requisite (or antecedent), b as the justification, and c as the consequent of the default rule.

Here all default theories will be assumed to be closed and consistent. This is not restrictive: inconsistent default theories are trivial (having a single inconsistent extension) and [Reiter, 80] also initially only deals with closed default theories, since the extension to more general default theories is straightforward.

Reiter's definition of extensions has a number of weaknesses. There are apparently sensible default theories which allow no extension. It means that Reiter's default logic lacks a proof theory (except for the special case of normal default theories), and lacks important and natural cumulativity properties.

2.1 Inference Rules and Default Theories

The approach to default logic developed here is based on the idea of adding inference rules to the logic. An inference rule, a / c (read 'if a then c') allows one deduce c if a is known.

For some set of closed wffs U and set of inference rules J we define $\text{Th}^J(U)$ to be the logical closure of U when all the inference rules in J are added to the logic i.e., the set of formulae obtained by applying all the inference rules in J repeatedly to U.

Definition 2.1.1 Let L be the language of a predicate calculus on a countable alphabet and let L' be the set of closed wffs in L. Let $U \subseteq L'$ be a set of closed formulae, and J be a set of inference rules (i.e. a set whose elements are of the form a / c where a and c are closed formulae in L).

(a) $\text{Th}(U)$, the logical closure (within L') of U, is defined to be $\{d \in L' : U \vdash d\}$, where $\vdash$ is entailment in predicate calculus.

(b) $\text{Th}^J(U)$ is the intersection of all sets $\Gamma \subseteq L'$ such that (i) $\Gamma \supseteq U$, (ii) $\text{Th}(\Gamma) = \Gamma$, and (iii) if $a / c \in J$ and $a \in \Gamma$ then $c \in \Gamma$.

Definition 2.1.2 A closed consistent default theory (abbreviated to 'default theory') is a pair (D, W) where $W \subseteq L'$ is a consistent set of closed wffs, known as the facts, and D is a countable set of default rules, each rule being of the form $a : b / c$ with $a, b, c \in L'$.

D will be labelled $\{a_i : b_i / c_i : i \in \delta\}$ where δ is either $\{1, \ldots, m\}$ for some $m \in \mathbb{N}$, or the set of natural numbers $\mathbb{N} = \{1, 2, 3, \ldots\}$.

2.2 A Rule-Based Approach to Default Logic

Reiter's default logic has a number of weaknesses. There are apparently sensible default theories that have no R-extensions. It also lacks other nice properties: it has no proof theory for general default theories (there is one for the special case of normal default theories), and lacks natural cumulativity properties.

In default logic the extensions are intended to be the different possible completions, using the default rules, of an incomplete set of facts about the world. Here a new, and in many ways simpler, definition of extension is suggested. This new type of extension enjoys these desirable properties. This definition differs from previous definitions such as those in [Reiter, 80; Lukacewicz, 84; Brewka, 91] in that it focuses on sets of default rules rather than sets of formulae.

For $\gamma \subseteq \delta$, let $I_\gamma = \{a_i / c_i : i \in \gamma\}$, and abbreviate $\mathrm{Th}^{I_\gamma}(U)$ to $\mathrm{Th}^\gamma(U)$ for $U \subseteq L'$. For $\gamma \subseteq \delta$, if we allow ourselves to use inference rules a_i / c_i for $i \in \gamma$, then we can deduce any formula in $\mathrm{Th}^\gamma(W)$ (and no others). However, if we can deduce $\neg b_i$ for some $i \in \gamma$ then this would seem to contradict the intention of the default rules, since b_i is inconsistent. This motivates the definition of Δ-consistent.

Definition 2.2.1 Let $\Delta = (D, W)$ be a default theory. $\gamma \subseteq \delta$ is said to be Δ-consistent if for all $i \in \gamma$, $\mathrm{Th}^\gamma(W) \not\ni \neg b_i$. Define $C^\Delta = \{\gamma \subseteq \delta : \gamma$ is Δ-consistent$\}$. γ is said to be an M-extension generator if γ is maximal in C^Δ. (M-extension generators are therefore maximal Δ-consistent sets). E is said to be an M-extension of Δ if $E = \mathrm{Th}^\gamma(W)$ for some M-extension generator γ.

The intuition behind the definition of an M-extension is that we accept as many of the rules as possible while maintaining the consistency of the corresponding justifications; 'accepting a rule' i means that we have to apply it if we can (so that c_i is deduced if a_i is known). Each set γ can be thought of as representing a 'belief state': where facts W are believed and rules corresponding to γ are accepted. M-extensions correspond to belief states which are maximal in the specified sense.

2.3 Properties of M-extensions

M-extensions have, for general closed consistent default theories, the nice properties that Reiter's extensions only have for closed consistent normal default theories: for example, every default theory has an M-extension. M-extensions, unlike Reiter's extensions are semi-monotonic [Reiter, 80]. Though mathematically this is a nice property, and might be viewed as an intuitive property, it appears to prevent an adequate solution to the famous 'birds fly, penguins don't fly, penguins are birds' example. When we extend this default logic by allowing orderings as described in [Wilson, 92, 93] we lose semi-monotonicity.

There is also a natural default proof theory, and the default logic has excellent cumulativity properties, including a choice function definition, as discussed in [Makinson, 90].

It can be shown that If E is a Reiter extension of default theory Δ then E is an M-extension of Δ. Furthermore, if Δ is a prerequisite-free normal default theory (which is equivalent to a Poole system without constraints [Poole, 88; Makinson, 90]), then these two definitions of extension are equivalent; (however the definitions differ on normal default theories, so the definition is not equivalent to that given in [Lukacewicz, 84]).

2.4 Jointly Consistent Justifications

An alternative definition of M-extension is achieved if we redefine Δ-consistent as follows: $\gamma \subseteq \delta$ is said to be Δ-consistent if $\mathrm{Th}^\gamma(W) \cup \{b_i : i \in \gamma\}$ is consistent.

This answers a criticism of Reiter's default logic made by Poole [88] and discussed further in [Brewka, 91] (who also solves it within his framework). M-extensions still have the above properties, such as semi-monotonicity, the same cumulativity properties and completeness of proof theory.

3 The Sources of Evidence Framework as a Logic

The Sources of Evidence Framework [Wilson, 89, 92], consists of a number of sources S_i, $i = 1, \ldots, m$, each of which give us some piece of evidence. Each source is taken to be either reliable or unreliable; if it is reliable then its statement is true; if unreliable, we know nothing about the truth of its statement. For each source S_i we make a judgement α_i of the chance that it is reliable.

A source and their evidence correspond essentially to Bernouilli's pure evidence [Bernouilli, 1713; Hacking, 75; Shafer, 78], and to a simple support function in Dempster-Shafer theory [Shafer, 76; Dempster, 67].

Let $\Omega = \{\varepsilon_\gamma : \gamma \subseteq \{1, \ldots, m\}\}$ where the proposition ε_γ refers to the event that sources $S_i : i \in \gamma$ are reliable and the others are unreliable. Natural assumptions lead to the choice of probability function $\mathbf{P}^{DS}$ on Ω. Measure of belief $\mathrm{Bel}(d)$ is defined to be the probability that d can be deduced (see below). Bel is then equal to the combination using Dempster's rule of the m simple support functions (corresponding to the sources).

To turn the Sources of Evidence Framework into a logic, roughly speaking, we tend the reliabilities of the sources (the α_is) to 1. B-extensions are the sets of formulae whose belief can be made to tend to 1. Bel will be considered as a function $\mathrm{Bel}_{\underline{\alpha}}$ where $\underline{\alpha} = (\alpha_1, \alpha_2, \ldots, \alpha_m)$ is the vector consisting of the reliabilities of all the sources.

Definition 3.1

An SE-structure is defined to be a function $K : \Omega \mapsto 2^{L'}$ such that for $\gamma, \psi \subseteq \{1, \ldots, m\}$, if $\gamma \supseteq \psi$, $K(\varepsilon_\gamma)$ consistent implies $K(\varepsilon_\psi)$ consistent.

For $\gamma \subseteq \{1, \ldots, m\}$, $K(\varepsilon_\gamma)$ will be abbreviated to K_γ.

SE-structures are a generalisation of Dempster's multivalued mappings [Dempster, 67]. K_γ is intended to be the set of formulae known (or believed) to be true if ε_γ is known to be true, i.e., if sources S_i for $i \in \gamma$ are known to be reliable. Other conditions on K seem natural, e.g., for any γ, K_γ is logically closed, and K_γ is monotonic with respect to γ. However, the following results do not require these extra conditions so they are not assumed here.

Definition 3.2

$E \subseteq L'$ is an M-extension of SE-structure K if $E = K_\gamma$ for some γ maximal such that K_γ is consistent.

M-extensions of SE-structures will be used as an intermediate step between the M-extensions of default theories defined in section 2.2 and the Belief Function based B-extensions of SE-structures defined below.

For reliabilities of sources $\underline{\alpha} = (\alpha_1, \ldots, \alpha_m) \in [0,1]^m$ the Dempster-Shafer probability function $P_{\underline{\alpha}}^{DS}$ on Ω is assumed, defined by

$$P_{\underline{\alpha}}^{DS}(\varepsilon_\gamma) = \begin{cases} \rho_\gamma/k, & \text{if } K_\gamma \text{ consistent;} \\ 0, & \text{otherwise,} \end{cases}$$

$$\text{where} \quad k = \sum_{K_\gamma consistent} \rho_\gamma \quad \text{and} \quad \rho_\gamma = \prod_{i \in \gamma} \alpha_i \prod_{i \notin \gamma} (1 - \alpha_i).$$

Definition 3.3

For SE-structure K, reliabilities vector $\underline{\alpha}$ and $d \in L'$,

$$\text{Bel}_{\underline{\alpha}}(d) = P_{\underline{\alpha}}^{DS}(K_\gamma \ni d) \quad \text{i.e.,} \quad \sum_{\gamma: K_\gamma \ni d} P_{\underline{\alpha}}^{DS}(\varepsilon_\gamma).$$

$\text{Bel}_{\underline{\alpha}}(d)$ can be thought of as the probability that d is known.

Example

This framework is a generalisation of the simple support function case of Dempster-Shafer theory. These definitions will probably make much more sense to the reader if considered in the light of this special case.

A single source S_i with reliability α_i, who says that proposition* p_i is true, corresponds to a simple support function Bel_i with corresponding mass function defined by $m_i(p_i) = \alpha_i$ and $m_i(\top) = 1 - \alpha_i$. In this case, if sources i for $i \in \gamma$ are reliable then we know that propositions p_i are true for $i \in \gamma$, so we know that $\bigwedge_{i \in \gamma} p_i$ is true. We would then set K_γ to be all the logical consequences of $\bigwedge_{i \in \gamma} p_i$. The function $\text{Bel}_{\underline{\alpha}}$ then turns out to be the belief function formed by combining the simple support functions Bel_i, $i = 1, \ldots, m$ using Dempster's rule [Shafer, 76].

To use the Sources of Evidence framework to produce a logic we require that for any closed wff p, $\text{Bel}_\alpha(p)$ tends to either 0 or 1. A B-extension is then the set of formulae whose Belief tends to 1.

---

* Usually presentations of the theory (e.g., [Shafer, 76]) represent propositions as subsets of a frame of discernment Θ, a set of mutually exclusive and exhaustive propositions. This, however, can be seen to make essentially no difference, using a standard correspondence between a finite propositional calculus and the boolean algebra of subsets of a set, e.g., via the sets of possible worlds in the semantics, or the Lindenbaum algebra. $\top$ corresponds to Θ, $\bot$ to $\emptyset$, conjunction to intersection, disjunction to union, negation to complement, entailment to 'is a subset of'.

Definition 3.4

$E \subseteq L'$ is a B-extension of SE-structure K if

for $i = 1, \ldots, m$ there exist monotonic functions $\alpha_i : [1, \infty) \longrightarrow (0, 1)$ with $\alpha_i(x)$ not tending to 0 as x tends to infinity, and given $\epsilon > 0$ there exists N_ϵ such that for all $x > N_\epsilon$ and for all $d \in L'$

$$\mathrm{Bel}_{\underline{\alpha}(x)}(d) > 1 - \epsilon \quad \text{if } d \in E$$
$$\mathrm{Bel}_{\underline{\alpha}(x)}(d) < \epsilon \quad \text{if } d \notin E.$$

Theorem 3.5

Let K be an SE-structure. Then $E \subseteq L'$ is a B-extension of K if and only if E is an M-extension of K.

Example continued

In the example above we had $K_\gamma = \mathrm{Th}(\{p_i : i \in \gamma\})$, for $\gamma \subseteq \{1, \ldots, m\}$. We can see that M-extensions are sets K_γ where γ is maximal such that $\{p_i : i \in \gamma\}$ is consistent. Theorem 3.5 shows that if we tend the reliabilities α_i in such a way that $\mathrm{Bel}(d)$ tends to either 1 or 0, then the set of propositions whose Belief tends to 1 is an M-extension. Conversely any M-extension can generated in this way. Therefore B-extensions of this SE-structure, which represents, roughly speaking, the sets of propositions whose Belief can be made (simultaneously) to tend to 1, are exactly the M-extensions (and hence the Reiter extensions) of the free normal default theory $\Delta = (\{\top : p_i / p_i : i = 1, 2 \ldots, m\}, \emptyset)$. This observation is the basis for the results in section 4.

4 Representing Default Rules in Sources of Evidence Framework

Default rules will be represented in the Sources of Evidence framework by treating them rather like numerical rules with a high, but unknown, certainty. The basic idea is to make the statement of the ith source be something like 'inference rule a_i / c_i should be accepted unless $\neg b_i$ is known'. To implement this the statement of the ith source is made to be that inference rules a_i / c_i and $\neg b_i / \perp$ are valid, so that knowing a_i will enable us to deduce c_i unless $\neg b_i$ is known, in which case inconsistency will ensue.

A Default theory (D, W) is said to be finite if D is finite.

Definition 4.1

For finite default theory $\Delta = (D, W)$, label D as $\{a_i : b_i / c_i, \quad i = 1, \ldots, m\}$. For $\gamma \subseteq \{1, \ldots, m\}$ let $J_\gamma = \{a_i / c_i, \neg b_i / \perp : i \in \gamma\}$.

For $E \subseteq L'$, E is said to be a B-extension of Δ if E is a B-extension of the SE-structure K^Δ defined, for $\gamma \subseteq \{1, \ldots, m\}$, by $K_\gamma^\Delta = \mathrm{Th}^{J_\gamma}(W)$.

Theorem 4.2

For finite default theory Δ,

E is an M-extension of Δ if and only if E is an M-extension of SE-structure K^Δ.

This leads, using theorem 3.5 to the following corollary, which is the central result of the paper, tying the default logic of section 2 to the SE-structures of section 3. It shows that this default logic can be viewed as the limit of the extended Sources of Evidence Dempster-Shafer framework.

Corollary 4.3

For finite default theory Δ and $E \subseteq L'$,

E is an M-extension of Δ if and only if E is a B-extension of Δ.

A consequence of this result is that it enables numerical and default rules to be used together within the same framework. This is discussed in [Wilson, 90b].

5 Discussion

This work shows a strong connection between a numerical and a logical framework, which are apparently quite different. Because this version of default logic was designed in order to show the relationship with Dempster-Shafer theory, it is perhaps surprising that it turned out to have such attractive properties, arguably better than any other equally expressive logic for default reasoning (if we take special cases, such as free-normal default theories, then of course we get better properties).

Another non-monotonic logic which is a limiting case of a probabilistic framework is Adams' logic of conditionals [Adams, 75] developed further by Geffner and Pearl (see e.g., [Geffner, 89; Pearl, 88]). This logic is not very closely related to the default logic developed here. Some discussion of this is given in [Wilson, 90b].

Acknowledgements This work was supported by the ESPRIT basic research action DRUMS (3085), and a SERC postdoctoral research fellowship. I am grateful to Jérôme Mengin for much enjoyable and useful discussion, and to Philippe Besnard, for some very useful comments on earlier versions of this work.

References

Adams, E., 75, *The Logic of Conditionals*, Reidel, Boston.

Bernouilli, J., 1713, *Ars Conjectandi*, Basel. Reprinted in 1968 by Culture et Civilisation, Brussels.

Besnard, Philippe, 89, *An Introduction to Default Logic*, Symbolic Computation—Artificial Intelligence, Springer-Verlag, Berlin, Heidelberg, New York.

Brewka, G., 91, Cumulative Default Logic: In Defense of Nonmonotonic Inference Rules, *Artificial Intelligence* 50, 183–205.

Dempster, A. P., 67, Upper and Lower Probabilities Induced by a Multi-valued Mapping. *Ann. Math. Statistics* 38: 325–339.

Geffner, H., 89, *Default Reasoning: Causal and Conditional Theories*, PhD thesis, Computer Science Department, UCLA, Los Angeles, CA90024, November 89.

Hacking, I., 75, *The Emergence of Probability*, Cambridge University Press, London.

Lukacewicz, 84, *Considerations on Default Logic*, Proc. Non Monotonic Reasoning Workshop, New Paltz NY, pp165–193; also, 1988, *Computational Intelligence 4*, pp1–16.

Makinson, D., 90, General Patterns in Nonmonotonic Reasoning, Chapter 2.2 of Vol II of *Handbook of Logic in Artificial Intelligence and Logic Programming*.

Pearl, Judea, 88, *Probabilistic Reasoning in Intelligent Systems: Networks of Plausible Inference*, Morgan Kaufmann Publishers Inc.

Poole, D., 88, A Logical Framework for Default Reasoning, *Artificial Intelligence*, 36: 27–47.

Reiter, R., 80, A Logic for Default Reasoning, *Artificial Intelligence* 13 (1, 2), pp81–132.

Shafer, G., 76, *A Mathematical Theory of Evidence*, Princeton University Press, Princeton, NJ.

Shafer, G., 78, Non-Additive Probabilities in the Work of Bernouilli and Lambert, *Archive for History of Exact Sciences* 19: 309-370.

Wilson, Nic, 89, Justification, Computational Efficiency and Generalisation of the Dempster-Shafer Theory, Research Report no. 15, June 1989, Dept. of Computing and Mathematical Sciences, Oxford Polytechnic., to appear in *Artificial Intelligence*.

Wilson, Nic, 90a, Default Logic and Belief Functions, *Proceedings DRUMS Workshop on Non-monotonic Logic*, Luminy, France, February 1990.

Wilson, Nic, 90b, Rules, Belief Functions and Default Logic, in Bonissone, P., and Henrion, M., 90, eds *Proc. 6th Conference on Uncertainty in Artificial Intelligence*, MIT, Cambridge, Mass.

Wilson, Nic, 92, Some Theoretical Aspects of the Dempster-Shafer Theory, PhD thesis, May 1992.

Wilson, Nic, 93, Default Logic and Dempster-Shafer Theory, unpublished manuscript (longer version of current paper).

Belief Revision by Expansion

Cees Witteveen[1] and Wiebe van der Hoek[2*]

[1] Delft University of Technology,
Dept. of Mathematics and Computer Science,
P.O. Box 356, 2600 AJ Delft, The Netherlands,
e-mail: witt@cs.tudelft.nl
[2] Utrecht University,
Dept. of Computer Science,
P.O. Box 80089,
3508 TB Utrecht, The Netherlands.

Abstract. We show that the standard framework for belief revision has to be adapted in order to deal with revision in non-monotonic theories. The reason is that sometimes *expanding* a theory seems to be more appropriate than *contracting* it in order to remove inconsistencies that occur as a consequence of adopting a non-standard semantics. We illustrate this approach by applying revision by expansion truth maintenance.

1 Belief revision in non-monotonic theories

We deal with belief revision in non-monotonic theories. Such a revision has to occur if the current theory becomes contradictory, i.e. has no acceptable model. In the dominant Alchourrón-Gärdenfors-Makinson (AGM-) framework ([1, 3]) the revision of such a contradictory theory is performed by applying a *contraction* operator in order to find a smaller but consistent (sub)theory.

In some cases, however, we propose not to contract, but to *expand* the current contradictory theory. The reason is that the AGM-approach deals with revision in classical theories, while we want to deal with revision in non-monotonic theories, too. We will argue that non-monotonicity requires an adaptation of the standard AGM-approach to theory revision.

First of all, while classically a theory is inconsistent iff it admits no models at all, for an inconsistent non-monotonic theory T it is perfectly possible to have classical models. The reason, of course, is that not every classical model of the theory is considered an *acceptable* model. So we distinguish for a given theory[3] T a subset of $Mod(T)$: its acceptable models and we call T *(non-monotonically) inconsistent* iff it has no acceptable models (allowing it still to have some classical models). So, classical inconsistency is a limiting case for inconsistent non-monotonic theories.

---

* This author was partially supported by ESPRIT Basic Research Action No. 6156 (DRUMS).

[3] Here, a *a theory* T is a set of sentences over a language $\mathcal{L}$. We use $Cn(T)$ to denote the deductive closure of T. In terms of the AGM-theory, T is a belief base and $Cn(T)$ the set of beliefs defined by it.

This notion of non-monotonic inconsistency has some important consequences: it disposes of the main rationale for applying revision by contraction if a theory is inconsistent. Whereas retraction in monotonic logic seems perfectly reasonable, if a non-monotonic theory is inconsistent it is not so obvious why we should apply it. For example, if the theory has classical models, we could adapt our notion of acceptability, and turn a classical model into an acceptable one. However, instead of changing the semantics, there is another way to solve a revision problem. For, our definition of non-monotonic inconsistency implies that:

> *for an* inconsistent *non-monotonic theory* T *there may exist* consistent *theories* T' *containing* T.

We call such a theory T' an *expansion* of T. Theory-expansion at least is an option in revising contradictory non-monotonic theories. To show that sometimes it is a better alternative, we will discuss a proposal for applying theory-expansion in *truth maintenance*. We will argue that whenever a truth maintenance theory is (purely) non-monotonically inconsistent, it is more appropriate to apply *theory expansion* than *theory contraction* to solve a revision problem. The reason for this is provided by the special nature of foundational reasoning in the semantics of truth maintenance, governed by the following meta-rule:

> *unless there is a* grounded reason *for a belief, assume it to be false.*

Then, applying revision by expansion is justified by the following consideration:

> *if in a theory* T *a contradiction arises as a consequence of making some assumptions, it is more adequate to revise the assumptions than the sentences of* T.

Revising these assumptions means that we have to state *explicitly* that some beliefs cannot be false. The only way to express such a statement in truth maintenance is to *add* a suitable argument for such a belief, i.e., to expand the theory.

2   Truth Maintenance Systems

A Truth Maintenance System (TMS) has to maintain a finite, propositional database of *beliefs* and *arguments for them*[4]. Usually, a TMS is considered to be a supporting system of a non-monotonic reasoning system R which queries the TMS for the status of some beliefs together with some arguments for them. (For an introduction into basic TMS-notions, see ([7, 11]).) Here, by a truth maintenance theory we mean a finite set T of *arguments* r, being formulas of the form $c \leftarrow \alpha$, with c an atomic proposition and $\alpha = \alpha^+ \wedge \alpha^-$ where $\alpha^+ = a_1 \wedge \ldots \wedge a_m$ is a conjunction of positive atoms and $\alpha^- = \sim a_{m+1} \wedge \ldots \wedge \sim a_{m+n}$ is a conjunction of negative atoms. Both α^+ and α^- may be empty. Such an

---

[4] We restrict ourselves to so-called Doyle-style systems: see [2, 7].

argument can be interpreted as: *c has to be believed if every a_i in α^+ is believed and there is no reason for believing any of the a_{m+j} in α^-* [5].

$\alpha(r)$ denotes the *antecedent* α of r and $c(r)$ the *consequent* c of r. We also use α^+ and α^- to denote the set of literals occurring in these conjunctions. For a wff ϕ and theory T, $At(\phi)$ $(At(T))$ denotes the set of atoms occurring in ϕ (in T, respectively).

The class of truth maintenance theories is denoted by TMS and a member of this class by tms. The class of tms theories with constraints, abbreviated TMSC, is the class of theories T containing a non-empty subset C_T of special arguments, called *constraints*, enabling it to declare that a given conjunction α of literals forms a *nogood*, i.e., that it is inconsistent to believe in all the literals of α simultaneously. Constraints are represented as $\perp \leftarrow \alpha^+ \wedge \alpha^-$.

As for the semantics, a (partial) interpretation I of a tms T is a consistent subset of $Lit(T)$, i.e., for no $x \in At(T)$, I contains both x and $\sim x$. A literal x is true, $I(x) = \mathbf{t}$, if it occurs in I; if $\sim x \in I$ then $I(x) = \mathbf{f}$; else $I(x) = \mathbf{u}$. With the *truth ordering* $<$, $(\mathbf{f} < \mathbf{u} < \mathbf{t})$, we can extend I to formulae over $(At(T), \wedge, \sim)$ using the strong Kleene truth-table definitions for $\wedge$ and $\sim$: $I(\phi \wedge \psi) = glb_<\{I(\phi), I(\psi)\}$ and $I(\sim \phi) = \sim I(\phi)$ where $\sim \mathbf{f} = \mathbf{t}$, $\sim \mathbf{u} = \mathbf{u}$ and $\sim \mathbf{t} = \mathbf{f}$. When we use $\mathbf{f}, \mathbf{u}$ and $\mathbf{t}$ in the antecedents of arguments, we use them as abbreviations and assume that interpretations respect their intuitive meaning. We say that I *respects an argument* $c \leftarrow \alpha \in T$ if $I(\alpha) \leq I(c)$. I is a *model* of T if I respects every argument in T. I *respects a constraint* $\perp \leftarrow \alpha$ if $I(\alpha) \leq I(\perp) < \mathbf{t}$. An interpretation is a *C-model* of a tmsc T if I is a model of T and I respects every constraint of T, i.e. $I(\perp) < \mathbf{t}$. If a tmsc theory does not have any *C*-model, it is called *C-inconsistent*, otherwise it is *C-consistent*.

Stable or *grounded* models of T capture the idea of only believing c if there is some grounded reason to believe c: a partial model M of T is said to be stable or grounded if there exists a partial ordering $\preceq$ of $At(T)$ such that for every atom x with $M(x) > \mathbf{f}$ there exists an argument $x \leftarrow \alpha^+ \wedge \alpha^-$ such that

1. $M(\alpha) = M(x)$, i.e., the belief in x is **supported** and
2. for every a in α^+, $a \prec x$, i.e., the support is **non-circular**.

For every T there is at least one stable model. These models are closed under intersection, so the *smallest* grounded model, also called the *well-founded* (wf) model ([6, 8]), is universally and uniquely defined for every T, and denoted by $WF(T)$. A model M is called the *wf_C-model* of a tmsc T iff $WF(T)$ is a *C*-model of T. This well-founded model semantics is generally considered to be a suitable semantics for TMS. (see e.g. [11]).

---

[5] Thus, $\sim$ has to be interpreted as *negation by default* or *negation as failure* instead of classical negation.

Revision in Truth Maintenance

In a standard tms T adapting the theory to new information is a simple process: since every tms has a wf-model, belief contravening arguments do not occur and basic reason maintenance can be performed simply by adding a new argument ϕ to the existing tms T and computing the resulting wf-model of $T \cup \{\phi\}$. Elsewhere, we have shown that such a revision process can be performed in $O(|c(T)| \times \|T\|))$ time, where $|c(T)|$ denotes the number of conclusions of arguments in T and $\|T\|$ the size of the tms theory ([11]).

The picture changes dramatically if we add constraints: consider the theory $T_1 = \{c \leftarrow a \wedge \sim b, \ a \leftarrow\}$. This theory has the wf-model $M_1 = \{c, a, \sim b\}$. However, if we add the constraint $\bot \leftarrow c$ to T_1, the resulting theory $T_1' = \{c \leftarrow a \wedge \sim b, \ a \leftarrow, \ \bot \leftarrow c\}$ has the wf-model $M_1' = \{\bot, c, a, \sim b\}$. Since $M_1'(\bot) = \mathbf{t}$, T_1' does not have a wf_C-model. So belief revision has to be performed. Before we try to solve this revision problem, let us look at a related theory $T_2 = \{c \leftarrow a \wedge b, \ a \leftarrow, \ b \leftarrow\}$: it has the wf-model $M_2 = \{c, a, b\}$ and if we add the constraint $\bot \leftarrow c$ to T_2, again the resulting theory does not have a wf_C-model. There is, however, an important difference between these two theories. In T_1 and T_1', b is assumed false as a result of applying negation by default: we have no grounded reason for b. This assumption in T_1' leads to an undesirable consequence: we reach a contradiction by making c true. T_1', however, is not classically inconsistent: for example, $\{a, b, \sim c, \sim \bot\}$ is a C-model for T_1'. The theory $T_2 \cup \{\bot \leftarrow c\}$, however, is classically inconsistent.

In the first case there is a natural solution to the problem. We assumed b to be false since we had no grounded reason for believing b. But, since this *assumption* that b is false leads us to the undesirable consequence that the constraint $\bot \leftarrow c$ is violated, we can now conclude that the derivation of this contradiction itself should be a perfect argument for believing b. Hence, the theory should be revised in such a way that in the resulting theory T' this assumption cannot be made. The easiest way to prevent this is to *add* an extra argument for b. Now, note that the theory $T_1'' = T_1' \cup \{b \leftarrow\} = \{c \leftarrow a \wedge \sim b, \ a \leftarrow, \ \bot \leftarrow c, \ b \leftarrow\}$ has the wf-model $M_1'' = \{a, b, \sim c, \sim \bot\}$ which is a wf_C-model of T''.

Of course, one could object and suggest that the theory T_1 should be contracted if T_1' is inconsistent. But, clearly, it seems not to be adequate to delete an *explicit argument* such as for example $a \leftarrow$, if it sufficient to prevent an *implicit argument* (b is false, since there is no reason to believe b) to occur. (We concentrate on cases where the theory is classically consistent, hence we will not consider T_2 any further.)

Summarizing, in TMSC the adoption of the grounded model semantics has some undesirable repercussions in the presence of constraints. These defects, however, can be easily repaired by (i) expanding the theory by adding additional arguments for atoms assumed to be false and (ii) determining the wf-model of the obtained *expansion* of the original theory.

We will call such an approach a *theory expansion approach*.

Notation: A theory T expanded by a set of rules R is denoted by $T + R$. If R is a singleton $R = \{r\}$, we will also use $T + r$.

3 A framework for revision by expansion

In [9, 10] we have formulated a general framework for theory expansion in truth maintenance and logic programming, based on the following notions:

Definition 3.1 (well-founded expansion, expansion function)
A **wf-expansion** *of a theory T is an expansion T' of T such that T' has a wf_C-model. Given a class of theories $\mathcal{T}$, a* **wf-expansion function** *is a (partial) computable mapping $E : \mathcal{T} \to \mathcal{T}$, assigning to every $T \in dom(E)$ a wf-expansion $E(T) = T'$ of T. $WF(T')$ is called the* **wf-expansion model** *returned by E.*

Not every expansion function will be acceptable to us. In particular, we will use the following criteria an expansion function E should satisfy:

1. *completeness*: E should return a wf-expansion whenever it exists.
2. *minimality*: E should be minimal in some respect.
3. *canonicity*: $E(T)$ should be canonical (in some respect).
4. *tractability*: the expansion function should be efficiently computable.

So *completeness* excludes functions which are too weak, *minimality* makes it possible to justify the choice for particular complete expansion functions and *canonicity* is in the spirit of a tms giving a canonical interpretation of arguments and beliefs.

Since a tms is a reasoner's assistant we will expect it to function smoothly and quickly. Therefore, we usually add the criterion concerning *efficiency*. We will now briefly discuss these criteria.

Completeness

Clearly, if a theory T is classically inconsistent, theory expansion makes no sense. So, let $CONS(\mathcal{T}) = \{ T \in \mathcal{T} \mid$ T is a C-consistent theory $\}$. where $\mathcal{T}$ is a class of tms-theories. Then we say that an expansion function $E : \mathcal{T} \to \mathcal{T}$ is *complete* with respect to $\mathcal{T}$ iff $dom(E) = CONS(\mathcal{T})$.

Clearly, it makes sense to concentrate on complete functions, since they can be considered as the most successful expansion functions, i.e. they fail to produce an expansion for a theory $T \in \mathcal{T}$ only if T is classically inconsistent. In the sequel, we assume expansion functions bo be complete with respect to TMSC. Such functions for TMSC do exist, in fact they can be constructed very efficiently, see [10]. As a simple example, consider the expansion function E returning for every C-consistent but contradictory theory T the following expansion $E(T)$:

$$E(T) = T + \{a \leftarrow\sim a \mid a \in At(T), WF(T)(a) = \mathbf{f}\,\}$$

Minimum and minimal expansion functions

We only expand a theory if it is necessary to do so. And if it is necessary it seems natural to try to change the theory as little as possible.
This idea of minimality can be specified either *syntactically* or *semantically*:

1. *Syntactically* , an expansion function is a minimum expansion if it minimizes the amount of expansion rules added to a theory T i.e., the *size* of the expansion, in order to obtain a contradiction-free expanded theory.
   Therefore, we will call an expansion function E a *minimum size expansion* function if for every E' and $T \in dom(E) \cap dom(E')$, we have $|E(T)| \leq |E'(T)|$ and E is called a *minimal size expansion* function if there is no expansion function E' such that for some T we have $E'(T) \subset E(T)$.
2. *Semantically*, an expansion function E is a minimum expansion if it effects the information conveyed by the original theory in a minimal way. Such a *minimum change* expansion can be defined as as a minimization of the model-difference between the (inconsistent) wf-model $WF(T)$ and the (consistent) wf-model $WF(E(T))$.
   More exactly, let $\Delta(T', T) = \{a \in At(T) \mid WF(T')(a) \neq WF(T)(a)\}$ then E is a *minimum change expansion* function, if for every E' and $T \in dom(E) \cap dom(E')$, we have $|\Delta(E(T), T)| \leq |\Delta(E'(T), T)|$.
   Likewise, we define E to be an (inclusion) *minimal change expansion* if there is no expansion function E' such that $\Delta(E'(T), T) \subset \Delta(E(T), T)$.

Canonicity

A tms has to inform a reasoning system about the status of its beliefs. The wf-model of a tms offers a canonical interpretation meeting the requirements of consistency and groundedness. Dealing with expansions, we prefer to preserve these properties: we like to get a canonical expansion of a theory, too.
Both completeness and minimality do not ensure canonicity: in general there is more than one expansion of a theory meeting these criteria.

In a three-valued setting, however, there is a natural solution to this problem if we use the *knowledge minimization* or *skeptical* approach. Viewing **u** as containing less knowledge than the classical truth-values **t** and **f**, knowledge minimization is realized by intersecting interpretations. Recall that the wf-model of a tms is the intersection of all partial stable models of T and can be characterized as the most skeptical (knoledge-minimal) partial stable model of the theory. Analogously, we can obtain a canonical expansion function by "intersecting" a set of expansion functions. In [10] we have shown that such an intersection always results in a (complete) expansion function and that a canonical expansion function E_{can} w.r.t. a class $\mathcal{E}$ of expansion functions can be obtained in a constructive way such that for every T and $E \in \mathcal{E}$, we have $WF(E_{can}) \subseteq WF(E)$. Although this operation preserves completeness, it does not preserve minimality. A solution to this problem is to compare canonical expansion functions of different natural classes of expansion functions w.r.t. these criteria.

Tractability

Since space is limited, we only mention some results already obtained. These results all occur in [10].

The problems to decide whether a theory has a consistent expansion and finding a complete expansion function are both tractable. We have proven that complete minimum size and minimum change expansion functions are difficult to compute: the problem to find a minimum size or change expansion is NP-Hard, but in $NP^{O(n)}$. On the other hand, finding a minimal size expansion is tractable, although finding a minimal change expansion is NP-Hard.

Compared to the use of two-valued approaches in other contexts, we can show that using three-valued semantics makes some problems significantly easier.

4 Analysis of some existing revision methods

One of the first belief revision methods used in truth maintenance is the well-known *dependency-directed backtracking* (ddb) method. While ddb was formulated mainly in procedural terms, it has been reconstructed in a more declarative setting in various ways[6]. Considered as an expansion method, a ddb method essentially adds logical contrapositives of tms-arguments occurring in the theory. A reconstruction shows that ddb methods can be complete expansion functions. Moreover, there is a canonical ddb method constructing for each contradictory tmsc theory T a canonical ddb-expansion in cubic time (see [11]). Other efficient variants of ddb-methods have also been investigated ([4, 10]).

Expanding a theory by a contrapositive of some argument does not change its class of propositional models. Moreover, it is easy to show that every stable model of a theory is also a stable model of such an expansion. Therefore, we can further characterize ddb expansions T' of a theory T as leaving invariant the space of propositional models of T but enlarging its space of stable models.

Ddb methods, however, generally do not satisfy minimality criteria: a canonical ddb-method may add arguments that do not occur in any minimal revision of the theory. Such arguments may be called *irrelevant*.

Recently, in ([5]) an elegant solution was proposed to the problem to find a canonical expansion method based on relevant arguments only, without first computing the set of all relevant arguments. Slightly generalizing their Contradiction Removal Semantics, we can describe it as follows:

1. Take the set of atoms A revised by some complete (but tractable) expansion function E applied to T; A is called the *candidate set*.
2. find the set A' of all $a \in A$ occurring as the conclusion of an additional argument in at least one *inclusion minimal size expansion* $E'(T) \subseteq E(T)$.
3. define the canonical expansion $E_{can}(T) = T + \{a \leftarrow \mathbf{u} \mid a \in A'\}$

---

[6] We refer to [4, 11] for a discussion of the original formulation of ddb and its logical reconstruction.

Whenever E is complete, E_{can} is also complete. So, if E is canonical, we could take E_{can} as a canonical refinement of E. Such a refinement, in general, will be more informative, i.e. $WF(E(T)) \subseteq WF(E_{can}(T))$. The bad news, however, is that we have to pay for this increase in strength: in [10] we have shown that in general, every derived canonical expansion method based on such a method is intractable.

5 Conclusion

We have shown that the standard framework for belief revision has to be adapted in order to deal with revision in non-monotonic theories. We proposed to replace *contraction* by *expansion* when non-monotonic inconsistency occurs and we illustrated this approach by showing how revision by expansion can be used in truth maintenance. As an application of the framework, we have shown that some earlier, procedurally formulated, ideas for belief revision in truth maintenance can be reconstructed and evaluated as specific revision by expansion functions.

Given the close relations between the stable model semantics of TMSC, the semantics of Default Logic and the stable expansions of auto-epistemic logic, we think that theory by expansion can be applied in these theories, too.

References

1. C. Alchourrón, P. Gärdenfors and D. Makinson, On the Logic of Theory Change: Partial Meet Contraction and Revision Functions, *Journal of Symbolic Logic*, **50**, 510–530, 1985.
2. J. Doyle, A Truth Maintenance System, *Artificial Intelligence* **12**, 1979.
3. P. Gärdenfors, *Knowledge in Flux*, MIT Press, Cambridge, MA, 1988.
4. C. M. Jonker, Cautious Backtracking and Well-Founded Semantics in Truth Maintenance. Technical Report RUU-CS-91-26, Dept. of Computer Science, Utrecht University, 1991.
5. L. M. Pereira, J. J. Alferes and J. N. Aparicio. The Extended Stable Models of Contradiction Removal Semantics. In: P. Barahona, L. M. Pereira and A. Porto, (eds.), Proceedings EPIA 91, Springer Verlag, Heidelberg, 1991.
6. T. Przymusinski, Well-founded semantics coincides with three-valued stable semantics, *Fundamenta Informaticae*, XIII:445–463, 1990.
7. M. Reinfrank, Fundamentals and Logical Foundations of Truth Maintenance, Linköping Studies in Science and Technology. Dissertations no. 221, Linköping University, 1989.
8. A. Van Gelder, K. A. Ross and J. S. Schlipf, The well-founded semantics for general logic programs. *Journal of the ACM*, 38(3), pp. 620–650, 1991.
9. C. Witteveen, Expansions of Logic Programs, in: D. Pearce and G. Wagner (eds), *Logics in AI*, Springer Verlag, Berlin, 1992.
10. C. Witteveen and C. M. Jonker, Revision by expansion in logic programs, Reports of the Faculty of Technical Mathematics and Informatics no. 93-02, Delft University of Technology, 1993.
11. C. Witteveen and G. Brewka, Skeptical Reason Maintenance and Belief Revision, *Artificial Intelligence*, **61** (1993) 1–36.

Author Index

Springer-Verlag
and the Environment

We at Springer-Verlag firmly believe that an international science publisher has a special obligation to the environment, and our corporate policies consistently reflect this conviction.

We also expect our business partners – paper mills, printers, packaging manufacturers, etc. – to commit themselves to using environmentally friendly materials and production processes.

The paper in this book is made from low- or no-chlorine pulp and is acid free, in conformance with international standards for paper permanency.

Lecture Notes in Computer Science

For information about Vols. 1–670
please contact your bookseller or Springer-Verlag